PSYCHOLOGICAL PERSPECTIVES ON CHRISTIAN MINISTRY

a reader

PSYCHOLOGICAL PERSPECTIVES ON CHRISTIAN MINISTRY

a reader

edited by

Leslie J Francis
D J James Professor of Pastoral Theology
Trinity College, Carmarthen, and
University of Wales, Lampeter

and

Susan H Jones
Centre for Theology and Education
Trinity College, Carmarthen, Wales

Gracewing.

First published in 1996

Gracewing
Fowler Wright Books
2 Southern Ave, Leominster
Herefordshire HR6 0QF

This publication of this book has been supported by a grant awarded by the Book Publishing committee of Trinity College Carmarthen.

ISBN 085244 332 3

Typesetting by
Action Typesetting Ltd, Gloucester, GL1 1SP

Printed by
Cromwell Press, Broughton Gifford, Wiltshire, SN12 8PH

Contents

Preface

Leslie J Francis and Susan H Jones

For some time we have been conscious of a growing interest in the contribution of psychological research to Christian ministry. Because of our own research initiatives in this area, a number of individuals have begun to seek our advice in reviewing existing knowledge in the field or in establishing new research projects. The recent establishment of the Centre for Theology and Education at Trinity College, Carmarthen, has given a fresh stimulus to new research in the psychology of Christian ministry.

One of the major difficulties in assessing and fostering psychological research on Christian ministry stems from the fact that the ongoing research is both diverse and scattered across a wide range of journals. This reader, therefore, attempts to draw together some of the initiatives published within the past twelve years.

The selection of material has not been easy to make. We have been guided by two main criteria. Each study included is grounded on empirical data. We have wanted to illustrate as wide a range of topics and methods as possible. These criteria mean that the selection of articles gives a fair representation of the current state of research in the field, illustrating both the strengths and weaknesses of empirical research concerned with the psychological study of Christian ministry. There are times when this research could have been improved by better conceptualisation, better measurement tools, better sampling, better response rates and better statistical analyses. All of these issues are proper challenges for the next generation of researchers to address. Whatever the weakness of individual studies, however, collectively the thirty-one articles reprinted in this reader clearly demonstrate that psychological research on Christian ministry is already a significant field of study in its own right.

Our hope for this reader is that it will now stimulate two positive developments. First, we hope that the insights already developed by research in this field may be constructively integrated into the development of the clerical profession and enhance the work of Christian ministry. Second, we hope that the existing body of research may stimulate and inspire new and improved studies.

We are grateful to many authors and publishers who have permitted their work to be republished in this reader, and to those who have helped in the processes of collating resources, compiling materials, copy-editing text, proof reading, word-processing, and seeking permissions, especially Anne Rees and Diane Drayson, to Dr William K Kay for compiling the index, and to the Right Reverend Peter Atkins, former Bishop of Waiapu and now Dean of the College of St John the Evangelist, Auckland, New Zealand, for providing the foreword.

Leslie J Francis
Susan H Jones
June 1994

Foreword

Peter G Atkins

For many years I have been involved in the selection, training and deployment of ordained ministers within the Anglican Church and more recently within an ecumenical setting. I have taught in different cultures within the Pacific Region and had the privilege of assisting with the preparation and in-service training of a number of bishops in a wider area within the Anglican Communion. From my experience, I have observed that the people who seek to undertake positions of service and leadership do not obviously fit into any particular stereotype of personality or gifts, but each has his or her own individual nature. Yet we still ask these questions about them. Why do some succeed at certain tasks and others fail? Why do some appear to relish certain parts of the job and others shrink from them? Why do some grow in the position and others just 'go through the motions'? What are the causes of burnout? All of those who, like me, have been supervisors and supporters of ministry, have to face such questions constantly. We even know that others sometimes ask them about us.

Pastoral theologians have written about some of the answers to those questions and the care that should be given to those in ordained ministry. They indicate that part of the answer may be in a loss of the core of faith, part in emotional trauma, part in the amount of support that the person receives or does not receive while doing the task.

However, the influence of Jung[1] and other psychologists has stimulated the pastoral theologians to look into the basic personality of each person to try to see how each approaches a range of tasks. Observation has led to a conclusion that, although each person in the end is unique, there are some basic patterns to personality which allow a measure of predictability and awareness to arise.

The use of personality typing has become a helpful tool for self-understanding and the awareness of how it would be easiest to approach a task. For example, the Myers-Briggs Type

Indicator[2] has now been developed and adapted to a number of cultures and allows a general shape of the personality to be defined. This shape should not be seen as rigid so much as a framework on which the unique gifts can be arranged. Another example uses the dimensional model of personality developed by Eysenck and Eysenck[3] and seeks to describe the location of the individual on the continua defined by three major dimensions of personality: extraversion, neuroticism and psychoticism. This measurement of *degree* is distinctive and is in contrast to the *type* defined in the Myers-Briggs Type Indicator.

For many years, such tools have been seen as useful in the system of selection and training for job placement in the secular world. More recently, the value of such tools has been recognised for the tasks of Christian ministry. It has also stimulated further thought as to what are the tasks or functions of Christian ministry in the cultures of the modern world.

It has become obvious that it is not sufficient to describe Christian ministry in terms of 'being' but that there are also definite functions that the ordained must carry out on behalf of the Christian community as a whole. Those responding to the church's call to service, be it as lay or ordained persons, want to know what they are expected to do. These questions continue throughout training and become more critical when assessment appraisal is undertaken.

Recent studies in the USA and Britain[4] have examined afresh the traditional roles and functions of Christian ministry and have put forward a renewed emphasis on leadership as one of the key functions of ordained ministry.

The way this function is exercised has also been the subject of discussion. The ideal is described in terms of collaboration rather than dominance, service rather than hierarchy.

As far as the accepted functions are concerned, three basic questions can be asked of the ministers:

>   Can they do it?
>   Will they do it?
>   How will they do it?

This approach highlights the inter-connectedness between ability, motivation and work style.

To respond to these questions it is very helpful to have the resources of awareness that arise from personality profiling and psychological assessment. Many within the church seem to be suspicious or anxious about using such resources. This anxiety may be on a personal basis – I wonder what will be revealed

about me which I would rather hide; or on an antiscience basis –
this will override the spiritual approach to personhood. A further
rejection may occur because of a theological principle
expounded – people can be changed by the gospel, so stereotyping is not permitted. I see such defensive attitudes as quite
unnecessary and similar to the spiritual healer rejecting the
contribution of scientific medicine and research to the health of
a person.

I see good reason why all those engaged in ministry formation
and oversight should listen carefully to the results of research in
this area. We should apply psychological insights to help us
respond to our questions about the way we carry out the functions within Christian ministry.

The articles in this reader cover a wide selection of topics
around the theme. They include the expectations held by various
groups of the role of the clergy, both women and men; the preferences those in ministry express for various functions in their jobs;
the effectiveness of ministry and how to measure it; the serious
issues of burnout and stress; and the mental health of clergy.

The middle articles in this book will be of special interest to
those of us within sight of retirement and those who would like
to leave a job for which they or others no longer feel they are
suitable. Ageing is a fact of life and an influence on ministry
fulfilment and it is good to see two articles on this topic. It is
helpful to identify differences due to gender and it is right that
this reader has articles exploring women in ministry and clergy
marriages.

My comments on the use of psychology make me welcome the
inclusion of articles on the facts about the clergy's use of various
methods and their attitudes to those of a kindred profession.

On a personal note, it is a delight to write this foreword to a
book edited by Professor Francis and his colleague in the Centre
for Theology and Education at Trinity College Carmarthen,
Susan H Jones. Recently Professor Francis and I worked
together in the production of a series of articles on Christian
leadership.[5] In his own person Leslie Francis brings together the
knowledge and skills of both the priest and the psychologist and
is thus in a unique position to set before us the relationship
between both disciplines.

I encourage you to study in detail these articles and for those
in positions of supervision and responsibility to use them as
springboards for action to enhance the quality of ministry and
the care of our ministers within the Christian family of churches.

Notes
1.   C G Jung, *Psychological Types*, London, Routledge, 10971; *Analytical Psychology: its theory and practice*, London and New York, Ark Paperbacks, 1986.
2.   I B Myers and P B Myers, *Gifts Differing*, Palo Alto, California, Consulting Psychologists Press, 1980.
     I Myers, *Introduction to Type*, Palo Alto, California, Consulting Psychologists Press, 1980.
3.   H J Eysenck and M W Eysenck, *Personality and Individual Differences: a natural science approach*, New York, Plenum, 1985.
4.   V A Rebeck, 'Gifted for ministry: setting up pastors for success,' *Christian Century*, June 30–July 7, 1993; M Grey, 'From patriarchy to beloved community: exploring new models of ministry for feminist theology,' *Feminist Theology*, 3, 1993, pp 116–129; Church of England Advisory Board of Ministry, *The Report of a Working Party on Criteria for Selection for Ministry in the Church of England*, London, Advisory Board of Ministry, 1993.
5.   Peter G Atkins with Leslie J Francis, *Training for Christian Leadership*, Auckland, St John's College, 1994.

Peter G Atkins
Auckland
October 1994

Introduction

Leslie J Francis and Susan H Jones

In common with a number of other professions, the clerical profession has become more conscious in recent years of the advantages of a solid research base for enhancing good professional practice. The discipline of psychology is central to the development of such a research base. As yet, however, the fostering of psychological research relevant for Christian ministry remains much less coordinated than in some other professional spheres, like teaching and nursing.

The present reader sets out to bring together in an accessible form some of the recent key articles which have made a significant contribution to psychological research into Christian ministry. The selection clearly displays the interdisciplinary, international and ecumenical context for this growing initiative. The one feature which all the thirty-one chosen articles have in common is a clear commitment to developing and testing psychological theory with empirical data. In order to begin to map the areas of Christian ministry currently illuminated by psychological research, the thirty-one chosen articles have been grouped within thirteen main chapters.

Chapter one opens the reader by recognising that Christian ministry is shaped not only by the skills and personal qualities of the ministers themselves, but also by the attitudes and expectations of those among whom they minister. The three articles in this chapter illuminate research into different aspects of *lay expectations*. First, Charles Burdsal, Robert Newton, Jeanne Burdsal and Kenneth Yates set out to identify and measure the dimensions considered important by Episcopalian parishes in the USA in evaluating their priest. In the second study, A Ward Jones examines the attitudes of general practitioners towards the involvement of clergy in patient care in the UK. In the third study, Edward C Lehman Jr undertakes a systematic evaluation of the ways in which lay members of the Baptist Church in England think and feel about the entry of women into the ranks of the ordained clergy. He sets these findings in the context of similar enquiries made among lay members of the Church of England, the Methodist Church and the United Reformed Church.

Chapter two turns attention away from the way in which the laity perceive the role of the clergy to the way in which the ordained clergy perceive their own *role preferences*. First, Alan Bryman's study enables two important comparisons to be made in interpreting the ways in which clergy understand their role. The first comparison is between two different denominations, namely the Church of England and the Methodist Church. The second comparison is between two different generations of clergy, studied in the early 1970s and again during the mid-1980s. In the second study, Leslie J Francis and Raymond Rodger explore the influence of personality on shaping role prioritisation, role influences, role conflict and dissatisfaction with ministry among Church of England clergy.

Chapter three is concerned with *ministerial effectiveness* and presents three different empirical perspectives on this question. First, Allen Nauss addresses the relationship between leadership styles and effective ministry among Lutheran parish pastors in the USA. In the second article, H Newton Malony and Laura Fogwell Majovski explore the role of psychological assessment in predicting ministerial effectiveness among United Methodist ministers in the USA. In the third article, Howard W Stone examines the extent to which seminary entrance test data can predict future effectiveness in ministry among Protestant clergy in the USA.

Chapter four focuses on *stress and burnout*, a subject recognised as an increasingly important area of research within the caring professions and already well documented among teachers, social workers, nurses and doctors. In the first article in this chapter, Carole A Rayburn, Lee J Richmond and Lynn Rogers administered four instruments concerned with different aspects of stress to a sample of priests, ministers, seminarians, nuns and brothers in the USA. In the second article, Philip J Dewe examines the sources of stress reported by a sample of Protestant clergy in New Zealand, together with the strategies they employ to cope with these problems. In the third article, Joseph H Fichter reports on a survey concerned with clergy health conducted among Catholic priests in the USA. In this report, he concentrates specifically on interpreting and evaluating the signs of psychological burnout. In the fourth article, Roger L Dudley and Des Cummings Jr report on the professional and personal morale of male Seventh-day Adventist pastors in the USA.

Chapter five turns attention from stress and burnout to wider issues concerned with the *mental health* of the clergy. Two studies illustrate different research perspectives taken on this issue. In the first study, Philip J Keddy, Philip Erdberg and Sean D Sammon describe the psychological problems of a group of Catholic clergy and religious who were referred for residential treatment. In the second study, Jayne Patrick explores the hypothesis that pathological narcissism is prevalent among the clergy, using a sample of United Church ministerial candidates in Canada.

Chapter six is concerned with clergy *ageing and retirement*. In view of the rising mean age of clergy within a number of denominations, research in this area is of growing importance. In the first, study Leslie J Francis and David W Lankshear examine the relationship between clergy age and certain quantitative indices of church life in two samples of Church of England parishes in order to compare the performance of ageing clergy in rural and suburban contexts. In the second study, Janet L Goodwin and Mervin Y T Chen investigate adjustment to retirement in a sample of Anglican, Baptist and United Church retired clergy from the Atlantic region of Canada.

Chapter seven focuses on *leaving ministry* and presents two studies which address the issues why some ministry candidates drop out of seminary or why some ordained clergy quit ministry. In the first study, Howard W Stone explores the combined ability of scores on the Minnesota Multiphasic Personality Inventory and the Theological School Inventory to distinguish between seminarians who graduated to ministry and those who failed to complete the course, within a mainline Protestant seminary in the USA. In the second study, Mary Jeanne Verdieck, Joseph J Shields and Dean R Hoge report on two surveys conducted among American Catholic diocesan priests in 1970 and 1985 in order to distinguish the characteristics of those most inclined to resign from ministry.

Chapter eight examines *male and female differences* among clergymen and clergywomen. Research in this area is illustrated by two rather different studies. In the first study, W Mack Goldsmith and Bonita Neville Ekhardt compare the response of male and female seminarians in the USA to the Bem Sex-Role Inventory. These responses are also compared with the responses of male and female masters of education students. The seminarians emerged as more androgynous and less same-sex typed than their education peers. In the second study, Edward C Lehman Jr reports on the findings of a telephone survey conducted among male and female pastors in four mainline Protestant denominations in the USA. The survey tested the theory that men approach the work of pastoral ministry using a masculine ministry style, while women perform the same work using a feminine ministry style.

Chapter nine follows on from the preceding chapter on male and female differences in ministry by focusing specifically on *women in ministry*. Again two different perspectives are presented. In the first study, Sue Webb Cardwell explores whether psychological factors can account for some of the differences between women who succeed in ministry and women who fail in ministry. She examines the test profile of women who entered Christian Theological Seminary in the USA between 1962 and 1976. In the second study, Lesley Stevens reports on a survey conducted among women ordained in the Anglican Church in Canada. She focuses particularly on the women's perceptions of gender differences in the concept and practice of ministry.

Chapter ten presents two studies concerned with monitoring *generational changes* among clergy. In the first study, Howard W Stone conducts an examination of data on students entering a mainline Protestant seminary in the USA between 1962 and 1986. He is particularly concerned to monitor changes in psychopathology and in cognitive abilities. In the second study, Lawrence A Young and Richard A Schoenherr engage in a debate interpreting the differences in theological attitudes found in two studies of Catholic clergy in the USA in 1970 and 1985. The problem concerns untangling the contribution of an ageing effect and of a cohort effect. The problem is made more complex by the way in which the overall attitudes of a cohort of clergy are affected by the withdrawal of resignees from the cohort.

Chapter eleven argues that research concerned with the psychology of Christian ministry would be incomplete without taking into account the home and *family life* of the minister. Two different examples of research in this area are presented. In the first study, Brent B Benda and Frederick A DiBlasio report on a study concerned with marital adjustment conducted among clergy who had attended a Presbyterian seminary in the USA and their spouses. In the second study, Diane L Ostrander, Carolyn S Henry and Charles C Hendrix report on the development, reliability and validity of the Stressors of Clergy Children Inventory, among a sample of clergy children in the USA. They are concerned to distinguish between three sources of stress defined as church stressors, family stressors and individual stressors.

Chapter twelve draws attention to a particularly fruitful field of psychological research which has concentrated on exploring specific areas of clergy *attitudes and knowledge*. Research of this nature is illustrated by three specific examples. In the first study, George Domino reports on the development of a multiple choice test to assess knowledge about psychopathology based on the material covered in abnormal psychology courses. He compares the responses of a heterogeneous group of clergy in the USA to this test with the responses of professional counsellors and undergraduate students attending psychology classes. In the second study, J Kirk Gulledge reports on the responses of Methodist, Baptist and Lutheran clergy in the USA to the Facts on Ageing Quiz in order to compare the level of gerontological knowledge of the clergy with the level of knowledge among other professional groups. In the third study, Alan Aldridge examines the attitudes of a sample of Anglican parochial clergy in England towards liturgical change.

Chapter thirteen is concerned with *counselling and psychology*. One of the most thoroughly researched aspects of the clerical profession concerns the role of the clergy as counsellor. Research in this field is illustrated by two very different studies. In the first study, Darrell Winger and Bruce Hunsberger report on a survey conducted among male clergy from ten Protestant denominations in Ontario to explore the relationship between clergy counselling practices, Christian orthodoxy and problem solving styles. They are concerned to discover the extent to which theological beliefs influence the ways in which clergy set about their work as counsellors. In the second study, Willa D Meylink and Richard L Gorsuch provide an overview of the empirical data concerned with the relationship between clergy and psychologists.

It is the editors' shared hope that this reader will now stimulate a wider interest in psychological perspectives on Christian ministry, both in the sense of applying the insights from such research to help shape the initial training and the in-service training of clergy and in the sense of fostering new research initiatives within this field of study.

1. Lay expectations

Christian ministry is shaped not only by the skills and personal qualities of the individual ministers themselves, but also by the attitudes and expectations of those among whom they minister. Failure to listen carefully to the attitudes and expectations of their congregations, of the wider local community and of the other professionals with whom they need to collaborate can lead to unrealistic strategies, inappropriate hopes and unnecessary feelings of disappointment and frustration. This opening chapter, therefore, begins by focusing on lay expectations of Christian ministry and illustrates how psychological research has focused on three specific topics in this area.

In the first article in this section, Charles Burdsal, Robert Newton, Jeanne Burdsal and Kenneth Yates set out to identify and measure the dimensions considered important by laity in evaluating their priest. Data are provided from 221 Episcopal parishes in the USA. Factor analysis identified eight usable factors which are described as follows: pastoral sensitivity, administrative skills, scholarship, personal integrity, innovation, personal spirituality, meaningfulness of services and laity involvement. The study provides a useful instrument capable of measuring these dimensions in future research.

Professor Charles Burdsal is Professor and Chairman of the Department of Psychology, the Wichita State University, Wichita, Kansas, USA. At the time of writing Robert Newton and Jeanne Burdsal worked in the same department. Kenneth Yates was a member of the Nashotah House Seminary faculty in Nashotah, Wisconsin. This article was first published in *Pastoral Psychology* in 1983.

In the second article, A Ward Jones examines the attitudes of general practitioners towards the involvement of clergy in patient care. Data are provided by 228 doctors in the UK about both their theoretical attitudes towards and practical involvement of clergy in relation to twenty specific concerns of patients, including areas like bereavement, divorce, depression and chronic illness. The doctors are also asked to explain from a series of options their reasons for referring or failing to refer patients to clergy. The findings demonstrate that the general practitioners perceived a significant role for the clergy in theory which was not matched in practice.

The Revd A Ward Jones is a Superintendent Minister in the Methodist church who also serves as a part-time chaplain at Victoria Hospital, Frome, England. This article was first published in *British Journal of General Practice* in 1990.

In the third article, Edward C Lehman Jr undertakes a systematic evaluation of the ways in which lay members of the Baptist Church in England think and feel about the entry of women into the ranks of ordained clergy. A sample of 360 church members indicated their level of agreement with stereotypical views of women clergy and expressed their preferences for men or women clergy in a variety of church positions and functions. Comparisons are then made with the responses of 347 members of the Church of England, 349 members of the Methodist Church and 358 members of the United Reformed Church.

Professor Edward C Lehman Jr is Professor of Sociology in State University of New York, College at Brockport, Brockport, New York, USA. This article was first published in *Baptist Quarterly* in 1986.

1.1 On the examination of the role of the Episcopalian priest in the pastoral ministry

Charles Burdsal, Robert Newton, Jeanne Burdsal and Kenneth Yates

Introduction

This research[1] was prompted by the need to understand in an empirical sense the role of the priest in the pastoral ministry. While in agreement with the concern expressed by Schuller, Brikke, and Strommen[2] that such an approach has a risk of introducing some aspects of the market mentality, that is 'What kind of minister do people wish to purchase these days?', realistically, the needs and concerns of the laity define at least a significant aspect of the role. The laity often have a very demanding image of what they expect from a parish priest. These expectations are not limited, as shown by Maddock, Kenny, and Middleton[3] to role functions, but include rather demanding personality characteristics. As in most instances, the laity control the employment of the priest either directly or indirectly, the needs and expectations of the laity are an important concern of the parish priest; an empirical examination as to the dimensionality of the role thus seems warranted. There have been several studies which have attempted to provide data concerning the role of priests and ministers. The emphasis of many of the studies has been in the area of role evaluation.[3-5] However, all of these studies have some major difficulties. The studies by Harris[4] and Umeda[5] barely touched on roles, and their criterion for success (the minister's and priest's self reports) is questionable at best. Weisgerber's[6] study unfortunately appeared quite weak in measurement methodology, making his conclusions suspect.

Probably the best empirical evidence of the priest's and minister's role can be found in Schuller, Brikke and Strommen.[2] The overall aim of their extensive research was to prepare a criteria-oriented measure aimed at determining an individual's readiness for the ministry. Schuller *et al.* initially did extensive research into developing a set of criteria by producing a questionnaire which utilised a broad sample including both ministers, priests, and the laity, who rated the importance of each item. However, several statistical problems were evident in the analysis performed on their data.[7]

Criticism notwithstanding, the study provides a wealth of data relating to the roles of ministers and thus provided considerable guidance for this research. In fact, one major logical question concerning their study helped set the direction of this research. Schuller *et al.* asked their subjects to rate the importance of each item on their questionnaire rather than actually rating the performance of each minister or priest. One wonders if an analysis of the interrelationships of the items based simply on importance would yield the same structure as an analysis based upon actual evaluations. It seems that ratings as to importance would be more likely to yield stereotypes.

This study, therefore, has two primary objectives:

    a.   to investigate the role of the priest as perceived by the laity; and
    b.   minimise the possibility of producing stereotypes by collecting actual ratings of priests by laity based upon many characteristics.

Method

Development of the instrument[8]

As the emphasis of this research was upon perception by the laity of the role of the parish priest, the lay people were used to generate the item pool. A nationwide sample of 508 Episcopal parishes was utilised. Meetings of laity highly involved in the church were held in each of the parishes by the parish priest. They were asked to discuss the question, 'What is most important in a parish priest?', and then to produce a list of the characteristics they agreed were important.

There was an amazing amount of agreement between parishes. A summary of the most common response may be found in table one as well as the percentage of the laity, clergy, and churches who participated in the survey and who regarded each particular as being of importance.

This information, together with reports on the evaluations by Dr Felix Lopez and the results of a survey on preparation for the ministry reported in the *Virginia Seminary Journal* in 1974, provided the basis for a questionnaire of 83 items. The responses for each item were a six-point Likert-like scale.

Questionnaire administration

Bishops in a statistical sample of Episcopal dioceses were asked to pick ten per cent of their active clergy, representing, insofar as possible, differing geographical and cultural situations, spanning the range from the least to the most effective, and representing accurately the educational background of the clergy of the diocese. Bishops were asked to pick priests of varying degrees of post seminary experience. Each priest selected received a letter explaining the research project. It was required that at least three of the vestry members or other exten-

Table 1: What is important in a parish priest? A comparison of areas from laity, clergy and churches involved in the survey

Role area	per cent considering area important		
	laity	clergy	church
a clear and obvious relationship with God, as expressed by joy, enthusiasm, openness, not just love for church	95	100	96
communication skills, everyday words, with meaning for people where they are: ability to communicate good news in a winning way	92	91	92
personal maturity and emotional security, shown by the absence of a holier-than-thou attitude or need to manipulate people; no tricks, no lies, no quiet stabbings	90	88	91
empathy, understanding, compassion, related to people and their situations	78	67	78
desire to be a pastor to all the congregation, and skills in working with all types and conditions of people	70	70	70
love for younger children, interest in them, skills in working with them for real goals, not playing church	66	0	64
business skills including decision making, planning, delegation of authority, financial planning, and general administration	62	82	61
a desire to build a real ministry by lay members, trust in their ability to minister, and skills in training and preparing people for lay ministry	59	55	57
skill and knowledge in the area of worship, to make the service come alive, and enable parishioners to know and worship God in and through the services	58	52	56
counselling skills; ability to work with people in crises, to support people pastorally, but to delegate to professional people the long term counselling role; the pastor is the first contact person in mental health but not a primary vendor	46	36	44
teaching skills; people felt the clergy know their subject, but need specific training in how to teach	42	40	40
evangelistic zeal; most comments included a willingness to experiment, to work in and through lay people. Urgency is central rather than method	36	21	35
concern for the community, both in terms of social action and in helping parishioners relate to their everyday world	28	15	27
additional broad liberal arts education	28	0	27
training and skill in time management	16	0	14
personal 'style'	10	21	9
ability to use supervision well	4	6	4
strong support for diocesan programmes	4	12	4
solid knowledge of bible and the tradition	0	82	—
acceptance of the discipline and routine of the parish ministry, the ability to find and work with God in the everyday life	0	42	—
priestcraft	0	42	—
leadership	0	33	—
skill as spiritual director	0	6	—

Note: While it may seem surprising at first that the laity seemed unconcerned with the priest's knowledge of the bible and tradition, further interviewing indicated that they simply assumed that any priest would have a solid knowledge of the bible and tradition.

sively involved church members rate their priest on the questionnaire.

In all, 221 parishes responded with complete data. The number of raters for each priest ranged from three to thirteen depending upon the parish. In addition demographic data was collected on each priest including her or his seminary, age at graduation, age at ordination, marital status, and number of children.

Results and discussion

The statistical technique of factor analysis was used in computing the results.[9] Twelve factors, of which eight were retained, were extracted in the analysis. A summary of the factors may be found in tables two and three.

Factor one: pastoral sensitivity. This factor was dominated by items involving the interpersonal relationship of the priest with the laity. It seemed to have a strong empathy component as seen in such items as: 'displays a comforting and friendly manner', 'is a good listener', 'is someone I talk with when I need to', 'accepts and appreciates the uniqueness of every person', etc. Also, there appeared to be an aspect of a comfortable personal demeanour. The priest who scored high on this factor would be one with whom his or her congregation would feel extremely comfortable. It seems that he or she would be of very low threat, and would be able to deal in a therapeutic manner with the problems of a parishioner, regardless of sex. It appeared to the authors to be a significant component of what the word 'pastoral' means. Thus, it is of little surprise that such a factor is a strong dimension of the role of the priest as viewed by the laity.

Factor two: administrative skills. This dimension represented the day-to-day functions of the parish, both long and short range. Many parish functions fall within the management and administrative realm. Thus, the parish priest could be regarded as an administrator or director for the parish. Any parish which functions reasonably smoothly would have to have at least one priest moderately high on this factor.

Factor three: scholarship. The degree to which the priest is a knowledgeable person is of concern to the laity. They are apparently sensitive to the extent to which the priest has as a value his or her personal education. Historically the priest has been among the few educated scholars in a community. Although the uniqueness of the pastoral role as a scholar no longer exists, the priest frequently is sought out by parishioners for instruction. The capability of the priest to impart guidance or counsel to parishioners is perceived as important.

Factor four: personal integrity. The degree to which the priest is a good moral model is of concern to the laity. The highest loadings clearly set the pattern: moderation, temperance, trustworthiness, personal integrity, and Godliness; all represent a unitary concern over

Table 2: Summary of factors by salient loadings

factor items	factor loadings
factor 1: pastoral sensitivity	
has a sense of humour	0.98
displays a comforting and friendly manner	0.89
is able to understand feelings of others	0.82
loves and cares for parishioners of all ages	0.80
is a good listener: 'someone I talk with when I have a need to'	0.74
deals well with young children	0.72
relates meaningfully to people and their situations	0.71
talks 'with' people and not 'at' them	0.67
accepts and appreciates the uniqueness of every person	0.63
understands emotions experienced by those of the opposite sex	0.60
deals capably with all types of conditions of people	0.60
demonstrates an ability to take and use constructive criticism	0.56
is socially active, participates in community planning and assists with community problems	0.53
uses authority without being authoritarian	0.51
is capable of dealing justly with those of the opposite sex	0.48
is able to express emotions appropriately	0.48
draws upon the disciplines of psychology and sociology to complement pastoral ministry	0.48
is accessible as opposed to being remote	0.45
is a skilful spiritual counsellor	0.45
factor 2: administrative skills	
is an effective administrator	0.81
keeps legible and accurate church related records	0.78
is a good planner	0.75
makes prudent use of time	0.57
gives appropriate leadership to fund raising activities in the parish	0.57
accepts the discipline and the routine of parish ministry	0.40
is a helpful adviser to those having trouble establishing a personal budget	0.38
is capable of motivating others	0.32
works industriously, is not lazy	0.28
mediates among groups inside the church	0.25
factor 3: scholarship	
is knowledgeable of the bible and theology	0.70
is appropriately educated	0.70
is a scholarly person	0.68
is a forceful and effective teacher, a person who has knowledge and imparts it to others	0.42
instructs helpfully in liturgical matters	0.36
draws upon the disciplines of psychology and sociology to complement pastoral ministry	0.34
seeks the benefits of continuing education	0.30
seems thoughtful and intelligent	0.25
factor 4: personal integrity	
demonstrates honesty and personal integrity	0.89
is a trustworthy person and priest	0.87
leads a godly life	0.81
has a moderate and temperate way of life	0.78
exercises discretion	0.63
has a pattern of life which complements the ministry	0.62
displays personal maturity and is a fine example for parishioners	0.54
evidences emotional security	0.53
practises stewardship	0.51
adapts well to the existing personal financial structures	0.48
celebrates the Eucharist in a meaningful way	0.45

Table 2: (continued)

factor items	factor loadings
is realistic – has feet on the ground	0.45
is reverent but real	0.44
wishes to be a pastor to all the congregation	0.42
factor 5: innovation	
is willing to experiment	0.87
is innovative and willing to try new things	0.84
makes appropriate use of innovative forms of public worship	0.63
accepts and appreciates the varieties of religious experience	0.49
is capable of dealing justly with those of the opposite sex	0.34
is an active supporter of diocesan programmes	0.30
factor 6: personal spirituality	
seems to have a strong personal prayer life	0.81
has an obvious personal relationship with our Lord	0.79
celebrates the joy of Jesus Christ and shares that joy with others	0.61
administers sacraments in a reverent and comforting manner	0.58
is concerned about the spiritual welfare of parishioners	0.54
seems charged with evangelical zeal	0.43
incorporates biblical perspectives when providing personal guidance	0.43
has a thorough knowledge of the faith and history of the church	0.31
factor 7: meaningfulness of services	
presents sermons with enthusiasm	0.98
gives sermons which have a 'living' quality, reflecting personal involvement and individual experience	0.89
gives 'life' to services of worship	0.81
communicates the Christian message in a winning way	0.58
has the ability to communicate the gospel in a winning way	0.57
enables members to know and worship God in and through the services	0.52
celebrates the Eucharist in a meaningful way	0.50
is capable of sharing problems with others	0.38
has and uses the ability to be clearly understood	0.36
is capable of motivating others	0.31
is able to involve youth in the spiritual life of the church	0.20
factor 8: laity involvement	
trusts lay members of the parish to share in the ministry	0.66
skilfully prepares members for their lay ministry	0.66
desires to build a strong ministry by lay members	0.62
enables parishioners to relate to the life in the community through insightful guidance	0.33
provides leadership	0.20

Table 3: Reliability of the factor scale

scale	alpha
pastoral sensitivity	0.969
administrative skills	0.935
scholarship	0.887
personal integrity	0.967
innovation	0.897
personal spirituality	0.903
meaningfulness of services	0.953
laity involvement	0.903

which the laity evaluated their priest. One of the lower loadings on this factor points to an interesting problem: 'adapts well to the existing personal financial structures.' This item's presence may well be a reflection of a common emotional quandary: while there is no doubt that a priest must be paid to be able to function, yet emotionally, members of the clergy feel that their priestly role makes it impossible for them to 'haggle' with the vestry about their pay. This conflict between what realistically must be, and what one feels somehow ought to be, probably results in some difficulty or uneasiness when it comes to dealings between the laity and their priest concerning salary. A priest high on this factor would probably be able to decide realistically and with moderation his or her financial needs, and also be able to decide realistically and with moderation his or her financial needs, and also be able to handle her or his interactions with the laity in such matters, in a manner that would reduce their discomfort.

Factor five: innovation. This factor represents the degree to which the priest is both willing to be innovative and supportive of others' original ideas.

Factor six: personal spirituality. It appeared that the laity recognises the degree to which the priest's focus of his or her role is based upon his or her calling from God, as opposed to approaching the role as one might the role of social service worker. In other words, does the priest's role reflect this calling from God, or are the role *functions* the centre of the role? In any case, the priest's personal friendship with God, and his or her ability to share the joy of such a relationship with others is the central theme of this dimension.

Factor seven: meaningfulness of services. Not surprisingly, the priest's ability to handle church services was a dimension of concern to the laity. The main thrust is the quality of the priest's preaching. Although other aspects of the service were also important, their loadings were lower. A priest would do well if a good preacher, even though his or her abilities with other aspects of the service were below average. On the other hand, being poor in sermons would likely result in a low view of his or her abilities with church services by the laity, even if he or she excels with the other aspects of the service.

Factor eight: laity involvement. This final factor implies that lay people see themselves as partners with the ordained clergy in the ministry of the church, which may reflect a change in the attitude of Episcopalians. The 1928 edition of the *Book of Common Prayer* says, 'What orders of ministers are there in the church? Answer: bishops, priests, and deacons.' The 1979 edition says,'Who are the ministers of the church? Answer: The ministers of the church are *lay persons*,[10] bishops, priests, and deacons.' Parishioners are concerned that their pastor wants to develop this lay ministry and that he or she both trusts and prepares them to carry it out.

These factors appear to represent an important if not exclusive set of dimensions in that the pool from which they were drawn resulted from

Table 4: Item scale means for all clergy

scale	mean
pastoral sensitivity	5.0
administrative skills	4.8
scholarship	5.2
personal integrity	5.4
innovation	5.1
personal spirituality	5.3
meaningfulness of services	5.0
laity involvement	4.9
all items	5.1

asking the laity what they thought was important in terms of the role of the parish priest. They are, by the nature of factor analysis, unitary *measurable* dimensions over which priests' activities are viewed.

Of the demographic variables examined, only years of experience showed significant differences on the eight factors. The years of experience were collected in five-year intervals (1 to 5, 6 to 10, 11 to 15, 16 to 20, 21 to 25, and 26 and over). An analysis of variance indicated a significant difference for all scales at the .01 level. It appeared that the priests with sixteen to twenty years experience were significantly higher on all factors than on the other levels of experience.

Finally, it is interesting to note the overall high ratings the Episcopal clergy received. The average item score per scale may be found in table four. As the possible item range was from 1–6 with 6 being the most desirable, and considering the fact that all scale/item means were greater than 4.5, it can be assumed that the laity had an overall positive opinion of the clergy.

There appeared to be little similarity in the results of this study and the factoring in the Schuller *et al.* study. Although it is possible that the differences could be the result of differences in methods of factoring, it is quite probable that many of the differences were caused by the use in the present study of actual ratings of the priests and the emphasis placed upon the view of the laity.

The dimensions found in this research provide a beginning insight into what the laity perceive as important aspects of the parish priest's role. As a number of the dimensions appeared to contain an aspect of personality, especially factors one (pastoral sensitivity) and four (personal integrity), support was lent to the assertion of Maddock, Kenny and Middleton[3] that personality is an important factor in the priest's role.

The fact that the factors found in this study are measurable provides a possible measure to gauge effectiveness of training for the ministry. Additionally, the results point to a combination of personality and learned skills as being desirable traits in a priest. The identification of those dimensions that are perceived as important by the laity can be used to augment the training currently received by students in the seminary.

A new study is underway to determine the relationship of personality and motivational traits of the priest measured upon entering seminary and ratings on the factors after he or she has been in a parish for at least a year. While the dimensions found do not represent all the important role factors of priests as seen by the laity, it is felt that a good beginning has been made into the understanding and *measurement* of what the laity see as important in their priests.

Notes

1. This research represents the initial results of a project funded by the Lilly Endowment in conjunction with Nashotah House Episcopal Seminary and Virginia Theological Seminary.
2. D Schuller, M L Brekke and M P Strommen, *Readiness for Ministry: volume 1, criteria*, Vandalia, Ohio, The Association of Theological Schools in the United States, 1976.
3. R Maddock, C T Kenny and M M Middleton, 'Preference for personality versus role-activity variables in the choice of a pastor,' *Journal for the Scientific Study of Religion*, 12, 1973, pp. 449–452.
4. W C Harris, 'The use of selected leadership, personality, motivational, and demographic variables in the identification of successful ministries,' *Dissertation Abstracts International*, 33, 1973, pp. 4133–4134.
5. J K Umeda and D H Frey, 'Life history correlates of ministerial success,' *Journal of Vocational Behaviour*, 4, 1974, pp.319–323.
6. C Weisgerber, 'The Theological School Inventory and some Roman Catholic and Protestant Differences,' *Counselling and Values*, 16, 1, 1971, pp. 54–65.
7. A cluster analysis was first performed on their data, followed by a factor analysis of the clusters. While such an approach was a worthwhile effort, several statistical problems were in evidence, not the least of which was the claim that cluster analysis and factor analysis were independent techniques, and that factoring clusters represents second order factoring. (See R B Cattell and C Burdsal, 'The radial parcel double factoring design: a solution to the item versus parcel controversy,' *Multivariate Behavioural Research*, 10, 1975, pp. 165–179.) Also, the method of factoring clusters which was determined by correlation coefficients is at best a questionable practice. Also insufficient detail was present to make a true evaluation of their use of either procedure, and in a number of cases they tried to describe factors as groups as opposed to dimensions.
8. A copy of the questionnaire may be obtained from the authors.
9. A matrix of correlations was computed between all pair-wise combinations of the items. All eigenvalues were extracted from the correlation matrix, and a scree test indicated twelve factors. The twelve factors were extracted utilising the principle axis method iterating until the communality stabilised in the third decimal place. A *varimax* rotation was then performed, followed by five graphical oblique hand rotations, finally ending with a *maxplane* clean up rotation yielding a 75.6% .10 hyperplane. Simple structure for each factor was significant at at least the .01 level. Such matrices as the correlation matrix, Vo. Lambda, Rf may be obtained from the authors. As the intent was to be able to measure each factor, scales were developed using unit weightings for items loading factors. Cronbach's alpha was computed for each factor. Only those factors whose alpha exceeded .80 were retained for interpretation. An analysis of the factor scores broken down by demographic variables was then done. For further information on the scree test see R B Cattell, 'The scree test for the number of factors,' *Multivariate Behavioural Research*, 1, 1966, pp. 245–276. For further information on the varimax rotation see R B Cattell and T Foster, 'The rotoplot programme for multiple single-plane visually guided rotation,' *Behavioural Science*, 8, 1963, pp. 156–165. For further information on the maxplane rotation see R B Cattell and J C Muerle, 'The maxplane programme for factor rotation to oblique simple structure,' *Educational and Psychological Measurement*, 24, 1960, pp. 3–30.
10. Italics added by the authors.

1.2 A survey of general practitioners' attitudes to the involvement of clergy in patient care

A Ward Jones

Introduction

In recent years interest in whole person medicine – recognising that health care involves treating people as body, mind and spirit – has greatly increased both within and outside the medical world. Ministering to the spirit has traditionally been left to the clergy and has generally been seen as separate from the treatment of body and mind, which has increasingly become the preserve of the health care professionals.

Last year saw the publication, after two years of meetings, of a joint working party report of the Royal College of General Practitioners (RCGP) and the Churches' Council for Health and Healing (CCHH) entitled *Whole person medicine.*[1,2] Seven recommendations were made in the report, including one which said:

> that both the college and the council should encourage closer cooperation between general practitioners and ministers of religion in the day-to-day care of patients.

This recommendation is supported by an approved statement of the British Medical Association, issued as long ago as 1947, which accepted:[3]

> There is no ethical reason to prevent medical practitioners from cooperating with clergy in all cases (concerned with the treatment of patients) and more especially those in which the doctor in charge of the patient thinks that religious ministrations will conduce to health and peace of mind or lead to recovery.

The BMA statement concluded by declaring, 'we welcome opportunities for discussion and cooperation in the future'.

In the light of these reports and the increasing attention now being given to whole person medicine,[4-8] a survey has been carried out to discover the attitudes of general practitioners towards involving the clergy in patient care and their actual practice of referring patients.

As both the RCGP/CCHH report and the BMA's approved statement were concerned with the involvement of Christian clergy, this survey was similarly restricted.

Method

Questionnaire

A questionnaire was compiled and pilot tested in the Swindon health district. It invited responses based on the theory and practice of involving clergy in patient care.

To look at the theoretical aspects twenty concerns were listed (for example, terminal illness, abortion, depression, retirement) and respondents indicated if they considered clergy could help in caring for the patient and for the person closest to the patient. This list was based on a similar one originally compiled at a course organised by the British Postgraduate Medical Federation, when 18 'rites of passage' were identified where it was felt clergy involvement would be beneficial.[9] In a second section four statements were presented about different degrees of relationship between religion and human illness and respondents were asked to tick one.

To look at practical aspects of referral to the clergy, respondents estimated the number of times in a year in which they referred patients and/or involved clergy in patient care. They were also asked to indicate which of the twenty theoretical concerns they had made referrals about. Next, a series of options was presented, reflecting possible positive and negative reasons for referral and respondents indicated why referrals were or were not made. These statements were compiled as a result of discussion with a number of doctors and clergy and were amended for the final survey to reflect additional factors which emerged from the pilot study.

Finally, the general practitioners were asked to state how many clergy they knew on first name terms.

Survey

An area within the Avon health district was chosen for the survey, consisting mainly of greater Bristol and including a cross section of social classes in the population. All active general practitioners in the area were mailed a questionnaire in the early spring of 1988 with a covering letter from the Bishop of Bristol's advisory group on health and healing (who wished to make use of the results).

Results

A total of 228 questionnaires were returned from the 410 mailed, a 55.6% response.

Clergy involvement: in theory

Table one reveals a very positive acceptance by general practitioners of

Table 1: Number of respondents believing that the clergy could be of help in caring for patients' concerns.

patients' concerns	GPs responding positively	
	N	%
terminal illness	225	98.7
bereavement	223	97.8
marriage	215	94.3
chronic illness	214	93.9
divorce	214	93.9
attempted suicide	205	89.9
depression	200	87.7
physical disabilities	195	85.5
alcohol/drug dependence	193	84.7
AIDS	192	84.2
big disappointment	184	80.7
abortion	182	79.8
getting older	182	79.8
major accident	174	76.3
unemployment/retirement	173	75.9
infertility	154	67.5
major surgical operation	152	66.7
new employment	118	51.7
childbirth	114	50.0
going on the 'pill'	103	45.2

Note: N = 228

the usefulness of clergy in theory in dealing with patients' concerns. In answer to the same question about the person closest to the patient, the responses were almost identical, except that clergy were deemed to be marginally more helpful to patients than to their partners. This positive response is underlined by the fact that 65 doctors (28.5%) recognised the potential of clergy for helping with all twenty concerns. The highest scoring concerns were those related to two of the issues traditionally associated with the clergy – marriage and death. The traditional 'hatch, match and dispatch' role was not, however, confirmed in 'hatch' concerns: abortion, infertility, childbirth and going on the 'pill' were not so frequently seen as areas in which clergy could help. While all the concerns were related to events which could radically affect people's lifestyle, a role was not easily perceived in new employment or after a major surgical operation. However, even here over 50% of respondents thought the clergy could be of help.

These positive attitudes are reinforced by 163 respondents (71.5%) confirming that religion has a specific contribution to make to the cure of illness for some patients and another 41 (18.0%) that it is of general relevance to the experience of illness and its treatment in all patients.

Clergy involvement: in practice

Referral rates to clergy are indicated in table two. It shows that 130 of the respondents (57.0%) have some contact with clergy over patient

Table 2: Number of times per annum when general practitioners referred patients and/or involved clergy in patient care.

no. of referrals annually	GPs referring	
	N	%
0	98	43.0
1–6	101	44.3
7–12	20	8.8
13–24	6	2.6
25–51	2	0.9
52+	1	0.4

Note: N = 228

care; this represents 31.7% of the total of 410 general practitioners in the health district. From this it is possible to define three groups of general practitioners apart from the 43.0% who were nil referrers: 44.3% who were occasional referrers (referring one to six cases per annum); 8.8% who were regular referrers (seven to 12 cases per annum); and 3.9% who were frequent referrers (13 + cases per annum).

Table three takes up the issue of why, if in theory clergy can potentially be so helpful, 98 (43.0%) of the respondents never make use of their services. There was little evidence that clergy were considered professionally incapable of helping or likely to misuse a referral. Only two doctors claimed any dissatisfaction with the outcome of previous referrals. Failure to refer was based on four factors: the assumption that the religious patient will self-refer and the non-religious patient will not want referral; the need for the 'right' clergy to be available; the lack of religious belief on the part of the general practitioner; the fact that referral had never occurred to a sizeable minority of doctors who felt they would have been prepared to consider the possibility.

Some of these factors are raised again in table four which records the attitude of occasional and regular referrers. Assumptions about the expectations of religious and non-religious patients are repeated. However, the claim of 41.3% of general practitioners that non-religious patients would not want to see the clergy is only partially borne out in practice where fewer doctors (31.4%) find the offer actually being declined, when made. The high proportion (52.1%) who encourage patients to self-refer is an indication that, if only indirectly, many occasional and regular referrers are actually using the services of the clergy more than they realise. Furthermore, 31.4% conceded they did not consider the possibility of referral even when it might have been useful. In table four the need of the 'right' clergy to be available is again acknowledged, while not knowing enough clergy acts as a controlling influence on the number of referrals. When doctors were asked how many clergy they knew, among the total 228 respondents only 28 (12.3%) knew four or more clergy on first name terms. This being so, referrals will inevitably be restricted.

Table 3: Reasons given for making no referrals to the clergy: responses of general practitioners who do not refer.

	GPs agreeing	
	N	%
patients who would accept help from the clergy would self-refer anyway	69	70.4
non-religious people would not want to see a clergyman	51	52.0
no clergy known	44	44.9
'right' clergyman was not available	25	25.5
no religious beliefs held	19	19.4
never considered the possibility, but will in future	17	17.3
not GP's responsibility to make or suggest referrals	11	11.2
clergy who are known could not help	9	9.2
clergy would regard referrals as 'souls for saving' rather than people to be helped	6	6.1
no wish to trouble busy clergymen	3	3.1
deterred by failure of a previous referral	2	2.0
clergy do not possess the necessary competence to be of any help	1	1.0

Note: N = 98

Table 4: Reasons given for not making more referrals to the clergy: responses of general practitioners who occasionally or regularly refer.

	GPs agreeing	
	N	%
usually suggest patients should self-refer, if they wish	63	52.1
most patients who would accept clergy help would self-refer anyway	62	51.2
only patients with known religious associations referred and few of these are seen	58	47.9
non-religious patients would not want to see a clergyman	50	41.3
not enough clergy known well to make referral a regular feature of patient care	47	38.8
referral not thought about when it might have been helpful for the patient	38	31.4
patients often decline the offer, when made, to involve a clergyman	38	31.4
more referrals possible if the 'right' clergyman had been available	37	30.6
clergy can help positively in only a few illnesses/problems	20	16.5
no wish to trouble busy clergymen	9	7.4

Note: N = 121

Table five shows that for the nine general practitioners who refer frequently, knowing a number of local clergy is important. They are, however, also prepared to make use of clergy they do not know, a confidence based presumably on their successful cooperation with known clergy. This confidence recognises the clergy's competence to deal with a wide range of concerns and that for some patients, including non-religious patients, such referral will be the most appropriate treatment. Eight of the group of nine considered themselves to be religious, and this must heighten their awareness of possible referral to the clergy.

The concerns for which referrals are actually made are detailed in table six. It can be seen that those referring regularly have a higher

Table 5: Reasons given for making frequent referrals to the clergy: responses of general practitioners who frequently refer.

	GPs agreeing N	%
clergy can be especially useful in a good number of illnesses/problems	9	100
hold personal religious belief and believe that religion has a part to play in health care	8	89
a number of local clergy known well	7	78
referral suggested to patients whether or not they are known to be religious	7	78
referral to a clergyman an appropriate treatment for some patients	7	78
clergy are competent to deal with referrals	5	56
one clergyman is known well and is worked with	4	44
prepared to make referrals whether or not clergyman known personally	4	44

Note: N = 9

Table 6: *Number of respondents who have actually referred patients to clergy for different concerns.*

	GPs who have made referrals					
	occasional		regular		frequent	
patients' concerns	N	%	N	%	N	%
terminal illness	49	49	16	80	7	78
bereavement	56	55	15	75	7	78
marriage	13	13	8	40	4	44
chronic illness	25	25	10	50	5	56
divorce	22	22	9	45	5	56
attempted suicide	7	7	5	25	2	22
depression	43	43	13	65	7	78
physical disabilities	4	4	1	5	1	11
alcohol/drug dependence	9	9	4	20	2	22
AIDS	0	0	0	0	0	0
big disappointment	1	1	3	15	2	22
abortion	11	11	4	20	5	56
getting older	3	3	0	0	0	0
major accident	2	2	0	0	0	0
unemployment/retirement	4	4	0	0	2	22
infertility	3	3	2	10	3	33
major surgical operation	3	3	4	20	3	33
new employment	0	0	0	0	0	0
childbirth	3	3	0	0	1	11
going on the 'pill'	6	6	0	0	2	22

Note: N of occasional = 101, regular = 20, frequent = 9

rate of referral and refer a wider range of concerns than those who only refer occasionally and this trend is further extended by the frequent referrers. When the relationship between the theory of table one and the practice indicated in table six is tested, there is a high positive correlation overall, the Spearman rank correlation coefficient produced being 0.72. Hence the referral pattern is not a random one, rather doctors actually refer more frequently patients with concerns for which in theory they also consider clergy best equipped to help.

Discussion

The fact that 44.4% of the general practitioners did not reply must be remembered in interpreting the responses of this survey. However, the data do indicate some of the trends in the thinking and practice of a not insignificant number of general practitioners within a prescribed area. The pilot survey in the Swindon health district produced a 65% response rate from a total of 210 doctors and the results there were similar to those reported here.

The views of this sample of general practitioners reveal that a role for the clergy could be envisaged across a wide range of life events, but that in practice referrals are mainly restricted to those situations associated with a more traditional view of the clergy's role and, perhaps, those concerns where doctors regularly find themselves at the limits of their own medical abilities. No reason is evident as to why involvement of clergy should not be across a broader spectrum of concerns and on a greater number of occasions. Almost one quarter of the total respondents conceded they did not think about involving the clergy even when the latter's help might have been useful. Over half of this sample (57.0%) made at least one referral a year, so for them positive contact with the clergy already exists. Other doctors suggested that patients will self-refer and 71.5% of respondents accept that religion has some specific contribution to make to the cure of illness for some patients. In practice, table six shows that the regular referrers and the frequent referrers refer over a wider range of concerns than do other doctors.

Knowing the 'right' clergyman matters across each of the referral groups. This is possibly the key to more doctor-clergy cooperation. 'Would like to meet local clergy' sums up a number of comments on the survey and indicates a need for a practical means of identifying clergy with whom doctors could work confidently. Better communications might accrue from joint meetings, professional lunches and any other opportunities for the professions to meet. Indeed these already happen in some areas, while the Institute of Religion and Medicine, founded in 1964, exists particularly to foster links between doctors and clergy.[10]

More cooperation would inevitably bring its own problems. Doctors may declare they do not limit referral because of a fear of troubling busy clergymen, but greater calls on limited clergy time would be inevitable. Awareness of the possibility of health centres where clergy too would have consulting times could be explored. Such centres already exist, as far afield as Scotland, the north east and the south west of England, building on the pioneering work of Dr Anthony Bird in Birmingham.[11]

One questionable assumption prevailing among general practitioners was the idea that clergy involvement would only be worthwhile for patients who have religious beliefs. A case against this assumption is offered in an editorial in the *Canadian Medical Association Journal* which also justifies the need to treat the whole person.[12] Personal experience, both in hospital and the community, leads the author to challenge the idea that only the religious will benefit. Some people who claim not to be religious are quite open to receiving the ministrations of a clergyman. As they get to know him better their attitude becomes more positive towards sharing a wide range of needs and concerns. Such a claim is supported by the pattern of referrals of the frequent referring group. If they were more confident about using clergy, general practitioners could advise patients who claim not to be religious of the possibilities of benefiting in some circumstances from referral to a clergyman.

The evidence of the survey indicates that the BMA approved statement of 1947 and the recommendation of the RCGP/CCHH working party would be acceptable to the sample of general practitioners surveyed. There is in theory a wide acceptance of the potential benefits of involving the clergy, but equally in practice a reluctance to test them. One respondent commented:

> Not being a Christian myself, I don't feel it my place to initiate such referral, but I'm very aware of the almost universal need for emotional and spiritual support in all sorts of life's problems.

It may be that doctors need to be more aware of the potential for using the clergy alongside other professionals, such as psychologists, psychiatrists, health visitors, social workers and surgeons. This is well accepted in parts of the United States of America where in some medical schools the role of religion in medicine is given a high profile which allows for the clergy to be recognised as representing one piece in the health care jigsaw.[13] The apparent willingness of general practitioners in the UK to consider greater involvement with the clergy suggests that greater cooperation between the two would lead to improvement in patient care within the context of the patient's whole person.

Notes

1. Churches' Council for Health and Healing and the Royal College of General Practitioners, *Whole Person Medicine: a Christian perspective*, London, Churches' Council for Health and Healing, 1989, p. 20.
2. M G Sheldon, 'The Christian approach to whole person medicine,' *Journal of the Royal College of General Practitioners*, 39, 1989, p. 166.
3. Anonymous, 'Medicine and the church,' *British Medical Journal*, 2, 1947, p. 112.
4. R Green, 'Healing and spirituality,' *Practitioner*, 230, 1986, pp. 1087–1093.
5. J H Hunt, 'Religion and the family doctor,' *Journal of the Royal College of General Practitioners*, 18, 1969, pp. 199–206.
6. E E J Martin, 'Healing and the Christian doctor,' *Update*, 38, 1989, pp. 179–184.
7. B Simsen, 'The spiritual dimension,' *Nursing Times*, 84, 1988, pp. 28–30.
8. L Swaffield, 'Religious roots,' *Nursing Times*, 84, 1988, pp. 28–30.
9. P C Pietroni, 'Without religion, science is lame,' *Health Healing*, 9, 1985, p. 5.
10. The Institute of Religion and Medicine has its headquarters at St Marylebone Parish Church, Marylebone Road, London, NW1 5LT.
11. A Bird, *The Search for Health: a response from the inner city*, Birmingham, University of Birmingham, 1981.

12. Anonymous, 'Clergy and physicians,' *Canadian Medical Association Journal*, 99, 1968, pp. 1205–1206.
13. D W Shriver, *Medicine and Religion*, Pittsburgh, Pennsylvania, University of Pittsburgh Press, 1980, pp. 49–76.
14. I would like to thank those general practitioners who took part in this survey. I also wish to express my appreciation to Dr Bernard Farr, Westminster College, Oxford and Dr David Millard, Department of Social and Administrative Studies, University of Oxford.

1.3 Reactions to women in ministry: a survey of English Baptist Church members

Edward C Lehman Jr

The feminist movement which gained so much notoriety in the late 1960s has influenced a variety of institutions. Now, some twenty years later, it has influenced our assumptions about our families, about who is supposed to do various kinds of work, involvement in the political process, the structure of formal education, and many other areas. While the events associated with this impact do not make the headlines as often today as they once did, with the obvious exception of women's involvement in the peace movement, the influence is still being felt.

The feminist movement has also had an impact on religion. It has long been recognised that religious institutions are among the slowest to change. Nevertheless, as new assumptions about appropriate roles of men and women have gained acceptance, some of these changes have spilled over into the churches. This article seeks to deal with one aspect of these changes: the entry of women into the ordained ministry and the reactions of lay church members to them.

To date the picture we have of the feminist movement in the churches is somewhat paradoxical. On the one hand, the movement of women into the ministry has been continuously reported in the media as controversial. Especially in the Church of England, the negotiations associated with this issue have involved intense internal political intrigue and manoeuvring. On the other hand, few lay persons seem to know a great deal about the debates, and even fewer seem to have thought seriously about the idea of having a woman specifically as their pastor. Each time the idea comes up in the context of a congregation searching for a new pastoral leadership, the reaction among the members is virtually always one of surprise, confusion and resentment.

The picture is also paradoxical in terms of the literature available which deals with the entry of women into ministry. The discussions produced by various religious presses included biblical treatises, theological discourses, and ethical discussions, all of which have been highly polemical in tone. But there have been no systematic studies of an empirical nature concerning just what changes are in fact taking place and just how church members are actually dealing with the problem. In short, we have a great deal 'more heat than light'. One thing that was needed was a systematic evaluation of the ways in which lay church members think and feel about the entry of women into the ranks of ordained clergy. This article seeks to report the results of such a study.

An empirical study of lay attitudes

During the academic year 1983–84, the author conducted a nationwide survey of lay church members in England. Four denominations participated in the study: the Baptist Union, the Church of England, the Methodist Church, and the United Reformed Church. The focus of the survey was the range of attitudes of lay church members towards the entry of women into the ordained ministry. One goal of the study was to obtain a sample of church members which would be representative of the entire nation. This was accomplished by means of probability sampling techniques. The sample was drawn in two stages. First, a systematic sample of churches was drawn from the yearbooks of each denomination involved. We drew equal numbers of churches in the three main cultural regions of the country, that is, the North, the Midlands and the South. Second, we telephoned the pastors of these churches and asked them to draw names from their membership lists in a specific way. The goal was to obtain lists of approximately 400 members in each of the four denominations.

The overall level of cooperation was very high. Better than 95% of the pastors cooperated and drew the list of lay members as specified. They also supplied basic information about their congregations. The level of cooperation among the lay church members was also very high. Table one portrays the numbers of members involved in each denomination. The overall response rate to the survey itself was about 91%. The figure for English Baptists was 92%. The regional distribution of the sample conformed almost exactly to the target figures. All told we can place a great deal of confidence in the representativeness of the sample which was ultimately drawn.

Lay perceptions of clergywomen

Social-psychological studies of attitudes have shown fairly conclusively that attitudes are very complex. They often involve many dimensions. This report deals with two such aspects of attitudes: first, the 'cognitive' dimension and second, the 'affective' or 'feeling' dimension.

The cognitive or perceptual dimension involves people's understandings of what the object of the attitude is like. It is a matter of 'head stuff'. It involves what people 'think'. In the case of lay church members' attitudes towards women in ministry, this is a matter of their understanding of 'what clergywomen are like'.

We approached this dimension of the members' attitudes toward clergywomen by examining the extent to which their images of women in ministry tended to take the form of stereotypes. As women have moved into various professions formerly dominated by men, they have typically encountered an identifiable set of stereotyped responses to them. The same stereotypes tend to appear in relation to women entering a variety of professions such as medicine, law, and higher edu-

Table 1: Sample size and rate of response from a survey of lay church members in four denominations in England

denomination	sample N	return N	response %
Church of England	400	347	87
Baptist Union	392	360	92
Methodist Church	390	349	89
United Reformed Church	375	358	95
total	1557	1414	91

Note: Regional distribution of sample: North 32%, Midlands 35%, South 33%.

cation. In general these stereotypes portray women as unreliable workers, overly emotional, unable to handle interpersonal conflict, etc.

Table two contains a listing of the questions that we used for this purpose. The members were asked to indicate the extent to which they thought each statement listed was 'true' or 'correct'. Table two also contains the percentages of church members responding to each question in various ways.

Several patterns are apparent in the table. First, it is clear that there is wide disagreement in the responses to each question. Regardless of which stereotype is involved, some church members tend to view clergywomen in a stereotyped way, while others do not. Second, some stereotypes appear to be held more widely than are others. For example, very few members see clergywomen as likely to change jobs very often. At the other extreme, a large proportion of members view women as temperamentally unfit for the pastorate and as subject to emotional problems because of the cross-pressures of demands from work and home. Slightly more than half of the members view women as basically weak church leaders. Third, nevertheless, on a majority of the stereotyping items, it is but a minority of church members who view women in ministry in such stereotyped terms. Most church members tend to have more open and positive perceptions of women in the role of ordained clergy.

Subdimensions of stereotyping

The next question we asked about these items was the extent to which church members answered each question in complete isolation from the others, or if they answered clusters of questions similarly. A statistical procedure that enables us to enquire about this is called 'factor analysis'. This approach allows us to compare the ways in which people answered each question, and then to identify subsets of questions which members seemed to answer in similar ways. By examining subsets of questions that appear to have been answered in the same way, we have an opportunity to check if those sets of questions have anything in common and thus to identify different themes or dimensions of stereotyping itself.

Table 2: Percent of English Baptist church members agreeing and disagreeing with stereotyped statements about women in ministry

	definitely true	probably true	probably false	definitely false
a woman minister who is married can fulfil her responsibilities as wife and mother just as well as if she were not working full time[1]	13	35	27	25
women ministers are likely to have higher levels of absenteeism from work than men	6	35	37	22
women ministers are likely to change pastorates more often than men	0	16	57	27
being divorced would impair the ministry of a woman more than of a man	13	28	26	33
women who try to be both full-time ministers and also wives and mothers are likely to have emotional problems due to all the demands placed on them	22	53	18	7
the children of women who are full-time ministers are likely to have personal problems due to lack of care and attention	7	33	36	24
most churches today need the strong leadership that a man is better able to give	28	26	21	25
a woman's temperament is just as suited for the pastoral ministry as is a man's[1]	41	37	13	8
a woman minister who openly questions the traditional male language about God will alienate many members of her church	24	46	26	5

Note: 1 Agreement with these items indicates the *non*stereotyped response. Agreement with the other items indicates the stereotyped response.

Table three contains the results of doing a factor analysis on the stereotyping questions. The results indicate that members tended to deal with each of these questions in terms of two basic underlying dimensions. The first and clearest dimension is that of 'role conflict'. That is, there is a subset of items which deal with members' perceptions of whether clergywomen can handle the cross-pressures of job and home. Among the total set of questions, the dominant concern clearly appears to have been this kind of issue: can the woman handle these cross-pressures?

The second dimension contained a subset of questions which have in common the concept of general 'reliability'. These items clearly tended to cluster together. But as an underlying dimension, the 'general reliability' theme was less clearly manifest than the 'role conflict' ethos.

Table 3: Dimensions of stereotyping women in ministry among
Baptist lay church members in England

	cluster on factor 1	cluster on factor 2
role conflict dimension[1]		
cannot handle home/work conflicts	0.72	0.03
children will be maladjusted	0.67	0.32
will have emotional problems	0.58	0.38
temperament not suited for pastorate	0.46	0.22
general reliability dimension		
divorce less acceptable for a woman	0.05	0.65
women are weak leaders	0.45	0.52
women likely to change pastorates	0.22	0.51
women high in absenteeism	0.30	0.41

Note: 1 Accounts for 83% of the explained variance.

The importance of this mode of analysis is two-fold: first, it demonstrates clearly that church members tend to apply underlying criteria to questions of this sort, that is, they do not answer the questions in isolation, and second, it demonstrates that among Baptist lay people the issue of whether the clergywoman will be a reliable church worker is less important to them than whether or not she can handle the conflicts associated with being a wife, mother, and professional church worker.

Preferences for men or women in church roles

The second general component of attitudes which the survey addressed is the 'affective' dimension. This second dimension focuses not on what people think but what they 'feel'. It is less a matter of 'head stuff', and more a matter of 'gut reaction'. In terms of clergywomen, the second dimension focuses not on what church members think of women in ministry, but rather more on their feelings about the idea.

We addressed this dimension of attitudes towards women in ministry by asking the church members about their preferences for men or women in a variety of church positions and functions. These items are listed in table four. For each position and activity on the list, the members were asked to indicate whether they preferred a man for that role, preferred a woman in it, or if it really made no difference to them. Thus the items give us an indication of what church members 'want' in terms of the gender of the person in a variety of clergy roles.

As was the case with the stereotyping questions, a number of patterns are observable in the table. First, the basic dividing line in most church members' minds appears to be between preferring a man on the one hand and the gender of the person making no difference on the other. Very few people indicated that they actually prefer a woman for any of these roles. The major exception to this has to do with the identity of the person from whom one might receive advice about a

Table 4: Percentage of English Baptist Church members indicating preferences for men or women in selected church roles

	prefer a man	no difference	prefer a woman
church positions			
senior or sole pastor	57	43	0
assistant pastor	28	67	5
denominational administrator	24	75	1
foreign missionary	7	87	6
college chaplain	51	49	0
pastoral activities			
performing a baptism	52	47	0
administering the Lord's Supper	35	65	0
preaching a sermon	29	71	0
conducting a funeral	44	56	0
advising you about a personal problem	28	60	12
conducting a business meeting of the church	36	63	1
guiding the church in a building programme	56	43	1
planning the congregation's annual budget	24	73	3
coordinate church staff as senior minister	46	53	1
performing a wedding	52	48	0
reading the scripture lesson during worship	6	91	3
leading a pastoral prayer	9	90	2

personal problem. More people indicated a preference for a woman on that question than on any of the others. However, it is clear that most of these people are themselves women, and this pattern is thus understandable. (Since more than half of the respondents were women, one might ask legitimately why the number indicating a preference for a woman was not greater.)

Second, it is instructive to examine the specific issues on which the most church members indicated that it made no difference if the functionary were male or female. These items are those dealing with reading the scripture lesson during worship, leading a pastoral prayer, and to a slightly lesser extent, being a denominational administrator, the one preaching a sermon, assistant pastor, or the one administering the Lord's Supper.

At the opposite extreme, the questions on which the members indicated the clearest preference for a man included the position of senior or sole pastor and the identity of a person guiding the church in a building programme.

The majority of church members tended to indicate that it made no difference whether the minister was a man or a woman in relation to most of these positions and activities.

Dimensions of gender preference

We subjected the members' answers to these preference questions to a factor analysis in the same way as we analysed the stereotyping questions above. Table five shows the results of this test. The factor analysis indicated that there were basically four dimensions of gender preference operating in the responses to these items.

Table 5: *Dimensions of preferences for men or women in ministerial roles among Baptist church members in England*

	factor 1	factor 2	factor 3	factor 4
sacramental dimension				
funerals	0.82	0.24	0.05	0.14
weddings	0.71	0.22	0.05	0.27
Lord's Supper	0.67	0.33	0.21	0.18
baptism	0.67	0.15	0.12	0.31
(preaching)	0.43	0.40	0.30	0.27
organisational dimension				
budget	0.15	0.72	0.10	0.07
business meeting	0.31	0.65	0.11	0.31
building programme	0.25	0.46	0.04	0.24
denominational administrator	0.16	0.44	0.17	0.33
counselling	0.15	0.34	0.19	0.18
(staff coordinator)	0.31	0.48	0.11	0.46
lay liturgy dimension				
read scripture	0.04	0.13	0.90	0.01
lead prayer	0.15	0.21	0.68	0.14
official authority dimension				
pastor	0.43	0.10	0.13	0.72
chaplain	0.36	0.26	0.01	0.48

The first and dominant dimension may be called a 'sacramental' dimension. That is, the questions which clustered together as the first and dominant factor included items which were largely sacramental or liturgical in nature. What this indicates is that the overriding concern in the minds of lay church members as they articulate preferences for men or women in clergy roles is the effect such women may have on the sacramental and liturgical life of the church.

The subdimension which emerged second in order of importance is the 'organisational' dimension. The items which clustered together on this component tend to be questions dealing with issues associated with running the organisational machinery of the congregation and the churches. In the minds of lay church members, their preferences for men or women for these activities are a 'different matter' from their preferences concerning liturgical roles.

The third dimension may be seen as a possible exception to the statement immediately above. That is, two items which are clearly liturgical in nature did not cluster with the first dimension but rather constituted a third factor in and of themselves. These two items are reading scripture and leading prayer during worship services. I have chosen to call these the 'lay liturgy dimension'.

The fourth and final factor is noteworthy, because it contains the position of senior or sole pastor. That item, combined with the question of the chaplaincy, constitutes the fourth dimension to come out of the factor analysis. I have chosen to label it the 'official authority' dimension, because of the presence of the senior pastor item and because of the few other questions which actually were correlated with it fairly highly. The position of 'staff coordinator' actually placed fairly strongly on this fourth factor (see table five), as did the position of 'denominational administrator', 'running a business meeting', and 'performing a baptism'. Most of these items also share the property of 'church authority'. What this pattern indicates is that, while the sacramental and organisational criteria for preferring men or women in various roles were obviously clearer and more primary in the minds of the lay members, their preference for a man or a woman in a position of authority – especially that of pastor – is again 'another matter'. The authority component stands out as a separate issue from the others. While it is not primary in the minds of the members, it is sufficiently important to stand relatively alone.

Willingness to accept a woman

At another point on the questionnaire, the church members in the survey were asked if they thought the members of their church would accept a qualified woman minister if she had been recommended to the congregation by the deacons. About 58% of the members indicated that they thought others in their congregation would accept such a person. We then asked them if they, themselves, would be willing to accept such a woman. Fully 74% indicated 'yes'. If a woman were recommended to the congregation by the deacons, about three-fourths of the laypersons were prepared to accept the idea.

This item was as close as we could get to a question about what members would actually do. How would they act? Would they accept the recommendation of a woman or not? Clearly most members would respond positively.

Comparisons with other denominations

With these patterns of receptivity amongst Baptist laypersons now before us, it is interesting to note how Baptist church members compare with members of other denominations participating in the study. Table six contains such comparisons for several dimensions of receptivity discussed above. Examination of the percentages in the table indicates several patterns in the responses. First, the denomination whose members tend to be the most resistant to women in ministry is the Church of England. These person tend to stereotype clergywomen the most, to prefer men in ministerial roles the most, and to be willing to accept a woman as priest the least. At the other extreme, members of United Reformed congregations tend to be the most receptive.

Table 6: *Comparison of Baptist church members with members of other denominations on selected indicators of receptivity to women in ministry*

	Anglican	Baptist	Methodist	URC
per cent willing to accept a qualified woman minister as pastor	61	74	93	92
per cent saying a woman minister can handle cross pressures of job and home[1]	54	48	60	67
per cent saying clergywomen who are also wives and mothers are *not* likely to have emotional problems[2]	29	24	27	36
per cent saying a woman's temperament is equally well suited for pastoral ministry[1]	76	79	89	89
per cent saying women equally able to provide strong church leadership[2]	44	45	66	64
per cent *not* preferring a man for senior pastor or parish priest[3]	38	43	58	65
per cent *not* preferring a man for assistant pastor[3]	63	73	90	88
per cent *not* preferring a man for administering the Lord's Supper[3]	51	65	77	80
per cent *not* preferring a man for preaching a sermon[3]	73	71	84	86
per cent *not* preferring a man for conducting a business meeting of the church[3]	71	64	77	81

Notes: 1 responding either 'definitely' or 'probably' true
       2 responding either 'definitely' or 'probably' so
       3 responding either 'no difference' or 'prefer a woman'

Second, the members of the four denominations tend to cluster into two groupings of two denominations each in terms of liberal/conservative tendencies. The Baptists tend to resemble the Anglicans in level of receptivity, whilst the Methodists compare favourably to the URC members. The Anglicans and Baptists constitute the more resistant denominations, and the Methodists and URC members comprise the more receptive bodies. There are greater differences in response patterns between these groupings than within them.

Patterns of receptivity: conclusions

The analysis of the survey data to this point will support the following generalisations:

a. church members are highly divided in their perceptions of women in ministry;
b. the main criterion underlying these differences in tendency to stereotype clergywomen appears to be whether women in ministry can handle the role conflicts associated with being working wives and mothers;

c. lay church members differ widely in the extent to which they actually prefer a man in a variety of church positions and activities;

d. church members' preferences for men or women in clergy roles are not monolithic;

e. to some extent, regardless of members' tendencies to stereotype women or to prefer a man in clergy roles, nearly three-fourths of the members indicated that in an appropriate search for pastoral leadership they would accept a qualified woman as pastor if she were recommended to the congregation by the deacons;

f. Baptist laypersons tend to resemble the Anglicans in their relatively conservative response to women in ministry, while the Methodists and URC members resemble each other in their greater willingness to accept women as ordained clergy.

Factors related to acceptance of women

The concluding section of this report focuses on explaining the differences in receptivity to women in ministry that we have described so far. The question now concerns why members differ in these ways. Is there any way in which we can identify church members who are more or less favourably disposed to the idea of women in the ministry? One approach to answering this kind of question is to compare the members' levels of receptivity to clergywomen with other characteristics that they manifest. We shall use that approach in the remainder of this report.

Demographic correlates

A number of observers (see for example, Allport, 1958) of various forms of prejudice in western society have noted that certain types of individuals are more or less predisposed toward prejudiced responses to others. With regard to 'sexism', the first of these correlates has to do with the sex of the respondent. As concerns sexism in general, other research (for example, Dempewolff, 1974) has indicated that males tend to be more prejudiced than females. Analysis of these data indicates a similar pattern. As shown in table seven, more females indicated a willingness to accept a woman as pastor than did males.

The second possible correlate concerns chronological age. In a number of previous studies (Lehman, 1981a; 1985a), prejudice and discrimination has been found to be characteristic more of older people than of younger ones. Such is not the case in our data from Baptist church members, however. The analysis of these data indicate that older church members tend to be more receptive than younger ones. This is a departure from the pattern that is

Table 7: *Percentage of English Baptist church members indicating they would accept a woman as pastor, compared with selected individual characteristics*

	demographic traits %		religiosity %	RO=1#	RO=2	RO=3	RO=4
by sex	males = 69 females = 78	by church attendance:	nearly every week = 73 once/twice a month = 100 few times per year = 100 rarely/never = 100				
by marital status: NS*	single = 80 married = 73 widowed = 74 sep/div = 57	by frequency of saying grace:	daily = 62 weekly = 72 special occasions = 82 never = 89				
by age:	younger = more opposed older = more receptive (correlation = .20)	by religious ideology:	importance of: worshipping community helping individuals traditional evangelism social reform	74 90 66 0	69 81 69 100	91 67 79 89	100(ns) 86 93 71
by formal education NS*	less than 'O' = 76 'O' levels = 74 6th form, no 'A' = 85 'A' levels = 73 univ. or polyt. = 67 post grad. = 68						
by type of occupation:	unstable = 88 unskilled blue collar = 81 skilled blue collar = 79 clerical/sales = 68 lo prof/mgrl = 72 hi prof/mgrl = 73						
by family income: (in thousands of pounds)	under £3 = 80 £3 - £6 = 81 £6 - £9 = 67 £12 - £15 = 58 over £15 = 67						

Notes: * NS indicates statistically *non*-significant differences.   # RO stands for 'rank order'.

typically found. (At this point we do not know why this pattern emerged.)

The third factor that is commonly taken into account is social class (Carroll, *et al.*, 1983; Lehman, 1979; 1985a). Most of the time in survey research social class is indicated by the respondents' education, occupation, and income. The survey questionnaire included questions dealing with those concepts. When we compare those answers to the answers on the question of whether or not they will accept the clergy-women, the results tend not to support patterns found in other research. That is, people in occupations characterised by a low degree of skill, power, and autonomy tend to be more accepting of women in ministry than those in high status occupations. The differences are not great, but they are real. The same pattern applied to family income. Members in families with low incomes tend to be more receptive of women in ministry than are those from families with high incomes. The results involving differences in formal education were inconclusive. That is, there was no clear indication that differences in formal education were predictive of differences in receptivity toward women in ministry.

We also asked the respondents about their marital status. This factor, like education, turned out to be unrelated to differences in attitude toward clergywomen.

Differences in religious commitment

Another possible factor determining attitudes toward women in the ministry is individual religiosity. We are talking, after all, about attitudes toward 'religious' leaders. There has also been a good deal of theological discourse on the issue. Do these data indicate that the religious factor makes any difference?

Table seven also contains the results of comparing differences in willingness to accept a woman as pastor and three indicators of differences in individual religious commitment. They are church attendance, frequency of praying at meals, and religious ideology. The measure of church attendance was highly skewed. That is, the survey turned up relatively few cases of low ritual involvement in church. Nevertheless, even those skewed patterns appear to be related to differences in receptivity to clergywomen. Members who report attending church every week were less inclined to accept a woman as pastor than were people who tend to attend church less frequently. In this case, degree of religious involvement is negatively related to acceptance of women in ministry. The more often people go to church, the less receptive they are to clergywomen.

A similar pattern emerged in the analysis of frequency of saying grace. As shown in Table seven, the more frequently people prayed at meals, the less likely they were to report accepting women as pastor. Combining this pattern with that involving church attendance (above), the picture emerges in which the more traditionally religious the member is, the less likely that person is to accept a woman as pastor. There appears to be something about traditional religious involvement that does not mix well with acceptance of clergywomen.

The third aspect of religious commitment that we looked at was religious ideology. The indicator of these differences was a set of questions which asked the church member to indicate which of four possible basic purposes of the church they thought was the most important (see table seven). They then were asked to indicate which of the remaining three was next in importance, then the next, and finally the least important. That is, we asked each member to rank-order four possible purposes of the church.

The results of this analysis indicate that the relative ranking of three of the four purposes of the church is predictive of receptivity towards women in ministry. People who ranked traditional evangelism high in importance tended to oppose women in ministry. On the other hand, people who ranked social reform high as a purpose of the church tended to accept women as pastors. People who viewed the church as working to help individuals who cannot help themselves also tended to be more in favour of clergywomen than did those who thought this was not important for the church to be doing. The extent to which the church as the worshipping community was considered important turned out to be unrelated to receptivity to clergywomen. Even though the worshipping community was listed as the most important purpose of the church by more people than anything else, this emphasis turned out to be not predictive of receptivity toward clergywomen. (Perhaps this purpose of the church is so commonplace as to be taken for granted and of little predictive utility.)

We also asked the lay members if they had ever known a woman minister. We thought perhaps those who had known a woman in the role of clergy would be more receptive to the idea than those who had not had such an experience. The data in table eight, however, indicate that such is not the case. There were no statistically significant differences in receptivity between those who had known a woman minister and those who had not. (See Lehman, 1985a, for other evidence and discussion of this point.)

Church characteristics

The next approach was to think not in terms of individual differences but rather in terms of differences between types of congregations. The question was whether people in one type of church would be more inclined to accept a woman as pastor than those in another type of congregation. The data in table eight indicate that such is indeed the case. The first such factor is community size. Members from churches located in large cities tend to be less willing to accept a woman as pastor than are those whose congregations are located in smaller places.

Table 8: Percentage of English Baptist Church members saying they would accept a woman pastor, compared with direct contact, church characteristics, and perceived tension

by contact		
ever known a woman minister?	yes	= 74
NS*	no	= 72
by church characteristics:		
community size:	large city	= 63
	small city	= 80
	small town	= 78
	village/rural	= 80
size of congregation:	200–500	= 63
	100–199	= 61
	50–99	= 79
	25–49	= 75
	less than 25	= 93
membership trend:	growing faster than community	= 54
	growing, but not that fast	= 71
	holding its own	= 77
	declining	= 90
budget trend:	increasing faster than inflation	= 68
	keeping up with inflation	= 74
	declining re: inflation	= 85
region of the country:	North	= 68
	Midlands	= 81
	South	= 73
by perceived tension:		
would woman candidate create tension?	yes	= 55
	no	= 96
how concerned over tension?	very	= 68
	slightly	= 87
	not very	= 83
	not at all	= 90

Note: *NS indicates statistically *non*-significant differences.

Size of congregation itself also turned out to be predictive of attitudinal differences. Members of small congregations tended to be more willing to accept a woman as pastor than were members of large churches. This pattern applied especially to members of very small churches.

The next factor concerned not absolute size but rather the trend in size of churches. Would it make any difference if a church were growing or declining? Again, the data in table eight indicate that the membership trend of the congregation is indeed predictive of receptivity to women in ministry. Members of declining churches tend to be more willing to accept a woman as pastor than are members of stable and growing churches. The same pattern applies to trends in the budget. Members of churches whose budgets are declining were more inclined to accept a woman as pastor than were those in churches which were prospering.

There were also some differences in receptivity with regard to the regional location of the church. Members of churches located in the Midlands tended to be the most receptive of women in ministry. Members of churches located in the North were the least willing to accept a woman as pastor. Evidently there is something in these regional subcultures which relates to these kinds of attitudinal differences.

Finally, we wanted to know if the way in which members expected others to react to women in ministry would be predictive of their own response. Other research in the United States (Carroll *et al.*, 1983; Lehman, 1981b; 1985a) has indicated that where the introduction of a woman is expected to introduce controversy and perhaps result in schism, receptivity to women as pastor is lower than where the member does not expect those consequences.

These patterns also emerged in this study (see table eight). Members who thought a woman candidate would create tension in their congregations were far less likely to indicate acceptance of a woman as pastor than were those who did not expect such tensions. The data in table eight also indicates that the more members were concerned about such tensions, the more likely they were to oppose having a woman as pastor.

Composite portraits

From this list of correlates, we are now in a position to extract a 'composite portrait' of the church member who is likely to accept a woman as pastor and the one who is not. The member who is likely to accept readily a woman as pastor is an older female whose family has relatively little income and whose members work in occupations involving little skill and prestige. She does not attend church as often as many of her neighbours, and she does not say grace at meals very often either. She does not think much of traditional evangelism. Instead she thinks the churches ought to be heavily involved in helping those who cannot help themselves and in trying to reform the structures of society. She is a member of a church located in a rather small community. Her congregation also tends to be rather small and has been struggling for some time. It tends to be in a pattern of losing members and declining financial resources. The church is located in the Midlands. She does not think that the introduction of a woman's name as a candidate in her congregation would create much tension, and she would not be unduly concerned even if it did.

By contrast the member who is likely to oppose women in ministry is a younger male who earns a fairly high income by working in a relatively high status occupation. He attends church quite often and says grace before most meals. He thinks the church should be heavily involved in evangelism, but he does not think much of programmes of social reform or helping the helpless. His church is located in a large city, and his congregation is quite large. It has been growing in relation to the community and its budget has been at least keeping up with inflation over the last several years. His church is located in the North. He is convinced that if a woman were introduced as a candidate for the pastorate of his church, it would create a great deal of tension in the congregation. This tension would make him very concerned about the future of the local church.

Predicting other dimensions of receptivity

Analysis of the survey data indicated that these same correlates of 'accepting a woman as pastor' tended also to be predictive of differences in stereotyping and preferences for men in clergy roles. With minor exceptions here and there, the same factors as those listed above tended to predict differences in stereotyping and in gender preferences for clergy roles.

The importance of organisational threat

Some of the patterns described above make sense when viewed from the perspective of the fact that churches are fragile voluntary organisations. In most instances they are not able to coerce their members into compliance with the wishes of leaders. Instead, members of congregations must be persuaded and cajoled into accepting structural and cultural innovations. The introduction of women into the ordained ministry is clearly such an innovation, and it is equally clear that it has the potential for generating controversy.

This pattern is especially evident in relation to the church characteristics which are associated with receptivity to clergywomen. Acceptance of women in ministry is associated with being in a small congregation whose membership roles and budgets are steadily shrinking and which is located away from the bustling and interesting large city. Why are members in this kind of church more prepared to accept a woman as pastor? One answer is clear. They have to. Members of small struggling churches do not have the organisational or financial resources with which to be choosy about pastoral leadership. They are in no position to complain. They must take what comes along. When the choice before them is between having either 'no pastor at all' or a 'poorly qualified pastor' on the one hand, and taking a non-traditional pastor such as a woman on the other, the choice becomes clear. They would rather have the qualified woman than the alternative.

This pattern exists because most church members will do almost anything to keep from having to close their church doors. Most members love the little communities of which they are a part and will work hard to keep them going. They will 'even take a woman'.

The same variable accounts for the relationships involving perception of tension in the congregation. Members who perceive a woman's candidacy as creating tension tend to prefer not to have a woman. The more this tension gives them concern about the future of their congregation, the less likely they are to accept a woman as pastor. The factor which lay beneath this set of responses is the same – concern for the viability of the congregation. If the congregation appears to be threatened by a change, members prefer to avoid that change. If the change is not threatening, even though it may be counter-attitudinal, they are more likely to accept it.

A similar interpretation may be placed on some of the ways in which religious commitment was related to acceptance of a woman as pastor. The more personal investment they have in their religious life, the less likely they are to be willing to risk change which could be disruptive of familiar patterns.

These patterns very closely resemble similar relationships observed among church members in the United States (Carroll *et al.*, 1983; Lehman, 1981b; 1985a). The more committed members were to their congregation, the less likely they were to be willing to accept a woman as pastor. The more their congregation was stable or growing, the less need they had to take innovation seriously, and the more they tended to oppose accepting a woman as pastor. Thus in two different societies involving the same denomination, very similar patterns have emerged. It appears that the factor or organisational concerns is a very important one concerning reactions to similar issues in both societies. If ways of addressing these organisational concerns cannot be developed it may become difficult to get lay church members to accept innovations such as the introduction of women into the pastoral ministry, no matter how well those changes are buttressed with theological argument and biblical scholarship. Most church members live out their religious life within their local congregation. That little community is what matters the most. The broader Christian community beyond it usually matters much less. Convincing them that accepting female leadership will benefit that little community is probably one of the major keys to getting lay church members to accept women in pastoral ministry. Research in the United States indicates that the 'horror stories' of congregational decline associated with the introduction of a woman as pastor simply do not materialise once she is on the scene (Lehman, 1985a; Royle, 1982). Similar studies in England will probably yield the same results – showing that congregations work as well under the pastoral leadership of a woman as of a man.

References

Adams, D W (1984) 'Parishioners' image of the ideal head of staff: a major impediment to equal opportunity for clergywomen in the United Presbyterian Church,' mimeographed.

Allport, G W (1958) *The Nature of Prejudice*, Garden City, New York, Doubleday and Company.

Beck, M (1978) 'Pluralist theory and church policy positions on racial and sexual equality,' *Sociological Analysis*, 39, pp. 338–350.

Bock, E W (1967) 'The female clergy: a case of professional marginality,' *American Journal of Sociology*, 27, pp. 531–539.

Carroll, J W, Hargrove, B and Lummis, A (1983) *Women of the Cloth*, New York, Harper and Row.

Charlton, J (1978) 'Women entering the ordained ministry: contradictions and dilemmas of status,' paper presented at the annual meeting of the Society for the Scientific Study of Religion, Hartford, Connecticut.

Colman, P M and Conrad, A D (1978) *Resource Book for Placement, Acceptance and Support of Clergywomen*, New York, Office for Women in Ministry, The Vocation Agency, United Presbyterian Church.

Commission on Women in Ministry (1976) *A Resource Guide for Women in Seminary*, New York, National Council of Churches.

Daly, M (1975) *The Church and the Second Sex*, New York, Harper and Row.

Dempewolff, J A (1974) 'Some correlates of feminism,' *Psychological Reports*, 34, pp. 671–676.

Driedger, L (1974) 'Doctrinal belief: a major factor in the differential perception of social issues,' *The Sociological Quarterly*, 15, pp. 66–80.

Gorsuch, R L and Aleshire, D (1974) 'Christian faith and ethnic prejudice: a review and interpretation of research,' *Journal for the Scientific Study of Religion*, 13, pp. 281–307.

Hacker, H M (1951) 'Women as a minority group,' *Social Forces*, 30, pp. 60–69.

Hale, H, King, M and Jones, D (1980) *New Witnesses: United Methodist Clergywomen*, Nashville, Board of Higher Education and Ministry.

Hale, H, King, M and Jones, D (1985) *Clergywomen: problems and satisfactions*, Lima, Ohio, Fairway Press.

Jacquet, C H Jr (1973) *The Status of Women in Various Constituent Bodies of the National Council of Churches: results of an enquiry*, New York, National Council of Churches.

Jacquet, C H Jr (1978) *Women Ministers in 1977: a report*, New York, National Council of Churches.

Jones, A R Jr and Taylor, L (1971) 'Differential recruitment of female professionals: a case study of clergywomen,' in A Theodore (ed.), *The Professional Woman*, Cambridge, Massachusetts, Schenkman.

Kasarda, J D and Janowitz, M (1974) 'Community attachment in mass society,' *American Sociological Review*, 39, pp. 328–339.

Klausner, S Z, (1984) 'Support for women rabbis is associated with declining home observance: why?' paper presented at annual meeting of Association for the Sociology of Religion, San Antonio.

Lehman, E C Jr (1979) *Project SWIM: a study of women in ministry*, a research report to the Ministers Council, American Baptist Churches, Valley Forge, Pennsylvania.

Lehman, E C Jr (1980) 'Placement of men and women in the ministry,' *Review of Religious Research*, 22, pp. 18–40.

Lehman, E C Jr (1981a) 'Patterns of lay resistance to women in ministry,' *Sociological Analysis*, 41, pp. 317–338.

Lehman, E C Jr (1981b) 'Organizational resistance to women in ministry,' *Sociological Analysis*, 41, pp. 101–118.

Lehman, E C Jr (1982) 'Changing receptivity to clergywomen: an application of the contact hypothesis,' paper presented at annual meeting of Association for the Sociology of Religion, Providence, Rhode Island.

Lehman, E C Jr (1984) *Women Clergy in England: the church members' response*, Brockport, New York.

Lehman, E C Jr (1985a) *Women Clergy: breaking through gender barriers*, New Brunswick, Transaction Publishers.

Lehman, E C Jr (1985b) 'Localism and sexism: do cosmopolitans do it better?' paper presented at annual meeting of Association for the Sociology of Religion, Washington DC.

Nason-Clark, N (1985) 'The sexual division of labour in British Protestant churches: an empirical study of the attitudes of clergy,' paper presented at annual meeting of Association for the Sociology of Religion, Wahsington DC.

Peek, C W and Brown, S (1980) 'Sex prejudice among white Protestants: like or unlike ethnic prejudice?' *Social Forces*, 59, pp. 169–285.

Peterson, L R and Takayama, K P (1984) 'Community and commitment among Catholics: a test of local/cosmopolitan theory,' *Sociological Quarterly*, 25, pp. 92–112.

Petty, R and Cacioppo, J T (1981) *Attitudes and Persuasion: classic and contemporary approaches*, Dubuque, Iowa, William C Brown.

Roof, W C (1978) *Community and Commitment: religious plausibility in a liberal Protestant church*, New York, Elsevier.

Royle, M H (1982) 'Women pastors: what happens after placement?' *Review of Religious Research*, 24, pp. 116–126.

Ruether, R R (1974) *Religion and Sexism: images of women in the Jewish and Christian tradition*, New York, Simon and Schuster.

Russell, L M (ed.) (1976) *The Liberating Word: a guide to non-sexist interpretation of the bible*, Philadelphia, Westminster.

Steward, M S, Steward, D S and Dary, J (1979) 'Women who choose a man's career: a study of women in ministry,' mimeographed.

Stromberg, A H and Harkess S (eds) (1978) '*Women working: theories and facts in perspective*, Palo Alto, California, Mayfield Publishing Company.

Tedin, K L (1978) 'Religious preference and pro-anti activism on the equal rights amendment issue,' *Pacific Sociological Review*, 21, pp. 55–56.

Weidman, J L (ed.) (1985) *Women Ministers: how women are redefining traditional roles*, New York, Harper and Row.

2. Role preferences

This chapter turns attention from the way in which the laity perceive the role of the clergy to the way in which ordained clergy perceive their own role. Psychological research in this area is illustrated by two different perspectives.

In the first article in this section, Alan Bryman's study enables two important comparisons to be made in interpreting the ways in which clergy understand their role. The first comparison is between two different denominations, namely Church of England clergy and Methodist ministers. The second comparison is between two different generations of clergy, studied in 1971–1972 and in 1985. The findings are based on 213 Anglicans and 100 Methodists in 1971–1972 and on 177 Anglicans and 68 Methodists in 1985.

Professor Alan Bryman is Professor of Social Research in the Department of Social Sciences at Loughborough University, Loughborough, England. This article was first published in *Sociology* in 1989.

In the second article, Leslie J Francis and Raymond Rodger explore the contribution made by individual differences in personality to role prioritisation, role influences, role conflict and dissatisfaction with ministry, among a sample of 170 male full-time stipendiary parochial clergy within the Church of England. Their data demonstrate that Eysenck's three major dimensions of personality (extraversion, neuroticism and psychoticism) are able to account for significant variations in all these key areas of ministry performance and assessment.

The Revd Professor Leslie J Francis is D J James Professor of Pastoral Theology at Trinity College, Carmarthen, and St David's University College, Lampeter, Wales. The Revd Canon Raymond Rodger is Personal Assistant to the Bishop of Lincoln, England. A slightly shorter form of this article was first published in *Personality and Individual Differences* in 1994.

2.1 The value of re-studies in sociology: the case of clergy and ministers, 1971 to 1985

Alan Bryman

This article reports some of the results deriving from a partial re-study of an investigation of the religious functionary in England conducted in the early 1970s by Ranson, Bryman and Hinings (1977). The bulk of the data collected for the original research was reported in a book, *Clergy, Ministers and Priests*, a title which reflected the researchers' empirical focus upon Church of England clergy, Methodist ministers, and Roman Catholic priests. The re-study reported below, which was carried out in 1985, is partial in at least three senses. First, data were only collected on clergy and ministers. Second, the re-study was conducted on far fewer respondents than was its predecessor. Precise details regarding these two points will be supplied below. Third, the re-study did not encompass all of the topics addressed in the original study, although the vast majority were re-examined.

In reporting the results of this research, the article has two chief objectives. Most obviously, there will be an attempt to chart some changes in the beliefs and attitudes of clergy and ministers. In particular, data relating to their views of their role and that of the church will be emphasised in the discussion. In addition, the article will seek to raise some methodological questions about the significance of change for sociological 'knowledge' and about the ways in which change may or may not be manifested.

Research on religious organisations

The first of this article's avowed aims – the presentation of data on the views of clergy and ministers regarding the church and their role – is potentially significant in view of sociologists' relative uninterest in the mainstream churches which nonetheless continue to have a fair degree of influence in national life and to attract a considerable following. Since the publication of *Clergy, Ministers and Priests* in 1977, there have been very few sociological studies of the church and the religious functionary.[1] Towler and Coxon (1979) and Aldridge (1986) are clear exceptions, though the former derives from research conducted before the investigations which formed the basis of *Clergy, Ministers and Priests* were underway. This state of affairs contrasts sharply with the substantial output associated with research on religious sects and cults. While research in the USA on ministers in various denominations has offset this trend to a certain degree (Mills, 1985), the emphasis in research on religious organisations still tends to be placed on cults and sects. For example, in his review of research on religious organisations, Beckford (1985a, p. 131) has remarked that: 'Studies of religious organisations in the 1970s and early 1980s have been dominated by considerations of a wide variety of new, minority and alternative religious movements.'

One can only speculate about the reasons for the relative inattention to the mainstream churches, especially in Britain. Demerath (1967, p. 83) remarked that sects are more 'exotic and erotic' than churches and hence more attractive objects of study. Further, sects and cults bespeak innovation and are often immersed in controversy (Beckford, 1985b), characteristics which almost certainly heighten their appeal. By contrast, mainstream churches may appear stodgy and inward-looking. There is little doubt that the influence of the churches continues to decline, but this influence has not dwindled to such a degree that the relative neglect by sociologists in Britain can be fully warranted. It is in this context that the research reported in this article will be addressed – to provide data relating to a neglected institution. Equally, in reporting the fruits of a re-study, the extent to which the churches and the views of their clergy and ministers are static or dynamic can be addressed. The changes which are reported reflect the ways in which religious functionaries and their churches respond to external and internal changes (such as secularisation and bureaucratisation respectively).

The manifestation of change: methodological issues

What are we looking for when we seek to gauge change? The research reported in this article derives from postal questionnaire surveys of clergy and ministers in which roughly identical instruments were administered to comparable samples in the early 1970s and in 1985. Changes over time are bound to be of interest when such a re-study is conducted, but the question of *what* it is that is being looked for when searching for evidence of change constitutes a methodological issue that is more complex than it appears to be at first glance. In other words, what kinds of findings should be taken as evidence of change? In fact, there are few methodological rules of thumb to assist the researcher in this connection.

In presenting the findings deriving from this research, three particular aspects of change will be distinguished: distributional, associational and constructional facets of change. These three aspects do not exhaust the full range that might be envisioned, but they constitute a useful heuristic.[2] First, distributional change is taken to refer to a clearly discernible change in the relative distribution of people in relation to different categories of a particular variable. This is the most obvious level of analysis when one seeks to gauge the amount of change manifested between two waves of observations. It results in statements to the effect that 'in time 1, 70% of Xs feel that a is the case, whereas in time 2, only 35% of Xs feel that a is the case; in time 2, Xs are more likely to feel that b is the case (45%)'.

Associational change refers to changes in the nature of, or the extent of, a relationship between two variables. Distributional change focuses upon one variable at a time, but precisely because change may occur in a variable the possibility of a change in the character of its relationship with other variables may change (especially since these other variables may themselves have changed over time).

Finally, constructional change refers to the possibility of a change in the nature and structure of the connection between a theoretical construct and its empirical indicators. Where a particular concept is being measured with a battery of indicators, its underlying factor structure may shift over time.[3]

These three aspects of change will form the basis for the presentation of the results below. Between them – to anticipate the discussion at the end of this article somewhat – these facets of change raise the spectre of the degree of consistency of sociological findings over time, and hence the degree to which such findings are at least in part historically specific.

Sampling

The fieldwork which provided the data for *Clergy, Ministers and Priests* was conducted over the years 1971 to 1973. Readers should consult *Clergy, Ministers and Priests* for full details regarding sampling and research instruments employed. For each of the three churches, samples of religious functionaries were selected from three administrative units. Thus, samples were drawn from three Church of England dioceses, three Methodist districts, and three Roman Catholic dioceses (that is, nine samples in total). While the three administrative units of each church were selected to reflect size and rural-urban coverage, the geographical coverage of one unit for each of the three churches coincided to a substantial degree. In other words, one Anglican diocese, one Methodist district, and one Roman Catholic diocese covered similar territory. It was these three units that it was intended to re-study. Unfortunately, it became apparent at an early juncture that access to the Roman Catholic diocese was unlikely to be forthcoming (since the author's correspondence was not answered), so the re-study is only of the Anglican clergy and Methodist ministers. In *Clergy, Ministers and Priests*, data deriving from the three samples for each church was aggregated. In order to provide direct comparisons with the specific diocese and district in question (rather than the aggregated data), information was culled from reports to the administrative units which the authors of *Clergy, Ministers and Priests* had prepared. The Church of England and Methodist administrative units which have been re-studied will be referred to as AnglDioc and

MethDist respectively. For one or two items of information, files had to be examined so that the necessary information could be gleaned for direct comparison with the 1985 re-study. However, there are two instances (both cross-tabulations of two variables) where the original results relating to AnglDioc and MethDist respectively are no longer available; they are only available in the aggregated form (that is, together with the two other dioceses and districts) in which they were presented in *Clergy, Ministers and Priests*.[4] This is not as great a limitation as it might appear. Although dioceses and districts differ from each other somewhat in their theological orientation (the former possibly more so), a major conclusion of *Clergy, Ministers and Priests* was that interdenominational differences were far more pronounced than were intradenominational differences. The two instances in which the aggregate data are employed will be clearly indicated below.

Thus far, the author has been referring to the samples that were drawn in this and the earlier research. It is not strictly accurate to refer to the respondents as constituting 'samples', because all clergy and ministers in AnglDioc and MethDist were sent questionnaires (in 1971 and 1972 respectively) in the original research. Similarly, in the re-study all clergy and ministers were sent questionnaires.[5]

Distributional change

The data presented in this section relates to the extent to which there have been clear changes in regard to particular variables. In dealing with the question of how far the views of clergy and ministers have changed over the period in question, variables which were emphasised in *Clergy, Ministers and Priests* will provide the focus for the present discussion. Where appropriate, data relating to both clergy and ministers will be presented side-by-side in the tables.

Conception of church: In *Clergy, Ministers and Priests* the authors were concerned to delineate the extent to which respondents conceptualised their church as 'having a responsibility to the whole population of an area regardless of people's religious or other affiliations' or as 'one denomination among many'. The data presented in table one do not indicate a profound shift in the views of clergy and ministers about the nature of their respective churches. The most striking change is that Methodist ministers are more likely to view their church as one denomination among many than in 1972, in that 62.7% view it in this way as against 37% in the initial research (that is, including those classified under 'both'). This change should not be exaggerated in that the bulk of this increase seems to derive from a smaller proportion classifying themselves as 'other' in the re-study. The authors of *Clergy, Ministers and Priests* pointed out that among those ministers classified as 'other' in 1972, a large proportion 'were merely elaborating the overriding denominational sentiment' (p. 48), citing annotated remarks written on the questionnaires as evidence. Thus, the shift towards a denomina-

Table 1: Conception of church

| | AnglDioc | | MethDist | |
	1971 %	1985 %	1972 %	1985 %
one denomination among many	10.8	13.0	27.0	40.3
special responsibility to the whole population of an area regardless of people's religious or other affiliations	71.2	60.5	26.0	17.9
both statements	16.5	20.3	10.0	22.4
other	1.4	6.2	37.0	19.4
	(N = 171)		(N = 67)	

tional view of the church implied by the data presented in table one may be less than is implied by the large percentage increase.

Conception of role: At the time of the initial research there was considerable discussion among sociologists of the role uncertainty from which many clergy were believed to be suffering (for example, Towler, 1969). The prime mover behind this uncertainty was deemed to be the continuing secularisation of the environing society which engendered doubt about the role of the religious professional. In addition, the growing bureaucratisation of the churches was seen as imposing a new set of demands on the clergy for which (in the view of many commentators) they were poorly trained and disinclined to meet. This view was shared by a number of commentators within the church. Leslie Paul, the author of an influential report on the state of the Church of England in the 1960s, remarked in a later work: 'there is much confusion in the minds at any rate of Church of England clergy about the roles they should play' (Paul 1973, p. 226). There is little doubt that the processes of secularisation and bureaucratisation have continued. The latter trend is likely to have had a more profound impact in the Church of England as a result of synodical government. The initial research was conducted shortly after the introduction of synodical government in 1970 and many commentators have argued that bureaucracy within the church has intensified in the succeeding years (for example, Moore, 1986). As regards secularisation, when a national sample of Anglican clergy was asked in 1985 about the degree of seriousness of 39 potential problems for the church in each clergyman's area, 'secularisation of the surrounding culture and people' was the third most frequently mentioned item by 42% of respondents (Heald and Rhodes, 1986). In addition, 'feeling of irrelevance of the church to the world around' was mentioned by 38%. Many commentators believe that role uncertainty is still pervasive. In 1983, the contributor to the preface of *Crockford's Clerical Directory* wrote of 'a crisis of confidence in the hearts of many ordained ministers who work hard but are not sure that it is work they should be doing' (p. xxiii).[6]

The issue of role uncertainty was not directly addressed by the authors of *Clergy, Ministers and Priests*, but they sought to contribute to the general issue through an examination of respondents' conceptions of their roles (pp. 61–2). Following the early leads of writers like Blizzard (1956) and Daniel (1967), the initial study sought to gain some leverage on the issue of how respondents viewed their role by asking them to rank the relative importance they attached to each of seven tasks (p. 62):

> the ordained minister as *administrator* (of church affairs); as *celebrant* (of sacraments and services); as *leader* (of the local community); as *preacher* (of the word); as *official* (of the church); as *pastor* (and father of the congregation); and as *counsellor* (adviser and confessor).

The respondents scored each task on a range from 1 (first priority) to 7 (lowest priority). The mean rank for each role was computed. When administering this question to Methodist ministers the term 'representative' was used instead of 'official', as this was deemed to be a more apt term for the Methodist tradition. The analyses of the data for the initial research and the re-study for the diocese and district in question are reported in table two. Note that a larger arithmetic mean indicates a lower priority.

For the Anglican clergy, the general pattern of the rankings has not changed at all between the two studies. The means are very similar too, except that the importance of the task of counsellor has waned in the second study, a point which will be taken up again below. There is much more pronounced evidence of change among the Methodist ministers. Both relative rankings and mean scores provide evidence of change. The task of preacher in 1972 had greater priority for ministers than in 1985; not only is the mean score attaching to this task higher, it seems to have become as important (if not more so) than the pastoral task. Even more striking is the relative change in the importance of the task of celebrant; the mean is much larger and of greater relative importance than in 1972. As with the Anglican clergy, there is some evidence of a diminution of the importance of the counselling task, as indicated by a higher mean and a lower rung on the ladder of priorities.

The authors of *Clergy, Ministers and Priests* emphasised the similarities and differences between the different views of the role of the religious functionary. They pointed to the considerable importance of the pastoral element among the three groups of respondents (that is, including the Roman Catholic priests). While table two confirms the continued relative importance of pastoral work, the 1985 means for both clergy and ministers are higher than in the early 1970s, suggesting some further evidence of change. The low rating of the celebrant task among Methodist ministers in 1972 was seen by the authors of *Clergy, Ministers and Priests* as a function of the evangelical tradition with its emphasis on simple worship and oratory and a corresponding dislike of ritualism. The shift among Methodist ministers suggests this explanation may have exaggerated the influence of theological doctrine

Table 2: Conception of role (arithmetic means)

| | AnglDioc | | | | MethDist | | | |
| | 1971 | | 1985 | | 1972 | | 1985 | |
	rank	mean	rank	mean	rank	mean	rank	mean
pastor	1	1.90	1	2.29	1	1.81	2	2.30
celebrant	2	2.60	2	2.54	5 =	5.30	3	3.49
preacher	3	3.12	3	2.79	2	2.88	1	2.27
counsellor	4	3.41	4	4.08	3	3.65	4	4.10
leader	5	4.50	5	4.38	4	3.91	5	4.44
administrator	6	5.17	6	5.52	7	5.73	7	5.94
official	7	6.52	7	6.34	5 =	5.30	6	5.08

upon role conception. Two possible explanations of the greater importance of the celebrant task among Methodist ministers can be proffered. One of the effects of secularisation has been that many of the tasks of the religious func-tionary are also carried out by others in the community. It may be that one effect of this is that ritual comes to be seen as the area in which the ordained minister is a specialist and hence achieves greater recognition. This contention is consistent with Aldridge's suggestion that: 'In a secular society, liturgical praxis is the only area in which clergymen exercise a largely unchallenged professional expertise' (Aldridge, 1986, p. 361). Alternatively, or possibly in addition, the anticipation of eventual union with the Church of England may have prompted a conception of ministry which has strong similarities to the Anglican tradition. In this context, it is striking that the Spearman rank correlation between the ordering of tasks by Methodist ministers in 1985 with that of Anglican clergy in 1985 is 0.86, whereas the correlation with the ranking by ministers in 1972 is 0.83, implying that the current role conception of Methodist ministers is factionally closer to that of Anglican clergy than to ministers in their own church in 1972.

The slightly lesser emphasis on the counselling task among both groups is also worthy of note. At the time of the initial research, there was evidence of greater attention being paid to counselling work in the churches (see, for example, Leat, 1973), so that the results relating to this task in 1971 and 1972 may in part have been a product of certain preoccupations in theological and ecclesiastical circles. One area which has scarcely changed at all is the low priority accorded administrative work. This finding was very much in accordance with the research in the USA of writers like Blizzard (1956) and Jud *et al.* (1970), all of whom found that ministers dislike administrative work and often feel over-burdened by it. Similarly, in the aforementioned national survey of clergy (Heald and Rhodes, 1986), 'the amount of administration' was the most frequently cited of the 39 problems facing clergy (mentioned by 53%).

Theological cosmology: Although a major theme of *Clergy, Ministers and Priests* was the significance of inter-denominational differences, the authors were simultaneously concerned to elucidate the implications of diverse theological strands (referred to as theological cosmologies) among clergy and ministers.[7] This emphasis was highly consonant with the recognition of different forms of 'churchmanship' within the Church of England (Coneybeare, 1853; Thompson, 1970). Anglican clergy were asked to locate themselves from among eight forms of churchmanship: anglo-catholic, 'prayerbook' catholic, central/broad church, modernist, new theology, liberal evangelical, conservative evangelical, and other. A different path had to be taken to extract data on churchmanship among Methodist ministers, since there are no clear theological parties within this tradition of the kind found in the Church of England. Respondents were asked to locate their theological positions, but the categories were left open. Many chose to identify themselves in terms of two or more categories. Churchmanship tended to be used by the authors of *Clergy, Ministers and Priests* as a correlate of a variety of other variables, as the discussion under 'associational change' below exemplifies.

Tables three and four report the degree to which there has been a change in the endorsement of different categories of churchmanship. Table three suggests that there has not been a great deal of change in the relative endorsement of particular categories of churchmanship among Anglican clergy. There are fewer subscribers to the central/broad church position and more conservative evangelicals than in 1971. The 'other' category has also been endorsed more frequently than in 1971. Table four portrays a similar absence of marked change when the data on churchmanship among Methodist ministers are examined. The clearest evidence of change is that considerably fewer respondents describe themselves as ecumenical than in 1972. As with the Anglican clergy the 'other' category was used to a greater extent in 1985. The greater endorsement of 'other' is of interest because it implies that the categories employed in the initial research do not have the same importance in 1985. Finally, the almost identical proportion of Methodist respondents who described themselves as catholic or sacrementalist in 1972 and 1985 is interesting in the light of the earlier finding in connection with the greater emphasis on the celebrant task (see table two). It might have been suggested that the greater priority accorded the celebrant task by Methodist ministers, when comparing the 1972 and 1985 data on role conception, was a product of a greater acceptance of catholic, sacramentalist or ritualistic notions among this group, but the absence of any change in the affirmation of this theological tendency belies this interpretation.

Ecumenism: Inter-church cooperation and even unity were prominent topics within the churches at the time of the original research, and were attracting a good deal of attention from sociologists (for example, Berger, 1963; Wilson, 1966). To a large extent, sociologists viewed the ecumenical movement as a response to the pressures imposed upon churches by continuing secularisation. The contemporary concern with ecumenism was mirrored in the initial research in that a variety of questions was asked

Table 3: Churchmanship in AnglDioc

	1971 %		1985 %	
anglo-catholic	12.1 }	31.7	14.3 }	31.4
prayer book catholic	19.6 }		17.1 }	
central broad church	33.2		21.7	
modernist	2.0 }	9.0	2.3 }	4.6
new theology	7.0 }		2.3 }	
liberal evangelical	13.1 }	18.1	9.1 }	22.8
conservative evangelical	5.0 }		13.7 }	
other	8.0		19.4	
			(N = 175)	

Table 4: Churchmanship in MethDist

	1972 %	1985 %
evangelical	49.5	43.5
ecumenical	60.2	41.7
liberal	34.4	41.7
middle of the road broad church	5.4	11.7
radical	32.4	28.3
conservative	2.2	1.7
catholic/ritualist/sacrementalist	19.4	20.0
other	9.7	18.3
		(N = 67)

Note: Percentages in each column add up to more than 100 because respondents were able to opt for more than one description.

of respondents regarding their support for various ecumenical ventures. In this article only data relating to the support of clergy and ministers for organic union with various churches will be presented.

Table five presents the findings related to the degree of change in support for organic union. The table is complicated by two factors. First, in the initial research on the Anglican clergy in this particular diocese, respondents were not asked about union with Pentecostal and Orthodox churches and 'all Christian bodies'. Consequently, it is not possible to indicate if support for union has increased in respect to these three items. Second, during the course of the initial fieldwork in the early 1970s, the Presbyterian and Congregational Churches amalgamated to form the United Reformed Church. Thus, while the initial research asked about support for union with each of these two churches, the re-study asked about the newly formed body. Consequently, in table five two percentages are provided for the degree of support in 1971 and 1972, the first in regard to the Congregational Church and the second for the Presbyterian Church.

Overall, the general impression provided by the data in table five is of relatively little change in degrees and patterns of support. Perhaps the major theme to emerge from the data is a general diminution of

Table 5: Support for eventual union with other churches

| | AnglDioc | | MethDist | |
| | 1971 | 1985 | 1972 | 1985 |
	%	%	%	%
Roman Catholic Church	87.7	84.2	73.2	63.6
Methodist Church/Church of England[3]	93.4	85.9	91.8	82.1
Baptist Church	73.9	77.1	91.7	83.6
United Reform Church	78.7/79.6[1]	82.4	95.9/80.0[1]	95.5
Pentecostal churches	*[2]	68.6	77.4	70.1
Orthodox churches	*[2]	84.1	67.7	66.7
All Christian bodies	*[2]	56.2	72.2	53.7
		(N = 170)		(N = 67)

Notes: 1 The two percentages refer to support for union with the Congregational and Presbyterian Churches respectively.
2 Not specifically asked in 1971.
3 Percentages under AnglDioc refer to Anglican support for union with Methodist Church; under MethDist they refer to Methodist support for union with the Church of England.

support among the Methodist ministers. With the exception of their support for union with the United Reformed Church, there has been a decline in ministers' support for union with each of the churches about which they were asked, as well as for 'all Christian bodies' (although the change in relation to the Orthodox churches is only 1%). The support of Anglican clergy for union with the Roman Catholic and Methodist churches appears also to have waned slightly, but very small increases in support are apparent in connection with the Baptist and United Reformed Churches. There is, then, some indication that support for organic union with other churches is not quite as pervasive as in 1971 and 1972, although the vast majority of clergy and ministers still appear to favour union. In the early 1970s ecumenical issues were more prominent than they were in 1985 when other matters, such as the ordination of women, were at the forefront of discussions about the direction of the churches. Equally, the data presented in table five provide a suggestion that the view that support for church unity grows as secularisation intensifies may need slight revision.

Patterns of influence: The impetus for the initial research derived from a concern to apply concepts drawn from organisation studies to the study of churches (Hinings and Foster, 1973). Accordingly, it is scarcely surprising that the research was concerned to elaborate respondents' perceptions of the structure of their dioceses and districts. One of the measures employed was the control graph scheme developed by Tannenbaum (1968) to assess control in organisations.[8]

The control graph approach was adapted by the authors of *Clergy, Ministers and Priests* so that respondents in each diocese or district were asked about the degrees of influence associated with a number of hierarchical positions, including decision-making bodies. Table six reports the data on patterns of influence in 1971 and in 1985 for AnglDioc. There has been little dramatic change, but there is evidence

Table 6: Pattern of influence in AnglDioc

	1971 mean	1985 mean
bishop	4.01	4.31
archdeacons	3.08	2.81
suffragan bishop	2.48	2.88
incumbents	2.17	2.17
laity	2.14	2.05
rural deans	1.98	2.12
provost	1.57	1.96
assistant curate	1.40	1.35
diocesan synod	2.69	2.69
deanery synods	2.06	1.67

that influence has become slightly more concentrated at the apex. In calculating the influence range for the diocese it is something of a moot point if the score for the laity or assistant curates should be subtracted from that of the bishop. In both cases the influence range has increased slightly: in the case of the laity from 1.87 to 2.26 and for curates from 2.61 to 2.96. These calculations imply that the growth of synodical government has intensified the amount of influence at the apex of the diocese (note also the increase in the score for suffragan bishops), while reducing the influence of the lower echelons. The greater bureaucratisation of the Church of England, which has accompanied synodical government (Moore, 1986), may have led to this greater concentration of influence. In any event, as Moore (1986) observes, centralisation within the Church of England has increased since the introduction of synodical government; this greater concentration of influence at national level may well have enhanced the influence of bishops within their own dioceses relative to curates and the laity (and indeed other positions).

The corresponding results for MethDist are presented in table seven. MethDist had a much flatter structure in 1972 than its Anglican counterpart. The influence range for ministers in 1972 was 0.88 and for lay members 0.93. In 1985, these figures were respectively 0.66 and 1.00. Thus, whereas there has been an intensification of centralisation in the Anglican diocese there has been little change in the Methodist district. The authors of *Clergy, Ministers and Priests* viewed the contrasting patterns in 1971/2 as a consequence of the episcopal tradition within the Anglican Church and the democratic, participative tradition within the Methodist Church.

Associational change

In this section will be considered the pattern of association between two variables which appear to have been of particular interest to the authors of *Clergy, Ministers and Priests*. It is not possible to provide the relevant tables for AnglDioc and MethDist in 1971 and 1972

Table 7: Patterns of influence in MethDist

	1972 mean	1985 mean
chairman	3.71	3.63
circuit superintendents	3.33	3.33
ministers	2.83	2.97
lay members	2.78	2.63
synod secretary	2.36	2.31
district synod	2.81	2.38
circuit quarterly meeting	2.60	2.55

respectively, since they are no longer available. Instead, the relevant tables in *Clergy, Ministers and Priests* will be referred to, but it is important to recognise that these tables are based upon the aggregate data for the three dioceses and the three districts.

The relationships between churchmanship and role conception: In table 4.2 in *Clergy, Ministers and Priests*, data were presented which showed a clear association between churchmanship and role conception among Church of England clergy. Churchmanship was found to be associated with the mean score obtained for each of the seven tasks examined. Further, the relative importance of each of the seven tasks varied according to churchmanship: those of central/broad church persuasion tended to rank the tasks in much the same way as the whole sample, but those who described themselves as catholics accorded first priority to the celebrant task; for evangelicals the celebrant task was of considerably lower priority and greater importance was attached to counselling and preaching; and those who described themselves as modernist/new theology emphasised counselling more than did any of the other groups.

Table eight provides the analogous table for the 1985 data. In *Clergy, Ministers and Priests*, most of the categories were combined and this procedure has been followed here. Thus, the two catholic groups are combined, as are the two evangelical groups, and those who subscribe to the labels of modernist or new theology are also combined. Two points stand out when this table is compared with its predecessor. First, in *Clergy, Ministers and Priests* all of the seven tasks were substantially associated with churchmanship in the sense that the means for each task varied considerably by churchmanship category, albeit in different degrees. Analyses of variance revealed churchmanship to have an impact upon each of the seven tasks. In the 1985 research, the impact of churchmanship is only really pronounced in regard to the means for the tasks of celebrant and preacher. In other words, the extent of the association between churchmanship and role conception is less clear-cut than in the initial research. Second, some of the patterns have changed. The patterns of relative priorities for catholics and evangelicals are the same as in 1971. Changes are most evident in the cases of those clergy who describe themselves as

Table 8: *Association between churchmanship and conception of role in AnglDioc in 1985*

	catholic		central/broad		modernist/ new theology		evangelical		other		F	P
	rank	mean	rank	mean	rank	mean	rank	mean	rank	mean		<
pastor	2	2.51	2	2.29	2	3.13	1	1.97	1	2.07	2.133	NS
celebrant	1	1.47	1	2.14	1	2.88	4	4.19	3	2.81	22.966	.001
preacher	3	3.24	3	2.80	4	3.63	2	2.03	2	2.67	7.031	.001
counsellor	4	4.08	5	4.40	3	3.50	3	3.97	4	3.96	1.095	NS
leader	5	4.55	4	4.00	5	4.25	5	4.87	5	4.44	0.553	NS
administrator	6	5.75	6	5.71	6	5.13	6	5.14	6	5.44	1.568	NS
official	7	6.40	7	6.51	7	5.50	7	6.22	7	6.44	1.759	NS

central/broad church and modernist/new theology. In the case of the former group, the task of celebrant tends to be accorded top priority (rather than second in 1971) and the leader task fourth priority (rather than fifth). For the modernist/new theology clergy, the role of celebrant is the first priority, whereas in 1971 it was fourth, and counselling is less important than in the initial research. Thus, the amount of associational change in regard to these two variables is quite considerable, since there has been a shift in both the extent and the character of the association between them.

In the initial research very little evidence of an association between churchmanship and role conception was found among the Methodist ministers (*Clergy, Ministers and Priests*, p. 70); indeed, the authors did not provide a table or any other statistical information to demonstrate the absence of an association. The 1985 study also found there to be very little evidence of an association between the two variables among Methodist ministers. However, the authors of *Clergy, Ministers and Priests* did find (following analyses of variance) that the age of ministers was associated with the ways they ranked the roles of preacher, counsellor, leader, and administrator. In asking about age, Ranson *et al.* (1977) asked respondents to locate themselves in one of nine age groups. In examining the association between age and a number of other variables the authors 'collapsed' responses into four age ranges: 39 and under, 40–49, 50–59, and 60 and over. In 1972, the proportions of respondents who fell into each of these four categories were 36%, 29%, 19% and 16% respectively; in 1985, the figures were 10.3%, 39.7%, 40.1%, and 8.8%. This change in the age distribution of the Methodist sample posed a problem for the presentation of a contingency table since the first and last age groups only comprise seven and six ministers respectively. In order to provide a table in which there was a much more even spread across the age categories, ministers' ages were bunched into three categories (see table nine).[9] Table nine strongly implies that the extent of these associations among Methodist ministers has diminished. There are still some differences: older ministers accord greater priority to the task of preaching and less

Table 9: Association between age and conception of role in MethDist in 1985

| | -45 | | 45–54 | | 55+ | | F | P |
	rank	mean	rank	mean	rank	mean		<
preacher	1	2.17	2	2.57	1	2.05	1.193	NS
pastor	2	2.44	1	2.22	2	2.27	0.149	NS
celebrant	3	3.39	3	3.52	3	3.56	0.043	NS
counsellor	4	4.06	5	4.09	4	4.14	0.018	NS
representative	5	4.56	6	4.91	6	5.68	1.688	NS
leader	6	5.17	4	3.91	5	4.41	2.277	NS
administrator	7	5.67	7	6.22	7	5.86	1.151	NS

priority to counselling than do their younger colleagues, as in 1972, but the extent of the differences is much less marked in 1985. Thus, while the absence of an association between churchmanship and role conception among Methodist ministers was confirmed, the presence of an association between age and some aspects of role conception was not.[10]

Constructional change: the case of professionalism

The degree to which the ordained ministry constitutes a profession has exercised a number of sociologists (for example, Gannon, 1971; Jarvis, 1975; Struzzo, 1970), and this concern is also evident in *Clergy, Ministers and Priests*. Many treatments of this topic entailed taking a formal model of professions and seeking to discern how well the clergy dovetailed with the model. The research on which *Clergy, Ministers and Priests* was based followed this approach in using Hall's (1968) 'Professionalism Scale' as a route to dealing with the issue of how far clergy and ministers exhibited the attitudinal features of a profession.[11]

It is striking how dated this aspect of the *Clergy, Ministers and Priests* research now appears. In a review of the relevant literature, Hall (1983, p. 11) has remarked that: 'The nature of the professional model, together with the more basic question of the nature of the professions, appears to be a dead issue in the sociology of work and occupations.' As Hall notes, the orthodoxy took root among sociologists in the 1970s (for example, Freidson, 1973; Johnson, 1972) that the notion of a formal professional model was theoretically arid, and that the critical focus should be on occupational strategies for the appropriation of power. However, as Hall also observes, the imagery of the formal model can often be discerned in many writings on professions and professionalisation. Certainly, there is evidence of continuing interest in the professionalisation of the clergy (for example, Mills, 1985, pp. 169–70).

A factor analysis of the original data for clergy, ministers and priests strongly implied that the resulting factor structure fitted Hall's dimensions very poorly. Since a number of writers have suggested that the

Table 10: Factor analysis of professionalism scale for AnglDioc in 1971 and 1985

	scale no.	factor one		factor two		factor three		factor four		factor five	
		1971	1985	1971	1985	1971	1985	1971	1985	1971	1985
professional	11	0.06	0.49	0.15	−0.13	0.19	0.14	0.06	0.29	−0.57	0.15
organisation	21	−0.33	0.60	0.23	−0.17	0.14	0.13	0.19	0.23	−0.52	−0.09
as reference	31	0.37	−0.04	−0.17	0.27	−0.21	−0.06	0.38	−0.17	−0.26	0.07
	46	0.41	0.30	0.22	0.12	0.31	0.17	0.23	−0.01	0.00	0.23
belief in service	2	0.46	0.07	0.48	0.69	−0.16	−0.04	−0.16	−0.13	−0.23	0.05
to public	7	0.05	−0.03	0.73	0.50	−0.05	0.19	0.05	0.42	−0.14	−0.19
	12	0.33	0.09	0.52	0.58	0.12	−0.25	0.01	0.13	−0.38	0.04
	22	−0.16	−0.15	0.66	0.45	0.09	0.02	0.23	0.38	−0.12	−0.16
colleague	3	0.08	−0.05	0.18	−0.07	0.18	0.11	0.74	0.40	−0.07	−0.01
control	8	−0.11	0.16	0.19	0.02	0.69	0.02	0.04	0.45	−0.15	−0.16
	23	−0.37	0.02	0.07	−0.03	−0.14	0.75	0.63	0.17	0.04	−0.05
	43	0.09	0.16	−0.14	0.08	0.77	−0.08	−0.05	0.03	−0.03	0.07
sense of	4	0.09	0.11	0.66	0.02	0.02	−0.01	0.17	0.42	−0.03	0.07
calling	19	−0.32	0.31	0.27	−0.21	0.32	0.46	0.25	0.41	−0.29	−0.01
	39	−0.11	0.07	0.31	0.06	0.27	−0.05	−0.21	0.26	−0.36	0.10
	44	−0.05	0.20	0.51	0.03	0.09	0.01	−0.08	0.42	0.07	−0.09
autonomy	5	0.11	−0.18	0.42	−0.06	0.25	0.08	0.01	0.33	0.59	0.48
	10	0.42	−0.02	−0.03	0.20	−0.15	0.07	0.12	−0.03	0.21	0.13
	15	0.72	0.09	0.05	0.07	−0.06	−0.02	−0.05	−0.01	0.11	0.72
	30	0.69	0.08	0.00	0.24	0.24	−0.28	−0.24	−0.31	−0.09	0.65
eigenvalues[1]			0.60		1.72		0.66		2.27		1.34

Note: 1 These are only available for the 1985 data.

clergy have become more professionalised (for example, Beckford, 1985a; Russell, 1980; Wilson, 1982), there might appear to be grounds for believing that in 1985 clergy and ministers would exhibit a better fit with the *de jure* dimensions of Hall's (1968) model.

Table ten provides the factor loadings for AnglDioc clergy in 1971 and 1985. The left-hand column provides the five dimensions of professionalism and their supposed scale items. The item numbers refer to the item numbers of the full inventory. Across the page are the factor loadings for five dimensions in both 1971 and 1985. The procedure was to request five factors to be extracted, using the SPSS-X PA2 procedure[12] with varimax rotation, which is roughly the same as the procedure used in the original research. The highest factor loadings should appear in those sectors of the table, for each of the two years, in which dimensions and factors correspond, that is, starting with the top left hand sector and descending diagonally to the bottom right hand sector. A similar analysis was not undertaken for the Methodist ministers since the small number of respondents could not sustain a factor analysis of twenty items adequately.

Interestingly, the factor structure in 1985 is 'cleaner' for three of the dimensions than in 1971. Three professional organisation as reference items (11, 21 and 46) load on factor I, without any other items loading on this factor (that is, coefficients in excess of 0.30); this contrasts with ten items loading on the corresponding factor in 1971. Second, all four belief in service to public items load on factor II and no other items. Again, this differs from the situation in 1971 which was a good deal less clean in that eight items loaded on this factor. Third, with factor V three autonomy items load on this factor (5, 15 and 30) and no others. This contrasts sharply with the 1971 analysis. However, the loadings for factors III and IV are very poor and at the very least are no better than was exhibited in 1971. Consequently, there is some evidence to support the notion that the structure of respondents' replies reflects the structure of the professional model to a greater degree than in 1971, although that evidence is not conclusive.

Discussion

The results which have been presented above imply that there has been both continuity and change in the views and perceptions of both clergy and ministers since the early 1970s. There is little change in their conception of the church and in the patterns of support for different types of churchmanship. The Anglican clergy exhibit little change in the ways in which they conceive of their role, an area in which Methodist ministers' views seem to have changed to a much more marked degree. Both groups seem to attach less emphasis to the counselling aspects of their work. In addition, ministers seem to be conceiving of their role in a manner which is much more similar to the Anglican clergy than in the early 1970s. It may be that secularisation and bureaucratisation in the mainstream churches have a 'standardising' effect, by virtue of imposing similar problems and similar contexts for the work of the religious functionary. The anticipation of organic unity between the Anglican and Methodist Churches may merely enhance this tendency. There was also some evidence to suggest a slight diminution of support among Methodist ministers for organic union with other churches; this point is underscored by the fact that fewer ministers described themselves as 'ecumenicals' in 1985 than in 1972 (41.7%, as against 60.2%). The perception of the pattern of influence in the Methodist district has changed very little, but there is clear evidence of greater centralisation of influence in AnglDioc. When examining the association between churchmanship and role conception, a change in both the extent and the character of this relationship was discerned among Anglican clergy. The absence of an association between these two variables among Methodist ministers was discerned in both the 1972 and 1985 studies, but the impact of age on role conception was far less pronounced in the re-study. Finally, there was evidence of change in the nature of the connection between the construct of professionalism and its associated indicators.

The primary aim of this re-study was to examine whether there has been significant change in some of the findings which were emphasised in the initial study. Certain areas of change have indeed been discerned in the data presented above. Sociologists are well aware that they study phenomena which are subject to substantial change in each of the ways articulated in this article. Some areas of the subject are repeatedly re-studied precisely because there is a recognition that different social conditions are likely to be associated with different configurations of findings. Social mobility research is a field in which there is strong recognition of the need to revise one's knowledge in the light of wider changes. Most recently, Goldthorpe and Payne (1986) have addressed the question of how far inter-generational mobility patterns have changed in the face of the inclement economic conditions that emerged since the Oxford Mobility research of 1972. The General Household Survey, by virtue of being an annual survey, can also be used as a data-base for inferring patterns of change over time (for example, Payne, 1985). The *British Social Attitudes* series of surveys is consciously committed to the strategy of 'by repeatedly asking the same carefully designed sets of questions of random samples of the population at intervals, we chart trends over the years' (Jowell *et al.*, 1987, p. ix). However, not all areas of sociology receive the attention that has char-acterised the study of social mobility; nor is every area of sociology catered for by ongoing surveys like the General Household Survey or *British Social Attitudes*. Instead, we are often forced in many areas of the discipline to rely on findings whose relevance and contemporary veracity are relatively unknown. There is also a sense in which partic-ular *zeitgeister* may have an impact upon facets of the results that are gleaned from an empirical study. In the research reported here there is the suggestion that in the early 1970s the interest in the counselling aspects of the role of the religious functionary may have been more prominent and that there was a greater preoccupation with the unity of the churches. Also, when examining the data on churchmanship in the re-study the greater use of the 'other' category was noted. Part of this greater use of 'other' can be attributed to changes in the theological fashions between the two time-periods. For example, ten of the thirty-four Anglican respondents who described themselves as 'other' used terms which were indicative of a commitment to the 'charismatic' movement which was scarcely on the agenda in the early 1970s. During this latter period, the 'new theology' was of greater interest (albeit for a small minority), but was scarcely mentioned by Anglican respondents in the re-study.

Thus, in presenting some findings relating to the contemporary reli-gious functionaries and their churches, this article has sought to draw attention to the possibility that configurations of findings from a piece of research may change in a number of different ways over time; in this instance a relatively short hiatus of thirteen to fourteen years. Yet if research is not re-studied the extent and ways in which such shifts take place may not be discernible. There are obvious barriers to re-studies.

Like replications in the natural sciences (Collins, 1985), conducting a re-study is often perceived as an intellectually unchallenging (and hence low status) activity. This is likely to be the case since for a re-study to enjoy a degree of credibility and legitimacy, it should depart from the original as little as possible, and therefore can easily be viewed as a mechanical application of someone else's procedures. If a re-study departs excessively from the original framework, too many alternative interpretations are possible of different results. Such excessive departures often characterise so-called 'replications' in sociology (for example, MacKinnon, 1980). Yet there may be entirely understandable compulsions to change techniques (such as the kinds of questions asked in a survey) in order to update them. In the case of the Middletown follow-up, which related to research undertaken fifty years earlier, the investigators felt compelled to update many of their instruments but regretted at a very early stage the changes that they had introduced (Bahr, Caplow and Chadwick, 1983). But precisely because issues and preoccupations change over time, the urge to tinker with research instruments is likely to be strong. In the research reported in this article, questions were not tampered with at all, in spite of a strong feeling that some questions and the pre-coded categories associated with them ought to have been changed slightly. In order to address issues of more contemporary relevance, additional questions were asked which were not meant to (and obviously could not) provide any kind of comparison with the 1970s research. However, as the Middletown researchers note, the urge to drift into topics not covered in the original research in order to expand the scope of the investigation and to instil an element of freshness is not without its drawbacks, since such a strategy may divert time and resources from the re-study component (Bahr *et al.*, 1983).

A further reason why re-studies do not take place more frequently is that sociological research is largely the product of changing theoretical and social concerns. Preoccupations in an earlier age will not have the same resonance at a later juncture when different issues are likely to prevail. One of the reasons why the field of social mobility enjoys the privilege of being the focus of re-studies is probably because it is a relatively enduring concern among sociologists (by virtue of their concern for inequality). It is significant in this context that much longitudinal research in both the USA and the UK has inequality as a root preoccupation (for example, Alexander and Eckland, 1980; Eckland and Alexander, 1980; Osborn and Milbank, 1987; Sewell and Hauser, 1980). Many other fields of research do not exercise such a hold over sociologists and are much more fleeting concerns. Nonetheless, such less privileged areas become a part of sociological knowledge; they even become enshrined in textbooks and hence imbibed by generations of students as 'findings'. The research reported in this article at the very least raises the question of how far the 'findings' on which students are weaned can still legitimately be called such. Since the research reported here suggests that there can be quite considerable change in patterns of association and correlation among variables with the passage of time, some findings in the literature may also be deemed to suffer from the same problem.

One implication of the foregoing discussion is that there is a case for more re-studies to be undertaken. However, sociologists' interests inevitably move into new areas of concern, while the abstemious funding of social scientific research in the UK means that re-studies are extremely unlikely to be favoured areas for support. Research funding bodies are largely concerned to fund 'relevant' research at the time of writing. Much of the research which has been carried out in the past, and which might be considered ripe for re-study, was carried out in periods of munificence during which 'relevance' was not as crucial as it is nowadays. Consequently, even if social scientists were so inclined, the amount of funding for re-studies would not be adequate. In the absence of more re-studies being undertaken, authors of textbooks in, and teachers of, sociology should make clear the limited generalisability and possibly relevance of findings over time. On occasions, this may entail attending to the historical context of the research, as recommended by Gergen (1973) in his discussion of social psychology as history. Attention to such issues is sometimes in evidence in connection with well-known studies like *The Affluent Worker* research on *embourgeoisement* (Goldthorpe *et al.*, 1969), with frequent mention of the 'Must Labour lose?' and 'You've never had it so good' themes which seem to have prompted the investigation. However, reference to such issues is not usual.

However, re-studies introduce a number of special research problems and dilemmas. One of the most intractable of these is the problem of time. How long is it appropriate to wait before conducting a re-study? There are no rules of thumb to guide the intending researcher who wishes to carry out a re-study. In the case of Middletown, the first re-study was conducted fairly soon after the initial research (Lynd and Lynd, 1937), but the second re-study had to wait many decades (Bahr *et al.*, 1983). But the length of time that is allowed to elapse between the original and a later investigation may well have a bearing on both the extent to which change is discerned and the patterns of results that are obtained. In a review of longitudinal research on leader reward behaviour, Sims and Szilagyi (1979) have noted that the extent of the time lag between waves of observations can affect the degree to which the leader's behaviour is found to have an impact on a variety of variables over time. While the research reported in this article is not longitudinal, the issue of the potential influence of the length of time lags on patterns of findings is relevant.

Further, as Burgess (1987) has observed in the context of his ethnographic re-study of Bishop McGregor school, the extent to which a particular locality or organisation is the same as it was when it was initially investigated is questionable. In the case of churches, substantial internal re-organisation, such as the closing and merging of parishes or circuits, is likely to have occurred. How far such developments render the 'sameness' of the organisational contexts of AnglDioc and MethDist questionable is an important consideration. A further problem for a re-study in which questionnaires are the main source of data collection is the extent to which questions ought to be changed to reflect contemporary concerns. The case of churchmanship illustrates this point. The churchmanship categories with which Anglican respondents were presented in 1971 were reasonable for that time; but in 1985 if the researcher wanted to reflect contemporary theological issues, the response categories would be different, probably reflecting the influence of the charismatic movement (as in Aldridge's, 1986, research). But if the question had been changed in the re-study the element of comparability would be lost. Herein lies a very considerable dilemma for anyone intending to conduct a re-study.

A semantic issue which is also relevant to the present discussion is the question of whether to use the term 're-study' or 'replication' to describe an investigation such as that reported in this article. In qualitative research, when an investigator returns to an area that has previously been studied (either by him/herself or someone else) the term 're-study' is invariably used (for example, Burgess, 1987; Smith *et al.*, 1987). In part, this tendency reflects the eschewal of a scientistic rhetoric, but it also denotes a belief that the study is not usually carried out to find out whether the initial findings were correct, but to determine how far observed patterns have changed. 'Replication' usually denotes an investigation in which the researcher aims to check the validity of certain findings. The two often shade into each other, but it is clearly the case that an investigation such as that reported in this article is not a replication since it is not possible to discern whether the results which derive from the 1970s research are 'correct'; rather the point has been to establish how far the results still obtain in 1985. Nonetheless, there is no agreed vocabulary for talking about replications and re-studies; Bahr *et al.* (1983), for example, observe from an examination of articles in the *Social Science Citation Index* that 'replication' is a term employed to cover studies that differ widely in terms of time, place, methods and subjects. It may be that the question of whether a particular investigation is a replication or a re-study is not a simple matter of the nature of the research design, but has much to do with the inferences that are derived from it.

It might be argued that the presentation of the results reported in this article has adopted a somewhat empiricist tone. However, it must be borne in mind that one of the main outcomes of *Clergy, Minister and Priests* was the development of a model of religious orientations out of the results which had been gleaned. To the extent that certain of the findings which derive from the 1970s research no longer obtain, the re-study reported in this article is locked into the wider theoretical considerations that *Clergy, Ministers and Priests* was seeking to address. In this sense, the empiricist cast is tempered by a grounding in the theoretical considerations which the authors of *Clergy, Ministers and Priests* developed.[13]

Notes

1. The somewhat clumsy term 'functionary' was often used in *Clergy, Ministers and Priests* to avoid terms like clergy or priest which were used to stand for the functionaries of the different churches. It has the advantage of not being associated with particular church traditions. The other possibility 'religious professional' somewhat pre-judges the issues of whether clergy, ministers or priests are members of a profession.
2. In longitudinal research, the additional possibility of addressing causal processes over time (as against cross-sectionally) is opened up.
3. Thus, when a piece of research is originally conducted, the factor loadings might point to a clear indication that x dimensions underpin the indicators; when a re-study is carried out, it might be found that the character of the factor structure has changed. Examples of such changes might be: the indicators might load on different dimensions, or there might be more (or fewer) dimensions, or the factor loadings might be similar but less 'clean' than in the initial research.
4. To the best of the author's knowledge, the original 'raw' data are no longer available either.
5. In 1971 all Anglican clergy in AnglDioc (257) were sent questionnaires, 213 of whom returned them, making a response rate of 83%. In 1985, 177 out of the 237 who were sent questionnaires returned them, making a response rate of 73%. The research in MethDist was carried out in 1972; all 112 ministers were contacted, of whom 100 returned questionnaires, making a response rate of 89%. In 1985, 68 out of the 83 ministers contacted returned questionnaires, making a response rate of 82%. It is striking that the later response rates are inferior to the earlier ones, reinforcing suggestions of a decline in survey response in recent years (Goyder and Leiper, 1985).
6. Interestingly, in Heald and Rhodes (1986) 'role uncertainty' was only mentioned as a problem by 11%, suggesting that the problem may have been wrongly diagnosed in the late 1960s and early 1970s, or that circumstances may have changed in the intervening years.
7. This strand of work was seen as contributing to the growing literature in the USA on the impact of different theological positions on orientations among the clergy and their congregations (for example Moberg, 1970; Spaulding, 1972; Stark, Foster, Glock and Quinley, 1971).
8. According to the Tannenbaum scheme, respondents in an organisation are presented with a number of hierarchical positions in their organisation. They are asked to indicate whether each position has very great, great, quite a bit, some, or little influence. Very great influence receives a score of 5; little influence a score of 1. Mean scores are then computed for each position, with higher scores connoting greater influence. A derivative of this computation is to calculate the influence range, the difference between the influence scores of the top and the bottom positions in the hierarchy; this calculation can be taken to provide a summary statement of the influence structure of an organisation, for example a small influence range betokens a 'flat' structure. Thus, in a diocese, the influence range can be computed by subtracting the score of assistant curates or the laity (representing the bottom of the hierarchy) from that of the bishop (representing the apex). For the Methodist district, the score for ministers or lay members would be subtracted from that of the chairman. This measurement scheme, often called the 'control graph', has been used widely in a variety of settings and countries (Tannenbaum and Cooke, 1979).
9. By contrast, the age distribution of Anglican clergy has hardly shifted.
10. However, an analysis was also carried out with the original age classification. The results were identical to those reported in table nine in that there was an absence of an association between age and role conception. Interested readers are welcome to contact the author for details.
11. Hall's (1968) scale proposed five dimensions of professionalism: the use of the professional organisation as a major reference, a belief in service to the public, a belief in self-regulation, a sense of calling to the field, and autonomy. The full scale comprises fifty items, with ten items per dimension. The *Clergy, Ministers and Priests* research employed an abbreviated version of this scale which contained twenty items, that is to say four per dimension. For a full account of the professionalism scale used and the results deriving from it, see Bryman (1985).
12. The PA2 procedure is a principal axis method of factor extraction which places an emphasis upon estimates of communalities. For a description, see Norusis (1985), p. 137.
13. The author wishes to express his gratitude to the Department of Social Sciences at

Loughborough University for financial assistance with the re-study and to Alan Aldridge for his comments on an earlier version of this article.

References

Aldridge, A (1986) 'Slaves to no sect: the Anglican clergy and liturgical change,' *Sociological Review*, 34, pp. 357–380.

Alexander, K L and Eckland, B K (1980) 'The explorations in equality of opportunity survey of 1955 high school sophomores,' in A C Kerckhoff (ed.) *Research in Sociology of Education and Socialization, volume 1*, Greenwich, Connecticut, JAI Press, pp. 31–58.

Bahr, H M, Caplow, T and Chadwick, B A (1983) 'Middletown III: problems of replication, longitudinal measurement and triangulation,' *Annual Review of Sociology*, 9, pp. 243–264.

Beckford, J A (1985a) 'Religious organizations,' in P E Hammond (ed.) *The Sacred in a Secular Age: toward revision in the scientific study of religion*, Berkeley, University of California Press, pp. 125–138.

Beckford, J A (1985b) *Cult Controversies: the societal response to the new religious movements*, London, Tavistock.

Berger, P (1963) 'A market model for the analysis of ecumenicity,' *Social Research*, 30, pp. 77–94.

Blizzard, S (1956) 'The minister's dilemma,' *The Christian Century*, 73, pp. 508–509.

Bryman, A (1985) 'Professionalism and the clergy: a research note,' *Review of Religious Research*, 26, pp. 253–260.

Burgess, R G (1987) 'Studying and restudying Bishop McGregor School,' in G Walford (ed.) *Doing Sociology of Education*, London, Falmer Press, pp. 67–94.

Collins, H M (1985) *Changing Order: replication and induction in scientific practice*, London, Sage.

Coneybeare, W J (1853) 'Church parties,' *Edinburgh Review*, 98, pp. 273–342.

Daniel, M (1967) 'London clergymen,' unpublished MPhil dissertation, University of London.

Demerath, N J (1967) 'In a sow's ear: a reply to Goode,' *Journal for the Scientific Study of Religion*, 6, pp. 77–84.

Eckland, B K and Alexander, K L (1980) 'The national longitudinal study of the high school senior class of 1972,' in A C Kerckhoff (ed.) *Research in Sociology of Education and Socialization, volume 1*, Greenwich, Connecticut, JAI Press, pp. 189–222.

Freidson, E (1973) *Professions and Their Prospects*, Beverly Hills, Sage.

Gannon, T M (1971) 'Priest/minister: profession or non-profession?' *Review of Religious Research*, 12, pp. 66–79.

Gergen, K J (1973) 'Social psychology as history,' *Journal of Personality and Social Psychology*, 26, pp. 309–320.

Goldthorpe, J H, Lockwood, D, Bechhofer, F and Platt, J (1969) *The Affluent Worker in the Class Structure*, Cambridge, Cambridge University Press.

Goldthorpe, J H and Payne, C (1986) 'Trends in intergenerational class mobility in England and Wales, 1972–1983,' *Sociology*, 20, pp. 1–24.

Goyder, J and Leiper, J M (1985) 'The decline in survey response: a social values interpretation,' *Sociology*, 19, pp. 55–71.

Hall, R H (1968) 'Professionalization and bureaucratization,' *American Sociological Review*, 33, pp. 92–104.

Hall, R H (1983) 'Theoretical trends in the sociology of occupations,' *Sociological Quarterly*, 24, pp. 5–23.

Heald, G and Rhodes, R (1986) *Gallup Survey of Church of England Clergymen with Particular Reference to Comparative Differences Between Urban Priority Areas and Elsewhere*, London, General Synod of the Church of England.

Hinings, C R and Foster, B D (1973) 'The organization structure of churches,' *Sociology*, 7, pp. 93–106.

Jarvis, P (1975) 'The parish ministry as a semi-profession,' *Sociological Review*, 23, pp. 911–922.

Johnson, T (1972) *The Professions and Power*, London, Macmillan.

Jowell, R, Witherspoon, S and Brook, L (eds) (1987) *British Social Attitudes: the 1987 report*, Aldershot, Gower.

Jud, G J, Mills, E W and Burch, G W (1970) *Ex-Pastors*, Philadelphia, Pilgrim Press.

Leat, D (1973) 'Putting God over: the faithful counsellors,' *Sociological Review*, 21, pp. 561–572.

Lynd, R S and Lynd, H M (1937) *Middletown in Transition*, New York, Harcourt, Brace and Jovanovich.

Mackinnon, M H (1980) 'Work instrumentalism reconsidered: a replication of Goldthorpe's

Luton project,' *British Journal of Sociology*, 31, pp. 1–27.

Mills, E W (1985) 'The sacred in ministry studies,' in P E Hammond (ed.) *The Sacred in a Secular Age: toward a revision in the scientific study of religion*, Berkeley, University of California Press, pp. 167–183.

Moberg, D O (1970) 'Theological positions and the institutional characteristics of Protestant congregations,' *Journal for the Scientific Study of Religion*, 9, pp. 53–58.

Moore, C (1986) 'The central organisation,' in C Moore, A N Wilson and G Stamp, *The Church in Crisis*, London, Hodder and Stoughton, pp. 9–68.

Norusis, M J (1985) *SPSS-X: advanced statistics guide*, New York, McGraw-Hill.

Osborn, A F and Milbank, J E (1987) *The Effects of Early Education: a report from the child health and education study*, Oxford, Clarendon Press.

Paul, L (1973) *A Church by Daylight*, London, Hodder and Stoughton.

Payne, J (1985) 'Changes in the youth labour market, 1974–1981,' *Oxford Review of Education*, 11, pp. 167–179.

Ranson, S, Bryman, A and Hinings, B (1977) *Clergy, Ministers and Priests*, London, Routledge and Kegan Paul.

Russell, A (1980) *The Clerical Profession*, London, SPCK.

Sewell, W H and Hauser, R H (1980) 'The Wisconsin longitudinal study of social and psychological factors in aspirations and achievements,' in A C Kerckhoff (ed.) *Research in Sociology of Education and Socialization, volume 1*, Greenwich, Connecticut, JAI Press, pp. 59–99.

Sims, H P and Szilagyi, A D (1979) 'Time lags in leader reward research,' *Journal of Applied Psychology*, 14, pp. 426–438.

Smith, L M, Prunty, J P, Dwyer, D C and Kleine, P F (1987) *The Fate of an Innovative School*, London, Falmer Press.

Spaulding, K E (1972) 'The theology of the pew,' *Review of Religious Research*, 13, pp. 206–211.

Stark, R, Foster, B D, Glock, C Y and Quinley, H (1971) *Wayward Shepherds*, New York, Harper and Row.

Struzzo, J A (1970) 'Professionalism and the resolution of authority among the Catholic clergy,' *Sociological Analysis*, 31, pp. 92–106.

Tannenbaum, A S (1968) *Control in Organizations*, New York, McGraw-Hill.

Tannenbaum, A S and Cooke, R A (1979) 'Organizational control: a review of studies employing the control graph method,' in C J Lammers and D J Hickson (eds) *Organizations Alike and Unalike*, London, Routledge and Kegan Paul, pp. 183–210.

Thompson, K A (1970) *Bureaucracy and Church Reform*, Oxford, Oxford University Press.

Towler, R (1969) 'The social status of the Anglican minister,' in R Robertson (ed.) *Sociology of Religion*, Harmondsworth, Penguin, pp. 443–450.

Towler, R and Coxon, A P M (1979) *The Fate of the Anglican Clergy*, London, Macmillan.

Wilson, B R (1966) *Religion in Secular Society*, London, Watts.

Wilson, B R (1982) *Religion in Sociological Perspective*, Oxford, Oxford University Press.

2.2 The influence of personality on clergy role prioritisation, role influences, conflict and dissatisfaction with ministry

Leslie J Francis and Raymond Rodger

Introduction

Personality theories have been shown by a number of studies to have considerable potential for predicting individual differences in a wide range of work related areas (Furnham, 1992). In particular Eysenck's dimensional model of personality (Eysenck and Eysenck, 1985) has been employed to explore variations in key areas of work performance and job satisfaction among such diverse groups as successful business-men (Eysenck, 1967b) card-punch operators (Savage and Stewart, 1972), chartered accountants (Granleese and Barrett, 1990), clerical employees (Sterns, Alexander, Barrett and Dambrot, 1983), commer-cial airline pilots (Evans, 1986), computer employees (Furnham and Zacherl, 1986), entrepreneurs (Lynn, 1969), gas fitters (Wilson, Tunstall and Eysenck, 1972), industrial managers (Henney, 1975), military pilots (Jessup and Jessup, 1971; Feggetter and Hammond, 1976; Bartram and Dale, 1982), female nurses (Loo, 1983; Bradley, 1986), male nurses (Brown and Stones, 1972; Gumley, McKenzie, Ormerod and Keys, 1979), offshore workers in the oil and gas industry (Sutherland and Cooper, 1991), personnel managers (Blunt, 1978), police officers (Gudjonsson and Adlam, 1983), psychiatric nurses (Jones, Janman, Payne and Rick, 1987), psycho-social workers (Kirkcaldy, Thome and Walter, 1989), school teachers (Innes and Kitto, 1989) and tobacco packers (Cooper and Payne, 1967).

Overall psychological research into the clergy is an underdeveloped field of study (Menges and Dittes, 1965; Bier, 1970; Dittes, 1971; Schuller, Strommen and Brekke, 1980; Malony and Hunt, 1991), and the role that personality plays in clergy development and functioning still remains comparatively uncharted (Nauss, 1973).

Eysenck's measures of personality have now been used among clergy or ordinands in England by six studies (Towler and Coxon, 1979; Francis and Pearson, 1991a; Francis, 1991, 1992a; Jones and Francis, 1992; Francis and Thomas, 1992). A major finding of these studies regarding the personality profile of the male clergy concerns their low scores on the extraversion scale. Although male clergy do not differ from the population norms in terms of their location on the neuroticism and psychoticism scales, they score significantly lower than men in general on the extraversion scale. Characteristically male clergy are introverts. Introverts are people who prefer to remain in the background on social occasions. They are shy in company, uneasy in taking social initiatives, uncertain in leadership, unwilling to take risks, uncomfortable with self-assertion, unhappy about meeting new people, reticent on public occasions. They are not people who would naturally choose to lead the dance, to knock on the door, to stand on the soap box, to rally the crowds, or to draw attention to themselves. Characteristically male clergy seem to possess the very mirror image of the personality qualities generally associated with the public and social profile of their occupation. Such incompatibility between personal preferences and public role expectations may lead to frustration, stress and sense of failure. Coping strategies developed to mediate between the requirements of the role and the personal difficulties in meeting these expectations may lead to shaping a public persona unhealthily detached from authentic human responses.

While some consensus is beginning to emerge from these studies regarding the *personality characteristics* of ordinands and clergy in England and some hypotheses are being generated regarding the possible implications of these personality characteristics for clerical role preferences and satisfaction with ministry, data are not previously available directly linking Eysenck's dimensions of personality and individual differences in clerical performance. The objective of the present study is to build on the existing research into clergy personality in four specific directions. The study is exploratory in nature.

The first aim is to chart the relationship between personality and the priority given by individual clergy to the different roles assumed within the clerical profession. While it is generally recognised that clergy perform a number of different roles, there is no generally agreed consensus regarding the most appropriate characterisation of these roles. For example, Nelsen, Yokley and Madron's (1973) study identified five functions, which are described as traditional, counselling, administration, community problem solving and Christian education. Blizzard's (1955, 1956, 1958a, 1958b) analysis, reflected by Coates and Kistler (1965), Jud, Mills and Burch (1970) and Towler and Coxon (1979), distinguished between six functions: teacher, organiser, preacher, administrator, pastor and priest. Reilly's (1975) analysis also identified six functions which are described as priest and teacher, prophet, pastor, administrator, organiser and priest-ritual. In their study of rural clergy, Davies, Watkins and Winter (1991) identified seven functions: sacerdotal or priestly, pastoral work, administration, private devotions and study, diocesan and deanery duties, travelling between events and other duties. In their comparative study of Catholic, Anglican and Free Church clergy, Ranson, Bryman and Hinings (1977) also identified seven functions which they characterise as pastor, celebrant, preacher, counsellor, leader, administrator and official/representative. Tiller (1983) spoke in terms of nine roles: leader, pastor, focus of the community, public spokesman, guardian of the tradition, professional minister, enabler of laity and church builder. Lauer (1973) listed ten roles: prayer and worship, preaching and teaching, care and comfort, evangelism and mission, organisation and administration, stewardship and finance, fellowship and service, publicity and promotion, public relations and personal counselling. There is at present no sound empirical basis on which to select between these and other competing suggestions. Discussions held with clergy themselves to help shape the present project led to the following list of roles being adopted: administrator, celebrant of sacraments, community leader, leader of public worship, pastor and counsellor, preacher and teacher.

The second aim is to chart the relationship between personality and the influences acknowledged as shaping the role priorities effective in current ministry. Little attention has been previously given to this issue. Discussions held with clergy themselves to help shape the present project identified the following five main areas of influence: congregation, church council, local community at large, family and church hierarchy.

The third aim is to chart the relationship between personality and the levels of conflict experienced by individual clergy between their preferred role prioritisation and the perceived expectations of others. Once again the key groups which may generate conflict are identified as congregation, church council, local community at large, family and church hierarchy.

The fourth aim is to chart the relationship between personality and dissatisfaction with ministry. While dissatisfaction with ministry may be expressed in a number of ways, one of the more salient indicators is likely to be thoughts of leaving the clerical profession for secular employment.

Method

Sample

A detailed questionnaire was distributed to all the 241 full-time stipendiary parochial clergy within one predominantly rural Anglican diocese, together with a stamped addressed envelope and assurances of anonymity and confidentiality. Thoroughly completed and usable questionnaires were returned by 170 male clergy and 13 female clergy, making an overall response rate of 76%. In view of the comparatively small number of women clergy in the diocese and the known personality differences between male and female clergy (Francis, 1991; 1992a), only male clergy were included in the subsequent analysis. The sample of male clergy included 33 men in their thirties, 47 in their forties, 56 in their fifties, 33 in their sixties and one in his seventies.

Questionnaire

Personality was measured by the short form Revised Eysenck Personality Questionnaire (Eysenck, Eysenck and Barrett, 1985). This instrument proposes twelve item indices of extraversion, neuroticism, psychoticism and the lie scale. This short form has been employed in a number of recent studies, including Raine and Manders (1988), Pearson (1989, 1990a, 1990b, 1993), Heaven (1990, 1993), Lester (1990, 1991) and Russell and Wells (1991), and is known to correlate highly with the longer and more established instruments.

Clergy role prioritisation was assessed by inviting the clergy to rate the priority they gave to each of the seven roles (administrator, celebrant of sacraments, community leader, leader of public worship, pastor and counsellor, preacher and teacher) on a seven point scale, ranging from 'very little' to 'very much'. Clergy were asked to rate these priorities for two different stages of their professional career, when they were first ordained and at the present time.

Clergy role influences were assessed by inviting the clergy to rate how much each of the five significant potential influences (congregation, church council, local community at large, family and church hierarchy of bishop and archdeacon) actually influenced their current ministry priorities on a seven point scale, ranging from 'very little' to 'very much'.

Clergy role conflict was assessed by inviting the clergy to rate how much they judge the role expectations put upon them by each of the five significant groups (congregation, church council, local community at large, family and church hierarchy of bishop and archdeacon) to be realistic on a seven point scale, ranging from 'very unrealistic' to 'very realistic'. An additional question invited the clergy to assess the overall conflict between how they see their role and how they perceive other people seeing their role on a seven point scale, ranging from 'very little conflict' to 'very much conflict'.

Dissatisfaction with ministry was assessed by asking the clergy whether they had ever thought of leaving the ministry, on a five point scale ranging from 'never', through 'once in my ministry', 'twice in my ministry' and 'often enough to be uneasy with my job', to 'often enough to look at alternative employment'.

Data analysis

The data were analysed by means of the SPSSX statistical package (SPSS Inc., 1988).

Results and discussion

Clergy personality profile

Before examining the relationship between personality and aspects of clergy performance, table one presents the functional properties of the personality scales themselves. Reliability, expressed in terms of the alpha coefficient (Cronbach, 1951), is well supported for the extraversion scale, the neuroticism scale and the lie scale. The lower alpha coefficient reported for the psychoticism scale is consistent with the psychometric difficulties still experienced in operationalising this more recent construct incorporated within the Eysenckian model of personality (Francis, Brown and Philipchalk, 1992) and indicates that findings associated with this scale need to be treated with more caution. Table one also presents the means and standard deviations for the four scale scores. The major disadvantage of employing the short form Revised Eysenck Personality Questionnaire (Eysenck, Eysenck and Barrett, 1985) rather than the more established Eysenck Personality Questionnaire (Eysenck and Eysenck, 1975) is that there are no secure published population norms against which the clergy personality profiles may be assessed. The scores published for men in the most recent test manual (Eysenck and Eysenck, 1991), based on 408 subjects for extraversion, neuroticism and the lie scale and 693 subjects for psychoticism, are not derived from a general population sample and cannot claim to be representative of the male population as a whole.

Clergy role prioritisation

Table two presents the role priorities as perceived by the clergy in their current ministry. In this table ratings of 1 and 2 have been characterised as 'low' priority, ratings of 3, 4 and 5 as 'medium' priority, and ratings of 6 and 7 as 'high' priority. The table also presents the mean rating for each role, together with the standard deviation. These figures make it clear that the highest priority is given to the two roles of celebrant of sacraments and pastor and counsellor. Both of these roles are highly consistent with the image of male clergy as tender-minded stable individuals who may prefer to relate to the outer world in a predominantly introverted manner. Placed lower on the list of role priorities are the three activities of leader of public worship, preacher and teacher. Men with introverted tendencies may feel less comfortable with these roles than with those of celebrant of sacraments and pastor and counsellor. Placed at the bottom of the list of role priorities are the two activities of administrator and community leader.

While table two presents the role priorities perceived by clergy in their current ministry, these current role priorities may differ from those anticipated by clergy at the time of their ordination. Table three,

Table 1: Reliability, means and standard deviations for the personality scales

personality dimensions	alpha	mean	st dev
extraversion	0.8160	6.83	3.25
neuroticism	0.7670	4.39	2.92
psychoticism	0.5419	2.28	1.71
lie scale	0.7431	4.35	2.73

Table 2: Role priorities in current ministry

role	low %	medium %	high %	rating mean	rating st dev
administrator	12	59	29	4.44	1.59
celebrant of sacraments	1	32	67	5.83	1.38
community leader	19	55	27	4.17	1.73
leader of public worship	2	38	60	5.73	1.27
pastor and counsellor	2	34	65	5.80	1.18
preacher	2	43	56	5.54	1.23
teacher	3	43	54	5.37	1.32

Table 3: Shifts in role priorities between ordination and current ministry through more than one scale point

role	less %	same %	more %	rating mean	rating st dev
administrator	1	52	47	1.47	1.58
celebrant of sacraments	7	86	7	0.07	1.06
community leader	6	70	24	0.53	1.40
leader of public worship	7	90	3	−0.21	0.95
pastor and counsellor	11	82	8	−0.07	1.16
preacher	9	86	5	−0.10	1.00
teacher	7	86	7	0.04	1.07

therefore, explores the shifts in role priorities which have taken place between ordination and the current experience of ministry. In designing this table a shift of just one scale point on the seven point continuum has been regarded as substantially insignificant. Individuals who have given a specific role the same rating on both occasions or who move their rating by only one point have been counted as giving the 'same' priority on both occasions. Those who have moved at least two points to the left of the scale have been counted as giving 'less' priority and those who have moved at least two points to the right of the scale have been counted as giving 'more' priority. From this table it becomes evident that comparatively little shift in role prioritisation takes place during ministry except in relationship to the two roles of community leader and administrator. In particular many men enter the clerical profession unprepared for the significant demands placed on them in the sphere of administration.

Table four presents the relationships between the perceived role priorities in current ministry and the four Eysenckian measures of

Table 4: Relationship between personality and role priorities in current ministry

role	E	N	P	L
administrator	+0.0118	+0.0114	−0.1867	+0.0786
	NS	NS	.05	NS
celebrant of sacraments	+0.1007	−0.0081	+0.0102	+0.0047
	NS	NS	NS	NS
community leader	+0.1733	−0.0818	−0.0322	−0.0557
	.05	NS	NS	NS
leader of public worship	−0.0572	+0.0004	−0.0936	−0.0235
	NS	NS	NS	NS
pastor and counsellor	+0.0988	−0.0397	−0.0878	+0.0754
	NS	NS	NS	NS
preacher	+0.0730	−0.1872	−0.0121	+0.1203
	NS	.05	NS	NS
teacher	+0.0559	−0.1091	−0.0006	−0.1056
	NS	NS	NS	NS

extraversion, neuroticism, psychoticism and the lie scale in terms of Pearson product moment correlation coefficients. Although the standard deviations presented in table two indicate a fairly high degree of consensus among the clergy in terms of role prioritisation, table four suggests that certainly some of the variation between clergy can be accounted for in terms of personality differences. Moreover, the small number of significant correlations which emerge between personality and role prioritisation are clearly consistent with Eysenck's model of the relationship between personality and individual differences.

According to the correlation coefficients, extraversion scores are irrelevant to individual differences in the priority given to the roles of administrator, celebrant of sacraments, leader of public worship, pastor and counsellor, preacher and teacher. Within the professional structure of ministry these are all tasks which may be accepted equally by introverts and extraverts. On the other hand, extraverts tend to give a higher priority to the role of community leader. These are the men who may well enjoy accepting a higher profile in the community at large. It is here that introverts may feel themselves to be disadvantaged and consequently prefer to invest their energy elsewhere.

According to the correlation coefficients, neuroticism scores are irrelevant to individual differences in the priority given to the roles of administrator, celebrant of sacraments, community leader, leader of public worship, pastor and counsellor and teacher. Within the professional structure of ministry these are all tasks which may be embraced by clergy who possess higher levels of neuroticism as readily as by clergy who possess lower levels of neuroticism. On the other hand, clergy who record a high level of neuroticism tend to give a lower priority to the role of preacher. These are the men who may well experience anxiety and unease about being required to preach. Such individuals may feel it necessary to invest disproportionate time and energy in sermon preparation and hence prefer to minimise this experience as far as possible.

According to the correlation coefficients, psychoticism scores are irrelevant to individual differences in the priority given to the roles of celebrant of sacraments, community leader, leader of public worship, pastor and counsellor, preacher and teacher. These all tend to be roles which clergy prioritise largely for themselves. In this sense they are fulfilling their own agenda. The role of administrator, on the other hand, is not one which is central in attracting vocations to the ordained ministry but which, as table three has demonstrated, needs to be recognised as a frequent and inevitable demand of ministry. The significant negative correlation between psychoticism scores and the priority given to the role of administrator indicates that the tenderminded men are more likely to accept this shift in their original views of what ministry should mean for them. Toughminded clergy, on the other hand, are more likely to resist accommodating their earlier established preferences to the demands made upon them by other individuals or by the institutional church. They are also more inclined to live with the conflict which may result from resisting such demands. This view is consistent with Eysenck's empirically derived theory that tendermindedness is associated with conditionability into socially accepted demands and behaviours (Francis, 1992b).

No significant correlations emerge between lie scale scores and clergy role prioritisation.

Clergy role influences

Table five presents the influences on current role priorities as perceived by clergy. In this table ratings of 1 and 2 have been characterised as 'low' influence, ratings of 3, 4 and 5 as 'medium' influence, and ratings of 6 and 7 as 'high' influence. This table also presents the mean rating for each influence, together with the standard deviation. These figures make it clear that the majority of clergy are not particularly conscious of any of the five potential influences listed in the questionnaire as exerting a high influence on setting their current role priorities. The two influences most frequently given a high rating are the groups with whom the clergy have to work most directly, the congregation and the church council. Family and the wider community are the next most frequently cited influences. The church hierarchy of bishop and archdeacon are geographically most distant from the individual clergyman and clearly exert the lowest influence on role prioritisation. The fact that the majority of clergy rate each of the potential sources of influence within the middle range of the seven point scale is consistent with the image of this group of men being sensitive to the expectations of others, but strong minded enough not to be overinfluenced by them.

Table six presents the relationship between the perceived influences on current role priorities and the four Eysenckian personality constructs. These correlation coefficients indicate that some of the

Table 5: Influences on current role priorities

influences	low	medium	high	rating	
	%	%	%	mean	st dev
congregation	3	59	38	5.08	1.23
church council	9	63	28	4.50	1.40
community at large	14	65	21	4.13	1.53
family	18	62	21	4.01	1.64
hierarchy (bishop/archdeacon)	28	62	10	3.50	1.58

*Table 6: Relationship between personality and influences on
          current role priorities*

influences	E	N	P	L
congregation	+0.1440	+0.0354	−0.1705	+0.0579
	NS	NS	.05	NS
church council	+0.0162	+0.0297	−0.1490	+0.0046
	NS	NS	NS	NS
community at large	+0.2041	−0.0528	+0.0179	−0.0068
	.01	NS	NS	NS
family	+0.1436	+0.1559	+0.0430	−0.0194
	NS	.05	NS	NS
hierarchy (bishop/archdeacon)	+0.0834	−0.1185	−0.2779	+0.2078
	NS	NS	.001	.01

variation between clergy can be accounted for in terms of personality differences, and interpreted within the framework provided by Eysenck's model of the relationship between personality and individual differences.

The amount of influence attributed to the hierarchy of bishop and archdeacon, while related to neither extraversion nor neuroticism, is negatively related to psychoticism scores and positively related to lie scale scores. The negative relationship with psychoticism scores suggests that toughminded clergy are least likely to take notice of the hierarchy. The positive relationship with the lie scale scores is perhaps best interpreted through the theory that the lie scale measures aspects of social acquiescence (Nias, 1973; Massey, 1980). Clergy who are more socially acquiescent are also more likely to allow themselves to be influenced by the expectations of the church hierarchy of bishop and archdeacon.

The amount of influence attributed to family, while related to neither extraversion, psychoticism nor lie scale scores, is positively related to neuroticism scores. The positive relationship with neuroticism scores suggests that clergy who score high on neuroticism may be more anxious about accommodating the needs and expectations of those personally closest to them. Consequently they are more likely to allow their personal relationships to influence their professional priorities.

The amount of influence attributed to the local community at large, while related to neither neuroticism, psychoticism nor lie scale scores, is positively related to extraversion scores. The positive relationship with extraversion scores suggests that clergy who score high on extraversion are more likely to engage with the wider community (as already demonstrated in table four), more likely to be in touch with the expectations of the wider community, and more likely to feel the need to appear responsive to that community. Introverts may more successfully ignore the demands and expectations of the wider community.

The amount of influence attributed to the congregation, while related to neither extraversion, neuroticism nor lie scale scores, is negatively related to psychoticism scores. The negative relationship with psychoticism scores suggests that toughminded clergy are least likely to take notice of the congregation, while tenderminded clergy are most likely to allow their priorities to be influenced by the expectations of the congregation.

Finally, the amount of influence attributed to the church council is related to none of the personality variables.

Clergy role conflict

Table seven presents the realism of role expectations held by others as perceived by clergy.

In this table ratings of 1 and 2 have been characterised as 'low' realism, ratings of 3, 4 and 5 as 'medium' realism, and ratings of 6 and 7 as 'high' realism. This table also presents the mean ratings and standard deviations. These figures make it clear that clergy feel most supported by the expectations of their immediate family. Next in line after their family they identify the church hierarchy of bishop and archdeacon as most realistic in their expectations. The congregation and church council are considered to be considerably less realistic in their role expectations. The wider local community is considered to be the least realistic of the nominated groups. Overall these figures indicate that clergy are aware of considerable disparity between their preferred role priorities and the expectations placed on their roles by others. Such disparity could lead to conflict and discontent.

Table eight present the relationships between the perceived realism or role expectations held by others and the four Eysenckian personality-constructs. These correlation coefficients indicate that some of the variation between clergy can be accounted for in terms of personality differences, and interpreted within the framework provided by Eysenck's model of the relationship between personality and individual differences.

Psychoticism scores emerge as the strongest predictor of the level of perceived realism of role expectations held by others. The correlation coefficients indicate that tenderminded clergy attribute greater realism to the role expectation held by bishop, archdeacon, congregation and church council. All four of these nominated bodies represent institutional authorities within the church. This finding is consistent with

Table 7: Perceived realism of role expectations held by others

expectations	low %	medium %	high %	rating mean	st dev
congregation	7	71	22	4.39	1.32
church council	5	72	23	4.51	1.27
community at large	24	64	12	3.65	1.49
family	3	41	56	5.41	1.39
bishop	5	49	46	5.12	1.36
archdeacon	4	56	40	4.94	1.35

Table 8: Relationship between personality and perceived realism of role expectations held by others

expectations	E	N	P	L
congregation	+0.1738	−0.1855	−0.2641	+0.1238
	.05	.05	.001	NS
church council	+0.1035	−0.1481	−0.2650	+0.0450
	NS	NS	.001	NS
community at large	+0.0839	−0.2287	−0.0990	+0.0536
	NS	.01	NS	NS
family	+0.1087	+0.0152	−0.1449	−0.0322
	NS	NS	NS	NS
bishop	+0.1443	−0.0750	−0.3247	−0.0708
	NS	NS	.001	NS
archdeacon	+0.1055	−0.661	−0.2942	−0.0568
	NS	NS	.001	NS

the view that toughminded clergy are more likely to reject authority and to criticise expectations associated with authority as unrealistic or inappropriate. The lack of significant relationships between psychoticism scores and the level of realism attributed to the role expectations of family and community at large adds further support to this interpretation, since neither of these groups represents authority within the local church.

Neuroticism scores emerge as a significant predictor of the perceived realism of role expectations held by the congregation and the local community at large. Both groups have immediate local impact on the life and wellbeing of clergy. The negative correlations suggest that clergy characterised by high neuroticism scores are more likely to attribute tension and conflict to these two groups.

Extraversion scores emerge as a significant predictor only of the perceived realism of role expectation held by the congregation. The positive correlation suggests that the more extraverted clergy perceive the role expectations of the congregation as being more realistic than the more introverted clergy. This is consistent with the view that introverted clergy may tend to minimise or avoid some of the socially oriented role expectations expressed by the congregations.

Lie scale scores emerge as a significant predictor in relationship to none of the six nominated sets of role expectations.

In response to the additional single question inviting clergy to assess the overall conflict between how they see their role and how they perceive other people seeing their role, 16% suggested there was little overall conflict by opting for a rating of 1 or 2 on the scale. Another 61% suggested that there was a moderate level of overall conflict by opting for a rating of 3, 4 or 5. Nearly one-in-four (23%) suggested that there was a high level of overall conflict by opting for a rating of 6 or 7.

Table nine presents the relationship between personality and perceived level of overall conflict between the role expectations held by others and the role preferences held by clergy themselves. These correlation coefficients demonstrate clearly that perceived conflict is positively associated with higher scores on both the neuroticism and psychoticism scales. Toughminded and neurotic clergy are more likely to experience tension and conflict between how they see their role and how they think other people see their role than tenderminded and stable clergy. Neither extraversion scores nor lie scale scores are significant predictors of the perceived level of overall conflict between the role expectations held by others and the role preferences held by the clergy themselves.

Dissatisfaction with ministry

Over a third (36%) of the clergy indicated that they had entertained thoughts of leaving the ministry. For 13% such thoughts had occurred at just one point in their ministry, and for 5% they had occurred twice. For 12% such thoughts had occurred 'often enough to be uneasy with my job', and for 6% 'often enough to look for alternative employment'.

Table nine also presents the relationship between personality and thoughts of leaving ministry. These correlation coefficients follow the same pattern as those presented in relationship to perceived levels of overall conflict between the role expectations held by others and the role preferences held by clergy themselves. Clergy who score higher on the neuroticism scale and clergy who score higher on the psychoticism scale are significantly more likely to have entertained thoughts of leaving the ministry than clergy who score lower on these personality dimensions. These findings are consistent with the views that toughminded clergy are more likely to experience dissatisfaction with the structures of ministry and neurotic clergy are more likely to experience higher levels of anxiety generated by the tensions and conflicts associated with ministry. On the other hand, neither extraversion scores nor lie scale scores are significant predictors of thoughts of leaving ministry. Although other studies suggest that the male clerical profession tends to recruit more introverts (Francis, 1991; Jones and Francis, 1992), the present data indicate that once ordained extraverts are no less content with remaining in ministry than introverts.

*Table 9: Relationship between personality and level of overall per-
ceived role conflict and thoughts of leaving ministry*

	E	N	P	L
perceived	−0.0814	+0.3719	+0.3045	−0.0449
role conflict	NS	.001	.001	NS
thoughts of	−0.0467	+0.2021	+0.1904	−0.0811
leaving ministry	NS	.01	.01	NS

Conclusion

This study has charted the personality characteristics of 170 full-time
male stipendiary Anglican clergy working within one diocese in the
Church of England, and explored the relationship between personality
and clergy role prioritisation, role influences, conflict and dissatisfaction with ministry. Four main conclusions emerge from this
exploratory study.

First, although there seems to be a general basic consensus among
male clergy regarding the level of priority given to different roles
within their current ministry, some of the variation between clergy in
role prioritisation can clearly be accounted for in terms of personality
differences. Clergy who score high on the extraversion scale tend to
give a higher priority to the role of community leader. These are men
who may well enjoy accepting a higher profile in the community at
large. Clergy who score high on the neuroticism scale tend to give a
lower priority to the role of preacher. These are men who may well
experience anxiety and unease about being required to preach. Clergy
who score high on the psychoticism scale tend to give lower priority to
the role of administrator. These are men who may well resist accepting
the expectations of their congregations and church councils that they
should take on more administrative responsibility than they would
freely choose for themselves. Clergy who score high on the lie scale
demonstrate no differences in role prioritisation from those who score
low on the lie scale. Overall these findings lend further support to the
view that personality differences may predispose individual clergy to
prioritise aspects of their ministry in different ways. Such information
should help both individual clergy and the church hierarchy to shape
more realistic expectations regarding potential ministry performance in
specific situations and contexts.

Second, some of the variation between clergy in the perceived influences on their current role priorities can be accounted for in terms of
personality differences. The amount of influence attributed to the hierarchy of bishop and archdeacon is negatively correlated with
psychoticism scores and positively correlated to lie scale scores. In
other words, toughminded clergy are less likely to be influenced by the
expectations of the bishop and archdeacon, while socially acquiescent
clergy are more likely to take notice of the views of the hierarchy. The
amount of influence attributed to family is positively correlated with

neuroticism scores. In other words, clergy who score high on neuroticism seem to be more anxious about accommodating the needs and expectations of those personally closest to them. The amount of influence attributed to the local community at large is positively correlated with extraversion scores. In other words, clergy who score high on extraversion seem to be more in touch with the expectations of the wider community and to feel the need to be responsive to those expectations. The amount of influence attributed to the congregation is negatively correlated with psychoticism scores. In other words, tenderminded clergy are more likely to allow their priorities to be influenced by the expectations of their congregation. Overall these findings support the view that personality differences may predispose individual clergy to allow different groups to influence their view of ministry and their role prioritisation. Such information should help to account for some of the differences in clergy performance and role prioritisation.

Third, some of the variation between clergy in their attitude toward the role expectations held by others can be accounted for in terms of personality differences. The data demonstrate that toughminded clergy judge the role expectations held by bishop, archdeacon, congregation and church council all to be less realistic than their tenderminded colleagues. Clergy who score high on psychoticism, therefore, seem to be more likely to reject authority and to criticise the expectations associated with authority as unrealistic or inappropriate. Clergy who score high on neuroticism judge the role expectations held by the congregation and the local community at large to be less realistic than their colleagues who score low on neuroticism. High neuroticism scores, therefore, seem to be associated with greater awareness of tension and conflict in relationship to the local groups among whom the clergy work. Clergy who score high on introversion judge the role expectations held by the congregation to be less realistic than their colleagues who score high on extraversion. Introverted clergy, therefore, seem more likely to reject the socially oriented role expectations held by their congregations. Overall these data support the view that personality differences predispose individual clergy to experience different levels of conflict within their ministry. The summary statistics make it clear that clergy who score high on neuroticism and on psychoticism experience significantly higher levels of role conflict than those who score low on these dimensions. Such information should help to explain some of the differences in clergy stress and dissatisfaction.

Finally, some of the variation between clergy in their thoughts of leaving ministry can be accounted for in terms of personality differences. The data demonstrate that clergy who score high on the neuroticism scale and clergy who score high on the psychoticism scale are significantly more likely to have entertained thoughts of leaving the ministry than clergy who score lower on these personality dimensions. Toughminded clergy may be more likely to experience dissatisfaction with the structures of ministry and neurotic clergy may be more likely to experience higher levels of anxiety generated by the tensions and conflicts associated with ministry. Such information should help to identify those clergy most likely to leave the ministry.

These conclusions have emerged from a relatively small exploratory study. They have, however, clearly demonstrated the value of extending this model of research. Future studies should attempt to refine more sophisticated measures of clergy role prioritisation, role influences, conflict and dissatisfaction with ministry and extend the population studied to include not only male Anglican clergy, but female Anglican clergy, male and female Free Church ministers and Catholic priests.

References

Bartram, D and Dale, H C A (1982) 'The Eysenck Personality Inventory as a selection test for military pilots,' *Journal of Occupational Psychology*, 55, pp. 287–296.

Bier, W C (ed.) (1970) *Psychological Testing for Ministerial Selection*, New York, Fordham University Press.

Blizzard, S W (1955) 'The roles of the rural parish minister, the Protestant seminaries and the science of social behaviour,' *Religious Education*, 50, pp. 383–392.

Blizzard, S W (1956) 'The minister's dilemma,' *The Christian Century*, 73, pp. 505–509.

Blizzard, S W (1958a) 'The parish minister's self-image of his master role,' *Pastoral Psychology*, 89, pp. 23–32.

Blizzard S W (1958b) 'The Protestant parish minister's integrating roles', *Religious Education*, 53, pp. 374–380.

Blunt, P (1978) 'Personality characteristics of a group of white South African managers: some implications for placement procedures,' *International Journal of Psychology*, 13, pp. 139–146.

Bradley, J (1986) 'Personality or performance?' *Nursing Times*, 82, 20, pp. 45–46.

Brown, R G S and Stones, R W H (1972) 'Personality and intelligence characteristics of male nurses,' *International Journal of Nursing Studies*, 9, pp. 167–177.

Coates, C H and Kistler, R C (1965) 'Role dilemmas of Protestant clergymen in a metropolitan community,' *Review of Religious Research*, 6, pp. 147–152.

Cooper, R and Payne, R (1967) 'Extraversion and some aspects of work behaviour', *Personnel Psychology*, 20, pp. 45–57.

Cronbach, L J (1951) 'Coefficient alpha and the internal structure of tests,' *Psychometrika*, 16, pp. 297–334.

Davies, D, Watkins, C and Winter, M (1991) *Church and Religion in Rural England*, Edinburgh, T and T Clark.

Dittes, J E (1971) 'Psychological characteristics of religious professionals,' in M Strommen (ed.) *Research on Religious Development: a comprehensive handbook*, New York, Hawthorn, pp. 422–460.

Evans, W (1986) 'Personality and stress,' *Personality and Individual Differences*, 7, pp. 251–253.

Eysenck, H J (1967) 'Personality patterns in various groups of businessmen,' *Occupational Psychology*, 41, pp. 449–450.

Eysenck, H J and Eysenck, M W (1985) *Personality and Individual Differences: a natural science approach*, New York, Plenum Press.

Eysenck, H J and Eysenck S B G (1975) *Manual of the Eysenck Personality Questionnaire (adult and junior)*, London, Hodder and Stoughton.

Eysenck, H J and Eysenck S B G (1991) *Manual of the Eysenck Personality Scales*, London, Hodder and Stoughton.

Eysenck, S B G, Eysenck, H J and Barrett, P (1985) 'A revised version of the psychoticism scale,' *Personality and Individual Differences*, 6, pp. 21–29.

Feggetter, A J W and Hammond, D R F (1976) 'The relationship between personality, flying aptitude and performance in rotary wing training,' *Journal of Naval Science*, 2, pp. 63–68.

Francis, L J (1991) 'The personality characteristics of Anglican ordinands: feminine men and masculine women?' *Personality and Individual Differences*, 12, pp. 1133–1140.

Francis, L J (1992a) 'Male and female clergy in England: their personality differences, gender reversal?' *Journal of Empirical Theology*, 5, 2, pp. 31–38.

Francis, L J (1992b) 'Is psychoticism really a dimension of personality fundamental to religiosity?' *Personality and Individual differences*, 13, pp. 645–652.

Francis, L J, Brown, L B and Philipchalk, R (1992) 'The development of an abbreviated form of the revised Eysenck Personality Questionnaire (EPQR-A): its use among students in England,

Canada, the USA and Australia,' *Personality and Individual Differences*, 13, pp. 443–449.

Francis, L J and Pearson, P R (1991) 'Personality characteristics of mid-career Anglican clergy,' *Social Behaviour and Personality*, 19, pp. 81–84.

Francis, L J and Thomas, T H (1992) 'Personality profile of conference-going clergy in England,' *Psychological Reports*, 70, p. 682.

Furnham, A (1992) *Personality at Work: the role of individual differences in the workplace*, London, Routledge.

Furnham, A and Zacherl, M (1986) 'Personality and job satisfaction,' *Personality and Individual Differences*, 7, pp. 453–459.

Granleese, J and Barrett, T F (1990) 'The social and personality characteristics of the Irish chartered accountant,' *Personality and Individual Differences*, 11, pp. 957–964.

Gudjonsson, G H and Adlam, K R C (1983) 'Personality patterns of British police officers,' *Personality and Individual Differences*, 4, pp. 507–512.

Gumley, C J G, McKenzie, J, Ormerod, M B and Keys, W (1979) 'Personality correlates in a sample of male nurses in the British Royal Air Force,' *Journal of Advanced Nursing*, 4, pp. 355–364.

Heaven, P C L (1990) 'Religious values and personality dimensions,' *Personality and Individual Differences*, 11, pp. 953–956.

Heaven, P C L (1993) 'Personality predictors of self-reported delinquency,' *Personality and Individual Differences*, 14, pp. 67–76.

Henney, A (1975) 'Personality characteristics of a group of industrial managers,' *Journal of Occupational Psychology*, 48, pp. 65–67.

Innes, J M and Kitto, S (1989) 'Neuroticism, self-consciousness and coping strategies, and occupational stress in high school teachers,' *Personality and Individual Differences*, 10, pp. 303–312.

Jessup, G and Jessup, H (1971) 'Validity of the Eysenck Personality Inventory in pilot selection,' *Occupational Psychology*, 45, pp. 111–123.

Jones, D L and Francis, L J (1992) 'Personality profile of Methodist ministers in England,' *Psychological Reports*, 70, p. 538.

Jones, J G, Janman, K, Payne, R L and Rick, J T (1987) 'Some determinants of stress in psychiatric nursing,' *International Journal of Nursing Studies*, 24, pp. 129–144.

Jud, G J, Mills, E W and Burch, G W (1970) *Ex-Pastors: why men leave the parish ministry*, Philadelphia, Pilgrim Press.

Kirkcaldy, B, Thome, E and Walter, T (1989) 'Job satisfaction among psychosocial workers,' *Personality and Individual Differences*, 10, pp. 191–196.

Lauer, R H (1973) 'Organisational punishment: punitive relations in a voluntary association: a minister in a Protestant church,' *Human Relations*, 26, pp. 189–202.

Lester, D (1990) 'Maslow's hierarchy of needs and personality,' *Personality and Individual Differences*, 11, pp. 1187–1188.

Lester, D (1991) 'Accuracy of recognition of genuine versus simulated suicide,' *Personality and Individual Differences*, 12, pp. 765–766.

Loo, R (1983) 'Nursing students: personality dimensions and attitudes toward women,' *Psychological Reports*, 52, pp. 504–506.

Lynn, R (1969) 'Personality characteristics of a group of entrepreneurs,' *Occupational Psychology*, 43, pp. 151–152.

Malony, H N and Hunt, R A (1991) *The Psychology of Clergy*, Harrisburg, Pennsylvania, Morehouse Publishing.

Massey, A (1980) 'The Eysenck Personality Inventory lie scale: lack of insight or . . .?' *Irish Journal of Psychology*, 4, pp. 172–174.

Menges, R J and Dittes, J E (1965) *Psychological Studies of Clergymen: abstracts of research*, New York, Nelson.

Nauss, A H (1973) 'The ministerial personality: myth or reality?' *Journal of Religion and Health*, 12, pp. 77–96.

Nelsen, H M, Yokley, R L and Madron, T W (1973) 'Ministerial roles and social actionist stance: Protestant clergy and protest in the sixties,' *American Sociological Review*, 38, pp. 375–386.

Nias, D K B (1973) 'Attitudes to the Common Market: a case study in conservatism,' in G D Wilson (ed.) *The Psychology of Conservatism*, London, Academic Press, pp. 239–255.

Pearson, P R (1989) 'Psychoticism and spiral maze performance in elderly psychiatric patients,' *Personality and Individual Differences*, 10, pp. 371–372.

Pearson, P R (1990a) 'Is personality related to behavioural disability in the elderly?' *Personality and Individual Differences*, 11, pp. 1189–1190.

Pearson, P R (1990b) 'Impulsiveness and spiral maze performance in elderly psychiatric patients,' *Personality and Individual Differences*, 11, pp. 1309–1310.

Pearson, P R (1993) 'Item endorsement of the short form of the EPQ-R among a group of elderly female psychiatric patients,' *Personality and Individual Differences*, 14, pp. 747–748.

Raine, A and Manders, D (1988) 'Schizoid personality, inter-hemispheric transfer, and left hemisphere over-activation,' *British Journal of Clinical Psychology*, 27, pp. 333–347.

Ranson, S, Bryman, A and Hinings, B (1977) *Clergy, Ministers and Priests*, London, Routledge and Kegan Paul.

Reilly, M E (1975) 'Perceptions of the priest role,' *Sociological Analysis*, 36, pp. 347–356.

Russell, R J H and Wells, P A (1991) 'Personality similarity and quality of marriage,' *Personality and Individual Differences*, 12, pp. 407–412.

Savage, R D and Stewart, R R (1972) 'Personality and the success of card-punch operators in training,' *British Journal of Psychology*, 63, pp. 445–450.

Schuller, D S, Strommen, M P and Brekke, M L (1980) *Ministry in America*, San Francisco, Harper and Row.

SPSS Inc. (1988) *SPSSX User's Guide*, New York, McGraw-Hill.

Sterns, L, Alexander, R A, Barrett, G V and Dambrot, F H (1983) 'The relationship of extraversion and neuroticism with job preferences and job satisfaction for clerical employees,' *Journal of Occupational Psychology*, 56, pp. 145–153.

Sutherland, V J and Cooper, C L (1991) 'Personality, stress and accident involvement in the offshore oil and gas industry,' *Personality and Individual Differences*, 12, pp. 195–204.

Tiller, J (1983) *A Strategy for the Church's Ministry*, London, Church Information Office Publishing.

Towler, R and Coxon, A P M (1979) *The Fate of the Anglican Clergy*, London, Macmillan.

Wilson, G D, Tunstall, O A and Eysenck, H J (1972) 'Measurement of motivation in predicting industrial performance: a study of apprentice gas fitters,' *Occupational Psychology*, 46, pp. 15–24.

3. Ministerial effectiveness

The discussion of ministerial effectiveness raises for psychological research both conceptual and methodological issues. What is meant by ministerial effectiveness? How can ministerial effectiveness be measured and assessed? This chapter presents three different perspectives on these questions.

In the first article in this section, Allen Nauss addresses the relationship between leadership styles and effective ministry. He selected parish office holders to rate the performance of 310 Lutheran parish pastors on the Ministerial Function Scale. The edition of the scale employed in the study included seven factors: preacher-priest, administrator, community and social involvement, personal and spiritual model, visitor-counsellor, teacher, and evangelist. The study also employs the Ohio State Leader Behaviour Description Questionnaire, slightly adapted to fit a congregational setting. The data demonstrate the relationship between differences in leadership style and different levels of effectiveness in different areas of ministry.

Professor Allen Nauss developed the Toward Excellence in Ministry research project at Christ College Irvine, Irvine, California, USA. This article was first published in *Journal of Psychology and Theology* in 1989.

In the second article, H Newton Malony and Laura Fogwell Majovski explore the role of psychological assessment in predicting ministerial effectiveness. The primary assessment tool employed in the study was the Minnesota Multiphasic Personality Inventory. The second objective assessment measure used was the Inventory of Religious Activities and Interests. Ministerial effectiveness was assessed by the Ministerial Effectiveness Inventory and by certain indicators of local church life, including membership, attendance, salary and giving. These data were coordinated for 71 United Methodist ministers. The results found that psychological evaluations at the time of ministerial selection were unrelated to ratings of job effectiveness.

Professor H Newton Malony is Professor of Psychology at the Graduate School of Psychology, Fuller Theological Seminary, Pasadena, California, USA. Laura Fogwell Majovski also worked at the Fuller Theological Seminary. This article was first published in *Review of Religious Research* in 1986.

In the third article, Howard W Stone also examines the extent to which seminary entrance test data could predict future effectiveness in ministry among a sample of 163 Protestant clergy. Test data included an intelligence test, a reading test, the Minnesota Multiphasic Personality Inventory and the Theological School Inventory. Ministerial effectiveness was established as the overall appraisal rating by judicatory supervisors. The results suggest that considerably more conceptual and methodological refinement is needed before psychological assessment can lead to efficient prediction of ministerial effectiveness.

Professor Howard W Stone is Professor of Psychology and Pastoral Counselling at Brite Divinity School, Texas Christian University in Fort Worth, Texas, USA. This article was first published in *Pastoral Sciences* in 1989.

3.1 Leadership styles of effective ministry

Allen Nauss

A number of major changes have appeared in our society within the past half century. The changes that have affected service in the parish ministry include, according to Schaller (1987), new media forms, new types of transportation, social change involving women, liberalised values, and socialistic trends. In order to meet these challenges effectively, clergy have had to adapt their ministry in different ways.

In this 'different world' Schaller (1987) has also observed increased expectations on the part of laity for competent performance of parish clergy. These expectations, as well as the societal changes, have placed greater demands on the clergy to display at least a satisfactory, if not a very effective, level of performance.

Research on effectiveness in ministry during the past 30 years has not elicited a clear picture of characteristics of the parish or the pastor. Previous research studies have highlighted only isolated aspects of the pastor's personality (Allen, 1955; Benson and Tatara, 1967; Breimeier, 1963; Carroll, 1970; Douglas, 1957; Ham, 1960; Harrower, 1964; Jackson, 1955; Nauss, 1973a, 1973b) as well as demographics of the pastor and the congregation (Allen, 1955; Ashbrook, 1967; Dyble, 1972; Ham, 1960; Jackson, 1955; Nauss, 1973b).

Malony (1976) has suggested that leadership is an essential factor in producing effective ministry. Several studies have dealt with the pastor's leadership and effective ministry, but only in a general sense (Ashbrook, 1967; Benson and Tatara, 1967; Free and Malony, 1982; Jackson, 1955; Luecke, 1973; Majovski and Malony, 1986; Nauss, 1973b; Sweeney, 1979). It would seem that studies should focus on the leadership of parish pastors regarded as effective in their ministry. Skills such as task-orientation and relations-orientation, considered to be primary factors in leadership (Bass, 1981), and others such as persuasiveness and goal-orientation, may likely be a part of the effective pastor's style.

Part of the problem in measuring ministerial effectiveness and obtaining associated results has stemmed from the use of a global assessment (Malony, 1984; Nauss, 1972). None of the studies that have used multi-dimensional performance measures have as yet presented a clear overall picture (Cochran, 1982; Dyble, 1972; Johnson, Lohr, Wagner and Barge, 1975; Nauss, 1983; Rader, 1969; Schuller, Strommen and Brekke, 1980). Only one has focused on leadership in particular. Moy and Malony (1985) used the LIFO survey (Atkins, 1981) and the Least Preferred Co-Worker Scale (Fiedler,

1967) as measures of leadership and found that the LIFO supporting-giving pattern proved to be the only style positively related to effectiveness overall, as well as to the visitor-counsellor and preaching roles.

It was hypothesised for this study that first, specific leadership skills as used by the parish pastor would be associated with ministerial effectiveness and second, effectiveness in each of the separate ministerial functions would be characterised by a different set or balance of the skills.

Method

Subjects

The ministry of clergy in congregations of three separate and somewhat contrasting districts of the Lutheran Church-Missouri Synod was rated by selected parishioners. In the Iowa West District (IA) 87 ministers (65% response) were included. A 58% response (91 clergy) was obtained from the California-Nevada-Hawaii District (CNH, including in California only the northern part). For the Southern California District (SOCAL), involving also parishes from Arizona and parts of Nevada, 132 ministers (61% response) were a part of the study. All clergy were male.

To rate the pastors, parish office holders who were presumed to be representative of the active members and also well acquainted with the pastor were selected from each congregation – congregation president, chairperson of the board of elders, women's group president, youth group president or representative, chairperson of the board of education, chairperson of the board of stewardship, Sunday School superintendent, and the parochial school principal (if available). When taken as a group the parish office holders' perceptions of the pastor's effectiveness and leadership skill may be regarded as equal to, or perhaps even more accurate than, self-perceptions or judgements by 'external' raters who are not in a position to observe the pastor over a long period of time. Response rates were 76% (IA), 68% (CNH) and 70% (SOCAL) with a required minimum of three to a maximum of eight raters for each pastor.

Instruments and Variables

The 30-item Ministerial Function Scale (MFS)[1] developed by Kling (1958) was used by the parishioners to rate the effectiveness of their pastor on five-point scales (1 = ineffective to 5 = outstanding). Each point was described in detail and the raters were also advised to avoid three rating problems (halo error, leniency error and similar-to-me error). The items in the original scale were factor analysed in the Growth in Ministry Study (Johnson *et al.*, 1975) and produced six factors with alpha reliability coefficients ranging from .70 to .88.

The preacher-priest factor includes six items referring to the leading of public worship services, preaching sermons, working with boards and committees and handling some pastoral care. The administrator develops plans and manages the church office and finances. Items for the community and social involvement factor involve participation in community and social affairs and agencies. The personal and spiritual model is concerned with the cultivation of the pastor's own home, and his personal and spiritual life. As a visitor-counsellor the pastor promotes and directs congregational fellowship and does counselling and visiting. The teacher factor includes the teaching of only children and youth.

A seventh set of items was added for this study to portray an evangelist function including such activities as being active in evangelism, setting membership goals, and promoting missions in the community and the world.

The evangelist factor was considered suitable for tentative use following a factor analysis involving a varimax rotation of principal components that was produced from a sampling of the ratings from each of the three districts.[2]

After rating the pastor's effectiveness in each of the functions, the parishioners assessed their pastors on the Ohio State Leader Behaviour Description Questionnaire (LBDQ), one of the most frequently used leadership measures. Reliability coefficients have ranged from .55 to .91 (Stogdill, 1963).

Eleven of the twelve subscales of the LBDQ were regarded as useful for assessing a pastor's leadership. Some of the items were changed slightly to fit a congregational setting. Ratings were made on a five-point scale (1 = never to 5 = always).

The titles of the subscales have been re-labelled in order to communicate the content more readily to clergy. Brief definitions are given as follows (LBDQ titles are given in the parentheses): *task-oriented* (initiation of structure): clearly defines own role, lets members know what is expected; *relations-oriented* (consideration): shows regard for the comfort, well-being, status and contribution of individual members; *controlling* (role assumption): actively exercises leadership role rather than surrendering it; *persuasive* (persuasion): uses persuasion and argument effectively, exhibits strong convictions; *integrative* (integration): maintains a closely knit group, resolves intermember conflicts; *goal-oriented* (production emphasis): urges members to work hard to improve their performance; *accurate in predicting* (predictive accuracy): exhibits ability to predict accurately potential problems and outcomes; *cool under pressure* (demand reconciliation): reconciles conflicting demands and reduces disorder to system; *prominent in representing congregation* (representation): speaks and acts as the representative of the congregation; *tolerant of freedom* (tolerance of freedom): allows members scope for initiative, decision and action;

tolerant of uncertainty (tolerance of uncertainty): is able to tolerate uncertainty and postponement without anxiety.

A total of 45 variables were used, including a measure of the pastor's personality (Myers-Briggs Type Indicator), self-ratings of the importance of the seven parish functions and several leader behaviours, and also an assessment of the parish and the congregational leaders (see table one for a listing of the variables assessed).

Procedure

An analysis of variance of the dependent and the primary independent variable ratings from the three districts was necessary first to determine if they could be legitimately combined (table one). Lack of significant differences among the districts for seven of the eight effectiveness variables and for ten of the eleven leader behaviours shows that the ratings were consistent from district to district and could be combined.

Multiple regression (MR) analysis was then employed to see if the LBDQ behaviours or any of the other variables, would be identified as predictors of effectiveness in any of the functions. However, the thrust of this study was upon the identification of effective leadership styles and included the first hypothesis which implied that the leader skills would outweigh the other variables as predictors. If some of the other variables listed in table one that reflect differences among the districts, such as age and parish experience of the pastor, would also prove to be highly significant as predictors of effectiveness, they might help explain any potential regional differences in leadership styles. Except for leader environment and worship attendance, the parish characteristic variables could not be admitted to the MR analysis programme employed in this study because they were recorded only as nominal data.

Results

Beta weights for the significant variables were translated into percentages of the total variance of the predicted variable (table two). This form of the results can help the reader understand the comparative importance of each of the characteristics predictive of a particular function.

In the preacher-priest function, as an example of one set of the results, five variables were selected to predict effectiveness. A squared multiple correlation (R squared) of .588 was obtained, indicating that the leader skills accounted for more than half of the variance.

For the seven functions, and also the overall effective pattern, 50 variables, including the same variable listings for several functions, were selected by the MR analysis as predictors of effectiveness. Of the 50 a distinct majority, 31, were leader behaviours. The number of

Table 1: ANOVA measures comparing three districts according to pastor and parish variables

	df	F
leader behaviours		
prominent in representing congration	2,307	1.88
cool under pressure	2,307	1.00
tolerant of uncertainty	2,307	0.00
persuasive	2,307	0.60
task-oriented	2,307	1.47
tolerant of freedom	2,307	5.17**
controlling	2,307	0.21
relations-oriented	2,307	0.14
goal-oriented	2,307	2.36
accurate in predicting	2,307	0.37
integrative	2,307	0.66
effectiveness ratings		
preacher-priest	2,307	0.50
administrator	2,307	0.50
community involvement	2,307	0.72
personal-spiritual model	2,307	0.72
visitor-counsellor	2,307	0.68
teacher	2,304	3.49*
evangelist	2,307	1.17
overall effective	2,305	0.96
pastor–background		
age	2,307	4.30*
present parish tenure	2,307	3.45*
parish experience	2,307	4.46*
parish characteristics		
size (baptised members)	2,292	4.84**
socio-economic status	2,290	3.51*
cultural mix	2,295	13.13***
age mix	2,295	3.14*
worship attendance	2,295	1.93
leader environment	2,305	2.14
pastor–self ratings		
extra–introverted	2,307	1.85
practical–theoretical	2,307	6.55**
thinking–feeling	2,307	1.07
structured–unstructured	2,307	0.44
task-orientation	2,307	0.32
relations-orientation	2,304	0.45
self–present level	2,304	2.49
self–expected level	2,304	2.88
parish–present level	2,304	5.79**
parish–expected level	2,304	9.03***
pastor–importance ratings		
preacher-priest	2,307	5.90**
administrator	2,307	0.32
community involvement	2,307	1.29
personal-spiritual model	2,307	6.97***
visitor-counsellor	2,307	0.26
teacher	2,307	7.99***
evangelist	2,307	4.10*

Note: $* p. < 05$ $** p. < 01$ $*** p. < 001$

leader skills that predicted functional effectiveness ranged from two for community and social involvement, evangelist, and teacher to five

Table 2: *Weights of leader behaviours and other variables for predicting effectiveness in ministerial functions*

predictor variables	preacher-priest	administrator	evangelist	visitor-counsellor	community involved	teacher	personal model	overall effective
leader behaviours								
representing congregation	96 (5.6)	145 (6.5)			371 (15.9)			.657 (6.2)
cool under pressure	121 (9.7)	195 (11.1)					476 (26.1)	1.162 (15.5)
tolerant of uncertainty								
persuasive	293 (22.3)		190 (7.2)	199 (12.3)				
task-oriented		310 (14.4)					553 (22.2)	.986 (11.4)
tolerant of freedom								
controlling							-217 (-7.9)	-.755 (-8.3)
relations-oriented	116 (7.5)		284 (9.6)	246 (15.1)	349 (12.2)	675 (16.2)		1.195 (13.7)
goal-oriented			574 (27.9)	205 (11.4)		190 (2.8)		1.508 (15.0)
accurate in predicting		369 (17.3)						
integrative	163 (13.9)	136 (8.6)		306 (25.9)				1.389 (19.7)
pastoral background								
age						-1.407 (5.2)		
present tenure			58 (1.5)				44 (0.6)	
parish characteristic								
leader environment			70 (1.8)					
personality								
introverted			202 (1.0)				306 (1.9)	
structured		-253 (3.0)						
unstructured					186 (0.9)			

Table 2: (continued)

predictor variables	preacher-priest	administrator	evangelist	visitor-counsellor	community involved	teacher	personal model	overall effective
				predicted variables: beta (%)				
self-rating								
Task-oriented		1.044 (2.3)						
pastor–importance ratings								
preacher-priest			-114 (0.8)	-101 (0.3)				
community involved					208 (10.8)			
personal model							123 (4.4)	
visitor-counsellor				122 (3.1)				
teacher						255 (15.0)		221 (1.4)
evangelist		78 (0.2)	217 (10.2)	–	-807 (0.1)			
Constant	105.894	62.305	-107.871	-10.691	7.595	-33.768	0.670	187.050
R squared	.588	.628	.573	.679	.396	.390	.466	.741

Note: Beta values are recorded without the decimal point except in the overall effective variable. The total of the percentage figures for each predicted variable does not always equal exactly the multiple correlation squared (R squared), because the percentage figures and the R squared amounts were computed from different sources, and because of rounding of data.

for preacher-priest and administrator. Seven of the eleven leader skills predicted overall effectiveness of the pastor. In only one function (teacher) did the weight of leader skills amount to less than half of the percentage of total variance accounted for (19% out of 39%). These results affirm the first hypothesis that specific leadership skills would be associated with effectiveness. In addition, the leader behaviours far outweigh the other variables in predicting effectiveness.

Prominent among the variables other than leader skills included in the MR analysis and also selected as predictors are the pastor's ratings of the importance of the several functions. For example, 10% of the variance for the effective evangelist may be explained by the high rating the pastor gave to the importance of that function. In only two of the functions, the preacher-priest and the administrator, was the self-rating of the importance of the function not included among its predictors.

When the sets of predictive skills for each function are compared, it is clear that different behaviours have been selected and when the same skills are listed for two functions they usually show different beta weights or percentages. For example, the effective preacher-priest is characterised by his use of persuasiveness (22%), integrativeness (14%), coolness under pressure (10%), relations-orientation (8%) and prominence in representing the congregation (6%). In some contrast, the effective visitor-counsellor uses three of the same skills as the preacher-priest but with different weights – persuasiveness (12%), integrativeness (26%), relations-orientation (15%), and goal-orientation (11%). Observation for these results affirms the second hypothesis that effectiveness in each of the functions would be characterised by a different set or balance of the skills.

Discussion

As noted above, previous research on ministerial effectiveness produced isolated results. From this study we have obtained sets of characteristics of one category, leadership, that are predictive of effectiveness. This offers us a sharper picture of effectiveness.

Again, since at least several leader skills are predictive of effectiveness for each function, it seems appropriate to apply the phrase 'leadership style' to the picture of effectiveness for the respective functions. However, an effective style requires more than just above average performance in a set of leader behaviours. The effective pastor is also able to apply the skills appropriately in a particular function and with a suitable balance.

To help explain the different styles of effective clergy according to each function, results of a factor analysis of the leader skills may be reviewed (table three). They reveal four secondary clusters or factors of the skills displayed by the clergy subjects of this study. First, the professional factor includes the behaviours of persuasiveness, coolness

Table 3: factor analysis of LBDQ scales for clergy sample

scale	factor one professional	factor two personal	factor three public image	factor four managerial
persuasive	0.86			
cool under pressure	0.62	0.64		
task-oriented	0.59			0.62
controlling	0.69			
accurate in predicting	0.56			0.42
relations-oriented		0.76		
integrative		0.57		0.58
tolerant of uncertainty		0.85		
tolerant of freedom		0.48		
goal-oriented				0.89
representing the congregation			0.92	

Note: A factor loading of .40 was established as the minimum for acceptance as part of a factor. A fifth factor derived from the original analysis was not included because the one accepted item, tolerant of freedom, was not a significant predictor of effectiveness.

under pressure, task-orientation, accuracy in predicting and control. The second factor is the personal approach characterised by being relations-oriented, integrative, cool under pressure, tolerant of freedom and tolerant of uncertainty. The third factor involves the presentation of a public image exhibited by only one skill, representing the congregation. A fourth factor, a managerial approach, requires that the pastor display skills in being goal-oriented, task-oriented, integrative and accurate in predicting.

The effective preacher-priest shows what is probably a traditional image with a modern flavour in using all four factors. He emphasises the professional (persuasive and cool under pressure) and personal approaches (relations-oriented, integrative, and cool under pressure), mixed with a slight use of the public image presentation. He also serves as a manager in a minor capacity by employing the integrative skill. The emphasis upon the personal approach affirms the relationship which Moy and Malony (1985) found between the supportive-giving style of leadership and the preacher-priest function.

The effective administrator also uses all four factors, but in a different balance. He is more businesslike in displaying primarily the professional and managerial approaches. However, he also mixes in a slight amount of the personal approach (the integrative skill) and represents the congregation as a part of its public image. The strong use of the businesslike approach may show some similarity to the lack of flexibility of Moy and Malony's (1985) subjects in the administrator function, but it would seem that the use of the integrative skill might tend to soften any excessive display of rigidity for the current clergy sample.

Although Ashbrook (1967) found that effective ministers combined instrumental and expressive leadership behaviours (similar to the professional and personal approaches noted above), leadership studies of other occupations within the past two decades have also pointed to the importance of looking at the needs of a particular situation and then determining an appropriate balance of the two approaches. This recent research has focused especially on the combination of the more specific task- and person-orientation behaviours (Bass, 1981; Fiedler, 1967; Hersey and Blanchard, 1982). The present study has identified the ministerial function as one primary indicator of the situation.

In a style different from that needed for the previous two functions, the effective evangelist is characterised primarily by the managerial approach (the goal-oriented skill), but also uses to a minor degree skills in the professional and personal approaches. This style would correspond somewhat to the rancher kind of leadership advocated by Wagner (1984) in his church growth studies. Free and Malony (1982) found that churches showing exceptional membership gain had ministers characterised by the use of task-oriented skills (as included in the professional and managerial approaches) and also by a supportive (or personal) approach.

In carrying out their tasks effectively, the visitor-counsellors show primarily a personal approach, as previous researchers have also found for the pastor in general (Benson and Tatara, 1967; Benton, 1964; Douglas, 1957; Ham, 1960; Jackson, 1955), for pastors in their counselling roles (Rader, 1969), and also specifically for the visitor-counsellor function (Moy and Malony, 1985). But to organise and direct the fellowship programme they use a similar degree of the managerial factor. A minor emphasis is shown in the use of the professional approach (persuasiveness).

Effective display of the other functions may be explained similarly with the help of the four factors (see table three) and the percentage weight given to the skill (see table two).

To the extent that the pastors in this study, in the execution of any function, emphasised the managerial approach, they might correspond to the entrepreneurial style that Schaller (1987) has observed in effective use, in contrast with the enabler style espoused so strongly in the 1950s and 1960s.

It should be remembered that effectiveness includes more than the skills and characteristics identified here. The unexplained variance in each function shows that other characteristics not yet identified need to be included if a complete picture is to be obtained. At the same time, the fact that certain measured leader skills were *not* included in the sets listed here for effective ministry means that they were likely used by a wide range of clergy and were displayed in varying degrees of performance by both effective and less than effective pastors. This may explain why the controlling behaviour, for one, was not included in a positive pattern in any of the functions. It is probable, too, that controlling, as a leader skill for the pastor, would become a hindrance to effective ministry if there should be too much or even too little.

The pastor who is effective overall reflects an exceptional use of a large number of leader behaviours. It is likely that only a few pastors would be included in such a category. The great majority of pastors would probably have developed themselves more than the average in just several of the skills, leading to effectiveness, therefore, in only one or two of the functions at most.

Personality variables as measured by the MBTI appeared as predictors in four functions, but each with 3% or less of the weight that could be predicted of effectiveness. The results are generally in accord with expectation in aligning a structured personality characteristic with the effective administrator, an unstructured trait with the community activist, and an introverted facet (I) with the personal and spiritual model and the evangelist. The meagreness of the effect of personality on leadership style may be due in part to the ability of pastors to adapt their personality, whatever type it may be, to the situation. In addition, a personality characteristic may have been reflected in a certain leader skill that became one of the listed predictors because it was a stronger, more inclusive variable.

The fact that effectiveness ratings for the teacher function reflected differences among the three districts suggests that it may be perceived differently in the three areas, and/or that the list of items may need to be revised and expanded. In addition, a single factor involving the teaching of adults may be worth considering for inclusion in a future Ministerial Function Scale, since that activity seems very prominent in many parishes.

Implications

To the extent that they may be generalised, these results would suggest consideration for both seminary and in-service training. It would appear that assistance should be provided for training in each of the skills. However, satisfactory performance in most or all of the skills should be complemented by an ability to arrange an appropriate balance for the skills according to function.

Results from the present study come from only one denomination. It is possible also that styles may vary according to region. Further research and analysis should be conducted to determine whether any denominational and regional differences exist.

Further discussions of the parish ministry should be benefited by employing the functions identified by the MFS and by concentrating upon styles of leadership characterised by the LBDQ skills.[3]

Notes
1. Copies of the Ministerial Function Scale and the modified Leader Behaviour Description Questionnaire are available from the author upon request.
2. A factor should regularly be cross-validated on another sample before being used. Interpretation of the results for the evangelist factor must therefore be regarded as only tentative in view of this principle.
3. The assistance of S I Moon and D R Halm in developing the Toward Excellence in Ministry research project and the financial support provided by Jon Pelzer are gratefully acknowledged. Kenneth Behnken assisted in selecting the evangelist items.

References

Allen, P J (1955) 'Childhood backgrounds of success in a profession,' *American Sociological Review*, 10, pp. 186–190.

Ashbrook, J B (1967) 'Ministerial leadership in church organization,' *Minstry Studies*, 1, pp. 1–32.

Atkins, S (1981) *The Name of Your Game*, Beverly Hills, California, Ellis and Stewart.

Bass, B M (1981) *Stogdill's Handbook of Leadership*, New York, Free Press.

Benson, J V and Tatara, M (1967) A longitudinal investigation of psychological test characteristics of LCA clergymen correlated with other criteria measures of effectiveness (unpublished confidential preliminary draft report), New York, Board of Theological Education, Lutheran Church in America.

Benton, J A Jr (1964) 'Perceptual characteristics of Episcopal pastors,' *Dissertation Abstracts International*, 25, p. 3963. (University Microfilms number 64–13188.)

Breimer, K (1963) The relation between selected personality, interest and ability measures and ministerial effectiveness, unpublished manuscript.

Carroll, D (1970) 'A follow-up study of psychological assessment,' in W C Bier (ed.) *Psychological Testing for Ministerial Selection*, New York, Fordham University Press, pp. 159–180.

Cochran, J D (1982) 'A study to identify critical elements associated with effective and ineffective behaviors of United Methodist ministers in performance of the pastoral ministry,' *Dissertation Abstracts International*, 43, pp. 398A–399A. (University Microfilms number 82–16532.)

Douglas, W G T (1957) 'Predicting ministerial effectiveness,' *Dissertation Abstracts International*, 17, p. 169.

Dyble, J E (1972) 'Report to ad hoc ministry study committee,' Office of Research, Board of Christian Education, United Presbyterian Church in the USA, Philadelphia.

Fiedler, F E (1967) *A Theory of Leadership Effectiveness*, New York, McGraw-Hill.

Free, J J and Malony, H N (1982) The incorporating body: how churches gain and hold members, unpublished manuscript.

Ham, H M (1960) 'Personality correlates of ministerial success,' *Iliff Review*, 17, pp. 3–9.

Harrower, M (1964) 'Mental-health potential and success in the ministry,' *Journal of Religion and Health*, 4, pp. 30–58.

Hersey, P and Blanchard, K H (1982) *Management of Organizational Behaviour* (4th ed.), Englewood Cliffs, New Jersey, Prentice-Hall.

Jackson, D E (1955) 'Factors differentiating between effective and ineffective Methodist ministers,' *Dissertation Abstracts International*, 15, p. 2320. (University Microfilms number 00–11633.)

Johnson, M, Lohr, H, Wagner, J, and Barge, W (1975) *The Relationship between Pastors' Effectiveness and Satisfaction and other psychological and sociological variables: the growth in ministry project research*, Philadelphia, Lutheran Church in America.

Kling, F R (1958) 'A study of testing as related to the ministry,' *Religious Education*, 53, pp. 243–248.

Luecke, D S (1973) 'The professional as organizational leader,' *Administrative Science Quarterly*, 18, pp. 86–94.

Majovski, L F and Malony, H N (1986) 'The role of psychological assessment in predicting ministerial effectiveness,' *Review of Religious Research*, 28, pp. 29–39.

Malony, H N (1976) 'Current research on performance effectiveness among religous leaders,' in J Donaldson (ed.) *Research in Mental Health and Religious Behaviour*, Atlanta, Psychological Studies Institute, pp. 242–261.

Malony, H N (1984) 'Ministerial effectiveness: a review of recent research,' *Pastoral Psychology*, 33, pp. 96–104.

Moy, A C and Malony, H N (1985) The relationship between leadership style and ministerial effectiveness, unpublished manuscript.

Nauss, A H (1972) 'Problems in measuring ministerial effectiveness,' *Journal for the Scientific Study of Religion*, 11, pp. 141–151.

Nauss, A H (1973a) *Perceptual Characteristics of More and Less Effective Ministers*, Springfield, Illinois, Concordia Seminary Studies, Concordia Theological Seminary.

Nauss, A H (1973b) *Toward Excellence in the Ministry*, Springfield, Illinois, Concordia Seminary Studies, Concordia Theological Seminary.

Nauss, A H (1983) 'Seven profiles of effective ministers,' *Review of Religious Research*, 24, pp. 334–346.

Rader, B B (1969) 'Pastoral care functioning,' *Ministry Studies*, 3, pp. 18–27.

Schaller, L E (1987) *It's a Different World!* Nashville, Abingdon.

Schuller, D S, Strommen, M and Brekke, M L (1980) *Ministry of America*, San Francisco, Harper and Row.

Stogdill, R M (1963) *Manual for the Leader Behaviour Description Questionnaire - Form XII: an experimental revision*, Columbus, Ohio, The Ohio State University.

Sweeney, J E (1979) 'Professional competencies for church ministry as perceived by seminary faculties, church lay leaders, and seminary seniors,' Dissertation Abstracts International, 39, p. 5298A. (University Microfilms number 79–05617.)

Wagner, C P (1984) *Leading your Church to Growth*, Ventura, California, Regal.

3.2 The role of psychological assessment in predicting ministerial effectiveness

H Newton Malony and Laura Fogwell Majovski

Introduction

While the initial intent of ministerial selection procedures was to screen out those unfit for ministry, more recently they have been directed toward choosing those who would be most effective. This study was an attempt to validate the utility of psychological assessments in making these predictions.

The selection of professional religion leadership has been a concern for almost fifty years. Various sources of information have been utilised in these endeavours: academic performance, interview, work-samples, supervisor evaluations, as well as psychological evaluations. Numerous studies were conducted using the Minnesota Multiphasic Personality Inventory (MMPI), projective tests, and other vocational tests to determine personality and interest differences between those who chose to enter the ministry and those who did not (Webb, 1968; Bowes, 1963; Harrower, 1964; and Douglas, 1957). Results suggested that consistent differences existed between these groups and that there was a need for special norms for religious populations (Bier, 1948, 1956; D'Arcy, 1962; Davis, 1963; and Fielder, 1964). A modified MMPI was developed in an attempt to account for these differences in profile elevations by religious populations (Bier, 1971).

One of the most recent studies of the role of psychological assessment in ministerial selection procedures was that of Haight (1980). She investigated the relationship of psychological evaluations of ordination decisions in the United Methodist Church. Her results indicated that while ordination decisions were in part determined by psychological assessment recommendations, other sources of information about a candidate were also significant determinants. Additional results indicated that MMPI items alone did not differentiate between recommended and non-recommended candidates. However, combinations of score patterns did relate significantly to the recommendations which emerged from the psychological evaluations.

Turning to the question of effectiveness, early researchers conceptualised success in terms of perseverance in seminary (Godfrey, 1955; Aloyse, 1961; Vaugh, 1963; and Weisgerber, 1962). Faculty and peer ratings of performance were also used (Ashbrook, 1962; Coville,

1962; and Cardwell, 1967). Results from these studies were mixed in terms of which variables, if any, predicted completion of seminary or better ratings of faculty and peers. These results highlighted the important issue of effectiveness in ministry and the difficult definitional problem of determining its criteria (May, 1934; Blizzard, 1956; Douglas, 1957; Dittes, 1962; and Nauss, 1970).

Subsequent research efforts have been directed toward defining these criteria (Kolarik, 1954; Kling, 1958; Nauss, 1970; Kleaver and Dyble, 1973; Lopez, 1973; and Johnson, 1975). Often, these studies included the development of behavioural descriptions of ministerial effectiveness by laity and clergy. Spiritual traits (May, 1934) and personal fulfilment of parishioners (Malony, 1976) have been suggested. A distinction between primary and secondary measures of effectiveness was made by Guion (1965). Nauss (1972) utilised this distinction and defined primary measures of ministerial effectiveness as specific observable behaviours while secondary measures were defined as consequences of pastoral leadership (Nauss, 1972).

The most recent comprehensive study of criteria for ministerial effectiveness was made by Schuller, Strommen and Brekke (1980). Over 5,000 laity and clergy from 47 denominations participated in their research. Beginning with 850 descriptions of ministry, participants rated the descriptions as to their importance in ministerial effectiveness. From these ratings, 64 dimensions of effectiveness emerged. Factor analytic procedures revealed eleven general areas of ministry contributing to ministerial effectiveness. These areas included: having an open, affirming style; caring for persons under stress; evidencing congregational leadership; being a theologian in life and thought; undertaking ministry from a personal commitment of faith; developing fellowship and worship; having denominational awareness; evidencing ministry to community and world; being priestly-sacramental in ministry; manifesting a lack of privatistic, legalistic style; and not having disqualifying personal and behavioural characteristics. The intention of the Schuller *et al.* (1980) research was to provide an evaluation tool for newly ordained ministers regarding their readiness for ministry. It was not utilised to assess later success in the profession.

Based on their research, Schuller *et al.* (1980) suggested that a minister's life is developmental. What is meant by this is that the behavioural competencies needed to begin a career of ordained ministry are not seen as significantly different from those expected of a more experienced minister (Schuller *et al.*, 1980). Therefore, the potential exists for those well-developed criteria of effectiveness to be applied to research predicting actual effectiveness in the parish setting. Prior to the present research this had not been attempted.

The purpose of this study was to extend the Haight (1980) research on the validity of psychological evaluations in ministerial selection and to address the larger issue of the role of psychological assessments in predicting ministerial effectiveness. In addition, the study applied the Schuller *et al.* (1980) readiness for ministry criteria to the Nauss (1972) model of effectiveness. The predictive relationship of psychological recommendations to measures of both primary and secondary criteria of ministerial effectiveness was surveyed.

Method

Eighty-seven United Methodist ministers in full time parish ministry of the Pacific-Southwest Conference were surveyed. Among this group there were 68 male and 3 female clergy who voluntarily participated in the study.

Psychological assessments of these ministers had been conducted over a five-year period (1973–1977) by the same psychological evaluator (PE) at the time they were being considered for final ordination. Recommendations from these evaluations were compared to ratings of effectiveness by the district superintendent, the Pastor-Parish Relations Committee, and the pastors themselves.

At the time of this study these minsiters had been in ministry between three and eight years. The following is a breakdown, by year of actual ordination, of the pastors in parish settings at the time of this research: 1973 (twelve of fifteen); 1974 (sixteen of twenty); 1975 (thirteen of fourteen); 1976 (nine of eleven); 1977 (fifteen of seventeen); 1978 (five of five); 1979 (one of one).

The two questions which were investigated were: first, what was the relationship between the psychological recommendations and ministerial effectiveness; and second, what was the inter-relationship of the primary and secondary measures of effectiveness?

Measures of effectiveness in this study included both primary and secondary criteria. The Ministerial Effectiveness Inventory (MEI) was developed to gather primary measures of ministerial effectiveness (that is, specific observable behaviours). The MEI is a 59-item Likert-type questionnaire derived from the comprehensive study of the characteristics of effective ministry in the United States as found by Schuller *et al.* (1980). The MEI items are descriptors of the eight main characteristics of effective ministry which were rated as 'quite' or 'highly important', or as 'quite' or 'highly detrimental' in the Schuller *et al.* research (1980). The eight areas included the following:

a. having an open, affirming style;
b. caring for persons under stress;
c. evidencing congregational leadership;
d. being theologian in life and thought;
e. undertaking ministry from a personal commitment of faith;
f. developing fellowship and worship;
g. having denominational awareness; and
h. not having disqualifying personal and behavioural characteristics.

A total of 24 MEI items were developed from these eight areas. An additional 35 items were derived from the important determinants of effectiveness identified by the United Methodist Church participants in the Schuller *et al.* research (1980) according to Trotter (1980). Only those items were included which met the criteria of being rated as 'quite' or 'highly' either important or detrimental. Thus, a 59-item questionnaire was developed which asked the rater: 'How characteristic is this [item] of your minister?' or '... of you?'

The MEI questionnaires were mailed to three types of raters for each of the 87 pastors: the pastor, the District Superintendent (DS), and the Pastor-Parish Relations Committee (PPRC). Members of the PPRC committee are from the local congregation and work closely with the pastor in all matters concerning the functioning of the church. The following return rates were obtained (N=71): self=93%; PPRC=83%; and DS=88%. The split-half reliability of the MEI questionnaire was evaluated by rating group and found to be: self r=0.82; DS r=0.96; and PPRC r=0.99. The possible range of MEI scores is 59 to 354, with 148 as the median score.

Secondary measures of ministerial effectiveness (that is, consequences of leadership) were also obtained. These included the following variables: membership (of total church); attendance (main weekly worship service); church school (weekly attendance, all ages); salary (including allowances); and giving (annual total, by congregation). These data were obtained from the annual conference journal. Secondary measures of effectiveness were incomplete for several subjects due to omissions in published data and inaccessible conference journals. For comparative purposes, the values of the secondary measures of effectiveness were computed as per cent-change for the length of current parish assignment, divided by the number of years in the current parish assignment.

Results

Table one provides the descriptive statistics for these primary and secondary measures of effectiveness. The relationship of the psychological recommendations to the measures of effectiveness was analysed by correlational statistics. At the conclusion of each assessment, the PE provided the annual conference board of ordained ministry with a written evaluation of findings and clinical impressions, including a recommendation concerning further action. The PE provided verbal feedback to the subject (and spouse when applicable).

The primary assessment tool was the Minnesota Multiphasic Personality Inventory (MMPI). This is a 566 true-false item, self-reference personality inventory. The MMPI provides a ten-scale clinical profile of dimensions of personality, as well as a three-scale profile as to the validity of the test. Ranges of significant psychopathology and normalcy are indicated with well-established norms

Table 1: Descriptive statistics of measures of effectiveness

variable	N	mean	SD	range
primary measures (MEI, possible range 59–354)				
self	66	298.62	26.20	188 to 344
DS	66	298.34	46.39	123 to 354
PPRC	59	289.32	35.55	178 to 343
secondary measures (% change)				
membership	64	-1.58	12.52	-42 to + 57
attendance	64	0.13	10.43	-53 to + 27
church school	64	5.55	32.05	-90 to +106
salary	58	27.31	32.58	-1 to +186
giving	63	19.24	25.82	-20 to +168

(Hathaway and McKinley, 1967). The MMPI was included on the theory that greater normalcy would be related to more effectiveness.

A configurational profile for the MMPI was obtained by using the following formula:

Invalid Profile: L$\geq$66 or F$\geq$70 or K$\geq$75.

Unhealthy Profile: Mf$\geq$80 or when any other clinical scale $\geq$70.

The second objective assessment measure used in the psychological evaluations was the Inventory of Religious Activities and Interests (IRAI, Webb, 1968). This is a 220 item inventory, developed from numerous role descriptions of ministry. Results provide a profile of preference for performing ten ministerial roles: counsellor; administrator; teacher; scholar; evangelist; spiritual guide; preacher; reformer; priest; and musician. The instrument ws designed primarily to be descriptive and only secondarily to be predictive. Its reliability ranges between 0.82 and 0.87 for the subscales, and it has been standardised on a national sample of seminary students (Webb, 1968). It was included on the theory that higher overall interest in ministerial roles would be related to greater effectiveness.

A configural profile for the IRAI was obtained by using the following formula:

Unsuitable Profile: 7 or more scales $\geq$90 or when 6 or more scale $\leq$50.

No significant correlations were found between primary and secondary effectiveness ratings and these profile configurations.

Multiple regression analysis was conducted to investigate further the relationship of the MMPI data and the measures of effectiveness. Several of the primary measures were negatively correlated with the MMPI scales. Results revealed that eight per cent of the variance of Pastor-Parish Committee ratings was accounted for by the scale Ma ($R=-0.29$, $F=4.000$, $df=1,91$; $p\leq0.05$). In addition, 11 % of the variance of the pastors' own ratings were accounted for by the scale PD ($R=-0.33$, $F=7.87$, $df=1,91$; $p\leq0.01$). No variables accounted for variance in the ratings of the district superintendent.

Only one secondary measure of effectiveness had a significant relationship with the MMPI data. The attendance variable had seven per cent of its variance accounted for by the social introversion scale ($R=0.27$, $F=4.81$, $df=1,91$; $p\leq0.05$).

The original psychological recommendations were transformed from written reports to descriptive codes. Each report was assigned an ordinal descriptor of the clinical opinion and recommendations of the PE:

8 = accept (without condition);
7 = accept (with counselling for spouse);
6 = accept (with counselling for self);
5 = accept (with counselling for both);
4 = defer (with counselling for spouse);
3 = defer (with counselling for self);
2 = defer (with counselling for both);
1 = reject (without condition).

No significant correlations were found between these recommendations and either the primary or secondary measures of effectiveness. Since the psychological evaluation was originally conducted for screening rather than predictive purposes, the PE reconsidered the reports and sorted them into a normal distribution in which 64% were rated likely, 14% were rated more likely, 14% were rated less likely, 4% were rated most and least likely to succeed. These ratings did not relate significantly to any of the primary or secondary ratings of effectiveness.

An additional analysis was conducted to investigate the role of the length of time since original psychological assessment and the measures of effectiveness. Results from the one-way ANOVA revealed only one significant difference between the evaluation groups. The most recent groups of subjects, those assessed in 1977, were evaluated by the District Superintendent significantly lower in effectiveness than the groups assessed between 1973 and 1976.

Correlational analysis of primary measures of effectiveness indicated a significant relationship between committee and superintendent ratings of subjects ($r=0.59$, $p\leq0.01$). Self ratings were not significantly correlated with either of these ratings.

Several analyses were conducted to investigate the inter-relationship of the primary and secondary measures of effectiveness. Table two presents these inter-relationships.

Correlational analysis of the secondary measure of effectiveness indicated high positive inter-correlations between membership, attendance, and church school. Membership and giving were also significantly positively correlated. Salary was significantly related only to church school.

Significant correlations were also found in the analysis of the inter-relationships of primary and secondary measures of effectiveness. Superintendent Committee ratings were significantly positively related

Table 2: *Correlations of measures of effectiveness*

variable	membership	attendance	church school	salary	giving
primary measures					
self	0.03	0.00	0.05	−0.03	−0.06
DS	0.26*	0.39**	0.41**	−0.03	0.01
PPRC	0.26*	0.39*	0.27*	0.10	0.11
secondary measures					
giving	0.22*	0.21	0.04	0.07	–
salary	0.18	0.08	0.37**	–	–
church school	0.54**	0.40**	–	–	–
attendance	0.54**	–	–	–	–
membership					

Note: * p < .05 ** p < .01

to three secondary measures: membership, attendance and church school. Self ratings evidenced no significant relationship to any secondary measures of effectiveness.

In sum, these results reveal the following: first, no significant relationship was found between the psychological recommendations and measures of effectiveness; and second, significant inter-relationships were found between the various measure of effectiveness.

The data indicated that psychological recommendations were largely dependent on personality data (the MMPI) and to a lesser degree on interest data (the IRAI). The significant use of the MMPI configurational profiles in determining these recommendations confirmed the previous findings of Haight (1980). However, in addition, several individual MMPI scales served as significant determinants of these recommendations. The negative relationship of certain elevated profiles to psychological recommendations was consistent with previously cited research relating various MMPI scale elevations to lack of perseverance in seminary (Godfrey, 1955; Aloyse, 1961; Vaugh, 1963; and Weisgerber, 1962).

Results also indicated a significant relationship between the recommendations and ordination decisions (r=0.86) confirming the Haight research (1980). However, this relationship was only significant when the recommendations and decisions were compared in general categories, namely: accept, defer and reject. Despite this demonstration of a significant relationship between psychological recommendations and ordination decisions, the value of the contribution of the psychological assessments is questionable. Basically, the psychological evaluator found little overall variance among the candidates and, of those evaluated, recommended 90% for ordination. The significant relationship between recommendations and ordination decisions resides in the fact that 74% of those recommended for ordination were ordained. However, for the remaining 26% of those recommended, other data outweighed the psychological recommendations. Furthermore, 71% of those recommended for deferral by the psychological evaluator were accepted for ordination. Only 67% of those who were recommended to be rejected without any reconsideration were actually deferred or rejected. One subject was ordained counter to the psychological recommendations not to be ordained under any conditions. Results indicate that the psychological recommendations were often questioned, and other data were considered to outweigh the evaluation of unsuitable/unstable personality traits. No significant determinants of ordination decisions were found in any of the psychological assessment data.

Discussion

A possible explanation for these results could be the lack of validity of the dependant variables. However, a wide variance of scores was found on both primary and secondary measures of effectiveness. Furthermore, significant positive inter-correlations were found between the measures of effectiveness and several raters. On the basis of these findings, the measures of effectiveness are assumed to be valid.

Another explanation for these results could be that the psychological recommendations were based on inappropriate measures for predicting actual ministerial effectiveness. Results indicated that psychological recommendations were significantly determined by various aspects of the MMPI data, and to a lesser degree IRAI data. However, the MMPI was designed as a measure of psychopathology, and Butcher and Tellegen (1978) have urged caution against using the MMPI as a measure of general personality. Considering the fact that 90% of the candidates evaluated were recommended for ordination, the assessment issue appeared to be one of evaluating general personality traits rather than psychopathology.

The use of the MMPI in ministerial selection procedures for ordination may be outdated. Its initital use was for the screening of entering seminary candidates (Bier, 1948). Recently, however, the MMPI has been used to evaluate candidates who are at the final stages of the selection process. These candidates have persevered several years beyond seminary and those with significant personality flaws may have already been selected out by the time of final ordination decisions. However, should this be the case, the abandonment of psychological assessments is not precluded. Rather the use of personality tests which evaluate more normal personality dimensions would be preferred. Interpersonal styles of relating may also be important to assess and the use of other instruments would provide insight into a candidate's style of leadership.

Results from the present study provide direction for future research. An improved research design might have psychological assessments completed on candidates but not used in ordination decisions. Follow-up prediction research would then have a wider range of persons for comparison. In terms of the measurement of ministerial effectiveness, several issues need to be highlighted. Pastor's self ratings of effectiveness were used in the present study. The results suggest that pastors respond to different indicators of personal ministerial effectiveness from their supervisors or their members. Therefore, future research could explore these differences.

Additional measures of effectiveness may also be needed. The high intercorrelations of several measures of effectiveness suggest that members and supervisors responded to visible 'people participation', that is, attendance, membership and church school, as a strong indicator of a pastor's effectiveness. Measures of intrapersonal satisfaction, that is, individual's change and fulfilment, may provide further evidence of ministerial effectiveness. Such measures are not presently available and need to be developed.

The present research found that psychological evaluations in ministerial selection procedures were unrelated to ratings of job effectiveness. The issue of how job evaluations are related to actual job performance is currently an important issue in job-related selection procedures. The field of ministerial selection needs to be guided by these larger concerns. When psychological evaluations are used in selection procedures, they are inherently predictive and, therefore, need to be validated (David, 1974). However, as noted earlier, psychological evaluations are only a part of the process of ministerial selection. The ordination decisions themselves need to also be validated as to their job-relatedness.

Thus, it would be of interest to investigate the ability of those making the ordination decisions to predict future ministerial effectiveness. The initial question of interest would be whether they are more accurate predictors of effectiveness than psychological assessments. Such comparisons could be made with other various aspects of data used to determine final ordination decisions.

References

Aloyse, M (1961) 'Evaluations of candidates of religious life,' *Bulletin of the Guild of Catholic Psychiatrists*, 8, pp. 199–204.

Ashbrook, J B (1962) Evaluating seminary students as potential ministers, unpublished MA dissertation, Ohio State University.

Bier, W C (1948) 'A comparative study of the seminary group and four other groups on the MMPI,' *Studies in Psychology and Psychiatry from the Catholic University of America*, 7, p. 107.

Bier, W C (1956) 'A comparative study of five Catholic college groups on the MMPI,' in G W Welch and W G Dahlstrom (eds) *Basic Readings on the MMPI in Psychology and Medicine*, Minneapolis, University of Minnesota Press, pp. 586–609.

Bier, W C (1971) 'A modified form of the Minnesota Multiphasic Personality Inventory for religious personnel,' *Theological Education*, 7, pp. 121–134.

Blizzard, S W (1956) 'The minister's dilemma,' *The Christian Century*, 73, pp. 508–510.

Bowes, N T (1963) 'Professional evaluation of religious aspirants,' New York, St Paul Publications.

Butcher, J N and Tellegen, A (1978) 'Common methodological problems in MMPI research,' *Journal of Counselling and Clinical Psychology*, 46, pp. 620–628.

Cardwell, S W (1967) 'The MMPI as a predictor of success among seminary students,' *Ministry Studies*, 1, pp. 3–20.

Coville, W J (1962) 'Future research,' in S W Cook (ed.) *Research Plans*, New York, Religious Education Association, pp. 175–188.

D'Arcy, P F (1962) 'Review of research on the vocational interests of priest, brothers and sisters,' in M B Arnold (ed.) *Screening Candidates for the Priesthood and Religious Life*, Chicago, Loyola Univeristy Press, pp. 1–63.

Davis, C E (1963) *Counseling Prospective Church Workers*, Pittsburgh, Board of Education of the United Presbyterian Church.

Davis, F B (1974) *Standards: for educational and psychological tests*, Washington DC, American Psychological Association.

De Wire, H A (1962) 'Psychological testing in theological schools,' *Ministry Studies Board Newsletter*, 1, pp. 2–4.

Dittes, J C (1962) 'Research on clergymen: factors influencing decisions for religious service and effectiveness in the vocation,' *Religious Education (Supplement)*, 57, S, pp. 141–165.

Douglas, W T (1957) Predicting ministerial effectiveness, unpublished doctoral dissertation, Harvard University, Massachusetts.

Fielder, D W (1964) A nomothetic study of the Southern California School of Theology Seminarian, unpublished ThD dissertation, Southern California School of Theology.

Godfrey, R J (1955) Predictive value of MMPI with candidates for religious brotherhood, unpublished MEd dissertation, Marquette University, Indiana.

Guion, R M (1965) *Personnel Testing*, New York, McGraw-Hill.

Haight, E S D (1980) Psychological criteria for the selection of ministerial candidates, unpublished PhD dissertation, Northwestern University, Illinois.

Harrower, M (1964) 'Mental health potential and success in the ministry,' *Journal of Religion and Health*, 4, pp. 30–58.

Hathaway, S R and McKinley, J C (1967) *The Minnesota Multiphasic Personality Inventory manual*, New York, Psychological Corporation.

Johnson, M, Lohr H, Wagner, J and Barger, W (1975) *Growth in Ministry*, Philadelphia, Lutheran Church in America.

Kleaver, G L and Dyble, J E (1973) Effectiveness of young pastors, unpublished manuscript, Office of Research, Support Agency of the General Assembly of the United Presbyterian Church USA.

Kling, F R (1958) 'A study of testing as related to the ministry,' *Religious Education*, 53, pp. 243–248.

Kling, F R (1970) 'Discussion: to testing for the Roman Catholic priesthood,' in W C Bier (ed.) *Psychological Testing for Ministerial Selection*, New York, Fordham University Press.

Kolarik, J M (1954) 'A study of the critical requirements of the Lutheran ministry,' *The Lutheran Quarterly*, 7, pp. 38–44.

Lopez, F M (1973) 'Pastoral planning: ministerial evaluation,' mimeographed paper, Felix Lopez and Associates, Port Washington, New York.

Malony, H N (1976) 'Current research on performance effectiveness among religious leaders,' paper delivered at a National Evangelical Conference on Research in Mental Health and Religious Behaviour, Atlanta, Georgia.

May, M A (1934) *The Education of American Ministers: volume II and III*, New York, Institute of Social and Religious Research.

Moore, T V (1936) 'Insanity in priests and religious: I. The rate of insanity in priests and religious,' *American Ecclesiastical Review*, 95, pp. 485–498.

Nauss, A (1970) 'Development of a measure of ministerial effectiveness: a preliminary draft,' mimeographed paper, Concordia Seminary, Springfield, Illinois.

Nauss, A (1972) 'Problems in measuring ministerial effectiveness,' *Journal for the Scientific Study of Religion*, 11, pp. 141–151.

Schuller, D S, Strommen, M P and Brekke, M L (1980) *Ministry of America*, San Francisco, Harper and Row.

Trotter, F T (1980) 'United Methodist Church,' in D S Schuller, M P Strommen and M L Brekke (eds) *Ministry in America*, San Francisco, Harper and Row, pp. 445–457.

Vaugh, R P (1963) 'A psychological assessment program for candidates to the religious life,' *Catholic Psychology Record*, 1, pp. 65–70.

Webb, S C (1968) *An Inventory of Religious Activities and Interests*, Princeton, Educational Testing Service.

Weisgerber, C A (1962) 'Survey of a psychological screening program in a clerical order,' in M B Arnold, P Hispanicus, C A Weisgerber and P R D'Arcy (eds) *Screening Candidates for the Priesthood and Religious Life*, Chicago, Loyola University Press, pp. 107–148.

3.3 Predicting ministerial effectiveness

Howard W Stone

Is there a way of knowing if a person entering seminary will make an effective minister? Are there indicators that can guide the church in their counselling with ministerial students and potential students? Is a candidate's personality or motivation to ministry sufficiently stable so that predictions at entrance to seminary are relevant for determining future performance in the profession?

In an attempt at answering these and similar questions, one hundred and sixty-three ministers in a mainline Protestant denomination were studied. Through the use of statistical procedures, the project undertook to determine if students' background information or seminary entrance test data – such as scores on an intelligence test, a reading test, the Minnesota Multiphasic Personality Inventory (MMPI) or the Theological School Inventory (TSI) – could predict their future effectiveness in ministry as defined by an overall effectiveness rating of their judicatory supervisor.

Obstacles to the study of effectiveness

There is increasing interest among researchers in determining ways to predict effectiveness in a career – any career – before one enters it. A number of such studies have looked at the ministerial personality (Bloom, 1971; Bowes, 1963; Brekke, Schuller, and Strommen, 1976; Dittes, 1962; Ekhardt and Goldsmith, 1984; Haight, 1980; Hjelle and About, 1970; Larsen and Shopshire, 1988; Nauss, 1973; Rayburn, Richmond and Rogers, 1986; Schuller, 1976; Webb, 1968.) In addition, there have been attempts to define what constitutes an effective minister (Cardwell, 1982; Johnson, 1975; Kleaver and Dyble, 1973; Kling, 1958; Kolarik, 1954; Lopez, 1973; Maloney, 1976; Nauss, 1970).

Significant challenges exist in any study that tries to predict the future effectiveness of ministers. The first hurdle in effectiveness studies is defining what constitutes a 'successful' or 'effective' minister. Some research has used quantitative criteria such as persistence in ministry, income level, size of church and the like (Aloyse, 1961; Godfrey, 1955; Vaugh, 1963; Weisgerber, 1962). The advantage of such indices is that they are easily ascertained and the data is quantifiable, but obvious problems exist. External measures do not examine the quality of one's ministry. A minister who is a skilful worship leader, preacher, teacher, administrator and pastoral carer may choose to serve a small rural parish that cannot afford a high salary. Such a person would not appear very 'successful' based on external criteria but may in fact be an extraordinarily effective pastor.

Other studies have tried to use more qualitative measures (Ashbrook, 1962; Ashbrook, 1967; Cardwell, 1967; Cardwell, 1982; Chalmers, 1970; Coville, 1962; Haight, 1980; Harris, 1973; Howard, 1986; Hutchison, 1984; Malony and Majovski, 1986; McGraw, 1969; Nauss, 1972; Schuller, Strommen and Brekke, 1980; Spiers, 1965; Weiser, 1987). Clarifying the components of an effective ministry has been the focus of some of these studies. Typically, ministerial self reports, judicatory supervisor ratings, and congregational evaluations have provided the material for ascertaining the attitudes and abilities of an effective ministry, and have helped to discriminate individuals' degrees of effectiveness. Some studies have used both quantitative indices and ministers' own self rating with the evaluations of others.

Intervening factors present a second impediment to effectiveness assessment. In the present study, typical subjects attended seminary for three-and-a-half years and had two to four years in the parish between the time they took the seminary entrance tests and the completion of the ratings. This time lag is beneficial because it allowed the subjects to mature in their ministry. On the other hand, intervening factors occurring during the time lag may not be accounted for by the instruments. For example, a marriage, the death of a parent, the birth of children, psychotherapy, the learnings in seminary, an unpleasant internship, or a forgiving first parish are all likely to shape how well a pastor functions; indeed, many intervening factors may affect the type of minister he or she is in the present.

The person who performs the rating, the criteria used for the rating, and the rater's interpretation of the criteria are additional snags in such studies. Who evaluates the minister's work – the minister, a senior pastor, a judicatory supervisor, or members of the congregation? Are ratings performed by persons other than the ministers themselves accurate? In addition, ratings most likely will not be uniform from one evaluator to another. The criteria (if any) used to discriminate levels of effectiveness, and how they are understood by the rater, will also determine what is valued and what is overlooked. Thus, uniformity of ratings is also at issue.

It is not difficult to see why many researchers have not undertaken such research into the prediction of future effectiveness in ministry. These complications, and numerous others, at best make such a study complex and the results tentative. Nevertheless, attempts at effectiveness research are being made. The following are several studies which relate to the present research. Each helps to form the hypotheses that emerge in this research and to provide a backdrop for the types of enquiry that are possible.

Jackson (1946, 1955) performed one of the early studies on effectiveness. He asked Methodist ministers from several conferences to provide him with a list of the ten most effective and the ten least effective ministers in their respective conferences. Jackson compared those lists with statistical data in the Methodist yearbook. He found that large churches are usually served by effective ministers; ineffective ministers do not increase membership appreciably; effective ministers are usually paid higher salaries; and tenures of four years or less are usually held either by those new to the ministry or by ineffective ministers.

Thirty-one Methodist ministers made up a study by Carr (1980) of the style and effectiveness of their ministry. Carr's assumption was that ministers bring to the parish a pattern of behaviour coming primarily from their own needs and personality characteristics rather than from the needs of the church. Carr demonstrated correlations between several subscales of the MMPI and effectiveness.

Cardwell (1982) argued that for women to be more fully accepted, identification of the characteristics which make successful women ministers would be required. In a study of 30 women students who entered Christian Theological Seminary from 1962–76, she demonstrated that successful women ministers had higher intelligence, better self-image, greater openness to feelings and acceptance of basic human weaknesses, stronger leadership skills, and the ability to take charge of their lives, as compared with less successful women ministers. T-tests were used to determine significance.

Hutchison (1983) studied 93 ministers. Through the use of the Pastoral Effectiveness Rating Form he divided them into those who were more effective and those who were less effective. Hutchison performed ANOVAs on 18 scales of the California Psychological Inventory and found that more effective ministers had higher scale scores on capacity for status, sociability, social presence, self-acceptance, tolerance, achievement via conformance, achievement via independence, and intellectual efficiency.

Weiser (1985) performed his research on 112 Lutheran clergy between the ages of 40 and 50. He administered the MMPI, the Millon Clinical Multiaxial Inventory, and a personal history questionnaire. A major focus of this study was narcissism and how it relates to effectiveness in ministry. Weiser found more succesful clergy to be more narcissistic and have greater ego strength, impulse control, and object relations. he also noted that more successful ministers had a strong, supportive father during their formative years.

Malony and Majovski (1986) studied 71 Methodist ministers in full time parish ministry. The ministers had been in the parish from three to eight years at the time of the research. Ratings of effectiveness were performed by the ministers themselves, by their district superintendents, and by members of the Pastor-Parish Relations Committee. Regression analysis was performed on MMPI scale scores and measures of effectiveness. Malony and Majovski's results indicated that eight per cent of the variation of the Committee ratings was accounted for by the MMPI Ma scale and eleven per cent of the pastor's own ratings were accounted for by the Pd scale. With the ratings of the minister's district superintendent no variables accounted for variance.

At the very least, the review of existing literature indicates that further research into the prediction of effectiveness in ministers is warranted.

Effectiveness study

For the past thirty years entering students at a mainline Protestant seminary have taken a series of tests during their first week of school. These tests, together with fifty-some demographic questions of Section I of the Theological School Inventory, served as the first set of data for comparisons in the present study. A second data set was comprised of the ratings of the students' judicatory supervisors. (Ratings were performed only after individuals had graduated and served in ministry for one year or longer.) Each minister was evaluated in the following thirteen areas: administration, Christian action, Christian education, evangelism, membership development, pastoral concern, preaching, staff/volunteer supervision, stewardship, teaching, world outreach, worship and youth work. A Likert-type scale was used with the following possible responses: excellent, above average, average, below average, inadequate, and don't know. A final question asked of the supervisor was, 'Overall appraisal: would you rate this person ...' followed by four options (excellent, above average, average, below average). An analysis was performed which determined that each of these thirteen areas accurately predicted the overall appraisal rating. All but thirteen responses to this final question fell within the 'above average' or 'average' category, thus providing the two groups for the analyses. For the present research the average ministers were defined as less effective and the above average ones as more effective.

After a review of the literature, and working within the limitations of the archival data available for study, a series of hypotheses were developed to guide the research. The hypotheses are:

1. The overall appraisal rating by judicatory supervisors will be predicted by tests taken by ministerial students at entrance to seminary.
2. Above average ministers will have greater academic abilities than average ministers.
3. Above average ministers will perform better in seminary classes and graduate with higher grade point averages than will average ministers.
4. On the MMPI, above average ministers will score higher on the Mf scale.
5. Above average ministers will have a different Theological School Inventory profile than will average ministers; above average minis-

ters will score higher on the FL, A and P scales and lower on the
I, F and R scales.
6. Above average ministers will describe themselves as having better
   personal relations while growing up than will average ministers.
7. Above average ministers will describe themselves as having better
   emotional adjustment than will the average minister.
8. Above average ministers will be more theologically conservative
   than their average counterparts.

Method

Subjects

One hundred and sixty-three M Div graduates entering a mainline
Protestant seminary program in the years 1962 through 1979 were
included in this study. Subjects, all members of the same Protestant
denomination, had completed a series of entrance tests during their
first week of school.

Materials

MMPI: The Minnesota Multiphasic Personality Inventory, probably
the most frequently used psychological inventory of personality,
contains 556 items. Although numerous scales can be applied to the
MMPI, the most important include three validity and ten clinical
scales. The control or validity scales are used to determine the attitude
of the person taking the test and to discern if there have been any
attempts to distort the clinical results by faking good, faking bad or
following a stylised response set. The ten clinical scales were
produced to diagnose individuals in ten separate areas of psychopathology.

TSI: The Theological School Inentory (TSI) is a self-report inventory designed to evaluate seminarians' decisions for the ministry. The
first section of the instrument asks 55 demographic questions about an
individual's family, religious, and church background. The second
section measures students' motivations for ministry, their certainty or
definiteness about entering it, and the strength of their natural and
supernatural leaning or inclination toward ministry.

Academic ability measures: Two tests were used with students to
measure their ability to think, study, and learn from materials they
read and lectures they hear: the Otis IQ, and a reading instrument.

The Otis Self-Administering Test of Mental Ability – Higher
Examination is comprised of 75 mixed verbal and numerical questions
that are arranged in order of difficulty. The types of items included in
the test are vocabulary, sentence meaning, proverbs, analogies, arithmetic problems, and number series.

The Diagnostic Reading Tests – Survey Section measures performance in three general areas: vocabulary, comprehension, and speed of reading. An interesting story-type selection measures the student's usual rate of reading; a 60-item vocabulary test includes English, mathematics, science, and social studies items; and a reading comprehension section measures study-type reading skills.

An overall academic ability measure was obtained for each individual by creating a composite score from the subject's reading speed, total reading, and IQ scores. This score was calculated by summing the subject's standardised score on each scale and dividing by the number of scales. This procedure is similar to creating a factor score, although each scale is assumed to have equal weight. Such a procedure avoids the problems associated with factor analysis (see Dillon and Goldstein, 1984; Stone, 1990).

Conservatism Measure: A theological conservatism/liberalism score was obtained for each subject. It was a composite score of the E, CC, SL, and FL scales on the TSI (same procedure as described in the previous paragraph). These particular TSI scales were used since in a previous study on conservatism using the same data base these scales loaded together when subjected to a Principle Components Analysis (Stone, 1990).

Procedure

Each year entering students completed the MMPI, TSI, IQ, and reading tests. All scores were recorded and placed in a permanent file. In addition, ratings by judicatory supervisors who knew the students after they had earned their M Div and worked in full time ministry for a minimum of one year were obtained. These ratings, like the test scores, consisted of archival information available to the researcher. All analyses were conducted based upon information retrieved from these two sets of files.

Results

The research project had two thrusts. First, from an exploratory perspective there was interest in determining if the information provided by the material administered to the students at the beginning of their schooling would be useful in predicting a later overall appraisal (OAP) rating by judictory supervisors of their effectiveness as ministers. The second component of the project was to test the research hypotheses outlined in the introduction.

Discriminant analysis

To test the ability of the data to predict OAP ratings, a series of stepwise discriminant analyses were conducted in an exploratory manner. Discriminant analysis was employed instead of a regression analysis since the OAP scores were basically categorical in nature. One major difference in the present research as compared with most previous studies is that it looked at a combination of variables rather than examining them individually. The genius of discriminant analysis over and against the use of a series of ANOVAs is that it considers how the disparate variables combine to influence each other, thus increasing the possibility of predicting future effectiveness.

Since discriminant analysis provides a way to statistically distinguish between two or more groups, it is a helpful technique in developing a picture of the effective minister. To differentiate between the average and the above average (defined as less and more effective) minister, the researcher selects a series of descriptive variables that measure characteristics on which the two groups are expected to differ. Mathematically the purpose of discriminant analysis is to weigh and linearly combine these descriptive variables in such a way that the two groups are differentiated as much as is possible. Discriminant analysis does not require that there be a statistically significant difference between the groups for any one variable. Rather, it is based upon how the variables combine differently for each group. The ratings of judicatory supervisors provided the two groups to be discriminated: 'above average' and 'average' ministers. Demographic data from section one of the TSI, the academic ability and conservatism composite scores, and scale scores from the entrance tests provided the descriptive variables.

As suggested above, discriminant analysis has two major abilities: the development of descriptive profiles, and the discrimination of individuals into different groups. It provides the researcher with information about the major dimensions in which the groups differ. In this study, the first task of discriminant analysis was to transform OAP scores into a dichotomous variable upon which persons with excellent or above average ratings comprised group one, and those with average or below average ratings comprised group two. This was necessary due to the relatively small number of subjects and the fact that almost all individuals fell into the 'average' or 'above average' ranges (only twelve of the 163 subjects were rated 'excellent', and one 'below average').

The selection of the variables for the stepwise procedure was based upon theoretical interests. The first analysis employed demographic information (including personal relationships, emotional adjustment, and encouragement to enter ministry) and academic ability and conservatism scores as the discriminating variables. No significant discriminant function was obtained from this analysis. The second analysis employed the scales of the TSI as the discriminating variables. While a significant discriminant function was found, the predictability of the TSI scales fell to the side when the scales of the MMPI were added to the discriminant function. In addition, the mean score for each TSI scale did not differ significantly between the above average and average groups. (It is also of interest to note that GPA correlated highly with the OAP [r=0.48] rating but did not significantly add to the discriminant function.) Finally, the best discriminant function came from including only the Mf, Pa, Pt, Sc, Ma and Si scales of the MMPI. This result indicates that the weighted combination of these scales provides the best distinction between the above average and average groups (see table one for the results of the discriminant analyses).

The accuracy of prediction can be seen in the classification matrix presented in table two. Sixty-eight per cent of the ministers were correctly classified. Only the univariate test for the Sc scale proved to be significant (F[1,155]=7.989, p < .01). The above average group scored significantly lower on the Sc scale (X=24.62) than did the average group (X=27.37). The means for all other scales were not significantly different. Such a result suggests that the distinction between the above average and average groups must be based upon a cluster of MMPI scales and cannot be made based upon the consideration of any scales separately.

Research hypotheses

Research hypotheses two through eight, listed in the introduction to this paper, were tested by a series of analyses of variance (ANOVAs). An analysis of variance is a statistical procedure which determines if any differences exist between groups. For example, ANOVAs help answer: 'Are above average ministers more theologically conservative than average ministers?' In the present study they sought to uncover significant differences between above average and average ministers when compared with TSI scores, the MMPI Mf scale score, academic ability and conservatism composite scores, GPA, emotional adjustment and quality of interpersonal relations while growing up. Significant ANOVAs were subjected to post hoc tests for mean differences.

ANOVAs were performed on research questions two through eight and only one, the GPA, turned up as significant. In that ANOVA, when students' grade point averages at graduation served as the dependant measure, a significant effect was found, F(1,136)=17.17, p < .001. Tukey post hoc analysis indicated that above average ministers (M=3.32) had higher graduating GPAs than did the average ministers (M=3.04). The results for the ANOVAs can be seen in table three.

Discussion

It would be particularly useful for denominational church occupations committees as well as seminary advisement counsellors to be able to forsee, from entrance test scores, which students will make effective ministers in the future. A primary interest of the present study was to determine how well one could predict a student's overall appraisal

Table 1: Discriminant analysis for the MMPI on overall appraisal

step entered	MMPI scale	Wilk's lambda	summary table P	loading
1	schizophrenia (Sc)	0.951	0.005	0.674
2	psychasthenia (Pt)	0.907	0.001	0.351
3	masculinity/feminity (Mf)	0.889	0.001	-0.612
4	hypomania (Ma)	0.874	0.001	0.322
5	social introversion (Si)	0.867	0.001	-0.023
6	paranoia (Pa)	0.860	0.001	0.114

canonical variate	Wilk's lambda	canonical discriminant function chi-squared	p	canonical correlation
1	0.860	22.88 (df. = 6)	0.001	0.374

Table 2: Classification matrix for the discriminant function of the MMPI on overall appraisal

actual group	predicted group above average	average
above average	86 (68.3%)	40 (31.7%)
average	10 (31.3'0)	22 (68.8%)

Total correctly grouped = 68.35%

Table 3: Univariate F-ratios for the seven research hypotheses

hypothesis number	dependant variable	F	P
1	academic ability	2.84	.09
2	GPA	17.17	.001
3	TSIFL	2.56	.11
3	TSIA	1.40	.24
3	TSIF	0.49	.48
3	TSIP	0.74	.39
3	TSII	0.12	.91
3	TSIR	0.31	.58
4	MMPI (Mf)	2.54	.11
5	theological conservatism	2.18	.14
6	personal relationships	0.24	.87
7	emotional adjustment	0.23	.63

Note: Degrees of freedom for all F-Ratios = 1,136.

rating from the demographic information and test scores recorded at entrance to seminary. The results of the discriminant analysis are statistically significant, however, they fail in the *degree* to which they distinguish effectiveness; that is, they do not differentiate the above average and average minister to an extent that would be useful for advisement of incoming seminarians. Although a correct classification of 68% of ministers into one of the two groups was achieved, the classification accounted for only 12 per cent of the variance.

While such results may not support the ability of present tests to provide sufficient discrimination of future effectiveness, they offer some interesting findings. Measures of academic ability at entrance to seminary were not as strong in predicting effectiveness as were personality tests. (This is true even though the above average OAP group at graduation had higher [M=3.32] GPAs than the average [M=3.04] group.) This result seems to suggest something other than academic skill as primary determinants of future effectiveness.

The MMPI and especially the paranoia (Pa), masculinity/femininity (Mf), psychasthenia (Pt), schizophrenia (Sc), hypomania (Ma) and the social introversion (Si) scales are the best predictors of effectiveness of the test and demographic data available in the present study. The MMPI scale scores are more useful than a series of demographic variables, the TSI or the classic measures of academic ability.

The other research hypotheses also found mixed support in analysis. As predicted, the above average OAP group had higher GPAs than did the average OAP group. However, there was no significant differences on any of the TSI scores, composite scores or any of the demographic information.

The present research demonstrates the difficulty of studies that try to predict future effectiveness. Several obstacles to such research were noted in the introduction to this paper. One thing is clear from the research: the archival data on background and demographics that seminaries generally retain on their students are not adequate for the prediction of ministerial effectiveness. Furthermore, most of the information on academic abilities and performance, although somewhat useful in suggesting which students will become more effective ministers, is not in and of itself sufficient. IQ scores and grades are not adequate predictors.

While MMPI scale scores appear more useful than academic measures, they also are insufficient. Statistically they are able to differentiate 68% of the ministers in the present study, but again the score differences are not great enough to be useful for advisement. This sometimes maligned personality instrument does, however, point out one direction in which future research ought to go, or at least a tack that may prove useful: the creation or discovery of more sophisticated measures of intrapersonal and interpersonal function.

Future research, it seems to this author, should take the following steps: first, work will have to continue in defining what constitutes an effective minister. Controversy will always exist over definitions of effectiveness; nevertheless, as much precision as possible is needed. Such definitions must be clear, measurable, and not so complex that they are not useful.

Career counsellors have been saying for years that many of the major difficulties which pastors experience in their work stem from interpersonal problems. The readiness for ministry work also has pointed out the importance of interpersonal skills (Schuller, 1976).

Ministerial work is interpersonal by its nature, yet few seminaries have developed ways to measure how people relate interpersonally. Tests and other measures of interpersonal function should be as important as the MMPI or the TSI for guidance of students.

The MMPI was developed to measure gross psychopathology. It is useful from that perspective at students' entrance to seminary. Nevertheless, measures of individual differences in personality that focus less on pathology are needed. Measures that cover such areas as coping skills, personal self-concept, potential for empathy, leadership ability, and the like must be discovered. Such measures, along with those testing interpersonal function, will certainly improve our ability to discriminate future performance in ministry.

Intervening variables, mentioned in the introduction, require further enquiry. Not only should studies be performed while students are in seminary and field education settings, but the first five years after graduation may serve as a primary influence in shaping pastors' career-long effectiveness. Also, the impact of marriage or divorce, financial difficulties, death of parents, or birth of children may significantly influence how well pastors do their ministry. In addition, how pastors deal with the loss of the idealism that is so often carried over from seminary, usually occurring after several years in the parish, may be a determinant of whether they remain hopeful and engaged with members in their parish, or become disillusioned and pull away from meaningful personal contact.

Finally, the use of more elegant procedures will be essential if clear distinctions are going to be drawn concerning ministers' future performance. Archival research like the present study is useful in a preliminary way since it points in directions to be followed by future studies, yet it is limited by the variables that are at hand. There are always other bits of data that the archival researcher recognises would make the research stronger. Long term longitudinal research will have to be accomplished if effectiveness research is to be accurate and useful in its predictions. In addition, discriminant analysis and sophisticated recently-developed models of statistical analysis will have to replace research that uses only t-tests and ANOVAs. The value of a procedure like discriminant analysis is that it is designed precisely to differentiate groups such as more and less effective ministers. The use of longitudinal research and other statistical procedures will help effectiveness research take the next step it must take in order to make accurate predictions.

The most important aspect of the present study was the general lack of discrimination between above average and average ministers. Variables thought to be influential failed to add to the prediction of OAP ratings. This suggests the need for new research designed to track individuals during seminary and in the first years of ministry to determine which variables cause the two groups to differ. It is hoped that such longitudinal studies will be undertaken. In addition, the present study has shown the need for more accurate instruments to be designed as constant measure of effectiveness in ministry. At present no fully adequate study of ministers had been undertaken. As research in the area continues, more and more pieces of the puzzle will fit together and a clearer picture of what constitutes effectiveness in ministry, and how to predict it, will evolve.[1]

Notes

1. This research project was made possible in part by grants from Lilly Endowment, Inc., and the Research Fund, Brite Divinity School, Texas Christian University. The Statistical Consultant for this project was Rick Clubb.

References

Aloyse, M (1961) 'Evaluations of candidates of religious life,' *Bulletin of the Guild of Catholic Psychiatrists*, 8, pp. 199–204.

Ashbrook, J B (1962) Evaluating seminary students as potential ministers, unpublished MA dissertation, Columbus, Ohio State University.

Ashbrook, J B (1967) *Ministerial Leadership in Church Organization*, Washington DC, Ministerial Studies Board.

Bloom, J H (1971) 'Who become clergymen?' *Journal of Religion and Health*, 10, pp. 50–76.

Bowes, N T (1963) *Professional Evaluation of Religious Aspirants*, New York, St Paul Publications.

Brekke, M L, Schuller, D S, and Strommen, M P (1976) 'Readiness for ministry: report on the research,' *Theological Education*, 13, pp. 22–30.

Cardwell, S W (1967) 'The MMPI as a predictor of success among seminary students,' *Ministry Studies*, 1, pp. 3–20.

Cardwell, S W (1982) 'Why women fail/succeed in ministry: psychological factors,' *Pastoral Psychology*, 30, pp. 153–162.

Carr, J C (1980) The MMPI, ministerial personality and the practice of ministry, unpublished PhD dissertation, Chicago, Northwestern University.

Chalmers, E M (1970) The relationship between personality characteristics and performance in the Seventh Day Adventist ministry, unpublished PhD dissertation, Knoxville, University of Tennessee.

Colville, W J (1962) 'Future research,' in S W Cook (ed.) *Research Plans*, New York: Religious Education Association, pp. 175–188.

Dillon, W R and Goldstein, M (1984) *Multivariate Analysis*, New York, Wiley.

Dittes, J E (1962) *Research on Clergymen: factors influencing decisions for religious service and effectiveness in the vocation*, New York, Religious Education Association.

Ekhardt, B N and Goldsmith, W M (1984) 'Personality factors of men and women pastoral candidates: 1. motivational profiles,' *Journal of Psychology and Theology*, 12, pp. 109–118.

Godfrey, R J (1955) Predictive value of MMPI with candidates for religious brotherhood, unpublished MEd dissertation, Milwaukee, Marquette University.

Haight, E S D (1980) Psychological criteria for the selection of ministerial candidates, unpublished PhD dissertation, Chicago, Northwestern.

Harris, W C (1973) The use of selected leadership, personality, motivational and demographic variables in the identification of successful ministers, unpublished PhD dissertation, Tulsa, The University of Tulsa.

Hjelle, L A and Aboud, J (1970) 'Some personality differences between seminarians and nonseminarians,' *Journal of Social Psychology*, 82, pp. 279–280.

Howard, D D (1986) The pastor as leader: personality strengths and church expectations, factors in pastoral length of ministry with the individual church, unpublished PhD dissertation, Tuscalossa, University of Alabama.

Hutchison, J K (1984) The development of an Exceptional Brethren ministers scale for the California Psychological Inventory, unpublished PhD dissertation, Williamsburg, College of William and Mary.

Johnson, M, Lohr, H, Wagner, J and Barger, W (1975) *Growth in Ministry*, Philadelphia, Lutheran Church in America.

Kleaver, G and Dyble, J E (1973) Effectiveness of young pastors, unpublished manuscripts, Office of Research, Support Agency of the General Assembly of the United Presbyterian Church USA.

Kling, F R (1958) 'A study of testing as related to the ministry,' *Religious Education*, 53, pp. 243–248.

Kolarik, J M (1954) 'Critical requirements of the Lutheran ministry,' *The Lutheran Quarterly*, 7, pp. 38–44.

Larsen, E L and Shopshire, J M (1988) 'A profile of contemporary seminarians,' *Theological Education*, 24, pp. 10–136.

Lopez, F M (1973) Pastoral planning: ministerial evaluation, unpublished paper, Felix Lopez and Associates, Port Washington, New York.

Malony, H N (1976) Current research on performance effectiveness among religious leaders, paper delivered at a National Evangelical Conference on Research in Mental Health and Religious Behavior, Atlanta, Georgia.

Malony, H N and Majovski, L F (1986) 'The role of psychological assessment in predicting ministerial effectiveness,' *Review of Religious Research*, 28, pp. 29–39.

McGraw, J P (1969) A comparison of MMPI scores and the variables with subsequent ratings of Nazarene ministers by their district superintendents, unpublished PhD dissertation, Lawrence, Kansas, University of Kansas.

Nauss, A (1970) Development of a measure of ministerial effectiveness a preliminary draft, unpublished paper, Concordia Seminary, Springfield, Illinois.

Nauss, A (1972) 'Problems in measuring ministerial effectiveness,' *Journal for the Scientific Study of Religion*, 11, pp. 141–151.

Nauss, A (1973) 'The ministerial personality: myth or reality?' *Journal of Religion and Health*, 12, pp. 77–96.

Rayburn, C A, Richmond, L J and Rogers, L (1986) 'Men, women and religion: stress within leadership roles,' *Journal of Clinical Psychology*, 42, pp. 540–546.

Schuller, D S, Brekke, M L and Strommen, M P (1976) *Readiness for Ministry: volume II assessment*, Vandalla, Ohio, Association of Theological Schools in the United States and Canada.

Spiers, D E (1965) A study of the predictive validity of a test battery administered to theological students, unpublished PhD dissertation, West Lafayette, Indiana, Purdue University.

Stone, H W (1989) 'Liberals and conservatives: differences in demographic characteristics, interests and service orientation among those entering ministry,' *Journal of Psychology and Christianity*, 8, 3, pp. 24–37.

Vaugh, R P (1963) 'A psychological assessment program for candidates to the religious life,' *Catholic Psychology Record*, 1, pp. 65–70.

Webb, S C (1968) 'An inventory of religious activities and interests,' Princeton, Educational Testing Service.

Weiser, C W (1987) Personality structure and success: a study of narcissism and related personality factors in successful Lutheran clergy, unpublished PhD dissertation, Philadelphia, Temple University.

Weisgerber, C A (1962) 'Survey of a psychological screening program in a clerical order,' in M B Arnold, P Hispanicus, C A Weisgerber and P R D'Arcy, (eds) *Screening Candidates for the Priesthood and Religious Life*, Chicago, Loyola University Press, pp. 107–148.

4. Stress and burnout

The assessment and prediction of stress and burnout is recognised as an increasingly important area of research within the caring professions. Research in this field is well established among teachers, social workers, nurses and doctors. This chapter introduces four studies which have researched stress and burnout among clergy.

In the first article in this section, Carole A Rayburn, Lee J Richmond and Lynn Rogers explore stress within religious leadership roles. They administered four instruments concerned with different aspects of stress to a sample of 250 priests, ministers, seminarians, nuns and brothers. The specially devised Religion and Stress Questionnaire focused on issues specific to Christian ministry. The Occupational Environment Scales allowed levels of stress within ministry to be compared with levels of stress within other occupational groups. The study concludes that religious leaders experienced lower overall occupational stress and personal strain and evidenced more personal resources than did the normative population.

Dr Carole A Rayburn is a Clinical and Consulting Psychologist at Silver Spring, Maryland, USA. Professor Lee J Richmond is on the staff of Loyola College of Maryland, USA. This article was first published in the *Journal of Clinical Psychology* in 1986.

In the second article, Philip J Dewe examines the sources of stress reported by a sample of 280 Protestant clergy in New Zealand, together with the strategies they employ to cope with these problems. Factor analysis of the thirty-eight work stressors included in the questionnaire revealed three main factors, which are described in the following terms: parish conflict and church conservatism, difficulties involving parish commitment and development, and emotional and time difficulties involving crisis work. Factor analysis of the sixty-five coping strategies included in the questionnaire revealed five main factors, which are described in the following terms: social support, postponing action by relaxation and distracting attention, developing capacity to deal with the problem, rationalising the problem, and support through spiritual commitment.

Professor Philip J Dewe is Head of Department, Department of Human Resource Management within the Faculty of Business Studies, Massey University in Palmerston North, New Zealand. This article was first published in *Work and Stress* in 1987.

In the third article, Joseph H Fichter reports on a survey concerned with clergy health conducted with a database provided by 4,660 Catholic priests in the USA. He concludes that a minority of 6.2% of the respondents may be termed candidates for burnout. They fit this category because they report being regularly overworked and because they also experience a great deal of emotional stress. The individuals most likely to fit this definition are diocesan parish priests in their mid-fifties who exhibit a high incidence of tension, worry and anxiety, have more physical ailments than other priests, are overweight and do not get enough physical exercise or restful sleep.

At the time of writing, Father Joseph H Fichter, SJ, was at Loyola University of the South, New Orleans, Louisiana, USA. This article was first published in *Sociological Analysis* in 1984.

In the fourth article, Roger L Dudley and Des Cummings Jr report on the responses of 172 male Seventh-day Adventist pastors to a simple twenty-one item questionnaire, The Pastor as Person and Husband. They found that, while most pastors were generally happy in their work, a substantial minority have had a variety of low morale experiences. A relationship was found between pastoral morale and pastor-spouse relationships.

Dr Roger L Dudley is Director of The Institute of Church Ministry, Seventh-day Adventist Theological Seminary, Andrews University in Berrien Springs, Michigan, USA. At the time of writing, Des Cummings Jr was in the same institute. This article was first published in *Review of Religious Research* in 1982.

4.1 Men, women, and religion: stress within leadership roles

Carole A Rayburn, Lee J Richmond and Lynn Rogers

Selye (1976) defined stress as 'the nonspecific response of the body to a demand' and discussed the physiological effects of the 'wear and tear' of stress. Osipow and Spokane (1981a, 1983) spoke of inadequate coping resources as leading to strain, and Cooper and Marshall (1976) linked coronary heart disease to stress. Epstein (1970), who studied stress and occupational leadership, found that many processes limited the participation of women at the highest levels. Such processes are especially evident among religious leaders. Women clergy are an extreme minority, with few empathetic mentors (Epstein, 1970; Rayburn, 1981a, 1981b, 1982). Further, women seminarians may question seriously the use of sexist noninclusive language in hymns, liturgy, and scripture (Rayburn, 1982, 1984, 1985a, 1985b). Goldsmith and Ekhardt (1981) found that women in seminary were stressed by the unrealistic expectations that others have of them. Hardesty (1979) suggested that as the numbers of women in seminary grow, attitudes and overall language in seminary may become increasingly more sexist, which would result in greater stress for both men and women.

Rayburn, Richmond and Rogers (1982, 1983) studied stress in religious leaders. A Religion and Stress Questionnaire was designed, and the Osipow and Spokane (1981b) Occupational Environment Scales, Personal Strain Questionnaire, and Personal Resources Questionnaire were used. The present study is an expansion of the two previous ones and affirms those results overall.

Method

Subjects and procedure

A total of 250 religious leaders were studied: 50 Roman Catholic priests, 50 brothers, 50 nuns, 50 ministers (25 females and 25 males), and 50 seminarians (25 females and 25 males). At the time of this study, not only was the religious population enlarged from the previous investigations, but the general population of the Osipow-Spokane normative group was broadened from 201 to 549 individuals. The minister group was added to ensure a more representative sample. The nuns and the brothers seemed to have comparable roles of teaching or working in hospital settings, and the seminarians and ministers had men and women whose situations appeared to be comparable within their groups. However, the priests were males and, as in the 1983 study, they mainly served in parishes or within orders.

All subjects completed the Religion and Stress Questionnaire and the Osipow-Spokane Scales and Questionnaires. Further, about 10% of the individuals were interviewed in depth.

Results

Religion and Stress Questionnaire

Need to excel: Half of the 250 subjects thought that women who were attending seminary sensed more need to excel than did their male counterparts. Subjects under 36 years of age tended to answer affirmatively to this more frequently than did older subjects. More priests (63%), ministers (59%), and seminarians (50%) than nuns (40%) and brothers (40%) answered 'yes' also. Nuns and brothers do not attend seminary, but go to a novitiate where goals are noncompetitive. About half of all women and all men answered 'yes'.

Recruitment and hiring opportunities: Almost half (46%) thought that women do not have equal recruitment and hiring opportunities. Ministers were more pronounced in this conviction; 73% agreed that women were at a disadvantage. Seminarians (50%) and priests (49%) were less apt to agree on this question. Perhaps the seminarians have not yet tasted as much of the 'real' world as the ministers had. Gender of the seminarians did not differentiate them on this question. While far more answered in the negative (50%) than in the affirmative (20%), 30% of the seminarians were not sure that recruitment and hiring opportunities were equally open to women.

Perhaps the most significant finding was that only 20% of the sample population and of each group said that they thought women *did* have equal access to jobs as religious leaders. In light of well-known facts about the inaccessibility of such job opportunities for women in fields far more open to women than that of religion (cf. Russo, Olmedo, Stapp and Fulcher, 1981), those who imagine that the situation is otherwise for women in religion are displaying considerable naiveté.

Suspicion and rejection: Sixty-seven percent of the subjects answered 'yes' to 'Do you think women experience suspicion or rejection from colleagues and/or congregation?' Females (71%) more than males (63%) and those under 36 years of age (74%) more than those over 36 (65%) were attuned more keenly to issues of suspicion and rejection. Ministers (half of whom were women) affirmed (92%) that the suspicion and rejection were real. Priests tended to concur (69%), and seminarians (half of whom were women) agreed at an even higher level (76%). However, brothers (48%) and nuns (52%) who affirmed this item showed less sensitivity and more distancing from the problem; perhaps this was due to the fact that they were not trained at seminary.

Blame: To the question, 'Because they dare to be female leaders in a predominantly male enterprise, do you think women get blamed for going against the tide of majority opinion?' 52% of the subjects answered 'yes'. More females (57%) than males (49%) answered in the affirmative. Further, more subjects under 36 (56%) than over 36 (51%) thought that women received blame. Of the five religious professional groups, ministers (65%) had the highest number of subjects who answered 'yes', followed by seminarians (60%), priests (53%), nuns (50%), and brothers (32%). There were no significant differences between males and females on this question.

Handling stress: Of the women interviewed, 52% responded 'yes' to 'Do you think women handle stress differently from their male counterparts?' About half of all subjects said 'no' (26%) or 'don't know' (24%), while 44% answered 'yes'. Women answered 'yes' about twice as frequently (52%) as men did (25%). Priests (49%), nuns (53%), and ministers (51%) tended to say 'no', while seminarians and brothers were split almost evenly on this question. Some of the seminarians, male and female, thought that men handle stress through more physical means, such as participating in sports. No significant differences were found between female and male seminarians on this question. Clergywomen more than clergymen saw women as handling stress differently from men ($t=3.37$, $p \leq 0.01$).

Pressures of leadership: In response to the question, 'What pressure do you think women feel who are in very high levels of leadership? Are there any pressures of leadership that one experiences just because one is female?' male seminarians thought that the pressures that women experience in leadership positions are more positive and helpful to the women. However, the women seminarians thought that such pressures are negative and detrimental ($t = \leq 2.84$, $p \leq 0.01$). In the group of ministers, there were no significant differences between women and men on this question.

Inclusive language: With regard to the question, 'What do you think about using language that is less gender-bound in church/synagogue texts and hymnals?' female seminarians more strongly and significantly favour less gender-bound language than do male seminarians ($t = 2.50$, $p \leq 0.05$). However, both male and female seminarians have more positive than negative views on using more inclusive language. Female ministers had more favourable responses to inclusive language than did their male counterparts ($t = 2.49$, $p \leq 0.05$).

Work-related stress: When asked 'How do you think women handle work-related stress?' clergywomen more significantly than clergymen thought that women handled work-related stress better or more effectively than did men. Clergywomen discussed the tendency of women to express their feelings more openly and to share with others, whereas men were seen by both sexes as holding in their feelings more frequently.

Occupational Environmental Scales

The Occupational Environment Scales, Form E-2 (Osipow and Spokane, 1981b) were designed to measure work stress. These scales measure role overload, role insufficiency, role ambiguity, role boundary, responsibility, and physical environment. Religious professionals experienced significantly less stress ($M=122.88$, $SD=23.54$) than did the normative population ($M=137.64$, $SD=26.59$); $t=9.91$, $p \leq .001$). Role insufficiency, role boundary, and physical environment seem to account for the difference. On role overload, role ambiguity, and responsibility, the religious professionals actually scored very slightly and statistically insignificantly lower than did the general population.

On role overload, a measure of how much job demands exceed resources, no significant differences were found between the subjects and the general population. Of note, however, were findings on the Religion and Stress Questionnaire item, 'How do you think women experience stress from institutional and personal pressure in your work?' in which both male and female ministers saw women as experiencing this kind of stress. (Clergywomen were the most aware of this.) Also, nuns significantly more than brothers were sensitive to such stress in women. Thus, on this Religion and Stress Questionnaire item, it is probable that with a greater number of ministers and nuns a higher loading on role overload might be expected.

On role ambiguity, the degree to which a person's expectations, priorities, and evaluation criteria are clear to her or him, and on responsibility (the degree to which individuals feel or have much responsibility for performance and welfare of others on the job), religious professionals were not significantly different from the general population.

The significant difference on role insufficiency (degree to which individuals' training, skills and education, as well as experience, are appropriate to their work) indicates that religious leaders far more than the general population see a fine fit between their job qualifications and their job performance, sense more that careers are progressing satisfactorily, and that their jobs have a good future. They would be apt to think that their needs for recognition and success are being satisfied and that they are being utilised appropriately in a job that maintains their interest.

The subjects were also significantly lower on role boundary (degree to which persons experience conflicting role demands and loyalties at work). This indicates that religious professionals sense less conflict in role demands and job loyalties, feel greater pride in their work, sense more personal investment in their work, and are clearer about lines of authority.

On physical environment (the extent to which persons are exposed to extreme physical conditions or elevated levels of toxins in the environment), religious professionals reported that they experienced better overall physical conditions on their jobs.

Overall, then, religious professionals experienced significantly less stress related to their occupational environments. Something within the religious work setting is working in favour of religious leaders in terms of greater peace of mind and job satisfaction. Nonetheless, the reported stress sensed by women religious leaders (especially by female seminarians and ministers) is both distressing and undeniable, as indicated on the Religion and Stress Questionnaire.

Personal Strain Questionnaire: The Personal Strain Questionnaire is designed to measure various types of strain: vocational strain, psychological strain, physical strain, and interpersonal strain. The subjects reported less strain ($M=73.43$, $SD=18.33$) than the general population ($M=86.26$, $SD=27.19$), with $t=11.06$, and $p \leq 0.001$. In the 1983 study, interpersonal strain was significant at the .01 level, but no significance was found in the current study; actually, interpersonal strain increased in the group of religious leaders and decreased in the general population. However, with the exception of Interpersonal Strain, the other four measures of personal strain not only maintained significance at the 0.001 level, but in each case did so at a T score that was higher. This fact gives greater assurance that the documented differences are truly significant.

Personal Resources Questionnaire: The extent to which resources are available to people to counteract the effects of occupational stress is measured by the Personal Resources Questionnaire. This questionnaire measures recreation, physical coping or self-care, social supports, and rational/cognitive coping. Total Personal Resources differentiated religious professionals ($M=137.93$, $SD=18.73$) from the general population ($M=134.53$, $SD=20.20$), with $t=2.85$ and $p \leq 0.01$.

There were no significant differences between the subjects and the general population on recreation. Religious leaders perceived that they have higher physical coping or self-care resources, more social supports, and higher overall personal resources than does the general population. However, they actually have fewer, but not significantly different, recreation resources. They are less apt to make use of and get pleasure from relaxation and regular recreational activities. Those in religious occupations have fewer rational/cognitive coping resources, and this was a significant difference. They are less apt to have a systematic approach to problem solution, less ability or willingness to set and follow priorities, are more distractible and less likely to be able to reorganise their work schedules, are less likely to put their jobs out of their minds when they go home, and are more apt to be bound to their job and to see it as the only really viable one for them. These findings are in general agreement with reports from many religious leaders that concern their needs for better learning to cope with and manage time constraints and demands upon their time and energy. Many religious professionals probably would agree that theirs is often a 24-hour job, something that their spouses, family, or friends are likely to substantiate.

Discussion

Within religious vocations, do men and women differ with regard to perceived stress, strain and resources? Within the Occupational Environment Scales, only role overload and role ambiguity significantly differentiated the women and men in this study. Men scored higher on role overload ($t=-2.68$, $p \le .01$), which indicates that their job demands more frequently exceed their resources. On role ambiguity, again the men were the high scorers, with $t=-3.13$, $p \le .01$. Men have a poorer sense of what is expected of them in their religious jobs and of how they should be spending their time.

Osipow and Spokane mentioned that high scorers on physical environment 'may report having an erratic work schedule or being personally isolated' (1981a, p. 15). While religious leaders scored lower on this question, ministers and seminarians often reported on the Religion and Stress Questionnaire that demands upon their time were great and that they needed to learn to schedule themselves and to manage time constantly. Ministers, especially those who were sole pastors at their churches, reported that they often felt isolated and had few people to turn to for direction. One male minister indicated that there was little confidentiality in the parish community, which had led him and his family to seek pastoral counselling outside his immediate environment in an exchange plan with other ministers. Priests and seminarians, though, enjoyed a supportive community of those like-minded, as did brothers and nuns. However, at times seminarians saw the seminary community as a mixed blessing, with the community's expectations seen as an intrusion into personal needs upon occasion; they described this as 'living in a fishbowl'. Ministers also may feel isolated from their congregations.

In terms of personal strain, religious leaders have fewer problems in work quality or output and have better attitudes toward their work; they show better psychological adjustment and a more positive outlook toward their jobs. They have fewer complaints about physical illness or poor health habits. While they showed insignificantly higher interpersonal stress than did the general population, the difference found may be related to the reported wish of seminarians and ministers to have more time outside the religious community, the congregation, or the community at large and to spend more time with family and friends. Ministers and seminarians expressed much concern about their need to learn to say no occasionally to others' demands on their time and stamina. Often, congregations persist in forcing a Rock-of-Gibraltar image upon clergy, and clergy are very unsure how to handle this problem. Because religious leaders may be set up by laity as 'the holy ones' and 'set apart' from the congregation and certainly from the population in general, they often may be presented with a lonely existence and sense a need to be guarded lest they be perceived as weak and vulnerable enough to slip off their pedestals. Little wonder, then, that they frequently spoke of not being allowed to be human, with even a few frailties of the species. Denial of any weakness may play a large part in some instances, especially for those who thought that their clerical roles depended upon maintaining a super-sacred, non-secular persona. These people may perceive demands upon them to be perfect as not even permitting them to express anger when it might be appropriate to do so; this tends not only to add to their discomfort, but to decrease their effectiveness in dealing with congregants on a day-to-day basis and in pastoral counselling. The ineffectiveness of clergy in general in pastoral counselling situations has been well documented (Dittes, 1962; Rayburn, 1985a; Virkler, 1979, 1980). Of course, such findings largely concern male clergy because men dominated the field of religion and pastoral counselling in most denominations until just recently. It would be interesting to test clergywomen on their effectiveness in pastoral counselling skills, even though they may be more subject to the fishbowl phenomenon and 'be perfect' demands than are their male counterparts. In addition, because women pastors are rather new to the sacramental and administrative roles within the clerical vocation, they may have been assigned to do pastoral counselling with children, youth, and women at the outset of their religious careers or even before then as advanced laity. Thus, they may have had more practice in this area.

Religious leaders did experience a much lower overall personal strain than did the general population. However, they may perceive that others demand or encourage them not to complain too much. It is possible that a noncomplaining attitude is circumscribed for religious professionals. Nonetheless, with the amount of stress and strain that women in seminary and clergy experience because of others' biases toward women, a larger study of seminarians and ministers might reveal more elevated Osipow and Spokane scores more in line with the stress reported by these groups of women on Religion and Stress Questionnaire. Women also tend to deny their problems less often than men do, and, thus, they may provide excellent role models of more realistic ways of dealing with being human and simultaneously seeking the divine.

Ministers and seminarians seem to have the most stress within the population of religious leaders. In order of most to least stress experienced are ministers, seminarians, priests, brothers, and nuns. Nuns have the least overall stress from occupational environment and also the highest score on total personal resources. Ministers, who have the greatest overall occupational environment stress and next to the lowest score on total personal resources, certainly appear to be a high-risk group in terms of stress and its detrimental aftermath. Similarly, seminarians, with the highest personal strain score, have the very lowest personal resources score and are at high risk also. Priests, with the next to the highest score in overall occupational environment stress and moderate personal strain, had the next hightest score on total personal strain. Brothers had next to the lowest score on overall occupational environment stress, the lowest score on overall personal strain, and moderate overall personal resources; they are involved mainly in nonadministrative and nonsacramental functions and may be able to avoid a lot of stress and strain.

When one-way analyses of variance were done, ministers were found to have the most work overload, the highest role insufficiency, role ambiguity, responsibility, overall occupational environment stress, and vocational strain; the second highest score on psychological, personal, physical, and overall personal strain; and the next to the lowest score in overall personal resources, social supports, and rational/cognitive coping resources.

Overall, on the Religion and Stress Questionnaire, seminarians and ministers (especially females) demonstrated more sensitivity to the needs of women religious leaders, as well as to stress factors that impinge upon religious leaders of both sexes, than did (in general order of awareness) Roman Catholic priests, nuns, and brothers. The seminarians and ministers had had experience with men and women co-existing in seminary, and most of the subjects came from mainline religious denominations in which women clergy had been a part of the leadership for at least a few years. The priests, who ranked next in degree of sensitivity to the issues, had stated that they had no direct experience of having women in the Roman Catholic seminaries, they were an older group, and they were men from a religious group not traditionally open to women in the priesthood. Yet, commendably, they were willing to deal with these issues and with sensitivity. The nuns and brothers, though, had no experience with seminaries or any religious educational setting in which there were men and women in training; they went through a novitiate. The brothers seemed to be the most unaware and least sensitive about the issues raised on the Religion and Stress Questionnaire. Perhaps this was due to their leaning toward ultra-conservatism; noncommitment with regard to matters not immediately within their purview; their being unaware or insensitive to the issues; their being unrealistic; their not really caring about social and personal issues of concern outside their immediate context of the classroom or the hospital setting, even though such matters were serious topics and situations within the larger context of their denomination; or they may have found the area very stressful and used a plausible excuse for not dealing with such issues. Further study with an even larger sample would help to resolve some of these questions.[1]

Notes

1. This research project was made possible in part by a grant from the Educational Foundation Program of the American Association of University Women.

References

Cooper, C L and Marshall, J (1976) 'Occupational sources of stress: a review of the literature related to coronary heart disease and mental health,' *Journal of Occupational Psychology*, 49, pp. 11–28.

Dittes, J E (1962) 'Research on clergymen: factors influencing decisions for religious service and effectiveness in the vocation,' *Religious Education*, 17, pp. 141–165.

Epstein, C F (1970) 'Encountering the male establishment: sex-status limits on women's careers in the professions,' *American Journal of Sociology*, 75, pp. 965–982.

Goldsmith, W M and Ekhardt, B N (1981) Personality differences between seminarians and secular education students, paper presented at the annual meeting of the American Psychological Association.

Hardesty, N (1979) 'Women and the seminaries,' *Christian Century*, 96, pp. 122–123.

Osipow, S H and Spokane, A R (1981a) *A Preliminary Manual for Measures of Occupational Stress, Strain, and Coping*, Columbus, Ohio, Marathon Consulting and Press.

Osipow, S H and Spokane, A R (1981b) *The Occupational Environment Scales, Personal Strain Questionnaire and Personal Resource Questionnaire, Form E-2*, Columbus, Ohio, Marathon Consulting and Press.

Osipow, S H and Spokane, A R (1983) *A Manual for Measures of Occupational Stress, Strain and Coping*, Columbus, Ohio, Marathon Consulting and Press.

Rayburn, C A (1981a) Further study of women seminarians' needs for counseling and consulting, paper presented at the annual meeting of the American Psychological Association, Los Angeles.

Rayburn, C A (1981b) 'Some reflections of a female seminarian: woman, whither goest thou?' *Journal of Pastoral Counseling*, 16, pp. 61–65.

Rayburn, C A (1982) 'Seventh-day Adventist women: values, conflicts, and resolutions,' *Journal of Pastoral Counseling*, 17, pp. 19–22.

Rayburn, C A (1984) 'Impact on nonsexist language and guidelines for women in religion,' *Journal of Pastoral Counseling*, 19, pp. 5–8.

Rayburn, C A (1985a) 'Prisons,' in R J Wicks, R D Parsons, and D Capps (eds) *Clinical Handbook of Pastoral Counseling*, New York, Paulist Press.

Rayburn, C A (1985b) 'Promoting equality for women seminarians,' *Counseling and Values*, 29, pp. 164–169.

Rayburn, C A, Richmond, L J and Rogers, L (1982) 'Women, men, and religion: stress within sanctuary walls,' *Journal of Pastoral Counseling*, 17, pp. 75–83.

Rayburn, C A, Richmond, L J and Rogers, L (1983) 'Stress among religious leaders,' *Thought: Fordham University Quarterly Review*, 58, pp. 329–344.

Russo, N F, Olmedo, E L, Stapp, J and Fulcher, R (1981) 'Women and minorities in psychology,' *American Psychologist*, 36, pp. 1315–1363.

Selye, H (1976) *The Stress of Life*, New York, McGraw-Hill.

Virkler, H A (1979) 'Counseling demands, procedures, and preparation of parish ministers: a descriptive study,' *Journal of Psychology and Theology*, 7, pp. 271–280.

Virkler, H A (1980) 'The facilitativeness of parish ministers: a descriptive study,' *Journal of Psychology and Theology*, 8, pp. 140–146.

4.2 New Zealand ministers of religion: identifying sources of stress and coping strategies

Philip J Dewe

In occupational stress research, considerable use has been made of the role conflict and role ambiguity scales first developed by Rizzo, House and Lirtzman (1970). Because these measures have been readily available and constantly used, their psychometric properties have been extensively researched. Psychometric evaluation of these measures suggests high construct validity (Schuler, Aldag and Brief, 1977). Recent reviews, however, have pointed up a number of problems, including:

a. inconsistencies in the wording of the scales (Tracey and Johnson, 1981);

b. the fact that few attempts have been made to evaluate the impact of role conflict and role ambiguity in organisations (Jackson and Schuler, 1985);

c. that the relationship between role conflict and role ambiguity and different cognitive, affective and health responses is still dependent upon a greater understanding of the constructs themselves (Van Sell, Brief and Schuler, 1981); and

d. that little recognition has been given to the fact that sources of stress are themselves subject to change as a result of changes in society (Glowinkowski and Cooper, 1985).

This is not to imply, however, that role-based stressors, in general, should be viewed as being of little practical importance or that other types of stressors have not been investigated and researched (Holt, 1982; Cooper, 1983). The point is that because measures of role *conflict* and role *ambiguity* have been so frequently used they have tended to overshadow the need to develop a better understanding of the nature and structure of actual role problems and the events which may now best describe them.

The criticisms raise a number of important methodological issues particularly in relation to how work role stressors should be best measured. Many established measures tend to be focused on specific concepts, such as conflict or ambiguity, but at the same time, generalise across occupational groups and organisations. Researchers should be aware that in doing so they may in particular cases overemphasise the importance of certain role stressors, ignore the presence of others or even measure irrelevant variables (Crump *et al.*, 1980;

Glowinkowski and Cooper, 1985; Handy, 1986). In addition, they limit the opportunity to identify and establish changes in the nature and structure of work role stressors.

What is needed is a new system of concepts and the development of alternative measures, based, for example, on behavioural indices or objective techniques (Crump *et al.*, 1980; Shaw and Riskind, 1983; Dougherty and Pritchard, 1985). One response has been to suggest that measures of role conflict and role ambiguity provide 'global perceptions' of work roles and that occupationally specific measures may be of practical advantage in identifying specific role problems and of greater predictive value (Dougherty and Pritchard, 1985). Studies by a number of authors (Koch, Tung, Gmelch and Swent, 1982; Shaw and Riskind, 1983; Cooper and Roden, 1985; Cooper and Sloan, 1985; Newton and Keenan, 1985) have tended to confirm the benefits of such an approach. They have highlighted the subtlety of different professional roles and indicated that while established scales may provide a good measure of 'global perceptions' they are not useful nor designed for evaluating specific role relationships or identifying the nature of conflicts and ambiguities (Jackson and Schuler, 1985; Dougherty and Pritchard, 1985). This study investigated the sources of role and general work stressors reported by a sample of ministers of religion.

Stress and burnout is now a recognised problem for those employed in the human service professions (Cherniss, 1980; Jackson, 1984) but little, if any, research has been published on ministers of religion. It would thus seem to be particularly important then to develop measures that identify specific sources of stress in this group, and thus offer a more practical basis for intervention.

This research also considered the coping strategies reported by ministers. Coping, as a number of authors have pointed out (Dewe, Guest and Williams, 1979; Parasuraman and Cleek, 1984; Newton and Keenan, 1985; Cox, 1987), has received a less than complete treatment in occupational stress research. This is partly because priority has been given to researching other aspects of the work–stress paradigm, and partly because, as House (1979) suggested, we have not been equipped to investigate the ways in which individuals respond to work stress. Although coping is not considered unimportant, only a few researchers (Burke, 1972; Burke and Belcourt, 1974; Pearlin and Schooler, 1978; Newton and Keenan, 1985; Latack, 1986) have attempted to understand the construct by examining and describing reports of specific behaviours individuals say they use. Most have preferred more general formulations, or simply selected, or grouped strategies on an *a priori* basis. What would appear to be the necessary first step, that of developing an understanding of the coping construct through determining a typology of the coping strategies individuals say they use in a work setting, has to a large extent been overlooked. This issue is addressed in the present study in relation to role and general work stress in ministers.

Method

In order to examine the stressors and coping strategies reported by ministers, a three-stage research programme was devised. In stage one a small sample of ministers ($N=38$) attending the ministry committee of a New Zealand Protestant church were interviewed. The interviews, which took on average 30 minutes to complete, consisted of a series of open-ended questions designed to elicit information on the causes and consequences of stress for ministers and the sorts of coping strategies they used to deal with such problems. From the content analysis of the interview data (stage two), a questionnaire was developed consisting of three sections. The first requested biographical information. The second section covered the sources of stress and their consequences while the third was concerned with the coping strategies that ministers used. In stage three the questionnaire was mailed to all ordained members of the church.

Questionnaire

The questionnaire consisted of three sections.

Biographical information

The first section requested biographical information regarding sex, age, marital status, length of service, number of appointments, time in current position, type of position, type of ministry work and whether full-time or part-time. All items in this section were forced-choice questions.

Sources of stress

In stage one, a group of ministers was asked to think of a time when they felt under stress and to describe 'the sorts of things which caused that stress'. All 38 subjects were able to recall situations and 59 events were collected. These responses were broadly grouped under six headings. These included work overload (too many meetings to the detriment of pastoral work; time pressures); role conflicts (balancing family and work priorities; conflicts between planned and crisis work; church conservatism); role ambiguity (uncertainty of job tenure; uncertainty surrounding important church issues – church union); dealing with grief and people in need (death of parishioner; troubled people who need constant help; welfare work); relationships with parishioners and parish (unrealistic demands of parish; motivating parishioners; lack of finances for parish); and self pressures (inability to say no; not appreciating one's own limitations; difficulties in delegating).

In stage two, a list of situations that best represented the six response categories was produced by the author. A second researcher then examined this list in relation to the original data noting differences in content and description, omissions and similarities between items. A final list of 48 items representing perceived sources of minister stress was then agreed. Respondents were then instructed to think about the occurrence of each of the items (events) during the last six months and to rate each on a five-point scale, first in terms of frequency ('never' to 'frequently'), then in terms of anxiety ('not at all anxious' to 'extremely anxious') and, finally, in terms of tiredness ('not at all tiring' to 'extremely tiring'). If any of the items (events) did not occur then the other two scales were left blank. Anxiety and tiredness were chosen as outcome measures following analysis of responses in stage one to the question 'One of the things we are interested in finding out, is the emotional impact that your job has on you. How did you find it affects you?'

The coping strategies

To collect information on the coping strategies ministers said they used, those taking part in stage one were asked 'to think of a time when you felt under stress' and then explain how they managed to cope with it. There were 73 coping actions described. Using the distinction developed by Lazarus (1975) between direct action (problem solving) strategies and palliative strategies (reducing the feelings of emotional discomfort), it was possible to classify 33% of the responses as direct actions (for example, keep committee work to a minimum; do one thing at a time; work out a systematic plan) and 67% as palliatives (for example, share with prayer group; quiet time every day; do what can be done and forget the rest; make use of hobbies – leisure).

In order that a wide range of coping strategies was gathered, two other questions were asked. These included 'How do you think others cope?' and 'If, like most people, you occasionally get fed up with your job and feel tense and frustrated, how do you cope with such feelings?' The responses to these two questions produced a pattern of coping strategies similar to that found in the earlier question. This time, perhaps because of the nature of the questions, a greater number of palliatives (70% and 88% respectively) were described. The procedure for item selection was identical to that described above and a list of 65 coping strategies was produced. Respondents were asked to consider each strategy and to indicate on a five-point scale ('never' to 'frequently') how often they used each strategy to deal with the problems in their job.

Analysis

Scores, denoting the frequency with which stressors occurred and coping strategies were used, were subject to 'principal component analysis'. This technique summarises the data to provide the best linear combination of items (variables). It is a descriptive, rather than an inferential, technique, providing a smaller set of components (factors) that may be taken as accounting for the observed interrelations in the data.

Factors with eigenvalues greater than or equal to one were first extracted using a varimax rotation and then considered in conjunction with the scree or discontinuity test. To minimise mis-specification, factor loadings were considered relevant if they achieved a value of [±]0.40.

Results

Sample

The sample was drawn from ordained members of a Protestant church. The questionnaire was mailed to all members ($N=468$) of the church throughout New Zealand and 280 completed questionnaires were returned, representing a response rate of 60%. There was no follow-up questionnaire and no attempt was made to investigate the non-responses. Of those who returned the questionnaire, 92% were men and 8% were women. Their average age was 46 years and 90% were married. Most had served at least 16 years in the ministry and during that time had averaged at least three appointments. Almost all (82%) described their type of ministry as 'parish work' and most (65%) were in single ministries.

The sources of stress

Principal components analysis of the 38 work stressors revealed three factors which accounted for 38.0% of the data variance. Eigenvalues for the three were 12.34, 3.60 and 2.28 respectively, explaining 25.7%, 7.5% and 4.8% of the variance. Each factor is described in table one and discussed below.

Factor one appears to describe parish conflicts and church conservatism. These include conflicts between the minister and the parish–parishioners, first in terms of expectations (for example, other people not accepting you for what you are) and second in terms of attitudes and values (for example, dealing with prejudice in others), conflicts between the church's teaching and personal beliefs (for example, being asked to make statements on questions you have not yet personally resolved), conflicts with church conservatism (for example, the feeling that you are continually propping up a cumbersome institutional structure) and conflict over administrative issues (for example, other people not meeing deadlines).

Table 1: Principal components analysis of the frequency scores of work stressors with varimax rotation

	component		
	one	two	three
parish conflicts and church conservatism			
conflict between the traditionally expected style of ministry and the way you see yourself using your skills and your gifts	0.6841	0.1954	0.1481
other people not accepting you for what you are	0.6713	0.2460	0.1412
church conservatism – the conflict between tradition and change	0.6307	0.1680	0.0246
the lack of acceptance of other person's point of view – bigotry	0.5979	0.2673	0.2083
people not realising that a minister also needs support	0.5860	0.3681	0.0983
dealing with prejudice in others	0.5708	0.2850	0.2285
the feeling that people forget that ministers are like anyone else – that they, too, have needs and desires	0.5698	0.3914	0.1840
expected to do things one way when they could be better done another way	0.5629	0.1263	0.0827
the feeling that society expects more from ministers – too much piety, too little reality of the minister's role	0.5625	0.3704	0.2133
meeting resistance to change	0.5406	0.5143	–0.0142
lack of recognition of the minister's role and its importance to parishioners and other people's lives	0.5337	0.3839	0.0712
the feeling that you are continually propping up a cumbersome institutional structure	0.5253	0.3741	–0.0013
parishioners who through their own exuberance put pressure on you	0.5084	0.0466	0.3401
other ministers and parishioners and the church's expectations of you	0.5046	0.3007	0.2354
uncertainty surrounding the resolution of major issues, for example, church union	0.5030	–0.0339	0.0924
the need to have endless self-control	0.4391	0.3208	0.1570
the feeling that society expects you to be able to help with all problems at all times	0.4316	0.2787	0.3025
inconsistency between your personal beliefs and the church's standard	0.4258	0.0594	0.0941
being asked to make statements on questions you have not yet personally resolved	0.4235	0.1265	0.0685
other people not meeting deadlines	0.4180	0.1183	0.1027
difficulties involving parish commitment and development			
the lack of commitment from parishioners	0.2428	0.7371	0.1123
the reluctance of parishioners to grow	0.3026	0.7158	0.0328
meeting apathy	0.3143	0.7018	0.756
the reluctance of members of the parish to take responsibility	0.2963	0.6493	0.1176
the feeling of inadequacy because not meeting the full pastoral needs of people	0.1332	0.5870	0.2681
a lack of contact with young people of the parish	0.1116	0.5419	–0.0857
lack of training in certain fields	0.2342	0.5237	0.1607
too little time to get to know people	–0.0321	0.4706	0.3472
inadequacy of parish finance	0.2116	0.4121	0.1275
the feeling that the church is becoming more and more isolated from the community	0.3553	0.4030	–0.0045
emotional and time difficulties involving crisis work			
dealing with others' marital problems	0.2477	–0.1270	0.6341
conflict between planned and crisis work	0.0840	0.0916	0.6321
too much work to do in the time available	–0.0566	–0.0085	0.6262
dealing with people in desperate need	0.1631	–0.0552	0.6176
troubled people who need more than it is possible to give	0.3650	0.0140	0.6118
dealing with the pastoral care of people in grief situations	–0.2047	0.3440	0.6083
the amount of time taken up dealing with people	0.7470	–0.0879	0.5937
dealing with funerals	–0.2478	0.3547	0.5199
committee work clashing with people's needs – do people come first or do deadlines?	0.1426	0.0943	0.5166
never being able to work to a set routine: someone always wanting something at inconvenient times	0.2093	0.2186	0.5050
necessary and important tasks being overshadowed because of the number of administrative duties to be carried out	0.2009	0.3214	0.4532
meeting deadlines	0.0647	0.1324	0.4397
having to move onto other tasks feeling that earlier tasks are still incomplete	0.2045	0.3757	0.4267
Eigenvalue	12.34	3.60	2.28
percentage of variance	25.7%	7.5%	4.8%

Factor two describes difficulties involving parish commitment and development. These are described in terms of the parish–parishioners (for example, the reluctance of parishioners to grow), self-development issues (for example, the feeling of inadequacy because not meeting the full pastoral needs of the people) and contact-isolation concerns (for example, too little time to get to know people). Factor three describes the emotional and time difficulties surrounding crisis work. These include administrative difficulties (for example, never being able to work to a set routine: someone always wanting something at inconvenient times), emotional demands (for example, dealing with people in desperate need) and time concerns (for example, necessary and important tasks being overshadowed because administrative duties have to be carried out).

The coping strategies

The principal components analysis of the 65 coping strategies revealed five factors accounting for 32.9% of the data variance. Eigenvalues for the five factors were 9.05, 3.93, 3.12, 2.95 and 2.29 respectively, explaining 13.9%, 6.1%, 4.8%, 4.5% and 3.5% of the variance. Each factor is set out in table two and discussed below.

Factor one describes social support. It includes talking it through (for example, talk about the situation with someone else); getting advice–help (for example, try to obtain advice and suggestions from someone else); and releasing the emotion (for example, express your irritation to other colleagues to be able to let off steam). Factor two involves postponing action by relaxation and distracting attention. There appear to be three aspects to this strategy: distracting yourself (for example, make a concerted effort to distract yourself with some fun or pleasurable activity); avoiding–ignoring the problem (for example, avoid the subject of contention); and distracting yourself until you feel ready to handle it (for example, simply drop what you are doing and take up something totally unrelated).

Factor three involves developing capacity to deal with the problem. It includes strategies for pacing yourself (for example, leave margins of time between activities); strategies which attempt to conserve energy (for example, do not work quite so hard or so long); strategies designed to enhance your capacity (for example, try to reduce the tension by taking physical activity); strategies which identify your own limits–capacity (for example, recognise your own limits and accept them); and strategies that identify the positive qualities of the situation (for example, try to see the humorous aspects of the situation). Factor four involves rationalising the problem. There appear to be three aspects to this strategy: putting things into perspective (for example, accept that it is your job and just do it); clarifying–explaining your position (for example, let people know where they stand) and using work itself as the means for rationalising work behaviour (for example, working harder and longer).

Table 2: Principal components analyses of the frequency scores of coping strategies with varimax rotation.

	one	two	component three	four	five
social support					
talk about the situation with someone else	0.7039	0.0438	−0.0112	−0.0347	0.0714
try to get advice and suggestions from someone else	0.6522	0.0157	−0.0038	0.1795	0.1782
share the problem with others – office bearers, personal friends, colleagues	0.6495	0.0490	0.0773	0.2624	0.2034
express your irritation to other colleagues to be able to let off steam	0.6389	0.1339	0.0738	0.0536	−0.1116
express your feelings and frustrations to others so that you can then think rationally about the problem	0.6208	0.1976	0.1410	0.2393	0.1239
draw on colleagues to develop one's own skills and beliefs	0.5198	−0.1323	0.2250	0.2645	−0.1035
have a few beers or other drinks	0.4462	−0.0683	0.1296	−0.0675	−0.2693
talk things over with your wife–husband at the end of the day	0.4121	0.2151	−0.0800	−0.0757	0.3826
try to find out more about the situation–seek out more information	0.4096	0.0005	0.0309	0.3540	0.2149
postponing action by relaxation and distracting attention					
simply drop what you are doing and take up something totally unrelated	−0.0423	0.6959	0.1361	−0.0012	0.0787
avoid the subject of contention	−0.2272	0.6498	−0.0487	0.0197	0.0469
do nothing and try to carry on as usual	0.2585	0.5742	−0.1096	0.1249	−0.0484
move onto some other work activity that you know you can get satisfaction from	0.1367	0.5485	0.0684	0.0001	0.0551
think of the good things in the future	0.0591	0.5119	0.0163	0.2347	0.1205
become more involved in family life, helping with wife–husband and children	0.0858	0.4969	0.0627	0.1061	0.0824
ignore for a time the apparent problem until you feel ready to handle it	0.1610	0.4935	0.2964	0.0391	0.1272
make a concerted effort to distract yourself with some fun or pleasurable activity	0.3399	0.4817	0.3166	−0.0499	−0.1056
just let the feeling wear off	0.0189	0.4382	0.0969	−0.0235	0.1295
leave the problem and try to solve it later by talking it through at home	0.3472	0.4210	−0.0584	0.0174	0.3097
developing capacity to deal with the problem					
leave margins of time between activities	0.0829	0.2519	0.5707	0.0195	0.0334
try to get as much rest as possible so you will be fresh and alert for work	−0.0003	−0.0016	0.5150	0.1100	0.1984
throw yourself into work and work longer and harder	0.1535	0.0963	−0.4917	0.4282	0.0851
try to reduce the tension by taking physical activity	0.2089	0.2749	0.4897	0.3130	−0.0237
become more involved in non work activities – hobbies, leisure etc.	0.1945	0.3551	0.4343	−0.1153	−0.1566
recognise one's own limitations and accept them	−0.0129	−0.0946	0.4335	0.2817	0.0296
try to see the humorous aspects of the situation	−0.0583	−0.1669	0.4258	0.2085	0.1740
do one thing at a time	0.1764	0.0952	0.4246	0.0278	−0.0002
make sure you have one day off a week	0.2196	0.0417	0.4106	−0.2219	0.0563
rationalising the problem					
simply remember that there are others in worse situations than yours	−0.0905	0.3469	−0.0167	0.5897	0.1538

Table 2: (continued)

	one	two	component three	four	five
get support from the fact that not all problems can be solved, even at a national level	0.0709	0.2912	0.1322	0.5882	0.0011
let people know exactly where they stand	0.2191	0.0316	0.0971	0.4854	−0.0067
accept that it is your job and do it	−0.0085	−0.1098	0.0143	0.4578	0.1568
throw yourself into work and work harder and longer	0.1535	0.0963	−0.4917	0.4282	0.0851
reconsider just how involved you are in your work	0.3388	0.1387	0.2276	0.4232	0.1161
make sure people are aware you are doing your best	0.2127	0.2089	−0.0223	0.4211	0.1263
support through spiritual commitment					
share problem with prayer group	0.0322	0.1432	0.0679	0.0854	0.5957
share in the support group of the church	0.2190	0.0693	0.0403	0.1579	0.5470
continually renew commitment to Christ	−0.0001	0.1415	0.0564	0.3528	0.5079
face the situation knowing that your family and wife–husband give you help and a sense of proportion to the problem	0.3375	0.0544	−0.0672	−0.0110	0.4612
take a break – have a quiet time every day	0.0279	−0.0041	0.3940	−0.0614	0.4478
try to think objectively about the situation and keep your feelings under control	0.0633	0.1504	0.1429	0.3075	0.4345
eigenvalue	9.05	3.93	3.12	2.95	2.29
percentage of variance	13.9%	6.1%	4.8%	4.5%	3.5%

Factor five involves support through spiritual commitment. This support comes through prayer (for example, share problem with prayer group); the family (for example, face the situation knowing that your family and spouse will give you help and sense of proportion to the problem); solitude (for example, take a break – have a quiet time every day); and through self-reappraisal (for example, try to think objectively and keep your feelings under control).

Factor scores were calculated for all eight factors. Means, standard deviations and correlational data are presented in table three. Mean scores indicate that the emotional and time difficulties surrounding crisis work are experienced more frequently than the other two stressors and frequent use is made of coping strategies that involve support through spiritual commitment, developing capacity to deal with the problem and social support. The correlation data indicate that low to moderate positive correlations exist between the perceived frequency of the stressors and the frequency with which the coping strategies are used. More particularly, significant relationships were present between all three stressors and two coping strategies (social support and rationalising the problem) and two of the stressors (parish conflicts and church conservatism, and difficulties involving parish commitment and development) and the coping strategy involving postponing action by relaxation and distracting attention.

Table 3: Intercorrelation matix and descriptive data for work stresses and coping variables

	mean	SD	1	2	3	4	5	6	7	8
1. parish conflicts and church conservatism	2.53	0.68	0.874[1]							
2. difficulties involving parish commitment and development	2.89	0.75	0.697**	0.870[1]						
3. emotional and time difficulties surrounding crisis work	2.95	0.60	0.450**	0.464**	0.837[1]					
4. social support	3.07	0.62	0.280**	0.137*	0.190**	0.799[1]				
5. postponing action by relaxation and distracting attention	2.42	0.54	0.318**	0.222**	0.097	0.265**	0.785[1]			
6. developing capacity to deal with the problem	3.07	0.45	0.043	0.055	0.090	0.373**	0.231**	0.655[1]		
7. rationalising the problem	2.10	0.57	0.250**	0.237**	0.205**	0.394**	0.397**	0.400**	0.659[1]	
8. support through spiritual commitment	3.14	0.71	0.014	-0.002	0.078	0.272**	0.315**	0.326**	0.370**	0.670[1]

Notes: 1 Cronbach alpha coefficients
$* p = <0.05$ $** p = <0.01$

Discussion

A number of issues emerge from these findings. Considering the data on stressors, the results of the principal components analysis revealed three stressor factors that related to the roles and duties of ministers of religion.

These results highlight the need to identify the specific nature and characteristics of role expectations experienced by different occupational groups. This does not mean that global measures should not be used. As Dougherty and Pritchard (1985) point out, they provide for commonality across studies. However, simply advocating their continual use on the grounds that they exhibit sound psychometric properties (Schuler *et al.*, 1977) may not be enhancing our understanding of stress at work. Obviously as the nature of work roles vary depending on the occupation being studied, then changes will occur in the items which best describe work stressors. The factor 'parish conflicts and church conservatism', for example, includes items that reflect both role conflict and role ambiguity. The factor 'emotional and time difficulties surrounding crisis work' includes what appears to be traditional quantitative work overload (Beehr, Walsh and Taber, 1976) in addition to experiences that reflect the emotional overload that accumulates from dealing with people in need. Ministers also appear to experience a stressor ('difficulties involving parish commitment and development') which cannot easily be described in terms of conflict, ambiguity or overload.

The principal components analysis of the data on coping strategies revealed five interpretable factors, seemingly more concerned with reducing the emotional discomfort rather than altering the source of that discomfort. One reason for this may be that the job of the minister and therefore the work stressors encountered are by their very nature more likely to be coped with by strategies which are emotion focused. This view is supported by the analysis of the relationship between the frequency of the stressors and that with which the different coping strategies were used. However, problem focused (direct action) strategies include not only active efforts to deal with the problems, but also cognitive strategies aimed at analysing the situation (Folkman, 1982). Thus, rationalising the problem (factor four) may represent the cognitive dimensions of a problem-solving strategy.

The relationship between the experience of stress and coping can also be explained in terms of the way in which such events are appraised (Lazarus, 1966; Folkman, 1984; Cox, 1987). The concern here is with how secondary appraisal (what can be done) influences the selection of a coping technique. A critical aspect of this part of the appraisal process involves the issue of control. In general terms where the situation is appraised as providing little or no possibilities for control, then it is more likely to generate 'higher levels' of emotion focused coping (Folkman, 1984). Problem focused coping is more likely in those situations where individuals perceive that something can be done. If, as one minister reported, 'most church work is emotional if you believe in what you are doing' and if, as another suggested, that society's view of ministers is that they should

> not rock the boat, know one's place, deal with social problems, relate to pastoral needs, be a religious guru, perform rituals, be a palliative

then it is reasonable to expect that in many situations emotion focused coping will be chosen over problem focused techniques.

These results highlight the role of palliative (emotion focused) strategies. Often when coping strategies are discussed little attempt is made to distinguish between the use of a strategy, on the one hand, and its impact or success, on the other (Folkman, 1984). This has resulted in problem focused strategies being emphasised at the expense of emotion focused strategies, because they can be more clearly identified with action or success. Consequently, palliative strategies have been viewed as inherently less successful or second best. Yet as these results suggest there may be little, if anything, many ministers can do to deal directly with certain stressors. Thus strategies which allow for the dissipation or regulation of emotional discomfort should be viewed as a legitimate part of coping and an important facet of our coping repertoire (Dewe, 1985; Dewe *et al.*, 1979).

It seems to be common practice in occupational stress research to focus on the relationship between stressor and stress. While this approach has yielded significant results it has meant that almost by default, current measures of role stressors have been accepted as adequate descriptions of the constructs being investigated. The methodology adopted in this study involved using in-depth interviews as the primary information base for questionnaire design and construction. This enabled 'more meaningful and precisely targeted questions to be developed' (Handy, 1986). It allows a challenge to the utility of universal measures and supports the view expressed by a number of authors that their application to specific individuals or occupations is problematic (Crump *et al.*, 1980; Fineman and Payne, 1981; Firth, 1985; Glowinkowski and Cooper, 1985) and that they now should be replaced by 'richer more context-specific theories and idiographic techniques' (Handy, 1986). In order to enhance our understanding, future research may wish to view role conflict and role ambiguity measures as they were first intended as heuristic devices providing conceptual boundaries (Kahn *et al.*, 1964), thus distinguishing between their usefulness at the global level and their structure and nature at the occupational level.

Similarly, it would seem that in order to explore the role that coping strategies play in the stress process, occupational stress research should, as a first priority, focus on the coping construct itself. Thus by identifying, describing and classifying specific strategies individuals say they use to cope with work stress, old ideas can be challenged and new directions identified which expand and develop our understanding of work related stress.

References

Beehr, T A, Walsh J T and Taber, T D (1976) 'Relationship of stress to individually and organisationally valued states: higher order needs as moderator,' *Journal of Applied Psychology*, 61, pp. 41–47.

Burke, R J (1972) 'Are you fed up with work? How can job tensions be reduced?' *Personnel Administration*, 34, pp. 27–31.

Burke, R J and Belcourt, M L (1974) 'Managerial role stress and coping responses,' *Journal of Business Administration*, 5, pp. 55–68.

Cherniss, C (1980) *Staff Burnout: job stress in the human services*, Beverly Hills, California, Sage Publications.

Cooper, C L (1983) 'Identifying stressors at work: recent research developments,' *Journal of Psychosomatic Research*, 27, pp. 269–376.

Cooper, C L and Roden, J (1985) 'Mental health and satisfaction among tax officers,' *Social Science and Medicine*, 21, pp. 747–751.

Cooper, C L and Sloan, S (1985) 'Occupational and psychosocial stress among commercial aviation pilots,' *Journal of Occupational Medicine*, 27, pp. 570–576.

Cox, T (1987) 'Stress, coping and problem solving,' *Work and Stress*, 1, pp. 5–14.

Crump, J H, Cooper, C L and Smith, M (1980) 'Investigating occupational stress: a methodological approach,' *Journal of Occupational Behaviour*, 1, pp. 191–204.

Dewe, P J (1985) 'Coping with stress: an investigation of teachers' actions,' *Research in Education*, 33, pp. 27–40.

Dewe, P, Guest, D and Williams, R (1979) 'Methods of coping with work related stress,' in C Mackay and T Cox (eds) *Response to Stress: occupational aspects*, Guildford, IPC Science and Technology Press Limited, pp. 69–84.

Dougherty, T W and Pritchard, R D (1985) 'The measurement of role variables: exploratory examination of a new approach,' *Organisational Behaviour and Human Performance*, 35, pp. 141–155.

Fineman, S and Payne, R (1981) 'Role stress, a methodological trap,' *Journal of Occupational Behaviour*, 2, pp. 51–64.

Firth, J (1985) 'Personal meanings of occupational stress: cases from the clinic,' *Journal of Occupational Psychology*, 58, pp. 139–148.

Folkman, S (1984) 'Personal control and stress and coping processes: a theoretical analysis,' *Journal of Personality and Social Psychology*, 46, pp. 839–852.

Folkman, S (1982) 'An approach to the measurement of coping,' *Journal of Occupational Behaviour*, 3, pp. 95–107.

Glowinkowski, S P and Cooper, C L (1985) 'Current issues in organisational stress research,' *Bulletin of British Psychological Society*, 38, pp. 212–216.

Handy, J A (1986) 'Considering organisations in organisational stress research: a rejoinder to Glowinkowski and Cooper and to Duckworth,' *Bulletin of the British Psychological Society*, 39, pp. 205–210.

Holt, R R (1982) 'Occupational stress,' in L Goldberg and S Breznitz (eds) *Handbook of Stress: theoretical and clinical aspects*, New York, Free Press.

House, R J (1979) *Occupational Stress And The Mental and Physical Health of Factory Workers*,' University of Michigan, Survey Research Center, Institute for Social Research.

Jackson, S (1984) 'Organisational practices for preventing burnout,' in A Sethi and R Schuler (eds) *Handbook of Organisational Stress Coping Strategies*, Cambridge, Massachusetts, Ballinger Publishing Company.

Jackson, S E and Schuler, R S (1985) 'A meta-analysis and conceptual critique of research on role ambiguity and role conflict in work settings,' *Organisational Behaviour and Human Performance*, 36, pp. 16–78.

Kuhn, R L, Wolfe, D M, Quinn, R P, Snoek, J D and Rosenthal, R A (1964) *Organisational Stress: studies in role conflict* and *ambiguity*, New York, John Wiley and Sons.

Koch, J L, Tung, R, Gmelch, W and Swent, B (1982) 'Job stress among school administrators: factorial dimensions and differential effects,' *Journal of Applied Psychology*, 67, pp. 493–499.

Latack, J C (1986) 'Coping with job stress: measures and future directions for scale development,' *Journal of Applied Psychology*, 71, pp. 377–385.

Lazarus, R S (1975) 'A cognitively oriented psychologist looks at biofeedback,' *American Psychologist*, 30, pp. 553–561.

Lazarus, R S (1966) *Psychological Stress and the Coping Process*, New York, McGraw-Hill Book Company.

Newton, T J and Keenan, A (1985) 'Coping with work-related stress,' *Human Relations*, 38, pp. 107–126.

Parasuraman, S and Cleek, M A (1984) 'Coping behaviours and managers' affective reactions to role stressors,' *Journal of Vocational Behaviour*, 24, pp. 179–183.

Pearlin, L I and Schooler, C (1978) 'The structure of coping,' *Journal of Health and Social Behaviour*, 19, pp. 2–21.

Rizzo, J R, House, R J and Lirtzman, S I (1970) 'Role conflict and ambiguity in complex organisations,' *Administrative Science Quarterly*, 15, pp. 150–163.

Schuler, R S, Aldag, R J and Brief, A P (1977) 'Role conflict and ambiguity: a scale analysis,' *Organisational Behaviour and Human Performance*, 20, pp. 111–128.

Shaw, J B and Riskind, J H (1983) 'Predicting job stress using data from the position analysis questionnaire,' *Journal of Applied Psychology*, 68, pp. 253–261.

Tracy, L and Johnson, T W (1981) 'What do the role conflict and role ambiguity scales measure?' *Journal of Applied Psychology*, 66, pp. 464–469.

Van Sell, M, Brief, A P and Schuler, R S (1981) 'Role conflict and role ambiguity: integration of the literature and direction for future research,' *Human Relations*, 34, pp. 43–71.

4.3 The myth of clergy burnout

Joseph H Fichter

Dr. Hans Selye (1978, pp. 60–69), the father of stress research, once wrote, 'We hear a great deal these days about the dangers of overwork and excessive striving, and of being the so-called Type A personality. But I think in many ways this is exaggerated and arouses unnecessary anxiety.' Even though much of the propaganda about clergy burnout can be dismissed for lack of evidence or for conceptual confusion, we should deal seriously with it for two reasons. The first is that bishops and religious superiors are disturbed by this phenomenon and think it is a cause for alarm. We owe them some reassurance. The second reason is the need to deflate the pop-psychologists and human relations experts who spread worrisome rumours. Every fad has to run its course, but we may be able to dampen some of this overheated enthusiasm.

I bring both scepticism and open-mindedness to the study of stressful working conditions among the priests. The term itself is suspect by researchers. Seymour Sarason (1980) is right when he remarks that 'professional burnout is a phrase that in a few short years has become part of our jargon. Some use it as an excuse, some as a badge of honour, and others as a negative symptom of our times and a fast changing society.' I am confident that the American Catholic clergy are not suffering an epidemic of overwork. As a group, the clergy probably work as hard and as long as men in other professions, but this does not mean that most of them are workaholics. When Marilyn Machlowitz (1980, p. 6) began her study of workaholics in the late 70s she said 'it wasn't easy' to find them. Her 'best estimate suggests that workaholics comprise no more than five percent of the adult population'. It appears to be no accident that we found only 6.2% of our clergy respondents who could be termed candidates for burnout.

When I say that the concept of clergy burnout is a myth, I do not belittle the anxiety expressed by the bishops or the discomfort of the men who experience burnout. The notion that overworked people who worry are heading for a nervous breakdown has been well-known for a long time. The man who first popularised the term, Herbert Freudenberg (1974), said it means 'to fail, to wear out, or become exhausted by making excessive demands on energy, strength, or resources'. Perhaps our research findings can help to demystify the subject, to recognise it as a legitimate concern of limited application, but not as a problem of epidemic proportions.

An ancient malady

Pasting a new label on an old package does nothing to change the contents. All through history and in all cultures – and long before the art of psychiatry was discovered – people have had old-fashioned nervous breakdowns, have cracked up and burned out. As Hans Selye (1956, p. 263) remarked, 'the existence of physical and mental strain, the manifold interactions between somatic and psychic reactions, as well as the importance of defensive-adaptive responses, had all been more or less clearly recognised since time immemorial'. Frustration is nothing new, nor is stress, nor is burnout. Perhaps Caligula was one of the early examples, and Judas Iscariot, and more recently the singer, Elvis Presley and the comic, John Belushi. The most obvious flame-outs become the most notorious burnouts. Graham Greene (1961) gave meaning to the label in his best-selling novel, *A Burnt-Out Case*. F Scott Fitzgerald recognised that he had all the modern symptoms when he 'cracked up' at the 'premature' age of thirty-nine years (Wilson, 1931). Wesley Shrader (1956) wrote a popular article for *Life* magazine explaining 'why ministers are breaking down', and described the same experiences that are now being rediscovered among the Catholic clergy. Veninga and Spradley (1981) suggest that 'everyone from clock puncher to chairman of the board is a potential victim of job burnout, a debilitating physical and psychological condition brought about by unrelieved stress on the job'. Alfred Kammer (1978), who is a social activist, is more selective of social-service professionals who burn out like 'poverty lawyers', physicians, prison personnel, social-welfare workers, clinical psychologists and psychiatrists in a mental hospital, child-care workers, and psychiatric nurses'.

If every person in every conceivable work situation is a candidate for burnour the definition probably has room for all of us. A lengthy litany of signs and symptoms that is said to emerge from clinical experience and research is recited by psychologist James Gill (1980): 'physical fatigue, exhaustion; insomnia; body tension; frequent sickness; backache or neckache; increased perspiration; migraine headaches; serious illness; worry about work or clients; difficulty making decisions; guilt feelings about work performance; preoccupation with problems; griping, cynicism; feeling frustrated, overwhelmed; loss of enthusiasm, feeling of stagnation; anger, resentment; blaming others and organisations; accident prone; hostile thinking and speech; yelling; impatient; irritated; uncharacteristic behaviour; loss of concern for others; treating clients coldly; stereotyping clients; communicating with clients impersonally; reduction of time spent with clients; mechanical performance of duties; excessive intellectualisation; repression of feelings'.

When an illness exhibits this enormous variety of signs and symptoms, it is either impossible to diagnose precisely, or it afflicts all of us at one time or another and in some form or other. Whatever else may be said of human beings in the work place, there is no question that stress and frustration are characteristic of everyone's life. Psychiatrist Paul Qualben (1982; Selye, 1969), writing for Lutheran clergy, wisely argues that stress is not the reason for burnout. Everybody is under stress. 'Most of the work in the church is done by people under stress. Stress is not the issue. The problem is rather distress. Distress is the product of frustration and repeated disappointment.'

The tendency among psychologists and psychiatrists is to emphasise both the novelty and the subjectivity of the burnout experience. The victim is often advised that he must cope with this subjective condition by learning to develop behavioural adequacy, or if this is not possible, simply to quit the job. The sociological perspective, however, encompasses the shifting environmental conditions of work as an important factor in burnout. Even Henri Nouwen (1972), without any data, suggests that the alienation of the clergyman is especially painful because 'he feels an added loneliness from the changing meaning of the ministerial profession itself'. Social science researchers have also found that 'in the vast majority of cases of burnout the major cause lies in the situation' (Pines and Aronson, 1981).

Some of the more conservative Catholic critics go even further when they trace the source of clergy stress and burnout to the *aggiornamento* introduced by the Second Vatican Council. They blame the American bishops for allowing environmental changes to 'take their toll on the physical, emotional and spiritual wellbeing of all the faith, and in a distinct way, of the priest'. In a sharply critical article, Eugene J Sweeney (1983), retired priest and ex-army officer, argues that the priest 'is suffering stress because he feels that the whole sense and direction of this priesthood has been changed, that for all practical purposes the priesthood for which he was ordained no longer exists in the United States'.

Sociological data base

The information we have here on so-called 'burnout' is really a spin-off for a survey conducted under the auspices of the National Conference of Catholic Bishops. Our mailed questionnaires were answered by 4,660 priests (a return rate of 58%). This is the first survey ever undertaken of the physical health of the clergy. Previous studies looked for psychoses and neuroses. Kind and Bailar (1969) searched through the literature and remarked that 'studies on illness among the clergy are almost entirely limited to mental disorders among priests'. Our current fixation on burnout falls into this tradition of psychological problems among the priests.

This research project is a sequel to the study on *The Priest and Stress* (1982, p. 9) as the initial phase of the American bishops' concern for the physical and emotional health of priests. 'It is evident that the high median age of priests and the demands made on their ministry posit the need for good health care in all facets of the life of the priest person: physical, emotional and spiritual.' The focus of the present survey is on the physical health of the clergy, but it quickly becomes apparent that emotional stress and physical fitness are closely intertwined. The bishops remark that 'the demands on a priest's time are burgeoning. Many over-zealous priests run great risks of suffering 'burnout', or emotional or physical illness.'

We did not ask the direct question: 'Have you been, are you now; or do you expect to become, a victim of burnout?' We did probe for signs of emotional stress and psychological disorders, and found a very small proportion (3.8%) of all respondents who report that they are troubled with mental illness, mainly in the form of depression. Other factors are mentioned that may have an association with mental illness, or even nervous breakdown, but attention is now fixed on the inter-relation of stress and burnout. We are reminded by the bishops that 'the growing awareness of the problem of stress among American priests has prompted many in the church to examine the extent of the problem, its threat to effective priestly ministry, and the critical importance of recognising the danger and taking positive steps to resolve it' (1982, p. 3). A quick overview of the research findings shows that the great majority of the priests consider themselves pretty healthy and are not likely candidates for burnout. Only one out of ten (9.8%) says that his health is worse now than it was two years ago, and a much smaller minority (3.2%) remark that ill-health 'greatly' affects the amount and quality of their ministry.

If they are fairly healthy we may expect that they work fairly hard. The average work week reported by these priests is fifty-six hours, which seems to be normal for most professional men. Approximately one-quarter of them (24.1%) say they work seventy hours or more a week, while a minority (14.4%), mainly the sick and elderly, work less than forty hours. The pressures of the ministry are not measured only by hours worked. Almost one-fifth (18.3%) report that they are 'regularly' overburdened (or 'swamped') by the work demands of their ministry, but less than ten percent (7.9%) say their current assignment is 'more than they can handle'.

Aside from physical fitness and work activities, there are also the psychological anxieties that are said to accompany burnout. About one-fifth (21.4%) of these priests say that a 'great deal' of emotional stress is associated with their life style and ministry, but less than ten percent (8.2%) experienced severe personal, emotional, or behavioural problems that required professional therapy. Stress is manifested in various ways, but we found that only a minority of priests say they 'often' have the following symptoms: worried about things (18.7%), were tense and nervous (16.5%), felt lonely (11.8%), or had feelings of depression (7.2%).

Candidates for burnout

Bishops and religious superiors are generally concerned about the health and fitness of their priests, but they have been led to believe that work and worry are threatening their men with burnout. Even though the demographic findings of this survey reveal a quite favourable state of physical fitness among Catholic clergy, there is a recurring and popular tendency to emphasise the strain and tension under which the priests live and work. It is thought that stress arises not only from overwork but also from an inability to cope with the demands of their assignment. The priest is trying to do too much, or is worrying about not doing enough, or is simply 'fed up' and ready to quit. There were many reasons given for the large exodus of Catholic priests in the decade following the Second Vatican Council, but there was no talk of burnout and hardly anyone suggested exhaustion from overwork and overstress. The phenomenon of the 'second career' has been noted when men leave one occupation for another, as many business and professional men did when they entered the seminary to become Episcopal priests. One does not necessarily say that they failed, or were burnt out, in the occupation they abandoned. Similarly we no longer speak of failure, or defection, among the many Catholic priests who turned to alternative careers in recent years.

Following the lead of the bishops we speculated that if there are any prospective, or actual, burnout victims among our clergy respondents, they ought to be found among the stressful hardworkers. If the bishops correctly interpret burnout as the consequence of 'burgeoning' demands on the 'overzealous' priest, they may well accept the definition provided by Cary Cherniss (1980, p. 21): 'Burnout is a process that begins with excessive and prolonged levels of job stress. This stress produces strain in the worker (feelings of tension, irritability and fatigue).' Almost one-fifth (18.4%) say they are 'regularly' overburdened with work, and a slightly higher percentage (21.4%) report that a 'great deal' of emotional stress is associated with their life and ministry. It is only when these two variables are combined that we can identify candidates for burnout. Most of those (66.0%) who are overburdened are not in great stress and most of those in stress are not overburdened. These combined criteria reveal a small minority of 291 priests, about one in sixteen (6.2%) of all respondents, who may be termed potential candidates for burnout.

The burnout candidates we uncovered in this research study do not fit the description given by Father Norbert Brockman (1978, p. 809) in *Review for Religious*, writing about priests who 'find themselves depleted, run out of energy, unable to reanimate themselves'. These priests are just the opposite. They are 'on the go' all the time. They are not the victims of the rapid pace of change and transition which is said to leave some church personnel bewildered and frustrated. It seems erroneous, or at least misleading, to suggest that stress and burnout inevitably accompany the adaptations required in a developing ministry and modernising church. The dynamic dedicated up-to-date priest thrives in this kind of situation. We are reminded by experts (Johnson and Goldfinger, 1981) that 'the person who works long hours and leads a busy life may be far less frustrated than the person trapped in a limited position with no sense of release or accomplishment'.

There is much supportive data to confirm their claim that they are regularly swamped with work, but we cannot tell whether this volume of work is imposed on them in their current assignment, or is the consequence of their own overzealous choice (as the bishops suggest). Perhaps many of them are the type of voluntary workaholics who, says Machlowitz (1980, p. 16), are a surprisingly happy group of people 'doing exactly what they love – work – and they can't seem to get enough of it'. From the perspective of sheer time devoted to their ministry, these busy priests are much more likely (73.8%) than the other priests (48.7%) to report that they work sixty hours or more a week; indeed, half of them say that their work week lasts seventy hours or more. The median for all respondents is 56.2 hours, but for these workaholics it is 65.8 hours. Two-thirds of them (65.3%) claim that they work harder than other professional men of their acquaintance (like engineers, lawyers, physicians). They are also much more likely than the others (47.0% to 21.3%) to report that the work they are expected to do is more than they can handle.

The comparative statistics of table one demonstrate that in the most pertinent types of psychological experiences they are enormously different from their fellow priests. Nine out of ten (91.8%) report that they are often tense and nervous, and approximately the same percentage (89.7%) say that they are often worried about things. Approximately eight out of ten (78.3%) have had some severe personal behavioural problem during the past twelve months, some of them (22.0%) so serious that they sought professional therapeutic counsel. They are also significantly more likely (46.4%) to admit that they often have feelings of loneliness, and of depression (44.0%), and finally that they are not happy (42.6%).

These research data, which show a definite correlation between overwork and overworry, are simply the logical demonstration of the fact that we selected the category of respondents who combine the criteria of regular overburden of work and of great emotional stress. At this point we have a kind of internal verification of the validity of the survey responses. From one point of view this is an artificial construct of a clergy type based on a deliberately contrived definition built on two selected criteria. From the point of view of the experts on burnout, however, this is simply a clear proof of their general speculation that too much work and too much worry combine to produce this debilitating psychological condition. It helps to explain also why the handling of burnout victims has been the concern of psychologists and psychiatrists rather than of medical doctors.

Table 1: Proportional categories of burnout candidates and others on selected manifestations of emotional stress

	burnout %	all others %
tense and nervous	91.8	16.6
worried about things	89.7	18.8
severe personal problems	78.3	39.8
feelings of loneliness	46.4	11.0
feelings of depression	44.0	7.3
not happy	42.6	9.8

Physical illness and burnout

The psychosomatic interpretation of illness tends to be holistic in the sense that the total human being is affected by any disorder or disability, whether psychological or physiological. Concepts like stress and burnout are so imprecisely used to cover a wide range of social and psychological phenomena, that many medical doctors seem reluctant to deal seriously with them. The practising physician who keeps office hours is sometimes annoyed by the large number of patients who have nothing wrong with them that is diagnosable by an internist (Fichter, 1981, pp. 30–32). As early as 1914, however, the Harvard physiologist, Walter B Cannon, recognised physiological response to external threats, and three decades later (1946) Hans Selye proved that 'psychological strain itself could cause dramatic hormonal changes and hence physiological symptoms' (Seyle, 1975). He showed that these biochemical changes then lead to a series of physical ailments which are now seen as symptoms of burnout. One of the central concerns of church leaders is the causal connection between the physiological and psychological, how the physical exhaustion of overwork leads to emotional stress, and how this stressful condition then becomes the cause of physical ailments.

A small proportion (7.6%) of the prospective burnout victims are free of all the ailments listed in the questionnaire, but the whole category reports an average of 3.2 maladies each while the other priests average 2.4 each. Other comparable statistics point to further manifestations of physical ill health. They are almost four times likely (30.9% to 7.7%) to say they are insomniacs. They are twice as likely (30.1% to 15.3%) as the others to have had three or more colds during the past year; and also twice as likely (42.3% to 20.6%) as the others to have suffered three or more severe headaches. They also have a higher percentage (40.8% to 25.1%) who report that they were confined to bed three or more days because of illness or injury.

While there continues to be much confusion in the literature on 'burnout', and while false diagnoses may be made in specific cases, there can no longer be doubt about the mutual influence of psychological processes and somatic processes (Levi, 1967, chapter 3). Without attempting to fix causality – much less explain it – we have several

Table 2: Proportional categories of burnout candidates and others on the incidence of selected physical ailments

	burnout %	all others %
back pains, or spine	52.2	38.3
sinus trouble	46.8	35.0
allergies	44.4	34.5
haemorrhoids, or piles	44.4	35.8
high blood pressure	30.6	29.5
stomach ulcers	19.3	14.1
mental illness	10.0	3.8
heart disease	8.5	13.4

clear examples in table two that the stressful hardworkers among the priests manifest a higher incidence of certain ailments: back pains (52.2% to 38.3%), sinus trouble (46.8% to 35.0%), allergies (44.4% to 34.5%) and haemorrhoids (44.4% to 35.8%). Everyone knows that ulcer of the stomach may be caused by emotional upset but in this study the differential incidence is only 19.3% to 14.1%. Perhaps the least we can say is that emotional stress is related to these physical ailments, if not as a cause, then as having a role in making things worse for the individual.

Some of our research findings, however, may help to restrain the exaggerated claims of burnout enthusiasts. We may legitimately raise the same kind of doubts that ultimately surrounded the popularity of the 'Type A' personality. In fact, some studies have shown that business executives with Type-A behaviour may have 'fewer heart attacks than less stressful employees at lower levels of the company' (Johnson and Goldfinger, 1981, p. 100).

The same kind of doubt arises about the physical effects of burnout that allowed us to question the hypothesis of the 'Type A' personality. We note in table two that the same proportion (30.6% to 29.5%) of both categories report high blood pressure, a fact that allows us to accept the caution that 'it would be misleading to automatically equate high-strung with high blood pressure'. The hypothesis becomes even more questionable when we note that the burnout candidates are even less likely (8.5% to 13.4%) to report having heart disease.

Portrait of the burnout candidate

We have no reliable statistical answer to the question how these particular priests will ultimately respond to the threat of burnout, and whether they are more able than other professionals to cope with this debilitating psychological condition. In the absence of comparable data about other adult males, we may presume that the proportion (6.2%) of potential clergy burnouts compares favourably with men in other professions. Our findings, compared with the general health statistics for educated adult males in the National Health Survey of 1979, indicate that the Catholic priests are in better health. Certainly we know that the clergy live longer than men in other professions. Given the superior spiritual and psychological training of the clergy, we may expect that they are better able to cope with the symptoms of burnout. After all, they are not routine job-holders; they are well-educated; they have long ago learned to exercise self control. It seems to me that we are selling the Catholic clergy short when we suggest that large numbers of them have not learned self control, are unable to cope with stress, that they let things get out of hand.

If we can safely extrapolate our statistical proportions to the total priest population in the United States, we estimate that there are about 3,500 Catholic clergymen who are potential victims of the burnout syndrome. The proportion of diocesan priests who fit this category is higher (6.7%) than that (5.2%) of religious order clergy. The diocesan clergy in much larger percentages are assigned to parish duties, and it is in the parish setting that we find a much higher incidence (7.5%) of burnout than in all other priestly ministries combined (4.5%). Since most clergymen do pastoral work in their congregations it is logical that anecdotes about clergy breakdown centre on the parish minister (Veninga and Spradley, pp. 22–23, 138–141).

The popularisers to the burnout syndrome like to focus attention on people at their most active stage in the so-called helping professions – and are themselves mainly psychologists in the human services. Their case studies do not include stories of elderly men and women – as though age is a variable of little consequence. In the present study we found a very low incidence (2.1%) of burnout candidates among the priests, age sixty-five and older. Even for the minority of candidates the hazardous years are during the first quarter century after ordination when the rate is 9.6%, which drops to 4.9% in the age category fifty to sixty-four years. Their average age is 44.7 years, an indication that they are over-worked and overstressed in the most active period of their priestly life.

One final question we may put to the research data is to ask if these candidates for burnout take the normal precautions to preserve their health, or even to restore health. Burnout is not a fatal illness and the assumption is that in all but the most extreme cases of clinical depression, the victim not only survives but has a good chance to recuperate. The research data allows us to investigate the so-called health habits of the clergy without judging whether these habits are either cause or effect of the psychological condition of the burnout candidate. We are not willing to judge if their neglect of the Alameda health practices contributed to their stressful condition, or resulted from it (Wiley and Camacho, 1980).

Our logical hypothesis is that the burnout syndrome is associated with general ill health and that a partial explanation – aside from work and stress – may be the extent to which these priests fail to observe the basic criteria for good health. In the comparisons of table three this

Table 3: Proportions of burnout candidates and others who obey the five Alameda health practices

	burnout %	all others %
no cigarettes	68.8	76.0
7–8 hours sleep	50.1	69.0
sufficient exercise	49.8	66.4
average bodyweight	45.0	56.1
no alcoholic drinks	34.7	37.4

means that the candidates for burnout ought to manifest a much lower incidence of the characteristic practices found among the physically fit. The most unexpected comparison is in the dangerous practices of smoking and drinking. Almost seven out of ten (66.8%) of the burnout candidates do not smoke cigarettes, as compared with three quarters (76.0%) of the others. There are less than three percentage points difference (34.7% to 37.4%) between them in abstinence from alcoholic beverages. It appears, therefore, that the stress and strain of overwork do not generally drive the clergy to these two common addictions.

The three remaining health habits listed in table three show a considerable difference between these two categories of priests. A much larger proportion (63.5% to 38.5%) appear to be insomniacs, reporting that they often or sometimes have trouble sleeping. The statistics show that only half of them get as much as seven or eight hours sleep a night. They are also three times as likely (15.3% to 5.2%) to say that they regularly or occasionally take sleeping pills or tranquilisers. Only half of them (49.8%) exercise regularly, and even fewer (45.0%) are able to maintain a normal bodyweight. We have seen in table one that they exhibit an extremely high incidence of tension, worry and anxiety. These manifestations of psychological distress combine with the facts of table three that they are overweight, do not get enough physical exercise, and do not get enough sleep.

In summary, we may claim in this research project to have placed the problem of clergy 'burnout' in proper perspective and have allayed the fears of bishops and religious superiors about the extent and intensity of the problem. We all know that some priests have a nervous breakdown, or a crack-up, and they deserve our deepest sympathy, but we have found them a relative minority (6.2%) and we deal with them in this study as candidates moving toward burnout, rather than as actual victims of the illness. The priest most likely to fit this category is a diocesan parish priest in his mid-forties who has more psychological problems than physical ills. We recognise him as fitting the definition accepted by the bishops: he is overburdened with work, putting in a longer work week than other priests and admitting to a great deal of emotional stress.

The great majority of priests, however, are not in such dire straits.

Like other adult Americans they are subject to the cultural and economic pressures of a narcissistic, consumer society. The notion that clergymen are suffering the fearful consequences of stressful overwork persists in the face of clear evidence that most Americans have long since abandoned the so-called Protestant work ethic. We have outlived our traditional reputation as a nation of industrious production workers and have moved toward an ethic of consumerism. Nevertheless, the normal and necessary work of the ministry goes on in the world's oldest institution that has survived many other fads over the centuries.

References

Brockman, N (1978) 'Burnout in superiors,' *Review for Religious*, 37, pp. 809–816.

Cherniss, C (1980) *Staff Burnout: job stress in the human services*, Beverly Hills, Sage.

Fichter, J (1981) *Religion and Pain*, New York, Crossroad.

Freudenberger, H (1974) 'Staff burnout,' *Journal of Social Issues*, 30, pp, 159–165.

Gill, J J (1980) 'Burnout: a growing threat in ministry,' *Human Development* 1, 2, pp. 21–27.

Greene, G (1961) *A Burnt-Out Case*, New York, Viking Press.

Johnson, G T and Goldfinger S E (eds) (1981) *The Harvard Medical School Health Letter Book*, Cambridge, Massachusetts, Harvard University Press.

Kammer, A C (1978) 'Burnout: contemporary dilemma for the Jesuit social activist,' *Studies in the Spirituality of Jesuits*, 10, 1, pp. 1–42.

King, H and Bailar, J (1969) 'The health of the clergy: a review of demographic literature,' *Demography*, 6, pp. 27–43.

Levi, L (1967) *Stress: sources, management and prevention*, New York, Liveright.

Machlowitz, M (1980) *Workaholics: living with them, working with them*, Reading, Addison-Wesley.

Nouwen, H J M (1972) *The Wounded Healer: ministry in contemporary society*, Garden City, Doubleday.

Pines, A M and Aronson, E (1981) *Burnout: from tedium to personal growth*, New York, Free Press.

Qualben, P A (1982) 'A psychiatrist looks at burnout,' *Partners*, 4, 6, pp. 13–16.

Sarason, S (1980) 'Foreword,' in Cary Cherniss, *Professional Burnout in Human Service Organizations*, New York, Praeger.

Selve, H (1956) *The Stress of Life*, New York, McGraw-Hill.

Selve, H (1975) 'Confusion and controversy in the stress field,' *Journal of Human Stress* 1, pp. 37–44.

Selve, H (1978) 'On the real benefits of stress,' *Psychology Today*, 1, pp. 60–69. Interview with Laurence Cherry.

Shrader, W (1956) 'Why ministers are breaking down,' *Life*, 41, pp. 95–104.

Sweeney, E J (1983) 'The Priest and Stress,' *Homiletic and Pastoral Review*, 73, 10, pp. 9–16.

Time Magazine, Cover Story (1983) 'Stress: can we cope?' June 6, pp. 48–54.

United States Catholic Conference (1982) *The Priest and Stress*.

Veninga, R and Spradley, J (1981) *The Work/Stress Connection: how to cope with job burnout*, Boston, Little Brown.

Wiley, J A and Camacho, T C (1980) 'Life-style and future health: evidence from the Alameda County Study,' *Preventive Medicine*, 9, 1, pp. 1–21.

Wilson, E (ed.) (1931) *The Crack-Up*, New York, Scribner's.

4.4 Factors related to pastoral morale in the Seventh-day Adventist Church

Roger L Dudley and Des Cummings Jr

This study addresses itself to the question of pastoral morale. There is concern that, in recent years, this has been slipping and that the pastoral ministry no longer holds the challenge and fulfilment that it once did.

Some years ago, Blizzard (1956) described the special characteristics of the pastor's position which create a high vulnerability to stress and discouragement. Since then a number of other studies (Jud, *et al.*, 1970; Mills and Koval, 1971; Smith, 1973) have investigated this theme. A recent report on clergy in the Penn Central Conference of the United Church of Christ (Hartley, 1980, p. 3) found that 84% of the respondents had had low morale experiences such as a sense of losing hope, a feeling of being overwhelmed, or an experience of futility in their ministry.

Of course there are still many pastors who love their work and who would not want to do anything else. They find their calling satisfying, rewarding, and joyous. But for an increasing number, the flame that once lighted their vision has flickered, burned low, or gone out. They find their daily routine to be drudgery. They have not found the success needed to fulfil their own expectations or those of their denominational administrations. They feel a sense of failure and of guilt. Some are hoping to find a 'promotion' into administrative work. Some seek to transfer to a teaching position. Others are simply leaving the ministry for secular callings. Many feel trapped and attempt to 'tread water' until retirement.

One theory is that the slippage in morale may be related to the stresses that the pastoral ministry places on family life, particularly on husband-wife relationships. Due to the high mobility of pastoral families and the supposed need to maintain impartiality, many wives have no close relationships in community or congregation. If, in addition, the husband devotes long hours, including evenings and weekends, to his profession, the wife may feel very alone indeed. Often the husband is better educated and much in the limelight, while she has neglected her personal development and sees herself as being left behind as the years pass. This situation may create strain and misunderstanding in the relationship and reinforce the pastor's doubts as to whether the pastorate is really where he ought to be after all. Two recent studies (Mace and Mace, 1980; Martin, 1980) discuss these issues.

The present research was designed to tap the depth and diversity of lowered morale among Seventh-day Adventist pastors in North America. It also allowed opportunity for the respondents to indicate what changes they would suggest to make the pastoral ministry a more fulfilling calling.

Methods

The Institute of Church Ministry at Andrews University designed a simple questionnaire called 'The pastor as person and husband'.[1] It consisted of twenty-one items on personal and pastoral morale and on husband-wife relationships. To each item the pastor could respond by disagreeing strongly, disagreeing somewhat, being neutral, agreeing somewhat, or agreeing strongly. In addition, open-ended questions asked for the areas of frustration and for the changes the pastor would like to see made in his profession.

For a sample we used the same group of pastors who had responded to a just-completed survey (Dudley and Cummings, 1981). In that study 295 churches were randomly selected from the entire North American Division (composed of United States and Canada, having 2,691 ordained and licensed ministers). A total of 238 pastors responded to the earlier study, and they were sent the questionnaire on morale in September 1980. Three follow-up letters were sent, and non-respondents were telephoned. By May 1981, 172 usable surveys (72%) were returned, and the present study is based on them.

Findings

A pastoral profile

The responses to the first twenty-one items will now be examined. The two disagree and the two agree positions have been combined. The mean score is based on assigning the numbers 1 to 5 to the positions ranging from strongly disagree to strongly agree. The higher the mean, the more agreement is indicated. It is important to note that in some cases the item is worded positively and in other cases negatively. Therefore the higher score may indicate high *or* low morale. The wording of the item must be considered. The results are displayed in table one.

The first impression that comes from an inspection of table one is that there is much reason for encouragement. The overall morale appears to be better than might have been expected. The item, 'I really enjoy being a pastor', received the second highest percent of agreement (94%) and the highest mean. Only 2% disagreed with the statement. Further, 95% are comfortable in one-to-one witnessing, 87% believe they are successful in their work, and 82% say that husband and wife are agreed that God wants them in the pastoral ministry.

Table 1: *Distribution of responses (in percent) to items on personal and pastoral morale and on husband-wife relationships*

item	disagree %	neutral %	agree %	mean
personal satisfaction				
My personal devotional life is satisfying.	17	9	74	3.78
We have regular family worship in our home.	16	14	70	3.88
Current internal theological challenges have caused me to question some of our teachings.	76	5	19	1.87
It would be good if a counsellor with no ties to administration were provided with whom pastors and their wives could discuss problems.	9	21	70	3.98
I sometimes feel a loneliness and isolation in the ministry.	34	8	58	3.24
I am disturbed by the fault-finding and criticism of some of the members toward me.	42	32	26	2.57
role and career				
I have an effective programme for my professional growth.	23	20	57	3.35
I would welcome a continuing education programme through which I could up-grade my ministerial skills.	1	7	92	4.53
I feel very comfortable in one-to-one witnessing.	1	4	95	4.58
I really enjoy being a pastor.	2	4	94	4.58
For the most part I believe I am a successful pastor.	3	10	87	4.22
I feel some concern that I may not meet the approval of my superiors in the conference office.	51	15	34	2.54
I hope eventually to be called into either an administrative, departmental, or teaching position.	51	28	21	2.30
Sometimes I feel as if I'd like to leave the pastoral ministry.	61	11	28	2.27
My wife and I have talked about the possibility of transferring to another type of ministry.	54	13	33	2.35
relationship with wife				
My wife and I often counsel together concerning the work of ministry in our area.	9	11	80	3.92
My wife and I always confer together before making a major decision (such as accepting a call).	0	5	95	4.70
My wife and I have a very open relationship and can freely discuss our deepest feelings with each other.	5	14	81	4.09
My wife encourages and supports me in the work of the pastoral ministry.	3	6	91	4.40
My wife and I are fully agreed that the pastoral ministry is where God wants us to be.	6	12	82	4.22
I regularly take time for my wife and children.	10	12	78	3.90

Note: The five response categories ranged from strongly disagree (1) to strongly agree (5). The means reflect this range. The categories were collapsed into disagree, neutral, and agree for the percentages shown in this table.

In the light of current theological controversies within the church, it may be encouraging to church officials that only 19% have had their faith in some of the church's historical teachings called into question (only 6.4% strongly agreed with the item) and that the mean (1.87) was the lowest of any of the item means.

The relationships between pastor and wife are generally positive. No one disagreed with the statement that 'My wife and I always confer together before making a major decision.' Other positive statements on spouse relationships drew from 78% to 91% agreement.

Yet a closer inspection of the table reveals some areas of concern. For example, 34% feel some concern that they might not meet the approval of their superiors in the conference office, 21% hope to be 'promoted' to some other form of ministry, 26% are disturbed by the fault-finding and criticism of members toward them, and 58% sometimes feel a loneliness and isolation in the ministry. Another 28% sometimes feel as if they would like to leave the pastoral ministry and 33% have discussed the possibility of a transfer with their wives.

Even in the generally positive areas of spouse relationships, there are some problems. Notice that in 3% of the cases, the wife does not encourage and support her husband in the ministry, in 5% there is not an open relationship between pastor and wife in which they can discuss their deepest feelings with each other, in 6% the couple is not agreed that the pastoral ministry is where God wants them to be, in 9% they do not counsel together concerning the work of ministry in their area, and in 10% the pastor does not regularly take time for his wife and children.

Husband-wife relationships and morale

Does this study lend any credence to the hypothesis that low pastoral morale might be related to stress in the pastor-wife relationship? All of the surveys of those who disagreed, strongly or somewhat, to one or more of three relationship-with-wife items, were singled out. These are the pastors who reported that they and their wives do not often counsel together concerning the work of ministry in their area, or do not have an open relationship where they can freely discuss their deepest feelings, or the wives do not encourage and support them in the work of pastoral ministry. There were twenty-three such surveys or about 13.4% of the total. We call them the marital-stress group. Table two reveals how these pastors compared with the others on nine key morale items.

It will be noted that chi-square analyses reveal significant differences between the two groups of pastors on five of the items with a sixth on the borderline. This seems to indicate that marital stress is related to lowered pastoral morale in at least some aspects. Especially noteworthy is the highly significant item, 'I believe I am a successful pastor.'

Table 2: Comparison of responses of marital-stress group with non-stress group on selected morale items

item	stress group % agree	non-stress % agree	chi square (2 df)	Cramer's V
satisfying personal devotional life	45	79	11.7**	0.26
regular family worship in home	52	75	10.6**	0.25
counsellor separate from administration				
needed for pastors and wives	91	66	6.0*	0.19
sometimes feel lonely and isolated	74	55	4.0	0.13
professional-growth programme effective	36	61	5.7a	0.18
believe I am a successful pastor	74	89	33.5**	0.44
hope to be called to administrative,				
departmental, or teaching position	35	19	2.8	0.13
sometimes want to leave the pastoral				
ministry	48	26	6.0*	0.19
wife and I have discussed transferring to				
another type of ministry	52	31	4.2	0.16

Note: * $p = <0.05$ ** $p = <0.01$ a $p=0.057$

A measure of morale

Thus far, morale has been considered as a collection of separate items. The analysis is now carried one step further to develop a morale scale on which every pastor may receive a score. The scale was constructed from eleven items: questioning some of the church's teachings, feeling a loneliness and isolation in the ministry, being disturbed by criticism, being comfortable in one-to-one witnessing, enjoying being a pastor, believing oneself to be a successful pastor, feeling concern for the approval of superiors, hoping for a call to an alternative type of ministry, wanting to leave pastoral ministry, discussing a transfer with wife, and being in agreement with wife that the pastoral ministry was God's will for them.

Each pastor was scored 1 to 5 on each item with 5 representing the hightest morale (reverse scoring was used with negatively worded items). The scores were totalled to yield a morale score which ranged from 27 to 55. This scale had a reliability coefficient alpha of 0.74. The scale scores were then correlated with several measures of pastor-wife relationships and with a number of items from the related data banks. The results are displayed in table three.

This approach substantiates the significant relationship between pastor-wife relationships and pastoral morale. It also indicates that it is the younger pastors who are more likely to be discouraged. Success as measured by church growth is significantly but weakly correlated with morale, but church size is not a factor. Several items indicate that an active laity that is responsible for adding new converts is a positive correlate of morale. All the items in this third table were then regressed on the morale scale using the SPSS multiple regression programme. Nine predictors, each contributing significantly at the 0.01 level, were identified with a multiple R of 0.54. The stepwise solution is shown in table four.

Table 3: Correlations of morale scale with selected items

item	r
marital factors	
pastor and wife counsel together on work of ministry	0.16*
pastor and wife have open relationship	0.25**
wife encourages and supports pastor in work in ministry	0.33**
regularly take time for wife and children	0.16*
personal factors	
age of pastor	0.35**
pastor has more organised work style[1]	0.19*
church characteristics	
18-month church growth rate	0.18*
18-month church growth rate adjusted to disregard transfers	0.16*
size of church	0.07
percent of members who set personal soul-winning goal in last year	0.19*
members rate their church as 'soul-winning'	0.33**
more converts added by efforts of lay members	0.21*
attractive church plant	0.23**
educational level of membership	0.23**
pastor rates his church 'united'	0.23**
church has complete ministry for all age groups	0.25**
church programme is highly focused on growth	0.25**

Note: * $p = < 0.05$ ** $p = < 0.01$
    1 Data for this and following items secured from related studies.

Table 4: Stepwise regression of selected items on morale scale

item	multiple R cumulative
wife encourages and supports pastor in work of ministry	0.352[1]
members rate their church as 'soul-winning'	0.447
pastor rates his church 'united'	0.478
church has complete ministry for all age groups	0.497
pastor has more organised work style	0.510
more converts added by efforts of lay members	0.517
pastor and wife counsel together on work of ministry	0.525
regularly take time for wife and children	0.535
age of pastor	0.540

Note: 1 Difference between this figure and the zero-order correlation on table 3 is due to lower-
    ing the number of cases to 129 because of missing items when interfacing several studies.

Source of low morale

One of the open-ended questions asked, 'Which areas of pastoral ministry furnish the most frustrations and disappointments for you?' A large variety of answers were given. They were classified in forty-four categories. The fifteen categories chosen by at least 4% of the pastors are shown in table five.

An inspection of this listing suggests that the sources of low morale might be encompassed in three themes:

   a.   the difficulties involved getting members to be and do what they
        should;

Table 5: Areas of frustration and disappointment

area	choosing %
motivation of laity for ministry, responsibility, discipling, or leadership	22
administrative work	17
dealing with members' problems	12
board, business, and committee meetings	10
poor inter-relationships between members	8
ingathering (a conference fund-raising programme)	8
church discipline	7
promotion of many conference programmes	7
lack of funds/poor stewardship of members	6
time pressures/managing time	6
seeing people reject the message after working hard to save them	5
too many churches or too large a territory to cover	5
conference administration	5
self-righteous attitudes of members	5
building programmes and fund-raising	4

b. the details of church administration which siphon off time from more 'pastoral' tasks;

c. the pressure of various kinds of goals from conference administrations.

Suggestions for changes

A second open-ended question asks, 'What changes would you like to see in the profession of pastoral ministry?' Approximately 25% of the pastors either did not answer the question or recommended no changes. The others gave a wide variety of suggestions which were placed in fifty categories. Those categories chosen by at least 4% of the pastors are displayed in table six.

Several general areas seem to emerge from the data:

First, pastors would like to see improvements in their own training, both pre-service and in-service, and in the development of their talents and abilities so that they can function more effectively in their ministerial duties.

Second, pastors would like relief from many tasks such as administrative minutiae, fund-raising, promotional programmes, and related duties that they perceive are draining their time and strength from high-priority ministerial functions.

Third, pastors would like to relate to conference leadership more on a basis of equals complementing each other than on an employer-employee relationship. They would like to have more input into conference programmes and would like administrators to be more sensitive to their needs and problems.

Some typical comments were:

'Realignment of priorities to make evangelism the most important.'

'Pastors trained so they might train their church instead of trying to do it all themselves.'

Table 6: Suggestions for change in pastoral ministry

change	choosing %
raise professional level with more continuing education and in-service education	14
less promotion of conference programmes	8
more emphasis on soul-winning	8
decrease pastor's multiple roles, less administrative work, and increase lay responsibility	7
more understanding and sensitivity from the conference	6
increase spiritual emphasis	6
reduce multi-church districts	5
less administrative direction	5
more opportunities for inter-relationships with other Adventist pastors	5
more input from pastors in setting conference goals	4

'A broader spectrum of spiritual credibility and spiritual concern versus self-preservation and promotion.'

'An atmosphere of openness, trust and trustworthiness.'

'Better job description. Why is it that the pastor has to perform duties which are not really in his calling?'

'More opportunity to be involved in decision-making on the conference level.'

'Opportunity to enhance pastoral skills.'

'I have often felt much like a herd animal or the victim of a high-pressure salesman at workers' meetings. Also the pressure of "Draw together to finish the work so Jesus can come."'

'Longer tenures (I've moved five times in three years).'

'Emphasis on quality not quantity in new members. Ministerial department focus on personal and professional growth of pastor.'

'Sometimes I literally get sick inside at the amount of continual *promotion*. It hardly leaves time for anything else.'

'More opportunities to get the D Min.'

'Make Ingathering an offering *not* a tax or a test of ministerial *ability*.'

'Eliminate professional barriers between ministers and lay members.'

'Having more time to spend with family.'

'Get back to the basics of the ministry.'

Conclusions

The findings which have been presented may be summed up in several conclusions:

First, most pastors are generally happy in their work, feel as if they are successful, and wish to remain in the pastoral ministry.

Second, a substantial minority do find discouragements from time to time and in certain areas. This lowered morale seems to result from a sense of powerlessness – the pastor is constantly being forced into roles different from the ones that he perceives as being basic to ministry. There is the occupational strain of trying to be too many things to too many people and, as a result, being sidetracked from following his own vision. He is the man-in-the-middle between conference and congregational demands.

Third, there does seem to be a correlation between pastoral morale and the quality of the relationship between pastor and his wife. We cannot say which is the causal factor or indeed if both are not produced by a third influence. No doubt the occupational pressures described create additional strains on the marriage by leading the pastor to neglect his wife and family. Perhaps she reacts by complaining or withdrawing. This may further heighten his sense of discouragement. Therefore, while the primary solutions to the morale problem must come in a restructuring of the job description of the pastor, emphasis on building the husband-wife relationship must also be a concern of conference leadership, not only because it is vital to the effectiveness of the pastor, but also because the pastoral home serves as a model to families in the church.

Fourth, pastoral morale could be raised by instituting certain changes in the structure of the pastorate. In addition to relieving pastors of the administrative minutiae of the church, these changes involve more continuing education with its development of talents and abilities and a more equal relationship with conference administrators including input by the pastor into goals and programmes.

Fifth, pastoral morale is likely to be higher in congregations in which the lay members take an active part in the mission of the church. Where the church is united in its purposes, where the members set personal 'soul-winning' goals, where members are actually responsible for bringing in new converts, and where the congregation has a self-image as a 'soul-winning' church, there is a higher probability of finding a happy and fulfilled pastor.

Notes
1. Very few pastors in the Seventh-day Adventist Church at the present time are females. All of the pastors in the sample for this study were males. Therefore the authors do not consider it sexist to refer to the 'pastor's wife' and to use the pronouns 'he', 'his', and 'him' in reporting this research.

References
Blizzard, S W (1956) 'The minister's dilemma,' *The Christian Century*, 73, pp. 508–10.
Dudley, R L and Cummings, D Jr (1981) 'A study of factors relating to church growth in the North American Division of seventh-day adventists,' research report, Institute of Church Ministry, Andrews University, Berrien Springs, Michigan.
Hartley, L H (1980) 'A study of clergy morale,' research report, Research Center in Religion and Society, Lancaster Theological Seminary, Lancaster, Pennsylvania.
Jud, G, Mills, E W and Burch G W (1970) *Ex-Pastors: why men leave the parish ministry*, Philadelphia, Pilgrim Press.
Mace, D and Mace, V (1980) *What's Happening to Clergy Marriages?* Nashville, Abingdon.
Martin, D (1980) 'Forgotten members: the pastor's family,' in T E Kadel (ed.) *Growth in Ministry*, Philadelphia, Fortress Press, pp. 141–142.
Mills, E W and Koval J P (1971) *Stress in the Ministry*, Washington DC, Ministries Studies Board.
Smith, D P (1973) *Clergy in the Cross Fire*, Philadelphia, Westminster Press.

5. Mental health

This chapter turns attention from stress and burnout to wider issues concerned with mental health. Two studies illustrate different research perspectives taken on this issue. One perspective describes the psychological assessment of clergy referred for residential treatment. The other perspective screens the general population of clergy for pathological symptoms.

In the first article in this section, Philip J Keddy, Philip Erdberg and Sean D Sammon describe the psychological problems of a group of 42 Catholic clergy and religious who were referred for residential treatment. The main tests used were the revised form of the Weschler Adult Intelligence Scale, the Minnesota Multiphasic Personality Inventory, and Exner's Comprehensive System approach to the Rorschach Inkblot Test. In discussing the findings from these tests, the authors give particular attention to problems concerned with sexual orientation.

At the time of writing, Philip J Keddy was based in Oakland, California; Philip Erdberg was based in Corte Madera, California; Sean D Sammon was based in Watertown, Massachusetts. This article was first published in *Pastoral Psychology* in 1990.

In the second article, Jayne Patrick explores the hypothesis that pathological narcissism is prevalent among the clergy. She reports on the administration of the Edwards Personality Preference Schedule and three subscales of the Minnesota Multiphasic Personality Inventory to a sample of 64 United Church ministerial candidates, 22 of whom also completed the pathological narcissism subscale of the Millon Clinical Multiaxial Inventory. The test findings did not confirm the majority of characteristics commonly associated with pathological narcissism, like lack of empathy, exploitativeness, intolerance of criticism, and grandiosity.

Dr Jayne Patrick works at McMaster University and the Department of Psychology, Hamilton Psychiatric Hospital in Hamilton, Ontario, Canada. This article was first published in *Pastoral Psychology* in 1990.

5.1 The psychological assessment of Catholic clergy and religious referred for residential treatment

Philip J Keddy, Philip Erdberg and Sean D Sammon

There have been few empirical studies of psychopathology among clergy and religious, especially in recent years. The pioneer in this area was a priest-psychiatrist, Father Moore, who reviewed the incidence of mental illness among clergy and religious as compared with the incidence among the general population in a 1938 article (Moore, 1938). In the early sixties, McAllister and VanderVeldt published two studies of psychiatric illness in hospitalised clergy and religious (1961, 1965). They examined diagnoses and reviewed case histories for factors that appeared related to the hospitalisations. Reviewing these and the few other studies available in 1974, Templer stated that methodological problems made the conclusions of the incidence studies highly questionable and that there were insufficient data to make any strong statements as to the types of psychological problems to which clergy and religious were prone. We agree with Templer's evaluations of these earlier studies. Templer also included studies done with seminarians and noted that 'the most salient and consistent finding' was that both Protestant and Catholic clergymen and seminarians tended to score in a feminine direction on psychological tests.

Kennedy, Heckler, Kobler and Walker undertook a large-scale study of the personalities of Catholic priests which was published in 1977. They obtained a randomly selected national sample of 271 subjects. A clinical interview was the principal instrument of investigation, plus several tests and scales. Standard diagnostic tests such as the MMPI were not used. They found it possible to group the priests into four categories along a continuum of development. Eight percent (8%) were considered maldeveloped, 57% underdeveloped, 29% developing, and 6% were seen as developed. Their definitions of maldeveloped and underdeveloped are given here because those are the groups from which applications to a residential treatment programme are likely to come. The 8% classified as maldeveloped had long histories of serious psychological problems, including underlying hostile feelings, poor self-esteem, and disruptive sexual conflicts. The underdeveloped, the category into which 57% were placed, were described as having an identity that related more closely to the role of the priesthood than to themselves as persons. Their lives seemed to be shaped by the expectations of others. These clergy had few, if any, experiences of intimacy and appeared to handle their feelings through repression and intellectualisation.

The purpose of the present study is to describe the psychological test characteristics of a group of Catholic priests, brothers, and nuns who were being evaluated at a residential treatment centre. By using standard psychological tests we planned to draw some conclusions as to the types of problems that a sample of Catholic clergy and religious were presenting in the 1980s. The use of standardised tests permits the possibility of future studies replicating these findings. These test data then also provide the basis for the discussion of the treatment and possible prevention of the types of problems identified.

Method

Setting

The data were collected at a residential therapeutic community for clergy and religious that was located in the San Francisco Bay Area. Data were collected between 1985 and 1987.

An assessment was required prior to admission to the programme. The assessee spent several days at the centre while undergoing a battery of psychological tests and two clinical interviews. While some clients simply came for an assessment to help determine the nature of their problems and to obtain a treatment recommendation, many came looking on the assessment as part of the application for residential treatment. The recommendation of residency was given to between 60 and 70% of those assessed. (This figure was based on an examination of statistics from all four centres around the country that were run by the same central organisation.) Assessees for whom the problem of substance abuse was found to be significant were referred to programmes specialising in the treatment of that problem.

The usual length of stay was between six and twelve months. Residential clients would meet with their primary therapist twice weekly, have small group therapy twice weekly, and community meetings three times weekly. There were also a variety of auxiliary therapies such as psychodrama, art, yoga, and dance. Liturgies and educational lectures addressing spiritual and psychological integration were also important programme components.

Subjects

The clergy and religious who came for an assessment did not represent a cross-section of clergy and religious seeking psychotherapy, but those for whom a religious superior had usually already concurred that a six to twelve month residential programme might be worthwhile. These were typically people seen as able to benefit from something more than outpatient psychotherapy, but not needing the kind of 24 hour monitoring that hospitals provide.

The participants in the study were 29 men and 13 women ranging in age from 29 to 64 years old. A signed release of the test data was obtained from each individual included in the study. For some participants, the assessment occurred at a situationally stressful time, while for others, the evaluation represented a well-planned step as they considered vocational and personal issues. For 52% of our participants, the superior initiated the referral; 33% were self-referred, and the rest referred by professional or unknown sources.

Although the age range of the sample was from 29 to 64, the distribution was not an even one. There were two major clusters; one in the mid-thirties and another in the mid-fifties.

The 13 women in the same sample were likely to have had a variety of assignments in teaching, hospital and parish work, with the older ones having moved as frequently as every four years. The male clergy were more likely to have been exclusively involved in parish ministry. Parish priests have faced increased isolation in recent years as their numbers have diminished. A parish that was staffed by a pastor and one or more associates may now be fortunate to have the pastor to itself. The brothers in the sample were more likely to have come from a community living situation. The ethnic background of the majority of assessees was caucasian.

Each participant was categorised according to the most readily apparent presenting problem. Consequently, the categories are not independent. The breakdown suggests that interpersonal problems, depression, sexual concerns, and vocational indecision were the major reasons for the referrals.

Assessment procedure and psychological tests used

The test battery that was given routinely included the Weschler Adult Intelligence Scale – Revised (WAIS-R), the Minnesota Multiphasic Personality Inventory (MMPI), the Rorschach Inkblot Test, the Bender-Gestalt, the Human Figure Drawing Test, and a structured autobiographical questionnaire. Other tests were administered on a non-routine basis.

The WAIS-R is the standard full-length measure of intelligence. We also used this test, as many clinicians do, to gain more information as to the person's personality and problems.

The MMPI is a 566-item true-or-false test that is the most commonly used and researched objective personality inventory (Greene, 1980, p. 1).

The Rorschach Inkblot test is a frequently used projective personality test (Lubin, Larsen, Matarazzo, and Seever, 1985). In this study the Comprehensive System approach (Exner, 1986) was used for the Rorschach. This is an empirical, atheoretical approach that has been developed through reliance on detailed computer analyses of research studies. As used in Exner's approach, the Rorschach is seen as a perceptual-cognitive task rather than a stimulus to fantasy. The scoring and interpretive system focuses on how the individual structures and organises the stimulus material. Many reliable points of relationship between behaviour on the test and behaviour in the everyday world have been established through studies on nearly 8,000 subjects. Exner (1986, pp. 267–295) compiled data on non-patient samples as well as various diagnostic-category patient samples. These data permit comparison with the data we are about to present. The administration, scoring, and interpretation of the test have all been standardised and a computer program (Exner, 1985) was used to assist in the calculation of ratios. In describing the comprehensive approach to the Rorschach we wish to emphasise that the validity of this system has been empirically demonstrated in contrast to earlier approaches that depended more on hypothetical statements and subjective judgements. The Rorschach was administered and scored by one of the researchers who has trained in the use of the Comprehensive System in graduate school and in numerous workshops.

The Bender–Gestalt was used as an organicity screening test, and the Human Figure Drawing Test was used clinically as a projective personality test. All of the above tests were used clinically, but only the results of the WAIS-R, the MMPI, and the Rorschach were statistically compiled for this research study. In addition to the formal testing, the assessee was interviewed by a psychologist other than the tester and by a psychiatrist. Faith life and spiritual issues were addressed in these interviews and in the structured autobiographical questionnaire.

Diagnostic from the third edition of the Diagnostic and Statistical Manual (DSM-III) (American Psychiatric Association, 1980) were assigned by the psychiatrist in consultation with the assessment team. A 'face sheet' was filled out that contained the diagnoses, recommendations, and key therapeutic issues if psychotherapy was indicated.

Results

Diagnoses

Occupational problems represented the most frequent DSM-III axis I diagnosis, with affective disorders and anxiety disorders also well represented. Mixed personality disorder was the most common axis II diagnosis.

Test results

The WAIS-R results indicate that this group is functioning in the average intelligence range overall, with the subtests that suggest an intellectualised orientation having the highest mean scaled scores. For example, the mean score for the vocabulary subtest equates with a full test score in the superior range as does the mean score on the comprehension subtest. In contrast, a subtest that is thought to be more indicative of social judgement, such as picture arrangement, had one of the lower mean scores, equivalent to a full scale score in the low average range.

On the MMPI we first examined the mean scores on the three validity scales to obtain information on test-taking attitude. The data indicated that our study participants presented themselves in a way that attempted to minimise difficulties, even to the extent of claiming unrealistically high standards. Graham (1987) has reported that the typical L scale score for college students equals zero or one while 70% of our participants endorsed more than two L scale items. In light of our group's advanced educational background, this signifies a naive, uninsightful defensiveness that would contribute to interpersonal tensions and difficulties.

Although the mean profile of the nine MMPI clinical scales was within normal limits, we were frequently struck by the degree of disturbance suggested by the significant individual elevations obtained. Seventy-eight percent of our study participants had a clinically significant elevation (greater than 70) on at least one scale.

On the masculinity-femininity scale, the mean score of our participants was 75.9 with a range from 59 to 104. As with the clinical scales, a score greater than 70 is considered significant. A high score for men suggests that they do not identify with the traditional masculine role. While interests that are not typical for one's gender cannot be assumed problematic, the possibility of sexual identity confusion or distress needs to be considered. The assessment team summary of key therapeutic issues on the face sheet was retrieved for 27 of the men in the study. Of these 27 men, 12 (44%) were considered by the assessment team to have a significant sexual problem. In eight cases (or approximately 30% of these men), the problem was distress or confusion about sexual orientation.

On the Rorschach Inkblot test, our participants tended to give a much larger than average number of responses. Although this initially gives the impression of greater involvement in the task, other factors serve to amend that interpretation. Their approach was characterised by ridding experience of its emotional components and attempting to deal with the world in an intellectualised and unambiguous way. This degree of attraction to structure is associated with rigidity. The Rorschach data further indicated that when confronted with emotionally charged situations, our participants are prone to losing control and having unmodulated outbursts of emotion. Considering these findings together, it appears that our participants approach situations trying to avoid emotional complexity, perhaps out of an awareness of difficulties in the handling of emotion. When unavoidably confronted with emotion, they do not handle it well, and are prone to outbursts.

Another striking finding was that many of this group would appear to have difficulty engaging in productive introspection. This portends some difficulty in starting an insight-oriented psychotherapy, although psychotherapy can help to promote introspective ability (Exner, 1986).

It was also apparent from the Rorschach that our participants have an idiosyncratic world view, that they intepret things in ways that could be confusing for those with whom they interact.

Discussion

As noted above, while the age range of our assessees was broad, there were two major clusters; one in the mid-thirties and the other in the mid-fifties. For the assessees in their fifties, our clinical impression is that many of them had longstanding personality problems that eventually brought them into conflict with superiors, peers, or parishioners. The increasing isolation of the priesthood and consequent morale problems may have contributed stress that brought these problems to light. In their study of the normal developmental stages in the adult life of men, Levinson, Darrow, Klein, Levinson and McKee did not follow their subjects beyond the late forties, but they did hypothesise an 'age fifty transition' (1978, p. 62). They thought the functions of this period to be similar to those of the age thirty transition. This is interesting in that this was the other age range of a number of our assessees. Levinson and associates suggested that the age fifty transition is a time to modify the life structure formed in the forties, and noted that it can be a time of crisis for those who have changed too little in the mid-life transition and have built 'an unsatisfactory life structure'.

We were initially surprised by the number of religious in their thirties who were coming for assessments with serious problems. In many cases we felt that thorough evaluations at the seminary or novitiate level could have identified the need for help then. There are, however, several reasons why the problems may only have gained attention when they did. Levinson and associates identified an age thirty transition when the first structuring of adult life that was done in the person's twenties is re-evaluated (p. 58). They found that a moderate or severe crisis was very common. The concept of the age thirty transition was clearly relevant to the experience of some of our assessees. For example, some priests who had made a commitment to become priests in their teens or even earlier were uncertain about their vocation. The assessees in their thirties would have gone through the seminary or novitiate in the first years after the Vatican Council II. We also speculate that seminaries in that period may have been overly accommodating to the expressed needs of seminarians and with regard to some behaviours previously judged unacceptable. Consequently, problems surfaced only when the realities of first assignments had to be confronted.

The data from all the tests employed presents a consistent constellation of problems. Beginning with the intelligence test, we saw an overemphasis on intellectual abilities that was not paralleled by skills on tasks reflecting social judgement. Again on the MMPI there were indications of rigidity and lack of insightfulness that would lead to interpersonal difficulties. The Rorschach data reiterates the intellectual orientation and lack of sophistication in the handling of emotional factors. Our assessees would try to avoid the emotional components of experience. When confronted with emotionally charged material, they reacted to it in an unmodulated way. This finding corresponded to the information we obtained as to the circumstances that led to the referrals, such as angry outbursts or sexual acting out.

Priests and brothers in our sample did not respond to the masculinity–femininity scale in a stereotypically male way. This was consistent with the findings of the many studies summarised by Templer (1974). The meaning of high scores for men on this scale has not been well established, partly due to a paucity of empirical research on it (Greene, pp. 89–92, 1980). Men scoring above a T-score of 70 are described by Greene as 'passive, inner-directed, and having aesthetic interests and activities. They do not identify with the traditional masculine role. Self-proclaimed homosexuals and persons willing to admit overtly their homosexual concerns will score in this range.' Among our assessees, with a mean score of 75, we found sexual orientation distress or confusion in approximately 30%. There were other sexual problems in 14.8% of these men.

The descriptors that emerged from our analysis correspond to our clinical impressions of the problems of other religious assessees and clients for whom we were not able to obtain test data. The types of problems that emerged from our data also correspond to the descriptions that Kennedy *et al.* (1977) gave of the underdeveloped and maldeveloped priests. Kennedy described the underdeveloped priests as handling their feelings through repression and intellectualisation, and as having few experiences of intimacy. Intellectualisation and difficulties in the handling of emotional factors that promote successful intimate relationships were seen among our assessees from the vantage points of the several tests employed. The characteristics Kennedy ascribed to the maldeveloped group – long histories of serious psychological problems, difficulties with anger, poor self-esteem, and disruptive sexual conflicts – were also found among our assessees, both on the test data and clinically.

The number of religious assessed for the present study was limited by the difficulty of collecting and compiling complete test batteries using the Exner Rorschach system, the Minnesota Multiphasic Personality Inventory including all the subscales developed for it, and the entire Weschler Intelligence Scale-Revised as opposed to brief measures of intelligence. The desirability of further research using equally detailed methods is obvious, and we believe that these findings have broader significance. A recent report from The Bishops' Committee on Priestly Life and Ministry stated that 'Many of the

53,500 Roman Catholic priests in the United States are overworked, lonely, and sexually troubled' ('US bishops assess loneliness of priests,' 1988). Among our sample of religious referred for psychological treatment, it is clear that some clergy and religious have developed personality problems that interfere with successful intimate relationships and thereby result in loneliness. The intellectualised orientation and difficulties in the handling of emotions that we found would most likely be channelled into an emphasis on work and an avoidance of deeper relationships. Lastly, we found a variety of sexual problems in our sample.

We see these findings as having implications for both treatment and prevention. These test data point to the need for therapeutic interventions emphasising emotional integration. By this we mean expressive, experiential psychotherapies that help people to learn to identify and appropriately voice their feelings. Therapies that would play into the intellectualising tendencies of this population would obviously be of little value. This is not to say that we are endorsing the anti-intellectual tendencies of some forms of therapy. The long-range goal is the integration of the intellectual, spiritual, and emotional. It was also our clinical impression that the underdeveloped emotional lives and interpersonal problems of our participants were paralleled by problems in their relationship to God. Successful psychotherapy often went hand-in-hand with a revitalisation of spiritual life, and spiritual direction complemented psychotherapy.

Because of the signs of longstanding personality problems among our assessees, we see a need for intensive, long-term psychotherapy to achieve genuine change and renewed growth. Psychotherapy of less than a year's duration, even intensive residential treatment, was unlikely to be adequate to address the personality problems we encountered. The residential period seemed most successful for helping people to acknowledge their problems and for initiating a commitment to the therapeutic relationship and the hard work of psychotherapy.

We also felt that many of the problems we assessed and treated could have been identified earlier. We believe that with thorough evaluations at the seminary or novitiate level the need for help could have been recognised in many cases. The need to leave an assignment and enter a residential treatment programme for six months to a year made for a period of great disruption and pain in the lives of many of our assessees. Breakdowns in assignments were also often deeply troubling for the religious superiors, peers, and relatives of our assessees. Identifying the need for help and beginning psychotherapy at the seminary or novitiate level would have undoubtedly prevented some of this suffering. We recommend that psychotherapy be considered as part of the formation of some religious professionals.

Given the diminished number of Catholic clergy and religious and the complexities of the situations they face in today's world, the need to promote the development of stable, well-integrated personalities is clearly evident. We hope we have provided some examples of how psychological assessment and psychotherapy can help.

References

American Psychiatric Association (1980) *Diagnostic and Statistical Manual of Mental Disorders*, Washington DC, American Psychiatric Association.

Exner, J E (1985) *Rorschach Interpretation Assistance Program* (Computer program), Asheville, North Carolina, Rorschach Workshops.

Exner, J .E (1986) *The Rorschach: a comprehensive system* (volume 1, 2nd edition), New York, John Wiley and Sons.

Graham, J R (1987) *The MMPI: a practical guide* (2nd edition), New York, Oxford University Press.

Greene, R L (1980) *The MMPI: an interpretive manual*, Orlando, Florida, Grune and Stratton, Inc.

Kennedy, E C, Heckler, V J, Kobler, F L and Walker, R E (1977) 'Clinical assessment of a profession: Roman Catholic clergymen,' *Journal of Clinical Psychology*, 33, pp. 120–128.

Levinson, D J, Darrow, C N, Klein, E B, Levinson, M H and Mckee, B (1978) *The Seasons of a Man's Life*, New York, Ballantine.

Lubin, B, Larsen, R M, Matarazzo, J D and Seever, M (1985) 'Psychological test usage patterns in five professional settings,' *American Psychologist*, 40, pp. 857–861.

McAllister, R J and Vanderveldt, A J (1965) 'Psychiatric illness in hospitalized Catholic sisters,' *American Journal of Psychiatry*, 121, pp. 881–884.

McAllister, R and VanderVeldt, A (1961) 'Factors in mental illness among hospitalized clergy,' *Journal of Nervous and Mental Diseases*, 132, pp. 80–88.

Moore, T V (1936) 'Insanity in priests and religious,' *American Ecclesiastical Review*, 95, pp. 485–498.

Templer, D I (1974) 'Review of personality and psychopathology research with clergymen, seminarians and religious,' *Catalog of Selected Documents in Psychology*, 4, p. 19.

The New York Times (1988) 'US bishops assess loneliness of priests,' December 25, p. 10.

5.2 Assessment of narcissistic psychopathology in the clergy

Jayne Patrick

In a recent article Meloy (1986) presents a rather startling and disturbing assertion, *viz.* that 'narcissistic character disorders are prevalent among members of the clergy' (p. 50). He bases this hypothesis on an analysis of factors endemic to the profession, which he regards as reinforcing narcissistic pathology. His illustrations of these factors include the experience of being personally chosen by God to exercise spiritual authority over others, the gratification derived from preaching to a (presumably) admiring congregation, and the role expectation of defining good and evil, which Meloy asserts functions as a source of external validation for the narcissistically disturbed minister's own proclivity to split reality into images of good and bad.

Meloy's characterological analysis of the narcissistically disturbed minister (his needs, conflicts, and the manner in which these would find expression in his ministry) incorporates aspects of both Kernberg's (1980) and Kohut's (1971) theories of pathological narcissism. At least in part Meloy's portrayal of the attraction which the ministerial role holds for the narcissistically-disturbed clergyman is plausible. However, his thesis is purely speculative. Meloy seems to be stating that because it could be so, it must be so.

Pathological narcissism has received considerable attention during the past two decades; it has been a focus in the work of the two major personality theorists cited by Meloy: Kernberg, and Kohut. The 1970s in fact came to be known as the 'me decade', reflecting the popular conception that excessive self-preoccupation and self-interest had come to dominate the consciousness of individuals in western society. These characteristics constitute a narcissistic orientation to the world. Since there is some element of narcissism in all individuals, pathological narcissism, to which Meloy refers, is first of all a matter of degree. Personality theorists such as Kohut and Kernberg, however, have also outlined specific dimensions of narcissistic pathology. Kohut (1978) emphasises these individuals' vulnerable self-esteem. In 1978 the American Psychiatric Association delineated the following diagnostic criteria for the narcissistic personality disorder:

a. grandiose sense of self-importance;
b. preoccupation with fantasies of unlimited success, power, etc.;
c. exhibitionism;
d. response to criticism characterised by indifference, rage, or

feelings of inferiority, shame, humiliation, or emptiness; and
e. interpersonal relationships characterised by lack of empathy, feelings of entitlement, exploitativeness, and vacillation between idealising and devaluating others.

The diagnosis of pathological narcissism rests not upon the identification of circumstances conducive to its existence. Psychiatric interviews and psychometric assessment are the recognised procedures which yield a diagnosis of this condition.

The issue which Meloy raises is one which can best be addressed empirically. Particularly over the past two decades, a number of psychometric measures have been developed to assess the presence of pathological narcissism. Three scales derived from the Minnesota Multiphasic Personality Inventory (MMPI) were selected to be utilised as measures of pathological narcissism in the present study.

The MMPI (Hathaway and McKinley, 1951) has been frequently employed with pastoral candidates to assess personality traits. The MMPI was standardised on a normal (that is non-psychiatric) population, and provides data on various aspects of personality functioning. A large number of research scales have been derived from combinations of the 566 items comprising the MMPI, to measure specific personality traits.

Three MMPI subscales which measure pathological narcissism were selected for inclusion in this study: The Narcissistic Personality Scale (Solomon, 1982), the Narcissism-Hypersensitivity Scale (Serkownek, 1973), and the Ego Inflation Scale (Harris and Lingoes, 1955). To date, validation studies for these measures have been limited. For this reason, no attempt was made to select which measure best addressed the concept of pathological narcissism as it is presently understood. There is no item overlap among these measures, therefore results obtained on each measure are independent.

A fourth measure of pathological narcissism which likewise derives from a self-report inventory, the Millon Clinical Multiaxial Inventory (MCMI) was also included. This measure (scale 5 on the MCMI) was developed to correspond with the construct of pathological narcissism (designated as narcissistic personality disorder) as identified by the American Psychiatric Association (1978).

The presence of narcissistic pathology can also be identified through inferential examination of scale scores on other measures of personality characteristics, such as the Edwards Personality Preference Schedule (EPPS, Edwards, 1957). The EPPS is a 225-item inventory derived from Murray's (1938) theory of need states. It yields a total of 15 scales which are measures of the following personality variables: achievement, affiliation, intraception, succorance, dominance, abasement, nurturance, charge, endurance, heterosexiality and aggression. Examination of the diagnostic criteria for narcissistic personality disorder developed by the American Psychiatric Association suggests that individuals who would receive this diagnostic classification would most likely obtain high scores on the following EPPS scales: achievement (ACH), exhibitionism (EXH), succorance (SUC), dominance (DOM), and aggression (AGG), and low scores on deference (DEF), intraception (INT), abasement (ABA), and nurturance (NUR). ACH, EXH, SUC, DOM, and AGG measure the following personality characteristics: ambition, competitiveness, desire for recognition, success (ACH); desire to be centre of attention (EXH); desire to receive support and attention from others (SUC); desire to be in control, make decisions, function in a leadership role (DOM); tendency to get angry, seek revenge, criticise those in positions of authority (AGG). DEF, INTRA, ABA, and NUR measure the following personality characteristics: tendency to defer to others' wishes, praise their work, solicit suggestions from others (DEF); capacity for self-reflection and for empathy/understanding of others' point of view (INTRA); willingness to accept blame, responsibility (ABA); compassion, caring, benevolence and altruism towards others (NUR). It is hypothesised that the pattern of high and low EPPS scores outlined typified pathological narcissism as reflected in the constellation of personality characteristics/symptoms identified by Kohut and Kernberg, *viz.* grandiosity, preoccupation with success and power, inability to tolerate criticism or blame, feelings of rage and hostility, lack of empathic capacity, need for validation, support and admiration.

Method

Subjects

The sample for this study consisted of 64 United Church candidates enrolled in the M Div programme. The sample included 34 males and 30 females. The mean age was found to be 37 (35 for males; 39 for females).

Procedures

All candidates referred for psychological assessment (a procedure required by many Conference Boards prior to ordination in the United Church of Christ) during the past 11 years (1977–1988) were included in this sample.

All candidates in the sample completed the MMPI and EPPS. Owing to its more recent development, MCMI results were available for only 22 subjects (12 males, 10 females).

Results

The means and standard deviations for males and females on the Narcissism-Hypersensitivity scale are as follows: males, $m = 54.97$ $(SD = 2.92)$; females, $m = 48.83$ $(SD = 2.07)$, total, $m = 52.09$

(SD=1.86). The mean score of the total candidate sample did not differ significantly from the mean (T score 50) of the MMPI normative sample. Likewise, no significant mean sex differences were obtained.

The means and standard deviations for males and females on the Ego Inflation scale were as follows: males, m=42.29 (SD=1.67), females, m=43.8 (SD=0.98). The mean T score of the total candidate sample (m=43, SD=0.77) was significantly lower (p= <0.01) than the mean (T score 50) of the MMPI normative sample. No significant mean sex differences were obtained on this scale.

The means and standard deviations for males and females on the Narcissism-Hypersensitivity scale were as follows: males, m=54.97 (SD=2.94); females, m=43.83 (SD=2.07). The mean score of the total candidate sample (m=52.09, SD=1.86) did not differ significantly from the mean of the normal population on the MMPI. Again, no significant sex differences were obtained.

The means and standard deviations for males and females on the NPD scale were as follows: males, m=6.09 (SD=0.36); females, m=6.00 (SD=0.31). The mean score of the total candidate sample (6.05, SD=0.24) differed significantly (p<0.001) from the means of both the normal sample (3.66) and the mean (10.00) of patients diagnosed as narcissistic personality disorders reported by Solomon (1982).

The means and standard deviations for males and females on the Millon Narcissistic Personality scale are as follows: males, 62.75 (SD=3.51); females, 75.1 (SD=3.82); total sample, 68.36 (SD=13.41). Males were found to score significantly lower (p<0.01) than the females on this scale. Only females in this sample obtained a mean score which fell into the interpretable range (74 and higher) for pathological narcissism.

Table one presents the mean percentile scores and standard deviations for the total sample on EPPS scales. It was predicted that the presence of pathological narcissism would be identified on the EPPS mean scores which were significantly higher than the norms on ACH, EXH, SUC, DOM, and AGG, and significantly lower than the norms on DEF, INT, and ABA.

The results of one-tailed t-tests (df 63) revealed that the means for this sample were not significantly higher than the norms on ACH, EXH, SUC, or AGG. The mean scores of this sample were, however, significantly higher (p<0.001) on DOM. No significant sex differences were noted in raw scale scores.

Results of one-tailed t-tests (df 63) indicated that the means for this sample were not significantly lower than the norms on DEF, INT, or NUR. In fact the sample means for NUR and INT significantly exceeded (p<0.001) general population means. On ABA, however, the sample mean was significantly lower than the norm mean. No significant sex differences were found on raw scale scores.

These findings indicate that ministerial candidates in this sample do

Table 1: EPPS percentile means and standard deviations

scales	males		females		total	
	mean	st dev	mean	st dev	mean	st dev
ACH	51.85	4.87	41.67	4.86	47.08	3.48
DEF	53.35	4.19	53.13	3.96	53.25	2.87
EXH	47.12	5.00	54.06	4.97	50.38	3.53
INT	81.27	3.64	80.93	2.94	81.11	2.36
SUC	54.32	4.73	51.63	4.45	53.06	3.24
AGG	32.06	0.71	36.37	3.89	34.08	3.21
DOM	65.32	3.58	77.27	3.68	70.92	2.66
ABA	31.29	4.50	27.97	4.98	29.73	3.32
NUR	20.62	0.69	60.47	5.58	70.47	3.37

not differ from the general population in the following characteristics: competitiveness, desire to be the centre of attention, willingness to praise others and defer to others' views. Their needs for support, praise, and recognition do not exceed those of the average individual.

Candidates in this sample, however, did demonstrate strong leadership tendencies, and a general unwillingness to feel guilty or inferior.

The purpose of this study was to empirically investigate Meloy's (1986) hypothesised high prevalence of narcissistic psychopathology among members of the clergy. The degree of pathological narcissism present in a non-self-selected sample of United Church of Christ ministerial candidates was assessed. Psychometric measures of personality characteristics associated with pathological narcissism (selected EPPS scales) and single scale measures of this construct *per se* (for example, the Narcissistic Personality Disorder scale) were administered to male and female M Div students.

The only positive EPPS findings in support of Meloy's thesis were that candidates in this sample tended to be far more dominant in their orientation (that is, striving for leadership and influence) than the average individual. As well, candidates in this sample were signficantly less inclined to blame themselves than individuals in the general adult population. There was no confirmation, however, of the other assessed characteristics which Meloy lists as salient to pathological narcissism (*viz*. exhibitionism, indifference to others, marked feelings of rage, inferiority, absence of empathy and altruism, ego inflation, etc.). In addition, candidates for the most part did not differ significantly from the general population norms on four specific measures of narcissistic pathology administered.

The results obtained from these measures which offered support for Meloy's hypothesis were limited to the findings that the mean NPD score for candidates somewhat exceeded the mean for the normal sample, and that female candidates scored just within the interpretable range on the MCMI narcissism scale. NPD results (and an examination of item content) would seem to indicate that candidates may be somewhat more self-focused than individuals in the general population, and more invested in self-esteem issues. This is in itself not surprising, in view of the leadership functions these individuals will need to perform; it is also important to note that this finding (in so far as the entire sample is concerned) is limited to results on one instrument, and more particularly that NPD scores for this sample fell well below the range of pathological narcissism reported for Solomon's (1982) sample.

It is generally recognised that women seeking ordination tend to have a greater struggle, compared with their male counterparts, in securing congregation acceptance (Ekhardt and Goldsmith, 1984; Hale, King and Jones, 1980; Tennis, 1979; Lehman, 1979). It is thus understandable that the anticipation of this type of non-affirmative experience could readily give rise (at least in the case of female candidates in this sample) to a type of defensive narcissism. This phenomena, fundamentally a self-protective stance, is typically manifested in hypervigilance to potential sources of narcissistic injury, together with various strategies (for example, exaggerated optimism and self-confidence) designed to restore and maintain narcissistic equilibrium. Thus, rather than the role of the minister lending support to an already existent grandiose self, in the case of women clergy it may be more accurate to state that the role of the minister compels the individual to adopt (hopefully temporarily) a defensive narcissistic stance, to ensure the survival of a pre-existing healthy self-structure.

These results strongly argue against a high prevalence of pathological narcissism among members of the clergy. Results on the EPPS in particular (significantly high scores on intraception and nurturance, for example), suggest that in comparison with the general population, prospective clergy in this sample are highly altruistic, compassionate, self-reflective, and genuinely empathic. Thus the present study would seem to support the conclusion that there exists in fact a *low* prevalence of pathological narcissism among members of the clergy. It is hoped that this investigation also serves to illustrate the fallacy inherent in reasoning, as Meloy does, that the mere existence of conditions seemingly conducive to the development or perpetration of pathological personality functioning, is sufficient to confirm its presence.

References

American Psychiatric Association (1978) *Diagnostic and Statistical Manual of Mental Disorders*, Washington DC, American Psychiatric Association.

Ashby, H, Lee, R and Duke, E (1979) A narcissistic personality disorder MMPI scale, paper presented at the meeting of the American Psychological Association, New York.

Edwards, A (1959) *Manual for the Edwards Personal Preference Schedule*, New York, The Psychological Corporation.

Ekhardt, B and Goldsmith, M (1984) 'Personality factors of men and women pastoral candidates: part 1, motivational profiles,' *Journal of Psychology and Theology*, 12, pp. 109–118.

Hale, H, King, M and Jones D M (1980) *New Witnesses: United Methodist clergywomen*, Nashville, Board of Higher Education and Ministry, The United Methodist Church.

Harris, R E and Lingoes, J C (1955) *Subscales for the MMPI: an aid to profile interpretation*, mimeographed materials, Department of Psychiatry, University of California.

Kernberg, O (1976) *Borderline Conditions and Pathological Narcissism*, New York, Jason Aronson.

Kernberg, O (1980) *Internal World and External Reality*, New York, Jason Aronson.

Kohut, H (1971) *The Analysis of the Self*, New York, International Universities Press.

Kohut, H (1976) *The Restoration of the Self*, New York, International Universities Press.

Lehman, E C (1981) 'Patterns of lay resistance to women in ministry,' *Sociological Analysis*, 41, pp. 317–338.

Meloy, J (1986) 'Narcissistic psychopathology and the clergy,' *Pastoral Psychology*, 35, pp. 50–55.

Millon, T (1983) *The Millon Clinical Multiaxial Inventory* (3rd edition), Minneapolis, Interpretive Scoring Systems.

Murray, H (1938) *Explorations in Personality*, Cambridge, Massachusetts, Harvard University Press.

Serkownek, K (1975) Subscales for scales 5 and 0 of the MMPI, unpublished manuscript.

Solomon, R (1982) 'Validity of the MMPI narcissistic personality disorder scale,' *Psychological Reports*, 50, pp. 463–466.

Tennis, G H (1979) Clergywomen in the United Presbyterian Church, USA, paper presented at the annual meeting of the Religious Research Association and the Society for the Scientific Study of Religion, San Antonio, Texas.

6. Ageing and retirement

In view of the rising mean age of clergy within a number of denominations, research concerned with clergy ageing and retirement is of growing importance. The two articles in this section focus first on the work performance of ageing clergy and then on the experience of clergy retirement.

In the first article in this section, Leslie J Francis and David W Lankshear employ path analysis to examine the relationship between clergy age and certain quantitative indices of church life in two samples of Church of England parishes: a sample of 1,553 villages and rural communities, and a sample of 584 suburban parishes. The data indicate that clergy aged sixty or over working in rural parishes tend to have contact with a smaller number of active church members than younger clergy working within comparable rural parishes, although they maintain contact with the same number of nominal church members. Clergy aged sixty years or over working in suburban parishes, on the other hand, have contact with the same number of active church members as younger clergy working within comparable suburban parishes.

The Revd Professor Leslie J Francis is D J James Professor of Pastoral Theology at Trinity College, Carmarthen, and St David's University College, Lampeter, Wales. David W Lankshear is Deputy Secretary of the National Society and Schools Officer of the General Synod Board of Education of the Church of England, in London, England. This article was first published in *Ageing and Society* in 1993.

In the second article, Janet L Goodwin and Mervin Y T Chen investigate adjustment to retirement in a sample of 185 Anglican, Baptist and United Church retired clergy from the Atlantic region of Canada. The data demonstrate that clergy maintain continuity of their lifestyles except when some situational factors force them to alter their way of life; that retired ministers tend not to develop new activities, but continue to participate in existing ones; that the occupational subculture of Protestant clergy has the function of facilitating their retirement; and that clergy appear to maintain a stability in the type of responses they have to change and crises.

Dr Janet L Goodwin is Research Coordinator, Intercultural Task Force, and Professor Mervin Y T Chen is Professor in the Sociology Department, Acadia University, Wolfville, Nova Scotia, Canada. This article was first published in *Journal of Religious Gerontolgy* in 1991.

6.1 Ageing Anglican clergy and performance indicators in the rural church, compared with the suburban church

Leslie J Francis and David W Lankshear

Introduction

Although two decades ago Heenan (1972) could speak in terms of 'fairly low research productivity' linking the fields of religion and ageing, in recent years there has been a growing research interest in the relationship between aspects of ageing and aspects of religion. Specific studies have explored the relationship of age and religion with such factors as life satisfaction (Guy, 1982; Hunsberger, 1985; Levin and Markides, 1988), loneliness (Johnson and Mullins, 1989), health (Idler, 1987; Broyles and Drenovsky, 1992), mental health (Reed, 1991), personal adjustment (Markides, 1983; Van Haitsma, 1986), depression (Nelson, 1990), coping strategies (Koenig, George and Siegler, 1988), complexity of thinking (Pratt, Hunsberger, Prancer and Roth, 1992), wellbeing (Mull, Cox and Sullivan, 1987; Koenig, Kvale and Ferrel, 1988), stress (Krause and van Tran, 1989) and mortality (Zuckerman, Kasl and Ostfeld, 1984). Other studies have explored the religious patterns and participation of older adults (Ainlay and Smith, 1984; Doka, 1986; Young and Dowling, 1987; Payne, 1988; Ainlay, Singleton and Swigert, 1992) or the changing roles of older adults in the church and synagogue (Dickerson and Myers, 1988).

By way of contrast, a significant research literature has not yet developed on the relationship between ageing and the professionally religious except, perhaps, in relationship to the specific phenomenon of the post-retirement experiences of priests and ministers (Nugent, 1976; MacGuigan, 1979; Fitcher, 1985; Goodwin and Chen, 1991; Chen and Goodwin, 1991). This may be accounted for, partially, in terms of the general lack of empirical research conducted into the clerical profession itself and, partially, in terms of the absence of general hypotheses relating ageing with the clerical profession generated by existing empirical research among male and female clergy in the UK (Ranson, Bryman and Hinings, 1977; Towler and Coxon, 1979; Fletcher, 1990), the USA (Carroll, Hargrove and Lummis, 1983; Fogarty, 1988; Malony and Hunt, 1991) and Australia (Blaikie, 1979; Hughes, 1989). So far, within the existing literature five main strands emerge in relationship to clergy age.

First, the most thoroughly explored set of hypotheses concerns the connection between clergy age and traditional or conservative attitudes towards issues like church authority, forms of ministry, lay involvement and liturgical change. Empirical data supporting the view that older clergy adopt more conservative attitudes in these areas are reported by several studies. Reidy and White (1977), in their study of Catholic priests in the Wellington diocese of New Zealand, found that 'increased age and higher status within the church hierarchy (at least somewhat related to age) are ... the biggest contributors to traditionalism' in attitudes to involvement in the parish community, morality and priestly life style, modernisation of the church, ecumenism, and the relaxation of the traditional Sunday mass obligation. Schoenherr and Sorensen (1982) and Hoge, Shields and Verdieck (1988) reported the findings of two national surveys of American Catholic diocesan priests, conducted in 1970 and replicated in 1985, using a twenty-one item Likert-type inventory, known as the 'modern values scale', to measure traditional versus modern theological attitudes. The traditional statements were taken from standard manuals of Catholic theology reflecting formulations prevalent before the mid-twentieth century, and the modern statements were taken from Vatican II and contemporary theologians. Their data demonstrated that the older clergy held significantly more conservative values both in 1970 and 1985. Four different explanations have been advanced to account for the clear association found between clergy age and conservative values in these two studies conducted in 1970 and 1985. Schoenherr and Sorensen (1982) argued that the differences between age groups were due to movement toward increasing conservatism throughout the ageing process. Hoge, Shields and Verdieck (1985) were critical of this ageing-effect assumption and argued that the differences between age groups observed in the 1970 data were due to cohort effects. In other words, they attributed the age differences 'to the different experiences of the generations, not due to attitude shifts with advancing age'. Reviewing the same data, Young and Schoenherr (1992) argue that the observed differences involved both an ageing and a cohort effect. They also posit as a third factor the impact of resignation, when a disproportionate number of resignees adhere to liberal views (Schoenherr and Greeley, 1974). Hoge, Shields and Verdieck (1992) add the fourth argument that those ordained later in life may enter the priesthood with more constructive attitudes and thus contribute to the conservative tendency of the older cohorts.

In their study of Methodist, Anglican and Catholic clergy in England, Ranson, Bryman and Hinings (1977) reported a clear association between age and conservatism within all three denominational groups. Regarding the Anglican clergy, they found that younger clergy, as well as being willing to support fundamental reform proposals, such as deployment, are also concerned to improve the participant activities of the laity and the equity of payment for clergy. By contrast, they concluded that 'the conservatism of the older clergy, of whom there are a large number (43% over fifty), is pronounced'. Regarding the

Methodist clergy, they found that 35% of ministers under forty believed the church greatly needed reform, as opposed to 11.4% of those over sixty. Regarding the Catholic clergy, they found that, whereas 28.2% of priests under the age of forty believed the church to be greatly in need of reform, 5.4% of those over sixty did so, and only 1% of the former believed it needed no reform, as against 12% of those over sixty. Aldridge's (1986) study of clergy attitudes towards liturgical change in the Church of England found that those who supported the traditional *Book of Common Prayer* were much more likely to be over the age of sixty. Similarly, in their study of the rural Anglican church, Davies, Watkins and Winter (1991) found that *Book of Common Prayer* services were 'far more common in rural areas under older priests than elsewhere'. On the other hand, Aldridge (1989) failed to support the view that older Anglican clergy take a less favourable attitude towards the ordination of women.

A second strand of research concerns the age-related differences in the religious beliefs and practices of priests and ministers. For example, De Jong and Donovan (1988) found that older priests expressed less doubt about the existence of God and tended towards reliance on logic more and on experience less than younger priests. While younger priests tended to find God most naturally through people and events, older priests tended more toward finding God through scripture or other writings and formal worship. Older priests had fewer transcendent experiences and less trust in dreams and imagination than did younger priests. Older priests tended to practise daily meditation and examination of conscience more frequently than did younger priests. Younger priests engaged in interpersonal religious practices more than did older priests, while older priests engaged in solitary religious practices more than did younger priests. De Jong and Donovan (1988) argued that these findings are consistent with Jungian developmental theory which suggests the return of the elderly to face the unconscious and the role of personal religion in this process (Jung, 1960). This interpretation, however, is confused by the significant structural changes experienced within the Catholic church during the period of time embraced by their study and the possible impact of these structural changes on the religious beliefs and practices of the younger cohorts of clergy (Hornsby-Smith, 1989).

Davies, Pack, Seymour, Short, Watkins and Winter (1990) also produced statistical evidence from their study of rural Anglican clergy that older clergy spend a greater amount of time, absolutely and proportionately, on private prayer and study than do their younger colleagues. Those over sixty-five years of age devoted 20% of their time to such activities, compared with 10% of those in their forties. According to this study, older clergy also spend significantly less time on pastoral duties and administration than do their younger colleagues. Similarly Brierley, Myers and Marshall (1991) found that clergy over the age of sixty gave more priority to sermon preparation and counselling and derived more satisfaction from their personal devotional lives than did their younger colleagues. According to this study, older clergy also gave a higher priority to conducting funerals.

A third strand of research concerns the relationship between clergy age and personal adjustment. For example, Jarvis (1976) found that older clergy displayed less dissatisfaction with the clerical profession than did their younger colleagues. Verdieck, Shields and Hoge (1988) employed path analysis in their study of American Catholic diocesan priests to demonstrate that older clergy are less inclined to complain of loneliness than are younger clergy. Brierley, Myers and Marshall (1991) found that clergy over the age of sixty were less likely to be troubled by professional conflict within their churches or by personal conflict within their families. Clergy over the age of sixty were also less likely to report difficulties in counselling relationships. Similarly, Carroll, Hargrove and Lummis (1983) reported better social and personal adjustment among older clergy in terms of experiencing fewer relationship difficulties within the parish and less tendency to complain of loneliness. In particular their findings suggested that older clergy perceived themselves as being seen as less of a threat to middle-aged parishioners who have leadership roles within the church, and that they have greater experience of finding supportive friends and effectively managing their professional and personal lives. These views are given further support by Davies, Pack, Seymour, Short, Watkins and Winter (1990) in their study of rural Anglican clergy. According to this study, older clergy found pastoral work particularly rewarding, compared with their younger colleagues. More than a third (38%) of clergy aged sixty or over mentioned pastoral work as a reward, compared with 21% of those under the age of forty. For clergy aged fifty or over, pastoral work was likely to be the most rewarding aspect of ministry. Other aspects of ministry which were more rewarding to older clergy included work with their congregation and cooperation and training. A substantially higher proportion (26%) of clergy under the age of forty reported problems connected with lay involvement than was the case among clergy aged sixty or over (16%). On the other hand, Reilly's (1975) study of Catholic priests in Massachusetts found generally lower levels of job satisfaction among clergy over the age of 55 years.

A fourth strand of research concerns the relationship between clergy age and the number of hours worked. For example, Davies, Pack, Seymour, Short, Watkins and Winter (1990) found that older clergy tend to work somewhat fewer hours than do their younger colleagues. This is demonstrated by two key statistical comparisons: 16% of clergy aged sixty or over worked less than forty hours a week, compared with 8% of those under fifty years of age; clergy aged over sixty-five worked about eight hours a week less than their younger colleagues. A similar conclusion can be drawn from Brierley, Myers and Marshall's (1991) study of church leaders in England and from Fichter's (1984) study of Catholic priests in the USA. Brierley *et al.* found that older clergy were less likely to feel pressured by time constraints or an excessive workload, and more likely to adopt a relaxed attitude towards taking time off. Fitcher found that older clergy were less likely to display symptoms of the burnout syndrome and concluded that older clergy were less likely to be overworked and over-stressed than in the earlier period of their priestly lives.

A fifth strand of research concerns the relationship between clergy age and work performance. For example, data reported by Brierley, Myers and Marshall (1991) indicated that older clergy were less willing to participate in in-service training courses and development programmes. Data reported by Francis (1985) and Rees and Francis (1991) suggest that older clergy may perform less efficiently in parish ministry. This view is supported by two kinds of evidence.

The first kind of evidence provided by Francis (1985) draws attention to the clear relationship between clergy age and the response rate to his questionnaire concerned with work-related perceptions. Within the overall response rate of 92%, the mean age of the clergy completing and returning the questionnaire was 52.6 years, compared with a mean age of 61.2 years among the clergy who did not complete the questionnaire. In the more general literature a number of studies point to the lower response rate among older people (Gannon, Northern and Carroll, 1971; Weaver, Holmes and Glenn, 1975; Hawkins, 1975; Van Westerhoven, 1978; O'Neil, 1979; De Maio, 1980; Smith, 1983; Herzog and Rodgers, 1988b). At the same time, the extent to which refusal rates are higher among older adults has been shown to vary both according to personal and demographic characteristics (Mercer and Butler, 1967) and according to the topics under review (McDaniel, Madden and Verilele, 1987). The lower response rate among older people has been explained in terms of less willingness to participate (Herzog and Rodgers, 1988a), a greater tendency to regard more questions as sensitive or threatening (Hoinville, 1983) and a susceptibility to a wider range of health problems (Herzog, Rodgers and Kulka, 1983). In line with this range of theories, Francis (1985) suggested that the higher mean age of the clergy not participating in his survey either reflected a general trend that older clergy are less willing to participate in surveys, or indicated a specific problem faced by older clergy working in the context of multi-parish benefices, now common in rural dioceses in England (Russell, 1986), who may feel particularly threatened by questionnaries reviewing aspects of their work.

The theory that older clergy may feel particularly threatened by questionnaires reviewing aspects of their work is consistent with recent discussion regarding the nature of professional burnout and stress. Sanford (1982), for example, in his study *Ministry Burnout* argued that one clear sign of this phenomenon is an unwillingness to face and to discuss the reality of the work situation.

Factors leading to or precipitating clergy stress (Dewe, 1987) and ministry burnout (Fichter, 1984) vary from situation to situation. Coate (1989), in her study of *Clergy Stress*, suggests that one significant source of pressure comes from the inevitable changes that have taken place in the task of ministry over recent years. Changes in the task of ministry may have been generated by growing secularisation (Gilbert, 1980), decline in membership (Francis, 1985), changes in the churches' relationship with the state maintained sector of education (Francis, 1987), shifts in theological perspective (Robinson, 1963), liturgical changes (Aldridge, 1986), financial stringency (Central Board of Finance and Church Commissioners, 1992), fewer vocations (Russell, 1980), the debate about the ordination of women to the priesthood (Aldridge, 1989) and the rethinking of parochial structure (Tiller, 1983).

In England the rural church in particular has undergone widespread and far-reaching changes during the past two or three decades (Russell, 1986). Following pastoral reorganisation, rural clergy often now find themselves responsible for four or more parishes. Not infrequently such pastoral reorganisation has been accompanied by considerable local discontent (Bowden, 1988). The different form of ministry which this involves may lead to a lower level of job satisfaction, a higher level of stress and a greater sense of failure, resulting in ministry burnout, especially among the older clergy who have themselves lived through and experienced the process of rapid change.

A second study by Rees and Francis (1991) compared the response rates of clergy to work-related questionnaires within two different kinds of parish ministry, single parish benefices (which tend to be mainly urban and suburban) and multi-parish benefices (which tend to be mainly rural). While, according to this study, there was no significant difference in the mean age of clergy working in these two kinds of ministry, there was a significant difference in their response rate to the questionnaire. Among the clergy working in single-parish benefices age made no difference to the response rate. In the multi-parish situation, however, the older clergy were much less likely to return their questionnaire. This point is illustrated by the example that among the clergy aged sixty years or over, 78% in single parish benefices returned their questionnaires, compared with 55% in multi-parish benefices. By way of contrast, among the clergy aged under sixty years, 80% in single-parish benefices and 86% in multi-parish benefices returned their questionnaires. These data lend further support to the two theories that rural clergy in multi-parish benefices may begin to experience premature ministry burnout around the age of sixty and adopt avoiding strategies to evade issues concerned with self- and work-appraisal, and that this phenomenon does not affect clergy working in single-parish benefices in non-rural environments.

The second kind of evidence provided by Francis (1985) drew attention to the clear relationship between clergy age and the size of the Sunday congregation, in a predominantly rural diocese, after controlling for differences in population and parish size by means of multiple regression and path analysis (Keeves, 1988). The path coefficients indicated that rural parishes within the care of clergy over the age of sixty had smaller congregations, although they had the same number of names on the electoral rolls. This means that if two clergymen, one aged fifty and the other aged sixty-five, have responsibility for the same number of parishioners and the same number of parishes, the older minister would be expected to have the same number of names on the electoral roll of the churches, but fewer people actually worshipping in those churches on a typical Sunday.

Francis' (1985) findings, however, are based on a relatively small number of clergy, namely 171, restricted to data from one diocese, calculated in relationship to one simple index of performance, namely adult Sunday worshippers, and concerned only with the rural church. Several subsequent studies have employed clergy age within overall regression equations concerned with markers of church life (Francis and Lankshear, 1990, 1992), but none has specifically set out to check and extend Francis' original conclusions. The present paper, therefore, proposes to do so.

At the same time, findings regarding the relationship between clergy work performance and age need to be seen in the wider context of other research concerned with work performance and age. Although several attempts have been made during the past fifty years to synthesise empirical findings in this area (McFarland, 1943; Welford, 1976; Baugher, 1978; Waldman and Avolio, 1986; McEvoy and Cascio, 1989), the consensus remains that this is a particularly complex and difficult field to synthesise due to the range of populations studied, the diverse measures of performance and performance-related attitudes employed, the various age groupings utilised in analysis and the host of cultural and generational variables which may contaminate the observed relationships between age and performance (Levine, 1980; Doering, Rhodes and Schuster, 1983; Davies and Sparrow, 1985; Avolio, 1991).

Some studies have concentrated on profiling the particular strengths and weaknesses of older workers in different spheres, including industry in general (Belbin, 1953; King and Speakman, 1953; Welford, 1966), heavy work (Belbin, 1955), heavy industry (Richardson, 1953), light engineering (Murrell and Tucker, 1960), coal mining (Powell, 1973), management (Singleton, 1983), law (Meltzer, 1981), music (Simonton, 1989), psychiatry (Weiner, 1990), and part-time occupations (Eichar, Norland, Brady and Fortinsky, 1991). Other studies have compared the performance or performance-related attitudes among different age groups of workers. For example, higher productivity and better performance is found from older employees among salesmen (Maher, 1955), factory workers and office workers (Greenberg, 1961), garment industry workers (Giniger, Dispenzieri and Eisenberg, 1983), para-professional programme assistants (Holley, Field and Holley,

1978), female civil service clerical workers (Arvey and Mussio, 1973) and workers in a large organisation (Bowers, 1952). On the other hand, lower productivity and inferior performance is found from older employees among women sewing machinists (King, 1956), footwear and furniture manufacturers (Mark, 1957), workers in the chemical industry (Chown, 1972) and printing workers (Clay, 1956). A third group of studies reports no relationship between age and productivity or performance among factory workers (Breen and Spaeth, 1960; Schwab and Heneman, 1977b), office workers (Kutscher and Walker, 1960) and academic scientists (Cole, 1979). Similarly, while Arthur, Fuentes and Doverspike (1990) found increased accidents with age among petroleum transport drivers, Barrett, Mihal, Panek, Sterns and Alexander (1977) found no relationship between accidents and age among commercial drivers and Root (1981) found fewer accidents and injuries among older workers in general. A greater consensus emerges, however, among studies reporting higher levels of job satisfaction among older workers, including both national samples of regularly employed workers (Glen, Taylor and Weaver, 1977; Janson and Martin, 1982; Kalleberg and Loscocco, 1983) and specific occupational groups like blue collar employees (Gibson and Klein, 1970; Schwab and Heneman, 1977a), city workers (O'Brien and Dowling, 1981), factory workers (Meltzer, 1958), hospital workers (Aldag and Brief, 1977), human service workers (McNeely, 1988), managers (White and Spector, 1987), regional officers within a social service agency (Snyder and Mayo, 1991), scientists (Arvey and Dewhirst, 1979) and white collar workers (Hunt and Saul, 1975). On the other hand, this positive relationship between job satisfaction and age is not supported by Bedeian, Ferris and Kacmar (1992) among non-academic university staff, or by Zeitz (1990) among some employees of a federal government agency.

Method

A detailed questionnaire was sent to every Anglican place of worship within 24 dioceses and one additional archdeaconry, a total of 9,909 centres, as part of a large scale enquiry into the Church of England's ministry among children and young people (Board of Education, 1988; Francis and Lankshear, 1991a). The questionnaire, based on the instrument originally designed by Francis (1985) asked each church to make a detailed profile of its activities over two Sundays and the intervening weekdays, carefully listing contact with the numbers of people in each age category. The questionnaire also requested key information about each church's activity throughout the year, including numbers of baptisms, confirmands, Easter communicants, Sunday school scholars, house groups and other activities, as well as the age of the minister 'responsible for leading the majority of Sunday services in this church'. For the purposes of analysis clergy ages were grouped into five year bands. The aim of the present analysis is to examine whether significant differences emerge between the clergy under sixty years of age and the clergy within the age bands sixty and over. Earlier exploratory analyses by Francis (1985) had indicated the predictive power of this particular age split.

A response rate of 72.2% produced completed information on 7,157 churches. The present analysis is conducted on two subsets of these data. The first subset of data identified the villages and rural communities with populations between 251 and 1,250 people within the nationally-based survey. In the database there are 1,553 communities within this category and for which there is a complete set of information. This subset of data was selected in order to provide a relatively homogeneous group of churches, excluding both the very small villages and hamlets at one end of the rural spectrum and the larger villages and market towns at the other end. The second subset of data identified the suburban communities. In the database there are 584 communities within this category and for which there is a complete set of information.

Before exploring the relationship between clergy age and numerical indicators of church life, it is necessary to take into account other factors which may also affect these outcomes. Previous research concerned with the urban and rural church has drawn particular attention to the predictive power of population size, electoral roll and multi-parish benefices (Francis, 1985; Francis and Lankshear, 1990, 1991b, 1992). It is particularly important to control for these variables, since the suspicion may still linger that bishops may choose to deploy older clergy in smaller parishes (less population), in less successful parishes (smaller proportion of population represented on the electoral roll) or in deeper rural areas (more churches per benefice). Before examining the relationship between clergy age and numerical indicators of church life, these potentially contaminating factors will be taken into account by means of multiple regression and path analysis (Keeves, 1988), using the SPSSX statistical package (SPSS Inc., 1988).

Results

The rural church

Inspection of the spread of communities within the rural sample indicated that 50% of them had popluations between 251 and 500, 23% between 501 and 750, 19% between 751 and 1,000 and 8% between 1,001 and 1,250. The number of names on the electoral rolls of these churches ranges from eight to 470, with 10% being between eight and 25, 34% between 26 and 50, 27% between 51 and 75, 14% between 76 and 100, and 15% over 100. The majority (90%) of the rural churches were within multi-parish benefices. Nearly three in every ten (29%) of the churches in the sample were served by clergy aged sixty years and over.

Inspection of the range of potential outcome variables included within the questionnaire indicated that many, like play groups, parent and toddler groups, church sponsored uniformed organisations, youth clubs and regular contact with cubs, brownies, scout and guides, were evidenced by such a small proportion of churches in rural communities of between 251 and 1,250 inhabitants that it was not sensible to employ path analysis to explore the impact of clergy age on such measures. The following outcome measures were, however, considered to be represented in sufficient churches to sustain careful analysis (the percentages refer to the proportions of rural churches reporting each form of contact): electoral roll (100%); Easter communicants (99%); Christmas communicants (98%); Sunday contact over two Sundays with 2–5 year olds (58%), 6–9 year olds (69%), 10–13 year olds (69%), 14–17 year olds (56%), 18–21 year olds (35%) and adults over the age of 21 (99%); 6–9 year olds attending Sunday school type groups (47%); church choir membership of 6–9 year olds (17%), 10–13 year olds (28%), 14–21 year olds (20%) and adults over the age of 21 (41%); infant baptisms (79%); and confirmation candidates under the age of 14 (27%), between the ages of 14 and 17 (21%) and over the age of 17 (23%).

Table one presents the multiple regression significance tests designed to explore the impact of clergy aged sixty years and over on each of these outcome variables within rural parishes, after taking into account population size, multi-parish benefices and the number of names on the elecoral roll, in that specified order. In the case of the rural church, the age of the minister contributes significant predictive information in respect of six of the eighteen listed outcome variables. The four outcome measures influenced negatively by the presence of an older minister all related to the normal Sunday church attendance, namely contact with 2–5 year olds, 6–9 year olds, 10–13 year olds and adults. The age of the minister has no significant relationship with the electoral roll, Easter and Christmas communicants, Sunday school, choir or baptisms. On the other hand, the older ministers generate significantly more confirmation candidates under the age of 14 and over the age of 17 than the younger ministers working in comparable parishes.

While table one presents the final conclusion of the regression analyses, it fails to make explicit the assumed causal paths being taken into account. Table two and figure one, therefore, make these paths explicit in relationship to just three of the significant outcome variables. In this model, electoral roll is first explored as a function of population, number of parishes in the benefice and the age of the minister. Then both adult Sunday church attendance and young confirmation candidates are explored as a function of population, electoral roll, number of parishes in the benefice and the age of the minister. When these relationships are found to be statistically significant, they are indicated in the path digaram by straight arrows.

Table 1: Multiple regression significance tests for rural parishes

dependent variables	total R^2	incr. R^2	F	P<
electoral roll	0.1951	0.0008	1.5	NS
Easter communicants	0.5147	0.0001	0.3	NS
Christmas communicants	0.3954	0.0004	1.0	NS
Sunday contact, 2–5 years	0.1411	0.0056	9.6	0.002
Sunday contact, 6–9 years	0.0973	0.0041	6.6	0.010
Sunday contact, 10–13 years	0.1174	0.0025	4.2	0.040
Sunday contact, 14–17 years	0.0244	0.0016	2.4	NS
Sunday contact, 18–21 years	0.1091	0.0006	1.1	NS
Sunday contact, over 21 years	0.4183	0.0031	7.7	0.006
Sunday school, 6–9 years	0.1126	0.0011	1.8	NS
church choir, 6–9 years	0.0287	0.0002	0.2	NS
church choir, 10–13 years	0.0816	0.0002	0.3	NS
church choir, 14–21 years	0.0844	0.0000	0.0	NS
church choir, over 21 years	0.2088	0.0004	0.8	NS
infant baptisms, under 2 years	0.1674	0.0000	0.0	NS
confirmands, under 14 years	0.0835	0.0037	5.9	0.015
confirmands, 14–17 years	0.0298	0.0006	0.9	NS
confirmands, over 17 years	0.0512	0.0032	5.0	0.026

Table 2: Multiple regression significance tests for path model I

dependent variables	independent variables	R^2	increase in R^2	F	P<	Beta	T	P<
electoral roll	population	0.1269	0.1269	213.4	0.000	+0.2919	+12.0	0.000
	multi-parish benefice	0.1943	0.0674	122.6	0.000	−0.2641	−10.8	0.000
	clergy aged 60+	0.1591	0.0008	1.5	NS	+0.0287	+1.2	NS
adult Sunday	population	0.2084	0.2084	386.6	0.000	+0.2646	+12.2	0.000
contact	electoral roll	0.4011	0.1927	471.9	0.000	+0.4349	+19.6	0.000
	multi-parish benefice	0.4152	0.0141	35.5	0.000	−0.1350	−6.3	0.000
	clergy aged 60+	0.4183	0.0031	7.7	0.006	−0.0560	−2.8	0.006
confirmands	population	0.0396	0.0396	60.5	0.000	+0.1238	+4.6	0.000
under 14	electoral roll	0.0781	0.0385	61.3	0.000	+0.1950	+7.0	0.000
years	multi-parish benefice	0.0798	0.0017	2.7	NS	−0.0368	−1.4	NS
	clergy aged 60+	0.0835	0.0037	5.9	0.015	+0.0616	+2.4	0.015

The suburban church

Inspection of the spread of communities within the suburban sample indicated that 10% of them had 3,000 or fewer inhabitants. A further 16% had between 3,001 and 5,000 inhabitants, 42% had between 5,001 and 10,000, 22% had between 10,001 and 15,000, and the remaining 10% over 15,000 inhabitants. The majority of the suburban churches (80%) were within single-parish benefices. The suburban churches were much less likely to be served by clergy aged sixty years and over (13%) than was the case for the rural churches (29%).

Inspection of the range of outcome variables employed in the rural analysis indicated that all of these variables were also well represented in sufficient suburban churches to sustain careful analysis. The following percentages refer to the proportions of suburban churches

Figure 1: Path model

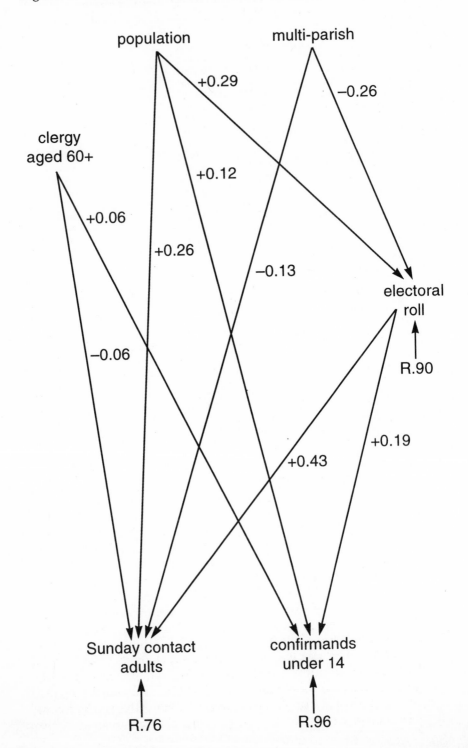

Table 3: Multiple regression significance tests for suburban parishes

dependent variables	total R2	incr. R2	F	P<
electoral roll	0.0668	0.0008	0.5	NS
Easter communicants	0.6567	0.0004	0.7	NS
Christmas communicants	0.5285	0.0021	2.5	NS
Sunday contact, 2–5 years	0.2749	0.0054	4.3	0.05
Sunday contact, 6–9 years	0.2941	0.0000*	0.0	NS
Sunday contact, 10–13 years	0.2738	0.0002	0.2	NS
Sunday contact, 14–17 years	0.2980	0.0000	0.0	NS
Sunday contact, 18–21 years	0.1255	0.0002	0.1	NS
Sunday contact, over 21 years	0.5022	0.0000	0.0	NS
Sunday school, 6–9 years	0.2217	0.0022	1.6	NS
church choir, 6–9 years	0.0931	0.0031	2.0	NS
church choir, 10–13 years	0.1231	0.0033	2.2	NS
church choir, 14–21 years	0.0466	0.0021	1.3	NS
church choir, adult	0.1534	0.0004	0.3	NS
infant baptisms, under 2 years	0.2076	0.0021	1.5	NS
confirmands, under 14 years	0.1177	0.0002	0.1	NS
condirmands, 14–17 years	0.1391	0.0017	1.2	NS
confirmands, over 17 years	0.0915	0.0048	3.0	NS

reporting each form of contact: electoral roll (100%); Easter communicants (100%); Christmas communicants (100%); Sunday contact over two Sundays with 2–5 year olds (94%), 6–9 year olds (98%), 10–13 year olds (97%), 14–17 year olds (95%), 18–21 year olds (89%) and adults over the age of 21 (100%); 6–9 year olds attending Sunday school type groups (91%); church choir membership of 6–9 year olds (41%), 10–13 year olds (65%), 14–21 year olds (58%) and adults over the age of 21 (85%); infant baptisms (92%); and confirmation candidates under the age of 14 (59%), between the ages of 14 and 17 (49%) and over the age of 17 (69%).

Table three presents the multiple regression significance tests designed to explore the impact of clergy aged sixty years and over on each of these outcome variables within suburban parishes, after taking into account population size, multi-parish benefices and the number of names on the electoral roll, in that specific order. In the case of suburban church, the age of the minister contributes significant predictive information in respect of only one of eighteen listed outcome variables. The one outcome measure influenced negatively by the presence of an older minister was the normal Sunday church contact with 2–5 year olds.

Discussion

These findings clearly demonstrate that there are significant relationships between clergy age and quantitative markers of rural church life and that these relationships are not found in suburban church life. The new data partially confirm Francis' (1985) earlier findings, but also extend and qualify them. Four features of these data are worthy of closer scrutiny and comment.

First, it is clear that rural clergy aged sixty years and over work with slightly smaller Sunday congregations than do younger clergy operating within similar rural contexts. By examining Sunday contact in terms of specific age groups, these data demonstrate that the older clergy attract fewer adults as well as fewer children to their churches. This comparison suggests that the quality of liturgy provided by the older clergy may be found less attractive to recruit new parishioners to regular worship or that the quality of pastoral care may be less attentive to the lapsation of regular worshippers from attending service.

Second, it is clear that, although the older rural clergy may have smaller congregations on a normal Sunday, their parishes continue to maintain a comparable level of names on the electoral roll, Christmas and Easter communicants and infant baptisms. This comparison suggests that the influence of clergy age on church life is seen in indices of regular commitment rather than in indices of more nominal practice. Similarly, although the older clergy may have smaller congregations on a normal Sunday, their parishes continue to maintain a comparable level of contact with young people through Sunday schools and choirs. This comparison suggests that the influence of clergy age on church life is not reflected in areas of ministry like Sunday schools and church choirs which are generally run by laity rather than the clergy themselves (Board of Education, 1988).

Third, it is clear that, while the older rural clergy may have smaller congregations on a normal Sunday, they actually present more young and adult confirmation candidates. This comparison suggests that the older rural clergy are more likely to conceptualise their ministry in terms of fulfilling traditional expectations to demonstrate signs of church growth, although they may fail to maintain the evidence of this growth in the Sunday services.

Fourth, it is clear that, while the older clergy working rural parishes tend to have smaller congregations on a normal Sunday than do their younger colleagues working in comparable rural parishes, the older clergy working in suburban parishes tend to have congregations of the same size as their younger colleagues working in comparable suburban parishes. This comparison suggests that the experiences of older clergy may differ significantly in rural and suburban parishes.

Taken in conjunction with the findings of earlier studies, these data suggest that the new patterns of rural ministry may now be over-stretching more elderly clergy. The key feature of these new patterns of rural ministry concerns the creation of multi-parish benefices, in which an individual minister may have the care of six or more parishes, without formal or informal, full-time or part-time, assistance from clerical colleagues (Russell, 1986). In an earlier generation many of the rural parishes currently organised within multi-parish benefices would have had their own parsonage and resident stipendiary incumbent. As yet very little is known from an empirical perspective regarding the practical consequences of this reorganisation of rural ministry. It is clear that the pattern of services available within rural parishes has been significantly reduced (Archbishops' Commission on Rural Areas, 1990). Francis (1985) demonstrated that there is a significantly lower level of church attendance within multi-parish benefices, in comparison with single-parish benefices which contain the same number of residents. Francis and Lankshear (1992) demonstrated that, within multi-parish benefices, the parishes which retain the parsonage maintain a higher level of church attendance in relationship to the overall population, than those parishes where there is no longer a resident incumbent.

While statistical evidence on the comparative functioning of multi-parish benefices remains scarce, evidence from participant observation, open-ended questionnaire data and interviews with rural clergy suggests that multi-parish benefices may generate five particular difficulties for their clergy, as well as unique opportunities (Francis, 1985; Archbishops' Commission on Rural Areas, 1990). First, the size of the geographical area covered by multi-parish benefices may lead to a high annual mileage in pastoral visiting and the conducting of services. Second, the desire of many rural parishes to retain their own pattern of Sunday services may lead to a tight and potentially exhausting liturgical schedule for the rural minister. Third, while contemporary ecclesiology emphasises the effective ministry of the laity (Board of Education, 1985), it may be more difficult for small rural parishes to generate this form of indigenous leadership than for larger suburban parishes (Wilson, 1989). Fourth, while the total number of inhabitants may appear small in many rural multi-parish benefices in comparison with urban and suburban benefices, this factor needs to be balanced against three other considerations. In rural areas the Anglican ministry is now unlikely to be supported by residential clergy from other denominations (Clarke and Anderson, 1986). In rural areas, parishioners may still have wider and deep-seated expectations regarding the involvement of Anglican clergy in local community life (Davies, Watkins and Winter, 1991). Each rural parish generally retains its own historic church building and local structure of church organisation and government, while the effective maintenance of both may make considerable demands on clerical time, energy and creativity. Fifth, the more general withdrawal of resources from rural areas may involve rural clergy in extra personal hassle in terms of access to such essentials as shops and medical facilities. All of these features of multi-parish benefices may generate additional personal and professional difficulties for older clergy.

In an earlier age small rural parishes may have provided an ideal context for what would in today's language be described as effective pre-retirement or post-retirement ministry. Now, however, pressures created by recruitment problems and falling income have removed from the rural church those 'light cure' parishes, described by Paul (1964) as ideal for sick, ailing or elderly clergy. Nevertheles, there still seems a tendency for older clergy to be concentrated in rural areas. According to the most recent diocesan analysis of clergy age published by the Central Board of Finance (1987), the eleven dioceses with the highest average age of clergy were all rural (Bath and Wells, Chichester, Ely, Exeter, Gloucester, Lincoln, Norwich, Peterborough, St Edmundsbury and Ipswich, Truro and Winchester). Unfortunately the more recent data published by the Central Board of Finance (1991) simply notes that between 16 and 17% of the total diocesan clergy were aged sixty years or over at 31st December, 1990, without providing a diocesan breakdown, although data provided by Davies, Watkins and Winter (1991) make it clear that the average age of the clergy is still higher in rural parishes.

The present data would suggest that the practical consequences of ageing may have significant implications on the deployment of Anglican clergy within the present structure and shape of the Church of England. Far from being an ideal context for pre-retirement ministry, the rural church should now be seen as offering challenges and presenting demands more appropriate to the ministry of younger clergy. Older clergy may now find a more professionally effective and personally satisfying ministry in areas which are able to generate more lay leadership, offer better social and medical facilities, and make gentler demands in terms of serving Sunday liturgy and undertaking pastoral visiting, as may be more frequently the case in suburban areas.

The main finding of this study that older clergy working in rural parishes perform less well than do their younger colleagues in rural parishes now needs further testing in a variety of ways. First, alongside the performance indicators of quantitative participation in local church life employed in the present study, it would be wise to explore a wider range of indicators, including measures of parishioner expectation and satisfaction, home visiting and effective ministry among the sick, elderly and bereaved. Second, alongside the present data collected among rural and suburban Anglican clergy in England, it would be helpful to explore whether similar trends emerge within other denominational and cultural contexts. Third, the theoretical explanation offered by the present study to account for the observed relationship between clergy age and performance in the rural church now needs to be examined more explicitly through a direct study of the relationship between type of ministry, stress and burnout. Meanwhile, however, the Church of England may be well advised to monitor carefully the strains placed on rural clergy during the years of ministry leading up to retirement.[1]

Note

1. We are grateful to the All Saints' Educational Trust, the Foundation of St Matthias, the Hockerill Educational Foundation, St Gabriel's Trust, the Sarum St Michael Educational Charity, St Christopher's Trust, the Central Church Fund of the Church of England and the Culham Trustees who provided funding for the original survey.

References

Ainlay, S C, Singleton, R and Swigert, V L (1992) 'Ageing and religious participation: reconsidering the effects of health,' *Journal for the Scientific Study of Religion*, 31, pp. 175–188.

Ainlay, S C and Smith, D R (1984) 'Ageing and religious participation,' *Journal of Gerontology*, 39, pp. 357–363.

Aldag, R J and Brief, A P (1977) 'Age, work values and employee reactions,' *Industrial Gerontology*, 4, pp. 192–197.

Aldridge, A (1986) 'Slaves to no sect: the Anglican clergy and liturgical change,' *Sociological Review*, 34, pp. 357–380.

Aldridge, A (1989) 'Men, women, and clergymen: opinion and authority in a sacred organisation,' *Sociological Review*, 37, pp. 43–64.

Archbishops' Commission On Rural Areas (1990) *Faith in the Countryside*, Worthing, Churchman Publishing.

Arthur, W, Fuentes, R and Doverspike, D (1990) 'Relationships among personnel tests, age, and job performance,' *Experimental Aging Research*, 16, 1, pp. 11–16.

Arvey, R D and Dewhirst, H D (1979) 'Relationship between diversity of interests, age, job satisfaction and job performance,' *Journal of Occupational Psychology*, 52, pp. 17–23.

Arvey, R D and Mussio, S (1973) 'Test discrimination, job performance and age,' *Industrial Gerontology*, 16, pp. 22–29.

Avolio, B J (1991) 'Levels-of-analysis perspective of aging and work research,' *Annual Review of Gerontology and Geriatrics*, 11, pp. 239–260.

Barrett, G V, Mihal, W L, Panek, P E, Sterns, H L and Alexander, R A (1977) 'Information processing skills predictive of accident involvement for younger and older commercial drivers,' *Industrial Gerontology*, 4, pp. 173–182.

Baugher, D (1978) 'Is the older worker inherently incompetent?' *Aging and Work*, 1, pp. 243–250.

Bedeian, A G, Ferris, G R and Kacmar, K M (1992) 'Age, tenure, and job satisfaction: a tale of two perspectives,' *Journal of Vocational Behaviour*, 40, 1, pp. 33–48.

Belbin, R M (1953) 'Difficulties of older people in industry,' *Occupational Psychology*, 27, pp. 177–190.

Belbin, R M (1955) 'Older people and heavy work,' *British Journal of Industrial Medicine*, 12, pp. 309–319.

Blaikie, N W H (1979) *The Plight of the Australian Clergy*, Brisbane, University of Queensland Press.

Board of Education (1985) *All are Called: towards a theology of the laity*, London, Church Information Office.

Board of Education (1988) *Children in the Way: new directions for the church's children*, London, National Society and Church House Publishing.

Bowden, A (1988) 'St Matthew's church, Coates, Gloucestershire,' in J Richardson (ed.) *Ten Rural Churches*, Eastbourne, MARC, pp. 15–34.

Bowers, W H (1952) 'An appraisal of worker characteristics as related to age,' *Journal of Applied Psychology*, 36, pp. 296–306.

Breen, L Z and Spaeth, J L (1960) 'Age and productivity among workers in four Chicago companies,' *Journal of Gerontology*, 15, pp. 68–70.

Brierley, P, Myers, B and Marshall, L (1991) *Leaders Under Pressure: postal survey*, London, MARC Europe.

Broyles, P A and Drenovsky, C K (1992) 'Religious attendance and the subjective health of the elderly,' *Review of Religious Research*, 34, pp. 152–160.

Carroll, J W, Hargrove, B and Lummis, A T (1983) *Women of the Cloth*, San Francisco, Harper and Row.

Central Board of Finance (1987) *Church Statistics: some facts and figures about the Church of England 1987*, London, Central Board of Finance of the Church of England.

Central Board of Finance (1991) *Church Statistics: some facts and figures about the Church of England 1991*, London, Central Board of Finance of the Church of England.

Central Board of Finance and the Church Commissioners (1992) *Still Giving in Faith*, London, Central Board of Finance of the Church of England.

Chen, M Y T and Goodwin, J L (1991) 'The continuity perspective of aging and retirement applied to Protestant clergy: an analysis of theory,' *Journal of Religious Gerontology*, 7, 3, pp. 55–67.

Chown, S M (1972) 'The effect of flexibility-rigidity and age on adaptability in job performance,' *Industrial Gerontology*, 12, pp. 105–121.

Clarke, J N and Anderson, C L (1986) *Methodism in the Countryside*, Horncastle, Clarke and Anderson.

Clay, H M (1956) 'A study of performance in relation to age at two printing works,' *Journal of Gerontology*, 11, pp. 417–424.

Coate, M A (1989) *Clergy Stress: the hidden conflicts of ministry*, London, SPCK.

Cole, S (1979) 'Age and scientific performance,' *American Journal of Sociology*, 84, pp. 958–977.

Davies, D, Pack, C, Seymour, S, Short, C, Watkins, C and Winter, M (1990) *The Clergy Life: rural church project volume two*, Cirencester, Centre for Rural Studies, Royal Agricultural College.

Davies, D, Watkins, C and Winter, M (1991) *Church and Religion in Rural England*, Edinburgh, T and T Clark.

Davies, D R and Sparrow, P R (1985) 'Age and work behaviour,' in N Charness (ed.) *Aging and Human Performance*, New York, John Wiley, pp. 293–332.

De Jong, J A and Donovan, D C (1988) 'Age-related differences in beliefs, attitudes and practices of priests,' *Journal for the Scientific Study of Religion*, 27, pp. 128–136.

De Maio, T J (1980) 'Refusals: who, where and why,' *Public Opinion Quarterly*, 44, pp. 223–233.

Dewe, P J (1987) 'New Zealand ministers of religion: identifying sources of stress and coping processes,' *Work and Stress*, 1, pp. 351–364.

Dickerson, B E and Myers, D R (1988) 'The contributory and changing roles of older adults in the church and synagogue,' *Educational Gerontology*, 14, pp. 303–314.

Doering, M, Rhodes, S R and Schuster, M (1983) *The Aging Worker: research and recommendations*, London, Sage Publications.

Doka, K J (1986) 'The church and the elderly: the impact of changing age strata on congregations,' *International Journal of Aging and Human Development*, 22, pp. 291–300.

Eichar, D M, Norland, S, Brady, E M and Fortinsky, R H (1991) 'Job satisfaction of older workers,' *Journal of Organizational Behaviour*, 12, pp. 609–620.

Fichter, J H (1984) 'The myth of clergy burnout,' *Sociological Analysis*, 45, pp. 373–382.

Fitcher, J H (1985) 'The dilemma of priest retirement,' *Journal for the Scientific Study of Religion*, 24, pp. 101–104.

Fletcher, B (1990) *Clergy Under Stress*, London, Mowbray.

Fogarty, J C (1988) *The Catholic Priest: his identity and values*, Kansas City, Sheed and Ward.

Francis, L J (1985) *Rural Anglicanism: a future for young Christians?*, London, Collins Liturgical Publications.

Francis, L J (1987) *Religion in the Primary School*, London, Collins Liturgical Publications.

Francis, L J and Lankshear, D W (1990) 'The impact of church schools on village church life,' *Educational Studies*, 16, pp. 117–129.

Francis, L J and Lankshear, D W (1991a) *Continuing in the Way: children, young people and the church*, London, National Society.

Francis, L J and Lankshear, D W (1991b) 'The impact of church schools on urban church life,' *School Effectiveness and School Improvement*, 2, pp. 324–335.

Francis, L J and Lankshear, D W (1992) 'The rural rectory: the impact of a resident priest on local church life,' *Journal of Rural Studies*, 8, pp. 97–103.

Gannon, M, Northern, J and Carroll, S (1971) 'Characteristics of non-respondents among workers,' *Journal of Applied Psychology*, 55, pp. 586–588.

Gibson, J L and Klein, S M (1970) 'Employee attitudes as a function of age and length of service: a reconceptualisation,' *Academy of Management Journal*, 13, pp. 411–425.

Gilbert, A D (1980) *The Making of Post-Christian Britain*, London, Longman.

Giniger, S (1983) 'Age, experience, and performance on speed and skill jobs in an applied setting,' *Journal of Applied Psychology*, 68, pp. 469–475.

Glenn, N D, Taylor, P A and Weaver, C N (1977) 'Age and job satisfaction among males and females: a multivariate, multisurvey study,' *Journal of Applied Psychology*, 62, pp. 189–193.

Goodwin, J L and Chen, M Y T (1991) 'From pastor to pensioner: a study of retired Canadian Protestant clergy from the continuity perspective,' *Journal of Religious Gerontology*, 7, 3, pp. 69–79.

Greenberg, L (1961) 'Productivity of older workers,' *Gerontologist*, 1, pp. 38–41.

Guy, R F (1982) 'Religion, physical disabilities, and life satisfaction in older age cohorts,' *International Journal of Aging and Human Development*, 15, pp. 225–232.

Hawkins, D F (1975) 'Estimation of non-response bias,' *Sociological Methods and Research*, 3, pp. 461–488.

Heenan, E F (1972) 'Sociology of religion and the aged: the empirical lacunae,' *Journal for the Scientific Study of Religion*, 11, pp. 171–176.

Herzog, A R and Rodgers, W L (1988a) 'Age and response rates to interview sample surveys,' *Journal of Gerontology*, 43, pp. S200–S205.

Herzog, A R and Rodgers, W L (1988b) 'Interviewing older adults: mode comparison using data from a face-to-face survey and a telephone survey,' *Public Opinion Quarterly*, 52, pp. 84–99.

Herzog, A R, Rodgers, W L and Kulka, R A (1983) 'Interviewing older adults: a comparison of telephone and face-to-face modalities,' *Public Opinion Quarterly,* 47, pp. 405–418.

Hoge, D R, Shields, J J and Verdieck, M J (1988) 'Changing age distribution and theological attitudes of Catholic priests, 1970–1985,' *Sociological Analysis,* 49, pp. 264–280.

Hoge, D R, Shields, J J and Verdieck, M J (1992) 'Response to Young and Schoenherr,' *Sociological Analysis,* 53, pp. 89–90.

Hoinville, G (1983) 'Carrying out surveys among the elderly,' *Journal of the Market Research Society,* 25, pp. 223–237.

Holley, W H, Field, H S and Holley, B B (1978) 'Age and reactions to jobs: an empirical study of para-professional workers,' *Aging and Work,* 1, pp. 33–40.

Hornsby-Smith, M P (1989) *The Changing Parish: a study of parishes, priests and parishioners after Vatican II,* London, Routledge.

Hughes, P J (1989) *The Australian Clergy,* Hawthorn, Christian Research Association.

Hunsberger, B (1985) 'Religion, age, life satisfaction, and perceived sources of religiousness: a study of older persons,' *Journal of Gerontology,* 40, pp. 615–620.

Hunt, J S and Saul, P N (1975) 'The relationship of age, tenure, and job satisfaction in males and females,' *Academy of Management Journal,* 18, pp. 690–702.

Idler, E (1987) 'Religious involvement and the health of the elderly,' *Social Forces,* 66, pp. 227–238.

Jenson, P and Mortin, J K (1982) "Job satisfaction and age: a test of two views,' *Social Forces,* 60, pp. 1089–1102.

Jarvis, P (1976) 'The potential resignee from the ministry,' *Contact,* 54, pp. 24–29.

Johnson, D P and Mullins, L C (1989) 'Subjective and social dimensions of religiosity and loneliness among the well elderly,' *Review of Religious Research,* 31, pp. 3–15.

Jung, C G (1960) 'The stages of life,' in *The Structure and Dynamics of the Psyche: collected works,* volume 8, pp. 387–403, New York, Pantheon.

Kalleberg, A and Loscocco, K (1983) 'Aging, values, and rewards: exploring age differences in job satisfaction,' *American Sociological Review,* 48, pp. 78–90.

Keeves, J P (1988) 'Path analysis,' in J P Keeves (ed.) *Educational Research, Methodology, and Measurement: an international handbook,* Oxford, Pergamon Press, pp. 723–731.

King, H F (1956) 'An attempt to use production data in the study of age and performance,' *Journal of Gerontology,* 11, pp. 410–416.

King, H F and Speakman, D (1953) 'Age and industrial accident rates,' *British Journal of Industrial Medicine,* 10, pp. 51–58.

Koenig, H G, George, L K and Siegler, I C (1988) 'The use of religion and other emotion-regulating coping strategies among older adults,' *The Gerontologist,* 28, pp. 303–310.

Koenig, H G, Kvale, J N and Ferrel, C (1988) 'Religion and well-being in later life,' *The Gerontologist,* 28, pp. 18–28.

Krause, N and van Tran, T (1989) 'Stress and religious involvement among older blacks,' *Journal of Gerontology,* 44, pp. S4–S13.

Kutscher, R E and Walker, J F (1960) 'Comparative job performance of office workers by age,' *Monthly Labour Review,* 83, pp. 39–43.

Levin, J S and Markides, K S (1988) 'Religious attendance and psychological well-being in middle-aged and older Mexican Americans,' *Sociological Analysis,* 49, pp. 66–72.

Levine, M (1980) 'Four models of age/work policy research,' *Gerontologist,* 20, pp. 561–574.

McDaniel, S W, Madden, C S and Verille, P (1987) 'Do topic differences affect survey nonresponse?' *Journal of the Market Research Society,* 29, 1, pp. 55–66.

McEvoy, G M and Cascio, W F (1989) 'Cumulative evidence of the relationship between employee age and job performance,' *Journal of applied Psychology, 74, 1* pp. 11–17.

McFarland, R A (1943) 'The older worker in industry,' Harvard Business Review, 21, pp. 505–520.

MacGuigan, J E (1979) 'The aging religious priest,' *Gerontologist,* 12, 11, pp. 19–20.

McNeely, R L (1988) 'Age and job satisfaction in human service employment,' Gerontologist, 28, pp. 163–168.

Maher, H (1955) 'Age and performance of two work groups,' *Journal of Gerontology,* 10, pp. 448–451.

Malony, H N and Hunt, R A (1991) *The Psychology of Clergy,* Harrisburg, Pennsylvania, Morehouse Publishing.

Mark, J A (1957) 'Comparative job performance by age,' *Monthly Labour Review,* 80, pp. 1467–1471.

Markides, K S (1983) 'Aging, religiosity, and adjustment: a longitudinal analysis,' *Journal of Gerontology,* 38, pp. 621–625.

Meltzer, H (1958) 'Age difference in work attitudes,' *Journal of Gerontology,* 13, pp. 74–81.

Meltzer, M W (1981) 'Reduction of occupational stress among elderly lawyers: the creation of a functional niche,' *International Journal of Aging and Human Development,* 13, pp. 209–219.

Mercer, J R and Butler, E W (1967) 'Disengagement of the aged population and response differentials in survey research,' *Social Forces,* 46, pp. 89–96.

Mull, C S, Cox, C L and Sullivan, J A (1987) 'Religion's role in the health and well-being of well elders,' *Public Health Nursing,* 4, pp. 151–159.

Murrell, K F H and Tucker, W A (1960) 'A pilot job-study of age-related causes of difficulty in light engineering,' *Ergonomics,* 3, pp. 74–79.

Nelson, P B (1980) 'Religious orientation of the elderly: relationship to depression and self esteem,' *Journal of Gerontological Nursing,* 16, 2, pp. 29–35.

Nugent, F M (1976) 'The disengagement theory of aging and retirement to clergymen,' *Dissertation Abstracts International,* 36, 10-B, p. 5358.

O'Brien, G E and Dowling, P (1981) 'Age and job satisfaction,' *Australian Psychologist,* 16, pp. 49–61.

O'Neil, M J (1979) 'Estimating the non-response bias due to refusals in telephone surveys,' *Public Opinion Quarterly,* 43, pp. 218–232.

Paul, L (1964) *The Deployment and Payment of the Clergy,* London, Church Information Office.

Payne, B (1988) 'Religious patterns and participation of older adults: a sociological perspective,' *Educational Gerontology,* 14, pp. 255–268.

Pwell, M (1973) 'Age and occupational change among coal-miners,' *Occupational Psychology,* 47, pp. 37–49.

Pratt, M W, Hunsberger, B, Pancer, S M and Roth, D (1992) 'Reflections on religion: aging, belief orthodoxy, and interpersonal conflict in the complexity of adult thinking about religious issues,' *Journal for the Scientific Study of Religion,* 31, pp. 514–522.

Ranson, S, Bryman, A and Hinings, B (1977) *Clergy, Ministers and Priests,* London, Routledge and Kegan Paul.

Reed, P G (1991) 'Spirituality and mental health in older adults: extant knowledge for nursing,' *Family and Community Health,* 14, 2, pp. 14–25.

Rees, R L D and Francis L J (1991) 'Clergy response rates to work-related questionnaires: a relationship between age, work load and burnout?' *Social Behaviour and Personality,* 19, pp. 45–51.

Reidy, M T V and White, L C (1977) 'The measurement of traditionalism among Roman Catholic priests: an exploratory study,' *British Journal of Sociology,* 28, pp. 226–241.

Reilly, M E (1975) 'Perceptions of the priest role,' *Sociological Analysis,* 36, pp. 347–356.

Richardson, I M (1953) 'Age and work: a study of 489 men in heavy industry,' *British Journal of Industrial Medicine,* 10, pp. 269–284.

Robinson, J A T (1963) *Honest tò God,* London, SCM.

Root, N (1981) 'Injuries at work are fewer among older employees,' *Monthly Labour Review,* 104, pp. 30–34.

Russell, A (1980) *The Clerical Profession,* London, SPCK.

Russell, A (1986) *The Country Parish,* London, SPCK.

Sanford, J A (1982) *Ministry Burnout,* London, Arthur James.

Schoenherr, R A and Greeley, A M (1974) 'Role commitment processes and the American Catholic priesthood,' *American Sociological Review,* 39, pp. 407–426.

Schoenherr, R A and Sorensen, A (1982) 'Social change in religious organisations: consequences of clergy decline in the US Catholic church,' *Sociological Analysis,* 43, pp. 23–52.

Schwab, D P and Heneman, H G (1977a) 'Age and satisfaction with dimensions of work,' *Journal of Vocational Behaviour,* 10, pp. 212–220.

Schwab, D P and Heneman, H G (1977b) 'Effects of age and experience on productivity,' *Industrial Gerontology,* 4, pp. 113–117.

Simonton, D K (1989) 'The swan-song phenomenon: last-works effects for 172 classical composers,' *Psychology and Aging,* 4, 1, pp. 42–47.

Singleton, W T (1983) 'Age, skill and management,' *International Journal of Aging and Human Development,* 17, 1, pp. 15–23.

Smith, T W (1983) 'The hidden 25 percent: an analysis of non-response on the 1980 general social survey,' *Public Opinion Quarterly,* 47, pp. 386–404.

Snyder, R A and Mayo, F (1991) 'Single versus mulitple causes of the age–job satisfaction,' *Psychological Reports,* 68, pp. 1255–1262.

SPSS Incorporated (1988) *SPSSX User's Guide,* New York, McGraw-Hill.

Tiller, J (1983) *A Strategy for the Church's Ministry,* London, Church Information Office Publishing.

Towler, R and Coxon, A P M (1979) *The Fate of the Anglican Clergy,* London, Macmillan.

Van Haitsma, K (1986) 'Intrinsic religious orientation: implications in the study of religiosity and personal adjustment in the aged,' *Journal of Social Psychology,* 126, pp. 685–687.

Van Westerhoven, E M C (1978) 'Covering non-response: does it pay? a study of refusers and absentees,' *Journal of the Market Research Society,* 20, pp. 245–247.

Verdieck, M J, Shields, J J and Hoge, D R (1988) 'role commitment processes revisited: American Catholic priests 1970 and 1985,' *Journal for the Scientific Study of Religion,* 27, pp. 524–535.

Waldman, D A and Avolio, B J (1986) 'Meta-analysis of age difference in job performance,' *Journal of Applied Psychology,* 71, 1, pp. 33–38.

Weaver, C N, Holmes, S L and Glenn, N D (1975) 'Some characteristics of inaccessible respondents in a telephone survey,' *Journal of Applied Psychology,* 60, pp. 260–262.

Weiner, F (1990) 'Older psychiatrists and their psychotherapy practice,' *American Journal of Psychotherapy,* 44, pp. 44–49.

Welford, A T (1966) 'Industrial work suitable for older people: some British studies,' *Gerontologist,* 6, pp. 4–9.

Welford, A T (1976) 'Thirty years of psychological research on age and work,' *Journal of Occupational Psychology,* 49, pp. 129–138.

White, A T and Spector, P E (1987) 'Investigation of age-related factors in the age-job-satisfaction relationship,' *Psychology and Aging,* 2, pp. 261–265.

Wilson, M (ed.) (1989) *The Rural Church: towards 2000,* Bulwick, The Rural Theology Association.

Young, G and Dowling, W (1987) 'Dimensions of religiosity in old age: accounting for variation in types of participation,' *Journal of Gerontology,* 42, pp. 376–380.

Young, L A and Schoenherr, R A (1992) 'The changing age distribution and theological attitudes of Catholic priests revisited,' *Sociological Analysis,* 53, pp. 73–87.

Zeitz, G (1990) 'Age and work satisfaction in a government agency: a situational perspective,' *Human Relations,* 43, pp. 419–438.

Zuckerman, D M, Kasl, S and Ostfeld, A M (1984) 'Psychosocial predictors of mortality among the elderly poor: the role of religion, well-being and social contacts,' *American Journal of Epidemiology,* 119, pp. 410–423.

6.2 From pastor to pensioner: a study of retired Canadian Protestant clergy from the continuity perspective

Janet L Goodwin and Mervin Y T Chen

Introduction

The continuity perspective in social gerontology states that, with consideration being given to those changes which occur with age, people endeavour to maintain unity in their lifestyles.[1] Unlike other gerontological theories, the continuity perspective views ageing as a life-long process, not one which begins at age sixty-five. Adjustment to retirement is affected by the long sequence of events which occur prior to that time. In a previous paper, Chen and Goodwin argue that situational factors, activity, occupational subculture, and psychological continuity are of particular importance to a continuity perspective.[2] An examination of these variables would enable a clearer understanding of retirement. This article reports some empirical findings of a study of Protestant clergy's retirement by using this framework.

Participants

The 185 participants in the study were both male and female, comprising 179 males and 6 females, these six females being pioneers in the field of women in pastoral ministry. At the time of their retirement all had been serving churches in the Atlantic region of Canada, therefore their names appear among the list of retirees printed in the annual yearbooks for each denomination in the region. These clergy were representative of three denominational groups: the Anglican Diocese of Nova Scotia, the Atlantic United Baptist Convention and the Maritime Conference of the United Church of Canada, the three largest Protestant groups in Atlantic Canada.

The average age of all participants was 75 years. The Baptist clergy averaged an older age of 78.5 years as compared with the Anglican or United Church clergy who averaged approximately 74 years. Average for entering the pastoral ministry was 29 years of age (Baptists 28.2 years, Anglican 29.4 years, United Church 29.4). The total sample averaged 36.9 years of service to the church. The Baptist clergy led in years of service (39.5 years) and were followed by Anglican clergy who averaged 37.3 years of service and the United Church clergy who served the shortest period, 34.8 years.

Data collection

The data were collected in two forms: mailed-questionnaires and semi-structured interviews. After two mailings of the questionnaire 84% of those who had received questionnaires returned them. In addition, there were 25 interviews which took place in the homes of the clergy. The process of selection for clergy to be interviewed was based on their proximity to the university. An analysis of both sets of data showed no significant differences between the questionnaire sample and the interview sample. Therefore all data were combined for analysis.

Background data

An analysis of the data showed that only two respondents in the entire sample had been retired less than one year, 47 had been retired between one and five years, 38 had been retired for six to ten years and the same number reported being retired between eleven and fifteen years. A small number (N = 4, 2.8%), had been retired 25 years or more.

Almost all, 139 (88%) of those who responded to the questionnaire, were married at the time of the survey; this also included those who were married for a second time. A greater number of the clergy were widowed (7.6%) compared with those never married (3.1%) or divorced (1.3%). No one in the sample was separated from their spouse at the time of the survey.

The average number of children for the three denominations is three. Only 8.3% of the clergy who responded to this question did not have any children. The majority of those who did have children reported that they were presently between the ages of 26 and 49 years of age.

Respondents were also asked to report the level of education they had completed. Over half, 55%, held a graduate degree. This included any theological training obtained after the Bachelor level (that is, Bachelor of Theology). A number of the respondents noted that they had been conferred with honorary doctorates. A greater number of Baptist clergy reported having less academic preparation, that is, 'some college' (22.4%) compared with Anglican clergy (4.2%) and United Church clergy (7.7%).

Findings

Situational factors

For this particular group of retired clergy it was found that adequacy of income (that being, enough income to support the style of life which was maintained prior to retirement) and good health (that being, a level of health which allows the individuals to participate in those things which they enjoy and are necessary for everyday living) were important situational factors which facilitated continuity of lifestyle.

When clergy were asked if their present income was adequate to meet their living expenses, 86% reported that it was. Furthermore, some of the participants reported that their income was greater now than it had been at any time prior to retirement. As well, a number commented that during their years of full-time ministry they had very small incomes and as a result led very frugal lives. There were those who spent years working overseas for modest pay, others were ministers in churches which could only afford small salaries. These factors had influenced the ability of clergy to cope more effectively, that is, to maintain continuity of lifestyle, with their retirement income.

Health status was also a situational factor which affected the life-styles of clergy in the retirement years. Over half of the sample (65%) reported their health to be good. The remainder, 26% reported their health as fair and 9% reported their health to be poor. Primarily, one's health condition affected the types and levels of activities pursued. For example, poor eyesight affected the ability of a person to read and write, whereas a weak heart restricted the number of physical activities which can be pursued. Therefore one's physical well-being has a significant impact on those activities which can be pursued and as a result has a direct effect on the continuity of lifestyle.

Activities

There were two reasons for examining the activities of retired clergy. One was to determine the effect of occupation on the tyes of activities engaged in during the retirement years. The other was to compare activities before and after retirement to find if they were similar or if there was a tendency to develop new ones. The data lent support to the prediction of the continuity perspective, that is, at retirement, individuals tend to carry on with activities which they previously had rather than creating new ones.

Among this particular group of clergy two trends with respect to activities emerged. First, clergy remained active in the church, but regarded retirement as a time to pursue those interests and activities which had been neglected because of their full-time commitment to ministry. The second trend was that of pursuing those interests and activities which had been neglected during full-time ministry, but separating themselves from the church after retirement. Of the 160 participants in the survey sample 22% indicated that they were no longer involved in the church, this being primarily for health reasons. Overall, the majority followed the first trend and found little difference in their lifestyles before and after retirement. This trend did not differ among the three denominations, a common saying among many of the participants being: 'Once a minister, always a minister.' These were people who had made a life-long commitment to their calling as a minister and therefore this influenced the extent to which they pursued various activities. For them, this stage of their career – retirement –

was a time to withdraw from full-time ministry and to engage in tasks within the church where they felt most effective. Therefore, in retirement these individuals tended not to develop new interests and hobbies, but to pursue those which had been of interest prior to retirement. However, the majority of clergy continued to work in the church in varied capacities. Clergy utilised the opportunities made available by the church in order to fulfil their needs to continue working.

The participants were questioned regarding their activities during 'free time'. Such activities were divided into four categories: domestic activities, entertainment activities, mental activities and social activities. Seventeen per cent (N = 27) of the sample reported being involved in a variety of sedentary activities from the various categories such as reading, writing, or playing table games. These participants reported being reduced to sedentary activities as the result of poor health conditions. At the opposite end of the spectrum, 20.1% (N = 32) of the sample were involved in active physical activities during their free time. This included such things as farm work, gardening, sports such as golf, hockey and tennis. It was found that those who were physically active were also participating in many domestic, entertainment, mental and social activities. Approximately 10.6% of the sample spent their free time participating in mental activities only. This included such tasks as reading or writing books, articles or poems, or simply sitting and thinking. The remaining 52.3% of the participants did not concentrate on one specific area of activity. Many participated in various domestic, entertainment and social activities. Some common recreational activities included sports such as fishing, swimming, curling, bowling and boating. Common hobbies were gardening and carpentry work. Like many other seniors, retired clergy enjoy spending time with their grandchildren. Many of the leisure time activities appeared to be a 'spill over' from their occupation, such as reading, writing, teaching, research and community work.

With regard to leisure activities the pattern appears to be the same among the three denominations of clergy. It could be speculated that the 'call' influences behavioural patterns in retirement considerably more than do denominational practices. Variations in activities by denomination appear when the retired clergy's activities within the church are examined.

All clergy, regardless of denomination, tended to be most active at the local level of the church. One activity common to all clergy was supply work; this involved preaching in various churches during the absence of the regular minister. Well over one-half, 65% (N = 104) reported that they still preached on a supply basis. Other activities included visitation to church members (particularly shut-ins), teaching (Sunday school or bible study), choir, attending or assisting in worship services. At the time of the survey, there were seven clergy maintaining a role in full-time ministry. There were those who desired a more structured role within the church. Many United Church clergy who desired this took on the role of Minister of Visitation. Still others were more inclined to be less committed and preferred to remain an inactive part of the congregation.

A smaller number, sixty three (39.4%) of the survey sample reported that they were active at regional levels of the church. United Church clergy were the most active at this level, by attending meetings of Presbytery (N = 36; 46.1% of the United Church sample). Presbytery is a group representing the various United Church congregations. Its work is to make sure that each pastoral charge has a minister and that both the minister and the congregation are doing the work of the church.[3] United Church clergy also reported being active in the Conference (N = 23; 29.5% of the United Church sample). The Conference serves as a supervisor to the Presbyteries, in this case the Atlantic Provinces. Conferences are responsible for overseeing all churches within its boundaries.[4] Only two of the respondents from this denominational group reported involvement in church activities at the national level.

Compared with United Church clergy, Anglican and Baptist ministers were not as active at the regional and national levels of their denominations. Only eight Baptist clergy (13.8% of the total Baptist sample) were active at the regional level. A smaller number of Anglican clergy (N = 3; 12.5% of the Anglican sample) were involved at the regional level of their denomination. Only one Baptist minister was actively involved with the denomination at a national level. Among Anglican clergy, no one was involved with the church at the national level. Thus, it seems that the organisational structure of the denominations influences which level of the church retired clergy continue to be most active in. In the United Church where the governing powers of the denomination are not placed within the autonomy of the local church, as is the case for the Baptists, but remain within a broader context, retired United Church clergy must remain active at the regional and national levels of the denomination if they wish to continue as part of the governing body of the church.

The activities of retired clergy have a sequential pattern. Those who had interests which were disrupted by the working years resumed these interests in retirement, rather than creating new ones. Those who were strongly dedicated to the church continued to remain active within it. Thus, looking at activity patterns from the continuity persepective reveals that clergy do maintain a continuity in activity patterns except when external factors, such as poor health, interfere.

Occupational subculture

Indeed, the occupation of clergy is unique. Upon retirement many of them still remain a part of the community in which they were once employed. It was anticipated that the clergy's occupational subculture would affect how they adjusted to retirement.

Well over half, 62% of all clergy, stated that their main reason for entering the pastoral ministry was because of a calling. For them the occupation of clergy was not a career which they had chosen for themselves, but one which they felt was chosen for them by God. The rest were motivated by a variety of reasons. Some expressed a desire to serve others and felt that being a minister was the most effective way to do so. Others were encouraged to enter the ministry by their family and friends. The influence of the church and other clergy was also mentioned as a reason for pursuing this specific occupation. It was clearly shown that clergy had a strong dedication to their occupation. Such a strong sense of commitment does not end at retirement. Retired ministers continue to remain part of the church community and serve the community in some capacity other than full-time ministry. It is therefore an expected phase in the life span of ministers.

Based on their strong sense of commitment to their profession, it was expected that clergy would retire much later than age sixty-five. However, the data did not bear this out. The average age of retirement for all clergy was 66 years. The Baptist clergy tended to remain in full-time service somewhat longer than did clergy of the other two denominations, with the average age of retirement being 67 years. The average age of retirement for Anglican clergy was 66 years. United Church clergy maintained an average retirement age of 65 years. Although the Anglican and United Church strictly enforced their mandatory retirement policies, all three denominations provided opportunities of service for retired clergy. Many took advantage of these opportunities to form the next phase of their careers as described above in the activity section. Clearly, the occupational subculture of clergy has the function of facilitating its members' transition to retirement.

The extent to which retired clergy remained active in the church was also influenced by their relationship with younger clergy. It was clear that positive attitudes and positive relationships between younger and older clergy benefited the young and the church community. Younger clergy profited from the experience and emotional support of retired clergy. They, in turn, provided retired clergy with the opportunity to continue using their occupational skills for the benefit of the church community.

A question regarding the role of retired clergy in ministering to older people in the church community was included in the questionnaire to gain some insight into the needs of elderly people in the church community and the role of retired clergy in meeting those needs. Overall, the data did not seem to show that retired clergy were working in roles, or felt they should develop roles, which helped to meet the needs of others their own age.

Psychological continuity

With regard to the psychological continuity of retired clergy, participants were asked to describe how they perceived themselves as responding to changes or crises which have occurred during their life-span. It has been suggested by Fox that examining an individual's perceptions of personality development in retrospect will assist in complementing a further understanding of continuity.[5] This was the approach taken to measure continuity of personality in this study. Respondents were asked how they felt they had responded to changes and crises which had occurred over their lifetime. Only 69% of the total sample answered this question. Almost all (80%) perceived them-selves as having accepted changes and coped quite effectively with crises in their lives. About one in five (18.8%) noted that they could not accept change easily. However, these individuals indicated that the most difficult changes to accept were the changing moral standards of society toward such things as marriage, abortion and moral conduct in general, as well as changing standards in the church, for example, the admittance of women for ordination.

Unfortunately the subjective measure of personality used in this study proved to be unsatisfactory. Although it did tap the participants' perceptions of their reactions to changes and crises, the question was too broad to provide a clear picture of continuity or discontinuity of personality. It would seem that the question employed in this study would be more effective in a longitudinal study. Possibly a more precise definition of personality and more specific questions could better direct the individual's thinking toward a clear perception of psychological continuity.

The information regarding personality provided by the clergy was useful. Close examination of the responses showed that no one indi-cated a difficulty in adjusting to the changes which were common with age (for example, retirement, lower income, loss of a spouse). This may indicate that the church, by accepting retired clergy and allowing them to continue working after retirement, is helping them to maintain a stability of self-concept. However, it was difficult to say with certainty that the individuals in this study had always responded in a similar way to change.

Conclusion

In conclusion, it has been shown that an effort was made to understand the transition of clergy into retirement by using the continuity perspec-tive. The findings revealed that clergy maintain continuity of lifestyle except when external factors such as poor health force them to alter their way of life. As well, the activity patterns of clergy lend support to the continuity perspective which states that after retirement individ-uals tend not to develop new interests and activities but to spend more time on those which already exist. It was also found that the attitudes, norms and policies of their occupational subculture help clergy to adjust successfully to retirement. Subjectively, clergy maintain a stability in the types of responses they have to changes and crisis situations. Together, the analysis of the four sets of variables has provided a comprehensive view of continuity of lifestyle for retired clergy. A significant number of areas remain to be researched. To provide further empirical support for the continuity perspective, the lifestyles of other occupational groups should be investigated for comparison. A comparative study of retired Catholic priests and Protestant clergy would provide a clearer understanding of clergy's adjustment to retirement.

Further research could include an enquiry into the role which a clergy's spouse plays, not only in retirement but also during the working years. Also it would be beneficial to examine more closely the clergy's level of activity in the church organisation before and after retirement. This could provide further explanation as to why some clergy are more active in the church than are others.

Finally, the continuity perspective itself merits closer scrutiny. With further development of its propositions and more empirical testing this approach has the potential to become a viable theoretical position in social gerontology.

Notes

1. R C Atchley, 'Retirement and leisure participation: continuity or crisis,' *The Gerontologist*, 11, 1971, pp. 13–19.
2. M Y T Chen and J L Goodwin, 'The continuity perspective of aging and retirement applied to Protestant clergy: an analysis of theory,' *Journal of Religious Gerontology*, 7, 3, pp. 55–67.
3. R Milton, *This United Church of Ours*, Winfield, BC, Wood Lake Press, 1981.
4. R Milton, *This United Church of Ours*, Winfield, BC, Wood Lake Press, 1981.
5. J H Fox, 'Perspectives on the continuity perspective,' *International Journal of Aging and Human Development*, 14, 2, 1981, pp. 97–115.

7. Leaving ministry

Understanding why some ministry candidates drop out of seminary or why some ordained clergy quit ministry is a matter of considerable practical and pastoral importance to the churches. This chapter presents two empirical studies which have addressed this question. One study focuses on seminary drop-outs, and the other study focuses on the decision to withdraw from or to continue in the active ministerial priesthood.

In the first article in this section, Howard W Stone explores the combined ability of scores on the Minnesota Multiphasic Personality Inventory and the Thelogical School Inventory to distinguish between seminarians who graduated to ministry and those who failed to complete the course. The data were provided by 552 students entering a mainline Protestant seminary programme between 1973 and 1986. Discriminant analysis using these scores was successful in correctly classifying 68% of the students as persisters or as leavers.

Professor Howard W Stone is Professor of Psychology and Pastoral Counselling at Brite Divinity School, Texas Christian University in Forth Worth, Texas, USA. This article was first published in *Journal of Psychology and Theology* in 1990.

In the second article, Mary Jeanne Verdieck, Joseph J Shields and Dean R Hoge report on two surveys conducted among American Catholic diocesan priests in 1970 and 1985. The 1970 analysis was based on 3,045 priests; the 1985 analysis was based on 729 priests. For both samples it was found that those most likely to report a higher probability of staying in the public ministry are older priests, those who have had religious experiences and those with high work satisfaction. Those most inclined to resign come from tense families, hold modern values, perceive loneliness as a problem and desire to marry.

At the time of writing, Dr Mary Jeanne Verdieck and Dr Joseph Shields were assistant professors in the School of Social Service at The Catholic University of America in Washington, DC, USA. Professor Dean R Hoge is Professor of Sociology at the same institution. This article was first published in *Journal for the Scientific Study of Religion* in 1988.

7.1 Seminary drop-outs: a study of predictability

Howard W Stone

Most of us who are ministers can remember the doubts we entertained in our anxious seminary years. Those doubts were not necessarily about the existence of God; more often, they had to do with whether or not we were meant to become pastors. It is such questions that the present study addresses. It attempts to understand what leads some people to drop out of seminary while others remain and become ministers.

A number of studies have tried to discriminate between persisters (those who remain in seminary and graduate) and leavers (those who drop out). The subject of persistence in ministry was of special import during the 1970s, and a majority of the existing research was performed during those years. More research took place at Roman Catholic institutions than at Protestant schools. In shaping a new study on persistence, a review of that literature is required. First Catholic and then Protestant studies will be considered.

Roman Catholic studies

Roman Catholic men training for the priesthood (60 persisters and 60 leavers) made up a study by Lee (1968). He considered 59 attitudinal responses regarding the individuals' understanding and relationship to God, 16 demographic variables, and 42 test scale scores from personality, appitude, interest, and achievement measures. He found persisters to be more submissive, and to have higher musical and social interests and lower literary and scientific interests than did levers. A regression analysis suggested that eight items predicted presisters: submissiveness; social, literary, musical and scientific interests; mechanical reasoning; intelligence; and self-esteem.

Several Catholic studies found no difference between those who graduated from seminary and those who did not. Crumbaugh, Raphael and Shrader (1970) used the Purpose-in-Life Test and discovered no difference between Dominican sisters who left or remained in the programme. Weisgerber (1962) used the major Minnesota Multiphasic Personality Inventory (MMPI) clinical and control scales in a study of seminarians and found no significant differences. In a later study Weisgerber (1966) used the Allport-Vernon-Lindzey Study of Values and again found no significant differences between Roman Catholic seminarians who stayed in school and those who dropped out. One research project that demonstrated some differences was by Murray and Connolly (1966). They discovered that persisters had lower MMPI schizophrenia (Sc) and mania (Ma) scale scores than did leavers.

Scordato (1976) studied 251 Roman Catholic seminary students, all graduates of a preparatory seminary in New York state. The Sixteen Personality Factor Questionnaire (16PF), the basic interest scales of the Strong Vocational Interest Blank (SBIB), and a biographical questionnaire were administered. Fourteen of the scales of the SVIB and 12 of the 16PF scales discriminated persisters from leavers. In addition, several of the biographic questions also distinguished the two groups. Persisters tended to be firstborn sons from middle-income families of immigrant or first generation Americans. Persisters more often experienced considerable influence to enter the ministry by a priest. Persisters were more conservative, outgoing, shrewd and venturesome. They were also more imaginative, tender-minded, conscientious, and stable.

Trachsel (1973) used the MMPI and the Behavioral Services data forms to differentiate persisters and leavers. The subjects were 80 Roman Catholic seminarians (40 who stayed and 40 who left). Analyses of Variance (ANOVAs) were performed on the thirteen main scales of the MMPI, and only the schizophrenic (Sc) scale was statistically significant. A discriminant analysis using the psychopathic (Pd), mania (Ma) and schizophrenic (Sc) scales of the MMPI showed a significant differentiation between persisters and leavers. There were 57 biographic variables, but only two showed any significant differences between the two groups. A study by Ogg (1975) of 203 Catholic seminarians at St Thomas Seminary used the MMPI, the SVIB, and a biographical questionnaire to differentiate those staying in seminary from those who left. Discriminant analyses were performed and realised two results: first, several MMPI scales combined to differentiate persisters and leavers; and secondly, a combination of the basic interest and occupational scales of the SVIB also differentiated the two groups.

Houck and Dawson (1978) studied 152 Roman Catholic seminarians, 54 leavers and 98 persisters. ANOVAs were performed on their responses to the Rorschach. Houck and Dawson's results implied that both groups showed considerable anxiety, differing only in the type of anxiety. Persisters had anxiety related to a lack of emotional fulfilment in their need for affection and interpersonal relationships. Leavers, on the other hand, had high anxiety related to aggression or destructive impulses. Their anxiety appeared to be more internally detrimental. There were no differences between persisters and leavers on the adjustment indicators, suggesting to the authors that neither group was better adjusted than the other.

Protestant studies

A study of 82 graduates and 85 nongraduates at a Protestant seminary by Ashbrook and Powell (1967) used the major scales of the MMPI to try to uncover significant differences. Chi-squares were used to test for significance. Their results were not able to support their hypothesis that MMPI scale scores could differentiate graduates from drop-outs. The authors suggested that both persisters and leavers presented a heterogeneous pattern of behaviour.

A number of the Protestant studies have used the Theological School Inventory (TSI). It consists of 12 scales which measure categories or components of motivation for ministry: acceptance by others (A), intellectual concern for theological issues (I), a drive for self-fulfilment (F), past leadership success (L), evangelistic witness (E), society-wide social reform (R), and individual service to persons (P). Three scales measure the strength of motivation for ministry: natural leading (NL), special leading (SL), and concept of call (CC). Two final scales measure the definiteness (D) and flexibility of call (FL).

Munger (1975) studied 150 students at Fuller Theological Seminary, half persisters and half leavers, using the TSI, the MMPI, and a demographic questionnaire. The MMPI scales did not discriminate between those who graduated and those who did not. The TSI, however, had quite the opposite results: 7 of the 12 scales differentiated persisters and leavers. Those who dropped out of seminary had lower evangelistic witness (E), definiteness (D), natural leading (NL), special leading (SL), and concept of the call (CC) scores. In addition, they had higher acceptance by others (A) and leadership success (L) scores.

Cardwell and Hunt (1979) performed follow-up research on 672 seminarians who took the TSI in 1962 and 574 students who took the TSI in 1973. Several of the items in the TSI correlated with persistence in seminary: definiteness of call, spouse's family and other's support for entrance in ministry, good health, being a younger member of a family (third, fourth, or fifth child), interest in parish ministry, positive role modelling of the father and ministers in the student's life, and a clear understanding of what a 'call' means. Cardwell (1974) also reported a 1970 study at Christian Theological Seminary using the TSI. In it she related that leavers had higher intellectual concern (I) and social reform (R), and lower evangelistic witness (E), acceptance by others (A), and leadership success (L) scores. Leavers were less definite (D) about entering ministry and had lower natural leading (NL) and flexibility (FL) scores. It appears from her research that only the L and R scales differed at a level of statistical significance.

It can be seen from the above studies that factors in persistence in seminary are not easy to isolate. A number of studies demonstrated little or no significant differences between the two groups. Studies utilising the TSI had results varying from one seminary to another. Only two scales, definiteness (D) and natural leading (NL), discriminated the persisters and leavers in all of the seminaries studied. Those not finishing their seminary training had lower scores on both of these scales. In other studies, hundreds of variables were required for significance to be elicited – raising a concern over the possibility of false positives.

Most of the researchers in these previous studies considered only individual scales of the instruments being used. Take, for example, the MMPI. Clinically, instead of looking at one scale separately from the others, the most accurate interpretation of the profile generally comes from examining the overall pattern of the scales. The proper use of the MMPI is to consider the total profile, as several of the Catholic studies demonstrated. The scales must be considered as part of the whole and not as separate items. Stone (1989b), for example, has demonstrated the ability to predict ministerial effectiveness when MMPI scales are employed together in a discriminant analysis. Ministerial effectiveness could not be predicted when the scales were considered separately.

After a review of the literature, and working within the limitations of the archival data available for study, two hypotheses were developed to guide the research. First, MMPI elevation will significantly distinguish graduates from nongraduates. Specifically, it is predicted that significantly more persons scoring highly on the MMPI than scoring low will fail to graduate from the seminary. Second, the best prediction of persistence will be obtained by combining both an elevated MMPI with scale scores and biographic items from the TSI.

Method

Subjects

The study included 552 MDiv students entering a mainline Protestant seminary programme in the years 1973 through 1986: 425 of the students were male and 127 female. The average age of the students was 27.9 years.

Materials

MMPI: The Minnesota Multiphasic Personality Inventory, probably the most frequently used psychological inventory of personality, contains 556 items. Although numerous scales can be applied to the MMPI, the most important include three validity and ten clinical scales. The control or validity scales are used to determine the attitude of the person taking the test and to discern if there have been any attempts to distort the clinical results by faking good, faking bad, or following a stylised response set. The ten clinical scales were produced to diagnose individuals in ten separate areas of psychopathology.

TSI: The Theological School Inventory (TSI) is a self-report inventory designed to evaluate seminarians' decisions for the ministry. The first section of the instrument asks 55 demographic questions about an individual's family, religious, and church background. The second section consists of twelve scales and measures students' motivations for ministry, their certainty or definiteness about it, and the strength of their natural and supernatural inclination toward ministry.

Cumulative MMPI score: An MMPI score was derived for each subject by creating a composite factor from the subject's scores on the H3 + .5K, D, Hy, Pd + .4K, Pa, Pt + 1K, and Sc. The score was calculated by summing the subject's K-corrected scores on each scale and dividing by the number of scales. (Note: A standard score is calculated by subtracting the mean of a variable from a subject's score and dividing by the standard deviation. This results in a distribution of scores with a mean of zero and a standard deviation of one.) This procedure is similar to creating a factor score, although each scale is assumed to have equal loadings (correlations) on the component factor. Such procedures avoid the problems associated with traditional principle component scores (see Dillon and Goldstein, 1984).

The selection of these scales to form the MMPI score was based upon earlier research by Stone (1989a). In applying principle components analysis it was determined that the above scales form a single cumulative score, defined as measuring 'the degree of psychopathology in students'.

Procedure

Each year entering students completed the MMPI, TSI, Concept Mastery, IQ, and reading tests. All scores were recorded and placed in a permanent file. All analyses were conducted based upon information retrieved from this file.

Results

In the initial analysis of this study, its investigator tried to determine if the MMPI score could distinguish between persisters and leavers. Students were first categorised into three groups: elevated MMPI, moderate MMPI, and low MMPI. The elevated MMPI group consisted of individuals whose score on the MMPI was at least one standard deviation above the mean (< 0.70). The moderate MMPI group had scores that were within one standard deiviation of the mean (-0.70 to 0.70), while the low MMPI group included students whose MMPI scores were one standard deviation below the mean (< -0.70). The selection of one standard deviation to determine the high and low scores on the MMPI was arbitrary because normative data on this cumulative score is lacking. The use of one standard deviation split, however, allowed for a clearer distinction of the high MMPI and low MMPI groups than would have been afforded by a median split.

The chi-square test of independence was used to determine the extent to which persisters and leavers could be predicted from their scores on the MMPI. Graduate/non-graduate served as one variable, and the low, moderate and elevated MMPI groups furnished the second variable. The results suggest that significantly fewer students in the low MMPI group (26%) and the moderate MMPI group (29%) failed to graduate, as compared with the students in the elevated MMPI group (47%), $\chi^2 (2, N = 552) = 10.74, p < 0.01$. Chi-square rather than a traditional analysis of variance (ANOVA) was the preferred method for testing the relationship between the MMPI factor and persisters and leavers. An ANOVA procedure would have tested the hypothesis that there exists a relationship between the MMPI score and persistence, but the goal of the present analysis was to determine the strength of this relationship. The chi-square test allowed the researcher to demonstrate the strength of this relationship by indicating the number of persisters and leavers who fit into the high and low groups based on the MMPI score (an ANOVA is conducted later in this section).

Discriminant analysis was employed in the second analysis. Since this procedure provides a way to statistically distinguish between two or more groups, it is a helpful technique in developing a picture of those who stay in seminary and those who leave. To differentiate between groups, the researcher selects a series of descriptive variables that measure characteristics on which the two groups are expected to differ. Mathematically, the purpose of discriminant analysis is to weigh and combine these descriptive variables in a linear equation such that the two groups are differentiated as much as possible. Discriminant analysis does not require that there be a statistically significant difference between the groups for any one variable. Rather, it is based upon how the variables combine to optimally distinguish the two groups. In the present case seminary graduates and seminary drop-outs made up the two groups to be discriminated.

Scores from entrance tests (MMPI and TSI) and several biographical items provided the descriptive variables. The first task was to distinguish which variables other than the MMPI score would be helpful in predicting persistence. The selection of variables in the present study used to predict persistence was based upon previous research, discussed earlier. Earlier research reported that the TSI was a useful instrument for measuring persistence (Cardwell, 1974; Cardwell and Hunt, 1979; Munger, 1975). The twelve scales of the TSI were included. In addition, several biographic items from section one of the TSI were used: the student's self-reported emotional stability, the quality of interpersonal relationships, physical health, and the marital status of the students' parents. The final variable to be included in the discriminant analysis was the student's MMPI score.

The results of the analysis employing these variables demonstrated that the MMPI score and six of the TSI scales – definiteness (D), flexibility (FL), special leading (SL), intellectual concern (I), leadership success (L), and natural leading (NL) – significantly added to the discriminant function. The resulting discriminant function correctly classified 68% of the students.

The data were further analysed through a series of one-way analyses of variance (ANOVAs) in which each of the variables included in the discriminant analysis (see table one) served as the dependent variable, and persistence served as the independent variable. Three ANOVAs yielded significance. The ANOVA for the MMPI score demonstrated that graduates scored significantly lower on the MMPI score ($M=0.106$) than did nongraduates ($M=0.242$), $F(1,550) = 24.23$, $p<0.001$. The ANOVA for the TSI Definiteness (D) scales showed that graduates scored significantly higher on the TSI-D scale ($M=55.05$) than did nongraduates ($M=52.2$), $F(1,550) = 13.20$, $p<0.001$. Finally, the ANOVA for the TIS flexibility (FL) scale demonstrated that the graduates scored significantly higher on the TSI-FL scale ($M=52.60$) than did the nongraduates ($M=50.08$), $F(1,550) = 10.48$, $p<.01$. No other variables showed significance. Only three variables were significant in predicting persistence when considered separately.

The high loadings ($r>0.40$) suggest that only the MMPI score, TSI-D scale, and TSI-FL scale correlated highly with the discriminant function. Furthermore, it indicates that the other variables in the discriminant function, although statistically significant, do not add to its predictive strength. The overall ability of the discriminant function to predict persisters and leavers is presented in table two. The discriminant function correctly classified 66% of the persisters and 71% of the leavers.

Discussion

It would be particularly useful for seminary advisement and for the church as a whole to be able to forsee, from entrance test scores, which individuals are likely to graduate and which are likely to drop out from ministerial training. The primary interest of the present study was, therefore to determine how well one could predict if a student would finish seminary, based on test scores recorded at entrance to school.

Although it is dangerous to generalise to all institutions from a study of persistence at one school, it is believed that the results suggest what is happening at other mainline Protestant seminaries. Even though these results must be treated tentatively, they can bear on the way we recruit for ministry, teach in seminaries, and offer pastoral care and counselling to those studying for church vocations.

In the first analysis the students were broken into three groups: low, moderate, and elevated MMPI score. The results demonstrated that almost one out of two students with an elevated MMPI score dropped out of seminary (47%), whereas seminarians with a low or moderate MMPI score left school only at a rate of 26% and 29% respectively. Elevated MMPI scores strongly predict drop-outs from seminary.

The purpose of the second procedure, discriminant analysis, was to consider if scale scores or a series of items from the biographic section of the TSI, along with the elevated MMPI score, could distinguish the two groups at a level of significance. The results are statistically significant, though they do not distinguish persisters from leavers to the

Table 1: Discriminant function loadings for predicting persistence

variables	discriminant loadings
MMPI score	0.59
TSI-D	−0.43
TSI-FL	−0.41
TSI-L	−0.23
TSI-I	0.13
TSI-SL	0.12
TSI-NL	−0.01

Note: Wilk's lambda = 0.863, $p < 0.001$
　　chi-square ($df = 8$) = 64.523, $p < 0.001$

Table 2: Classification matrix of persisters and leavers based upon the resulting discriminant function

	actual group	
	persisters	leavers
predicted group		
persisters	252 (66%)	127 (34%)
leavers	50 (29%)	123 (71%)

Note: correctly classified: 375 (67.8%)

degree needed for advisement purposes. A correct classification of 68% of students into one of the two groups was achieved.

More studies of persistence have been done at Roman Catholic seminaries than at their Protestant counterparts. Although some studies were not able to differentiate persisters from leavers using the MMPI, the work of Ogg (1975) and Trachsel (1973) reported discriminations with the MMPI. It is the author's belief that there are some important differences between the Catholic and Protestant populations of those studying for ministry (Weisgerber, 1971). As a result, direct comparisions between the two traditions have to be made with caution.

Though more is certainly needed, noteworthy research has been done on persistence of Catholic students in seminary. The same area of study among Protestant students is as yet wide open. Little has been accomplished and many questions remain to be answered. Earlier Protestant research on persistence using the MMPI has not been successful. Ashbrook and Powell (1967) and Munger (1975) did not discover differences using comparisons of individual MMPI scales. Several researchers, though, have been able to show differences in Protestant students using the TSI (Cardwell, 1974; Cardwell and Hunt, 1979; Munger, 1975). A difference in the present study from previous Protestant work was that *both* the MMPI and TSI proved useful for differentiating graduates from nongraduates.

One of the major advantages of the present research, compared with most previous Protestant studies, is that it looked at a combination of variables rather than examining them individually. The genius of discriminant analysis over and against a series of ANOVAs is that it considers how the disparate variables combine to influence each other, thus increasing the possibility of predicting future persistence. In most previous research, the MMPI has not been able to discriminate persisters and leavers. Although these studies were performed on different sets of data, it is very possible that the reason they failed was that they considered the scales individually rather than as a whole. The present study suggests that the MMPI is able to differentiate seminary graduates from nongraduates. This study and earlier research (Stone, 1989) demonstrates that MMPI scales must be considered together. The subject's profile is what is significant, not individual scales. In addition, the results suggest that this cumulative MMPI score used in conjunction with items from the TSI provide the best predictor of persistence.

A second difficulty with previous research has been its reliance upon univariate statistics, primarily chi-square, *t*-test, and ANOVAs, when analysing data. These procedures are eminently useful, but lack the power and sophistication required to investigate complex phenomena such as persistence in seminary. Complex phenomena require more elegant research methods. A weakness of the earlier studies was that they concluded, before exhausting their analytical options, that a relationship between test data and persistence did not exist. It is possible that significant differences between persisters and leavers do exist in the data of these previous studies and that alternate statistical procedures are needed to ferret them out.

The results of the present study are statistically significant but presently are not very useful for making seminary admissions decisions. More research is required to refine analytic methods of discrimination before such procedures can inform seminary entrance decisions. The present study is one step in that direction. In addition, greater theological reflection will have to be given to the practice of using psychological tests to determine a person's suitability in the ordained ministry. Indeed, additional research is necessary for clearer distinctions to be confirmed between persisters and leavers. Future study, it seems to this author, should take the following directions. First, the Readiness for Ministry work has pointed out the importance of interpersonal skills for ministerial practice (Schuller, Brekke and Strommen, 1976). Ministry work is interpersonal by its nature. It is believed that students who begin to recognise this fact but experience a lack of such skills are more likely to drop out. Few seminaries have developed ways to measure how people relate interpersonally. Tests and other measures of interpersonal function may be as important to persistence in seminary as the TSI and MMPI for student guidance. Studies of the interpersonal skills of persisters and leavers are required.

Intervening variables are another area demanding enquiry. The impact of marriage or divorce, financial difficulties, death of parents, or birth of children may significantly influence how well individuals persist in seminary. Such intervening variables may determine whether students remain hopeful and engaged in school or become disenchanted and pull away from seminary contacts and ultimately from the school itself.

The 'fit' between seminarian and institution is another subject that has not been adequately reviewed. Some of those preparing for ministry may feel a loss of call, not because they do not belong in ordained ministry but because they did not make a good match with the school. This is especially evident when it comes to theological position. Theological liberals in a conservative seminary or, conversely, theological conservatives in a liberal seminary will experience considerable dissonance with those around them, both students and faculty. Such individuals may be more likely to move on to another school or cease their preparation for ministry.

Finally, the use of more elegant investigation procedures will be essential if clear distinctions are going to be drawn concerning persistence. Archival research like the present study is useful in a preliminary way, since it points out directions to be followed by future studies, yet it is limited by the variables that are at hand. There are always other bits of data that the archival researcher recognises would make the study stronger. Longitudinal research with variables chosen ahead of time by the investigator will have to be accomplished if persistence research is to become more accurate in its predictions. In addition, discriminant analysis and other multivariate statistical analyses will have to replace research using only t-tests and ANOVAs.

In the present research, the MMPI and especially the paranoia (PA), schizophrenic (Sc), psychasthenia (Pt), psychopathic (Pd), hysteria (Hy), Hypochondriasis (Hs), and depression (D) scales considered as one cumulative score along with the TSI definiteness (D) and flexibility (FL) scales proved to be the best predictors of persistence. It demonstrated that persistence in seminary is not primarily an element of demographics or biographic items; rather, it is especially one of personality characteristics. Even the definiteness (D) and the flexibility (FL) scales of the TSI do not describe a specific motivation to ministry but suggest how ministerial students feel about their decision to enter ministry. Hunt, Cardwell and Dittes (1976) put it this way: 'These scales refer more to how the respondent feels about structure, ambiguity, and decisions in general (FL) and about the more specific decision concerning the ministry as a career (D)' (p. 58).

Seminarians with elevated MMPI profiles and less flexibility and definiteness about their call to ministry certainly need to be tracked. They are a population at great risk of dropping out of school. Such students require extra attention on the part of seminary personnel. They need assistance in their exploration of the career of ministry. In addition, it is surmised that students with such scores will have more difficulty fitting into their particular school and will require extra measures to help them feel 'at home'.

In the end, however, no seminary wishes to retain students who lack the gifts or the vocation to become ordained pastors. With the help of findings from the present study and future research like it, those who are merely unsettled or anxious can be supported in their commitment to finish seminary, while those who are certain to find themselves unsuited for full-time ministry can be guided from the start toward more fitting occupations in which to answer God's call to faithful service.[1]

Note

1. This research project was made possible in part by grants from Lilly Endowment Inc., and the Research Fund, Brite Divinity School, Texas Christian University. The Statistical Consultant for this project was Rick Clubb.

References

Ashbrook, J B and Powell, R K (1967) 'Comparison of graduating and non-graduating theological students on the Minnesota Multiphasic Personality Inventory,' *Journal of Counseling Psychology*, 14, pp. 171–179.

Cardwell, S W (1974) 'The Theological School Inventory: after ten years,' *The Journal of Pastoral Care*, 28, pp. 267–279.

Cardwell, S W and Hunt, R A (1979) 'Persistence in seminary and in ministry,' *Pastoral Psychology*, 28, pp. 119–131.

Crumbaugh, J R, Raphael, M and Shrader, R R (1970) 'Frankl's will to meaning in a religious order,' *Journal of Clinical Psychology*, 26, pp. 206–207.

Dillon, W R and Goldstein, M (1984) *Multivariate Analysis*, New York, Wiley.

Houck, R L and Dawson, J G (1978) 'Comparative study of persisters and leavers in seminary training,' *Psychology Reports*, 42, pp. 1131–1137.

Hunt, R A, Cardwell, S W and Dittes, J E (1976) *Theological School Inventory Manual*, Dallas, Texas, Ministry Studies Board.

Lee, J L (1968) An exploratory search for characteristic patterns and clusters of seminary persisters and leavers, unpublished doctoral dissertation, University of Michigan.

Munger, E (1975) Personality, motivation and experience in their effect on persistence in a theological seminary, unpublished doctoral dissertation, Fuller Theological Seminary.

Murray, J B and Connolly, F (1966) 'Follow-up of personality scores of seminarians: seven years later,' *Catholic Psychological Record*, 4, pp. 10–19.

Ogg, T G (1975) A descriptive study of student persisters and nonpersisters at St Thomas Seminary from 1969 to 1973, unpublished doctoral dissertation, University of Wyoming.

Schuller, D S, Brekke, M L and Strommen, M P (1976), *Readiness for Ministry: assessment volume 2*, Vandalia, Ohio, Association of Theological Schools.

Scordato, A J (1976) A comparison of interest, personality and biographical characteristics of seminary persisters and nonpersisters from St Pius X Preparatory Seminary, unpublished doctoral dissertation, University of Wyoming.

Stone, H W (1989a) 'Female and male called to ministry,' *Journal of Pastoral Psychotherapy*, 2, pp. 27–43.

Stone, H W (1989b) 'Predicting ministerial effectiveness,' *Pastoral Sciences*, 8, pp. 81–97.

Trachsel, M D (1973) Survival and attrition among seminarians, unpublished doctoral dissertation, Marquette University.

Weisgerber, C A (1962) 'Survey of psychological screening program in a clerical order,' in M B Arnold, P Hispanicus, C A Weisgerber and P R D'Arcy (eds) *Screening Candidates for the Priesthood and Religious Life*, Chicago, Loyola University Press, pp. 107–148.

Weisgerber, C A (1966) 'The study of values in screening for a religious order,' *Journal of Religion and Health*, 5, pp. 233–238.

Weisgerber, C A (1971) 'The TSI and some Roman Catholic and Protestant differences,' *Counseling and Values*, 16, pp. 54–65.

7.2 Role commitment processes revisited: American Catholic priests 1970 and 1985

Mary Jeanne Verdieck, Joseph J Shields and Dean R Hoge

In the twenty-two years since the closing of the Second Vatican Council, the American Catholic Church has witnessed a great deal of religious and social change. Researchers and church commentators have documented shifts in religious practice and beliefs among lay Catholics. The introduction of democratic or quasidemocratic structures such as parish councils and priests' senates has had an impact on the structural configuration of the church at the parish as well as the diocesan level. Vocational recruitment to religious life and priesthood has declined significantly, and resignations from the active priesthood persist (Hoge, Potvin and Ferry, 1984; Neal, 1984; Schoenherr and Sorensen, 1982; Shields and Verdieck, 1985).

Given the hierarchical structure of the church and the importance of the role which priests occupy in this structure, the issue of declining priesthood vocations and continuing priest resignations is viewed by many as one of the more serious problems facing the church today. In 1970 the large number of priest resignations prompted research on the reasons why many priests were suffering morale problems. In 1985 the question of ministerial commitment was again being urgently asked because of its importance for recruiting new seminarians.

Between 1970 and 1985 the number of priests in the United States declined from 59,192 to 57,317, an overall loss of 3.2% (Kenedy, 1970 to 1985). However, these figures are somewhat misleading since they do not take into consideration the age structure of the population. In 1970 approximately 7% of the diocesan priests and 8% of religious priests were 66 years of age or older compared with 16% and 28% in 1985 (Hoge, Shields and Verdieck, 1986). The number of resignations has had an impact on the structure of the priests' population. In the two decades prior to the Second Vatican Council the number of priest resignations was quite small, amounting to approximately one-tenth of one percent per year (Fichter, 1968; Schoenherr and Greeley, 1974). Since the closing of the council the number has increased dramatically. It is estimated that approximately 12.5% to 13.5% of all diocesan priests active in 1970 resigned in the following ten years (Schoenherr and Sorensen, 1982) and that approximately 15% to 17% of all religious priests active in 1970 had resigned by 1980 (Shields and Verdieck, 1985). Most priests who resigned were under 45 years of age.

Most past research in the area of priesthood resignations has tended to focus on personality and psychological factors and has been based on data collected from relatively small and/or non-representative samples. An exception to this trend is the research conducted by Schoenherr and Greeley (1974). Because the present research is a partial replication of Schoenherr and Greeley's work, we summarise their study.

Schoenherr and Greeley examined commitment to the priesthood role from a social exchange perspective. They argue that 'role commitment is a process which links a person to a position in a social system to the extent that the position provides him a favourable net balance of rewards over costs' (Schoenherr and Greeley, 1974, p. 407). Thus, a priest will be more likely to continue in the role if the perceived rewards are greater than the perceived costs. In order to test this proposition the authors analysed data collected in 1970 from a national representative sample of American Catholic priests (NORC, 1972). The major dependent variable in their study was 'decision to continue' and they attempted to explain the variation in this by means of an eight-variable path model. The variables included in the model were age, family tension, inner directedness, religious experience, modern values, work satisfaction, loneliness and desire to marry. The authors report that decision to continue is influenced most directly by desire to marry, loneliness, work satisfaction and modern values. The authors further report that much of the impact of the earlier variables in the model is channelled through desire to marry, indicating that the cost of foregoing marriage was a major consideration affecting decision to continue in the priestly role. Overall, the eight-variable model was able to explain 50% of the variance in decision to continue.

In order to understand role commitment processes further, the authors examined the model in the context of variables measuring societal and regional influences as well as organisation and group influences. With the exception of one factor, the effects of contextual factors were non-significant. The authors conclude that higher level influences such as regional environment, organisational context and group climate are too remote and too dispersed to affect strongly a priest's personal decision to continue in ministry. The sole exception was that the variable 'average decision to continue' had an impact indicating that priests who resided in a diocese which had a high average 'decision to continue' score were more likely to report that they would probably continue in the formal priesthood.

Schoenherr and Greeley conclude that the commitment model based on the social exchange theoretical perspective was very effective for explaining their data. Celibacy was viewed as the major 'cost' and work satisfaction as the major 'reward'. When desire to marry outweighs the rewards of ministry the probability of continuing in the ministry is minimised.

Changes since 1970

The data on which Schoenherr and Greeley based their analysis were collected in 1970. In interpreting these data it is important to keep in mind the religious and social atmosphere of 1970. It was five years after the closing of the council; the initial exuberance generated by the council was beginning to wane. Issues of sexuality and authority were openly being debated in the Catholic and secular press. Newspapers were filled with accounts of priest resignations, former priests, and priests who wanted to get married. In his discussion and reflection on the future of the priesthood Greeley (1970) referred to 1969 as 'the year of the priest' because of the tremendous amount of press coverage given to the priesthood and the problems of priests. Data on priest resignations indicate that the years 1969 through 1971 represent the highpoint (Hoge, Shields and Verdieck, 1986; Shields and Verdieck, 1985).

Data on priests collected in 1985 inidcate that certain shifts have occurred. Priests in 1985 as compared with their counterparts in 1970 report higher levels of morale and work satisfaction and are less likely to report authority and relationships with pastors and superiors as being major problems. Celibacy is still regarded as a major frustration; however, fewer men report that they probably or certainly would get married if celibacy were optional (Hoge, Shields and Verdieck, 1986).

In order to see whether or not the role commitment model developed in 1970 is still relevant in the mid 1980s, we will replicate in a partial manner the model developed by Schoenherr and Greeley (1974).

Data and methods

The 1970 data were collected by the National Opinion Research Center at the request of the National Conference of Catholic Bishops (NORC, 1972). The researchers used a stratified two-stage cluster sample with probabilities proportional to size. In the first-stage sample, 85 of the 155 American dioceses and 91 of the 252 self-governing units of religious institutes were selected. In the second-stage sample 7,260 of the approximately 64,000 American priests were selected, 5,155 of whom returned usable questionnaires, yielding a response rate of 71%. The analysis on which the role commitment model was developed was based on the responses of the 3,045 diocesan priests.

The data for the 1985 analysis were collected during the spring and summer of 1985. The study was designed to be a partial replication of the 1970 study, involving a smaller sample and shorter questionnaire. From the dioceses and religious institutes contained in the first-stage of the 1970 survey approximately one-third were randomly sampled. From the lists of priests they supplied, 12.5% were selected randomly, resulting in a total of 1,244. Of these, 1,062 returned usable question-naires resulting in a response rate of 87%. As in the 1970 survey, the analysis of the role commitment model will be based on the responses of the diocesan priests (N = 729).

The model developed by Schoenherr and Greeley (1974) included nine key variables: age, family tension, inner-directedness, religious experience, modern values, work satisfaction, loneliness, desire to marry, and decision to continue in the ministry. All of these measures, with the exception of inner-directedness, are contained in the 1985 analysis. In the 1970 study inner-directedness was operationalised by means of the Personal Orientation Inventory (POI), a 150-item person-ality test developed by Shostrom (1966). One-fifth of the respondents in the 1970 study received the Personal Orientation Inventory. Because of the length of the POI and the cost of analysing the results, a deci-sion was made to omit this variable from the 1985 study. Thus, in order to maintain comparability the 1970 data were reanalysed with the inner-directedness measure excluded. The Appendix contains the means, standard deviations and case bases of all measures used in the 1970 and 1985 surveys. Actual items are contained in NORC (1972, pp. 333–45). Brief definitions of the measures, with the exception of age, are contained in the Appendix.

In analysing the 1970 data Schoenherr and Greeley used multiple regression and path analysis methods. They established the rule of thumb criteria of $r > 0.20$ for examining the interrelationships of the many variables and of beta > 0.10 for retaining paths in the path models. The final path model represented an over-identified linear recursive system in which the regression equations were recomputed after eliminating those terms in which the beta weights were < 0.10. In analysing the 1985 data identical procedures are used.

The findings

Table one presents the zero-order correlations for all of the variables in the models for 1970 and 1985. For both samples it is found that those most likely to report a higher probability of staying in the public ministry are older priests, those who have had religious experiences and those with high work satisfaction. The negative coefficients show that those most inclined to resign come from tense families, hold modern values, perceive loneliness as a problem and desire to marry. When the coefficients for both samples are compared for statistical significance, utilising the Fisher log transformation technique (Hinkle, Wiersma and Jurs, 1979), it is found that only coefficients for modern values and desire to marry with decision to continue are significantly different at $p < .05$. In 1970 modern values and desire to marry are more strongly correlated with decision to continue than they are in 1985.

Table 1: Correlation matrix of selected characteristics of American diocesan priests: 1970 and 1985 (1985 above the diagonal; 1970 below the diagonal)[1]

variable	age	family tension	religious experience	modern values	work satisfaction	loneliness	desire to marry	decision to continue
age	–	–0.15	0.10	–0.55	0.08	–0.37	–0.37	0.43
family tension	–0.16	–	–0.13	0.18	–0.08	0.14	0.10	–0.14
religious experience	0.10	–0.20	–	–0.15	0.31	–0.23	–0.12	0.19
modern values	–0.64	0.22	–0.14	–	–0.02[2]	0.37	0.38	–0.42
work satisfaction	0.07	–0.13	0.19	–0.10	–	0.28	–0.11	0.24
loneliness	–0.34	0.21	–0.22	0.37	–0.30	–	0.44	–0.43
desire to marry	–0.48	0.16	–0.17	0.48	–0.19	0.50	––	–0.47
decision to continue	0.45	–0.20	0.22	–0.50	0.29	–0.47	–0.64	–

Note: 1 Pearson r; the number of cases is given in table A.1.
2 Not significant at .05 level.

Table 2: Explanation of variance on the decision to continue in the ministry: 1970 and 1985

variable	1970		1985	
	R^2	R^2 change	R^2	R^2 change
age	0.20	0.20	0.18	0.18
family tension	0.22	0.02	0.19	0.01
religious experience	0.24	0.02	0.21	0.02
modern values	0.30	0.06	0.25	0.04
work satisfaction	0.35	0.05	0.28	0.03
loneliness	0.39	0.04	0.32	0.04
desire to marry	0.50	0.11	0.37	0.05

Note: The mutiple R^2 corresponding to each variable is derived from the regression equation estimating the effects on the decision to continue of that variable and all others antecedent to it (above it in the table). The value reported for age is thus the r^2. Any apparent errors in subtraction are due to rounding.

Table two, a summary table, contains the estimates of the explained variance each antecedent variable contributes to decision to continue for 1970 and 1985. It should be noted that the independent variable, decision to continue in the priesthood, is skewed. In 1970, 13% were inclined to resign or were uncertain, and in 1985, this had dropped to 8%. The skew is worse in 1985, which weakens the entire model. Also, the desire to marry variable is slightly more skewed in 1985 than in 1970; in 1970 22% said they would probably or certainly like to get married if priests were allowed to, and in 1985 18% said this. (The 4-point reduction is mostly traceable to the youngest priests; in 1970 37% of those 26 to 35 wanted to get married, but in 1985 it was only 25%). In 1970 age accounts for 20% of the variance, with family tension adding 2%, religious experience 2%, modern values 6%, work satisfaction 5%, loneliness 4%, and desire to marry 11%. In 1985 age accounts for 18%, with family tension adding 1%, religious experience 2%, modern values 4%, work satisfaction 3%, loneliness 4%, and desire to marry 5%. Overall, in 1970 the model explains 50% and in 1985 37% of the variance in decision to continue. The major difference between the two samples is the contribution of desire to marry.

In order to understand how the variables' interrelationships explain the commitment process we turn to the path diagrams contained in figure one and figure 2.

Figure one contains the path diagram relating decision to continue in the ministry to prior variables for the 1970 sample, and figure two contains the diagram for the 1985 sample. The diagrams include only betas equal to or greater than 0.10. The corresponding B's for each reported beta are contained in table A.2 in the Appendix.

For both the 1970 and 1985 samples, age and family tension are negatively correlated. The younger men are slightly more likely to report experiencing tense family relationships.

The negative impact of family tension on religious experience is unaffected by age for both samples. Those who come from tense families are somewhat less likely to have felt personal contact with God. This negative effect is slightly stronger in the 1970 sample (−0.20) as compared with the 1985 sample (−0.13).

In the 1970 sample 42% of the variance in modern values is explained by age and family tension. The principal explanatory variable is age. The direct path between age and modern values is −0.62, while the path between family tension and modern values is 0.12. In the 1985 sample the effect of family tension on modern values is diminished and age alone explains 31% of the variance in modern values. The differences between samples in the relationship between age and modern values may be attributed to changes that have occurred in theological thinking over the fifteen year span. Values that may have been considered modern in 1970 may not be considered modern in 1985 and are thus less likely to be affected by age.

In the 1970 sample 4% of the variance in work satisfaction is explained by the model, compared with 10% in 1985. In both models the principal explanatory variable is religious experience. The impact of religious experience is stronger in 1985 (0.31) compared with 1970 (0.18). Those respondents who report having felt a personal contact with God are more likely to be satisfied with their work.

In both 1970 and 1985 the factors affecting loneliness are quite similar. In both models approximately 25% of the variance in loneliness is explained by age, modern values, religious experience, and

Figure 1: Path diagram relating decision to continue in the ministry to prior variables, 1970

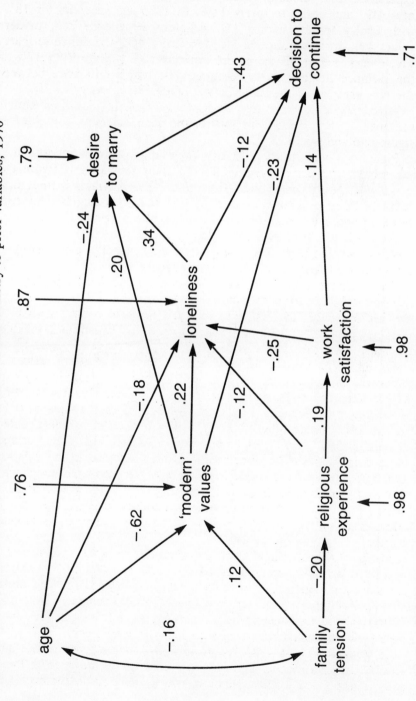

Note: All paths below .10 have been ommitted from this figure

Figure 2: Path diagram relating decision to continue in the ministry to prior variables, 1985

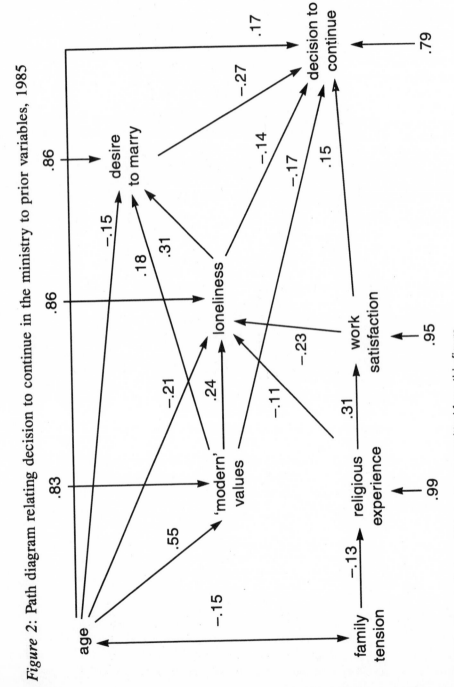

Note: All paths below .10 have been ommitted from this figure

work satisfaction. Age has a direct impact on loneliness (-0.18, 1970; -0.21, 1985) and an indirect effect through modern values (-0.14, 1970; -0.13, 1985). Modern values is positively related to loneliness in both samples (-0.22, 1970; .24, 1985). In both samples a weak relationship exists between religious experience and loneliness (-0.12, 1970; -0.11, 1985). Work satisfaction is negatively related to loneliness (-0.25, 1970; -0.23, 1985). The findings indicate that for both samples, younger priests are much more likely to feel the costs of loneliness because of their youth and their more modern values. Also, those having fewer religious experiences and those less satisfied with their work are more apt to find loneliness a problem.

In the 1970 sample, 38% of the variance in desire to marry is explained by the preceding six variables, as compared with 26% in the 1985 sample. This variable is an indicator of the degree to which a priest has considered the costs of foregoing alternative roles. As noted, the desire to marry is weaker in 1985 than in 1970. In both samples the most important factor related to desire to marry is loneliness (-0.34, 1970; -0.31, 1985). Age has a direct effect on desire to marry (-0.24, 1970; -0.15, 1985) and an indirect effect through loneliness (-0.06, 1970; -0.07, 1985). Modern value has a direct effect on desire to marry (0.20, 1970; 0.18, 1985), and on indirect effect through loneliness (0.07, 1970; 0.07, 1985). Both work satisfaction and religious experience have an indirect effect on desire to marry which is mediated by loneliness (religious experience: -0.04, 1970; -0.03, 1985; work satisfaction: -0.9, 1970; -0.07, 1985).

The findings indicate that priests who are young, hold modern values, and report loneliness as a personal problem are more likely to desire marriage. Also, the impact of age, modern values, religious experience and work satisfaction on desire to marry is heightened when loneliness is perceived as being a personal problem.

The final segment in the model, decision to continue, is influenced directly by four variables in 1970 and five variables in 1985. In both samples decision to continue is directly influenced by desire to marry (-0.43, 1970; -0.27, 1985), loneliness (0.12, 1970; 0.14, 1985), modern values (-0.23, 1970; -0.17, 1985) and work satisfaction (-0.14, 1970; -0.15, 1985). In the 1985 sample, age has a direct influence on decision to continue (-0.17). Besides these direct effects age, modern values and loneliness influence decision to continue through desire to marry (age -0.10, 1970; -0.04, 1985; modern values -0.09, 1970; -0.05, 1985; loneliness -0.15, 1970; -0.08, 1985).

The findings indicate that for both the 1970 and the 1985 sample, the impact of modern values, loneliness and work satisfaction on decision to continue is similar. Priests who hold traditional values, are satisfied in their work, and do not perceive loneliness as a personal problem are more likely to continue in ministry. The influence of age and desire to marry on decision to continue are different for the two samples. In 1970 age did not directly influence decision to continue but was related indirectly through modern values, loneliness and desire to marry. In 1985 age has a direct impact on decision to continue and an indirect effect through modern values, loneliness, and desire to marry. The direct effect of desire to marry on decision to continue is substantially reduced in 1985 as compared with 1970 (-0.43, 1970; -0.27, 1985).

Conclusions

In general, the overall 1985 findings are similar to the 1970 findings. The commitment model based on social exchange theory is effective for explaining both data sets.

In 1970, the single most important variable related to decision to continue in the priesthood was desire to marry. In 1985 this was still the case, but the strength of the relationship weakened. As indicated there is a slight decline in the percentage of priests who report a desire to marry in 1985, as compared with 1970. This produces more skew. However, it seems unlikely that this increased skew is great enough to account for the weakened relationship. We hypothesised that the difference might be due to the overall age distributions in the 1970 and 1985 data. In order to test for this interpretation we weighted the 1985 sample to reinstate the 1970 age distributions and reconstructed the path model. The findings indicated no differences between this model and the 1985 model reported above. Thus, the differences cannot be attributed to the different age distributions.

The weakened impact of desire to marry on decision to continue may be, in part, a function of changed social norms regarding the legitimacy of various life style alternatives. In 1970 priests may have viewed marriage as the only alternative to priesthood, whereas in 1985 other alternatives may be viewed as acceptable. This finding may also be a result of the supposed increase in homosexuality among the clergy. Although no large scale social science study has focused on homosexuality among priests, recent popular and religious journalistic efforts have highlighted this issue (Woodward, 1987).

In 1970, age had an indirect effect on decision to continue through modern values, loneliness and desire to marry. In 1985, age has a direct effect on decision to continue as well as the same indirect effects. This indicates that regardless of personal values, experiences of loneliness or seriously entertaining an alternative role, older priests are more likely to report a higher desire to continue in the priest role. It may be argued that the older priests in the 1985 study have weathered the storm of seeing many of their friends and colleagues resign from the active priest role and are thus more certain in their own personal decision to continue in the priest role. Also, during this time period a larger number of older men have entered seminaries and as a result are being ordained at older ages. These men may also be more certain in their decisions than are their younger counterparts.

During the period of time encompassed by this study (1970 to 1985) a great deal of change has occurred in the Catholic Church. However, the dynamics underlying the role commitment process have changed very little. The cost of celibacy, although weaker than in 1970, is still a priest's principal consideration in the commitment process. This finding has implications for church policy-making as well as for the future of Catholic leadership. The data on which this study is based, as well as other studies on personnel projections for Catholic priests in the United States, indicate that the number of priests available for active ministry will continue to decline. Concurrently, the number of Catholics in the United States will continue to increase. Thus, if nothing is done to reverse these trends a crisis is inevitable. Hoge (1987), in a thorough study of the various options available to address this coming crisis, considers the option of opening the priesthood to married as well as celibate men to be viable. The restrictions against married priests is a matter of church discipline, not church doctrine. It doen not involve a theological change. Opening the priesthood to married men will produce quantitative as well as qualitative outcomes. Quantitatively, the number of priests available for active ministry will increase and by enlarging the eligibility pool the quality of priests can be enhanced.

It has been argued that by accepting a policy of optional celibacy the church would be embarking on a path of radical change. However, to some this represents the least radical of all options currently being debated (for example, combining or restructuring parishes; or delegation of deacons or laity to preside at Eucharist) because it implies a change within the system rather than a change in the total system. According to Broccolo (1986, p. 23) 'to have change within the structure is less radical than changing our whole structure of church life'. Celibacy is and will continue to be a major issue for Catholic priests. The present study documents empirically the role it plays in the overall commitment structure for currently ordained Catholic priests.

References

Broccolo, G T (1986) 'Can we have prayer without Father?' *Journal of the Catholic Campus Ministry Association,* 1, pp. 22–24.

Fichter, J H (1974) *Organization Man in the Church,* Cambridge, Massachusetts, Schenkman.

Greeley, A M (1970) *New Horizons for the Priesthood,* New York, Sheed and Ward.

Hinkle, D E, Wiersma W and Jurs S G (1979) *Applied Statistics for the Behavioural Sciences,* Boston, Houghton Mifflin Company.

Hoge, D R (1987) *Future of Catholic Leadership: responses to the priest shortage,* Kansas City, Missouri, Sheed and Ward.

Hoge, D R, Potvin, R H and Ferry, K M (1984) *Research on Men's Vocations to the Priesthood and the Religious Life,* Washington DC, United States Catholic Conference.

Hoge, D R, Shields, J J and Verdieck, M J (1986) 'Attitudes of American priests in 1970 and 1985 on the church and the priesthood,' *Report #4, Study of Future Church Leadership,* Washington DC, The Catholic University of America.

Kenedy, P J (1970–85) *The Official Catholic Directory,* New York, P J Kenedy and Sons.

Neal, M A (1984) *Catholic Sisters in Transition,* Wilmington, Delaware, Glazier.

National Opinion Research Center (1972) *The Catholic Priest in the United States: sociological investigations,* Washington DC, United States Catholic Conference Publications.

Schoenherr, R A and Greeley, A M (1974) 'Role commitment processes and the American

Catholic priesthood,' *American Sociological Review,* 39, pp. 407–425.

Schoenherr, R A and Sorensen, A (1982) 'Social change in religious organizations: consequences of clergy decline in the US Catholic church,' *Sociological Analysis,* 43, pp. 23–52.

Shields, J J and Verdieck, M J (1985) 'Religious life in the United States: the experience of men's communities,' Washington DC, Center for Applied Research in the Apostolate.

Shostrom, E L (1966) *EITS Manual for the Personality Orientation Inventory (POI),* San Diego, Education and Industrial Testing Services.

Woodward, K L (1987) 'Gays in the clergy,' *Newsweek,* February 23, pp. 58–60.

Appendix

Definitions of variables

Family tension: Recollection of mostly tense and strained rather than close and intimate relationships between one's parents and between oneself and each parent; continuous 3-item scale with a range of 1.0 to 5.0.

Religious experience: Frequency of having felt close to God or Christ in the past two or three years; an integer 3-item scale with range of 3 to 12.

Modern values: Agreement with few 'traditional' and many 'modern' beliefs and values regarding twenty-one aspects of God, Jesus and the church; a continuous 21-item scale with a range of 1.0 to 5.0.

Work satisfaction: Of seventeen short phrase descriptions, agreement with few unpleasant and many pleasant sounding phrases; an integer scale with a range of 1 to 52.

Loneliness: High personal importance ascribed to the problem of loneliness of priestly life on a day to day basis; a single item with a range of 1 to 4.

Desire to marry: High certainty of wanting to marry if celibacy for priests became optional; a single item with a range of 1 to 5.

Decision to continue: High certainty regarding one's decision to stay in the public ministry; a single item with a range of 1 to 5.

Table A.1: *Means and standard deviations of personal characteristics of diocesan priests: 1970 (N = 3,045) and 1985 (N = 729)*

	1970		1985	
	mean	st dev	mean	st dev
age	45.6	12.54	50.6	13.39
family tension	2.0	0.83	1.7	0.88
religious experience	9.7	2.01	10.0	1.79
modern values	2.9	0.97	3.0	0.86
work satisfaction	34.6	9.86	35.9	9.18
loneliness	2.4	1.02	2.4	0.97
desire to marry	2.4	1.25	2.3	1.18
desire to continue	4.4	0.83	4.5	0.68

Table A.2: Regression coefficients (Bs) for the path models presented in figures 1 and 2

	1970	1985
family tension from age	-0.01	-0.01
religious experience from family tension	-0.48	-0.26
'modern' values from age	-0.05	-0.04
family tension	0.15	—[1]
work satisfaction from religious experience	0.93	1.56
loneliness from age	-0.01	-0.02
religious experience	-0.06	-0.06
'modern' values	0.23	0.26
work satisfaction	-0.03	-0.02
desire to marry from age	-0.02	-0.01
'modern' values	0.26	0.25
loneliness	0.42	0.38
decision to continue from age	—[1]	0.01
'modern' values	-0.20	-0.13
work satisfaction	0.12	0.11
loneliness	-0.10	-0.10
desire to marry	-0.29	-0.15

Note: 1 Path not included in figure; beta is less than 0.10.

8. Male and female differences

The role of women in ministry has expanded considerably in recent years within a number of denominations. This has led to a set of research questions concerned with the ways in which women clergy differ from clergymen in their approach to ministry. At the same time a number of studies have begun to draw attention to the feminine characteristics of some male clergy. Research in this field is illustrated by two rather different studies.

In the first article in this section, W Mack Goldsmith and Bonita Neville Ekhardt compare the responses of 90 male and 114 female seminarians and of 26 male and 82 female masters of education students to the Bem Sex Role Inventory. The data demonstrated that the male seminarian responses on the Bem Sex Role Inventory did not differ from the female seminarian responses. At the same time the male seminarians scored higher in femininity and the female seminarians scored higher in masculinity than the college men and women, respectively, reported by other studies. The seminarians were more androgynous and less same-sex typed than their education peers.

Professor W Mack Goldsmith is Professor of Psychology, Emeritus, in Department of Psychology, California State University, Stanislaus, Turlock, California, USA. Bonita Neville Ekhardt is at the Kern County School District, Bakersfield, California. This article was first published in *Journal of Psychology and Theology* in 1984.

In the second article, Edward C Lehman Jr reports on the findings of a telephone survey among 517 women and men comprising a national sample of pastors in four mainline Protestant denominations in the USA. The survey tested the assertions of religious feminists that men approach the work of the pastoral ministry using a masculine ministry style, while women perform the same work using a feminine style. The analysis indicated that the emergence of male-female differences in ministry style depended on which of nine dimensions of approach to ministry style was under consideration. The emergence of male-female difference in ministry style was also contingent on other contextual variables, including race and ethnicity, seminary cohort, and type of placement.

Professor Edward C Lehman Jr is Professor of Sociology in State University of New York, College at Brockport, Brockport, New York, USA. This article was first published in *Sociology of Religion* in 1993.

8.1 Personality factors of men and women pastoral candidates: sex-role preferences

W Mack Goldsmith and Bonita Neville Ekhardt

Within the last ten years, increasing attention has been focused on the roles of men and women in our society. Much of this attention has sought to increase the options available to men and women – to give them access to the rights and responsibilities previously held by the opposite sex. Changes in openness to nontraditional choices of men and women have been measured by indices such as job opportunities, pay scales, and social approval of nontraditional choice (Gallup Poll, 1976).

These changes have been felt in the religious realm as well. In 1975 Paul Jewett published a controversial book on the importance of both elements of masculinity and femininity in our view of humanity and God. At the same time, psychologists were exploring the possibility of individuals incorporating both masculine and feminine traits into their personality structure. Bem, in 1974, published the Bem Sex-Role Inventory (BSRI), a test which was able to measure masculinity and femininity as two orthogonal dimensions rather than opposite poles of the same scale. She described individuals who showed both high masculinity and high femininity as androgynous. Individuals might also be either masculine or feminine. Those low in both masculinity and femininity were called undifferentiated. Bem theorised that individuals who were androgynous would be better able to act appropriately in response to a variety of situations, and would even be able to blend these complementary modalities in a single act.

The BSRI has been surrounded by controversy since its inception. The issues have been concerned with both theoretical questions about the nature and applicability of the concept of androgyny and with the methodology of the test itself. In this article, we have explored the applicability of the BSRI and the concept of androgyny to religious persons. We were also concerned about a possible bias of the BSRI toward religious subgroups. One possible bias, for example, concerns the frequent claim in the literature that religiosity is a feminine characteristic (for example, Nelsen and Potvin, 1981; McCready and Greeley, 1976). Thus, the first purpose was to determine if people with strong religious commitments, Christian seminarians in this case, respond differently to the BSRI than do people whose religious values are more representative of the general population.

Controversy over the methodology of the BSRI has focused on the best method for scoring it, the social desirability of the items on its two scales, and other methodological issues (for example, Jackson and Sampo, 1980; Spence and Helmreich, 1979). Recently Bem (1979b) has replied to some of the criticism and proposed a shorter version of the test, which she says has been refined as the result of factor analyses. Items dropped were those associated with a gender factor and a group of feminine items with relatively low social desirability. The revised scales are described in Bem's (1981) manual. We have seen no studies using the new scales with religious subjects. However, Lorr and Diorio (1978) used a shortened version of the original BSRI in a study of 678 students in Catholic high schools. Their feminine scale was identical to Bem's new feminine scale. Their masculine scale contained six of her ten new masculine items plus four others. They found the new scales were able to define four androgyny groups – masculine, feminine, undifferentiated, and androgynous. With discriminant analysis they were able to identify both a masculine and a feminine function. We have found no studies making comparisons between the original and the new forms of the BSRI. We thought it would be important to make this comparison, particularly as a guide to anyone who must decide which form of the test to use with religious subgroups.

A question naturally arises about possible differences and similarities in personality between men and women clergy and seminarians. Barry and Bordin (1967) describe the ministerial role as one of service (nurturance) with a 'mixed masculine-feminine modality'. Nauss (1973), in reviewing 12 studies which tested male seminarians using the MMPI, found that these men scored high on the MMPI *Mf* scale, indicating strong attraction to interests typical to women. This was the most strikingly consistent finding of the twelve studies.

One difficulty with the MMPI *Mf* scale, though, is that it is a unidimensional scale; that is, it is a single bipolar scale with 'maleness' at one end and 'femaleness' at the other. Bem (1974) and others have attacked the unidimensional concept of sex-roles and sexual attitudes. She has proposed that some people may be 'androgynous', meaning that they simultaneously express balanced levels of both masculinity and femininity. For example, a person might be very dominant (traditionally a male trait) but also very tender (a female one). Others, she said, will be sex-typed, either masculine or feminine in the traditional way, or even cross-identified. Bem (1977) later admitted yet another type opposite to the androgynous person, an 'undifferentiated' style low on both masculine and feminine traits. The BSRI was a test designed with separate, indepenent masculinity and femininity scales and is used to classify people into the four sex-role types. We know of no studies of clergy or seminarians' sex-role attitudes done with the BSRI, or any other inventory, which allows the assessment of androgyny, and we know of no studies – even with the older, unidimensional scales – done on women clergy or seminarians.

Tangri (1975), among others, reported that women choosing careers in male-dominated fields are more autonomous, individualistic, internally motivated and achievement oriented than women choosing traditionally feminine occupations. All of these characteristics suggest that these women role-innovators should score higher on the BSRI masculinity scale. Women planning to enter the pastoral ministry are, of course, role-innovators in a traditionally all-male field; as such they, too, should score more masculine than the average woman. Conversely, the findings of Barry and Bordin (1967) and of Nauss (1973) suggest that male seminarians should score higher on the BSRI femininity scale than does the average male. These predictions can be combined into a hypothesis that seminarians of both sexes should score very similarly to each other on the two BSRI scales and also be more androgynous, respectively, than men and women from the general population.

Method

Subjects

Subjects were students in either seminary Master of Divinity (MDiv) or university graduate education programmes. Graduate education students were used as a comparison group to seminarians for several reasons. Both groups are in professional graduate programmes requiring the same level of education. Both professions are service oriented, but graduate education programmes have been traditionally more open to women than have seminary programmes. Seminarians were limited to those within M Div programmes because we were interested specifically in those students planning careers in pastoral ministry.

Subjects were recruited in two stages. First, a large number of seminaries and universities were asked to supply mailing lists of their students in MDiv or graduate education programmes, respectively. From these mailing lists, all of the women seminarians and male education majors, as well as approximately equal randomly selected numbers of the opposite sexes within the programmes, were contacted. One seminary gave contact letters to all their students through the use of campus mail boxes. Of those students who agreed to participate, only those seminarians who indicated a career goal of pastoral ministry and those education majors who indicated an educational career goal were selected. The percentages of those contacted who responded and met the selection criteria were 18% of male seminarians, 24% of female seminarians, 10% of male education students and 21% of female education students.

Our four groups ranged in age from 22 to 56, with mean ages of 28.56 for male seminarians, 31.15 for male education students, 31.79 for female education students, and 31.85 for female seminarians. Analysis of variance indicated that there were significant differences between these means, $F=3.983$ $p<0.01$. A Scheffé test indicated that the male seminarians were significantly younger than both groups of females, but not younger than the male education students. The other three groups did not differ significantly.

The seminary sample included 90 males and 114 females for eleven Protestant seminaries, ten of which were denominationally affiliated. The denominational affiliations in rank order were Presbyterians (42.6%), Methodists (28.9%), United Church of Christ (8.3%), Lutherans (8.3%), Baptists (2.8%), and miscellaneous others (8.8%). The seminarians were about equally distributed within the three year programme. Seventy-two percent were full-time students, although many had part-time jobs within churches. Ninety-three percent were seeking ordination to pastoral ministry, and another five percent were already ordained.

The education sample consisted of 26 males and 52 females from two secular schools, one in Minnesota (53.8%) and one in southern California (47.2%). Only 24% were full-time students, with 53.8% employed full-time in education fields. Half had completed two-thirds or more of their graduate programme. The religious beliefs and affiliations reported indicated that 68.4% had religious beliefs and affiliations, 22.4% had beliefs but no affiliations, and 9% had neither beliefs nor affiliations. Those claiming religious belief were also asked to rate the 'strength of your personal involvement in your religion'. The mean rating of strength with which religious beliefs were held was 3.83 on a five point scale, where 1 was very weak and 5 was very strong. (SD = 1.09)

Procedure

Subjects responding positively to the initial contact letter were mailed a questionnaire containing personal data items, the Bem Sex-Role Inventory (BSRI), and the Personality Research Form (PRF-E), along with the PRF-E test booklet, instructions and return envelope. The questionnaire was to be completed anonymously, but subjects were asked to mail a separate card to confirm that they had returned the data. They were also offered the option of receiving their PRF profiles, and most requested them.

The personal data contained questions about the subjects' seminary or education programme, career choices, religious affiliations, and so forth. The BSRI (Bem, 1974, 1977) is a 60 item list of adjectives which the subjects rated as like or unlike themselves on a seven-point scale. Twenty of these adjectives comprise the BSRI masculine scale (MASC) which includes items such as self-reliant, assertive, analytical. The BSRI feminine scale (FEM) has 20 items such as yielding, sympathetic, warm. The remaining 20 items are intended as fillers.

Results and discussion

The analyses of the BSRI data reported here had three goals:

a. to determine if the BSRI items are biased for subjects with deep religious commitments;
b. to compare the usefulness of the original long-form of the BSRI described by Bem (1974) with that of the revised short-form version (New BSRI) described by Bem (1979a, 1981); and
c. to compare the sex-role responses of the seminarians with those of comparison groups religiously more similar to the general population.

With respect to the first of these goals, we hypothesised that people whose self-concepts centre on their religious identity would stereotype themselves differently from those who do not. Since the BSRI items were selected by Bem to represent social stereotyping, the test must be considered biased for members of any subculture – religious, in this case – which includes distinctive values and ideals in its stereotypes.

With respect to the second goal, we had no hypotheses about religious differences but simply wished to test if the New BSRI was superior to the original. Superior, in this case, was taken to mean better psychometric qualities.

With respect to the third goal, we hypothesied: first, that male and female seminarians would not differ much from each other on the two BSRI scales but second, that male seminarians would score more feminine than comparison men, but not differ from them on the masculine scale, while female seminarians would score higher on the masculine scale than comparison women, while not differing from them on the feminine scale; and finally that proportionally more seminarians would be classified as androgynous and fewer as same-sex stereotyped than comparison subjects.

The subjects responded to all 60 of the original BSRI items, and their scores on the original masculine (MASC) and feminine (FEM) scales were based upon the summed responses to 20 items per scale. Nine of the 282 subjects were missing one or at most two of the 40 items. Their scores on both scales were weighted to adjust for the missing data. Scores on the new masculine (New MASC) and new feminine (New FEM) scales were computed similarly but using only the ten items for each scale designated by Bem (1979a, 1981) for the short form. The original 60 items, arranged according to the respective scales, are shown in table one. Items included on the New BSRI scales are so marked.

Table 1: Bem Sex Role Inventory (BSRI) Items

masculine	feminine	neutral
B01 self-reliant	B02 yielding	B03 helpful
B04 defends own beliefs*	B05 cheerful	B06 moody*
B07 independent	B08 shy	B09 conscientious*
B10 athletic	B11 affectionate*	B12 theatrical
B13 assertive	B14 flatterable*	B15 happy
B16 strong personality*	B17 loyal	B18 unpredicatable
B19 forceful*	B20 feminine	B21 reliable*
B22 analytical	B23 sympathetic*	B24 jealous*
B25 has leadership abilities*	B26 sensitive to the needs of others*	B27 truthful*
B28 willing to take risks*	B29 understanding*	B30 secretive*
B31 makes decisions easily	B32 compassionate*	B33 sincere
B34 self-sufficient	B35 eager to soothe hurt feelings*	B36 conceited*
B37 dominant*	B38 soft-spoken	B39 likeable
B40 masculine	B41 warm*	B42 solemn
B44 willing to take a stand*	B43 tender*	B45 friendly
B46 aggressive*	B47 gullible	B48 inefficient
B49 acts as a leader	B50 childlike	B51 adaptable*
B52 individualistic	B53 does not use harsh language	B54 unsystematic
B55 competitive	B56 loves children*	B57 tactful*
B58 ambitious	B59 gentle	B60 conventional*

Note: The item numbers indicate the position of the item on the original BSRI as answered by the subjects.
    * Items on the respective masculine, feminine or neutral scales of the short-form test (New BSRI).

Use of the BSRI with religiously distinctive groups

Our first major concern was if the seminarians, a group with distinctive religious values, differed in responses to the BSRI from the graduate education students, a group whose religious values were assumed to represent the general poplulation. A discriminant analysis was performed using all 60 BSRI items as predictors to membership in the two groups. This analysis controlled for age differences and used Rao's *V* as the criterion for stepwise inclusion or removal. The resulting discriminant function was highly significant (χ^2 [29] $=$ 139, p < 0.001) and its canonical correlation $= 0.65$. This function correctly classified 85% of the subjects as seminarians or education students on the basis of different patterns of responses to the BSRI items. Of the 60 items, 35 were entered into the equation and eighteen significantly increased Rao's *V.* Table two lists these eighteen items in the order of their ability to discriminate between the seminary and education samples. The table also shows whether the item was a masculine (M), feminine (F) or filler (N) item and whether the seminarians scored higher or lower on it than did the education students.

A similar discriminant analysis was performed using only the 30 items from the New BSRI scales. The results were essentially the same as with the full 60 items. The analysis computed a discriminant funcion with a canonical correlation of 0.47 which could correctly classify 80% of the subjects into their respective groups. Of eight significant discriminators, six were from the New MASC scale and two from the New FEM scale.

Table 2: BSRI items that discriminate best between seminarians and education students

item	scale	seminarians %
B25 has leadership abilities	M	high
B50 childlike	F	high
B58 ambitious	M	low
B23 sympathetic	F	high
B51 adaptable	N	low
B24 jealous	N	low
B28 willing to take risks	M	high
B13 assertive	M	low
B19 forceful	M	high
B56 loves children	F	low
B31 makes decisions easily	M	high
B52 individualistic	M	low
B12 theatrical	N	high
B53 does not use harsh language	F	high
B57 tactful	N	low
B32 compassionate	F	high
B29 understanding	F	high
B41 warm	F	high

The clear conclusion from these discriminant analyses is that the seminarians responded to the BSRI items in ways different from the education students. This was true for both the old and new forms of the test. Because we cannot assume that the seminarians are typical of all deeply religious people or that the graduate education students do not differ from other secular groups that might have been chosen out of the general population, we have not attempted to interpret just what the pattern of highs and lows in table two mean. We would suggest, however, that any researcher or clinician who wishes to use the BSRI with highly religious subjects or clients should be wary. There appears to be a powerful set of response biases in religious subjects which affects many of the BSRI items. Further exploration of these different patterns of responses must await less specialised samples than these, however.

There were religious differences among the education students, of course. Of these, 32% rated themselves as non-religious or weak in the strength of their beliefs, 18% considered themselves average and 50% as strong or very strong. We wondered if the more religious education students would show a pattern of responses to the BSRI items similar to that of the seminarians. A multiple regression analysis with age controlled showed that some of the same BSRI items which characterised the seminarians (for example, 'has leadership ability' B25) also correlated significantly with the religious education students' rating of the strength of their beliefs. However, the overall pattern of responses was by no means the same as that of the seminarians.

Comparison of the original BSRI and the new form (New BSRI)

The masculinity and femininity scales of both the BSRI and the New BSRI were item analysed using the SPSS Reliability subprogramme (Hull and Nie, 1979), and *alpha* coefficients were computed, using the total sample of 281 subjects. These results are summarised in table three, which shows the scale means, standard deviations, and mean inter-item correlations. It also shows the *alpha* coefficients and lists of items which would lower the *alpha* coefficient of the scale and thus weaken its reliability. It is clear that the New BSRI scales are better than the original BSRI ones, both in terms of higher *alpha* coefficients and fewer bad items in the scales. The one 'bad' item in the New MASC scale, 'independent' (B07), just barely met the critierion of lowering the *alpha*. On the other hand, the 'bad' item in the New FEM scale, 'loves children' (B56) was clearly worse than the other items in that scale. Its item-to-total correlation was only 0.28.

Table four shows the correlations between the three subscales of the original BSRI and the corresponding three of the New BSRI based on the total sample. The 'neutral' scales (NEUT and New NEUT) contain filler items. We have included them in this paper because we wondered if religious people might respond differentially to some filler items. In fact, there was a high and undesirable correlation ($r = 0.51$) between the FEM and NEUT scales of the BSRI. The corresponding correlation between the feminine and neutral scales of the New BSRI is much lower ($r = 0.15$), although it is still significant. We also found that the negligible correlation between the MASC and FEM scales from the long form increased to a low but significant correlation ($r = 0.12$) on the corresponding scales of the New BSRI. In general, however, we feel that the scales of the New BSRI show greater reliability and independence than do those of the older and longer BSRI, and we would recommend use of the new form by other researchers.

We factored both the original set of 40 BSRI items comprising the MASC and FEM scales and the 20 corresponding new BSRI items. The factor analyses were principle components analyses (SPSS PA1) with varimax rotation. Using a criterion of latent roots equal to one or greater, 11 factors were extracted when the 40 BSRI items were analysed. These accounted for 62.7% of the total variance, but only two factors accounted for more than 6% of the variance. Factor one accounted for 16% and factor 2 for 12%. Table five lists these two factors and the BSRI items having factor loadings of 0.5 or greater on each.

Factoring the items of the New BSRI masculinity and femininity scales with the new criterion yielded four factors which accounted for 56% of the variance. Again, there were only two factors accounting for more than 6% of the variance: factor one accounted for 26%; factor two for 19%. Table five also shows the New BSRI items with factor loadings of 0.5 or greater. An examination of the items in table five

Table 3: Comparison data for the masculine and feminine scales of the original BSRI and the shortened form (New BSRI)

	median	mean	SD	mean inter-item correlation	alpha coefficient	bad items
BSRI masculine	101.00	100.57	11.32	0.20	0.81	B10, B22, B40
BSRI feminine	99.06	99.36	9.41	0.16	0.74	B08, B14, B20, B50, B53
New masculine	51.01	50.84	6.97	0.33	0.83	B07
New feminine	57.08	56.51	6.35	0.39	0.86	B56

Note: These medians were used to determine membership in the four androgyny groups.

Table 4: Correlations of BSRI and New BSRI scales

	BSRI MASC	BSRI FEM	BSRI NEUT	New MASC	New FEM	New NEUT
BSRI MASC	1.00	-0.08	0.14*	0.89*	0.12*	0.12*
BSRI FEM		1.00	0.51*	-0.06	0.86*	0.24*
BSRI NEUT			1.00	0.14*	0.42*	0.67*
New MASC				1.00	0.12*	0.02
New FEM					1.00	0.15*
New NEUT						1.00

Note: $*p < 0.05$

clearly shows that the two factors for both the BSRI and New BSRI correspond to their respective masculine and feminine scales. This finding is similar to that reported by Lorr and Diorio (1978) and by others, as well. More to the point, it is clear that the factorial structure of the New BSRI is superior to that of the original BSRI and again suggests that future researchers use the new scales.

Sex-role responses

Our first hypothesis concerning sex-role responses was that men and women seminarians would not differ in responding to the BSRI masculine and feminine scales. This prediction was based upon accumulated evidence of similarity on other personality measures, the mixed sex-role model of the ministry and the fact that the women were role-innovators in a traditionally masculine field. Consistent with this prediction, the means for the two sexes of seminarians did not differ on either the New MASC or New FEM ($t[202] = -0.46$ and -0.77, respectively).

The next hypothesis addressed was that the men and women seminarians would combine masculinity and femininity in their sex-role attitudes more than does the general population; that is, that men seminarians would score more feminine and the women seminarians more

Table 5: Factor loadings (.5 or higher) on major facors for 40
MASC and FEM items and 20 New MASC and New FEM
items

	factor one		factor two	
BSRI items				
MASC	B13	0.65		
	B16	0.69		
	B28	0.52		
	B44	0.63		
	B49	0.60		
FEM	B08	−0.50	B23	0.64
	B32	0.50	B26	0.52
			B29	0.55
			B32	0.64
			B35	0.51
			B41	0.61
			B43	0.56
			B59	0.59
New BSRI items				
New MASC			B13	0.69
			B16	0.64
			B19	0.77
			B25	0.53
			B37	0.68
			B46	0.73
New FEM	B11	0.69		
	B23	0.68		
	B26	0.74		
	B32	0.78		
	B41	0.72		
	B43	0.75		
	B59	0.75		

masculine than average. The most appropriate general group for whom data are available on the BSRI is college students. The means of the present samples on the New BSRI masculine and New BSRI feminine scales were compared with data collected on 169 male and 206 female college students at Washington State University and reported by Kimlicka, Wakefield and Friedman (1980). The male seminarians did not differ from the college males on the New MASC scale (seminarians' M = 50.74; college males' M = 50.01) but differ from them significantly in the predicted direction on the New FEM scale (seminarians' M = 56.69; college males' M = 54.16; $t[257] = 2.302$, $p < 0.05$). The results were symmetrically opposite for the women. The female seminarians did not differ from the college women on the New FEM scale (seminarians' M = 57.07; college females' M = 56.93) but they did differ as predicted on the New MASC scale (seminarians' M = 51.45; college females' M = 45.08; $t[318] = 6.51$, $p < 0.01$). These data support our prediction that seminary men would have more feminine traits and seminary women more masculine traits than do students from the general population. What is equally interesting, however, is that the masculinity of the men and the femininity of the women was not decreased.

Androgyny classifications

The similarity of the male and female seminarians to each other and their differences from the college students of the same sexes suggested a further hypothesis. We predicted that proportionately more seminarians would be classified as androgynous and fewer as same-sexed typed than a comparison sample whose sex-role attitudes should be similar to those of the general population, in this case, our sample of graduate education students. First we used the New BSRI scales to classify all seminarians and education students of both sexes into the four androgyny groups. Subjects were scored as androgynous if they scored above the total sample on both medians of the New MASC and New FEM scales, undifferentiated if they scored below both and as masculine or feminine sex-typed if they scored above the New MASC and below the New FEM medians, or vice versa, respectively. This classification method is suggested by Bem (1977).

Membership in these four groups was then cross-tabulated with membership in the seminarian or education student groups to test if there was an association between these variables. Of the seminarians, 27% were classified as androgynous (vs 15% for education), 28% as undifferentiated (vs 30% for education), 22% as masculine (vs 30%) and 23% as feminine (vs 26%). Thus, there was a slight tendency in the predicted directions, but the association was not significant, $\chi^2(3) = 4.73$.

This procedure does not test the actual prediction, however, because it does not consider the actual sex of subjects classified as masculine or feminine. A male who is classified as masculine shows characteristics stereotypically associated with his sex and he should experience relatively little conflict with conventional social values. A female who is classified as masculine, however, shows characteristics sharply different from society's expectations. Similarly, of course, a female who is classified as feminine fits the common stereotype but a male who is classified as feminine may be seen as effeminate. Therefore, we reclassified all subjects who fell into the masculine and feminine groups to reflect whether their classification fit with their actual sex or was opposite to it. These classifications were called same-sex and cross-sex categories. This way of classifying subjects has been used by previous researchers, for example, Bem and Lenny (1976).

The specific prediction was now testable. We cross-tabulated the 134 subjects who were classified either as androgynous or as same-sex typed. Of these, 55 seminarians were androgynous and 41 were same-sex typed. There were 12 androgynous education students and 28 same-sexed typed. Clearly there were more androgynous seminarians and fewer same-sex typed ones than would be expected by chance, $\chi^2(1) = 8.41$, $p < 0.01$. The hypothesis was confirmed.

We believe that men and women now preparing for the ministry will face graver stresses from sex-role conflicts than will their peers preparing for vocations in education and other secular professions in which there is less demand for a blending of masculine and feminine personality traits and activities. We expect these conflicts to be especially severe for the women who will enter ministry because they perceive a lack of successful role-models, according to Hale, King and Jones (1980).

Conclusions

The BSRI is a very widely used and influential instrument, as is the theory of androgyny which underlies it. Our comparison of the responses of seminarians and education students shows a pervasive pattern of differences. These differences indicate that the BSRI may be biased in as-yet unkown ways when used with distinctively religious groups. Nevertheless, the general structure of independent masculine and feminine scales did appear in our samples essentially as Bem's theory claims and as other research has confirmed. In addition, we showed that the new, short form of the BSRI is clearly superior to the old form with respect of better reliabilities, better factor structure, and other psychometric properties. It may be less biased for religious groups as well, but it is not unbiased. Finally, our results support the hypothesis of greater androgyny in seminarians and less stereotypic sex-role patterns.

References

Barry, W A and Bordin, E S (1967) 'Pesonality development and the vocational choice of the ministry,' *Journal of Counseling Psychology,* 14, pp. 395–430.

Bem, S L (1974) 'The measurements of psychological androgyny,' *Journal of Consulting and Clinical Psychology,* 42, pp. 155–162.

Bem, S L (1977) 'On the utility of alternative procedures for assessing psychological androgyny,' *Journal of Consulting and Clinical Psychology,* 45, pp. 196–205.

Bem, S L (1979a) *Administration and Scoring Guide for the BEM Sex-Role Inventory,* Palo Alto, California, Consulting Psychologists Press.

Bem, S L (1979b) 'Theory and measurement of androgyny: a reply to the Pedhazur-Tetenbaum and Locksley-Colten critiques,' *Journal of Personality and Social Psychology,* 37, pp. 1047–1054.

Bem, S L (1981) *Bem Sex-Role Inventory: professional manual,* Palo Alto, California, Consulting Psychologists Press.

Bem, S L and Lenny, E (1976) 'Sextyping and the avoidance of cross-sex behaviour,' *Journal of Personality and Social Psychology,* 33, pp. 48–54.

Gallup Poll Organization (American Institute of Public Opinion) (1976) *Women in America,* Report No. 128.

Hale, H, King, M, and Jones, D M (1980) *New Witnesses: United Methodist clergywomen,* Nashville, United Methodist Church.

Hull, C H and Nie, N H (1979) *SPSS Update,* New York, McGraw-Hill.

Jackson, D N and Sampo, V P (1980) 'Personality structure and assessment,' *Annual Review of Psychology,* 31, pp. 503–551.

Jewett, P (1975) *Man as Male and Female,* Grand Rapids, Eerdmans.

Kimlicka, T M, Wakefield, J A and Friedman, A F (1980) 'A comparison of factors from the Bem Sex-Role Inventory for male and female college students,' *Psychological Reports,* 47, pp. 11–17.

Lorr, M and Diorio, M (1978) 'Analysis and abbreviation of Bem's Sex-Role Inventory,' *Psychological Reports,* 43, pp. 879–882.

McCready, W C and Greeley, A M (1976) *The Ultimate Values of the American Population,*

Beverly Hills, California, Sage Publications.

Nauss, A (1973) 'The ministerial personality: myth or reality,' *Journal of Religion and Health*, 12, pp. 77–96.

Nelsen, H M and Potvin, R H (1981) 'Gender and regional differences in the religiosity of Protestant adolescents,' *Review of Religious Research*, 22, pp. 268–285.

Spence, J T and Helmreich, R L (1979) 'On assessing "androgyny",' *Sex Roles*, 5, pp. 721–738.

Tangri, S S (1975) 'Implied demand character of the wife's future and role innovation: patterns of achievement orientation among college women,' in M T Mednick, S S Tangri, and L W Hoffman (eds) *Women and Achievement*, Washington, Hemisphere.

8.2 Gender and ministry style: things not what they seem

Edward C Lehman Jr

Remember the lines from the Broadway musical (Berlin, 1971), *Annie Get Your Gun*, when Annie exclaims to her bragging cowboy:

'Anything you can do, I can do better!
I can do anything better than you!'
'No, you can't!' was the reply.
Then – 'Yes, I can!'
'No, you can't!'
'Yes, I can! Yes, I can! Yes, I can!'

The dialogue usually brings a smile to our faces, because it calls to mind some delightful musical entertainment, and it lets us safely poke fun at ourselves as participants in the longstanding competition between the sexes.

There is no way that Irving Berlin could have anticipated that the lines would also come to symbolise an important difference of opinion in the current women-in-ministry movement over a pair of assertions: first, that women and men by nature take divergent approaches to the pastoral ministry (including the priesthood and the rabbinate) – a traditional 'masculine' style and a recently unveiled 'feminine' approach, and second, that the 'feminine' mode is much more desirable than the 'masculine' stance. Some religious feminists charge that men are responsible for the masculine approach and its resultant 'patriarchy', a ministry style steeped in impersonal hierarchies, segmental relationships, hypercompetitiveness, power over people, authoritarian decision making, mastery over nature, rigid theology, legalistic ethics, and exclusion of women and minorities – traits considered 'pathological' (Ice, 1987, pp. 6–7).

By contrast, the feminine approach that women bring to ministry incorporates personal communities, holistic relationships, egalitarianism, empowerment of lay people, democratic decision making, cooperation with nature, open and flexible theology, existential ethics of responsible caring, and inclusion of women and minorities (Ice, 1987; Nason-Clark, 1987, pp. 332–33). This feminine mode is described as healthy, an important corrective in ministry style (Ice, 1987, pp. 6–7; see also Christ and Plaskow, 1975; Meyers, 1988; Weidman, 1985; Hahn, 1991; Ochs, 1983; Franklin, 1986; Collins, 1974; Christ, 1977; Maitland, 1983; Russell, 1974; Daly, 1973; Fiorenza, 1983).

These assertions parallel recent discussions of gender and approach to work on other occupations as well – medicine, law, corporate administration, advertising, higher education and even mortuary work (for example, Lunneborg, 1990; Eagly and Johnson, 1990; Epstein, 1988; Maccoby and Jacklin, 1974; Tavris and Offir, 1977). In each instance, some feminists have charged that women can do it better. The confrontation is a sign of the times, a manifestation of the boast of the 'generalised' Annie, 'We can do it better! Yes, we can; yes, we can; yes, we can!'

It is important to remember, however, that not all religious feminists accept these assumptions. The movement speaks with many voices. The argument for feminine superiority represents but one segment of a complex constellation of perspectives. The particular individuals who are impressed by possible female-male differences have been called maximalists – persons who postulate clearly identifiable cognitive, affective, and behavioural uniquenesses endemic to women and men – *as women and men* (for example, Gilligan, 1982; Lunneborg, 1990; Ice, 1987; Meyers, 1988; Stevens, 1989; Weidman, 1985; Christ and Plaskow, 1979).

Arguing in opposition to such axioms, by contrast, are other feminists labelled minimalists. The minimalist stance contends that there are far more similarities than differences between male and female ministers, and that the proposed grounds for significant gender-specific ministry styles are spurious (Robb, 1985). To the minimalists, gender is not a trait possessed by males and females (for example, Stoltenberg, 1990; Hare-Mustin and Marecek, 1989; Mednick, 1989). Rather, it is a social construction that organises relations between women and men, a concept that evolved from the experience of hierarchy. They argue, for example, that analyses of the structural location of women and men as social actors indicate that those external circumstances are the major sources of any seemingly unique social characteristics manifested by the sexes. Men and women in similar positions of power and authority, for example, tend to think and act more like each other than do persons of the same sex but who differ in power and authority. Thus to the minimalists any cognitive, affective, or behavioural differences perceived in men and women are not artifacts of sex-specific personality traits, but instead are epiphenomenal of their place in a social structure. These opposing assumptions appear in many facets of religious scholarship and polemics (for example Daly, 1975; Fiorenza, 1984, 1983; Ruether and McLaughlin, 1979; Weidman, 1985).

An empirical study

Who is right? Until recently few people asked if we could obtain any empirical evidence to support one position or the other (for related studies see Ekhardt and Goldsmith, 1984; Carroll *et al.*, 1983;

Stevens, 1989). This is what I tried to do in a recent study (Lehman, 1993).

The research involved interivew data from national samples of women and men ordained as pastors (or senior ministers, co-pastors, etc) of local congregations (or parishes). These clergy belonged to one of four Protestant denominations taking part in the project, that is, the American Baptist Churches, the Presbyterian Church (USA), the United Church of Christ, and the United Methodist Church. The 517 interviews of roughly equal numbers of men and women were completed mostly during February, 1990.

The focus of the undertaking was the respondents' approach to their work as local pastors. The project was introduced to the clergy simply as a study of different ways in which ministers confront their work. The respondents were not aware of our primary interest in gender. Telephone interviews produced good levels of cooperation, and the numbers in the ultimate sample generally represented the initial targets.

The primary technique for measuring differences in ministry style was to present to each pastor a series of 48 statements describing specific actions, values, orientations, or attitudes, each one representing some aspect of approach to parish ministry (Lehman, 1993, chapters 2, 3). Respondents were asked to indicate how much each statement was 'like them personally'.

The analysis involved combining those items to construct nine composite measures, each one tapping differences in a specific dimension of ministry style. Those nine dimensions, as defined by religious maximalists, were:

1. Willingness to use coercive power: Wishing to have power over the congregation is a 'masculine' trait. Men, more than women, seek to 'lord it over' their lay members.

2. Striving to empower congregations: Giving away power, the 'flip side' of coerciveness, is something that men find hard to do. Women, on the other hand, based on their experiences of lack of power over their own lives, strive to enhance the power their members have over their individual and collective lives. This is a 'feminine' trait.

3. Desire for formal authority: Like power, wishing to be in positions of authority is defined as a 'masculine' trait. Men are more concerned about such positions than are women.

4. Desire for rational structure: Rationality, science, and formal logical structure are aspects of the traditional patriarchal system. It has been primarily a sphere of male activity. Women's approach is more intuitive, integrative, inductive, and holistic.

5. Ethical legalism: The traditional masculine approach to ethics and morality is based on rules, precedents, authority, and similar legalistic principles. The feminine stance, by contrast, is founded on a

principle of responsible caring. Men lean toward a deontological approach, while women prefer more teleological criteria.

6. General interpersonal style: Men tend to be status-conscious, defensive, aloof, and formal in general interpersonal relations. Women, on the other hand, are more egalitarian, willing to be vulnerable, close, and informal.

7. Orientation to preaching: The masculine approach to preaching uses it as a vehicle for telling people what is so – to pontificate, prescribe and proscribe. It is usually an important role to men. The feminine approach to homiletics, by contrast, focuses on sharing experiences and feelings with others. It is not as central an activity for women as for men.

8. Criteria of clergy status: Clear criteria for making invidious distinctions between self and other are important to persons participating in the masculine system – educational pedigree, size of congregation, size of local budget, having the 'right' people as members. Religious maximalists argue that such status systems are unworthy of Christian service; there is no place for them in the feminine approach to ministry.

9. Involvement in social issues: Working to address social issues usually involves seeking what is good and helpful for others – not oneself, not one's own congregation or one's own 'kind of people'. This orientation does not fit well into the patriarchal system. It is more compatible with the feminine approach.

Again, these male-female differences are as defined by maximalists. The minimalists deny that any such divergences exist.

Results

According to the frequency distributions of these scores, we succeeded in measuring differences on each dimension – some clergy appeared more 'masculine' in orientation, and others displayed more 'feminine' characteristics (see Lehman, 1993, chapter 3). Gender differences in ministry style did exist. The next question – the one central to the study – was whether the men manifested the more 'masculine' approaches to ministry, while the women displayed the more 'feminine' styles.

When we compared scores on these indices to sex of clergy, the results were not as conclusive as one would like. Maximalists and minimalists alike were to be disappointed. Things were not what they seemed to the protagonists. Do men and women differ in their approach to ministry? The answer was, 'It depends!'

Bivariate relationships

It depends, first of all, on the dimension of ministry style. Only four of the nine dimensions of ministry style were associated with differ-

ences in clergy sex – using coercive power, congregational empowerment, rational decision making, and ethical legalism. As the
maximalists would predict, proportionately more men than women
were willing to use coercive power over the congregation, preferred
rational and formally structured modes of decision making, and dealt
with ethical situations legalistically. Likewise more women than men
sought to empower their congregation. The correlations were not very
strong. They ranged from 0.15 to 0.40. Yet they are consistent with
the maximalist position. We did find differences.

However, the maximalist assertions were not supported on the other
five dimensions of ministry style. There were no significant sex differences in clergy wanting formal authority, openness of interpersonal
style, approach to preaching, acceptance of traditional ministerial
status criteria, and involvement in social issues. These patterns tend to
support the minimalist argument – no difference between men and
women. Is approach to ministry based on gender? It depends on which
aspect of ministry style one is considering.

Multivariate relationships

Whether clergy sex was predictive of ministry style depended, next, on
a number of identifiable conditions, background factors that appeared
to be causally necessary for the relationships. Three of those specifying conditions were the ministers' race or ethnicity, their seminary
cohort, and the type of placement they had.

Race and ethnicity: Clergy racial-ethnic status was more consistently predictive of approch to ministry than any other single factor.
Members of racial-ethnic minority groups tended to be more masculine in ministry style than members of the white majority, a pattern
that also applied separately for both sexes – that is, minority men
manifested more masculine approaches to ministry than did white-
majority men, and minority women likewise displayed more masculine
ministry styles than did white-majority women. The *sex* differences in
use of coercive power, congregational empowerment, preference for
rationality, and legalism appeared among white-majority clergy but not
the minority ministers (which supports Andolsen, 1986; and Grant,
1989; see also Lincoln and Mamiya, 1990). Sex differences? It
depends on race and ethnicity. They showed up among white majority
clergy but not among minority clergy.

Seminary cohort: The appearance of sex differences in the white
pastors' ministry style depended, in the second place, on seminary
cohort. The general pattern was for sex differences to appear among
white ministers who had completed seminary since about 1970.
Among pastors who completed seminary education prior to 1970, sex
differences in ministry style involved only immersion in social issues.
Women were more involved than men. The sex differences in coer-
cion, empowerment, rationality, and legalism appeared only among

clergy who completed seminary training since 1970 (and in some cases since 1980).

Why was this so? The keys to this pattern seem to be shifts in seminary education that began roughly with the 1970s: first, the introduction of feminist concerns into the routinised cultural and structural patterns of seminary life, and second, selective enrolment of feminist women in seminary (for example, Charlton, 1987). It was roughly in the 1970s that religious feminist concerns began to be accepted and institutionalised in seminary culture and social structure. That was when feminist literature joined the reading lists, feminist courses were added to the curriculum, feminist issues were integrated into segments of existing courses, and more women appeared on the faculty and in higher levels of seminary administration. If we can assume that female seminarians participated in these curricular innovations more fully than did men, then one would expect to see more sex differences in approach to ministry style among those ministers than among persons who finished seminary prior to the feminist innovations. Carroll (1992) suggests that the pattern is not unlike the self-fulfilling prophecy. Add to this situation the likely selective enrolment of more feminist women in the seminary after roughly 1970, and there is even more reason to expect greater sex differences in ministry style in the more recent cohorts.

Type of placement: The third factor influencing relationships between ministry style and sex was the kind of pastoral position held by the white respondents. This was especially the case when comparing solo pastors to senior ministers in multiple-staff situations. Male-female differences in ministry style emerged primarily among senior ministers, where the men were more clearly 'masculine' in approach and the women were more clearly 'feminine'. That is, among senior ministers only, more men than women used coercive power over the congregation, sought positions of formal authority, preferred rational structure for decisions, and manifested ethical legalism. In the same group, more women than men sought to empower their congregations and manifest an open interpersonal style. Those differences did not show up among the solo pastors, that is, ministers serving a congregation as the only salaried religious professional on the staff. The solo pastorate, of course, is the modal pattern.

Furthermore, when we controlled for sex and compared the senior/solo dichotomy with scores on the indices of ministry style, type of placement was predictive of approach to ministry primarily among the women. Female solo pastors tended to manifest a more 'masculine' ministry style than did female senior ministers. For females, more solo pastors than senior ministers used power over the congregation and wanted formal authority, while they were less inclined than senior ministers to empower their congregations, to report an open interpersonal style, and to be strongly oriented toward social issues. Sex differences in ministry style depend on what kind of minister one is describing.

Summary

The general empirical conclusions of the study are that:

a. there are some gender-specific approaches to pastoral ministry among female and male Protestant pastors, more than the minimalists say but clearly less than proposed by the maximalists, depending on which dimension is under consideration;
b. the strength of those differences tends to be weak, suggesting that the differences that do exist in ministry style of men and women are not as great as has been argued;
c. whether any differences in women's and men's ministry style appeared at all was dependent on identifiable cultural, structural, and biographical conditions.

The reasons for those results and their interpretations are important. Unfortunately, we cannot deal with that material within the limits of this article, so I must refer you to the one complete report for that discussion (Lehman, 1993). Instead, let me point out some general methodological ramifications that this work may have for social-scientific analysis of these kinds of issues.

Discussion

Why did something that seemed so simple at the outset turn out to be so complicated? To address that question, it is useful to return to the events and issues that gave rise to the research in the first place. Frequently the meanings of patterns in research results have hints in the social milieu from which they sprang. In this instance the point where it all started is the fact of women suffering discrimination and exclusion from ordained ministry. It is important to remember that the assertions of sex differences in ministry style flowed initially from concern about that resistance to change. They derived from the heat of institutional struggle. It seems that this is the same pattern as has been observed in challenges to sexism in other institutions (Bacchi, 1990). Women seeking ordination and placement as pastors (and other church-related positions) had experienced prejudice, discrimination, humiliation, and rejection in response to their efforts to expand their roles in the church. Even in these denominations where women's ordination is formally endorsed, often also reinforced by some form of affirmative action policy, women are still usually not welcome as pastoral candidates, especially at the level of the local congregation. Churches have to be persuaded to 'do the right thing'.

How do women seeking ordination and placement deal with that? One thing they do is seek legitimations for their cause. One legitimation, which is also a strategy for allaying lay members' fears of possible negative consequences they expect from female pastoral leadership (see Lehman, 1981), is to indicate ways in which accepting women as ordained church leaders will improve the situation in the churches. In this mode, adopting the maximalist stance, one tactic has been to argue that a woman's way of ministering is more consistent with basic Christian values than is the traditional men's way, and that the situation for the churches will be better under the pastoral leadership of women than men. 'Anything they can do, we can do better!'

Thus a significant background to these assertions about sex differences in ministry style is the need for a rationale by the women-in-ministry movement to legitimate their demands. Whatever else they are, gender-specific descriptions of ministry styles are legitimations for change. This simple observation has important methodological implications. Viewed in this light, the source, objectives, and logic underlying the argument about sex differences take on a unique character.

1. The source: The major concern behind the maximalists' assertions of sex differences in the way pastors approach their work was not a theoretical enquiry into the social psychology of gender. Instead, the basis of the propositions was the agenda of a social movement pressing for changes in sexist religious institutions.
2. The objectives: The basic objectives of the persons proposing sex differences was not a programme of study to explain patterns of human functioning. Rather, the purpose was to criticise the male-dominated world of religious leadership and to motivate religious decision makers to question their sexist assumptions and open up church structures to broader female participation.
3. The logic: The logic in the predictions of sex-specific ministry styles did not derive from social-scientific theory. Instead, the rationale behind those expectations flowed from the political strategy of one branch of the women-in-ministry movement. What we may be dealing with, then, is a social agenda in search of a theory.

In this sense the statements by maximalist religious feminists about male and female clergy are not unlike those made of opponents in the heat of political campaigns. They are intended to attain social objectives by casting one's antagonists, not present analytically useful descriptions of them. They portray the opponent as the bad guy while depicting themselves as more closely approximating the ideal. Whether those contrasting images are accurate representations of reality is not the central question. That may be irrelevant. The major issue is what will bring about the desired result? This is not to say that the maximalists are being insincere. It seems quite clear that they firmly believe what they say. Rather, it is to suggest that the force of cultural values and social objectives have an almost irresistible power to structure perceptions of reality, especially where one's interests are at stake – a proposition enjoying wide acceptance in social and behavioural science. In such circumstances, things may not be what they seem.

Statements by the minimalists participate in some of the same dynamics. Rather than being primarily theoretically or empirically-based statements of reality, the minimalists' discourse is also largely strategic. Their contentions of 'no difference' often are intended to avoid having women ministers shoot themselves in the foot by stigmatising themselves in the eyes of persons whose acceptance they think they need.

Accordingly, the results of this investigation take on a new light when viewed from this perspective. The empirical patterns imply that we may have been asking the wrong question! We began with a naive query – do women and men manifest divergent ministry styles? In the results, the straightforward assertion with which we started – that 'women and men do ministry differently' – has been transformed into an analytical question. Now we must ask instead 'Under what conditions do women and men do ministry differently?' This analysis suggests that to identify those conditions one must examine racial-ethical identity, seminary subcultures, and the social structure associated with different kinds of pastoral positions. No doubt there are many other specifying conditions as well. Nevertheless, in the process of this research, what to some was an obvious truth, a matter of dogma, became a complicated conceptual puzzle. That kind of metamorphosis almost always occurs during careful examinations of accepted wisdom – 'what everybody knows'. Research almost always tells us that things are not what they seem.

The distinctions betweeen argument as legitimation and as theory can be characterised in terms proposed by Alfred Schutz (1967), who delineated the difference between social and scientific discourse in terms of different orders of concepts. Concepts shared by actors in the concerns of everyday living Schutz called first-order constructs. These are the typifications of the objects and events by which ordinary people make sense out of their experiences. They are the shared constructs of the taken-for-granted culture that pattern people's thoughts and deeds – the 'folk concepts'.

Social science, says Schutz, is concerned with making sense out of those systems of concepts. In that enterprise, scientific discourse creates second-order constructs, theoretical fabrications designed to explain the first-order constructs, to account for the systems of meaning of everyday life – the folk concepts. Social science involves constructs about other constructs.

The criterion of validity (or success) of first-order constructions is simply whether they work for the purpose of organising individual and social action. The criterion of validity of second-order constructs is whether their theoretical propositions can be supported by replicated empirical research. In these terms making sense out of one's life goals and experiences rests on selective observation and consensual validation, while systematically explaining those ways of making sense out of life rests on formal social-scientific discourse – two quite different enterprises.

To the extent that assertions of sex-specific approaches to pastoral ministry derive from perceptions of useful strategy for broadening women's roles in the church, the arguments involve basically first-order constructs, the meaning systems of the participants. They are the language of the social actors – political statements. As such their criterion of validity is simply if they work, if they actually serve to open up church structures to broader female participation. It matters little if they can be confirmed by empirical evidence. And in the end it may make little sense to expect them to conform to the rules of logic and evidence comprising the canons governing second-order constructs in social-scientific research. Some of the ambiguity and confusion about gender-specific approach to ministry could derive from our misinterpreting first-order constructs by expecting them to be useful as second-order constructs.

Finally, viewing statements about gender-specific ministry styles as legitimations may also have implications for the strategic importance we place on them. The assertions may be less important than they seem. Bacchi points out that feminists have not always divided into two camps, one emphasising sameness and the other focusing on difference. She shows that such a split did not occur until about the turn of the century. The divisions that occurred in the feminist movement even at that time were primarily a result of divergent perceptions of what strategy could best improve women's situation (1990, p. 104) – the same kind of objective as we see in the women-in-ministry movement. The debates within feminism along sameness/difference lines typically arose only where there appeared to be but two options for women, joining the male-dominated system on its own terms or remaining outside of it. From a historical perspective, she says, 'the debates dissolve, or never even surface, when it is possible to expect humane living conditions for everyone' (1990, p. 259).

Furthermore, the debates about similarity and difference have not always involved the same substantive issues. There have been at least three distinct questions in the history of the discussions. One issue has been metaphysical, asking about the fundamental nature of men and women. A second focus has been functional, where the question has been whether or not men and women should play distinct roles in society. The third question was institutional, asking if women need special institutions or legislation to meet their needs. Proponents of the interests of women stressed either sameness or difference from men as it appeared useful strategy to bring about arrangements helpful to women in these specific terms, and each type of issue has been dominant in specific historical struggles of women for social participation and change (Bacchi, 1990, p. 2). Translated into these terms, the arguments about male and female clergy have been whether a metaphysical stance would best promote a functional objective.

Bacchi points out that up to now neither strategy has really worked very well for women (1990, p. xiii). The gains in creating societal structures to allow women (and men) to participate in the economic and political life of the society and still deal adequately with other needs seem to have been rather small. And whether the actual change we have seen was due to the effects of arguments based on sex similarity or difference is almost impossible to determine. The particular type of argument may have had little to do with the eventual outcome. Bacchi says that we need to move beyond the dichotomous debate and focus instead on how society is orgainized and how we should live, work, and care for our families. To overemphasise the sameness/difference framework 'does feminism a disservice since it mystifies these political issues' and distracts us from the real problems associated with contemporary social organisation (1990, p. 265). It derails discussion from a main-track focus on ways to eliminate sex discrimination and sidetracks it on the spur of possibly unproductive arguments about sex differences.

Could the women-in-ministry movement benefit from Bacchi's argument? It is probably far too early to tell if the religious maximalists or minimalists have been more successful in bringing about institutional change in access to the ministry in these denominations. Perhaps the structural alterations that have taken place to date would have happened regardless of whether the pressure for change involved an emphasis on sameness or difference. In the long run of history, those distinctions may prove to have been important in dealing with religious sexism, or they could turn out to have been irrelevant. Only time will tell. Nevertheless, if there is a chance that the debate between maximalists and minimalists on the nature of male and female clergy is focusing attention away from the central issue of equal participation in ministry, perhaps the antagonists will want to reconsider the importance of the entire discussion. The question of masculine and feminine approaches to pastoral ministry is still wide open. It remains to be seen if the issue will be as important in the future as it seems now.

References

Andolsen, B H (1986) *Daughters of Jefferson, Daughters of Bootblacks: racism and American feminism,* Macon, Georgia, Mercer University Press.
Bacchi, C L (1990) *Same Difference: feminism and sexual difference,* Sydney, Allen and Unwin.
Berlin, I (1971) 'Anything you can do, I can do better!' *Annie Get Your Gun,* Universal City, California, Decca.

Carroll, J W (1992) Personal correspondence.

Carroll, J W (1983) *Women of the Cloth: a new opportunity for the Churches,* New York, Harper and Row.

Charlton, J C (1987) 'Women in seminary: a review of current social science research,' *Review of Religious Research,* 28, pp. 305–318.

Christ, C P (1977) 'The new feminist theology: a review of the literature,' *Religious Studies Review,* 3, pp. 203–212.

Christ, C P and Plaskow J (1979) *Womanspirit Rising: a feminist reader in religion,* New York, Harper and Row.

Collins, S (1974) *A Different Heaven and Earth: a feminist perspective on religion,* Valley Forge, Pennsylvania, Judson Press.

Daly, M (1973) *Beyond God the Father: toward a philosophy of women's liberation,* Boston, Beacon Press.

Daly, M (1975) *The Church and the Second Sex,* New York, Harper and Row.

Eagly, A H and Johnson, B T (1990) 'Gender and leadership style: a meta-analysis,' *Psychological Bulletin,* 108, pp. 233–256.

Ekhardt, B N and Goldsmith, W M (1984) 'Personality factors of men and women pastoral candidates,' *Journal of Psychology and Theology,* 12, pp. 211–221.

Epstein, C (1988) *Deceptive Distinctions: sex, gender and the social order,* New York, Russell Sage Foundation.

Fiorenza, E S (1983) *In Memory of Her: a feminist theological reconstruction of Christian origins,* New York, Crossroads.

Fiorenza, E S (1984) *Bread Not Stone: the challenge of feminist biblical interpretation,* Boston, Beacon Press.

Franklin, M A (1986) *The Force of the Feminine,* Sydney, Allen and Unwin.

Gilligan, C (1982) *In a Different Voice: psychological theory and women's development,* Cambridge, Massachusetts, Harvard University Press.

Grant, J (1989) *White Women's Christ and Black Women's Jesus: feminist Christology and womanist response,* Atlanta, Scholars Press.

Hahn, C A (1991) *Sexual Paradox: creative tensions in our lives and in our congregations,* New York, Pilgrim Press.

Hare-Mustin, R T and Marecek, J (1988) 'The meaning of difference: gender theory, postmodernism and psychology,' *American Psychologist,* 43, pp. 455–464.

Ice, M L (1987) *Clergywomen and Their World Views: calling for a new age,* New York, Praeger Publishers.

Lehman, E C Jr (1981) 'Organizational resistence to women in ministry,' *Sociological Analysis,* 41, pp. 101–118.

Lehman, E C Jr (1993) *Gender and Work: the case of the clergy,* Albany, State University of New York Press.

Lincoln, C E and Mamiya, L H (1990) *The Black Church in the African-American Experience,* Durham, North Carolina, Duke University Press.

Lunneborg, P W (1990) *Women Changing Work,* New York, Bergin and Garvey.

Maccoby, E E and Jacklin, C (1974) *The Psychology of Sex Differences,* Stanford, California, Stanford University Press.

Maitland, S (1983) *The Map of the New Country: women and Christianity,* London, Routledge and Kegan Paul.

Mednick, M T (1989) 'On the politics of psychological constructs: stop the bandwagon, I want to get off,' *American Psychologist,* 44, pp. 1118–1123.

Meyers, E S (1988) Searching for feminist ecclesial forms of power and authority: a sociological perspective, paper presented at the annual meeting of the Society for the Scientific Study of Religion, Chicago, Illinois.

Nason-Clark, N (1987) 'Are women changing the image of ministry? a comparison of British and American societies,' *Review of Religious Research,* 28, pp. 331–340.

Ochs, C (1983) *Women and Spirituality,* Totowa, New Jersey, Rowman and Allanheld.

Robb, C S (ed.) (1985) *Making the Connections: essays in feminist social ethics,* Boston, Beacon Press.

Ruether, R R and McLaughlin, E (eds) (1979) *Women of Spirit,* New York, Simon and Schuster.

Russell, L (1974) *Human Liberation in a Feminist Perspective,* Philadelphia, Westminster Press.

Schutz, A (1967) *The Phenomenology of the Social World,* Evanston, Illinois, Northwestern University Press.

Stevens, L (1989) 'Different voice/different voices: Anglican women in ministry,' *Review of Religious Research,* 30, pp. 262–275.

Stoltenberg, J (1989) *Refusing to Be a Man: essays on sex and justice,* Portland, Oregon, Breitenbush Books.

Tavris, C and Offir, C (1977) *The Longest War: sex differences in perspective,* New York, Harcourt, Brace, Jovanovich.

Weidman, J L (ed.) (1985) *Women Ministers: how women are redefining traditional roles* (revised edition), New York, Harper and Row.

9. Women in ministry

Following on from the preceding chapter on male and female differences in ministry, the present chapter focuses specifically on women in ministry. One study concentrates on the differences between women who succeed or fail in ministry. The other study concentrates on clergywomen's self-understanding of ministry.

In the first article in this section, Sue Webb Cardwell explores whether psychological factors can account for some of the differences between women who fail or succeed in ministry. She examined the test profile of 30 women who entered Christian Theological Seminary between 1962 and 1976, 15 of whom had succeeded in ministry and 15 of whom had failed. The test instruments employed were the Theological School Inventory, the Minnesota Multiphasic Personality Inventory, the Adjective Check List and the California Test of Mental Maturity. The successful women ministers were characterised by higher intelligence, a better self-image, more openness to feelings and to general human faults, greater alternative viewpoints, more leadership ability and greater ability to take charge of their own lives.

Professor Sue Webb Cardwell is Professor Emeritus, Pastoral Care and Counselling, and sometime Director of Pastoral Counselling Service at Christian Theological Seminary, Indianapolis, Indiana, USA. This article was first published in *Pastoral Psychology* in 1982.

In the second article in this section, Lesley Stevens reports on a survey conducted among 108 women ordained in the Anglican Church of Canada. Quantitative and qualitative data are discussed in three sections. First, a demographic portrait is presented of the respondents. The second section summarises the women's perceptions of gender differences in the concept and practice of ministry. The third section defines a sub-group of clergywomen who are described as radical. The findings provide some support for the thesis that clergywomen share an orientation that is relational and centred on care for others, but at the same time the findings also reveal striking differences among clergywomen.

Lesley Stevens is a doctoral student and sessional lecturer in the Department of Religion at Concordia University, Montreal, Quebec, Canada. This article was first published in *Review of Religious Research* in 1989.

9.1 Why women fail or succeed in ministry: psychological factors

Sue Webb Cardwell

Today women are entering the ministry in increasingly larger numbers. The percentage of women working on professional degrees in seminaries has more than doubled from 1972 to 1979 – from 9.8 % to 21.1% according to the Association of Theological Schools. However, women are experiencing difficulty in being accepted and placed in congregations. During this period of working toward full acceptance on equal terms by the church, women need to be extra effective in order to establish and prove themselves. Women who fail or who are very mediocre only hurt this cause. Therefore, if factors which contribute to success or failure can be isolated, it makes it possible for remedial or potentiating measures to be taken. Seminaries, regional and national staffs could know how to be of help to women as they prepare for and enter into ministry.

Christian Theological Seminary has administered a battery of psychological tests to entering students since the mid-1950s, with test results on file in the pastoral care office since 1959. So, test data on women through the years are available, making it possible to do a study of some of the psychological factors involved in their success or failure in ministry. The study was limited to women students at CTS and therefore included only a small sample of women ministers and used only the tests administered there. However, it can be suggestive.

Method of the study

A list of women students from 1959 on was prepared. Of these, women who graduated with preferably the Master of Divinity degree were selected. Then this list was gone over carefully with Dr Vinton Bradshaw, Director of Field Education at CTS since 1958. He had worked closely with these women in placement and supervision through their seminary years, and had kept in touch with their careers since. They were divided into two groups, first, those clearly successful in ministry, and second, those either having failed and having moved into another occupation because of lack of success, or those still in ministry experiencing little success. There were fifteen placed in each group. Six others who were difficult to place, as they were in the middle, were not used.

Subjects

The subjects of the study then were 30 women who entered Christian Theological Seminary between the years of 1962 and 1976. Of these, 25 received the Master of Divinity degree, three the MA with Specialisation, one the Master of Ministry, and one the STM. As to demomination, eighteen are Christian Church (Disciples of Christ), four are Methodist, two are Presbyterian, one is Roman Catholic; others are United Church of Christ, Baptist, and Christian Church Independent. Twelve of these women are single, fourteen are married and four are divorced. Currently nine are serving as Pastors of a church, six are Associate or Assistant Pastors, two are on regional or institutional staffs, two are working with their minister husbands but on a nonsalaried basis, three are serving on team ministries with their husbands, four are involved in social service occupations and the four others are in other secular work. In both groups they have been out of seminary for one to thirteen years, for an average of 5.64 years for the more successful goups, and of 6.75 years for the other.

Tests

The tests used included the scales of the Theological School Inventory, the MMPI (Minnesota Multiphasic Personality Inventory), the Adjective Check List and the California Test of Mental Maturity (CTMM). These will be briefly described later. The scores of the two groups on the various scales of these tests were entered, the means found, and the differences between the means tested for significance. Also the adjectives of the ACL checked by the two groups were compared for differences in self-descriptions. For all but one person the scores as seniors were used except for the CTMM, which is administered only on entrance.

Results of the study

Intelligence

The successful women ministers as a group were most intelligent, as shown by their scores on the CTMM. Their average score on the total mental factors was 119.4 vs 114.7 for the less successful ones. This difference did not quite reach significance. However, their mean score of 127.67 on the language factor was significantly ($p \leq 0.05$) higher than the 119.80 of the less successful group. This means their verbal ability is significantly greater – and the ministry *is* a verbal profession! Scores of 120 to 130 are in the superior range of intelligence, in comparision with the general population. Also, the range of scores of the less successful was greater – 97 to 138 vs 114 to 138. So we see that higher intelligence contributes to success in ministry as a 'necessary but not sufficient' condition, since three of the less successful scored above 130. There are many ways to fail, but all necessary elements must be there for success!

Motivation for ministry

The TSI measures the relative strength of various motivations for ministry, but there were no significant differences in these motivations. The strongest motivations for both groups were service to persons – pastoral care and counselling – and leadership in the programme of the church, followed by concern for social reform. The successful ones expressed more confidence in their leadership ability and had had more positive encouragement for ministry. They were less conservative, and more flexible and open to new ideas, though these differences did not reach statistical significance.

Self-image

The Adjective Check List consists of 300 adjectives. The instructions are to check those which are self-descriptive – so it gives a self-image in terms of scales for personal adjustment, for self-control, for mood swings, for self-confidence, and for sixteen needs, such as achievement, dominance, affiliation, nurturance, heterosexuality, deference, etc. Also the number of favourable and unfavourable adjectives give an indication of the relative favourableness of self-image.

Three of these scales showed significant differences between the most and least successful women ministers: personal adjustment (0.02 level of significance), affiliation (0.01), and heterosexuality ($p \leq 0.02$), while a fourth almost reached significance – number of favourable adjectives (0.10).

The personal adjustment scale was based on subjects rated higher and lower on personal adjustment and personal soundness. Both groups of women scored in average range, but the more successful ones scored significantly higher (at the .02 level, meaning only twice out of a hundred times could this difference have happened by chance). These could be expected to have more of the characteristics of high scorers on this scale: 'optimism, cheefulness, interest in others and readiness to adapt'; 'seen as dependable, peaceable, trusting, friendly, practical, loyal and wholesome'; 'fits in well, asks for little, treats others with courtesy, and works enterprisingly toward (her) own goals'; 'possesses the capacity to love and work'. Lower scorers would tend to be 'at odds with other people, moody, dissatisfied' – problems in interpersonal realtionships.

The need affiliation is defined as a need 'to seek and sustain numerous personal friendships'. High scorers on affiliation are 'adaptable, anxious to please, ambitious and concerned with position'. (The descriptions apply to both men and women.) Low scorers tend to be 'more individualistic, less trusting, more pessimistic, and restless in prolonged contacts with others'. While both groups of women scored in average range, the more successful women ministers scored significantly higher and would tend to resemble high scorers, and therefore have better interpersonal relationships.

The need, heterosexuality is defined as 'to seek the company of and derive emotional satisfactions from interactions with opposite sexed peers'. High scorers are also interested in life and experience in a healthy, direct, and outgoing manner. This would tend to characterise the more successful women ministers – of whom nine are married, one is divorced and five are single. Low scorers tend to 'think too much, dampen vitality, be dispirited, inhibited, shrewd and calculating in interpersonal relationships'. This would only represent tendencies, and only part of this might be descriptive. However, five (vs nine) of the less successful women are married, and three (vs one) divorced and seven are single. On the whole, then, the more successful group do seem to have better heterosexual relationships – as well as being more outgoing and interested in life. The difference between the two groups was significant at the 0.02 level.

The number of favourable adjectives gives an indication of the favourableness of self-description. Both groups scored above the mean, but with the more successful scoring higher at the 0.10 level of significance. They would be likely to have more of a 'desire to do well by hard work and conventional endeavour' and not egotistical or self-centred – a generally better self-image.

When the adjectives themselves were tallied for the two groups, for thirteen of the fifteen in each group, some adjectives were checked by eleven, twelve or all of one group but several fewer of the other group. These suggest real differences in self-image. The more successful women ministers described themselves more frequently as: active, affectionate, attractive, fair-minded, feminine, gentle, good-looking, intelligent, and wholesome. Less successful ones described themselves more frequently as: cooperative, clear-thinking, individualistic, sentimental, and serious. In addition, there were other adjectives checked by over half of one group but by several (three to five) fewer of the other. In this category more successful women ministers checked complicated, pleasure-seeking, poised, sharp-witted, soft-hearted, talkative, and witty. Similarly the less successful women checked hard-headed, impatient, inventive, quiet, shy and another five to zero checked silent. Though many of the adjectives were endorsed by both groups in equal or almost equal numbers, just reading these lists endorsed differently gives a feel for very real differences in self-image between the two groups. It fleshes out the differences indicated by the scales discussed above.

In sum, the more successful women ministers seem to have better self-images, more self-esteem. They would be better adjusted, have more friendships, better personal relationships in general as well as with the opposite sex, be interested in life and experience in a more healthy, direct and outgoing manner. They tend to see themselves more frequently as attractive, feminine, active, affectionate, intelligent and verbal.

On the other hand, the less successful women ministers tend to have less favourable self-images in the ways listed above, and also are more likely to see themselves as individualistic, impatient, quiet and shy – even for one-third of them, silent.

The MMPI

The Minnesota Multiphasic Personality Inventory, one of the most widely used of standardised tests, consists of a pool of 550 items which have been used to develop over 450 different scales. However, the usual scoring is for four validity scales useful for indicating test-taking attitude, ten clinical scales developed originally to place people in various diagnostic categories but also useful as indicators of problem areas, and eleven new scales which indicate additional problem areas, but also some areas of strength. These were the scales used in this study.

Three of these scales showed significant differences between the two groups, and five others approached significance.

The more successful women ministers scored significantly lower on the R (conscious repression) scale (0.01), and on the L (lie) scale (0.05), and significantly higher on the Cn (control) scale (0.02). Approaching significance were the K (correction) scale, the Dy (dependency) scale and the Ma (hypomania), the A (conscious anxiety) and the Re (social responsibility) scale ($p \leq 0.10$).

The R scale measures conscious repression (suppression), the extent to which a person uses denial and rationalisation as coping behaviours and also a lack of effective self-insight. The less successful ones on the average do use a mild amount of conscious repression of feelings, and are reluctant to discuss some topics. The most successful women ministers score in the range indicating that they are not trying to repress consciously any of the topics covered by the MMPI, but are willing to be open and self-disclosing to others. They are likely to be outgoing, emotional and spontaneous. This would be helpful in interpersonal relationships.

Interacting with this is the *A (conscious anxiety)* scale, on which the more successful women ministers scored higher (almost significantly so) though both groups scored in the low average range. This means that because they use less repression, they are more aware of situational anxiety when they feel it than are the less successful women ministers.

The Cn (control) scale is a measure of personality control, the extent to which the person can control problem behaviour. The more successful women ministers scored significantly higher on this scale, indicating more ability to control problem behaviour from being exhibited in the presence of others. In this range the score also indicates realistic self-appraisal.

The L (lie) scale measures the degree to which a person is trying to look good in an obvious way, by not admitting to human foibles. The less successful presented themselves as virtuous, conforming and self-controlled, while the more successful ones were more willing to admit to general human faults, more relaxed, significantly so.

The K (correction) scale measures defensiveness and guardedness, but much more subtly than the L scale. Both groups of women scored in the range denoting the 'healthy defensiveness' of normal college-educated populations. They see their lives as generally satisfactory, themselves as basically competent, and able to manage their lives. However, again the more successful women were less defensive.

The Dy (dependency) scale measures the extent to which one would like to or actually is leaning on others. Both groups scored in the mentally healthy range, but with the more successful women admitting to more dependency on others. Both groups again score in the range on the *Do (dominance) scale* which indicates a tendency to take charge of their own lives, but with the more successful scoring higher. Thus the more successful women ministers seem to be better able to both take charge of their own lives and at the same time to be more dependent on others, healthily so. (Only one of this group was divorced as compared with three of the other.) The higher Do score also indicated more leadership ability.

The Ma (hypomania) scale measures psychic energy – both mental and physical activity. The less successful groups scored in the high average range, in the range for average college students. The more successful scored higher, in the typical range for graduate students, tending to be more active, with more projects they tend to complete. They are likely to get more done.

The Re (social responsibility) scale seems to measure the degree to which persons accept the values with which they were reared, parental values or, if over 25, their own present value system. The less successful group seemed to have a greater acceptance of parental/own present value system, while the more successful scored on the average just on the borderline between questioning/exploring alternative viewpoints and accepting present value systems. In other words, they seemed more open to alternative viewpoints without being rebellious against parental values.

In sum, looking back over the differences as shown by the MMPI, more successful women ministers seem to:

a. use less repression, but be more open and self-disclosing, more outgoing, emotional and spontaneous.
b. be better able to control any problem behaviour, do more realistic self-appraisal;
c. be more willing to admit to general human faults, more relaxed;

d. be less defensive, while seeing their lives as generally satisfactory, themselves as basically competent, able to manage their lives;

e. be more (healthily) dependent on others while at the same time better able to take charge of their own lives, more leadership ability;

f. have more psychic energy, more active both mentally and physically, tend to get more done;

g. be more open to alternative viewpoints without rebelling against parental/own present value systems.

The Terman Study has followed over 1,500 gifted children since 1921 – six decades. It is interesting to compare some of the findings as reported in the February, 1980 issue of *Psychology Today* with ours on women ministers. In the Terman Study the most and least successful in work were compared – men only, since so few women were employed full time. Though hundreds of variables were included, the differences seemed to be in attitude and adjustment. Ratings by others and themselves revealed differences in only three traits, in that the most successful were more goal-oriented, had greater perseverance and more self-confidence. However, the study of life satisfaction for the women revealed similar factors involved in greater satisfaction: favourable self-concept, high in confidence, and in ambition for excellence. These indeed correspond closely to the findings of women ministers and confirm their importance.

The area of interpersonal relationships so important to success in ministry was only indirectly reported for the Terman Study, but the most important sources of life satisfaction for women were family, friends, work, since less than half of them were employed full time. (For men, the order was family, work, friends, etc.) The least successful men were the least likely to marry and close to half were divorced compared with 16% of the most successful. Successful women ministers were also more likely to be married and less likely to be divorced. They had higher needs for interpersonal relationships with persons of both sexes.

So what?

Now that we know all this, what difference does it make? Does it give us clues as to interventions that could be helpful in increasing the effectiveness and success of women ministers? Yes, indeed! Attitudes and adjustment can be changed.

However, all that follows is based on real openness to growth and motivation to change on the part of the person herself. No one outside can do it for her or make her do it. However, there are ways of increasing motivation, including making opportunities available, encouragement, support and, where needed, negative feedback that may be necessary, but painful. Most frequently the negative feedback comes from congregations, peers, others around them. The specific intervention needed depends on at which end of the continuum the person is. As for instance, the overly inhibited needs to be helped to loosen up, be more spontaneous, while the overly impulsive needs to learn to use more conscious, rational control. Or the overly submissive woman who swallows her anger needs to learn to use it constructively and be more assertive. The hostile woman needs to work through the faulty childhood learning experiences to greater acceptance of self and others. It can be done!

Helpful experiences

Clinical pastoral education

It would help if CPE were required for all seminary students. It is a watershed experience for a great many. It provides for many their first experience of an open, confrontive yet supportive group. It fosters openness to honest sharing, to acceptance of human foibles in others and in oneself, to corrective feedback, to constructive handling of anger. It helps the overinhibited to loosen up, the submissive to become more assertive, etc. One gets feedback on blocks to good interpersonal relationships as well as help with intrapsychic conflicts and self-image. In addition, the learning of skills in ministering is invaluable. At least nine of the more successful women ministers has CPE vs two of the less successful.

Counselling

Some have personal pain, internal conflicts, and problems in self-concept that need more than CPE can offer – longer term, perhaps even in-depth counselling. This can be tremendously helpful, can make deep, long-lasting changes. The Terman Study of both men and women found the relationship with parents extremely important to success and life satisfaction. Women handicapped by faulty learning or painful experiences in childhood can be helped to work these through to better relationship with parents and better interpersonal relationships in general, plus better self-image and self-confidence. Of the successful women, nine had counselling (that I know of) vs four of the less successful. These four ended up functioning at least acceptably, whereas without it, they would have really failed.

Other group or growth experiences

There are many other kinds of these that can be helpful, from a good prayer group that really shares, to Mid-West and Southern Academies, to National Training Labs, TA, Gestalt, or other therapy groups, etc. The leadership is the most important variable in any of these, and should be carefully chosen.

Special mention should be made of the SCOFE groups at CTS which provide the helpful sharing, feedback and support mentioned plus actual supervision of ministry. Nine of the more successful were in SCOFE. Parish relations committees and 'mentor' relationships are invaluable. These suggestions represent only a few of many possibilities.

Assertiveness training

The recent distinction between submissiveness, aggressiveness and assertiveness is a very helpful one. The workshops and other training experiences in how to be effectively assertive are particularly important for women who are acculturated to being nonassertive if not submissive, and who are so quickly negatively labelled 'aggressive female'.

Conclusion

The fortunate women ministers are those who are endowed with high intelligence and favourable family experiences so they come to ministry with good self-concepts, with motivation to competency, and good interpersonal relationships, well adjusted. And, in 'Cotton Patch' type language, 'Them what has, gits', as we have seen. They are also more open to and take more advantage of growth-enhancing experiences. However, intelligence is used more efficiently if interfering anxiety is lessened. And poor self-images – translated as lack of love of oneself – can melt away in the warmth of loving, caring relationships in one to one or group. The love of neighbour that wells up then means better interpersonal relationships. These, then, can be made more effective by training skills. So the gospel message can become, to a greater degree, incarnate. Than this, nothing is more important – or more urgent.

References
Dahlstrom, W G, Welsh, G S and Dahlstrom, L E (1972) *An MMPI Handbook,* volumes 1 and 2, Minneapolis, Minnesota, University of Minnesota Press.
Duckworth, J (1979) *MMPI Interpretation Manual for Counselors and Clinicians* (2nd edition), Munice, Indiana, Accelerated Development.
Glass, G V and Stanley, J C (1970) *Statistical Methods in Education and Psychology,* Englewood Cliffs, New Jersey, Prentice Hall.
Harrison, G G and Heilbrun, AB (1965) *Adjective Check List Manual,* Palo Alto, California, Consulting Psychologists Press.
Hunt, R A, Cardwell, S W and Dittes, J E (1976) *Theological School Inventory Manual and Guide to Interpreting the TSI,* Dallas, Texas, Ministry Studies Board.
Sullivan, E T, Clark, W W and Tiegs, E W (1963) *Examiners Manual, California Short-Form Test of Mental Maturity,* Monterey, California, McGraw-Hill.

9.2 Different voice, different voices, Anglican women in ministry

Lesley Stevens

The different voice hypothesis and clergywomen

In her book *In a Different Voice: psychological theory and women's development,* Harvard psychologist Carol Gilligan argues that there is a distinctively feminine mode of reasoning about self and morality which constitutes a 'different voice'. It values personal relationships over abstract principles, responsibility and care for others over universal rights, and is centred on women's knowledge of 'the importance of intimacy, relationships, and care' (Gilligan, 1982, p. 17). Gilligan contrasts this approach, also termed the 'ethic of care' with the 'ethic of justice' associated with 'mature' male morality as described by moral development theorists. The ethic of justice applies universal principles of rights and justice equally to all persons and is informed by 'the formal logic of fairness' rather than 'the psychological logic of relationships' (Gilligan, 1982, p. 73).

Though careful not to claim that the different voice or ethic of care is exclusive to women, Gilligan does state that its association with women is an empirical observation, and calls for research that 'delineates in women's own terms the experience of their adult life' (Gilligan, 1982, p. 73).

The different voice hypothesis invites application to a female population professionally concerned with people and morality: clergywomen. The research reported here examines two types of data (from a survey of Canadian Anglican clergywomen) in light of the different voice hypothesis; first, the clergywomen's perceptions of gender difference in ministry and second, their responses to a range of social-ethical issues.

The research confirms the general applicability of the different voice hypothesis outside the actual field of moral development studies: clergywomen do appear to believe that they share a pastoral approach that is more relational, caring and less hierarchical than that of most of their male colleagues. However, the research findings also suggest that a shared perception of a different voice in pastoral ministry can go hand in hand with sharply divergent views on social-ethical issues. Such intra-gender differentiation raises questions about the application of the different voice hypothesis in research on women in ministry.

Research sample, method, and reporting

This paper is based on data from a 110-item questionnaire eliciting both quantitative and anecdotal information, which was mailed to 180 of a total population of 185 women ordained in the Anglican Church of Canada. The number of completed returns is 108; these were analysed in conjunction with background material from interviews with five clergywomen not included in the questionnaire sample.[1]

Section one of the paper summarises key demographic characteristics of the respondents with reference to comparative data drawn principally from a large sample (N = 1374) American survey of Protestant clergymen and women (Carroll, Hargrove and Lummis, 1983).

Section two analyses the clergywomen's perceptions of gender difference in ministry and assesses the extent to which they correspond to Gilligan's notion of a different voice or ethic of care.

Section three identifies and defines a sub-group of radical clergy-women who, though they share with their colleagues the sense of a different voice in pastoral ministry, differ in their application of a social justice perspective to questions of social ethics. In a concluding section, I discuss implications of this differentiation in ethical approach among clergywomen, both for the church and for research on women in ministry.

Demographic portrait of the questionnaire respondents

Regional distribution

The regional distribution of respondents is within 2% of the actual distribution of ordained Anglican women by region, indicating that there is no regional bias in the sample that does not reflect social reality. The largest single group of respondents (54%) is from the Central region, where in fact 54% of Anglican clergywomen reside.

Age

The relative maturity of clergywomen and their late entry into the profession has been noted by previous research. Carroll *et al.* (1983, pp. 68–71) found that twice as large a proportion of women as men entered seminary at age 29 or older, and that the Episcopal Church had the highest proportion of 'second-career' women among Protestant denominations. This is confirmed by another more recent study which reports a mean age at ordination of 41 years for a sample of Episcopal clergywomen, compared with 25 years for men (Morgan, 1985, pp. 14–17).

The mean age of respondents in this survey is 46 years and mean age at ordination 41 years. Only 22% were aged under 30 years at ordination and thus presumably entering the ministry as a first career.

Social class

Researchers suggest that clergywomen tend to come from higher status family backgrounds than their male counterparts. Carroll *et al.* (1983, p. 52) found that 41% of clergywomen, compared with 28% of clergymen, had fathers in professional or executive occupations. That finding is replicated in this survey, in which 47% of respondents had professional or executive fathers. However, this leaves a majority of clergywomen with other than professional family backgrounds. Given the weight of common wisdom that the Anglican/Episcopal tradition represents the upper middle class and the 'Tory Party at prayer', it is worth noting that 27% of this sample had fathers with working class occupations, and one-half of the respondents' mothers working outside the home were non-professional.

Civil status

The higher proportion of singles among clergywomen, compared with clergymen, is well documented. Carroll *et al.* (1983, p. 251) found 45% of clergywomen and only 6% of clergymen were single, divorced or widowed; Morgan (1985, p. 17) notes that while 40% of his sample of clergywomen were single, divorced or widowed, only 12% of Episcopal clergymen in a 1979 study were single, and a 'negligible' number divorced.

In this sample 49% are married, 34% single (never married), 13% divorced, and 4% widowed. Thus, close to half of the clergywomen surveyed are unmarried, and this represents a shift away from the traditional clergy household and lifestyle.

Education, job status, and income

Most of the respondents (85%) have one or more university degrees and 69% hold the Master of Divinity degree, which has become an educational norm for Anglican clergy only in the past ten years.

Despite generally high educational qualifications, however, Anglican clergywomen are not filling high-status positions ten years after the first ordinations of women to the priesthood. Of those presently working in parish ministry, less than one-half (47%) are in charge as sole or senior minister. The typical parish clergywoman in this sample is either rector in charge of a small, non-urban parish or assistant in an urban or suburban parish; while a majority have salaries in the $10,000–$16,000 (US) range, 39% earn less than $10,000 (US) yearly.

These figures compare closely with those in the survey by Carroll *et al.* (1983, p. 230), in which 49% of clergywomen were sole or senior pastors, compared with 88% of clergymen. While 39% of clergywomen in that study earned $10,000 or less yearly, only 10% of clergymen were in that category.

Place and type of employment are key issues for the clergywomen in this survey, 30% of whom work in non-parish ministry and thus do not fit the cultural norm identifying clergy as those in charge of congregations. At least one subject of women in ministry research has remarked upon the hidden assumption that success equals full time work as head of a parish and asks, 'Is parish ministry, solo, the measure of women's success and acceptance?' (Hiatt, 1985).

A different experience, a different voice

The experience of discrimination

Gilligan's different voice hypothesis depends in part on the assumption that the origins of many gender differences lie in the different life experience of women: 'women not only reach mid-life with a psychological history different from men's and face a different social reality ... but they also make a different sense of experience, based on their knowledge of human relationships' (Gilligan, 1982, p. 172).

The reported experience of some respondents in this study includes discrimination based on gender, resulting from the male domination of the profession. The most commonly cited discriminatory experiences include the absence of female role models, discrimination in education, selection and placement processes, difficulty in getting ordained, and opposition to ordained women encountered on the job.

The absence of female role models contrasted to the wealth of models for male ministers is frequently noted in research on women in ministry (see Carroll *et al.,* 1983; Charlton, 1985; Nason-Clark, 1985). The 35% of respondents in this survey who had female role models are younger, and most come from three dioceses with more than token numbers of ordained women. Respondents' comments point both to the drawbacks of male-only models ('man can teach you the trade, but not the role') and to the responsibility of clergywomen to act as models for younger women.

Direct discrimination in preparation for ministry was experienced by one-third of the respondents, who cite a male-biased curriculum, all-male faculty, lack of financial support for seminary women, preferential selection of male candidates, difficulty finding first or second placements, discrimination in salary benefits, resistance to clergy couples and in some cases to divorced women. Getting ordained was 'somewhat' or 'very' difficult for 54% of respondents; in contrast, Carroll *et al.* (1983, p. 225) report only 7% of their male sample experienced any difficulty getting ordained.

There is a higher level of reported discrimination post-ordination, in parish work, than for the pre-ordination situations, with 80% of respondents reporting that they have encountered some opposition to ordained women on the job. The majority mentioned clergymen as the most persistent opponents. This is consistent with other research evidence that Episcopal clergymen are both more likely than other Protestant clergymen and more likely than lay people to be 'anti-feminist' (Carroll *et al.*, 1983, p. 101). A recent study (Lehman, 1985) employs the 'contact hypothesis' to predict reductions over time in lay opposition to women leaders; Anglican clergymen may indeed remain opposed longer because, unlike most lay people, they are able to effectively avoid contact with women performing a clerical role.

Clergywomen's concepts of ministry: issues of power, authority and leadership

In support of the different voice hypothesis, Gilligan links such experiences of male domination and consequent discrimination to the formation of a distinctively feminine orientation to power. A principal source for this insight is the work of Jean Baker Miller (1976), who concludes that because of their experience of subordination in relationships of inequality with men and of temporary dominance in the parenting role, women are more sensitive than men to the potential for abuses in the exercise of power and authority. Gilligan puts forth literary and other evidence to show that men and women employ contrasting images of 'hierarchy' and 'web' to convey their different senses of the structuring of relationships, with women preferring a 'non-hierarchical vision of human connection' (Gilligan, 1982, p. 62).

The women in this study do express ambivalence about their authority and desire to rework it into non-hierarchical forms. The clerical collar and shirt, for example, symbols of traditional male clerical authority, are the focus of ambivalent feelings for the majority of respondents. The 43% who wear clerical dress 'often' see it as necessary less because of the need to denote authority than because of the need to counteract the expectation that clergy are male, and to 'make a statement about women's ordination'. Many of these frequent wearers, however, express ambivalence about clerical dress as a power symbol by adapting its design and colour in a variety of non-traditional ways.

Clergywomen who compromise and wear clerical dress 'occasionally' (31%), are uncomfortably aware both of the need to make clergywomen visible, and of the drawbacks: 'You're caught – if you don't wear it, you aren't seen. If you do, you may be seen, but seen as masculine, competitive, and threatening to other women.' For the 26% of respondents who 'rarely or never' wear clerical dress, it is unequivocally regarded as a symbol of patriarchal power. Their position compares with the 20% of clergywomen and 6% of clergymen in the survey by Carroll *et al.* (1983, p. 172) who reported that they 'never wear a collar outside of church services'.

Respondents also reveal a pre-occupation with the question of power and authority in their anecdotal statements about the impact of women on the ministry of the church. More than one-half (53%) cited 'leadership style' as the locus of the greatest change in the church resulting from the presence of ordained women. In terms which echo Gilligan's description of the different voice, they describe female leadership as: 'more personal', 'less authoritarian', 'inclusive of others', 'collegial', 'facilitative', 'non-hierarchical', and 'the exercise of authority without power-seeking'. Though the clergywomen must often regard this style as a matter of principle, some are conscious of its origins in the negative experience of subordination: 'Women have a particular sensitivity to the experience of being oppressed and are exploring new patterns of using and sharing power.'

More than two-thirds of the respondents (73%) responded affirmatively to the question: 'Does being a woman affect the way you understand or perform the following activities of ministry: celebration of the Eucharist, preaching, and pastoral work?' The subjective judgement of most respondents that there are significant gender differences in ministry mirrors Gilligan's different voice, principally in the emphasis placed on relationships, care, inclusiveness, and the use of non-hierarchical structures and language.

Eucharistic celebration

Clergywomen's comments about perceived gender difference in liturgical celebration fall into three thematic categories: physical presence, nurturing, and authority. Comments of the first type draw attention to surface effects of female presence such as voice, gesture, and attention to detail; several note that they recite the liturgy slower than their male colleagues in order to ensure that everyone is able to follow the words. In addition, some speculate that a female body at the altar has significant symbolic impact on Anglican congregations, 'giving a whole new meaning to Christ's words "This is my body" '.

A second theme involves the image of the Eucharist as family meal, and some female celebrants describe their role as explicitly maternal, 'a mother nourishing her children'. Others use the language of nurturing but try to avoid the connotation of a mother-child relationship with the laity.

The third type of comment focuses on the preference for an egalitarian style of authority in ritual, and describes the celebrant's role as shared with the whole community. 'Horizontal' is the term most often employed to describe this approach, 'where the focus is communal, not on the priest'. 'Sarah's circle' is both an image and an actual ritual format employed by clergywomen concerned to avoid hierarchical structures in worship.

Preaching

Comments about gender difference in preaching concern both the content and style of sermons. The major content differences reported by respondents are the use of feminine life experiences and images as illustrations, and the use of inclusive language. Examples of the former are the use of pregnancy and childbirth images and experiences, and increased reference to biblical texts featuring women.

The 69% of respondents who unequivocally favour inclusive language are regularly using it and provide examples, such as a blessing which refers to God as both Mother and Father, and avoids traditional sonship language by calling Jesus 'Redeemer'. A further 24% express conditional support, with reservations because of concern not to offend parishioners. Only 7% are definitely opposed to the use of inclusive language. In comparison, 88% of clergywomen and 53% of clergymen in the major American survey favoured inclusive language (Carroll *et al.*, 1983, p. 149).

Respondents echo Gilligan's description of the different voice in their use of contrastive pairs to convey their sense of gender difference in their preaching style. The feminine approach to preaching is described as: 'more personal, less theoretical', 'more relational, less dogmatic', 'more circular, less linear', 'the we instead of the you perspective'.

Pastoral work

Two themes emerge in respondents' comments about perceived gender differences in pastoral work: clergywomen believe that they have both special, gender-specific qualities as pastoral care-givers, and a unique relationship to both women and men as clients. Again, the language used reflects the different voice. Clergywomen describe themselves as 'more emotionally available', 'relational', and 'easier to approach' than clergymen. Touch is mentioned as a sign of female pastoral care – respondents observe that they are 'freer to hug, touch and hold people' than are clergymen. Because they 'speak the same language' as girls and women, they feel they are better able to respond to their concerns. While some clergywomen report a corresponding lack of affinity with men as pastoral clients, others observe that men find it easier to open up to a female minister: 'Men find they are able to show their feelings, and even cry – we see more male vulnerability than clergymen do.'

Summary

The subjective sense of a different voice in the practice of ministry which is reported by more than two-thirds of the respondents is effectively summarised by an observer's report on a 1981 conference of Anglican clergywomen: 'Women are aware of their ministry as different because of their powerlessness and vulnerability, their valuing of the basic emotional connections between people' (Tetrault, 1981, p. 5). Many of the clergywomen in this survey who perceive gender differences in ministry also desire to integrate their gender characteristics with the clerical role, and to 'be a woman priest, not a woman playing at a male role'. One respondent suggests: 'The church should decide if it wants women priests or male priests with breasts!'

A minority of respondents (less than one-third) do not agree or are not sure that gender shapes their practice of ministry. They tend to adopt a non-sexual concept of personhood and priesthood: 'I think the person is more important than his or her sex – women should concentrate on being priests and not women priests.' An underlying concern of such women is their wariness of the feminism that they feel is implicit in discussions of gender differences. Rejection of feminism by clergywomen has elsewhere been attributed to 'generational rift' (Anderson, 1986), or the non-assertive personalities of some clergywomen, which leave them 'vulnerable to negative social pressures' (Ekhardt and Goldsmith, 1981). This is echoed in the clergywomen's conference report cited above, which noted that clergywomen fear being labelled and isolated if they assert themselves (Tetrault, 1981).

However, the responsibility may lie less with clergywomen's personalities than with their real professional vulnerability to backlash from conservative clerical authorities and colleagues. The relative conservatism of Episcopal clergymen on feminist issues is documented by Carroll *et al.* (1983, p. 101). That study reports that while 24% of their general Protestant sample of clergymen support strong feminist positions, only 15% of Episcopal clergymen do so.

The positive side of vulnerability to negative social pressures is the very quality of sensitivity and the sense of responsibility to others which is central to Gilligan's characterisation of the different voice: 'Assumption of responsibility for taking care lead women to attend to voices other than their own ... women question the normality of their feelings and alter their judgements in deference to the opinions of others' (Gilligan, 1982, p. 16). Even clergywomen who consciously oppose the notion of gender difference in ministry may, according to Gilligan's standard, be manifesting such a difference in their concern not to offend conservative communities and colleagues.

A voice within the different voice: radical clergywomen

The self perceptions of clergywomen that they are centrally concerned with relationships, care, responsibility to others, and with non-hierarchical leadership appear to fit well with the different voice hypothesis. So far, though, the investigation has been limited to the personal and immediate pastoral sphere of clergywomen's lives. Gilligan has been criticised for employing an exclusively individualist and not a societal perspective in her investigation and thus her theorising about women's moral reasoning. She is charged with ignoring the influence of social factors (such as class and political ideology) which can contribute to divisions among women (as among men) in ethical orientation (see Auerbach *et al.*, 1985, and Stack, 1986). Moreover, Gilligan's approach to the choice and definition of the moral problems to be investigated reveals a personalist bias: even the abortion studies, which provide much of her data on women's moral reasoning, present abortion as a personal, and not a societal dilemma. The role of a societal perspective in the thinking of clergywomen warrants attention, then, if the different voice hypothesis is to be fully explored in relation to women in ministry.

In fact, the clergywomen in this survey display considerable differentiation in ethical approach when confronted with questions of societal or political import. One priest, asked to compare her position on social issues with that of her colleagues (male and female), replied: 'I think I'm way out on a limb!' The sense of marginality, which other clergywomen described as 'being on the fringes' or 'at the edges' of the church, marks the experience of a distinctive sub-group of respondents. I have termed these clergywomen 'radicals' because they integrate a feminist and social justice perspective with their vocation to ministry.

The radical clergywomen are defined statistically by their scores on a 60-point radicalism scale. The scale is composed of 20 items measuring social-ethical attitudes and participation or willingness to participate in activities related to social justice. Items in the radicalism scale asked respondents: to describe themselves as theologically conservative, moderate, liberal, or radical; how often they participate in a social justice group; if they read feminist theology; to indicate levels of agreement or disagreement with a series of statements on feminist issues in the church (ordination rights, election of women bishops, equal representation on all church decision-making bodies, inclusive language, maternity policies and conferences for clergywomen); to indicate agreement or disagreement with statements on abortion rights, homosexual rights, nuclear arms and economic justice; and finally to indicate willingness to participate in public actions related to these issues. The coherence and reliability of the scale was tested and confirmed (Cronbach's Alpha = 0.9094).

While the mean and median score on these items for the entire sample is 44 out of 60, thirty-five clergywomen scored 51 or higher (85% or more of the total score). These clergywomen are defined as radical in their orientation to church and society.

The radical clergywomen, 32% of the sample, differ from their non-radical colleagues across the range of social-ethical issues explored in the survey (summarised in table one). Almost all (97%) of the radicals, compared with 31% of the non-radicals, describe themselves as liberal or radical in theological orientation. They are more likely than non-radicals to support feminist positions on matters pertaining to women in the church, and to opt for unilateral nuclear disarmament, a pro-choice position on abortion, and the right to ordination for sexually active homosexuals.

Practically, radical clergywomen are more likely than non-radicals

Table 1: Responses of non-radical/radical clergywomen to selected questionnaire items (measures of radicalism)

	nonradicals %	radicals %	N
liberal or radical in theology	31	97	96
participate in social justice group	18	74	98
read feminist theology	8	80	90
strong agreement that:			
'women should be eligible for ordination in all dioceses'	97	100	98
'the Anglican Church should encourage the ordination of more women'	52	90	99
'women should be eligible for election as bishops'	75	100	99
'the Anglican Church needs special maternity leave policies for clergywomen'	54	90	98
'the Anglican Church should fund an annual conference for clergywomen'	10	50	97
'there should be equal representation for women on church decision-making bodies'	57	81	98
'the church should use inclusive language in worship'	55	97	98
'Canada should not produce, test, or use nuclear weapons'	85	100	98
'the church should take stronger public stands and action on issues of economic and social justice'	73	93	98
'abortion should be a decision of a woman and her doctor'	15	68	97
'the church should consider recognising homosexual marriages as legitimate Christian unions'	4	77	97
strong disagreement that:			
'the church should not ordain active homosexual/lesbian persons'	9	90	97
would participate in a demonstration against Cruise Missile testing in Canada	40	93	92
would participate in a demonstration against government cutbacks in welfare and social services	44	93	91
would consider asking her church to provide (illegal) sanctuary to a refugee threatened with deportation to El Salvador or Guatemala	42	87	94
would participate in a demonstration to defend access to legal abortion services	6	41	93
would actively sponsor a qualified homosexual/lesbian parishioner as a candidate for ordination	14	83	92

to participate in a social justice group, to read feminist theology, and to express willingness to participate in public action on social issues. Radicals, for example, are more likely to say they would participate in a demonstration against nuclear arms testing or welfare cutbacks or to defend access to abortion services, provide sanctuary for a Central American refugee, or publicly sponsor a homosexual/lesbian candidate for ministry.

Radical clergywomen and non-parish ministry

A cluster of demographic differences between radical and non-radical clergywomen point to some future implications for the shape of ordained ministry in the Anglican Church (see table two). Four demo-

Table 2: Comparative demographic characteristics of clergywomen

	nonradicals %	radicals %	N
age under 40 years	27	74	97
Master's degree	61	87	98
urban location	35	72	92
non-parish employment	18	42	99

graphic variables show a strong relationship with radicalism scores: age ($X = 19.64$; $p < 0.001$) educational level ($X = 9.57$; $p < 0.02$), urban or non-urbanlocation ($X = 18.65$; $p < 0.0003$) and parish or non-parish employment ($X = 6.65$; $p < 0.01$). Radical clergywomen are more likely than non-radical clergywomen to be younger, to have a Master's degree, to live in an urban or suburban environment, and to be employed in non-parish work.

More than twice as many radicals (42%) as non-radicals (18%) are in non-parish jobs. This fact, combined with the relative youth of the radicals, points to growth in non-parish ministries as a possible outcome of the ordination of women and particularly of more socially radical women. Other research findings suggest that this may be a general trend in North American Protestant churches. Carroll *et al.* (1983, p. 235), though they found a smaller proportion of clergy-women in non-parish work (9%, compared with 3% of clergymen), did report that 26% of the women (compared with 14% of the men) would prefer a non-parish position for their next appointment. Morgan (1985, p. 41) found a high proportion of Episcopal clergywomen in non-parish jobs, but concluded negatively that women are being 'directed' into specialised ministries to their disadvantage.

There is no indication in my data that the high incidence of non-parish employment is not a deliberate choice and preference for the clergywomen concerned. For some of the radicals, a shift in church resources not only to non-parish, but also to new and innovative ministries, is a structural condition for the development of a positive social role for the church: 'Clergywomen need to define new ways and places of being a priest, to bring down structures by living out a commitment to non-traditional forms of ministry.'

Over half of the radicals in non-parish ministry are employed in new or innovative forms of ministry, rather than the more traditional chap-laincies in hospitals, universities and prisons. Non-traditional ministries represented in this sample include an urban storefront ministry, an advocacy organisation for the inner-city poor, a food bank, educational and community work among native people, coun-selling work with battered, sexually abused and homeless women, and ministry to the gay community.

The common element in these ministries is a deliberate shift away from both the traditional locations and clientele of the church. While much of the mainstream of the Anglican Church is concerned with evangelism programmes aimed at 'inactive' members (see Bibby, 1986), these initiatives represent a small but significant move towards the 'unchurched' (and indeed, towards those least likely to become traditional church members). One radical clergywoman succinctly expressed the ethos of non-traditional ministries: 'I try to be the church in a new way, for those to whom it's irrelevant.'

The social justice perspective of radical clergywomen

The anecdotal statements of radical clergywomen about their concepts of ministry reveal the social justice perspective underlying their support for radical positions on particular isues of social ethics. These statements go several steps beyond support for lay ministry and non-authoritarian leadership by fully integrating a commitment to social justice into the vocation to ministry.

Content analysis shows that two-thirds of the radicals explicitly mention the pursuit of social justice as an essential component of their concept of ministry. Typical statements both recall key elements of the different voice (relationships, care, responsibility for others), and include the call for justice:

> I see unity between worship, spirituality, care of persons, and connections to the larger call to justice.
> We need to be a caring nurturing community that moves outside the church to the marginalised, to create change.
> I believe in the integrity of worship and social action ... a special responsibility to the poor and powerless.

The radicals, then, share an orientation with their colleagues within the realm of pastoral relationships, but differ in their commitment to broadening the focus of ministry to take in the social and political spheres.

An additional difference is that radical clergywomen apply their social justice principles consistently across a range of issues (in this study, the issues of nuclear disarmament, economic justice, abortion and homosexual rights). Non-radicals, on the other hand, are significantly more conservative in their response to sexuality issues, which are most controversial in the parish context. Most notably, radical clergywomen do not exclude the issue of homosexual/lesbian rights from submission to the social justice perspective, and 90% of the radicals (compared with 9% of non-radicals) support the right of sexually active homosexuals/lesbians to be ordained. Moreover, 83% of the radicals (compared with 14% of non-radicals) say they are definitely willing to sponsor a homosexual/lesbian candidate for ordination. The radicals' positions are striking in light of indications that conservatism prevails in their church on this issue. Bibby (1986, p. 85) reports that 90% of his sample (N = 1720) of Toronto Anglican laypersons think that homosexuality is 'wrong', and 60% oppose the ordination of homosexuals, whether sexually active or not.[2]

Since the non-radicals show considerable support (though less than the radicals) for nuclear disarmamnet and economic justice, it is clear that the radical/non-radical difference in ethical approach pertains especially to questions of sexuality. The feminist and social justice viewpoint is radically distinct from the view of sexuality as a matter of personal morality and convention.

The social justice perspective and the different voice: implications for research

The evidence of differentiation among clergywomen in their approach to certain ethical issues has implications for the use of the different voice hypothesis in research. That hypothesis draws heavily on Kohlberg's six stages of moral development, though Gilligan disputes the hierarchical arrangement of his stages in terms of more or less mature morality. In Kohlberg's schema (Kohlberg, 1981), women are frequently placed at stage three, where morality is conceived in interpersonal terms or in terms of conventional norms and rules. In mature moral reasoning (stages five and six), relationships are subordinated to universal principles of rights and justice. Gilligan's opposition of the feminine ethic of care to the masucline ethic of justice reflects her assimilation of Kohlberg's stages: 'The moral imperative that emerges repeatedly in interviews with women is an injunction to care, a responsibility to alleviate the real and recognisable trouble ... in men the moral imperative appears rather as an injunction to respect the rights of others' (Gilligan, 1982, p. 100).

Given this definition of gender-linked morality, the near-unanimity of clergywomen on issues of peace and poverty is understandable as an example of the different voice or ethic of care in operation. In the area of sexuality, however, the non-radicals appear to uphold conventional rules of morality, while radicals apply an approach which resembles the ethic of justice in its respect for rights without regard for personal feelings or conventions.

Gilligan does allow for a form of female moral maturity which integrates responsibility and care with rights and justice. However, the title of her concluding chapter (Vision of maturity) indicates that the integrated morality is a thing of the future, and she describes its actualisation in very few of her research subjects. Moreover, the vision of moral maturity which integrates care and justice is defined in very individual terms: women's acquisition of the rights and justice perspective is to be applied principally to the attainment of 'integrity of the self'. The goal is: 'including in the network of care not only the other but also the self' (Gilligan, 1982, p. 173). This morality of self-realisation fails to encompass the central concern of radical clergywomen with a social and not just an individual definition of rights and justice. In particular, the social justice perspective seeks to link sexuality issues to other justice issues: 'Establishing the connection between "personal" issues of human sexuality and justice is essential to a social ministry, which can challenge and transform abuses of patriarchal power, the undergirding of injustice' (Gross, 1985, p. 138).

Critics have drawn attention to the absence of a social or political dimension to Gilligan's schematisation of gender and morality. They note that she neglects 'the importance of race, class, consciousness and generation in theory building and the construction of gender' (Stack, 1986, p. 323), and that because her book lacks a political perspective it 'ignores differing and often opposing interests that divide not only women and men but also some women against others' (Auerbach *et al.*, 1985, p. 154).

Consequently, the different voice hypothesis is most useful for delineating and explaining perceptions of gender difference in the interpersonal realm, and in the case of clergywomen, the realm of traditional pastoral work. However, its applicability is limited by its own personalist and relational framework. The ethic of care which the clergywomen feel they share may operate in the territory of immediate pastoral relationships, but rarely be extended to the pursuit of change at institutional or societal levels. There is a need for more research into the moral universes of women and men, but with attention to moral questions both personal and political in nature. As the evidence from this study suggests, uncritical use of the different voice hypothesis as it now stands risks glossing over very real differences in moral thinking within groups of women who otherwise share many personal and professional traits.

Notes

1. The survey was carried out with financial assistance from the FCAR (Quebec). Special thanks to Professors Fred Bird and Lynn Teskey of Concordia University, for their help and advice, and to the editor and associate editors of the *Review of Religious Research* for guidance in revising the original manuscript.
2. The current official position of the Anglican Church of Canada is that sexually active homosexual/lesbian persons are not eligible for ordination. In a highly publicised case early in 1986, two lesbian women were removed from their functions as deacons by the Diocese of Toronto.

References

Anderson, G (1986) Lutheran seminary women, unpublished manuscript, Wilfred Laurier University.

Auerbach, J, Blum, L, Smith, V and Williams, C (1985) 'Commentary: on Gilligan's *In a Different Voice,' Feminist Studies,* 11, pp. 149–161.

Bibby, R (1986) *Anglitrends: a profile and prognosis,* Toronto, Synod of the Anglican Diocese of Toronto.

Carroll, J, Hargrove, B and Lummis, A (1983) *Women of the Cloth,* New York, Harper and Row.

Charlton, J (1985) Seminary experiences of women in ministry, paper presented at the Annual Meeting of the Religious Research Association, Savannah.

Ekhardt, B M and Goldsmith, W M (1981) Personality differences between seminarians and secular education students, symposium on problems of female seminarians, American Psychological Association, Division 36, Los Angeles.

Gilligan, C (1982) *In a Different Voice: psychological theory and women's development,* Cambridge, Massachusetts, Harvard University Press.

Gross, R (1985) 'The embodied church,' in J Weidman (ed.) *Women Ministers,* San Francisco, Harper and Row, pp. 135–157.

Hiatt, S (1985) 'Women in research: a subject's reflections,' remarks presented at the Annual Meeting of the Religious Research Association, Savannah.

Kohlberg, L (1981) *The Philosophy of Moral Development,* San Francisco, Harper and Row.

Lehman, E C (1985) *Women Clergy: breaking through gender barriers,* New Brunswick, Transaction Publishers.

Miller, J B (1976) *Toward a New Psychology of Women,* Boston, Beacon Press.

Morgan, J (1979) *The Diaconate Today,* Bristol, Wyndham Hall Press.

Morgan, J (1985) *Women Priests,* Bristol, Wyndham Hall Press.

Nason-Clark, N (1984) Clerical attitudes towards appropriate roles for women in church and society, unpublished PhD dissertation, London School of Economics.

Nason-Clark, N (1985) Experience in ministry, paper presented at the Annual Meeting of the Religious Research Association, Savannah.

Stack, C (1986) 'On *In a Different Voice:* an interdisciplinary forum,' *Signs,* 11, pp. 304–333.

Tetrault, G (1981) Plain talk: Anglican clergywomen, unpublished report, Anglican Clergywomen's Conference, Winnipeg.

10. Generational changes

Empirical research into the psychology of Christian ministry has now been well established for a sufficient period of time to permit some precise questions to be asked about the ways in which clergy may be changing over time. This chapter presents two studies concerned specifically with monitoring the changing face of Christian ministry.

In the first article in this section, Howard W Stone conducts an examination of data on 1,139 students entering a mainline Protestant seminary between 1962 and 1986. Data were available from the Minnesota Multiphasic Personality Inventory, the Theological School Inventory, the Otis Self-Administering Test of Mental Ability and the Diagnostic Reading Tests. The data demonstrate no changes in levels of psychopathology over this period of time. The academic ability factor, however, shows a significant linear decline in the cognitive abilities of those entering ministry since the late 1960s.

Professor Howard W Stone is Professor of Psychology and Pastoral Counselling at Brite Divinity School, Texas Christian University in Fort Worth, Texas, USA. This article was first published in *Journal of Pastoral Psychotherapy* in 1989.

In the second article, Lawrence A Young and Richard A Schoenherr engage in a debate interpreting the differences in theological attitudes found in two studies of Catholic clergy in the USA in 1970 and 1985. The problem concerns untangling the contributions of an ageing effect and of a cohort effect. Furthermore, the ageing effect includes two components. First, individual priests may become more conservative as they age. The second component of ageing involves the structural effect of resignation. That is to say, cohorts of priests may become more conservative in their theology as they age, if a disproportionate number of resignees adhere to liberal views.

Dr Lawrence A Young is Assistant Professor in the Department of Sociology at Brigham Young University, Provo, Utah, USA. Dr Richard A Schoenherr is at the University of Wisconsin-Madison. This article was first published in *Sociological Analysis* in 1992.

10.1 A twenty-five year study of the changes in those who enter ministry

Howard W Stone

Most seminary faculty members, church judicatory officials, other ministers, and even lay people will say that those who are now entering ministry have changed from those of years past; that there is a new breed of student entering ministry. But is this assumption true? If individuals attracted to ministry today are different from their colleagues of the past, how are they different? In what ways have they changed?

The purpose of the present research was to study demographic data and psychological tests for students entering a mainline Protestant theological seminary over a 25-year span (1962 to 1986) to determine what changes, if any, existed in the overall type of individuals attending seminary. Statistical procedures are performed to determine if any such changes were evident, if existent changes indicated linear or nonlinear trends, and if any such changes were statistically significant.

The population for the study was 1,139 entering students at a Disciples of Christ seminary. All were enrolled for the MDiv degree; special students and candidates for other degree programmes were excluded.

The study of the character of ministerial students by the use of psychological tests is not new; such research has been going on for over 50 years (Bloom, 1971; Brekke, Schuller and Strommen, 1976; Dittes, 1962; Ekhardt and Goldsmith, 1984; Hjelle and Aboud, 1970; Larsen and Shopshire, 1988; Nauss, 1973; Schuller, 1976). Numerous studies have tried to describe components of the ministerial personality. Researchers such as Jack Bloom (1971) or Allen Nauss (1973) have summarised a number of the studies and attempted to draw schemes of what such a personality is like. Few studies, though, have attempted to note the changes over time in the character of those who choose the ministry. This, therefore, is the focus of the present study.

In order to evaluate changes in those preparing for ministry, a number of assumptions were made about changes in the seminary population over the 25 years. These assumptions served as research questions to be answered.

1. It was believed that students were more liberal during the years of 1967 to 1971 but returned to their previous level on a liberal-conservative scale.
2. It was assumed that the academic ability of students had slowly deteriorated over the past 25 years.

3. It was thought that the degree of certainty or definiteness about entering ministry was at its lowest during 1967 to 71 but returned to the previous degree of certainty after that period.
4. It was believed that recent students would show greater elevation in the clinical scales of the MMPI and thus show a greater level of mental/emotional disturbance.
5. It was assumed that students during 1967 to 71 had a higher natural leading and a lower supernatural or special leading to ministry.
6. It was thought that students in 1967 to 71 were motivated more by intellectual concerns and less by personal service, and that after that period students would return to previous levels on those indicators.
7. It was believed that there was a higher evangelistic motivation for ministry prior to 1967 to 71, and that the evangelistic concern was lowest during 1967 to 71 but has increased since, though not to previous levels.
8. Finally, it was assumed that the motivation for social reform in ministry was highest during 1967 to 71 and has decreased since then.

Method

Subjects

One thousand, one hundred and thirty-nine first year regularly enrolled students in a seminary MDiv programme from the years 1962 through 1986 served as the subjects in this study. The mean number of students per year was 45.56. These numbers ranged from a low of 21 in 1967 to a high of 78 in 1978. Eighty-five per cent of the students were male, while 15 per cent were female. Sixty-five per cent were Disciples of Christ students, 18 per cent were Methodist and 17 per cent represented other denominations.

Materials

MMPI: The Minnesota Multiphasic Personality Inventory (MMPI), probably the most frequently used psychological test of personality, contains 556 items. Although numerous scales can be applied to the MMPI, primary ones include three control and ten clinical scales. The control of validity scales are used to determine the attitude of the person who took the test and discern if there have been any attempts to distort the clinical results by faking good, faking bad or following a stylised response set. The ten clinical scales were produced to diagnose individuals in ten separate areas of psychopathology.

TSI: The Theological School Inventory (TSI) is a self-report inventory designed to evaluate seminarians' decisions for the ministry. The first section of the instrument asks 55 demographic questions about an individual's family, religious, and church background. The wording of some of the questions in this section was changed in 1973. The second section tests students' motivations for ministry, their certainty or definiteness about entering it, and the strength of their natural and supernatural leading or inclination toward ministry. The questions and scales of the second section have remained constant during the 25 years of this study.

Academic ability measures: Four tests have been used with students to measure their ability to think, study, and learn from materials they read and lectures they hear. Two instruments are not used in the present study (the Miller Analogies and the Concept Mastery tests) since they were not given in the entire period of the study. The other two tests are the Otis IQ and a reading instrument.

The Otis Self-Administering Test of Mental Ability: Higher Examination is comprised of 75 mixed verbal and numerical questions that are arranged in order of difficulty. The types of items included in the test are vocabulary, sentence meaning, proverbs, analogies, arithmetic problems, and number series.

The Diagnostic Reading Tests: Survey Section measures performance in three general areas: vocabulary, comprehension, and speed of reading. An interesting story-type selection measures the student's usual rate of reading; a 60-item vocabulary test includes English, mathematics, science, and social studies items; and a reading comprehension section measures study-type reading skills.

Procedure

Beginning students from each year completed the MMPI, TSI, IQ, Concept Mastery, and reading test during the week which preceded the beginning of classes.

Results

Overview of analyses

Initially students' scores on the scales of the MMPI and TSA – as well as their IQ and reading scores – were subjected to a principal components factor analysis. This type of analysis considers relationships (correlations) between these variables and returns a smaller number of variable groups (factors). If too many different variables were tested, by the law of probability a few items would show up as significant, whether they were significant or not. The purpose of the factor analysis is to reduce the number of variables that will be tested while at the same time retaining as much of the pertinent information as possible. For example, three different tests could have been performed to see if there were significant changes in students' reading speeds, their overall reading scores, and their IQs. Instead, the factor analysis demonstrated that these three items were highly correlated, and therefore they served as one factor score (the academic ability factor).

Due to the logical nature and clear differentiation of variable groups, a ten factor solution with a varimax rotation was selected. In order to facilitate simplicity of interpretation, factors were employed to create composite scores, rather than factor scores. The use of composite scores avoids some of the associated problems in using factor scores for subsequent analyses (see Dillon and Goldstein, 1984). The composite scores were created by first standardising each of the variables, summing the standardised scores for each variable that loaded on a given factor and dividing by the number of variables in that factor (for example, theological conservatism = TSIE + TSICC + TSISL – TSIFL/4). *A priori* interests and interpretability of the factors resulted in the creation of four composite scores to be used for year-group comparisons. The scores were: theological conservatism, academic ability, elevated MMPI, and intellectual/service orientation. (See table one for the scales that constituted these scores and their loading.)

These composite scores and four TSI scale scores (natural leading – TSINL; supernatural leading – TSISL; evangelism – TSIE; and social reform – TSIR) then served as dependent measures in a series of one-way analyses of variance (ANOVAs). The analysis of variance is a statistical procedure to determine if differences exist between groups. For example, ANOVAs help answer the question, 'Are seminary students more theologically conservative now than they were 25 years ago?' In the present study it helped to uncover if there had been significant changes over the 25-year period in any one or all of the eight TSI scales or factors.

Significant ANOVAs were subjected to *post hoc* tests for mean differences and tests for linear and nonlinear trends (Hays, 1981). The former simply tests to determine which individual groups were significantly different from one another. The latter tests for trends across the five groups.

Linear trends note a significant straight line increase or decrease of, for example, conservatism, over the 25-year period. A quadratic trend shows one peak, and a cubic two peaks, over a particular time span. If the theological conservatism at the beginning of the study were low but increased during the years of the Vietnam war and then immediately returned to the prewar level, a quadratic trend would exist. If there were a second swell of conservatism, a cubic trend would exist.

Longitudinal group comparisons

In order to examine longitudinal seminarian changes, five five-year groups were created: 62 to 66, 67 to 71, 72 to 76, 77 to 81 and 82 to 86. These groups served as the independent variable in a series of analyses of variance, each corresponding to one of the experimental

Table 1: Variables employed to create the theological conservatism, academic ability, elevated MMPI and intellectual/service factors

	variables	factor loading
theological conservatism: the degree of conservatism of students' theological beliefs		
	TSII	−0.72
	TSIE	0.65
	TSIFL	−0.60
	TSID	0.54
	TSINL	0.49
	TSISL	0.42
academic ability: the degree of students' abilities to think, study, and learn from lectures and material they read		
	IQ	0.85
	reading total	0.84
	reading speed	0.66
elevated MMPI: the degree of psychopathology in students		
	MMPIScK	0.85
	MMPIPtK	0.76
	MMPIPdK	0.73
	MMPIHsK	0.67
	MMPIHy	0.62
	MMPID	0.48
	MMPIPa	0.36
intellectual/service: the intellectual over against service interest of students		
	TSII	0.87
	TSIP	−0.46

hypotheses: conservatism factor; academic ability factor; TSID; elevated MMPI; TSINL; TSISL; intellectual/service factor; TSIE; and TSIR. (See table two for cell statistics for the ANOVAs in which a significant main effect was found.)

In the first ANOVA, in which theological conservatism served as the dependent measure, a significant effect for year group was found, $F(4,978) = 4.60$, $p < 0.01$. Tukey *post hoc* analysis indicated that the 1967 to 71 group scored significantly lower, and therefore less theologically conservative, than all other groups except the 1972 to 1976 group. Tests for trend indicated both significant quadratic, $F(1,978) = 4.59$, $p < 0.05$ and cubic, $F(1,978) = 9.94$, $p < 0.01$ trends (see figure one).

In the second ANOVA, academic ability was the dependent variable. Asignificant effect was found, $F(4,1047) = 3.37$, $p < 0.01$. Tukey *post hoc* analysis found that the 1967 to 71 group had superior academic ability to the 1977 to 81 and 1982 to 86 groups. In addition, a significant linear trend was found, demonstrating a lowering of academic ability over time, $F(1,1046) = 10.03$, $p < 0.01$ (see figure one).

A significant effect, $F(4,979) = 9.36$, $p < 0.0001$, was found in the third ANOVA in which the TSID scale (definiteness or certainty about becoming a minister) served as the dependent measure. Tukey *post hoc*

Table 2: Changes in seminary students as a function of year group

scales/factors	1962–66	1967–71	year group 1972–76	1977–81	1982–86
theological conservatism factor					
mean	0.14	–0.19	0.02	0.03	0.03
st dev	0.72	0.76	0.86	0.79	0.78
academic ability factor					
mean	0.09	0.15	0.00	–0.07	–0.06
st dev	0.77	0.76	0.77	0.75	0.86
TSID					
mean	56.37	54.56	55.48	57.28	56.67
st dev	4.96	5.23	5.06	5.25	5.20
TSINL					
mean	51.91	51.13	51.36	53.20	53.45
st dev	7.38	6.86	7.11	7.02	7.01
TSISL					
mean	48.15	45.37	46.81	46.35	46.67
st dev	8.77	8.13	9.22	8.90	8.32
TSIE					
mean	13.02	10.22	11.06	11.12	10.62
st dev	6.29	6.71	6.90	6.64	6.47
TSIR					
mean	12.14	12.98	11.56	10.85	10.33
st dev	4.20	4.45	4.50	4.45	4.36

Note: The theological conservatism and academic ability factor represent standardised variables.

tests indicated that the 1967 to 71 group scored significantly lower, or less definite, than the 1962 to 66, 1977 to 81, and 1982 to 86 groups. In addition, the 1972 to 76 group scored significantly lower than the 1977 to 81 group. Significant linear $F(1,979) = 10.26$, $p < 0.01$, quadratic $F(1,979) = 5.58$, $p < 0.05$, and cubic $F(1,979) = 21.47$, $p < 0.0001$ trends also were found.

No significant effects were found for the fourth ANOVA in which elevated MMPI scores served as the dependent measure.

In the fifth TSINL (natural leading) ANOVA, which determines to what degree individuals feel their own talents and abilities qualify them to serve as ministers, a significant effect was found, $F(4,981) = 4.57$, $p < 0.01$. Tukey *post hoc* tests indicated that the 1967 to 71 group scored significantly lower than the 1977 to 81 and 1982 to 86 groups, while the 1972 to 76 group scored significantly lower than the 1982 to 86 group. Tests for trend yielded a significant linear trend, $F(1,981) = 11.13$, $p < 0.001$.

The TSISL (special leading) scale constituted the dependent measure for the second part of the fifth assumption ANOVA. Students with high scores considered an immediate, direct intervention by God in their life as a primary motivator for their entrance into the ministry

Figure 1: Academic ability vs theological conservatism by year group

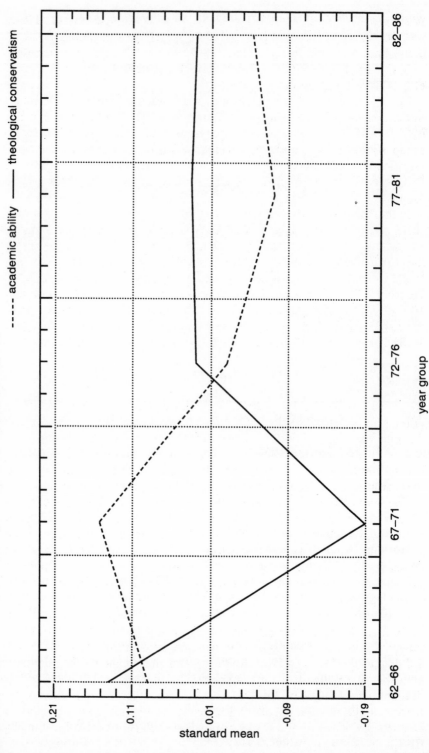

A significant effect, $F(4,979) = 2.51$, $p < 0.05$, was found. Tukey *post hoc* analysis found that the 1962 to 66 group significantly scored higher than the 1967 to 71 group. No significant trends were found.

In the sixth (intellectual/service factor) assumption, no significant effects were found in the ANOVA.

The TSIE (evangelistic motivation) scale was the dependent variable in the next ANOVA. Again, a difference was found, $F(4,981) = 4.86$, $p < 0.001$. Tukey *post hoc* comparisons found that the 1962 to 66 group scored significantly higher than all other groups. In addition, significant linear, $F(1,981) = 5.52$, $p < 0.05$, quadratic $F(1,981) = 4.40$, $p < 0.05$, and cubic $F(1,981) = 8.11$, $p < 0.01$, trends were found.

In the final ANOVA, the TSIR (strength of social reform motivation) scale was the dependent measure. A significant effect was found, $F(4,981) = 11.49$, $p < 0.0001$. Tukey *post hoc* analysis indicated that the 1982 to 86 group scored significantly lower and thus had less social reform motivation than the 1962 to 66, 1967 to 71, and 1972 to 76 groups. The 1977 to 81 group scored lower than the 1962 to 66 and 1967 to 71 groups. Further, the 1967 to 71 group scored higher than the 1972 to 76 group. Tests for trend found significant linear, $F(1,981) = 35.15$, $p < 0.0001$, and cubic $F(1,981) = 6.30$, $p < 0.05$ trends.

Discussion

It is always dangerous to generalise from the study of one seminary to other seminaries and ultimately to all people entering ministry. It is difficult to cross denominations or different parts of the country. All results have to be treated tentatively. Nevertheless, some conclusions can be drawn about a particular Disciples of Christ seminary, and these findings may generalise to other mainline Protestant seminaries.

The assumptions upon which this research was developed came from a survey of the literature and from interviews with seminary professors who had taught over most or all of the 25-year period of the study. The picture that was drawn, though noting such linear trends as decreases in academic abilities and motivation for evangelism, pointed to social activism and the resistance to the Vietnam war in the late 60s as *the* significant influence during the 25-year period.

At the beginning of the study in 1962, the effect of social activism in ministry upon the motivation to bring about change to social structures and address social problems was strong. This influence, though, did not reach its peak until near the end of that decade. The seminary also was a place where those opposed· to the war could avoid being drafted. The years 1967 through 1971 was the peak period when alternatives to the military draft were being sought. It was a period of heightened idealism, and the church was seen as a vehicle for altering the ills of society.

Those years of social activism had a profound effect on the church in the second half of this century and those who were attracted to the seminary at that time were somewhat different from those who preceded or followed them. Theologically they were less conservative than their predecessors, and no group of seminarians since has been as theologically liberal. What is interesting, as can be seen from table two and as indicated by the significant quadratic trend, is that the level of theological conservatism of present seminarians is approaching a return to the level found prior to the late 60s. In other words, those entering ministry now are more theologically conservative than their 1967 to 71 counterparts.

During the period of heightened social activism, those attending seminary felt less definite in their decision about entering ordained ministry. They were less certain whether they should be ministers than at any period prior or since. Table two shows that the level of definiteness dropped in 1967 to 71 but has returned to similar levels that existed prior to the late 60s. (It is also supported by a significant quadratic trend.) The research also suggests that the call to ministry of those entering seminary in 1967 to 71 was motivated less by both natural and special leading. Students during that period considered an immediate and compelling direct intervention by God less crucial to their call to ministry. This was a distinctive break with those who came to seminary before them.

It was hypothesised that of these motivators for ministry, the evangelism drive would be lowest with people entering seminary in 1967 to 71 but would increase again, if not to previous levels. This study noted that of the 25 years studied, the early 60s found students more strongly motivated by a desire to evangelise than at any other time. Although no other significant group differences were found, a significant quadratic trend indicates that evangelistic motivation has rebounded somewhat since the low point of 1967 to 71.

The motivation to bring about social reform to the structures of society, as might be guessed, was highest during the 1967 to 71 period. This motivation was reasonably high in the early 60s and in the five-year period after the late 60s. Since that time, however, the image of ministry as an important way in which people can bring about change to social structures and to remediate social problems has continued to decline. It is presently at its lowest point in the last 25 years.

Although the entering grade point averages of college graduates going to seminary increases each year, their academic abilities are decreasing. The academic ability factor shows a significant linear decline in the cognitive abilities of those entering ministry since the late 60s.

The abilities required to think and to study are now at an all-time low over the 25 years of the research. This is the bad news of the study. At this seminary, students do not show greater levels of psychopathology, but cognitively they cannot stand shoulder to shoulder with their peers from the past.

The lower academic abilities of recent seminarians is suggested by other indices. For example, the percent of college graduates later going into ministry who were Phi Beta Kappa members in 1945 to 49 was 3.9% while in 1980 to 83 it was 0.8% (*Key Reporter*, 2). Now more than ever before, top college students are choosing professions other than ministry.

There have been critical changes in the character of those who are entering ministry over the last 25 years. The shifts appear to reflect some of the changes in our society. They also may reflect the view of academically superior college students who see ministry as a less viable career option than in the past. Although these trends are from one study at one particular seminary, there is reason to believe that such trends may also reflect other mainline Protestant seminaries in other parts of the country. Longitudinal research is presently going on at other schools and in other denominations; from such research we will be able to gain an even clearer and more detailed picture of the changes in those who now enter ministry. Only when a more complete image of these changes has been formed will it be possible to consider strategies for improving the overall quality of ministry in the 90s and beyond.[1]

Note

1. This research project was made possible in part by grants from Lilly Endowment, Inc. and the Research Fund, Brite Divinity School, Texas Christian University.

References

Bloom, J H (1971) 'Who become clergymen?' *Journal of Religion and Health*, 10, pp. 50–76.
Brekke, M L, Schuller, D S and Strommen, M P (1976) 'Readiness for ministry: report on the research,' *Theological Education*, 13, pp. 22–30.
Dillon, W R and Goldstein, M (1984) *Multivariate Analysis*, New York, Wiley.
Dittes, J E (1962) *Research on clergymen: factors influencing decisions for religious service and effectiveness in the vocation*, New York, Religious Education Association.
Ekhardt, B N and Goldsmith, W M (1984) 'Personality factors of men and women pastoral candidates: 1, motivational profiles,' *Journal of Psychology and Theology*, 12, pp. 109–118.
Hays, W L (1981) *Statistics*, New York, Holt, Rinehart and Winston.
Hjelle, L A and Aboud, J (1970) 'Some personality differences between seminarians and nonseminarians,' *Journal of Social Psychology*, 82, pp. 279–280.
The Key Reporter (1985), 2.
Larsen, E L and Shopshire, J M (1988) 'A profile of contemporary seminarians,' *Theological Education*, 24, pp. 10–136.
Nauss, A (1973) 'The ministerial personality: myth or reality?' *Journal of Religion and Health*, 12, pp. 77–96.
Schuller, D S, Brekke, M L and Strommen, M P (1976) *Readiness for Ministry: assessment (statistics)*, volume 3, Vandalia, Ohio, Association of Theological Schools.

10.2 The changing age distribution and theological attitudes of Catholic priests revisited

Lawrence A Young and Richard A Schoenherr

We read with great interest the article on the changing age distribution and theological attitudes of Catholic priests by Hoge, Shields, and Verdieck published in *Sociological Analysis* in 1988. We wish to explore two aspects of their analysis.

First, Hoge *et al.* set out to test earlier projections concerning the age distribution of Catholic priests made by Schoenherr and Sorensen (1982). Hoge *et al.* conclude that 'the Schoenherr-Sorensen projections over-estimate the number of older priests and underestimate the number of younger priests' (1988, p. 269). We wish to present newly available data which will help assess whether the Schoenherr-Sorensen projections or the Hoge *et al.* survey results provide a more accurate estimate of the age distribution of the active clergy.

Second, Hoge *et al.* correctly point out that 'contrary to the (Schoenherr-Sorensen) projection, theological attitudes did not shift in the conservative direction' between 1970 and 1985 (1988, p. 264). However, we believe that explaining the source of the error in the original Schoenherr-Sorensen projections of theological attitudes requires a more complex analysis than provided by Hoge *et al.*

Comparing the age distributions

Figure two in the Hoge *et al.* article shows the Schoenherr-Sorensen projected age distributions in 1970, 1980, and 1990 (1988, p. 269). It also includes the age distributions of surveyed priests in the 1970 NORC survey of priests (1972), which Schoenherr and Sorensen utilised, as well as the age distribution of priests in the Hoge *et al.* 1985 survey study. Hoge *et al.* concluded that Schoenherr and Sorensen overcorrected for the higher nonresponse of older priests in the 1970 NORC study. According to Hoge *et al.*, this led Schoenherr and Sorensen to overestimate the age shift toward an older clergy.

The new data we present allow us to assess whether the Schoenherr-Sorensen projections were correct in adjusting for the nonresponse of older priests or if Hoge *et al.* are correct in concluding that the Schoenherr-Sorensen projections overestimate the extent of ageing within the population of active diocesan clergy.

Our data come from an on-going study of the impact of the demographic transformation of the diocesan clergy on the organisational structure of Roman Catholic dioceses (see Schoenherr *et al.*, 1988;

Schoenherr and Young, 1990). In the study, which is funded by Lilly Endowment and sponsored by the United States Catholic Conference, we have returned to the stratified weighted sample of dioceses in the original 1970 NORC study (see the discussion of methods in Hoge *et al.*, 1988, p. 268). Because of the creation of new dioceses, this sample of dioceses had grown to a total of 89 by 1984, which was the beginning year of our data collection. Of the 89 sample dioceses, 86 agreed to participate in our study. Within each of the participating dioceses, a census registry was constructed containing the name and demographic history of each diocesan priest who had lived within the diocese for any period of time between January 1, 1966 and January 1, 1985. Consequently, we have complete population data concerning priests in each of the 86 dioceses. Furthermore, we can obtain accurate estimates of the national diocesan clergy population parameters by assigning a weight to each priest in our study based upon the probability of his diocese being selected in the original 1970 NORC sample of dioceses. We think that the estimate of the national age distribution of diocesan priests obtained from our census registry provides the baseline necessary to evaluate the Schoenherr-Sorensen projections and the Hoge *et al.* survey results.[1]

Why do we think that our estimates of the 1985 age distribution of diocesan priests are more reliable than either the Schoenherr-Sorensen projections or the Hoge *et al.* survey results? First, we were able to obtain 1985 estimates based on demographic data gathered for that year. On the other hand, the Schoenherr-Sorensen projections are just that – projections based on historical data gathered for the period between 1966 and 1973. Obviously, population estimates are more reliable than population projections when both are based on similar samples. Second, while our estimates and the Hoge *et al.* survey results started with the same sample of dioceses, our estimates are based on complete population level data within 86 dioceses ($N = 33,510$), while Hoge *et al.* rely on a much smaller sample of priests drawn from 28 dioceses ($N = 796$). Furthermore, while we have weighted our data to reflect the probabilities of the various dioceses being included in the original NORC sample, Hoge *et al.* have not done the same for their survey data (see NORC, 1972 for a discussion of the original weighted sample of dioceses).

Table one shows a comparison of the 1985 age distributions in the Hoge *et al.* article. Hoge *et al.* obtained the Schoenherr-Sorensen 1985 age distribution by taking the mean of the 1980 and 1990 age distributions provided by Schoenherr and Sorensen. In comparing the Schoenherr-Sorensen projection with their own survey results, Hoge *et al.* concluded that the diocesan clergy population was becoming older, as indicated by the Schoenherr-Sorensen projections, but they also concluded that the extent of the ageing process was less than that projected by Schoenherr and Sorensen. Note, however, that in our estimate of the 1985 age distribution, listed as the Young-Schoenherr

Table 1: 1985 age distribution of diocesan priests (percent)

	age group			
Source	26–35	36–45	46–55	56–75
Hoge *et al*. survey results[1]	17.0	26.0	26.0	31.0
Schoenherr-Sorensen projection[1]	19.5	19.5	26.5	35.5
Young-Schoenherr census estimate	12.4	23.9	26.4	37.3

Note: 1 From Hoge *et al*., 1988, p. 268.

census estimate in table one, the ageing process had progressed even further than Schoenherr and Sorensen had projected.

For example, while 43% of the Hoge *et al*. sample were 45 or younger, only 39% of the priests in the Schoenherr-Sorensen 1985 projection fell into the 45 or younger age group. This led Hoge *et al*. to conclude that the Schoenherr-Sorensen estimates of ageing were too drastic. Note, however, that the Young-Schoenherr census estimate of the 1985 age distribution indicates that only 36% of diocesan priests were 45 or younger. In other words, based on the newly available data, we may conclude that the Schoenherr-Sorensen projections of ageing were not drastic enough.

Underlying dynamics governing theological attitudes

Hoge *et al*. have shown that the Schoenherr-Sorensen projections of theological attitudes over-estimated the growth of conservatism. In trying to analyse the source of the error in the Schoenherr-Sorensen projections, Hoge *et al*. (1988, pp. 265, 274–5) summarise the assumptions governing the Schoenherr-Sorensen projection of theological attitudes. Hoge *et al*. are in general agreement with all but one of the assumptions posited by Schoenherr and Sorensen – the ageing-effect assumption. Schoenherr and Sorensen observe large differences in theological attitudes between age groups in the 1970 NORC data. They argue that the differences between age groups were due to movement toward increasing conservatism throughout the ageing process. Thus, if one focuses on any given cohort of priests and follows them across time, they will become increasingly conservative as they become older. At the same time, Schoenherr and Sorensen assume that theological attitudes were stable within age groups. That is, Schoenherr and Sorensen argue that as cohorts of priests entered older age groups, they would adopt the attitudes of the older age groups – an ageing effect.

Hoge *et al*. are critical of this ageing-effect assumption and argue that its incorrect application is the source of error in the Schoenherr-Sorensen projections of theological attitudes. Hoge *et al*. argue that the differences between age groups observed in 1970 were due to 'cohort effects; that is, young-versus-old differences in attitudes are due to the different experiences of the generations, not due to attitude shifts with advancing age' (1988, p. 276). They go on to argue that comparing their 1985 survey data with the 1970 NORC data suggests that old priests die and young priests grow older while carrying their attitudes largely unchanged (1988, pp. 279–80).

We think that a comparison of the 1970 NORC data and 1985 Hoge *et al.* data ought to lead to a different conclusion. Namely, the replication data lead us to conclude that the underlying dynamics governing the theological attitudes of the clergy are more complex than either Schoenherr and Sorensen or Hoge *et al.* have described, and involve both an ageing and a cohort effect. Furthermore, the ageing effect potentially includes two components, with only the first having been identified by Schoenherr and Sorensen – namely, that individual priests become more conservative as they age. The second component of ageing involves the structural effect of resignation. That is, cohorts of priests may become more conservative in their theology as they age due to the structural ageing process of resignation, when a disproportionate number of resignees adhere to liberal views (Schoenherr and Greeley, 1974).

If the Schoenherr and Sorensen assumption of the ageing process were correct, then the distribution of attitudes within each age group would be the same at time one and time two. Comparing the theological attitudes of age groups in 1970 and 1985 clearly shows that Schoenherr and Sorensen incorrectly assumed that theological attitudes within age groups were stable over time. For example, comparing 1970 and 1985 attitude scores in tables one to six of Hoge *et al.* would show equal attitude scores in both years within each age group if Schoenherr and Sorensen were correct (that is, the 26 to 35 year old age group in 1970 would have scores identical to the 26 to 35 year old age group in 1985). Note, however, that in the large majority of cases, the theological attitudes of priests within each age group in 1970 differs from the theological attitudes in 1985. Another demonstration of the weakness in the Schoenherr-Sorensen ageing-effect assumption is that figures three and four in the 1988 Hoge *et al.* article differ from what the Schoenherr and Sorensen assumption would predict. If the ageing-effect assumption were correct, the 1985 timeline in figures three and four would be superimposed upon the 1970 timeline. Visual comparison of the two timelines in each figure indicates that the two lines are not identical. Based on this analysis, Hoge *et al.* conclude that priests do not adopt the attitudes of each succeeding age group as they go through the ageing process.

We must be careful, however, not to interpret the lack of complete correspondence between the ageing-effect assumption and Hoge *et al*'s survey data as an indication that priest attitudes form independently from an ageing effect. In fact, we believe that the Hoge *et al.* data lend strong support to the notion that an ageing effect leads to changing attitudes over time, although the data do not allow us to disaggregate this effect into its component parts of individual change and structural change due to resignations. The ageing effect is demonstrated by the reanalysis of their data which we present in table two. The table follows three cohorts of priests across fifteen years. This allows us to see if the attitudes of each entering cohort remained stable, as predicted by Hoge *et al.*, or if the attitudes of each cohort were transformed as the cohort went through the ageing process, as predicted by Schoenherr and Sorensen.

Hoge *et al.* did not perform this analysis because they concluded that cohort analysis was too risky due to the instability of cohorts between 1970 and 1985 (1988, p. 273). Specifically, they argue that ordinations of older priests coupled with resignations have created movement into and out of the cohorts first observed in 1970. While Hoge *et al.* are correct in drawing attention to the fluidity of membership within cohorts, we think that their rejection of cohort analysis in favour of comparing age-groups over time is flawed for the following reasons.

First, age-group analysis, as performed by Hoge and his colleagues, is just as risky as cohort analysis. Hoge *et al.* document that age at ordination is increasing and the crude resignation rate is decreasing (1988, pp. 266–67). Consequently, the dynamics of membership within age groups also demonstrates fluidity. For example, the 1970 age groups in Hoge *et al*'s analysis would have relatively more seniority in the priesthood due to earlier average age at ordination and higher exit rates due to resignation than the 1985 age groups.

Second, while Hoge *et al.* argue that the fatal flaw in the Schoenherr-Sorensen analysis is the ageing-effect assumption, Hoge *et al.* have not performed the appropriate analysis to support their position. That is, because both the Schoenherr-Sorensen ageing-effect assumption and the Hoge *et al.* cohort-effect assumption are based upon what happens to cohorts over time, they can be evaluated only through cohort analysis.

Third, Hoge *et al.* reject cohort analysis because resigning priests have exited cohorts between 1970 and 1985. While resignations have certainly had an impact upon the theological attitudes within cohorts, we will argue that this impact is one component of a more complex understanding of the ageing process.

Finally, Hoge *et al.* are concerned about the possible impact of increasingly conservative and older seminarians on cohort analysis. While this anticipated impact might help us understand why cohorts, defined by age rather than date of ordination, are more conservative than initially expected, it provides no more of a reason to drop cohort analysis than does the fact that 'young priests in the late 1970s and 1980s (are) more conservative theologically' (Hoge *et al.*, 1988, p. 280) provide a reason for dropping age group analysis.

Our position is that cohort analysis is no more risky than age group analysis. While we agree with Hoge *et al.* that membership in cohorts was not stable between 1970 and 1985, the dynamics governing

Table 2: Reanalysis of fifteen statements of theological attitudes in table 1 of Hoge et al.[1] (percent saying 'agree strongly' or 'agree somewhat')

item in Hoge et al. table 1	cohort A	Cohort[2] cohort B	cohort C
1. 1970 observed score	76.0	83.0	94.0
1985 observed score	83.0	90.5	94.0
1985 cohort-effect score[3]	76.0*	83.0**	94.0
1985 ageing-effect score[3]	88.5*	95.5**	98.0***
2. 1970 observed score	18.0	37.0	60.0
1985 observed score	21.0	44.5	62.0
1985 cohort-effect score	18.0	37.0*	60.0
1985 ageing-effect score	48.5***	67.0***	79.5***
3. 1970 observed score	17.0	35.0	57.0
1985 observed score	25.0	43.5	65.5
1985 cohort-effect score	17.0**	35.0*	57.0*
1985 ageing-effect score	46.0***	65.0***	79.0***
4. 1970 observed score	86.0	64.0	50.0
1985 observed score	77.0	61.5	42.5
1985 cohort-effect score	86.0***	64.0	50.0
1985 ageing-effect score	57.0***	41.0***	26.0***
5. 1970 observed score	89.0	71.0	54.0
1985 observed score	65.5	55.5	41.0
1985 cohort-effect score	89.0***	71.0***	54.0**
1985 ageing-effect score	62.5	48.0*	39.0
6. 1970 observed score	91.0	77.0	55.0
1985 observed score	87.5	73.0	56.5
1985 cohort-effect score	91.0	77.0	55.0
1985 ageing-effect score	66.0***	50.5***	47.5***
7. 1970 observed score	78.0	64.0	40.0
1985 observed score	74.0	55.5	33.0
1985 cohort-effect score	78.0	64.0*	40.0
1985 ageing-effect score	52.0***	31.5***	21.0***
8. 1970 observed score	5.0	17.0	35.0
1985 observed score	9.5	21.5	32.5
1985 cohort-effect score	5.0**	17.0	35.0
1985 ageing-effect score	26.0***	43.0***	51.0***
9. 1970 observed score	33.0	53.0	75.0
1985 observed score	48.5	58.0	73.5
1985 cohort-effect score	33.0***	53.0	75.0
1985 ageing-effect score	64.0***	82.0***	91.5***
10. 1970 observed score	38.0	59.0	79.0
1985 observed score	55.0	69.0	82.0
1985 cohort-effect score	38.0***	59.0**	79.0
1985 ageing-effect score	69.0***	84.5***	92.5***
11. 1970 observed score	36.0	59.0	79.0
1985 observed score	59.0	71.5	85.0
1985 cohort-effect score	36.0***	59.0***	79.0
1985 ageing-effect score	69.0**	85.0***	94.5***
12. 1970 observed score	21.0	41.0	58.0
1985 observed score	35.0	48.0	65.0
1985 cohort-effect score	21.0***	41.0	58.0
1985 ageing-effect score	49.5***	65.5***	79.5***
13. 1970 observed score	87.0	72.0	56.0
1985 observed score	77.5	62.0	42.5

Table 2: (continued)

item in Hoge et al. table 1	cohort A	cohort B	cohort C
		Cohort[2]	
	cohort A	*cohort B*	*cohort C*
1985 cohort-effect score	87.0***	72.0**	56.0**
1985 ageing-effect score	64.0***	50.0**	38.0
14. 1970 observed score	13.0	22.0	35.0
1985 observed score	25.5	35.5	48.5
1985 cohort-effect score	13.0***	22.0***	35.0***
1985 ageing-effect score	28.5	41.0	56.5
15. 1970 observed score	28.0	46.0	63.0
1985 observed score	41.0	51.0	68.5
1985 cohort-effect score	28.0***	46.0	63.0
1985 ageing-effect score	54.5***	68.0***	78.5**

Notes: 1 The Ns are based upon data in table 1 of Hoge *et al.* (1988). The Ns for the 1970 NORC sample were, for cohort A, $N = 759$; for cohort B, $N = 901$; for cohort C, $N = 662$. The Ns for the 1985 observed scores were derived from the Hoge *et al.* sample by taking the mean of Ns for the two age strata which overlap each cohort: for cohort A, $N = 190.5$; for cohort B, $N = 178$; for cohort C, $N = 143$.

2 The age strata corresponding to each cohort were: for cohort A, 26–35 in 1970 and 41–50 in 1985; for cohort B, 36–45 in 1970 and 51–60 in 1985; for cohort C, 46–55 in 1970 and 61+ in 1985.

3 The 1985 cohort-effect scores are expected scores based on Hoge *et al*'s assumption concerning cohort effects. The 1985 ageing-effect scores are expected scores based on Schoenherr and Sorensen's assumption concerning the ageing process. Difference of proportion tests were computed between each of these scores and the corresponding 1985 observed scores.

* Difference is significant at .05, 2-tailed.
** Difference is significant at .01, 2-tailed.
*** Difference is significant at .001, 2-tailed

membership within age groups – especially those dealing with the seniority or experience of priests within each age group – were also fluid during the same period. Furthermore, given Hoge *et al*'s desire to compare the ageing-effect assumption with the cohort-effect assumption, cohort analysis is the *required* approach, since the central issue in this comparison is what happens to cohorts over time. While we recognise the risks involved in cohort analysis given the fluidity of cohort membership, we believe even *greater* risks are introduced by reaching conclusions concerning the competing hypotheses of ageing effects versus cohort effects without performing the more appropriate test.

Table two, which is based upon recalculations of the data provided in table one of Hoge *et al.* (1988, pp. 270–71), presents a cohort analysis of fifteen statements of theological attitudes. Cohort A is the group of priests who were 26 to 35 in 1970 and 41 to 50 in 1985. Cohort B is the group of priests who were 36 to 45 in 1970 and 51 to 60 in 1985. Cohort C is the group of priests who were 46 to 55 in 1970 and 61 to 70 in 1985. The scores of the attitudes of priests in these cohorts for 1970 is taken directly from table one of Hoge *et al.*

Since the cohorts fall midway between two age groups in 1985, the actual attitudes of priests in these cohorts is estimated by taking the mean score of the two age groups.[2] For example, the mean age of priests in cohort A in 1985 would be approximately 45.5. Since the mean age falls midway between the 36 to 45 age group and the 46 to 55 age group, we estimate the actual attitude score for cohort A by taking the mean score of the 36 to 45 age group and 46 to 55 age group in 1985.

The next step in the analysis is to obtain the expected attitude score of each cohort in 1985 based upon the Hoge *et al.* assumption of unchanging attitudes during the ageing process (the cohort effect) and then the expected attitude score of each cohort in 1985 based upon the Schoenherr and Sorensen assumption of stable attitudes within age groups (the ageing effect). The Hoge *et al.* expected scores (hereafter referred to as the cohort-effect scores) are easy to obtain since they argue that the attitudes of cohorts will not change from time one to time two. Hence, the cohort-effect score for each cohort in 1985 is equal to the actual attitude score for each cohort in 1970. Thus, if Hoge *et al.* are correct in asserting a cohort effect instead of an ageing effect, the 1970 and 1985 attitude scores should be equal for each cohort.[3]

The Schoenherr and Sorensen expected attitude scores (hereafter referred to as the ageing-effect scores) are based upon stability of attitude scores within age groups. Thus, the 1985 ageing-effect score for cohort A, which is currently in the 41 to 50 age group, is equal to the actual attitude score of the 41 to 50 age group in 1970. This score is obtained by taking the mean score of the 36 to 45 and 46 to 55 age groups in 1970. If the Schoenherr and Sorensen ageing-process assumption is correct, then the 1985 actual attitude scores should equal the 1985 ageing-effect scores.

Tables two to four provide a reanalysis of data contained in Hoge *et al.* As indicated, each table includes the observed attitudes of each cohort in 1970 and 1985, as well as the expected outcomes in 1985 based on the Hoge *et al.* cohort-effect assumption and the Schoenherr-Sorensen ageing-effect assumption. In addition, we have included the results of the difference of proportion tests based on the comparison of the expected outcomes with the observed outcomes. The difference of proportion tests provide a way of assessing whether either the cohort-effect assumption or the ageing-effect assumption accurately predicted the actual outcomes in 1985. If the difference between one of the expected scores and the observed score, which is based on the Hoge *et al.* survey data, is sufficiently large, then the difference of proportion test will be statistically significant. Thus, statistical significance indicates that the underlying assumption upon which the expected score is based is incorrect.

Table five summarises the results of the statistical tests. For each cohort, we were able to compare 27 expected outcomes based on the

Table 3: Reanalysis of ten statements about the priesthood in table 5 of Hoge et al.[1] (percent saying 'agree strongly' or 'agree somewhat')

item in Hoge et al. table 1	cohort A	Cohort[2] cohort B	cohort C
1. 1970 observed score	44.0	38.0	23.0
1985 observed score	27.0	22.5	17.0
1985 cohort-effect score[3]	44.0***	38.0***	23.0
1985 ageing-effect score[3]	30.5	18.0	10.0**
2. 1970 observed score	51.0	66.0	78.0
1985 observed score	64.0	77.5	85.5
1985 cohort-effect score	51.0***	66.0**	78.0*
1985 ageing-effect score	72.0*	84.5**	93.0***
3. 1970 observed score	81.0	74.0	64.0
1985 observed score	71.0	63.0	50.0
1985 cohort-effect score	81.0***	74.0***	64.0***
1985 ageing-effect score	69.0	60.0	49.0
4. 1970 observed score	30.0	19.0	13.0
1985 observed score	23.5	16.0	10.5
1985 cohort-effect score	30.0*	19.0	13.0
1985 ageing-effect score	16.0**	10.5*	8.5
5. 1970 observed score	49.0	39.0	27.0
1985 observed score	29.5	24.5	23.0
1985 cohort-effect score	49.0***	39.0***	27.0
1985 ageing-effect score	33.0	23.0	18.5
6. 1970 observed score	77.0	86.0	94.0
1985 observed score	72.0	83.5	91.5
1985 cohort-effect score	77.0	86.0	94.0
1985 ageing-effect score	90.0***	95.5***	97.0***
7. 1970 observed score	85.0	67.0	41.0
1985 observed score	64.0	44.0	30.5
1985 cohort-effect score	85.0***	67.0***	41.0*
1985 ageing-effect score	54.0**	32.5**	20.0**
8. 1970 observed score	25.0	40.0	70.0
1985 observed score	40.5	65.0	84.5
1985 cohort-effect score	25.0***	40.0***	70.0***
1985 ageing-effect score	55.0***	77.5***	88.0
9. 1970 observed score	70.0	64.0	41.0
1985 observed score	67.5	56.0	41.0
1985 cohort-effect score	70.0	64.0*	41.0
1985 ageing-effect score	52.5***	36.0***	26.0***
10. 1970 observed score	78.0	63.0	43.0
1985 observed score	57.0	45.0	34.5
1985 cohort-effect score	78.0***	63.0***	43.0**
1985 ageing-effect score	53.0	36.0**	26.5**

Notes: 1 See table 2, footnote 1 for *N*s.

2 See table 2, footnote 2 for age strata corresponding to cohorts.

3 See table 2, footnote 3 for explanation of cohort-effect scores and ageing-effect scores.

*   Difference is significant at .05, 2-tailed.

**   Difference is significant at .01, 2-tailed.

*** Difference is significant at .001, 2-tailed.

Table 4: Reanalysis of two statements on happiness and probability of leaving in table 6 of Hoge et al.[1]

| item in Hoge et al. table 1 | cohort[2] | | |
	cohort A	cohort B	cohort C
percent 'very happy'			
1970 observed scores	23.0	22.0	29.0
1985 observed score	35.0	40.5	42.5
1985 cohort-effect score[3]	23.0**	22.0***	29.0***
1985 ageing-effect score[3]	25.5**	30.0**	37.0
percent 'uncertain about my future',			
'probably will leave', or			
'definitely decided to leave'			
1970 observed score	23.0	17.0	7.0
1985 observed score	10.0	4.5	1.0
1985 cohort-effect score	23.0***	17.0***	7.0**
1985 ageing-effect score	12.0	4.5	1.5

Notes: 1 See table 2, footnote 1 for *N*s.
      2 See table 2, footnote 2 for age strata corresponding to cohorts.
      3 See table 2, footnote 3 for explanation of cohort-effect scores and ageing-effect scores.
     *   Difference is significant at .05, 2-tailed.
    **   Difference is significant at .01, 2-tailed.
  *** Difference is significant at .001, 2-tailed.

Table 5: Summary of statistical tests in tables 2–4

| | cohort-effect score vs 1985 observed score[1] | | | ageing-effect score vs 1985 observed score[1] | | |
cohort	*1* number of tests	*2* number of tests with significant differences	*3* percent of expected scores that are correct	*1*	*2*	*3*
A	27	22	18.5	27	20	25.9
B	27	19	29.6	27	22	18.5
C	27	11	59.3	27	18	33.3
total	81	52	35.8	81	60	25.9

Note: 1 See table 2, footnote 3 for explanation of cohort-effect scores and ageing-effect scores.

cohort-effect and ageing-effect assumptions with the corresponding actual outcomes. As table five indicates, the Hoge *et al.* assumption of a cohort effect produced expected outcomes that did not differ significantly from the observed or actual outcomes in 36% of the tests. That is, the cohort-effect assumption correctly predicted the actual outcome about one-third of the time. The Schoenherr-Sorensen assumption of an ageing effect produced expected outcomes that did not differ significantly from the observed or actual outcomes in 26% of the tests. That is, the ageing-effect assumption correctly predicted the actual outcome about one-fourth of the time. While the cohort assumption produced slightly better expected outcomes, neither Hoge *et al.* nor Schoenherr and Sorensen were particularly effective in predicting theological attitudes over time. We anticipate that one reason for the weakness of each model is that both cohort and ageing effects were operating simultaneously. We explore this issue in greater detail later.

The summary of test results in table five shows that it is only for cohort C that the predictions based on Hoge *et al*'s cohort-effect assumption seem to do a consistently better job than the predictions based on Schoenherr and Sorensen's ageing-effect assumption. The accuracy of the Hoge *et al*. predictions is much weaker for cohorts A and B – evidence of stable theological attitudes within these cohorts is much weaker.

Is there a possible explanation for the greater stability of attitudes in cohort C, which was the cohort that fell between the ages of 46 and 55 in 1970? We think that the impact of resignations probably explains the greater accuracy of cohort-effect scores for cohort C. Why? First, we know that age-specific resignation rates begin to taper off by age 46 and are relatively low by age 55 (Schoenherr and Sorensen, 1983, pp. 28–29). Second, we know that resigning priests tend to be more liberal (Schoenherr and Greeley, 1974). Thus, between 1970 and 1985, cohort C would experience a much more limited resignation effect than either cohorts A or B, since priests in cohorts A and B were more likely to resign. Consequently, it is likely that at least part of the greater instability of theological attitudes in cohorts A and B is due to the structural ageing process of resignation. That is, as the cohort ages, it will become more theologically conservative due to the structural effects of resignation, even if individual priests remain stable in their theological attitudes. We would suggest that one reason the model based on Hoge *et al*'s cohort assumption does better in cohort C is that the effects of the ageing process on theological attitudes due to resignation did not have much of an impact on cohort C after 1970, since this cohort of older priests was no longer subject to high rates of resignation. Since the NORC and Hoge *et al*. data do not allow us to disaggregate the degree to which growing conservatism within cohorts is due to the structural impact of resignations during the ageing process and the degree to which it is due to growing conservatism of individual priests during the ageing process, researchers and theorists should continue to give emphasis to the possible impact of both aspects of the ageing process in understanding the underlying dynamics of priests' attitudes over time.

Although we are unable to perform a statistical test on the data contained in the Hoge *et al*. article concerning the modern values index, table six presents comparisons of the accuracy of the cohort-effect scores with the ageing-effect scores. Once again, while the expected outcomes based on the cohort effect are somewhat more accurate than the expected outcomes based upon the ageing effect, the differences do not warrant either the unabashed acceptance of the cohort-effect assumption or the wholesale rejection of the ageing-effect assumption.

Table 6: Reanalysis of scores on modern values scale in table 2 of Hoge et al.[1]

	cohort A[2] differences from 1985		cohort B differences from 1985		cohort C differences from 1985	
	score	observed score	score	observed score	score	observed score
1970 observed scores	3.74		3.19		2.60	
1985 observed scores	3.30		2.89		2.40	
1985 cohort-effect score[3]	3.74	0.44	3.19	0.30	2.60	0.20
1985 ageing-effect score[3]	2.90	-0.40	2.39	-0.50	2.04	-0.36

Notes: 1 See table 2, footnote 1 for Ns.
    2 See table 2, footnote 2 for age strata corresponding to cohorts.
    3 See table 2, footnote 3 for explanation of cohort-effect scores and ageing-effect scores.

The most significant flaw in Hoge *et al*'s analysis is that they incorrectly conceptualised the cohort-effect assumption and the ageing-effect assumption as competing assumptions. Reanalysis of their data suggests that elements of both assumptions ought to be integrated into an understanding of the dynamics governing theological attitudes over time. That is, there is greater stability in the theological attitudes of individual priests than assumed by Schoenherr and Sorensen in their 1982 article. However, there is also more of an ageing effect than assumed by Hoge *et al.* in their 1988 article. Furthermore, the degree to which the ageing effect is a function of the structural transformation of cohorts of priests through resignation and the degree to which it is a function of the transformation of the theological attitudes of individual priests has yet to be determined. Schoenherr and Sorensen alerted their readers to the potential need to integrate both ageing and cohort effects into their analysis when they suggested that their 'projections ignore the fact that beliefs and values of the Catholic clergy may be undergoing or have undergone notable changes owing to identifiable period effects, which might warrant a more complex set of assumptions' (1982, p. 48).

Table seven illustrates the need to integrate the two assumptions. It shows that in 81% of the specific comparisons of the cohort-effect scores with the ageing-effect scores contained in tables two to four and table six, the actual outcomes fall somewhere between the competing expected outcomes. In addition, when the cohort-effect scores and ageing-effect scores are either both above or below the actual outcomes, as was the case in the remaining 19% of the comparisons, the closest estimate of the theological attitude is evenly divided between the expected outcomes based on Hoge *et al*'s cohort assumption and the expected outcomes based on Schoenherr and Sorensen's ageing-process assumption.

Table 7: Summary of the location of the cohort-effect scores and ageing-effect scores relative to the 1985 observed score in tables 2–4 and 6[1]

	cohort A	cohort B	cohort C	total
number of cases where 1985 observed score fell between the cohort-effect score and the ageing-effect score	23	25	20	68 (81.0%)
number of cases where the cohort-effect scores and the ageing-effect scores were either both above or below the 1985 observed scores but				
cohort-effect scores were closer	1	1	6	8 (9.5%)
ageing-effect scores were closer	4	2	2	8 (9.5%)

Note: 1 See table 2, footnote 3 for explanation of cohort-effect scores and ageing-effect scores.

Conclusions

We set out to accomplish two tasks in this reanalysis of the data reported in Hoge *et al*. First, we wanted to assess if they were correct in concluding that the Schoenherr-Sorensen projections over-estimated the number of older priests and underestimated the number of younger priests due to the overcorrection for the higher nonresponse of older priests in the 1970 NORC study. We think that the analysis surrounding table one indicates that the Schoenherr-Sorensen projections of the age distribution are superior to the survey results of Hoge *et al*. and that Schoenherr and Sorensen did not overcorrect for the higher nonresponse of older priests.

Second, we wanted to show that neither Hoge *et al*. nor Schoenherr and Sorensen had provided a sufficiently complex explanation of the underlying dynamics governing priests' theological attitudes over time. On the one hand, the inadequate explanation provided by Schoenherr and Sorensen led them to project overly conservative theological attitudes among priests. On the other hand, the inadequate explanation provided by Hoge *et al*. led them incorrectly to reject Schoenherr and Sorensen's assumption concerning the impact of the ageing process on theological attitudes. Additionally, neither Schoenherr and Sorensen nor Hoge *et al*. gave sufficient attention to the structural effect of resignation on theological attitudes in developing their explanations of the ageing and cohort effects.

Had there been no ageing effect, the theological attitudes observed by Hoge *et al*. would have been notably more liberal. Had there been no cohort effect, the theological attitudes observed by Hoge *et al*. would have been notably more conservative. Our analysis suggests that the ageing process (including the effects of resignation) leads to a more conservative priesthood. This process of growing conservatism is critical given the transformation of the Roman Catholic clergy from a younger to an older population (Schoenherr and Sorensen, 1983; Schoenherr *et al.*, 1988; Schoenherr and Young, 1990). However, the impact of an increasingly older clergy on the degree of conservatism in theological attitudes has been minimised due to cohort effects in which relatively conservative older cohorts of priests have been replaced by the more progressive younger cohorts of priests who first entered the clergy during the 1950s and 1960s.

Note, however, that if Hoge *et al.* are correct in suggesting 'that young priests in the late 1970s and 1980s have been more conservative theologically' (1988, p. 280), then there is every reason to expect the cohort effect to be transformed into a conservative effect over the next few decades. If such a transformation takes place, then we can expect the coupling of the ageing process with a conservative cohort effect to produce an increasingly conservative clergy.

Notes

1. In the response that follows this article, Hoge, Shields and Verdieck argue that there is no basis for concluding whether the Young-Schoenherr or Hoge, Shields and Verdieck estimates of the clergy age structure are more reliable. Based on probability theory, which provides the theoretical foundation for statistical analysis, we strongly disagree with their conclusion and are concerned by the potential confusion that their response may produce. We reemphasise three points which establish the greater reliability of our estimates. First, since the standard error of the mean is equal to the estimated standard deviation divided by the square root of the sample or n, the impact of differences in sample size can be estimated by taking the square root of the larger sample and dividing it by the square root of the smaller sample. Based on this simple calculation, we can assume that the estimated standard error of the mean for our sample will be approximately 6.5 times smaller than the estimated standard error for the Hoge, Shields and Verdieck sample. Thus, probability theory indicates that the Hoge, Shields and Verdieck estimates of the population age structure are at much greater risk of deviating from the true population values. Second, probability theory suggests that since our sample was drawn from 86 dioceses as contrasted to the 26 dioceses used in the Hoge, Shields and Verdieck sample, the Hoge, Shields and Verdieck sample is at greater risk of encountering sampling bias. Finally, and perhaps most important, Hoge, Shields and Verdieck failed to weight their survey data to reflect the probabilities of the various dioceses being included in the original NORC sample. Given this failure, there is no question but that the Hoge, Shields and Verdieck survey data are contaminated by sampling error. Based on these considerations, we think that the Hoge, Shields and Verdieck response confuses a clear cut issue; namely, that our data provide a much more reliable basis for estimating the age distribution of priests than do the Hoge, Shields and Verdieck survey data.
2. This technique is similar to the one utilised by Hoge, Shields and Verdieck (1988, pp. 268–269) in obtaining the 1985 Schoenherr-Sorensen age distribution estimates.
3. On one level, we have oversimplified the argument put forward by Hoge, Shields and Verdieck. They acknowledge that resignations have had an effect on theological attitudes that would undermine the stability of cohort scores. We have ignored this fact when we suggest that cohort scores are expected to be stable based on Hoge, Shields and Verdieck's cohort assumption. The fact that resignations introduced instability in cohort scores is precisely why Hoge, Shields and Verdieck have chosen not to undertake cohort analysis. We have attempted to circumvent the problem of unstable cohorts so that the appropriate analysis could be performed. Our strategy involves conceptualising resignations as a structural component of the ageing process. This approach allows us to move the analysis of changing theological attitudes one step forward, but we must still concede two weaknesses in our analysis. First, we are unable to disaggregate the structural and individual components of the ageing process. Second, when we refer to Hoge, Shields and Verdieck's cohort assumption, we ignore their acknowledgement that resignations undermine the stability of cohort scores. Notwithstanding these weaknesses, the theoretical question raised by Hoge, Shields and Verdieck concerning cohort and ageing process effects dictates cohort analysis. Consequently, we think the cohort analysis we have undertaken is superior to the age group analysis undertaken by Hoge, Shields and Verdieck.

References

Hoge, D R, Shields, J J and Verdieck, M J (1988) 'Changing age distribution and theological attitudes of Catholic priests, 1970–85,' *Sociological Analysis*, 49, pp. 264–280.

National Opinion Research Center (1972) *The Catholic Priest in the United States: sociological investigations*, Washington DC, United States Catholic Conference Publications.

Schoenherr, R A and Greeley, A M (1974) 'Role commitment processes and the American Catholic priesthood,' *American Sociological Review*, 39, pp. 407–426.

Schoenherr, R A and Sorensen, A (1982) 'Social change in religious organizations: consequences of clergy decline in the US Catholic church,' *Sociological Analysis*, 43, pp. 23–52.

Schoenherr, R A and Young, L A (1990) 'Organizational demography and structural change in the Roman Catholic church,' in C Calhoun, M W Meyer and W R Scott (eds) *Structures of Power and Constraint: papers in honor of Peter M Blau*, Cambridge, Cambridge University Press, pp. 235–270.

Schoenherr, R A, Young, L A and Vilarino, J P (1988) 'Demographic transitions in religious organizations: comparative study of priests decline in Roman Catholic dioceses,' *Journal for the Scientific Study of Religion*, 27, pp. 499–523.

11. Family life

Research concerned with the psychology of Christian ministry would be incomplete without taking into account the home and family life of the minister. This chapter presents two examples of research in this area. The first example focuses on clergy marriages. The second example focuses on clergy children.

In the first article in this section, Brent B Benda and Frederick A DiBlasio report on a study of marital adjustment conducted among 247 clergy who had attended a Presbyterian seminary and among the spouses of these clergy. The study employed Spanier's Dyadic Adjustment Scale to assess marital adjustment and Brogan and Kutner's Sex-Role Orientation Instrument. The data demonstrated that marital adjustment decreased with greater perceived stress from work and family, with fewer children five years old and younger, with greater perceived stress from family, and with single earners, compared with dual earners.

Dr Brent B Benda is at the Department of Social Work, University of Arkansas at Little Rock, Little Rock, Arkansas, USA. Dr Frederick A DiBlasio is at the University of Maryland at Baltimore, Baltimore, Maryland, USA. This article was first published in *Journal of Psychology and Theology* in 1992.

In the second article, Diane L Ostrander, Carolyn S Henry and Charles C Hendrix report on the development, reliability and validity of the Stressors of Clergy Children Inventory, among a sample of 85 clergy children in the age range 15 to 42 years. This instrument distinguishes between three types of stressors defined as follows: church stressors, for example, 'how people in my father's congregation think I should behave'; family stressors, for example, 'my mother works because we need the money'; and individual stressors, for example, 'feeling all alone or different from my friends'.

Dr Diane L Ostrander is Assistant Professor, Family Sciences, in the Department of Human Development, Consumer and Family Sciences at South Dakota State University, Brookings, South Dakota, USA. Carolyn S Henry and Charles C Hendrix were in the Department of Family Relations and Child

Development, Oklahoma State University, Stillwater, Oklahoma, USA. This article was first published in *Psychological Reports* in 1990.

11.1 Clergy marriages: a multivariate model of marital adjustment

Brent B Benda and Frederick A DiBlasio

This study examined a theoretical model of marital adjustment of couples within the profession of clergy. Of particular interest were the effects of earner status (dual or single earner families) and role orientation on marital adjustment. While there is a burgeoning literature on marital adjustment among various sociodemographic groups (see Fuller, 1988; Spanier and Lewis, 1980), and increasing attention is being given to how earner status and role orientation may influence this adjustment (for example, House, 1986; Keith and Schafer, 1984; Yogev, 1982), there is a paucity of research that investigates these issues among clergy (Dunlap and Kendall, 1983; Hartley, 1978; Niswander, 1982; Roth, 1988). However, clergy marriages represent a 'classical example' or 'ideal type' (Weber, 1949; Zetterberg, 1963), in which these issues become particularly salient.

Historically, most clergy have been in two-person single careers (Dunlap and Kendall, 1983), where both spouses perform the duties of one position. Hence, separate careers for clergy spouses and egalitarian role orientations present an especially ominous challenge to marriages within this profession. Due to expectations arising out of church heritage, spouses' refusal to assist in the performance of the clerical role in favour of pursuing their own career can be tantamount to clergy being unable to successfully fulfil their professional role.

On the other hand, traditional expectations that both spouses will function in one clerical role can cause persons with non-traditional role orientations to perceive the clerical position as troublesome and to feel resentment toward it. Resentments between spouses build over the years and begin to fracture the marital relationship (Worthington and DiBlasio, 1990). This problem could be especially true for spouses who are inclined towards pursuing their own career. These problems arise not only for lay/clergy couples, but also for dual clergy partners (Warner and Carter, 1986).

Aside from the threat that dual careers pose to marriage, clergy marriages are also imperilled by strain resulting from monumental demands upon clergy's time and skills. Within the purview of the typical clergy position is a wide range of different specialised skills (for example, teaching, family counselling), and persons occupying the position usually spend long hours, extending into late evenings, studying and ministering to hurting people. The demands on knowledge, skill and time can cause clergy to come to perceive their work as very stressful, and this stress often precipitates a chain of events leading to marital maladjustment (Cooper, Chassin, Braver, Zeiss and Khavari, 1986; Dunlap and Kendall, 1983; Kingston and Nock, 1987).

Work-induced stress and familial stress are interrelated; their mutual influence produces a complicated stress cycle. Moreover, in addition to the common pressures experienced in family living, the unusually high standards of conduct to which clergy family members are held in combination with their 'fishbowl' existence only serve to exacerbate the level of stress of events such as financial problems or even small infractions such as traffic violations.

Because of unique stresses faced by clergy in their work and in their families, and the possible interrelatedness of these stresses, the authors decided that the effects of stress on marital adjustment among clergy needed to be examined along three dimensions: first, perceived stress from work, second, perceived stress from family, and third, perceived stress from work and family. The hypotheses were that each of these dimensions of perceived stress would reduce marital adjustment. In the present study, perception of stress was investigated instead of actual stressful events because prior research has demonstrated that these events are often independent of subjective impressions of stress (Runciman, 1966; Stouffer *et al.*, 1949). Indeed, Barnett and Barach (1982), in a study of multiple-role strain and psychological well-being, found that qualitative aspects of one's experience with roles was more relevant to stress than were more objective aspects of these roles. More specifically, Yogev (1986; Yogev and Brett, 1985) found that perceived stress was a stronger predictor of marital adjustment than were many objective conditions of marriage.

This study was also based on the assumption that perception of stress and marital adjustment among clergy and their spouses would be affected by earner status and role orientation. Whereas the multiple-role demands of dual earners might serve to increase perceptions of stress in their work and in their family, and thereby diminish marital adjustment, prior research (House, 1986; Pleck, 1977; Thomas, Albrecht and White, 1984; Yogev, 1982) suggests that the stress of these demands is often tolerated or overcome by the increased mental satisfaction derived from the congruence between non-traditional role orientations and the dual earner lifestyle (Cooke and Rosseau, 1984; Cooper *et al.*, 1986). Apparently, the personal meaning and satisfaction derived from pursuing valued career endeavours compensates for role strain and actually enhances marital adjustment. Hence, in the present study, it was hypothesised that dual earners and persons with nontraditional role orientations would report higher marital adjustment than would single earners and persons with traditional role orientations.

Finally, the present study was based on the assumption that clergy spouses would be likely to report higher marital adjustment than clergy because they are the more direct beneficiaries of dual earner situations. Clergy are more likely to experience stress in their work, and therefore in their family and marriage, when their spouse is unavailable to assist them because of the spouse's career responsibilities.

While the theoretical framework undergirding this study implies reciprocal interactions between factors relevant to marital adjustment among clergy couples, these hypothesised reciprocal effects are not specifically examined in this preliminary investigation due to the lack of theoretical or empirical precedent. As stated earlier, there have been very few articles published on clergy marital adjustment. Hence, the purpose of the present study was to see if the hypothesised theoretical factors were relevant to, or predictive of marital adjustment among clergy and their spouses.

Method

Subjects

The sample for this study consisted of former students of a theological seminary and their spouses. Subjects were drawn from a Presbyterian seminary, offering different concentrations and degrees, including Doctor of Theology (ThD). Using a list obtained from the registrar of all former students who attended that seminary during the period from 1974 to 1978, a simple random sample (Smith, 1981) was drawn, the response rate was 65%. Two questionnaires (one for each spouse) were sent to each household and 286 individuals responded; however, since 32 persons had never been married, they were eliminated from the analyses along with 7 respondents who failed to provide enough information.

To ensure confidentiality and anonymity, respondents were asked to record a four-digit code (three numbers and one letter) of their choosing so that surveys from husbands and wives could be matched without names (the same code was recorded for both spouses). Self-addressed, stamped envelopes were provided to potential respondents along with a cover letter on seminary stationery from one of the prominent professors of marriage and family counselling at the seminary. The cover letter addressed the importance of the survey to planning for future courses and workshops at the seminary, and assured respondents of anonymity as well as the fact that information would only be shared in the form of statistical tables. Finally, respondents were asked to complete the questionnaire without consulting their spouse in order to ensure independent responses.

Data

The questionnaire (Benda and Osmer, 1989) from which data were analysed in the study, consisted of demographics (see table one) and scales measuring marital adjustment (dependent variable) and sex-role orientation. The two scales used will be discussed in detail separately. Also included on the questionnaire were questions concerning beliefs about clergy and spouse roles, perceptions of stress related to work and family, and seminary's effect on the respondents' marriage, including the marriage and family workshops and counselling. The analyses of seminary's effect on marriages is not presented in this study since this information was collected for the seminary's use.

Taking each of these items one at a time, respondents were asked to record their percentage (0% to 100%) of agreement with statements such as:

a. the bible says that the final authority for decision-making within the family is the husband;
b. the spouse of a minister is called to assist the minister in the performance of ministerial duties; and
c. the role expectations of clergy spouses are burdensome and cause conflict and resentment.

Three items taken from Yogev (1986) measured perceived stress within family, work, and work and family. All three stress items were worded according to the following example, except that the source of the stress was changed: How often do you feel overloaded or stressed because of your work responsibilities? (The choices presented were never, seldom, often and almost always.)

Finally, earner status was dichotomised as: first, when both spouses worked 35 or more hours weekly (dual earners); or second, any other situation (single earners). Average hours over the past year were used.

Marital adjustment

To operationalise the dependent variable, Spanier's Dyadic Adjustment Scale (Spanier, 1976, 1979; Spanier and Filsinger, 1983) was used. This frequently used scale consists of 32 items, thirty of which are Likert items presenting five or six options, measuring dyadic cohesion (for example, relates sexually), dyadic satisfaction (for example, regrets), dyadic consensus (for example, agreement on finances), and affectional expression (for example, kisses often). Reliability and validity coefficients of this scale are in the .80 to .90 range (Spanier, 1976, 1979; Spanier and Filsinger, 1983). Parameters of this study's sample were: mean (111.5), median (113), mode (115 – 5%), range (49–144), and standard deviation (13.9).

Role orientation

To measure role orientation, the normative approach was taken by using the 36-item scale introduced by Brogan and Kutner (1976). This approach takes both sexes into account and is based upon a gender-role continuum where lesser or greater degrees of gender differentiation and typing are expressed. This scale reflects a multidimensionality of sex-role orientation that was particularly relevant to this study and sample. Reliability and validity coefficients of the scale range in the .80s (Brogan and Kutner, 1976), and in this sample, parameters were: mean (188.7), median (195), mode (216 – 11%), range (80–216), and standard deviation (24.1).

Bivariate analyses were done with Pearson's Product Moment Correlation (Pearson's Rho), whereas the theoretical model was tested with hierarchical regression procedures. In the hierarchical regression procedures, the amount of variance accounted for by control or sociodemographical factors was examined. In a second entry, the amount of explained variance was computed for control and theoretical factors. Prior to using these regression procedures, scatter plots and an intercorrelational matrix were examined to test the assumption of linear, normally distributed data, and the lack of multicollinearity. Data were normally distributed, highly linear, and intercorrelated variables were not considered together in analyses. For example, age and years of marriage ($r = .82$) were not analysed together.

These regression procedures were selected because they permit an examination of the relative amounts of variance explained by control variables and by theoretical factors, and this was important in a preliminary study that proposed a theoretical model. Also, these procedures have the advantage of disentangling reciprocal effects by controlling for spuriousness in nonrecursive systems that result from variables having opposite or incongruent effects on each other. Several analyses of variance were performed to check for statistical interactions between independent variables, but none were found.

Results

Sample characteristics

Major characteristics of the sample of clergy and spouses are displayed in table one. There were 127 males and 120 females, 145 of whom graduated from the seminary, and 135 (55%) of the total subjects were in church-related employment. In fact, 81 respondents (33% of the sample) were senior or solo pastors, 18 (7%) were associate pastors, 10 (4%) were in other staff positions, and 23 (9%) performed in specialised ministries, leaving 112 (46%) who were not employed by a church. Moreover, 36 of the respondents reported that neither spouse was ordained as a clergy, while 161 answered that one member of the couple was a clergy, and 37 persons said that both were clergy.

The average age of the study's participants was 37 (75% $\leq$ 40), a large percentage were highly educated (93% $\geq$ 16 years of education), and most (73%) had been away from the seminary 10 years or less.

Table 1: Sample characteristics

demographics (frequencies)
1. gender: 127 males, 120 females
2. seminary graduate: 145 yes, 99 no
3. church-related employment: 135 yes, 109 no
4. church position: 81 senior or solo pastors, 18 associate pastors, 10 other staff, 23 specialised ministry
5. number of clergy in couple: 36 none, 161 one, 37 two

	means	range
6. age	37.3	25–59
7. education	19.1	8–28
8. hours employed weekly	38.8	0–120
9. years since graduation	6.7	0–18
10. years of marriage	12.8	1–37
11. children ≤ age 5	0.6	0–3
12. children ≥ age 6	0.8	0–4
13. annual income	$41,049	$2,500–333,000
scales		
14. marital adjustment	111.5	49–144
15. role orientation	188.7	80–216

The years of marriage showed considerable variance, but 44% had been married 10 years or less. As noted in table one, the average number of children aged five and younger (mean = 0.6) or six and older (mean = 0.8) was not large; actually, 21% of these couples consisted only of spouses, while 86% of the families were composed of four or fewer persons. Moreover, the mean annual income of respondents was $41,049, which included dual incomes. Finally, the racial composition of this sample was predominantly white (only six minorities), which reflected the racial make-up of the seminary's enrolment.

Bivariate and multivariate findings

The statistically significant bivariates (Pearson's *r*), displayed in table two, show that marital adjustment scores declined as

a. perceived stress from work and family increased;
b. perceived stress from the family alone increased;
c. we considered single-earner families (instead of dual-earner families); and
d. couples were married longer.

Other bivariates were not significant at $p \leq .05$. All statistical analyses in the study were computed using the SPSS-X Data Analysis System (Statistical Package for Social Sciences, 1990).

To test the theoretical model proposed in the introduction to this article, hierarchical regression (Wonnacott and Wonnacott, 1970) procedures were employed. These procedures examined control or sociodemographic factors first, to determine the amount of variance

Table 2: Bivariate correlations and hierarchical regression results of controls and theoretical variables on marital adjustment

variable	Pearson's r	B	Beta	t
1. education	0.006	-0.176	-0.039	-0.612
2. children ≤ age 5	0.016	3.469	0.197	2.841**
3. children ≥ age 6	-0.062	1.167	0.082	1.172
4. years of marriage	-0.130*	-0.197	-0.104	-1.482
5. perceived stress from family/work	-0.234**	-5.458	-0.246	-2.958**
6. earner status	0.148*	4.200	0.149	2.322*
7. role orientation	0.108	0.060	0.106	1.697
8. gender	-0.035	-0.287	-0.010	-0.158
9. perceived stress from family	-0.221**	-3.999	-0.170	-2.395*
10. perceived stress from work	-0.124	-1.888	-0.090	-1.082
(constant)		109.491		11.023**

entry 1 (variables 1 through 4):
$F = 1.46$ *Multiple R* $= .151$ R^2 *changed* $= .023$

entry 2 (variables 5 through 10):
$F = 4.13^{**}$ *Multiple R* $= .381$ R^2 *changed* $= .122$

Total $R^2 = .145$

Notes: B was the unstandardised regression coefficient, whereas Beta was the standardised.
  Only earner status (1 = single earner; 2 = dual earner) and gender (1 = male; 2 = female) were dichotomies; all other variables were continuous.
  $*p \le .05$ $** p \le .01$

they explained in the dependent variable. In a second entry, the amount of explained variance was determined for both control and theoretical-variables. Control factors were selected on the basis of consistently high correlations with marital adjustment in the literature (see Fuller, 1988; Spanier and Lewis, 1980).

The hierarchical regression analysis is displayed in table two. In the first entry (step 1), control factors were examined, and it was observed that they accounted for only 2% ($R^2 = .023$) of the total variance in marital adjustment among clergy and their spouses. When theoretical factors were added to control variables (step 2), together they explained 15% of the variance. The standardised *beta* coefficients, because they are based on standard scores or Z scores, allowed a deter-mination of the relative predictiveness of each predictor in the equation. For example, the significant beta coefficients ($p \le .05$) showed that the strongest predictor was perceived stress from work and family (-0.25), followed by number of children age five and younger (0.20), perceived stress from family (-0.17), and earner status (0.15). The positive and negative coefficients revealed that all relationships were congruent with the proposed theoretical framework undergirding this study. Perceived stress levels were inversely related to marital adjustment, and dual earners reported higher marital adjustment than did single earners. However, two theorised factors, gender and role orientation, were not significant contributors to the variance in marital adjustment scores within the sample. Contrary to the more typical finding in the literature (see Fuller, 1988), this study's results indicated that marital adjustment increased 3.47 points with each additional child who was five years of age or younger.

Discussion

In this study ($N = 247$) of clergy and their spouses, a proposed theoretical model was tested to investigate its utility in explaining the variance in marital adjustment. The hypothesised model included earner status, role orientation, perceived stress related to work, perceived stress from family, perceived stress from work and family combined, and gender.

In bivariate analyses, four of the ten factors examined were significantly correlated with marital adjustment. Hierarchical regression procedures identified four statistically significant predictors of marital adjustment (in order of predictiveness): first, perceived stress from work and family combined; second, number of children five years old and younger; third, perceived stress from family; and fourth, earner status. Specifically, marital adjustment decreased with greater perceived stress from work and family, with fewer children age five and younger, with greater perceived stress from family, and with single earners (compared with dual earners). The control factors together accounted for very little (20%) of the total variance in marital adjustment, whereas control and theoretical variables accounted for 15% of the variance.

These results indicate that the proposed theoretical model has limited utility in explaining marital adjustment among clergy and their spouses. On the other hand, three theoretical factors were identified that are useful for developing an explanation of their marital adjustment. Perceived stresses from work and family, as well as from the family alone, along with earner status, are important influences on marital adjustment. This study's results, of course, need to be verified in other samples. Future clergy samples should include a wider variety of sociodemographic and racial groups. This will require large, multiple sampling from several schools, as these institutions tend to be homogeneous in personal characteristics. Comparison samples of non-clergy and/or longitudinal data would be necessary in order to establish causal events, processes, and sequences.

Meanwhile, this study's data provide support for the theoretical perspective that perceived stress in the life arenas of work and family do affect one's sense of marital adjustment. This observation holds for men and for women; gender was irrelevant to marital adjustment in the present study. That dual earners reported higher marital adjustment than did single earners supports the assumption that multiple-role strains in clergy marriages are often overcome by the satisfaction gained from pursuing valued career objectives. It should be noted at this juncture that this study's sample was largely young, highly educated persons, and thus the results pertaining especially to earner status may be peculiar to this type of sample. Further analyses showed that dual earners were younger than single earners; however, it should also be pointed out that age and number of years of marriage were not predictive of marital adjustment. The level of education in this sample was likely the reason that role orientation was not related to marital adjustment; that is, the vast majority of the sample scored in the nontraditional range (or the upper quartile of role orientation scale), indicating little variability in role orientation.

Due to the possible peculiar and individual properties of the present study's sample, the findings on earner status and role orientation need to be replicated in a more diverse population, and particularly among other denominations. It is plausible that role orientation is more homogeneous among seminary-educated, Presbyterian clergy and their spouses than among other sociodemographic groups. The relationships between role orientation, earner status, and marital adjustment need to be examined further in future research, according to such nuances as whether or not couples had free choice in selecting earner status and the relationship between this choice and role orientation. Also important would be research that would investigate all these factors in relation to contingencies such as spouses' shared responsibilities for child care, for domestic duties, and for ministerial opportunities (Hulme, 1985; Keith and Schafer, 1984; Kingston and Nock, 1987; Niswander, 1982; Portney, 1983).

Summarily, the findings of this study indicate that while useful factors for theory development have been found, other theoretical ingredients must be integrated to explain the variance in marital adjustment among clergy and their spouses. An immediately obvious theoretical possibility is that the amount of congruence in beliefs between spouses concerning biblical injunctions about marital obligations may have a real impact on adjustment in marriage. In this regard, the few items that were used to operationalise aspects of spirituality were dropped from the present study because of validity concerns; however, a more complete scale of spirituality could prove highly productive (for example, Roth, 1988). Conceptual literature suggests that the degree of isolation, amount of congregational support, and the extent to which spouses must rely solely on each other for emotional support are also relevant to marital adjustment (Dunlap and Kendall, 1983; Hartley, 1978; Mace and Mace, 1980; Rediger, 1982; Richmond, Rayburn and Rogers, 1985; Warner and Carter, 1986). These factors appear to contribute to clergy 'burn out', and then to marital problems (Hulme, 1985; Mace and Mace, 1980; Rediger, 1982; Sandford, 1982; Warner and Carter, 1986).

The primary influences on marital adjustment in this study were perceived stress (that is, in work and in family) and number of young children. The positive correlation between number of young children and marital adjustment would need further empirical investigation to provide a satisfactory explanation. For example, it may be that better adjusted couples have more young children, or that young children enhance marital adjustment among clergy couples. Scripture informs us that children are a blessing in life (for example, Psalm 127:3–5).

Perceived stress was the most important finding of the present study. This factor remained important even when a number of objective conditions were taken into account such as age, number of children, years of marriage, income, and gender, and these conditions are well-established influences on marital adjustment (see Fuller, 1988; Spanier and Lewis, 1980). The clerical role is highly demanding and typically encompasses a wide range of responsibilities requiring diverse skills and long hours that extend into late evenings. Given these realities, it is not surprising to learn that clergy and their spouses perceive stresses from work and from their families, and that these stresses decrease marital adjustment. Perceived stresses from work and from the family should be included in future conceptualisation efforts to explain marital adjustment in clergy marriages.

In conclusion, to assert that perceptions, thoughts, and feelings are purely a product of mental processes is tantamount to confessing that one has not yet undergone the 'trials and tribulations' (for example, 1 Peter 1; James 1; Job) that gives us deep personal experience with external forces. These experiences acquaint us with the fact that there are some events in life that are forced upon us, over which we exert little if any control. And yet, how people perceive and evaluate adverse circumstances is critical to their feelings and thinking. Cognitive therapeutic approaches (Foreyt and Rathjen, 1980) maintain that humans choose how they characterise and respond to circumstances (Burns, 1980). Hence, while some affliction and pain are beyond our control, there is a considerable margin within which we can regulate our thoughts about and emotional reactions to those experiences.

In recent years, various cognitive therapeutic approaches have been formulated (for example, Backus, 1985a; 1985b; Backus and Chapian, 1985; Beck, 1976; Beck, Rush, Shaw, and Emery, 1979) and there is empirical support for their effectiveness (Foreyt and Rathjen, 1980). These approaches are easily taught, can be self-administered, and entail the restructuring of one's thoughts. They are based on a foundational assumption that if thoughts are changed, perceptions and emotions (and even behaviour) will change as well. Cognitive restructuring would seem to offer a particularly useful therapeutic strategy for alleviating or ameliorating perceived stresses in clergy families and in their work. These cognitive restructuring strategies are biblically-based (for example, Corinthians 10:1–6; Joshua 1:8; Philippians 4:8), could easily be incorporated into seminary courses and workshops on marriage and the family, and could be used in marital and family therapy sessions (for example, DiBlasio, 1988). By familiarising students with cognitive restructuring practices, seminaries could assist future clergy and their spouses in preventing stressful perceptions of work and family. As stated earlier perceptions tend to be more influential in feeling stress than are more objective conditions of the situations (Runciman, 1966; Stouffer *et al.*, 1949; Yogev and Brett, 1985).[1]

Note

1. The authors would like to express their deep appreciation to Sarah J Osmer for her very able direction of the project, and to reviewers for their helpful comments in revising this manuscript.

References

Backus, W (1985a) *Telling each Other the Truth*, Minneapolis, Minnesota, Bethany House.

Backus, W (1985b) *Telling the Truth to Troubled People*, Minneapolis, Minnesota, Bethany House.

Backus, W and Chapian, M (1980) *Telling Yourself the Truth*, Minneapolis, Minnesota, Bethany House.

Barnett, R C and Barach, G K (1982) *On the Psychological Well-being of Women in mid years* (working paper number 85), Wellesby, Massachusetts, Wellesby College, Center for Research on Women.

Beck, A T (1976) *Cognitive Therapy and the Emotional Disorders*, New York, International Universities Press.

Beck, A T, Rush, A J, Shaw, B F and Emery, G (1979) *Cognitive Therapy of Depression*, New York, Guilford Press.

Benda, B and Osmer, S (1989) Marital satisfaction, sex-role orientation, and stress in dual-earner and single-earner couples: a study of clergy marriages, unpublished manuscript, Virginia Commonwealth University, Richmond.

Brogan, D and Kutner, N G (1976) 'Measuring sex-role orientation: a normative approach,' *Journal of Marriage and the Family*, 38, pp. 31–40.

Burns, D D (1980) *Feeling Good: the new mood therapy*, New York, Signet.

Cooke, R and Rosseau, D (1984) 'Stress and strain from family roles and work-role expectations,' *Journal of Applied Psychology*, 68, pp. 19–25.

Cooper, K, Chassin, L, Braver, S, Zeiss, A and Khavari, K (1986) 'Correlates of mood and marital satisfaction among dual-worker and single-worker couples,' *Social Psychology Quarterly*, 49, pp. 322–329.

DiBlasio, F A (1988) 'Integrative strategies for family therapy with evangelical Christians,' *Journal of Psychology and Theology*, 16, pp. 127–134.

Dunlap, P C and Kendall, K H (1983), 'Two-career clergy/lay couples: problems and possibilities,' *Quarterly Review*, 12, pp. 3–17.

Foreyt, J P and Rathjen, D P (1980) *Cognitive Behavior Therapy: research and application*, New York, Plenum Press.

Fuller, J W (1988) Shared care-giving in traditional dual-career families: implications for marital quality and family competence, unpublished doctoral dissertation, Virginia Commonwealth University, Richmond.

Hartley, S F (1978) 'Marital satisfaction among clergy wives,' *Review of Religious Research*, 19, pp. 178–191.

House, E A (1986) 'Sex role orientation and marital satisfaction in dual- and one-provider couples,' *Sex Roles*, 14, pp. 245–259.

Hulme, W E (1985) *Managing Stress in Ministry*, San Francisco, Harper and Row.

Keith, P M and Schafer, R B (1984) 'Role behavior and psychological well-being: a comparison of men in one-job and two-job families,' *American Journal of Orthopsychiatry*, 54, pp. 137–145.

Kingston, P W and Nock, S L (1987) 'Time together among dual-earner couples,' *American Sociological Review*, 52, pp. 391–400.

Mace, D R and Mace, V C (1980) *What's Happening to Clergy Marriages?* Nashville, Tennessee, Abingdon.

Niswander, B J (1982) 'Clergy wives of the new generation,' *Pastoral Psychology*, 30, pp. 160–169.

Pleck, J H (1977) 'The work-family role system,' *Social Problems*, 24, pp. 417–427.

Portney, J (1983) 'Work/family: keeping a balance,' in C R Figley and H I McCubbin (eds) *Stress and the Family: volume 1 coping with normative transitions*, New York, Brunner/Mazel.

Rediger, G L (1982) *Coping with Clergy Burnout*, Valley Forge, Pennsylvania, Judson Press.

Richmond, L J, Rayburn, C and Rogers, L (1985) 'Clergymen, clergywomen and their spouses: stress in professional religious families,' *Journal of Career Development*, 12, pp. 81–86.

Roth, P (1988) 'Spiritual well-being and marital adjustment,' *Journal of Psychology and Theology*, 16, pp. 153–158.

Runciman, W G (1966) *Relative Deprivation and Social Justice: a study of attitudes toward social inequality in twentieth-century England*, London, Kegan Paul.

Sandford, J A (1982) *Ministry Burnout*, New York, Paulist Press.

Smith, H L (1981) *Strategies of Social Research: the methodological imagination* (2nd edition), Englewood Cliffs, New Jersey, Prentice Hall.

Spanier, G B (1976) 'Measuring dyadic adjustment: new scales for assessing the quality of marriage and similar dyads,' *Journal of Marriage and the Family*, 38, pp. 15–28.

Spanier, G B (1979) 'The measurement of marital quality,' *Journal of Sex and Marital Therapy*, 5, pp. 288–299.

Spanier, G B and Filsinger, E E (1983) 'The dyadic adjustment scale,' in E E Filsinger (ed.) *Marriage and Family Assessment: a sourcebook in family therapy*, Beverly Hills, California, Sage, pp. 34–47.

Spanier, G B and Lewis, R A (1980) 'Marital equality: a review of the seventies,' *Journal of Marriage and the Family*, 43, pp. 825–839.

Statistical Package for the Social Sciences (1990) *SPSS-X Data Analysis System*, release 4.0 (computer programme), Michigan, SPSS.

Stouffer, S A, Suchman, E A, De Vinney, L C, Star, S A, Williams, R M Jr, Lumsdaine, A A, Lumsdaine, M H, Smith, M B, Janis, I L and Cottrell, L S Jr (1949) *The American Soldier* (volumes 1–4), London, Oxford University Press.

Thomas, S, Albrecht, K and White, P (1984) 'Determinants of marital quality in dual-career couples,' *Family Relations*, 33, pp. 513–521.

Warner, J and Carter, J D (1986) 'Loneliness, marital adjustment, and burnout in pastoral and lay persons,' *Journal of Psychology and Theology*, 12, pp. 125–131.

Weber, M (1949) *From Max Weber: essays in Sociology*, New York, Oxford University Press.

Wonnacott, R J and Wonnacott, T H (1970) *Econometrics*, New York, John Wiley.

Worthington, E L Jr and DiBlasio, F A (1990) 'Promoting forgiveness in the fractured relationship,' *Psychotherapy*, 27, pp. 219–223.

Yogev, S (1986) 'Happiness in dual-career couples: changing research, changing values,' *Sex Roles*, 8, pp. 593–605.

Yogev, S (1986) 'Relationships between stress and marital satisfaction among dual-earner couples,' *Women and Therapy*, 5, pp. 313–330.

Yogev, S and Brett, J (1985) 'Perceptions of the division of housework and childcare and marital satisfaction,' *Journal of Marriage and the Family*, 47, pp. 609–618.

11.2 The Stressors of Clergy Children Inventory: reliability and validity[1]

Diana L Ostrander, Carolyn S Henry and Charles C Hendrix

In recent years scholars have become increasingly aware of the importance of the family as a context of adolescent development (Leigh and Peterson, 1986). Researchers have sought to understand and assess factors in the family and broader social environment that are stressful for adolescents (Boss, 1987; McCubbin and Patterson, 1987). Although such approaches have made significant contributions to the measurement of adolescents' perceptions of stress, they do not focus on the unique factors that have the potential to cause change, or *stressors*, for youth in specific family situations. Recent literature, for example, indicates that youth in ministerial families experience a distinct set of stressors (that is, beyond the normative stressors of adolescence) that have developmental consequences for them both during adolescence and adulthood (Lee and Balswick, 1989; Moy and Malony, 1987). The purpose of this report was to describe the development and preliminary evaluation of the Stressors of Clergy Children Inventory, an instrument designed to measure perceptions of adolescent stress among the offspring of clergy members.

According to family stress theory, the extent to which the offspring of clergy experience stress associated with the ministerial lifestyle is dependent not only on the particular stressor events they face, but also upon the ways they perceive and define the stressors (Boss, 1987; Burr, 1973; McCubbin and Patterson, 1983, 1986; McCubbin, Thompson, Pirnet and McCubbin, 1988). It has been suggested that the offspring of clergy members face a variety of church, family, and individual stressors. Church stressors include the direct impact of the ministerial occupation on family members, frequent moves, and the church's interference in parent-child relationships (Gibb, 1986; Graham, 1982; Hartley, 1978, Lee and Balswick, 1989; Niswander, 1982). In addition, family stressors for offspring include the nonministerial parent's work roles, family resilience, and threats to family security (Mace and Mace, 1980; Slack, 1979). Further, individual stressors such as feelings of alienation from peers, health concerns, and personal issues may be perceived as stressful (Gibb, 1986; Hsieh and Rugg, 1983; Niswander, 1982).

Although specific stressors among the offspring of clergy members have received increasing attention, minimal empirical documentation is found that addresses which events are perceived as stressful by the offspring of clergy themselves (Moy and Malony, 1987). The absence of such research may be due to a greater focus on general measures of stress for children (Yamamoto, 1979) and adolescents (McCubbin and Patterson, 1987), neglecting measures of stress for unique groups of adolescents such as the offspring of clergy members. In contrast, Daniels and Moos (1990) proposed that specific measures of adolescents' stress are necessary for divergent groups to understand adequately and develop interventions for particular groups of adolescents.

Method and results

A national sample of adolescent and adult children of clergy members within an evangelical Protestant denomination was used to investigate both current and earlier definitions of adolescent stress. Through use of the denomination's yearbook of ministerial families' addresses and ordination records, it was estimated that approximately 1,500 families in this denomination might have an eligible offspring to participate in the study. Three hundred, or about 20% of these ministerial families, were selected using a stratified random sample procedure to ensure equal representation of the population throughout the United States. The families were contacted by mail to ask if they had offspring between 15 and 42 years of age who were available to participate in the study. Of these, 127 responded. Twenty-eight reported no offspring between 15 and 42 years, fourteen questionnaires were completed by children outside the specified age range or incomplete, and 85 in the age range, for an effective response rate of 37%.

Age groups of the subjects were as follows: 15 to 22 years (43.5%) and 23 to 42 years (54.1%), while 2.4% did not report age. The sample included 53% women ($n = 45$) and 47% men ($n = 40$). Thirty-five (41.2%) were currently living in the clergy home, while 49 (57.6%) were no longer in the home, and one person (1.2%) did not indicate current residence. Given the few female ministers within this denomination (less than one percent), the sample included only offspring with fathers in the clergy.

The initial over-all instrument contained 58 theoretically-based items scored on a Likert scale of 0 to 5 (does not apply, not concerned, a little concerned, somewhat concerned, quite concerned, and very, very concerned). Given the nature of the sample, questions in the inventory were worded to refer to the clergy 'father' and nonclergy 'mother'. For samples including the offspring of both male and female clergy members, gender-nonspecific wording such as 'clergy parent' and 'nonclergy parent' would be used in the items. Several researchers were asked to examine and comment on the clarity and appropriateness of the 58 items. Next, 30 local church members were given the inventory to check for the readability and clarity of the questions. Based upon these preliminary reviews, three questions were rewritten.

Table 1: Principal components factoring followed by varimax rotation for Church Stressors Scale

church stressors: items	1	2	3
1. direct impact			
people criticising me	0.75	0.10	-0.01
how the people in my father's congregation think I should behave	0.73	0.11	0.07
how our town/neighbourhood people think ministers' children should behave	0.71	0.23	0.15
lack of privacy for our family – the feeling that people can see into our home and watch our family	0.64	0.42	-0.04
the amount of time I am expected to work at church – singing, cleaning, etc.	0.62	0.17	0.00
the number of services I am expected to attend	0.61	0.17	0.36
missing out on things because my father is a minister	0.54	0.04	0.39
2. moving concerns			
the number of times we have moved	0.19	0.73	0.26
whether or not I feel I have one place I can call my hometown – where I am from	0.10	0.66	0.20
missing out on things other kids do because of moving often	0.17	0.64	0.17
my father is gone a lot on weekends and evenings when I am home	0.36	0.64	0.01
the house we live in is not large enough for our family's needs	0.11	0.53	-0.12
3. church interference in parent-child relationship			
whether or not my father practises what he preaches	0.05	-0.06	0.79
whether or not the church or the family is more important to my father	0.08	0.20	0.71
the way my father talks to me as compared with the way he talks to the church people	0.39	-0.13	0.69
the time our family spends praying and/or reading the Bible together	- 0.11	0.38	0.55
eigenvalue	6.51	2.09	1.80
% of variance	27.10	8.70	7.50
Cronbach alphas	0.84	0.78	0.71

Note: Kaiser-Meyer-Olkin Measure of Sampling Adequacy = .76, Bartlett Test of Sphericity = 744.80, $p < .001$, Off-diagonal Elements of AIC Matrix $> 0.09 = 116$ (21%), Residuals Above Diagonal [ea] 0.05 = 106 (38%).

For the initial over-all instrument internal consistency was high based on estimations using the SPSS[x] (SPSS, 1988) reliability analysis. Cronbach alpha = .93 (Cronbach, 1951). The inventory was divided into three scales based on the type of stressor (that is, 24 church items, 15 family items, and 19 individual items). To establish the appropriateness of the data for factor analysis, the Bartlett Test of Sphericity (that is, a test for the adequacy of the correlation matrix for factor analysis [Bejar, 1978]), was conducted and found to be significant for the Church Stressors Scale ($p < .001$, see table one), the Family Stressors Scale ($p < .001$, see table two), and the Individual Stressors Scale ($p < .001$, see table three). The correlation matrices upon which the factoring was performed were as follows: 24 by 24 for the Church Stressors Scale, 15 by 15 for the Family Stressors Scale, and 19 by 19

Table 2: *Principal components factoring following by varimax rotation for Family Stressors Scale*

family stressors: items	1	2	3
1. family work			
my mother works because we need the money	0.88	0.21	-0.01
my mother works	0.84	0.24	0.03
the amount of time my mother is home when I am home	0.66	0.31	0.15
my father's second job*	0.57	-0.17	0.03
2. family resilience			
another family member's emotional/mental health	0.04	0.78	0.23
the death of a close relative	-0.14	0.72	-0.12
a family member's physical health	0.26	0.61	0.26
the church people's help, or lack of help when one of us is sick	0.30	0.57	0.21
3. family security			
my parents' divorce, or talk of divorce	0.01	-0.02	0.83
my parents' fighting	-0.01	0.05	0.81
having to leave my pet when we move	0.07	0.14	0.58
eigenvalue	3.98	1.96	1.50
% of variance	26.50	13.00	10.00
Cronbach alphas	0.88	0.72	0.67

Notes: Kaiser-Meyer-Olkin Measure of Sampling Adequacy = .65, Bartlett Test of Sphericity = 475.76, $p < .001$, Off-diagonal Elements of AIC Matrix > 0.09 = 52 (24.8%), Residuals Above Diagonal > 0.05 = 53 (50%).
* Item deleted from the final scale, due to low internal consistency reliability with the Family Work Subscale.

for the Individual Stressors Scale. Measures of off-diagonal elements in the anti-image covariance matrix and the reproduced correlation, the residuals above the diagonal greater than .05 (Norusis, 1988), and the Kaiser-Meyer-Olkin measure of sampling adequacy (Kaiser, 1970) were all deemed acceptable for factor analysis for all three scales; see tables one, two and three. The large percentages of residuals for church (38%), family (50%), and individual (47%) factors greater than .05 would not normally be an acceptable result. In these cases, however, as the range of the residuals (-.19 to .14, -.21 to .18, and -.22 to .14, respectively) was narrow, the averages of the absolute values (.08, .10, and .09, respectively) were low, and the study was exploratory, the authors concluded that the fit was adequate.

Construct validity for the church, family, and individual stressor scales was established through the use of SPSS[x] (SPSS, 1988) principal components factoring followed by varimax rotation. This factor analytic procedure was used because the study was exploratory and an attempt was made to reduce improper solutions resulting from maximum likelihood estimation factoring (Jackson and Chan, 1980; Kim and Muellet, 1978). Tabachnick and Fidell (1983) suggested that, when factor loadings are at least .30, the level at which factors should be deleted is a matter of the researchers' discretion. The authors, therefore, chose a .50 cut-off because Comrey (1973) suggested that factor loadings between .45 and .55 were fair to good, explaining 20

Table 3: Principal components factoring followed by varimax rotation for Individual Stressors Scale

individual stressors: items	1	2	3
1. alienation			
feeling all alone or different from my friends	0.72	−0.02	−0.07
not having close friends	0.67	−0.11	0.06
whether or not I can ask for help for my emotional/mental health	0.64	0.53	−0.08
having to be the new kid in school	0.59	0.09	0.10
the way I am allowed/not allowed to express my anger and other negative emotions	0.59	0.31	0.07
the things I do to get attention at school	0.50	0.20	0.30
2. health concerns			
whether or not I can ask for help for my physical health	0.01	0.75	0.13
my health in general	0.46	0.73	−0.03
my physical health	−0.01	0.67	0.11
my emotional/mental health	0.43	0.63	0.09
whether or not I have an adult I can talk to	0.31	0.60	0.20
3. personal concerns			
career decision-making	−0.08	0.11	0.69
extracurricular activities	0.02	−0.06	0.69
school grades	−0.10	0.10	0.67
things I do to get attention	0.31	0.08	0.54
dating	0.27	0.01	0.54
eigenvalue	4.74	2.46	1.66
% of variance	25.00	12.90	8.70
Cronbach alphas	0.75	0.78	0.66

Note: Kaiser-Meyer-Olkin Measure of Sampling Adequacy = .72, Bartlett Test of Sphericity = 491.88, $p < .001$, Off-diagonal Elements of AIC Matrix > 0.09 = 84 (24.6%), Residuals Above Diagonal > 0.05 = 81 (47%).

to 30% overlap in the variance between the variable and the factor.

Three subscales (factors) emerged from the Church Stressors Scale factoring: direct impact on offspring, moving concerns, and church interference in parent-child relationship; see table one. The amounts of variance in the Church Scale accounted for by the direct impact, moving concerns, and church interference in the parent-child relationship subscales were 27.1%, 8.7%, and 7.5%, respectively; see table one. The Family Stressors Scale factoring gave three subscales (factors) identified as family work, family resilience, and family security, which accounted for 26.5%, 13%, and 10% of the respective variance; see table two. Alienation, health concerns, and personal concerns emerged as subscales (factors) as a result of the Individual Stressors Scale factoring; see table three. The amounts of variance in the Individual Stressors Scale accounted for by the three subscales were 25%, 12.9%, and 8.7%, respectively; see table three.

After the 15 items with low factor loadings were deleted, SPSS[x] (1988) reliability analysis was used to estimate internal consistency (Cronbach alpha) for the final over-all 42-item inventory, scales, and subscales. The Cronbach alpha for the final 42-item over-all inventory yielded an internal reliability coefficient of .91. The Church Stressors, Family Stressors, and Individual Stressors Scales and their

Table 4: Values of Cronbach Alpha, means, and standard deviations for Church, Family, and Individual Stressors Scales and subscales

Scale	no. of items	Cronbach alpha	M^1	M^2	SD
Church Stressors total scale	16	0.85	27.93	1.75	15.47
direct impact issues	7	0.84	14.49	2.07	8.77
moving concerns	5	0.78	7.31	1.46	6.23
church interference/parent-child relations	4	0.71	6.39	1.60	5.02
Family Stressors total scale	10	0.77	13.12	1.31	9.63
family work	3	0.88	4.59	1.53	4.64
family resilience	4	0.72	7.01	1.75	5.60
family security	3	0.67	1.54	0.51	1.60
Individual Stressor total scale	16	0.81	31.54	1.97	13.93
alienation	6	0.75	9.72	1.62	7.42
health concerns	5	0.78	7.87	1.57	6.24
personal	5	0.66	13.96	2.79	4.86

Note: M^1 = subscale mean, M^2 = individual item within the subscale mean, SD = standard deviation within the subscale mean.

respective subscale Cronbach alphas are reported in table four. Means and standard deviations for the subscales are also presented in table four. Bivariate correlations of age with the scales and subscales showed no significant differences between younger (15 to 22 years of age) and older (23 to 42 years of age) subjects.

In addition to the factoring followed by varimax rotation, concurrent validity was established based on correlations between the inventory and the A-FILE Total Recent Life Changes Scale, a 50-item self-report measure of perceived individual and family stressors occurring in the previous 12 months, which has an established Cronbach alpha of .69, and test-retest reliability of .82 (McCubbin and Patterson, 1987). The over-all inventory, along with the three scales, showed positive correlations with the over-all Recent Life Changes Scale on the A-FILE (McCubbin and Patterson, 1987), that is, for the Recent Life Changes Scale and the over-all Inventory $r = .53$ ($p < .01$), for the Church Stressors Scale $r = .53$ ($p < .001$), for the Family Stressors Scale $r = .32$ ($p < .05$), and for the Individual Stressors Scale $r = .48$ ($p < .01$).

Discussion

The preliminary evaluation of the Stressors of Clergy Children Inventory supports the validity and reliability of the instrument as a means of measuring adolescent stressors among the offspring of clergy. Specifically, the Church Stressors, Family Stressors, and Individual Stressors Scales and their associated subscales all had acceptable internal consistency. Construct validity was established through principal components factoring followed by varimax rotation with each scale.

Concurrent validity was estimated in relation to the A-FILE Recent Life Changes Scale (McCubbin and Patterson, 1987). Consistencies of the factor loadings and Cronbach alphas indicate the 42-item instrument is suitable for research use. The Church Stressors, Family Stressors, and Individual Stressors Scales are sixteen-, ten-, and sixteen-item scales respectively. These scales measured diverse areas of potential change that the offspring of clergy members perceived as stressful.

Further studies of validity and reliability of the inventory among the offspring of clergy members from additional religious groups (including those with more female clergy members) and younger adolescents are required. The reliability of the three stressor scales should be interpreted with greater confidence than the over-all estimate until replication with other groups of larger sizes. Despite these limitations, however, the present study indicates the inventory shows considerable promise as a means of assessing the extent to which offspring of clergy define aspects of the ministerial lifestyle as stressful during adolescence.

References

Bejar, I I (1978), 'Comment on Dzuiban and Shirkey's decision rules for factor analysis,' *Psychological Bulletin*, 85, pp. 325–326.

Boss, P (1987) 'Family stress: perceptions and context,' in M B Sussman and S Steinmetz (eds) *Handbook of Marriage and the Family*, New York, Plenum, pp. 695–824.

Burr, W R (1973) *Theory Construction and the Sociology of the Family*, New York, Wiley.

Comrey, A L (1973) *A First Course in Factor Analysis*, New York, Academic Press.

Cronbach, L J (1951) 'Coefficient alpha and the internal structure of tests,' *Psychometrika*, 16, pp. 297–334.

Daniels, D and Moos, R (1990) 'Assessing life stressors and social resources among adolescents: applications to depressed youth,' *Journal of Adolescent Research*, 5, pp. 268–289.

Gibbs, B (1986) 'Children of the parsonage,' *Ministry: International Journal for Clergy*, 59, pp. 18–19.

Graham, P (1982) 'The pastor's problems: part 13, the pastor and his family,' *The Expository Times*, 93, pp. 359–362.

Hartley, S F (1978) 'Marital satisfaction among clergy wives,' *Review of Religious Research*, 19, pp. 179–191.

Hsieh, T Y and Rugg, E F (1983) 'Coping patterns of ministers' wives,' *Journal of Psychology and Christianity*, 2, pp. 73–82.

Jackson, D N and Chan, D W (1980) 'Maximum-likelihood estimation in common factor analysis: a cautionary note,' *Psychological Bulletin*, 88, pp. 502–508.

Kaiser, H F (1970) 'A second generation little jiffy,' *Psychometrika*, 35, pp. 401–416.

Kim, J and Mueller, C W (1978) *Introduction to Factor Analysis: what it is and how to do it*, Beverly Hills, California, Sage.

Lee, C and Balswick, J (1989) *Life in a Glass House*, Grand Rapids, Michigan, Zondervan.

Leigh, G K and Peterson, G W (eds.) (1986) *Adolescents in Families*, Cincinnati, Ohio, South-Western.

Mace, D and Mace, V (1980) *What's Happening to Clergy Marriages?* Nashville, Tennessee, Abingdon.

McCubbin, H I and Patterson, J M (1983) 'Family transitions: adaptation to stress,' in H I McCubbin and C R Figley (eds) *Stress and the Family: coping with normative transitions* (volume 1), New York, Brunner/Mazel, pp. 5–25.

McCubbin, H I and Patterson, J M (1986) 'Adolescent stress, coping, and adaptation: a normative family perspective,' in G K Leigh and G W Peterson (eds.) *Adolescents in Families*, Cincinnati, Ohio, South-Western, pp. 256–276.

McCubbin, H I and Patterson, J M (1987) 'A-FILE: adolescent family inventory of life events and changes,' in H McCubbin and A Thompson (eds) *Family Assessment Inventories for Research and Practice*, Madison, Wisconsin, University of Wisconsin-Madison, pp. 101–111.

McCubbin, H, Thompson, A, Pirner, P and McCubbin, M (1988) *Family Types and Strengths: a life cycle and ecological perspective*, Edina, Minnesota, Burgess International.

Moy, S and Malony, H N (1987) 'An empirical study of ministers' children and families,' *Journal of Psychology and Christianity*, 7, pp. 52–64.

Niswander, B (1982) 'Clergy wives of the new generation,' *Pastoral Psychology*, 30, pp. 160–169.

Norusis, M J (1988) *SPSS Advanced Statistics Guide* (2nd edition), Chicago, Illinois, SPSS, Inc.

Slack, S L (1979) 'Clergy divorce,' *The Christian Ministry*, 10, pp. 22–26.

SPSS (1988) *SPSS User's Guide* (3rd edition), Chicago, Illinois, SPSS.

Tabachnick, B G and Fidell, L S (1983) *Using Multivariate Statistics*, New York, Harper and Row.

Yamamoto, K (1979) 'Brief reports: children's ratings of the stressfulness of experiences,' *Developmental Psychology*, 15, pp. 581–582.

12. Attitudes and knowledge

A particularly fruitful field of psychological research has concentrated on exploring specific areas of clergy attitudes or knowledge. Greater understanding in this area can help to structure developments in initial clergy training and in-service clergy training. Research of this nature is illustrated by three specific examples, concerned with clergy's knowledge of psychopathology, clergy's gerontological knowledge, and clergy's attitudes towards liturgical change.

In the first article in this section, George Domino argues that although clergy provide a substantial amount of psychotherapeutic counselling, little is known about the degree of knowledge that clergy have about basic psychopathology. He reports on the development of a 120 item multiple choice test to assess knowledge about psychopathology based on the material covered in Abnormal Psychology courses. This test was administered to 23 clinical psychologists, 75 graduate students in Clinical and Counselling programmes, 279 undergraduate students in Abnormal and in Introductory psychology classes, and to 157 clergy including Catholic priests, Jewish rabbis, Protestant ministers, Eastern religious leaders and those in non-traditional ministries. Clergy scored lowest of all groups.

Professor George Domino is Professor in the Department of Psychology within the Faculty of Social and Behavioural Sciences, College of Arts and Sciences, University of Arizona, Tucscon, Arizona, USA. This article was first published in *Journal of Psychology and Theology* in 1990.

In the second article, J Kirk Gulledge reports on the responses of 76 Methodist, 71 Baptist and 74 Lutheran clergy to a questionnaire containing the updated version of the Facts on Ageing Quiz and two scales related to attitudes and training needs. He found that clergy demonstrated a relatively high level of gerontological knowledge in comparison with other reference groups, but that their concepts of ageing were affected by a number of consistent stereotypes and inaccuracies that may negatively influence their ministry among older adults.

Dr J Kirk Gulledge is Managing Director of Force Services

Ltd, Jacksonville, Florida, USA. This article was first published in *Educational Gerontology* in 1992.

In the third article, Alan Aldridge examines the attitudes of a sample of 178 Anglican parochial clergy in one English diocese towards liturgical change. He found that the great majority of respondents approved of the new forms of service and frequently used the new service book for the conduct of worship. At the same time he found no evidence to support the theory that support for liturgical change was associated with a sectarian view of the Church of England.

Alan Aldridge is Senior Lecturer in the School of Social Studies, University of Nottingham, Nottingham, England. This article was first published in *Sociological Review* in 1986.

12.1 Clergy's knowledge of psychopathology

George Domino

From a theoretical point of view, the link between religion and psychotherapy has been a rather stormy one, probably beginning with Oskar Pfister, a Swiss Protestant clergyman, who was a friend of Freud and corresponded with him (Irwin, 1973). Freud's strong antireligious posture is well known and created considerable difficulties for the Reverend Pfister. At the other end of the historical continuum, one can point to the rise of the third force in psychology in the 1950s, the existentialist-humanistic approach to psychotherapy that provided a rapprochement and a multitude of bridges between religious thinking and psychological principles (Quackenbos, Privette and Klentz, 1986). In between these two poles there have been numerous religious and secular writers and a corresponding multitude of viewpoints on the relationship between religious concepts and psychotherapeutic process. Among the better known psychotherapists who have made a strong case for the interrelationship of religion and psychotherapy are Mowrer (1961), Frankl (1969), Peck (1978), Lovinger (1984), and Propst (1988); and the efforts to continue building those bridges seem to be increasing (for example, Ahlskog, 1987; Bergin, 1980; Schlauch, 1987).

From an empirical point of view, the link between religion and psychotherapy is both a *fait accompli* and a problematic issue. A number of studies have shown that in the United States a substantial number of individuals seek therapeutic services from the clergy rather than from more formally designated mental health providers.

In the well-known study by Gurin, Veroff and Feld (1960), the University of Michigan's Survey Research Centre interviewed 2,460 American adults, representative of the normal, stable, adult population of the United States. The most frequently consulted source of help for a personal problem was the clergy, chosen by 42% of the respondents, followed by 29% who went to a physician. Slightly less than one-third (31%) went to some practitioner or agency subsumed under the heading of mental health professional. As Gurin *et al.* (1960) pointed out, those institutions explicitly created to provide psychological guidance were consulted less often than those for which psychological guidance is not a major function.

A subsequent replication of this study by Veroff, Kulka and Douvan (1981), covering the period 1957 to 1976, yielded somewhat similar results: 39% of people who sought help for their problems went to the clergy, 21% to a family physician, 29% went to psychiatrists and psychologists, and 20% to other mental health sources. These percentages need, however, to be interpreted in light of several factors: the reported categories are not mutually exclusive, respondents mentioned more than one source of help, and there are distinct interactions of categories of help providers with variables such as gender and age. The results, however, do indicate a general decline from 1957 to 1976 in the mention of clergy as a source of professional help, particularly on the part of younger people. Yet Veroff *et al.* (1981) do report that young men and older women are distinctly more likely to turn to the clergy for personal problems; in their sample 41% of men aged 21 to 34 and 51% of women aged 55 and over did so.

The findings from other studies support this pattern of seeking help from the clergy. For example, Quackenbos, Privette and Klentz (1985) surveyed 126 residents of a Florida county through a mail questionnaire. Of the 86 individuals who responded, 53% indicated that if a pastoral counselling centre were available they would seek therapy there. Of those respondents who would seek psychotherapy, the largest number (26%) selected the clergy, 23% chose psychiatrists, 20% a community mental health centre, and 13% a psychologist. Similarly, Posavac and Hartung (1977) found that 20% of their sample had sought pastoral counselling, while Clemens, Corradi and Wasman (1978) found that 42% of their sample turned to clergy when in psychological difficulties.

Furthermore, there is evidence that prospective clients either do not or are not able to differentiate fully among various mental health professionals. For example, Posavac and Hartung (1977), in a survey of 133 lower division students of a Catholic University, found no differences in stereotypes related to type of psychotherapy and discipline of mental health provider (including clergy) but did find that students expected complete recovery in thirteen sessions with a psychiatrist versus nineteen sessions with other counsellors!

Clergy do in fact spend a fair amount of their professional time doing counselling that is primarily of a psychological nature. Lowe (1986) found that ministers spend between four and ten hours a week in counselling activities; these figures are very similar to those reported by other investigators (for example, Abramczyk, 1981; Bell, Morris, Holzer and Warheit, 1976; Gilbert, 1981; Givens, 1976; Virkler, 1979).

Although one would expect that much of the counselling done by clergy focuses on spiritual problems, and that indeed is the case, the literature also suggests that the problems clergy are consulted for do not seem to be drastically different from those seen by other mental health professionals. In addition to spiritual concerns, marital problems, depression, anxiety and guilt seem to be the most common presenting symptoms (Lowe, 1986; Ruppert and Rogers, 1985; Virkler, 1979).

Given the substantial mental health problems currently experienced in the United States, the availability of such a large pool of potential mental health providers could be viewed as a major resource and perhaps even an embarrassment of riches. The fly in the ointment, however, is that most clergy have rather little, if any, training in psychotherapy. Linebaugh and DeVivo (1981) surveyed 76 accredited Protestant seminaries in the United States. They found that 53% required only one course within the area of pastoral counselling, and there seemed to be no consensus of opinion on number and type of either required or elective courses. The authors concluded that counselling is gaining importance in the seminary curriculum, and that seminarians were interested in obtaining further pastoral counselling training. Yet a number of seminary directors were concerned about this trend, and some administrators saw counselling as a potential threat to the historical role of the ministry.

Some studies (for example, Lowe, 1986; Ruppert and Rogers, 1985), also indicate that the types of counselling techniques used by ministers are related to the amount of education and academic counselling training received by those ministers. The less education and training, the more likely are ministers to use bible reading, prayer, or confrontation of sin as psychotherapeutic techniques. Other studies (for example, Clark and Thomas, 1979) have shown that a minister's religious affiliation (for example, whether the minister belongs to a conventional denomination such as Episcopalian, a conservative one such as Baptist, or a fundamentalist one such as the Church of God) influences that minister's view of the role as counsellor, and the amount of emphasis attached to that role.

Finally, the literature has fairly well documented the fact that ministers make few client referrals to mental health professionals, and mental health professionals make even fewer referrals to ministers (Abramczyk, 1981; Bell *et al.*, 1976; Cummings and Harrington, 1963; Gilbert, 1981; Lowe, 1986; Virkler, 1979). For example, Bell *et al.* did a tripartite study that involved the examination of the records of over 17,000 patients from psychiatric and mental health centres, interviews with a random sample of 2,029 normal individuals, and a survey of 278 clergy. One of the questions asked concerned the referral sources used by the various components of the mental health systems studied. The answers indicated that the clergy accounted for less than 3% of the referrals, although almost 12% of the normal sample had consulted clergy to resolve a personal problem. Meylink and Gorsuch (1988) summarised twelve studies which assessed either clients, clergy, or psychologists as to referral patterns of clergy. The results appear reasonably consistent, with clergy referring approximately 10% of those who seek their services.

What has not been well studied is the degree to which clergy can provide positive therapeutic assistance, and perhaps more basically, their capacity to recognise the nature and degree of morbidity evidenced by symptoms of psychopathology. In one of the few studies on this topic, Domino (1985) administered to 112 clergy, as part of a study of attitudes towards suicide, the Recognition of Suicide Lethality Scale (Holmes and Howard, 1980). This scale presents thirteen signs of suicidal ideation and/or risk in a multiple choice format. The results clearly indicated that clergy were not able to recognise the signs of suicide lethality any better than were educated laypersons, and substantially less well than were other mental health professionals such as psychiatrists, psychologists, and social workers. In addition, degree of accurate recognition was related to attitudes towards suicide, such that those clergy who had a higher degree of suicide symptom recognition had attitudes that more closely resembled those to be expected of a sophisticated and knowledgeable mental health professional.

Since suicidal behaviour represents a phenomenon with a relatively low base rate, this study was undertaken to assess the clergy's knowledge of psychopathology more broadly defined.

Method

Subjects

The clergy in this study consisted of 41 Catholic priests, 27 Jewish rabbis, 36 Protestant ministers, 23 religious leaders affiliated with Eastern religions (such as Hinduism and Buddhism) and 30 nontraditional ministers representing ministries not affiliated with any traditional denomination, such as humanistic and charismatic centres and nondenominational churches. In addition, five samples of subjects were utilised as comparison groups: 23 doctoral level clinical psychologists; 32 graduate students in clinical psychology; 43 graduate students in counselling psychology; 114 undergraduates enrolled in Abnormal Psychology; and 165 undergraduates enrolled in Introductory Psychology. These samples are described more fully later in this article.

Of the 157 clergy, 145 were male and twelve were female; their mean age was 47.6 years ($SD = 3.1$). All clergy were contacted individually in person, by letter, or phone, with names of potential subjects obtained through a variety of contacts. Approximately 180 clergy were contacted individually: eighteen declined to participate, four did not show up at testing times despite repeated invitations, and one produced a nonusable protocol. Geographically, they represent a wide range of locations with sixteen from the Northeast, eighteen the Southwest, 29 the West Coast, 23 the Southeast, eighteen the South, 22 the Midwest, and 31 the East Coast of the United States.

Instrument

A Knowledge of Abnormal Psychology (KAP) test was constructed for this study by first developing, in consultation with various colleagues and current Abnormal Psychology textbooks, a taxonomy of the major content categories covered in the typical undergraduate Abnormal Psychology course. This yielded fifteen content areas: nomenclature and taxonomy; dynamic theories and principles; behaviour therapy theories and principles; childhood disturbances; neurotic behaviour; personality disorders; alcohol and drug abuse; psychophysiological aspects; schizophrenia; affective disorders; organic disorders; psychological assessment; psychotherapy; mental retardation; and sexual functioning.

The next step was to select multiple choice items from course examinations, test item banks provided by book publishers and instructors' manuals, that would fall in these content areas. Each item was read by at least three instructors of Abnormal Psychology to assure that the items were appropriate, clearly written, reflective of basic material, not tied to a particular textbook, and germane to the specific content area. These items were incorporated into midterm and final examinations in six Abnormal Psychology courses (*N*'s ranging from 65 to 231) and Kuder-Richardson (1937) reliabilities were determined for each item within each content area. Those items with a K-R reliability of .65 and above were retained. Thus, the final form of the KAP used in this study contained 120 multiple choice items, and eight items for each content area.

Because the KAP was constructed especially for this study, additional reliability and validity data were obtained where possible. For a sample of 114 undergraduates enrolled in Abnormal Psychology, K-R reliability coefficients were computed for each of the fifteen content areas; these coefficients ranged from .73 to .91, with a median of .86. Also for these Abnormal Psychology undergraduates, scores on the KAP correlated at .48 ($p < .01$) with midterm grades and .62 ($p < .01$) with final course grades, although KAP scores were not made available to the instructor until after course grades had been assigned. For a sample of 32 doctoral graduate students enrolled in Clinical Psychology programmes, KAP scores correlated at .59 ($p < .01$) with instructor's ratings of 'knowledge about psychopathology' and .36 ($p < .05$) with clinical supervisors' global ratings of therapeutic competence, both expressed on nine-point rating scales.

Procedure

The KAP was administered to the following groups of subjects: 23 (twelve males, eleven females) doctoral level clinical psychologists in full-time private practice; 32 (eleven males, 21 females) advanced (that is, beyond the second year) doctoral graduate students in two APA-approved Clinical Psychology programmes; 43 (eighteen males, 25 females) advanced (that is, beyond the second year) doctoral graduate students in four APA-approved Counselling Psychology programmes; 114 (51 males, 63 females) undergraduates in Abnormal Psychology, as part of a final course exam; 165 (86 males, 79 females) undergraduates in Introductory Psychology (administered as part of a required experiment participation, in the last two weeks of the semester); and the 157 (145 males, twelve females) clergy that form the focus of this study. All administrations were monitored group administrations.

Scores on the KAP consisted of total number of items correct; because each content area was based on too few items, subscores were not generated or considered.

Results

Table one presents the means and standard deviations for each of the groups tested. Scores are given as *t*-scores with a mean of 50 and *SD* of 10, using the two undergraduate groups as the normative groups.

An analysis of gender differences indicated no significant gender differences in any of the groups where this could be tested (that is, all except the Catholic priests, Jewish rabbis, and Protestant ministers, who were all males) so gender was not considered further. An ANOVA across the six main groups yielded a significant F value ($F[5, 528] = 13.9$, $p < .001$; $\Omega^2 = .68$); Scheffe's test indicated that all group means were significantly different from each other. An ANOVA using only the data from the five clergy subgroups also yielded a significant F value ($F[4, 152] = 5.3$, $p < .01$; $\Omega^2 = .42$); Scheffe's test indicated that priests, rabbis, and ministers scored significantly higher than Eastern and nontraditional ministers, and that nontraditional ministers scored significantly lower than all other clergy subgroups.

Discussion

The results indicate a clearly delineated continuum of knowledge with doctoral clinical psychologists scoring highest, then doctoral students in clinical psychology, doctoral students in counselling psychology, undergraduate students enrolled in abnormal psychology, undergraduate students enrolled in introductory psychology, and lowest of all clergy. Within the clergy subgroups, Catholic priests scored highest, then Jewish rabbis, Protestant ministers, Eastern religious leaders, and finally nontraditional ministers.

These results coincide with the results reported by Holmes and Howard (1980), who found that their 30 clergy scored lowest on recognition of suicide lethality among various professional mental health groups, and with the results reported by Swain and Domino (1985) on the same scale who found that psychologically oriented mental health workers, such as crisis-line workers, psychologists, and social workers, scored higher than medically oriented personnel (such as psychiatrists, psychiatric nurses, and physicians) and these in turn scored higher than clergy. Thus, what Holmes and Howard labelled as a disturbing result, namely that clergy are not able to recognise signs of suicide lethality

Table 1: Participants' knowledge of abnormal psychology

group	N	mean	SD
doctoral clinical psychologists	23	66.8	6.9
graduate students – clinical	32	62.3	8.4
graduate students – counselling	43	58.1	9.3
undergraduates – abnormal psychology	114	56.3	9.7
undergraduates – intro. psychology	165	49.9	10.6
Clergy: Catholic priests	41	48.3	8.3
Jewish rabbis	27	47.1	9.5
Protestant ministers	36	46.6	10.2
Eastern religious leaders	23	39.3	11.6
nontraditional ministers	30	33.5	12.3

Note: Means and SDs are given in t-scores, with an expected mean of 50 and SD of 10.

any better than educated laypersons, can now provisionally be expanded to include signs of psychopathology.

A key question is whether knowledge of psychopathology *per se* is determinant of psychotherapeutic competence, and at one level we can easily answer no. Much more is required to be a skilful and effective therapist than mere knowledge of what schizophrenic behaviour is, or what the clinical features of depression are. On the other hand, the findings of this study suggest that at least in doctoral clinical psychology students there is indeed a relationship, albeit modest, between KAP scores and psychotherapeutic competence, even though psychotherapeutic competence was assessed indirectly through supervisors' global ratings. In this context, it is interesting to note that Garfield and Bergin's (1978) monumental review of psychotherapy was singularly silent as to the nature of such a relationship. Therapists' level of experience has been discussed (Parloff, Waskow and Wolfe, 1978), and despite the fact that several comprehensive reviews of this area (for example, Auerbach and Johnson, 1977; Bergin, 1971; Luborsky, Chandler, Averbach, Cohen and Bachrach, 1971) suggested that there is a relationship between level of experience and outcome, the reviewers concluded that the available data was not sound enough to permit any firm conclusions.

Veroff *et al.* (1981) reported that clergy are in fact evaluated as a very helpful source of psychological assistance by those who seek their services, but that the 1976 responses showed less unqualified endorsement and less unqualified devaluation than the 1957 responses. One would expect, however, that the process of psychotherapy is likely to be more effective if the client's difficulties are correctly identified by the mental health service provider.

There appears to be almost no empirical evidence on the effectiveness of religious counselling. Worthington (1986) reviewed the literature on religious counselling between 1974 and 1984. Few studies are reported on training and effectiveness and these include surveys of clerics' self-reports, which usually conclude that the clergy themselves feel underprepared, or Clinical Pastoral Education training, which Worthington (1986) concluded may produce change in trainees, but the permanence of this change is suspect (p. 424).

Quackenbos *et al* (1986) suggested that the coming rapprochement between religion and psychotherapy will affect both sides. They stated that clergy 'must have rigorous preparation in counselling' and suggested that secular psychotherapists should consider specialised education or certification in religious counselling. The results of this study are certainly consonant with their first suggestion, and under-score the need for education and regulation of those practitioners who provide mental health services, whatever their designated vocation may be.

Quite clearly, clergy have been intimately involved with the psychotherapeutic enterprise for quite some time; and as Veroff *et al.* (1981) concluded, the clergy plans a continuing critical role in assist-ing lay people with personal problems. In part this role seems to be a function of the perception that consulting a clergy member may be less stigmatising than seeking help from a professional counsellor (Sell and Goldsmith, 1988). Gorsuch and Meylink (1988) suggested that the 'gatekeeper' model, wherein the clergy are seen as occupying a pivotal role that involves identifying clients with potential psychological diffi-culties and referring these clients to mental health practitioners, is less useful than a co-professional model wherein both clergy and mental health professionals are involved in a true partnership. Such a partner-ship would require additional educational efforts on the part of both clergy and mental health professionals.

The discussion of these results must be tempered by a number of considerations. The instrument used in this study was developed for this study and lacks the extensive psychometric data ordinarily required. The indications are, however, that the KAP had adequate content validity, that it is reliable, at least from an internal consistency point of view, and that there is some evidence for at least modest concurrent validity. Using Gough's (1965) terminology, the KAP seems to show adequate primary validity.

More problematic is the reality that all the samples tested were samples of convenience, none selected in a truly random fashion. Especially in the case of the clergy, their participation was voluntary and often the result of a referral from a mutually known cleric; although perhaps because of this there was a high participation rate (157 out of 180). Thus the results obtained are not necessarily gener-alisable to all clergy. Yet the author's impression was that these clergy were better educated and more interested in psychotherapeutic issues than a 'random' group of clergy; certainly their voluntary participation suggests a positive stance towards 'science' and a willingness to be assessed as to their knowledge. As Lowe (1986) indicated, the compo-sition of the ministers used in a given study may have a significant impact on the findings.

For the purposes of this study, clergy were considered as one occupational group. This is not a defensible assumption since there is a wide spectrum of differences in training, education, religious beliefs, and so forth, so that clergy are in fact more heterogeneous *vis-à-vis* those psychological variables related to therapeutic effectiveness than other mental health practitioners. Finally, most clergy were males simply because there are relatively few female clergy, and the anonymous, voluntary aspect of this study made the collection of additional demographic data (for example, amount of pastoral counselling done, degree of training, etc.) not feasible. A pilot study indicated that such information would be difficult to obtain in a reliable manner, and almost impossible to translate into numerically objective data (how are we to compare a one-day workshop with a three-day convention?).

Given these caveats, the results strongly support the notion that clergy, as a group, are not well trained in basic psychopathological principles, a fact of which, according to Linebaugh and DeVivo (1981), many seminarians are well aware.[1]

Note

1. I am greatly appreciative of the assistance received from Dr Larry Aleamoni, Director of IRAD and his staff; from Gary Blair, Chris Almli, Sheri Aldrich and Jim Campbell in various phases of this project; and from a variety of colleagues at the University of Arizona, Fordham University and UCLA.

References

Abramczyk, L W (1981) 'The counseling function of pastors: a study in practice and preparation,' *Journal of Psychology and Theology*, 9, pp. 257–265.

Ahlskog, G R (1987) 'The paradox of pastoral psychotherapy,' *The Journal of Pastoral Care*, 41, pp. 311–318.

Auerbach, A H and Johnson, M (1977) 'Research on the therapist's level of experience,' in A S Gurman and A M Razin (eds) *Effective Psychotherapy: an handbook of research*, New York, Pergamon, pp. 154–173.

Bell, R A, Morris, R R, Holzer, C E and Warheit, G J (1976) 'The clergy as a mental health resource: parts I and II,' *The Journal of Pastoral Care*, 30, pp. 103–115.

Bergin, A E (1971) 'The evaluation of therapeutic outcomes,' in A E Bergin and S L Garfield (eds) *Handbook of Psychotherapy and Behavior Change: an empirical analysis*, New York, Wiley, pp. 217–270.

Bergin, A E (1980) 'Psychotherapy and religious values,' *Journal of Consulting and Clinical Psychology*, 48, pp. 95–105.

Clark, S A and Thomas, A H (1979) 'Counseling and the clergy: perceptions of roles,' *Journal of Psychology and Theology*, 7, pp. 48–56.

Clemens, N, Corradi, R and Wasman, M (1978) 'The parish clergy as a mental health resource,' *Journal of Religion and Health*, 17, pp. 227–232.

Cummings, E and Harrington, C (1963) 'Clergyman as counselor,' *American Journal of Sociology*, 69, pp. 234–243.

Domino, G (1985) 'Clergy's attitudes toward suicide and recognition of suicide lethality,' *Death Studies*, 9, pp. 187–199.

Frankl, V (1969) *The Will to Meaning*, New York, New American Library.

Garfield, S L and Bergin, A E (1978) (eds) *Handbook of Psychotherapy and Behaviour Change: an empirical analysis* (2nd edition), New York, Wiley and Sons.

Gilbert, M G (1981) 'The decision of Assemblies of God pastors to counsel or refer,' *Journal of Psychology and Theology*, 9, pp. 250–256.

Givens, R J (1976) 'The counseling ministry of the Churches of Christ,' *Journal of Psychology and Theology*, 4, pp. 300–303.

Gorsuch, R and Meylink, W D (1988) 'Toward a co-professional model of clergy-psychologist referral,' *Journal of Psychology and Christianity*, 7, 3, pp. 22–31.

Gough, H G (1965) 'Conceptual analysis of psychological test scores and other diagnostic variables,' *Journal of Abnormal Psychology*, 70, pp. 294–302.

Gurin, G, Veroff, J and Feld, S (1960) *Americans View their Mental Health*, New York, Basic.

Holmes, C B and Howard, M E (1980) 'Recognition of suicide lethality factors by physicians, mental health professionals, ministers, and college students,' *Journal of Consulting and Clinical Psychology*, 48, pp. 383–387.

Irwin, J (1973) 'Oskar Pfister and the Taggart report: the 'first pastoral counselor' and today's role problem,' *Journal of Pastoral Care*, 28, pp. 189–195.

Kuder, G F and Richardson, M W (1937) 'The theory of estimation of test reliability,' *Psychometrika*, 2, pp. 151–160.

Linebaugh, D E and DeVivo, P (1981) 'The growing emphasis on training pastor-counselor in Protestant seminaries,' *Journal of Psychology and Theology*, 9, pp. 266–268.

Lovinger, R J (1984) *Working with Religious Issues in Therapy*, New York, Jason Aronson.

Lowe, D W (1986) 'Counseling activities and referral practices of ministers,' *Journal of Psychology and Christianity*, 5, 1, pp. 22–29.

Luborsky, L, Chandler, M, Averbach, A H, Cohen, J, and Bachrach, H M (1971) 'Factors influencing the outcome of psychotherapy,' *Psychological Bulletin*, 75, pp. 145–185.

Meylink, W D and Gorsuch, R L (1988) 'Relationship between clergy and psychologists: the empirical data,' *Journal of Psychology and Christianity*, 7, 1, pp. 56–72.

Mowrer, O H (1961) *The Crisis in Psychiatry and Religion*, Princeton, New Jersey, Van Nostrand.

Parloff, M B, Waskow, I E and Wolfe, B E (1978) 'Research on therapist variables in relation to process and outcome,' in S L Garfield and A E Bergin (eds) *Handbook of Psychotherapy and Behaviour Change: an empirical analysis* (2nd edition), New York, Wiley and Sons, pp. 233–282.

Peck, M S (1978) *The Road Less Traveled*, New York, Simon and Schuster.

Posavac, E and Hartung, B (1977) 'An exploration into the reasons people choose a pastoral counselor instead of another type of psychotherapist,' *Journal of Pastoral Care*, 31, pp. 23–31.

Propst, R L (1988) *Psychotherapy in a Religious Framework: spirituality in the emotional healing process*, New York, Human Sciences Press.

Quackenbos, S, Privette, G, and Klentz, B (1985) 'Psychotherapy: sacred or secular?' *Journal of Counseling and Development*, 63, pp. 290–293.

Quackenbos, S, Privette, G and Klentz, B (1986) 'Psychotherapy and religion: rapprochement or antithesis?' *Journal of Counseling and Development*, 65, pp. 82–85.

Ruppert, P P and Rogers, M L (1985) 'Needs assessment in the development of a clergy consultation service: a key informant approach,' *Journal of Psychology and Theology*, 13, pp. 50–60.

Schlauch, C R (1987) 'Defining pastoral psychotherapy II,' *The Journal of Pastoral Care*, 41, pp. 319–332.

Sell, K L and Goldsmith, W M (1988) 'Concerns about professional counseling: an exploration of five factors and the role of Christian orthodoxy,' *Journal of Psychology and Christianity*, 7, 3, pp. 5–21.

Swain, B J and Domino, G (1985) 'Attitudes toward suicide among mental health professionals,' *Death Studies*, 9, pp. 455–468.

Veroff, J, Kulka, R A and Douvan, E (1981) *Mental Health in America: patterns of help-seeking from 1957–1976*, New York, Basic.

Virkler, H A (1979) 'Counseling demands, procedures and preparation of parish ministers: a descriptive study,' *Journal of Psychology and Theology*, 7, pp. 271–280.

Worthington, E L Jr (1986) 'Religious counseling: a review of published empirical research,' *Journal of Counseling and Development*, 64, pp. 421–431.

12.2 Gerontological knowledge among clergy: implications for seminary training

J Kirk Gulledge

Introduction

The fastest growing section of the US population is the group of persons over 65 years of age (Clements, 1981). With an estimated net increase of more than 1,400 per day, the growth rate of the elderly is twice as high as that of the general population (Gorry, 1980). Demographic projections indicate that the elderly will comprise almost 20% of the population within the next 30 years (Schick, 1986).

Nowhere has this 'graying' of America been felt more intensely than in local church congregations. A study by Ellor and Coates (1986) found that the proportion of seniors in the average church is approximately ten percentage points higher than the proportion of seniors in the community. Some churches may, however, have considerably higher proportions of older members. It has been estimated that 40% of the membership of the United Methodist Church is over the age of 65 (Hopkins, 1982), and many rural churches may be comprised of 70 to 80% elderly members (Oliver, 1984).

In view of the dramatic demographic shift in both the general population and most local churches, it is appropriate to ask whether the clergy who are responsible for ministry to these increasingly elderly congregations are adequately prepared to provide sensitive and meaningful leadership. Do they have sufficient knowledge of the ageing process to understand, counsel, encourage, and inspire their older parishioners? Much of the previous literature relative to this question suggests that clergy may be neither adequately prepared nor motivated to meet the needs of their elderly church members.

Review of the literature

A number of writers have suggested that many clergy tend to hold negative stereotypes about old age and ageing (Cole, 1981; Ford, 1981; Maves, 1980; Moberg, 1975; Tillapaugh, 1985; Willimon, 1983). Stereotypical attitudes towards old age may result in avoidance of contact with older parishioners (Wallace and Wallace, 1982); monolithic thinking and characterisations, such as 'Old people are all alike' (Cole, 1980); condescension toward or oversight of elderly in ministry plans (Russell, 1985); or discrimination against older members in appointments to church leadership roles (Moberg, 1981). Hammond,

(1970) suggests that ministry with the elderly may be regarded as an unpleasant necessity by many clergy.

Despite the prominence of elderly members among most church congregations and parishes, ministers receive virtually no specialised training in gerontology or ministry with older persons during their seminary education (Byrd, 1980; Clark, 1982; Kimble, 1981). A national study of seminary curricula found that most seminaries did not have a single course relating to ageing (Watkins, 1975). The number of seminaries adding optional gerontology courses in recent years has been increasing (Carlson, 1985), but because of the demands of other required courses, few ministerial students choose to take the elective courses related to senior ministries (Ziegler, 1980). A study by Wallace and Wallace (1982) suggested that clergy as a group may have less knowledge about ageing than do other similarly educated professional groups. This conclusion was confirmed by Levy and West (1985), who found that clergy possessed a level of gerontological knowledge equivalent to that of undergraduate college students.

Method

A questionnaire containing the updated version of the Facts on Ageing Quiz (Palmore, 1988), several demographic questions, two scales related to attitudes and training needs, and five open-ended questions was mailed to 289 clergy who were randomly selected from three major denominations: United Methodist, Southern Baptist, and Evangelical Lutheran. Each of the questionnaires was accompanied by a letter of endorsement from a representative of the respective denomination. Two follow-up mailings were sent to nonrespondents at one-month intervals.

The Facts on Ageing Quiz (FAQ) was scored according to the key provided by Palmore (1988), and the scores were then converted to percentages in order to compare them with the scores of other reference groups reported in the literature. The open-ended questions were summarised by category of response and denomination of respondent to provide greater understanding and elaboration of the FAQ scores.

Results

A total of 221 responses were received, representing a response rate of 76.5%. The responses were distributed by denomination as follows: Methodist, 76; Baptist, 71; and Lutheran, 74. Almost 92% (203) of the respondents reported that they were the pastors or senior pastors of their respective churches; 5% were assistant pastors, and the remainder occupied other positions. A total of 204 respondents were men and 17 were women. All age levels from 20 through 70 years of age were represented, with an average age of approximately 46. Educational levels of respondents were reported as follows: high school, 1; associate degree, 3; bachelor's degree, 16; master's degree, 150; doctorate, 42; postdoctorate, 9.

The average FAQ score for this group of clergy respondents was 68.21, which is somewhat higher than the results previously reported by Wallace and Wallace (1982) and Levy and West (1985). Both of the previous studies had resulted in an average score of 66, which is at the knowledge level of undergraduate students (Courtney and Weideman, 1985; Dail and Johnson, 1985; Palmore, 1977). However, this study found that the gerontological knowledge level of ministers was equivalent to that of other groups with graduate-level educational degrees (Barresi and Brubaker, 1979; Broder and Block, 1986; Coe, Miller, Pendergast, and Grossberg, 1982; Hannon, 1980).

Misconceptions about ageing

The FAQ identified nine stereotypes or misconceptions about ageing and older adults that were believed to be true by more than half of the respondents. Each of these areas could influence the effectiveness of the clergy in ministering to older parishioners. These misconceptions were as follows:

a. fifty-two percent of the respondents believed that the majority of old people say they are bored;
b. fifty-four percent of the respondents believed that old people are often irritated or angry;
c. fifty-five percent thought that more than 10% of older adults live in long-term-care institutions;
d. fifty-five percent did not believe that medical practitioners give low priority to the aged;
e. fifty-seven percent believed that the majority of elderly people live below the poverty line;
f. sixty-one percent believed that older adults tend to become more religious as they age;
g. sixty-three percent did not believe that old people usually take longer to learn something new;
h. sixty-four percent did not believe that the relative health and socio-economic status of older people will change in the next ten years;
i. ninety-four percent thought that more than 15% of the US population is over the age of 65.

These misconceptions paint a composite picture of older adults as being generally poor, sick, bored, frustrated, and increasingly dependent upon religion. To the extent that the stereotypes are believed, they can cause the minister to relate to older persons as objects of ministry who need help but who are themselves unable to make any meaningful contributions to the life and ministry of the church.

Gerontological training needs

Of the 153 respondents who answered an unstructured question regarding the need for gerontology as part of seminary education, 151 (68.3% of the respondents) felt that additional training in gerontology was both desirable and necessary. Many of the comments received were quite emphatic, such as, 'Anything would be helpful! We have none!' and 'Several courses needed. They're the future.'

Approximately 40% of the respondents expressed an interest in knowledge of ageing dynamics and the needs of the elderly. Areas that were most frequently mentioned included dynamics of human development, stages of life, psychological changes related to ageing, intergenerational relationships, Alzheimer's disease, and spirituality among the elderly.

Many of the respondents linked their interest in the needs of older persons with their desire for skills and training to address those needs. Most frequently mentioned were interest in learning about government and community resources, training in how to help with financial problems, and knowledge of the health-care system and how to access it to benefit older persons.

More than half of the respondents indicated interest in developing ministry and counselling skills with older persons. Specific areas mentioned included communicating and listening ('how to hear the older generation – needs and advice'), coping with losses and grief, ministering to homebound persons and nursing home patients, and 'preaching to the needs of seniors'.

The Baptist and Methodist ministers expressed the need for training in the area of church programming for seniors; they mentioned specific Christian education courses, skills in networking among seniors, 'forming effective core units', retirement and financial planning courses, and biblical studies for seniors. The Lutheran pastors were unified in their desire to keep seniors in the mainstream of church activities without targeting them with age-related programming.

A significant area mentioned by more than one third of the respondents was the need to recognise the worth and talents of older adults in the church. A number of respondents suggested courses that emphasised the leadership and decision-making roles of the elderly, 'utilising their spiritual and practical resources', 'empowerment of senior adults to be in ministry', 'affirming the worth of older adults', and 'convincing older persons that they are needed and not washed up'.

Educational implications

The findings of this study provided some important implications for the place of gerontology within seminary educational programmes. These include the following:
1. Studies in gerontology should be a vital component of seminary

training. The overwhelming majority of respondents strongly advocated that all seminary students be exposed to the needs of older persons and ministerial approaches to meeting those needs.

2. A one-semester required overview course is the preferred educational framework for gerontology in seminary training. Although several respondents suggested the inclusion of a gerontology emphasis within other courses (such as pastoral care or death and dying), the majority of persons who addressed this issue felt that a general introductory course would be the most efficient means of transmitting the needed information and awareness.

3. The myths and realities of ageing should be addressed and clarified by the survey course. These misconceptions include such areas as the demographics of ageing, socioeconomic trends among older persons, learning abilities, incidence of institutionalisation among older people, and social behaviours among the elderly.

4. Gerontology courses should be practice-oriented. Although the need for a general understanding of the physical, psychological, social, emotional, and spiritual needs of the elderly was suggested by many respondents, the theoretical perspectives of gerontology were seen as only foundational to identifying actual needs that could be addressed through ministry. The survey course should introduce practical approaches and programmes for meeting needs.

5. Opportunities for contact with older persons should be provided. Experiences of interaction and discussion with the elderly themselves exert a greater influence on the development of knowledge and attitudes toward ageing and are more often remembered than other academic treatments of ageing concepts and stereotypes.

6. Students should be introduced to the private, community, and government resources available to provide assistance to older persons. Information should be provided on both the sources of help and the practical means of accessing the help when needed.

7. Emphasis should be placed on the value and worth of older people as full participants in the life and programme of the church. Ideas should be offered for approaches to challenge, enable, and utilise the elderly in ministry and leadership.

8. Issues of intergenerational relationships, needs, and programmes should be discussed. These include mutual understandings among age groups, parent and adult child relationships, and ways to provide a balance in programming and ministry.

9. The attitudes of pastors toward their own ageing, death, and dying should be addressed during the seminary educational programme. (The survey results showed that pastors become less receptive to these topics at later stages of their ministry.)

Summary

In contrast to the negative speculation by earlier writers, this study found that clergy exhibit as high a degree of gerontological knowledge as that shown by similar professional groups with graduate-level education. Nevertheless, stereotypes and misconceptions about ageing are common among this group, and many clergy appear to maintain the common image of older people as poor, sick, and helpless.

Very few of the respondents had had any type of training in gerontology, but the overwhelming majority felt that some sort of training was needed as part of regular seminary education. A one-semester required overview course that could help students identify the major needs of older persons and practical pastoral approaches to senior ministry was the most frequently suggested educational format.

References

Barresi, C and Brubaker, T (1979) 'Clinical social workers' knowledge about ageing: responses to the 'Facts on Aging Quiz',' *Journal of Gerontological Social Work*, 2, pp. 137–146.

Broder, H and Block, M (1986) 'Effects of a geriatric education on the knowledge of dental students,' *Special Care in Dentistry*, 6, pp. 177–179.

Byrd, J (1980) 'Pastoral care: a Christian perspective,' *Gerontology and Geriatrics Education*, 1, pp. 129–132.

Carlson, R (1985) 'The Episcopal seminaries and aging: a survey of Episcopal seminaries and schools of theology as to teaching and training in the field of ministry to the aged,' *Journal of Religion and Aging*, 1, 4, pp. 1–12.

Clark, C (1982) 'Pastor's personal preparation for ministry to the aged,' *Church Administration*, 24, 10, pp. 26–28.

Clements, W (1981) 'The new context for ministry with the aging,' in W Clements (ed.) *Ministry with the Aging: designs, challenges, foundations*, San Francisco, Harper and Row, pp. 1–17.

Coe, R, Miller, D, Pendergast, J, and Grossberg, G (1982) 'Faculty resources for teaching geriatric medicine,' *Journal of the American Geriatrics Society*, 30, pp. 63–66.

Cole, E (1980) 'Spiritual and religious dimensions of aging: applications,' in J Thorson and T Cook (eds) *Spiritual Well-being of the Elderly*, Springfield, Illinois, Charles C Thomas, pp. 214–217.

Cole, E (1981) 'Lay ministers with older adults,' in W Clements (ed.) *Ministry with the Aging: designs, challenges, foundations*, San Francisco, Harper and Row, pp. 250–265.

Courtney, B and Weideman, C (1985) 'The effects of a "don't know" response on Palmore's Facts on Aging Quizzes,' *The Gerontologist*, 25, pp. 177–181.

Dail, P and Johnson, J (1985) 'Measuring change in undergraduate students' perception about aging,' *Gerontology and Geriatrics Education*, 5, 4, pp. 61–67.

Ellor, J and Coates, R (1986) 'Examining the role of the church in the aging network,' in M Hendrickson (ed.) *The Role of the Church in Aging: implications for policy and action*, New York, Haworth Press, pp. 99–116.

Ford, S (1981) 'The social process of aging: its implications for pastoral ministry,' *Pastoral Psychology*, 29, 3, pp. 213–215.

Gorry, E (1980) 'The parish includes the elderly,' *New Catholic World*, 223, pp. 109–112.

Hammond, P (1970) 'Aging in the ministry,' in M Riley and A Foner (eds) *Aging and Society: volume 2 aging and the professions*, New York, Russell Sage Foundation, pp. 293–323.

Hannon, J (1980) 'Effects of a course on aging in a graduate nursing curriculum,' *Journal of Gerontological Nursing*, 6, pp. 604–615.

Hopkins, J (1982) 'Seminar stresses appreciation for the aged,' *The United Methodist Reporter*, April 22.

Kimble, M (1981) 'Education for ministry with the aging,' in W Clements (ed.) *Ministry with the Aging: designs, challenges, foundations*, San Francisco, Harper and Row, pp. 209–219.

Levy, W and West, H (1985) Knowledge of aging in human service professions, paper presented at the annual meeting of the Texas Chapter, National Association of Social Workers, Dallas, Texas.

Maves, P (1980) 'Spiritual well-being of the elderly: a rationale for seminary education,' in J Thorson and T Cook (eds) *Spiritual Well-being of the Elderly*, Springfield, Illinois, Charles C

Thomas, pp. 51–58.

Moberg, D (1975) 'Needs felt by clergy for ministry to the aging,' *The Gerontologist*, 16, pp. 283–293.

Moberg, D (1981) 'What graying of America means to the local church,' *Christianity Today*, 25, pp. 30–33.

Oliver, D (1984) 'Gerontology in a graduate theological seminary,' *Journal of Religion and Aging*, 1, 1, pp. 87–101.

Palmore, E (1977) 'Facts on Aging Quiz: a short quiz,' *The Gerontologist*, 17, pp. 315–320.

Palmore, E (1988) *The Facts on Aging Quiz*, New York, Springer.

Russell, W (1985) 'Relating to senior adults,' *Church Administration*, 27, 5, pp. 26–27.

Schick, F (1986) *Statistical Handbook on Aging Americans*, Phoenix, Arizona, Oryx Press.

Tillapaugh, F (1985) 'Pastor to pastor: targeting seniors for ministry,' *Moody Monthly*, 85, 7, pp. 58–60.

Wallace, R W and Wallace, R K (1982) 'Assessing clergy's knowledge of aging: suggestions for training,' *Gerontology and Geriatrics Education*, 2, pp. 285–290.

Watkins, D (1975) 'Seminary instruction in gerontology,' *NICA Inform*, 1, pp. 2—3.

Willimon, W (1983) 'Aging and changing in the church,' *The Christian Ministry*, 14, 2, pp. 5-6.

Ziegler, J (1980) 'Strategies in seminary curricula,' *Theological Education*, 16, 3, pp. 349-351.

12.3 Slaves to no sect: the Anglican clergy and liturgical change

Alan Aldridge

The significance of liturgical change

Decades of struggle by the Church of England to wrest from the state the power to determine its own corporate worship and doctrine culminated in the Worship and Doctrine Measure of 1974, which was passed by Parliament despite vocal opposition. This reversed the humiliations of 1927 and 1928, when the House of Commons twice rejected a new prayer book which the church had produced as an alternative to the 1662 *Book of Common Prayer*. The 1974 measure authorised the General Synod of the Church of England to approve, amend, continue or discontinue forms of service without Parliamentary sanction. The *Book of Common Prayer* appeared, nevertheless, to have an assured future in the corporate worship of the church. Under the measure, the *Book of Common Prayer* was to remain permanently available for use; the canons of the Church of England would continue to treat the *Book of Common Prayer* as the doctrinal and liturgical bedrock, with newer services as permitted alternatives; the form of service used in parishes was to be jointly decided by the incumbent and the Parochial Church Council, and in the event of disagreement the PCC would be able to insist on retention of the *Book of Common Prayer*. (For a summary of this measure see Welsby [1984].)

Many churchmen were, however, alarmed at the pace and scope of liturgical change. In 1975 the Prayer Book Society was founded 'to uphold the worship and doctrine of the Church of England as enshrined in the *Book of Common Prayer*' and to ensure that the book remained 'a major element in the worshipping life of the Church of England'. The publication in 1980 of the *Alternative Service Book 1980* and its rapid adoption in many parishes caused alarm to the society, which claimed that the safeguards built into the 1974 measure had been inadequate. Some went further, arguing that the safeguards had always been a sham. C H Sisson writes (1981, p. 228):

> It would certainly have surprised the ordinary churchgoer, in 1974, to learn that what was being plotted under the guise of a measure to allow the church to manage its own affairs, was a complete change in the character of the Church of England.

At the instance of the Prayer Book Society the first steps were taken in 1981 to introduce to Parliament a bill seeking to ensure that, if a requisite number of people on the electoral roll of any church so wished, the liturgy of the *Book of Common Prayer* would be used for the principal Sunday service of that church at least once a month. The bill attracted widespread publicity. Some Parliamentarians displayed an eloquence almost worthy of Cranmer, but no political party was keen to pursue the matter: the church had, after all, fought hard for the right to regulate its own worship and doctrine, so for some churchmen now to urge Parliament to intervene seemed ironic. Parliamentary action was renewed in 1984, the campaigners having decided that their earlier warning shot had produced little deterrent effect. They still made it clear that they would abandon the campaign if the diocesan bishops acted decisively to protect the *Book of Common Prayer*.

The Prayer Book Society has been very active, but has had difficulty in determining the means to its ends. Its members and sympathisers have mobilised distinguished people to sign petitions to the General Synod in defence not only of the *Book of Common Prayer* but also of the Authorised Version and of the church's musical heritage; they have cited opinion polls which show the public's affection for the *Book of Common Prayer*, and have brought forward evidence to suggest that the 1662 liturgy commands larger congregations than does the *Alternative Service Book 1980*; they have castigated the theological colleges for their neglect of the *Book of Common Prayer*, which has meant that young clergymen are unfamiliar with it; and they have condemned the clergy's zeal for the new services and determined manipulation of reluctant congregations. Some of those supporting the campaign, including many who signed the petitions, are neither communicating members of the church nor even professed Christian believers. This is not seen as a weakness but rather a point of pride: the church serves the nation, and should be responsive to the expert opinions and spiritual needs of this wider constituency (Sisson, 1981; Brewer, 1981). The Archbishop of Canterbury, in an interview in 1981, endorsed this view, which he saw as characteristically Anglican.

The case for the defence of the Prayer Book

The defence of the *Book of Common Prayer* has typically involved a trenchant attack on the new services in the *Alternative Service Book 1980*. The case made out by the critics is as follows (see Martin, 1979; Morris, 1980; Martin and Mullen, 1981).

The *Alternative Service Book 1980* offers an extensive menu of variants to suit most tastes, provided they are not too discerning. The language of the book is uninspired and not even truly contemporary, but a mishmash of ancient and modern. The majestic prose of Cranmer has been 'hustled and shoved into the museum' (Martin, 1979, p. 1), to be supplanted by the inferior efforts of multinational bureaucracies. The language of the new book is unpoetical and unmusical, lacking rhythm, movement and cadence. Not one poet has praised it. Its flat-footed sentences, often slackly constructed, fail to convey a sense of the numinous. The irony is that the new liturgies are quite unnecessary, a wanton 'spitting on one's luck' as Auden said; for the language of Cranmer, far from being impenetrably alien, is still easily 'understanded of the people'.

Nor do the new liturgies express a profound theology. They do not convey God's transcendence, the sinfulness of humankind and the need for penitence, individual confession and personal commitment. Difficult disciplines are replaced by the cosy glow of collective self-righteousness: all is celebration, all compulsory joy in a psuedo-community of the like-minded.

There are two divergent strands in the campaign that need to be distinguished. The first, concerned that the *Book of Common Prayer* may fall into disuse, centres on the insistence that it be widely and regularly used in the Church of England alongside other authorised liturgies. This was, of course, the aim of the Prayer Book Protection Bill. Many church leaders have voiced their sympathy for this view. In a newspaper article in 1984 the Archbishop of Canterbury commended the 1662 liturgy and encouraged the laity to be bold in asking for it. He also stressed that he did not intend the *Book of Common Prayer* to suffer neglect. The Archbishop of York published a book in 1983 in which he suggested that the church should consider 'planned pluralism', to make sure that all traditions of worship were adequately represented in every local area. Despite the obvious difficulties he hoped this might mean 'passing beyond sterile controversy about styles of worship into an actual enjoyment of human diversity' (Habgood, 1983, p. 143).

In this strand of argument the call is for fair competition and an effective voice for the consumer. The Prayer Book Society is fighting a similar battle to its secular counterpart, the Campaign for Real Ale. Both are attacking the marketing policies of allegedly complacent bureaucratic organisations, and their demands express the principles of competitive consumerism. Provided such campaigns are well managed and persistent they are likely to enjoy some success. However, the crucial problem facing the Prayer Book Society is the autonomy and symbolic power of the parochial clergy and of the theological colleges that train them. One widely recognised feature of the campaign has been its anti-clericalism (Homan, 1979; Homan, 1983; Sisson, 1981). Yet the clergy are not necessarily hostile to liturgical variety; in my survey, outlined below, 55.1 per cent denied that there are too many liturgies in contemporary use. One reaction is to insist that all churches provide *Book of Common Prayer* services if there is a local demand for them, the other is some scheme of planned diversity as suggested by Habgood. It is predictable that eventually the situation will stabilise, and that most lay people will be able to get the services they want, though not necessarily from their parish church.

The second strand of argument goes further than and is ultimately incompatible with the first. Liturgical revision on the scale undertaken by the Church of England is seen as foolhardy and quite unnecessary. Some minor alterations to the *Book of Common Prayer* may well be in order, but that is all. The revised services are theologically impoverished when compared with Cranmer, and linguistically disastrous. Cranmer's english is easily understood today, and the few difficulties that present themselves are an occasion not for unresolved bewilderment but for enquiry, discovery and reflection (Martin, 1980, p. 102). The only sensible thing for the church to do would be to return to the *Common Book of Prayer* as the norm. There would still be individual churches specialising in particular forms of worship and attracting commuters across parish boundaries, but in all the rest the *Book of Common Prayer* would prevail. Excessive liturgical variety undermines the parish system and encourages inward-looking congregationalism: each church has its own pattern of worship with which only its own regular votaries are familiar. Cranmer's great achievement was to produce a book of common prayer, creating unity in place of division. A truly national church demands a fundamental uniformity in worship. The distinctive identity of the Church of England should continue to be defined by the *Book of Common Prayer*, the Authorised Version, the Establishment, the Canons and the Thirty-Nine Articles. Although this inheritance of faith, order and worship is not treated in a fundamentalist fashion, ecumenical ventures that threaten the Church of England's historic identity should be rejected.

If the critique stands, why have the clergy been so foolish as to desert the glory of 1662 for the banality of 1980? Critics have suggested several reasons for this, all of which can be related to one master theme: the lure of sectarianism as a refuge in a secular society.

In a secular society, liturgical praxis is the only area in which clergymen exercise a largely unchallenged professional expertise. In Wilson's words, 'Liturgicalism reasserts the monopoly of the professional, by providing him with the equivalent of skills and techniques which he alone is licensed to practise' (1966, pp. 134–8). This view is strongly supported by Russell's historical study of the clerical profession (1980, pp. 108–10). From the nineteenth century onwards the profession has been divested of many of its social functions, while other professions have become ever more closely defined by their respective specialisms. In this light, the growth of ritualism in the church is one example of the general pattern of change in the professions. Russell points out that one characteristic of church life in the late nineteenth century was the clergy's enthusiasm for liturgical science and their preoccupation with the minutiae of ceremonial and sanctuary design. Clergy were seeking 'to reinterpret their role and to centre it around a new spiritual technology'. The growth of sacramentalism and the elevation of the sacerdotal role of the clergyman emphasised the irreducible priestly functions upon which no lay person could legitimately encroach. 'At the same time', Russell concludes, 'the new sacramental theology contained the means by which the clergy could appeal to a new source of authority which invested their role with a greater significance than any appeal to social position or social utility could give.' Thus when lay people, however eminent, seek significantly to influence the course of liturgical events, they are likely to be seen as encroaching on clerical professional prerogatives.

As religion has lost its grip over the hearts and minds of most adult citizens, and as religious institutions have been divested of most of their social functions, so, it is argued, the Church of England has turned in on itself without realising that it has done so. It retains, even emphasises, the rhetoric of the church while moving inexorably in the direction of the sect, a process captured in clerical enthusiasm for the *Alternative Service Book 1980*. No one has put this case with greater force and clarity than David Martin.

A drift to sectarianism?

One striking manifestation of the drift to sectarianism that Martin emphasises is the alienation of the clergy and church leaders from high culture. They do not see themselves as fortunate heirs to a great tradition, and do not welcome being reminded of their responsibilities to their inheritance. Anyone who does this is treated as a trespasser on areas of clerical professional expertise. So it was that when the Prayer Book Society presented to the General Synod its petitions in defence of the *Book of Common Prayer* and the Authorised Version, they had a frigid reception. Aesthetic criticism of the new forms, however distinguished its source, has been impatiently dismissed as irrelevant. Of this tendency Martin writes: 'as we begin to use words like 'aesthetic' and 'culture' as terms of abuse we are ceasing to be a church and commencing a career as a sect' (Martin and Mullen, 1981, p. 12). It is not only that the church is careless of its inheritance, it is also reluctant 'to tap the creative genius available to the church' (Martin, 1979, p. 12), and has therefore failed to enlist any of this century's great Christian poets in the task of liturgical change or to inspire contemporary composers to set the new offerings to music.

Impoverishment of the liturgy is also sectarian, Martin argues (Martin and Mullen, 1981, p. 20), 'because it narrows down the range of response evoked by worship, above all feelings of awe, immensity and the numinous created by heightened language and profound music'. The sense of the transcendent is eroded 'in favour of an impoverished sectarianism and a clerically orchestrated conviviality'. The new texts lend themselves to the promotion of shallow camaraderie and pseudo-community. This sectarian element is 'a Christian variant of the touchy-feely culture', in which intrusion upon personal sensibilities is encouraged.

Paradoxically, the spiritual narrowness of the new services is accom-

panied by a wide diversity of forms of worship. Not only does the
Alternative Service Book 1980 contain two forms of communion
service, Rite A in 'modern' English and Rite B in modified
Cranmerian, but each of these, especially Rite A, permits multiple
choice at many points. This means that each parish church will have
chosen, from the extensive menu offered, a particular combination that
especially suits its, or perhaps the incumbent's, idiosyncratic preferences. There is no norm of common prayer, but rather an
inward-looking congregationalism. The sense of being receptive to a
wider public is gradually whittled away; thus Series Three, the precur-
sor of Rite A, often became in Martin's view 'the semi-private rite of
an episcopal sect' (1980, p. 96).

As the gathered remnant draws in on itself, links with the wider
society are necessarily severed. 'The sectarian element is symbolised
in the closed or semi-closed circle, where the faithful set their backs to
the world' (Martin and Mullen, 1981, p. 20). The new services
strongly emphasise commitment, and in so doing a sharp line is drawn
between the remnant inside the church and the world outside, a world
whose inhabitants are unfamiliar with and thus estranged from the new
rites. Only the remnant can recite the Lord's Prayer in any of its
revised versions: everyone else relies on the traditional form. This
explicit and deliberate breach with tradition cannot but move the
church towards sectarianism. The Church of England is becoming a
voluntary organisation with a core of activists and a shrinking periph-
ery of the less committed, many of whom feel uncomfortable with the
new moralising insistence on community and spontaneity. The significance of civic ties dwindles with 'the slow but tangible movement away
from a civic church to a small semi-sectarian cell' (Martin, 1980, p.
96). Nothing less than a sea-change in the Church of England's identity is foreshadowed: 'From being a church with roots, possessing
identity and conferring identity, the Church of England, Ecclesia
Anglicana, could end up as a featureless international sect' (Martin
and Mullen, 1981, p. 22).

For Martin, then, the church's sectarian withdrawal from the world
is composed of the following elements: alienation from high culture;
repudiation of the aesthetic; abandonment of the historic in favour of
the sham contemporary; promotion of a pseudo-community of the
committed few; intrusiveness; loss of a sense of a wider constituency;
rejection of civic responsibilities; congregationalism; and rootless,
featureless internationalism.

Liturgical revision to the degree seen in the Church of England is
not, if the Prayer Book Society is to be believed, a minor technicality
interesting only to specialists in ecclesiastical ritual. Rather, it is 'the
touchstone for testing all other aspects of the current crisis' of the
Church of England (Mullen, 1983). The wholesale abandonment of the
Book of Common Prayer for the *Alternative Service Book 1980* has
completely transformed the church's character. Brewer has expressed

this forcefully. He argues (1981, p. 242) that:

> just as the *Book of Common Prayer* marked the full emergence of the
> Church of England, so the ASB will mark its disappearance. The feeble-
> ness and lack of urgency of expression, the facile and evasive optimism
> of its theology, the bewildering multiplicity of its practices, will encour-
> age the proliferation of churches that are minor sects of local quietist
> groups, constituency parties run by enthusiasts. They will be populist in
> intended appeal, tiny in actual membership, autocratic in practice,
> hostile to the traditional virtues, hospitable to passing fashions and with
> about as much significance for the majority of English people as any
> other local group.

Clergymen and liturgical change: survey evidence

The evidence to be presented was gathered from a postal questionnaire
sent in November and December 1983 to all the Anglican parochial
clergy in one English diocese. Replies were received from 178 respondents, 82.4% of the target population. Even though the rate of
response was high, care must be taken in generalising from the sample
to the parochial clergy as a whole. The diocese has a rather conservative cast, and in statistical terms the evangelical tradition is probably
over represented and the catholic under represented. However, the fact
that the diocese is not in the vanguard of ecclesiastical fashion
strengthens the arguments put forward here.

It is hard to see, in the clergymen's responses, anything less than a
widespread approval of the *Alternative Service Book 1980*. 83.1% of
the respondents gave their overall opinion of the book as favourable;
only 5.1% were unfavourable and 9% neutral. Clear majorities also
assented to a variety of statements defending the new book. 68%
agreed that the ASB services were 'more meaningful to the majority of
churchgoers than those of the *Book of Common Prayer*'; 67.4% agreed
that the *Alternative Service Book 1980* 'reflects more accurately than
does the *Book of Common Prayer* the faith of the church today'; 73.6%
denied that the ASB services were 'theologically inferior to those of
the *Book of Common Prayer*', and 64.6% did not believe that the use
of the ASB services made it 'more difficult for those who are not
regular churchgoers to maintain contact with the church'.

Preference for the *Alternative Service Book 1980* is expressed in
liturgical practice: 122 respondents, 68.5% of the sample, gave an
ASB liturgy as the one they used more often than any other for the
main Sunday service. Rite A, the modern language liturgy, was by far
the most frequent, being cited by 43.2%. Only sixteen respondents,
9% of the sample, gave the 1662 liturgy as the one they used most
often for the principal service on Sunday. Many did indicate that they
use the *Book of Common Prayer* for other services, such as early
morning communion (which in most churches would be sparsely
attended), Mattins and Evensong. To this the Prayer Book Society

would certainly reply that in a church in which mid-morning celebration of the Eucharist has become by far the most important liturgical act, to reserve the *Book of Common Prayer* for other services is indeed to ensure its slide into oblivion.

Clerical approval of the *Alternative Service Book 1980* cuts across divisions of churchmanship. In this study, eight categories of churchmanship were distinguished: Anglo-Catholic, Liberal Catholic, Catholic Charismatic, Central/Broad Church, Modernist/New Theology, Liberal Evangelical, Conservative Evangelical and Evangelical Charismatic. With the exception of those identifying with Modernism/New Theology (the smallest category, with only three respondents), the majority in each tradition favoured the *Alternative Service Book 1980*, ranging from 75% of the Central/Broad Churchmen to all the Catholic Charismatics. In all traditions, the ASB liturgy was the one used most frequently for the main Sunday service.

The survey contained a battery of questions designed to uncover aspects of the respondents' basic theological position. Their opinion of the relationship between the Christian faith and secular thought and values was sought, as was their view of the historic creeds and bible fundamentalism, and their general orientation to theology. Answers to these questions were not only highly intercorrelated but were also significantly related to other factors such as questions of discipline and membership principle, the ordination of women to the priesthood, church-state relations and other political issues. In the case of the *Alternative Service Book 1980*, in contrast, its supporters were drawn almost equally from the different theological positions, radical, liberal and conservative. They made extensive use of the ASB liturgies, particularly Rite A.

Some respondents who were unenthusiastic about the *Alternative Service Book 1980* were also critical of the *Book of Common Prayer*. Several Anglo-Catholics had little affection for either book, while other respondents preferred the new book but deplored its bulk, poor pagination and complexity: 'Liturgy: okay, book: lousy' epitomised this school of thought. Even on a generous interpretation, there were only seventeen respondents, 9.6% of the sample, identifiable as men both unimpressed by the *Alternative Service Book 1980* and supporting the defence of the *Book of Common Prayer*.

In broad theological terms, these seventeen men are in the mainstream of the Church of England. What stands out is their resistance to changes in the church that are advocated by most of their brother clergy. The majority of these seventeen are against the ordination of women to the priesthood, less on purely theological grounds than through fear that it would cause a major schism in the Church of England and also undermine the ecumenical movement. They were opposed to the 'Covenanting for Unity' scheme, under which it was hoped that a gradual growth toward union would take place between the Church of England, the Methodists, the United Reformed, the

Moravians and the Church of Christ. Most are against the remarriage of divorcees in church, the ordination of divorced men and the admission of children to holy communion before confirmation. They also dislike the General Synod. The majority are content with current practice in regard to baptism, and do not favour restricting infant baptism to the children of churchgoers or moving to adult baptism as the norm. They believe that the rites of passage provided by the church should in effect be open to all who request them. They are also loyal supporters of the establishment.

The most striking characteristic of the seventeen is, however, demographic. Eight of them are over sixty, none under thirty. Only one had been in holy orders for less than ten years. Those recently ordained, perhaps because their training had not familiarised them with the *Book of Common Prayer* – a point pressed by the Prayer Book Society – were overwhelmingly in favour of the *Alternative Service Book 1980*. Of the 56 men ordained within the previous ten years, 51 gave their opinion of the new book as favourable.

This evidence suggests that if clerical opinion prevails, the *Book of Common Prayer* is indeed likely to become more marginal to the corporate worship of the Church of England. The clergy themselves believe this to be so. When asked for their judgement of the probable role of the *Book of Common Prayer* at the end of this century, only 3.9% of the sample saw it as central to the church's life; 36.5% saw it as a significant option in worship and 50.6% foresaw its role as minor. A few were more dismissive: one thought it would be consigned to the dustbin, another that it would survive merely as a socio-liturgical curio.

Indirect evidence from the survey points to the great confidence of clergymen in judging the merits and impact of liturgical change. Levels of uncertainty and non-response on these issues were low, especially on the basic question of opinion of the *Alternative Service Book 1980*, where only three respondents were uncertain. The section of the questionnaire on liturgical change was one about which the respondents appeared to have few reservations. They did not indicate, as some did elsewhere, their own lack of experience, interest or expertise. They were also rather confident in looking ahead to the end of the century, and more than half of them expected the *Book of Common Prayer* to play a minor or even negligible role in the church's corporate worship. Granted they may be mistaken: opinions may be revised, expectations may be frustrated, but there is nevertheless little reason to believe that clerical opinion on liturgical change is hesitant or volatile. These are matters of which the parochial clergy have day-to-day experience and on which they are widely though not universally regarded as the experts. Here, even if nowhere else, they are professionals among amateurs.

The evidence presented above is congruent with many of the claims made by the Prayer Book Society. Most clergymen are indeed favourably inclined to the *Alternative Prayer Book 1980* and use it extensively. They do not see it as an inferior alternative to the *Book of Common Prayer* even if they recognise its faults. Those who do clearly deplore the new book are a small minority of disproportionately older men. More than half of the respondents saw at most a minor role for the *Book of Common Prayer* in the corporate worship of the Church of England in the next century. There was some support for the principle of protecting the *Book of Common Prayer*, but the problem remains how such protection is to be secured in an organisation where the relative autonomy of the priest is guarded jealously. Only a minority supported a reduction in liturgical variety, and in any case the *Alternative Service Book 1980* rather than the *Book of Common Prayer* is the standard to which most would rally.

Even though the fact of clerical approval of the *Alternative Service Book 1980* is confirmed, the interpretation of it remains to be resolved. Why do the clergy welcome the new services, and are they, as their critics allege, pushing the church down the road to sectarianism?

A sectarian clergy?

In everyday usage, and among churchmen, the terms 'sect' and 'sectarian' are irretrievably pejorative. They carry associations of narrowness, intolerance, bigotry, self-righteousness, and an evasion of engagement with the outside world. These terms are applied to others: we are a church, you are a denomination, they are a sect. Many movements aspire for varying reasons to the name of church. A church is, above all, a highly respectable body. Churches enjoy charitable status and the tax advantages that flow from it. It may be important in some contexts for a minority movement to establish for itself a 'religious' rather than a 'political' or 'therapeutic' identity, to escape the attention of the state or entrenched professional interest groups. The claim to churchly status may symbolise the movement's fidelity to the example and teaching of its founder.

There is an embarrassment of self-proclaimed churches but not one group that calls itself a sect. To suggest that fellow churchmen are sectarians inevitably invites a rebuttal; clergy who are in favour of the new services reject the diagnosis of sectarianism. For them, liturgical change has brought not sectarian narrowness but vitality, commitment and a renewal of the church's mission to the world.

There is a good deal of evidence from my survey that clergymen do not express, indeed repudiate attitudes and opinions characteristic of sectarian forms of organisation. The majority of respondents oppose changes which would make initiation into the church more demanding and exclusive. On the sensitive question of the remarriage of divorcees in church, most respondents have tolerant, inclusive views, rather than calling for strict discipline. Anglican theologians have not, in their view, had too much freedom of expression. They look favourably on and participate in ecumenical ventures with other denominations. The majority do not support the exclusiveness, the strictness of membership discipline and the sense of a unique religious legitimacy that typify the sect (see especially Robertson, 1970, pp. 117–42; Wallis, 1976, pp. 11–18; Wilson, 1982, pp. 89–120).

First, let us consider baptism, which is theologically and socially the principal rite of initiation into the Church of England. The baptism service in the *Alternative Service Book 1980* stresses very heavily the incorporation of the individual into the church. The responsibilities of parents and godparents are underlined: they promise to use prayer, example and teaching to ensure that their charges are raised 'as Christians within the family of the church'. If the child is old enough to understand, the priest explains that he or she is God's child and is joining a family in which all Christians are brothers and sisters. The congregation says a prayer of welcome to the initiate, and the priest reinforces this in a prayer of thanksgiving for 'our fellowship in the household of faith with all those who have been baptised in your name'.

The practice of infant baptism is a sensitive issue, and it has had stern critics in the church. Very few churchmen today would justify it by the claim that the sacrament of baptism is necessary to salvation (a belief manifest in the *Book of Common Prayer*). In the *Alternative Service Book 1980*'s rubric on emergency baptism the priest is called on to assure parents 'that questions of ultimate salvation or of the provision of a Christian funeral for an infant who dies do not depend upon whether or not he had been baptised'. Some churchmen have argued that infant baptism is not consonant with the practice of the early church, for arguably the New Testament gives no warrant for anything other than adult believers' baptism. Others argue that infants obviously cannot make the vows and commitments demanded of them in baptism, and that it is absurd to suggest that someone else can do so vicariously. Even among those who are prepared to allow infant baptism there is widespread condemnation of 'indiscriminate baptism', in which the priest makes no serious effort to ensure sincere Christian commitment on the part of parents and godparents but instead acquiesces in a socially acceptable 'folk religious' rite of passage.

In the survey, respondents were asked a number of questions about Christian initiation. Not one of them thought that the church's baptism policy was too strict; on the contrary, 53.4% thought it too lax and 42.7% about right. When pressed more specifically, however, many respondents drew back from rigorist, exclusive policies: 50.6% were against confining infant baptism to the children of regular churchgoers, and 66.3% disagreed that the practice of adult baptism should be the norm; 61.2% favoured the admission of children to holy communion before they had been confirmed – a clear indication of the declining significance of confirmation. More generally, 60.1% of the sample supported the present practice under which, in effect, clergy are expected to provide the rites of baptism, marriage and burial to all parishioners who request them. If respondents had been determined sectarians, they surely could not have countenanced inclusive provision of the rites of passage.

As well as imposing strict criteria of admission, sects exert tight internal discipline, exacting from their members relatively high levels of participation and performance. In the survey there were a number of questions bearing on this. One highly controversial area is the remarriage in church of divorcees during the lifetime of their former partner. The majority of respondents in my survey, 60.1%, would accept the remarriage of divorcees in church in some situations: 2.8% said there should be no barrier to remarriages, 18% said they should normally be allowed and 39.3% said they should be granted only after a careful enquiry into the couple's circumstances. In contrast, 28.7% of the sample did not think the church should conduct remarriages: this was made up of 7.3% who said the church should give no approval to the remarriage of divorcees, and 21.3% who preferred a service of blessing, or of prayers and dedication, after a civil ceremony. The majority of clergymen did not, then, support the indissolubility of marriage, as one would expect sectarians (though not only sectarians) to do. Furthermore, 51.7% agreed and only 28.7% disagreed that men who remarry during the lifetime of their former partner may be ordained as priests. (This is not to deny that the position of the divorced priest is often made uncomfortable. In his report of 1982 the Clergy Appointments Officer said that some dioceses would not accept divorced men for any clerical appointment while others, showing more tolerance, would offer them only unbeneficed posts.)

There is one other area of membership discipline on which the respondents had the chance to express sectarian opinions and yet failed to do so. Since the Second World War there has been a succession of highly publicised controversies about allegedly extravagant interpretations of the Christian faith by theologians and church leaders, including the late Bishop John Robinson's *Honest to God*, the writings and broadcasts of Don Cupitt, the collection entitled *The Myth of God Incarnate*, the television series *Jesus – the Evidence*, and the debate provoked by the Bishop of Durham's approach to the doctrines of Virgin Birth and Resurrection. In reply to the question, 'Have Anglican theologians in recent years had too much freedom of expression?', 61.2% said no and 25.3% yes. Tolerance of theological exploration has never been considered a sectarian trait.

Data from other parts of the questionnaire appear not to support the assertion that most respondents had a sectarian orientation to the Church of England. For example, ecumenical ventures were broadly favoured: 86.5% were in favour of eventual union with the Methodist Church, 81.5% with the United Reformed Church, 71.9% with the Orthodox Church, 71.3% with the Baptist Church and 70.2% with the

Roman Catholic Church; 55.6% had been in favour of the Covenanting for Unity proposals; 83.1% were in favour of local ecumenical projects and 40.4% had participated in one; 92.1% had preached in a church of another denomination, 88.2% had invited a minister of another denomination to preach in their own church, and 67.4% had taken part in a service of intercommunion. If the sect is a body with a strong sense of its unique legitimacy and monopoly of the truth, then these clergymen are not sectarians. It may be, as Wilson has argued (1966, pp. 225–33), that both ecumenism and sectarianism are responses to secularisation – but they are diametrically opposite responses.

Nor is there much evidence to suggest that respondents wanted the church to disengage from the world or radically to reorder its place in national life. On the general question of disestablishment, 27% were in favour and 48.3% against, with 24.7% uncertain. Several respondents indicated that much turned on the way in which the state used its power in future. Fifty-nine per cent were opposed to the state's continued involvement in the appointment of bishops. On the other hand, 51.7% would favour allowing clergymen to serve in the House of Commons as elected Members of Parliament, 69.1% agreed with the present representation of bishops in the House of Lords (6.7% said the number should be increased), and 85.4% rejected the view that church leaders should not intervene in politically controversial subjects. Opinion was almost equally divided on whether parochial clergymen should avoid being publicly identified with one political party: 43.8% thought they should; 44.9% disagreed.

The established church

The importance of establishment to the identity of the Church of England was shown in a comparative study of Anglican clergymen, Methodist ministers and Roman Catholic priests carried out in the early 1970s by Ranson, Bryman and Hinings (1977, pp. 46–51). Respondents were asked whether they thought of their church as one denomination among many or as having a special responsibility to the whole population of an area regardless of people's religious or other affiliations. The Methodist ministers, the authors conclude, 'clearly view their church as one denomination among others' sharing in mission to the whole community: the denominational sentiment was overriding. This denominational view was taken by only 7.5% of the Roman Catholic priests and 10.7% of the Anglican clergy, and by 12.4% of my own respondents. Conversely, 63% of the Roman Catholic priests, 69.2% of the Anglican clergy and 53.9% of my respondents saw their church as having a special responsibility for the whole community. For many of the Roman Catholics, as Ranson *et al.* emphasise, their church is seen as having a theologically unique legitimacy as the one true Catholic and Apostolic Church founded by Christ: respondents annotated their questionnaires with comments whose degree of certainty and theological unanimity was striking. In the case of the Anglican clergy, in contrast, 'there is a substantial secular element', in that 'because theirs is the national church, clergy see themselves as having a responsibility to all the members of their parish whatever their religious belief' (1977, p. 48). The establishment – as John Habgood, the Archbishop of York, has argued – conveys privileges and responsibilities on the Church of England but does not signify that it has a unique religious legitimacy (Habgood, 1983, pp. 93–112).

Given this, there is something odd in the proposition that the established Church of England is in danger of becoming a sect. Surely establishment and sectarianism are incompatible? A sect's indifference or hostility to the world is not to be reconciled with the national position of power, privilege and responsibility which establishment entails. Is, then, the establishment itself under attack from sectarians in the church? Three aspects of this question will be examined. First, what is the overall pattern of response to the prospect of disestablishment? Second, do those who favour disestablishment display any sectarian characteristics? Finally, are the seventeen men identified as *Book of Common Prayer* supporters significantly different in their view of establishment from those who favour the *Alternative Service Book 1980*?

Among my respondents there is far more support for establishment than for disestablishment, but there is also some uncertainty and divergence of opinion about which particular aspects of establishment should be retained and which modified or abolished. In reply to the general filter question, 27% said that the church should seek disestablishment, 48.3% disagreed and 24.7% were uncertain; several commented that disestablishment might be forced on the church by overweening state power. Age was a very significant factor: 40.4% of those under forty favour disestablishment and 25% definitely oppose it, whereas among men of forty and over only 21.8% favour disestablishment, and 58.1% oppose it. Among the seventeen senior clergymen in my sample (defined here as canons and above) not one was in favour of disestablishment and only two were uncertain. This pattern is reflected at national level, where few church leaders are calling for disestablishment: it is not a live issue, as even so fierce a critic as Peter Cornwell is forced to concede. The case for disestablishment is weakened by the fact that many ostensible disestablishers would be glad to retain those features of establishment which appeal to them. None of the respondents who said they supported disestablishment thought that the state should be involved in any way in the appointment of bishops, yet 50% believed that the representation of Anglican bishops in the House of Lords should be retained or even expanded.

There is evidence from my survey that those who favour disestablishment are more inclined to seek stringent membership criteria, as sects do. Comparing the views of the opponents of establishment with its supporters shows a sharp difference of opinion over baptism: 83.3% of opponents and 31.4% of supporters think the church's policy on baptism is too lax; 68.7% of opponents as against 24.4% of supporters would like infant baptism confined to the children of regular churchgoers, and 52.1% of opponents as against 14% of supporters hold that the practice of adult believers' baptism should be the norm.

Although it has a critical importance as the church's principal initiation rite, baptism should be seen as one facet of a wider pattern of relations between the church and the world. The Canon Law of the Church of England places on the clergy certain specific responsibilities towards the parishioners within their cure. Only under fairly closely defined circumstances can the clergy refuse to provide baptism, marriage and funeral services, and some parishioners are assertive about their rights. Respondents were therefore asked whether or not they thought they should be free from the obligations placed on them by Canon Law concerning the rites of passage. Once again, those favouring disestablishment took the more exclusivist view: 64.6% said clergy should be released from these obligations and only 16.7% thought the obligations should be retained. In complete contrast, 87.2% of the supporters of establishment were in favour of the retention of these Canon Law provisions, and a mere 8.1% favoured their removal.

The dilemmas that clergy face are mirrored in debates among leading churchmen, where disagreements about the identity of the church and its operative membership principle are very evident. Peter Cornwell's attack on establishment faces these issues squarely. For him the fundamental question is 'whether Christianity is based on the religious aspirations and search of men or on the movement of God towards us in self-disclosure' (1983, pp. 36–37). He firmly opts for the latter, and draws this conclusion (1983, p. 39):

> If the church is shaped by the gift and call of God then it is less an institution existing to provide religious ceremonies for the nation than a community which has to be joined. No one has a right, by virtue of being English, to be a member of it. No one is born into the church.

Establishment dissolves the church in the world, yet the world is no longer Christian if indeed it ever was. The proponents of establishment are fostering a sentimental fiction about English society (1983, p. 57):

> If the symbols of establishment suggest that the nation deep down holds Christian beliefs, affirms Christian values and offers Christian worship when, for the most part, it does none of these things, then the symbols frankly encourage delusion, and delusion is always a barrier to spiritual advance.

Cornwell argues that in a secular society there is not a simple choice between established church or sect, since all religious bodies are dissenting minorities and many churches are open and inclusive yet not established (1983, pp. 34–5). In May 1985 Father Cornwell left the Church of England: he did not join a sect, but was received into the Roman Catholic Church.

In comparing the seventeen supporters of the *Book of Common Prayer* with the 148 men who gave a favourable opinion of the *Alternative Service Book 1980* some differences do emerge, though they are not very striking. Among both groups disestablishment is supported by only one person in four. The *Book of Common Prayer* supporters seem more content with the establishment as it is at present, whereas among those favouring the new book there appears to be a little more disquiet, especially about the state's involvement in the appointment of bishops. Conversely, those favouring the *Alternative Service Book 1980* are more willing to see clergymen identified with party political positions, and to have ordained priests free, as they are not at present, to stand for election to the House of Commons.

The evidence gathered supports the following conclusions. Disestablishment is favoured only by a minority in the sample, and even among these men there is approval of some of the current features of establishment. They do express a wish for stricter criteria of church membership, and this is indeed a characteristic of sects; however, it is likely that what they seek is a different kind of church, one that would be less bound up with national identity without being in any serious sense sectarian. The minority of men who appear loyal to the *Book of Common Prayer* are supporters of the establishment as presently constituted – but then so are those who warm to the *Alternative Service Book 1980*, albeit to a lesser degree. Thus although establishment is a safeguard against sectarianism it is not a necessary one.

The church in a secular society

Many commentators have diagnosed a crisis of identity in the Church of England. (See Mol, 1976, this theme in general; on the Church of England see Sykes, 1978; Gilbert, 1980; Kilmister, 1983; Martin, 1980). One recent collection of writings that argues this position very forcefully is *When Will Ye Be Wise?* edited by Anthony Kilmister, one of the Prayer Book Society's most articulate members, who says in the book's preface that he hopes to see 'our national church returning more clearly to its historic mission'. The contributors identify a variety of ways in which the church has precipitated the crisis. Liberal theologians and bishops have relativised central elements of the Christian faith; the church's leaders have politicised it, aligning it with fashionable causes, usually leftist ones; ill-conceived ecumenical ventures have generated enthusiasm followed by frustration and recriminations; neo-pentecostalism in the form of the charismatic movement has been disruptive, facile and spurious; Christian morality has been subordinated to secular permissiveness; the ordination of women to the priesthood not only threatens to divide the church into rival factions, jeopardising its character as both Catholic and Reformed, but arguably transforms Christianity in to paganism; the church is embarrassed by its historic link with the state and is thus becoming an increasingly disregarded dissident organisation; and finally, the church's shabby desertion of the *Book of Common Prayer* betrays an institutional bad faith that may even be irreversible.

A fundamental weakness of these arguments, I suggest, is that they exaggerate the extent to which the church has been responsible for its own declining social significance. Even if the church had been 'wise' in the sense intended by the critics, it is doubtful how much difference this would have made. In the case of the *Book of Common Prayer*, its advocates tend to overstate the degree to which it penetrates English culture. Their argument that people who are not regular churchgoers are alienated by the new services while being conversant with the *Book of Common Prayer* is not very convincing. Familiarity with the *Book of Common Prayer* comes for most people through regular churchgoing; but since the statistics of declining church attendance are incontrovertible (Currie *et al.*, 1977), it follows that fewer and fewer people are acquainted with the *Book of Common Prayer*. The decline was under way well before the church introduced modern language liturgies (Series Three Holy Communion was authorised in 1973). Most adult English men and women are admittedly far more familiar with the Authorised Version than with any other bible translation, and if asked to recite the Lord's Prayer most would do so in the traditional form given in the *Book of Common Prayer*, or a close variant of it (as in Rite B of the *Alternative Service Book 1980*). This familiarity, however, has been developed not simply through church attendance but also through reception and rote learning at school, a point which does not apply to the *Book of Common Prayer* as a whole.

Supporters of the *Book of Common Prayer* campaign, including sociologists, have used the term 'sect' in a frankly evaluative way and usually without any clear definition. Over the years sociologists have suggested very many characteristics as distinctively sectarian, yet few of these accurately describe the Church of England today. The church is not epistemologically authoritarian, but on the contrary allows a wide diversity of belief; it does not apply stringent tests of membership but continues to baptise infants and opens its rites of passage to parishioners without pressing awkward questions very far; it does not seek a totalitarian hold over members, does not impose strict discipline on them, is extremely reluctant to exclude them and is tolerant of their failings; and its members are not seen as an elect or elite but more as representatives of a wider constituency of infrequent attenders. Most clergymen want the Church of England to be open and inclusive in evangelism, to play an active, critical role in national affairs, to co-operate locally and nationally with other mainstream churches and to work towards eventual reunion with them. Adherence to the *Book of Common Prayer* has not been shown to be vital to any of these objectives.

In urging on the Church of England a stark choice between church and sect, defenders of the *Book of Common Prayer* are invoking a conceptual framework that has diminishing relevance for contemporary Britain. As both Beckford (1975, p. 125) and Wilson (1982, p. 89 *et seq.*) have argued, the classic contrast of church and sect to be found in the works of Max Weber, his pupil Ernst Troeltsch and countless successors, greatly oversimplifies the variety of religious expression in modern industrial societies, even in ones where an established church enjoys legal privileges and responsibilities that are not shared with other religious movements. On the one hand, sects do not now arise from schisms or protests against a church, nor do they take a church or the church as the point of reference for their own separate identity. To understand their distinctive commitment it is no longer necessary to focus on their relationship to a church: as Wilson says, 'this exercise of comparison may now be regarded as more of a hindrance to sociological analysis than a help'. In a pluralist society there is also a tendency for erstwhile sects to become institutionalised, reaching a *modus vivendi* with the wider society. On the other hand, social changes have undermined the preeminence of the Church of England. The assumption that English people are 'born into' the Church of England unless they opt out of it has become less and less valid, for their membership is indeed more of a voluntary choice than an ascribed status. The Church of England is dealing with other denominations on a more equal footing than before, is engaging in ecumenical ventures at local level and has pursued though ultimately drawn back from the Covenanting for Unity proposals and the earlier scheme for union with the Methodist Church. The legal privileges enjoyed by the established church have become fewer, the Free Churches no longer define their identity in terms of 'dissent' or 'nonconformity', and discrimination against other churches has shrunk to a tiny residuum.

A major theme of the Prayer Book Society's campaign has been to apply the term 'sectarian' and its cognates to the processes of liturgical change that are taking place in the Church of England. In this respect the campaign has been hyperbolic. Although there are sectarian tendencies within the church and among some clergymen, there is little evidence to suggest that sectarianism is characteristic of those – the clear majority – who favour and use the *Alternative Service Book 1980*. The social significance and cultural supremacy of the Church of England have been undermined not by a misguided commitment to new liturgies, but by social changes that are largely beyond the church's control. In part, the Prayer Book Society's rhetoric has been a cry of pain at the inroads of secularisation.

References

Beckford, J A (1975) *The Trumpet of Prophecy*, Oxford, Blackwell.
Brewer, D (1981) 'Letters to the editor,' in D Martin and P Mullen (eds) *No Alternative*, Oxford, Blackwell, pp. 191–202.

Cornwell, P (1983) *Church and Nation*, Oxford, Blackwell.

Currie, R, Gilbert, A and Horsley, L (1977) *Churches and Churchgoers*, Oxford, Oxford University Press.

Gilbert, A D (1980) *The Making of Post-Christian Britain*, London, Longman.

Habgood, J (1983) *Church and Nation in a Secular Age*, London, Darton, Longman and Todd.

Homan, R (1979) 'Noli me tangere,' in D Martin (ed.) *Crisis for Cranmer and King James*, Manchester, Carcanet Press.

Homan, R (1983) 'Machiavelli and the sacred ministry,' in C A A Kilminster (ed.) *When Will Ye Be Wise?* London, Blond and Briggs.

Kilmister, C A A (ed.) (1980) *When Will Ye Be Wise?* London, Blond and Briggs.

Martin, D (ed.) (1979) *Crisis for Cranmer and King James*, Manchester, Carcanet Press.

Martin, D (1980) *The Breaking of the Image*, Oxford, Blackwell.

Martin, D and Mullen, P (eds) (1981) *No Alternative*, Oxford, Blackwell.

Mol, H (1976) *Identity and the Sacred*, Oxford, Blackwell.

Morris, B (1980) *Ritual Murder*, Manchester, Carcanet Press.

Mullen, P (1983) 'The end is nigh . . .,' *Manchester Guardian*, 8 January.

Ranson, S, Bryman, A and Hinings, B (1977) *Clergy, Ministers and Priests*, London, Routledge and Kegan Paul.

Robertson, R (1970) *The Sociological Interpretation of Religion*, Oxford, Blackwell.

Russell, A (1980) *The Clerical Profession*, London SPCK.

Sisson, C H (1981) 'Bogus contemporary' and 'A warning to the Church,' in D Martin and P Mullen (eds) *No Alternative*, Oxford, Blackwell, pp. 114–121 and 227–230.

Sykes, S W (1978) *The Integrity of Anglicanism*, London, Mowbray.

Wallis, R (1976) *The Road to Total Freedom*, London, Heinemann.

Welsby, P A (1984) *A History of the Church of England, 1945–1980*, Oxford, Oxford University Press.

Wilson, B R (1966) *Religion in Secular Society*, London, Watts.

Wilson, B R (1982) *Religion in Sociological Perspective*, Oxford, Oxford University Press.

13. Counselling and psychology

One of the most thoroughly researched aspects of the clerical profession concerns the role of the clergy as counsellor. Research in this field is illustrated by two very different studies. One study reports a specific enquiry into the way in which theological position is reflected in counselling practices. The other study provides an overview and synthesis of a number of studies.

In the first article in this section, Darrell Winger and Bruce Hunsberger report on a survey conducted among 127 male clergy from ten Protestant denominations in Ontario to explore the relationship between clergy counselling practices, Christian orthodoxy and problem solving styles. The findings confirmed that clergy's views of mental illness and their approaches to counselling are related to their religious orthodoxy and their approaches to problem solving. For example, clergy who tended to view both the individual and God as active in problem solving tended to report using both psychological and spiritual techniques in their counselling. Clergy who tended to view the individual as passive and God as active in problem solving were more likely to use spiritual techniques in their counselling.

Dr Bruce Hunsberger is in the Department of Psychology, Wilfrid Laurier University, Waterloo, Ontario, Canada. Darrell Winger was studying in the same department. This article was first published in *Journal of Psychology and Theology* in 1988.

In the second article, Willa D Meylink and Richard L Gorsuch provide an overview of the empirical data concerned with the relationship between clergy and psychologists. The authors conclude that, although approximately 40% of people seeking help first approach clergy, less than 10% of those help seekers are referred to mental health professionals. Psychologists refer even fewer clients to clergy or other religious resources.

Professor Richard L Gorsuch is Director of Research and Evaluation and Professor of Psychology at the Graduate School of Psychology, Fuller Theological Seminary, Pasadena, California, USA. Dr Willa D Meylink was studying in the same department. This article was first published in *Journal of Psychology and Christianity* in 1988.

13.1 Clergy counselling practices, Christian orthodoxy and problem solving styles

Darrell Winger and Bruce Hunsberger

This study is concerned with relationships among religious orientation, problem solving styles, and the counselling attitudes and practices of Protestant clergymen. It has been well established that members of the clergy are quite active in the area of counselling (Bell, Morris, Holzer and Warheit, 1976; Virkler, 1979; Wright, 1984; Wright, Moreau and Haley, 1982). Bell *et al.* have emphasised that the clergy are an important 'front-line' mental health resource. Estimates of the average amount of time spent counselling each week have ranged from 2.5 hours (Bell *et al.*) to 7 hours (Wright). In Wright's study 97% of the Protestant and Catholic clergy sampled reported at least some counselling contacts. There is evidence that clergy also refer some of their clients to others, including mental health agencies, psychologists, psychiatrists, physicians, social agencies, and the like (Bell *et al.*; Wright).

Contrary to what one might expect, much of the counselling that clergy engage in is not of a spiritual nature. Wright (1984) found that marriage and family problems were most commonly encountered, followed by 'emotional difficulties' and alcohol and drug problems. Only 4.9% of the problems cited were of a spiritual nature. Virkler (1979) reported that depression, premarital counselling, marital communication problems, guilt, spiritual concerns, and feelings of inadequacy were all encountered by clergy ten or more times a year.

However, in spite of the relatively few 'spiritual' problems reported, there is apparently a strong emphasis on 'spiritual counselling'. For example, Bell *et al.* (1976) found that 40% of their sample of clergy usually suggested bible reading during their counselling sessions, and 69% usually prayed with their clients. Similarly, Virkler (1979) reported that 85% of his sample used scripture and 82% reported that they prayed aloud in their sessions.

One might suspect that clergy members' religious affiliation or orientation would have some relationship to their understanding of problems and their causes, as well as to their approach to counselling. Wright *et al.* (1982) did find that fundamentalists were more likely to attribute mental illness to spiritual causes, but orthodoxy did not seem to affect counselling and referring in general. In addition, while Wright *et al.* concluded that clergy saw the causes of mental illness primarily in psychological terms, Virkler (1979) concluded that his clergy believed that spiritual, psychological and physical forces interact to contribute to one's personal difficulties.

Recently, Pargament *et al.* (1985) have provided a framework which could contribute to our understanding of the relationship between religion and counselling. They developed scales to measure three styles of 'problem solving'. The first style 'involves active efforts by the individual him/herself to solve problems without the help of God (active person/passive God). The second style involves a passive approach to the solution of problems by the person him/herself, and a reliance on God for problem solutions (passive person/active God). The third style involves a process of collaboration between the person and God in solving problems (active person/active God)' (p. 3).

Pargament *et al.* (1985) found that scores on the Problem Solving Scales were correlated with measures of religiousness for lay church members, such that the active person/passive God scale scores were negatively correlated (from -.24 to -.60) with measures of religiousness (including church attendance, frequency of prayer, religious salience, God control, and doctrinal orthodoxy). A positive relationship existed between both the passive person/active God and active person/active God scales, and the measures of religiousness (with all correlations between .20 and .62). Although research with the Problem Solving Scales has focused on samples of laypersons, there would seem to be considerable potential in applying these measures to the clergy, particularly as aids in understanding clergy approaches to counselling. For example, those clergy who view the *person* as active in the problem solving process (that is, active person/passive God, or active person/active God) would be expected to focus on counselling strategies which actively involve the client (that is, 'psychological techniques') rather than those which appeal more to God for solutions to problems (that is, 'spiritual techniques').

In light of the above literature, several hypotheses were examined in the present study: first, those clergy who score high on active person/passive God or active person/active God scales are more likely to use psychological techniques than spiritual techniques in counselling; second, less orthodox clergy are less likely to use spiritual methods of counselling and are more likely to use psychological techniques than the more orthodox clergy; and third, clergy from less orthodox denominations score higher on the active person/passive God scale, while clergy from more orthodox denominations score higher on the passive person/active God scale. In addition to these specific hypotheses, the role of clergy's education and psychological or counselling training on counselling attitudes and approaches was explored.

Method

A seven-page questionnaire was sent to 178 Protestant ministers in southern Ontario, Canada, with a self-addressed, stamped envelope. Completed questionnaires were received from 127 clergy (all male, with a mean age of 45.4 years) yielding a return rate of 71.3%.

Denominations represented included Anglican (fifteen), Brethren in Christ (fifteen), Mennonite (fifteen), Mennonite Brethren (fourteen), Missionary (fourteen), Lutheran (thirteen), Baptist (twelve), Presbyterian (twelve), Pentecostal (eleven), and United Church of Canada (six). On average, 17.9 years had been spent in the pastorate. Of the sample, 53% had obtained a postgraduate degree, 20% had done some postgraduate work, and 19% had a Bachelor's degree (or equivalent).

The questionnaire included the Christian Orthodoxy (CO) scale (Fullerton and Hunsberger, 1982) (a scale based essentially on Christian credal beliefs), Religious Problem Solving (RPS) scales (Pargament *et al.*, 1985) and items to assess issues related to pastoral counselling such as techniques used by the clergy in their counselling sessions, types of problems counselled, referral practices and perceived causes of mental illness. Copies of the questionnaire are available from the authors. All statistical analyses were conducted using the Nie, Hull, Jenkins, Steinbrenner, and Bent (1975) SPSS programmes.

Results

In this study, 61% of the clergy reported spending 0 to 4 hours per week in counselling, 17% reported 5 to 8 hours, 16% reported 9 to 10 hours, and the remaining 6% reported over 10 hours per week ($M = 5$ hours per week). The problems reportedly dealt with most frequently were spiritual concerns, premarital counselling and bereavement, with average ratings of 7.2, 7.1 and 6.9 respectively on the 0 to 10 response scale used.

The problems most frequently referred to other professionals were various mental disorders (21.2%), severe depression (16.1%), marital problems (12.3%) and addiction problems (including alcoholism) (8.5%). Referrals were most frequently made to psychiatrists (18%), psychologists (14.5%), medical doctors (8.3%), Christian counselling clinics (8.3%) and Christian psychologists (7.3%). The clergy generally viewed the causes of mental illness to be equally a result of spiritual, psychological and social factors, with respective means of 6.5, 6.2 and 6.1 on the 0 to 10 response format. Physiological factors, although reported to contribute as well to the cause of mental illness, were seen as playing a lesser role ($M = 4.6$).

With respect to the psychometric properties of the RPS scales, 30% of the clergy in the present study reported that they had some difficulty, usually in terms of redundancy of items and inappropriate and/or rigid wording. However, psychometric analyses of the RPS scales seemed to indicate at least adequate psychometric properties. For example, Cronbach alphas (measuring internal consistency) for the three scales were .90 (active person/active God), .88 (passive person/active God), and .87 (active person/passive God) for our sample of clergy.

There were few significant Pearson product-moment correlations between the RPS scales and the items relating to psychological techniques used in counselling (designed to tap Rogerian, behaviouristic, Freudian, and Rational-Emotive approaches to counselling). Low positive correlations were significant ($p < .05$) between the item, 'I point out "problem" behaviours that are the "root" of my clients' problems, and how to change these behaviours to ones that are beneficial and healthy' and both the active person/active God ($r = .20$) and passive person/active God ($r = .18$) scales; between the item, 'I point out to my clients how present problems are a result of childhood experiences' and the active person/active God scale ($r = .20$); and between the item, 'I challenge and attempt to correct my clients' faulty or inaccurate ways of thinking concerning their specific problems' and both the active person/active God ($r = .18$) and passive person/active God ($r = .21$) scales. None of the other correlations between items and RPS scales (or the CO scale) even approached significance. Other items were, 'I attempt to empathise with my client and provide a warm, non-judgemental atmosphere', 'I do most of the talking and direct the conversation during counselling sessions with my clients' and 'The clients set the agenda for the session through whatever they choose to discuss.'

Table one shows the correlations between RSP scales and spiritual counselling techniques. Overall, the various spiritual counselling techniques were positively and significantly correlated with active person/active God and passive person/active God scores, while such items tended to be negatively related to active person/passive God scores (although only one of four of the latter correlations was significant). Although no significant correlations emerged between CO scores and psychological technique items, orthodoxy was significantly positively correlated with spiritual technique items (table one).

Table two shows the results of t-tests indicating that clergy from less orthodox denominations (Anglican, Lutheran, United Church, Presbyterian) scored higher than those from the more orthodox denominations (Mennonite, Mennonite Brethren, Brethren in Christ, Missionary, Baptist, Pentecostal) on active person/passive God measures while scoring lower on the active person/active God and the passive person/active God measures.

Further analyses indicated that the clergy's general level of education was not correlated with their views on the cause of mental illness or the problems which they counselled. Also, correlations between clergy's level of counselling or psychology education and their views on the causes of mental illness or the problems which they counselled were generally non-significant. However, *graduate* training in counselling or psychology did correlate with a view of mental illness as psychological ($r = .28, p < .01$).

Graduate level education in counselling or psychology (as defined by number of courses taken at the graduate level) correlated positively

Table 1: Correlations between spiritual counselling technique items, Religious Problem Solving Scales and the Christian Orthodoxy Scale

spiritual counselling technique items	scales			
	AP/PG	AP/AG	PP/AG	CO
I incorporate prayer into my counselling sessions	-0.10	0.23**	0.26**	0.22**
I incorporate scripture into my counselling sessions	-20.05	0.22**	0.24**	0.21*
I present clients with relevant scripture, and pray for and with my clients to the exclusion of any other methods	-0.18*	0.25**	0.56***	0.31***
I attempt to show my clients that their problems are mainly due to some problem in their spiritual life	-0.02	0.21*	0.29**	0.18*

Note: * $p < .05$ ** $p < .01$ *** $p < .001$

Table 2: T-Tests for religious problem solving styles: liberal versus conservative denominations

problem solving style	group	N	M	t	df	p
active person/ passive God	liberal	43	22.98	2.00	118	.047
	conservative	77	20.79			
active person/ active God	liberal	43	40.02	-3.28	118	.001
	conservative	77	44.58			
passive person/ active God	liberal	44	20.75	-4.75	120	.000
	conservative	77	27.06			

with the item tapping a Rogerian approach ($r = .20$, $p < .05$) but negatively with the use of spiritual techniques. That is, clergy with more graduate training were less likely to use prayer in counselling sessions ($r = .28$, $p < .01$); use scripture in counselling sessions ($r = .27$, $p < .01$); use scripture, and pray for and with their client, to the exclusion of any other methods ($r = -.28$, $p < .01$); and show clients that their present problems are mainly due to some problem in their spiritual life ($r = -.27$, $p < .05$).

Graduate training was also related to RPS scores, correlating positively with active person/passive God scores ($r = .25$, $p < .05$) and negatively with passive person/active God scores ($r = -.24$, $p < .05$). There was no significant correlation for active person/active God scores.

Orthodoxy was found to be only weakly correlated with views on the causation of mental illness or the problems counselled. Orthodoxy was negatively correlated with the view that the cause of mental illness was psychological ($r = -.19$, $p < .05$) and with the view that it was due to societal factors ($r = -.16$, $p < .05$). There were no significant correlations between orthodoxy scores and a view of mental illness as caused by psychological or spiritual factors, but orthodoxy was negatively correlated with level of education ($r = -.26$, $p < .01$).

Discussion

Our finding that the clergy sample was averaging five hours per week counselling is consistent with previous research (Virkler, 1979; Wright, 1984). Contrary to Wright's findings, however, our clergy indicated that considerable counselling does involve spiritual concerns, and there was more emphasis on premarital and bereavement counselling reported here than in previous research (Bell *et al.*, 1976; Wright, 1984). Results regarding referrals were quite consistent with previous findings (Bell *et al.*, 1976; Wright, 1984) that clergy refer a wide variety of problems, primarily to mental health professionals.

Problem solving scores and counselling techniques

The prediction that RPS scores would be related to counselling techniques was partially supported. Active person/active God scores did correlate significantly and positively with the use of three psychological techniques. However, the fact that passive person/active God scores were positively correlated with two of the same psychological approaches (behavioural and Rational-Emotive) contradicts, to some degree, the hypothesis.

It is possible that the item that taps a more behaviouristic approach (pointing out 'problem' behaviours) may be viewed from the perspective that such problem behaviours are actually 'sinful' behaviours, and therefore the clergy might perceive that they have a responsibility to reveal this to their clients and explain necessary changes to behaviours that are not sinful. Similarly, the item that taps a more Rational-Emotive approach (challenging inaccurate ways of thinking) could be viewed from the standpoint of sinful thoughts or inaccurate conceptions of God. Thus, these clergy (passive person/active God) may see themselves as using spiritual rather than psychological techniques. It is also possible that clergy who score high on the passive person/active God scale see themselves as God's emissaries on earth, and thus feel responsible (acting on God's behalf) to point out problem behaviours or faulty ways of thinking. More research is needed to investigate these possibilities.

As expected, passive person/active God scores were positively correlated with spiritual counselling techniques. Apparently clergy members who see themselves as passive and God as active in solving their own problems would tend to help others solve their problems from a more spiritual, God-oriented perspective. However, contrary to expectations, active person/active God scores were also positively correlated with all spiritual items. One might speculate that the emphasis here is on active *God*, regardless of whether the person is viewed as passive or active. This is supported by Pargament *et al.*'s (1985) finding that active person/active God scores correlated positively with measures of God control. Since clergy who score high on this scale also tend to use psychological techniques, as mentioned above, this presents a consistent approach to their counselling style (that is, they employ *both* spiritual and psychological techniques).

Contrary to expectations, active person/passive God scores did not correlate positively with the use of psychological techniques. One might expect that those especially who exclude God from the problem solving process would then use more psychologically-oriented counselling techniques, techniques which do not directly include a spiritual component. Of course, 'excluding God' from the problem solving process is a relative statement, since each ministerial participant undoubtedly includes God in the process to some degree.

Overall, it would seem that RPS scores did correlate, at least to some degree, with counselling techniques, although not as clearly as predicted in our first hypothesis. Clergy who scored high in the active person/active God scale were more likely to use both spiritual and psychological techniques, and clergy who scored high on the passive person/active God scale were more likely to use spiritual techniques and some psychological techniques. However, contrary to expectations, active person/passive God scores did not correlate positively with psychological techniques.

Religious orthodoxy and counselling techniques

As predicted, orthodox clergy did employ spiritual techniques more than less orthodox clergy. This seems to contradict Wright's (1984) finding that there were no significant differences between liberal and conservative Protestant denominations in counselling or referral variables. However, contrary to our prediction, orthodoxy was not related to reported use of psychological techniques. Thus it appears that orthodoxy is related to the use of spiritual, but not psychological, counselling techniques. This may have implications for effectiveness or outcome of counselling, but research has not yet addressed this issue.

Religious problem solving scores and denomination

As predicted, clergy from less orthodox denominations did score higher on active person/passive God measures than did those from the more orthodox denominations. Thus it would appear that clergy from less orthodox denominations are less likely to see God as active in solving problems. Rather, they apparently hold the individual more responsible for problems and their solutions. This is consistent with Pargament *et al.*'s (1985) findings that active person/passive God scores correlated negatively with doctrinal orthodoxy and God control.

Also, as predicted, clergy from more orthodox denominations scored higher on passive person/active God measures than did those from less orthodox denominations. Apparently, more orthodox clergy were more likely to view God as active in solving problems, and the person as less active or responsible. This, too, is consistent with Pargament *et al.*'s (1985) findings that passive person/active God scores correlated positively with doctrinal orthodoxy and God control.

Taken together, the findings that first, clergy from more orthodox denominations score higher on the passive person/active God scale, second, passive person/active God scores are positively correlated with spiritual counselling techniques, and third, more orthodox clergy are more likely to use spiritual counselling techniques, add strength to the proposition that clergy from orthodox denominations engage in a different style of counselling than those from less orthodox denominations.

Additional findings

The overall level of education of our sample of clergy was not correlated with any particular view of the causes of mental illness. Although Larson (1967) had found that more 'realistic' opinions about the causes of mental illness were associated with increased level of education, he failed to specify what a realistic opinion was, making comparisons with his research difficult.

As expected, clergy who had taken courses in counselling or psychology at the graduate level tended to see the cause of mental illness in more psychological terms, and were also more likely to use a Rogerian method of counselling. These results suggest that graduate work in psychology or counselling (rather than general education) is related to ministers' attitudes and approaches. However, graduate level training did not correlate positively with the reported use of other (non-Rogerian) psychological techniques.

The finding that orthodoxy and views of the causation of mental illness are related is consistent with earlier research (Larson, 1967; Wright, 1984), although in our study orthodoxy was negatively correlated with two causes – psychological and societal. Comparable correlations for spiritual and physiological causes were not significant. It is interesting to note that although the orthodox clergy apparently did not perceive the cause of mental illness or the problems which they counsel to be of a spiritual nature alone, they did reportedly tend to use spiritual techniques to counsel clients.

Larson (1967) stated that religious affiliation (which might imply varying levels of orthodoxy) was a key variable in shaping attitudes about mental health. Our results support this notion, but avoid Larson's ambiguous use of the terms realistic and unrealistic.

Wright's (1984) finding that nonfundamentalist clergy were less likely to attribute mental illness to spiritual causes was supported by our research. Further, our results are consistent with Virkler's (1979) finding that clergy supported an interactional model of the causation of mental illness. They perceived spiritual, psychological and physical factors as interacting. Our sample of clergy reported that spiritual, psychological and social factors were all moderately important in this regard.

Summary

Overall, this study confirmed that, as in previous research, the clergy spend a significant amount of time counselling a wide variety of problems and they also refer a variety of clients, primarily to mental health professionals.

Second, there was a relationship between RPS styles and counselling techniques, such that those clergy who scored high on the active person/active God scale were more likely to use both psychological and spiritual techniques. Those clergy who scored high on the passive person/active God scale were more likely to use spiritual techniques. Apparently, a clergyman's personal approach to problem solving is related to his choice of counselling technique. Similarly, the more orthodox clergy employed spiritual counselling techniques more than did less orthodox clergy. Apparently a clergyman's personal theological orientation is related to his choice of counselling techniques.

Also, clergy from less orthodox denominations tended to score higher on the active person/passive God scale than did the clergy from more orthodox denominations, while those from more orthodox denominations scored higher on the passive person/active God scale. Knowing that RPS scores correlated with counselling techniques, it is possible that the clients (parishioners) of clergy from more orthodox denominations are receiving a different type of counselling than are the clients of clergy from less orthodox denominations.

Education was related to counselling such that clergymen who had taken counselling or psychology courses at the graduate level tended to view the cause of mental illness as psychological and also used a psychological (Rogerian) approach to a greater extent than those who had no comparable experience in graduate courses.

Finally, the clergy in this study seemed to espouse an interactional type of model of causation of mental illness, viewing psychological, spiritual and social factors as approximately equally important in contributing to the cause of mental illness.

Overall, this study confirms and further specifies the relationships between religious orientation and counselling, and extends this to include problem solving styles as a potentially valuable predictor of approaches to counselling. Much research remains to be done in this area to further clarify the relationships between theological orientation and approaches to problem solving on the one hand, and views of mental illness and approaches to counselling, on the other. Some of the 'muddiest' findings in this study involved the RPS scales – more work needs to be done investigating the scales themselves (and their relationship to counselling practices). Further, this study was limited to self-reports of Protestant clergy. Future research might examine the *client*'s perceptions and expectations of counselling from the clergy and the effectiveness of counselling done by the clergy from different theological and psychological perspectives.

References

Bell, R A, Morris, R R, Holzer, C E and Warheit, G J (1976) 'The clergy as a mental health resource: parts I and II,' *The Journal of Pastoral Care*, 30, pp. 103–115.

Fullerton, J T and Hunsberger, B (1982) 'A unidimensional measure of Christian orthodoxy,' *Journal for the Scientific Study of Religion*, 21, pp. 317–326.

Larson, R F (1967) 'Denominational variations in the clergymen's attitudes concerning mental health,' *Mental Hygiene*, 51, pp. 185–191.

Nie, N H, Hull, C H, Jenkins, J G, Steinbrenner, D H and Bent, D H (1975) *Statistical Package for the Social Sciences*, New York, McGraw-Hill.

Pargament, K I, Kennell, J, Hathaway, W, Grevengoed, N, Newman, J and Jones, W (1985) Religion and the problem solving process: three styles of coping, paper presented at the Society for the Scientific Study of Religion meetings, Savannah, Georgia.

Virkler, H A (1979) 'Counseling demands, procedures, and preparation of parish ministers: a descriptive study,' *Journal of Psychology and Theology*, 7, pp. 271–280.

Wright, P G (1984) 'The counseling activities and referral practices of Canadian clergy in British Columbia,' *Journal of Psychology and Theology*, 12, pp. 294–304.

Wright, P G, Moreau, M E and Haley, G M (1982) 'The clergy's attitudes about mental illness, counseling and the helping professions,' *Canadian Journal of Community Mental Health*, 1, pp. 71–80.

13.2 Relationship between clergy and psychologists: the empirical data

Willa D Meylink and Richard L Gorsuch

Both clergy and psychologists are often involved with people in need of help, but to what extent are they involved with each other and to what extent should they be involved with each other? The answers to such questions lie in part in data showing the interactions of the professions. This paper will review empirical literature on the relationships between clergy and mental health professionals such as psychologists.[1]

The second purpose of this paper is to provide a basis from which to reflect upon views of the clergy's role in light of the data and the possibilities that do exist. The literature review forms the basis for such a discussion.

Empirical data exist on a number of topics relevant to the relationship between clergy and psychologist. First is the basic question of whether clergy are involved in the mental health process in the contemporary era. For those who are, the question then arises of the degree to which these clergy refer clients to psychologists. Fortunately, there has been considerable research on clergy variables relating to referral, including the perceptions of the role of the clergy relevant to counselling and the impact of variables such as age of the clergy involved and their education. Another clergy variable is that of their theological orientation and how that influences the process.

Clergy mental health activities usually occur in some type of church context, and the characteristics of the context may be influential on the clergy-psychologist interaction. Both the size of congregation and the congregational income have been investigated for their relationship of clergy referrals to psychologists.

Another important set of variables revolves around those who are seeking help from clergy or mental health professionals. What type of presenting problems are they most likely to confront? What are the implications of the type of problems taken to clergy for interaction between clergy and other mental health professionals?

Finally, studies of this relationship between a particular member of the clergy and a particular mental health professional are reviewed. These studies were concerned with the degree to which personal acquaintance influenced that interaction, as well as such variables as clergy awareness of mental health professionals and to whom do clergy refer and how referrals to and from clergy influence the professional interaction.

Clergy involvement in mental health process

Gurin, Veroff and Feld (1960) interviewed a stratified random sample in the United States on a wide spectrum of mental health issues, one of which was to whom a person turned for help for an emotional problem. They found that 42% of people requesting help for mental problems first turned to a member of the clergy. Also in 1960, the final report of the Joint Commission on Mental Illness and Health noted the important role of clergy in the mental health process. The survey was replicated some two decades later by Veroff, Kulka and Douwan (1981). In this replication of the earlier national interview survey, similar results were found with 39% of those who sought help for an emotional problem turning first to clergy. These studies have thus documented in the area of mental health what most churches have long claimed, namely, that their clergy are there in part to help people with problems. The Veroff *et al.* (1981) conclusion appears to ably summarise the situation: 'In spite of the clear and important shift of 1976 toward the consultation of mental health professionals for personal problems, one cannot fail to be impressed by the continuing critical role that clergy play in assisting many Americans in dealing with personal problems' (p. 134).

Clergy referrals

Since clergy are seldom trained in mental health treatment as a primary focus, the question arises as to the degree to which clergy, seeing numerous people who are seeking help for an emotional problem, refer these on to other mental health professionals. Some studies ask the clients themselves whether they were referred by clergy to a mental health resource. Other studies interviewed clergy, asking what percentage they referred, whereas still other researchers interviewed psychologists for the source of their referrals. The research on this topic is summarised in table one, which is subdivided according to the source of the information.

Major studies have used the client report method to evaluate clergy referrals to mental health professionals. These include Gurin *et al.* (1960) and Veroff *et al.* (1981), both using national samples and including much the same questions in their interviews. Additional major studies include Bell, Morris, Holzer and Warheit (1976) and Morris, Bell and Holzer (1976) who reviewed the client files of 17,723 patients and Mannino, Rooney, and Hassler (1967) who reviewed some 1500 cases from mental health clinics. As table one shows, the studies consistently show some 2 to 3% of psychologists' and psychiatrists' clients had, according to the client, been referred by clergy. The figure is higher when a wider range of mental health resources is included, being some 15% in that case. Not surprisingly, Rumberger and Rogers (1982) found somewhat more referrals when the clients examined were

Table 1: Clergy referrals

study	sample	location	method[1]	data
client report				
Gurin *et al*. (1960)	2,460	national	interview	of all those referred to psychiatrist or psychologist, 2% were referred by clergy
				of all those referred to another mental health resource, 14% were referred by clergy
Mannino *et al*. (1967)	1,500 clients	Maryland	review of clinic records from '52–61	3% of contacts with mental health clinic were from clergy referral
Bell *et al*. (1976)	17,723 patients	SE states	review of records	3% of private practice patients referred by clergy
				2.2% of rural-urban mental health clinics referred by clergy
				1% of urban mental health clinics referred by clergy
Veroff *et al*. (1981)	2,267	national	interview	of all those referred to psychiatrist or psychologist, 2% were referred by clergy
				of all those referred to another mental health resource, 16% were referred by clergy
Rumberger and Rogers (1981)	146 clients	Southern California	37% return	8% of clients were referred by clergy to a Christian mental health centre
clergy report				
Piedmont (1968)	242 clergy	St Louis, Missouri	52% return	clergy refer 6% of parishioners consulting them
Bell *et al*. (1976)	178 clergy	SE states	64% return	clergy refer 10% of their clients, clergy counsel and refer another 10%
Kevin (1976)	94 clergy	Austin, TX	69% return	clergy refer 10.2 clients/year
Virkler (1979)	54 clergy	1 Northern and 1 Southern city	50% return	majority of clergy refer 0–10% of clients
Gilbert (1981)	74 clergy (Assembly of God)	West Texas	67% return	clergy refer 6.5% of clients
Elkins (1983)	107 clergy (United Meth.)	Middle Tenn.	37% return	clergy refer 16% of clients
mental health resource report				
Kevin (1976)	30 psychologists	Austin, TX	73% return	psychologists reported 2.2 clergy referral/year
Tryon (1983)	165 psychologists	national	55% return	26% of psychologists reported clergy as a referral source (clergy ranked 9th)
Inman and Bascue	222 psychologists	Philadelphia	59% return	4% of psychologists reported clergy as an important referral source (clergy ranked 8th)

Note:1 When a 'per cent return' is given, data were collected by mail questionnaire.

from a Christian mental health facility, but even in that case only 8% of the clients had been referred by clergy (a finding which is more suggestive than conclusive due to the study being limited to one clinic and the study's having a low rate of return of mail questionnaires).

When clergy reports are considered, the data are somewhat different, as can be seen by examining the second section of table one. First, the studies are much more limited in that each had a small to moderate sample, was from a specific region, and was sometimes from one particular denomination. Generally these studies were also mail surveys with limited rates of return. Given the wide range of types of samples, the results are reasonably consistent: clergy report referring approximately 10% of those who seek them out to other mental health professionals. The clergy report figures are consistent with the client reports. Assuming that 39% go first to clergy and that clergy refer 10% of them, the psychologists would receive 39% times 10% of their clients from clergy referral. Since 39% times 10% is 4%, this agrees closely with the 3 to 4% reported by psychologists as being referred to them by clergy.

The studies asking psychologists regarding clergy as a source of referrals are difficult to compare with the other reports because the studies are asked in such a radically different way. Kevin (1976) asked how many clergy referrals there were each year, whereas Tryon (1983) and Inman and Bascue (1983) asked psychologists to list important sources of referrals. But those reports also suggest that the clergy referral rate is low.

Personal characteristics of referring clergy

Several studies have related the personal characteristics of the clergy to the degree to which they refer clients to other professionals. Major variables investigated are summarised in table two, and include clergy age, education, counselling related education, and theological orientation.[2]

The scattered studies which have looked at the age of clergy have seldom found much relationship to whether the clergy refer. As can be seen from table two, most of these studies were so small that age may not have had a chance to be significant. The one study sufficiently large to detect minor influences did find that younger clergy were more likely to counsel than to refer. Whether this is a function of differential patterns of education associated with age will be examined below.

The research on the relationship of clergy's total education to referral is again spotty with most studies being small, of non-representative samples, and having such low returns in mail surveys as to be questionable. There are some slight tendencies in these studies for greater education to be related to more referral, but, due to the limited nature of the studies conducted, such a conclusion may be somewhat premature.

Table 2: Personal characteristics of a referring clergy

study	sample	location	method[1]	data
clergy age				
Cumming and Harrington (1963)	59 churches	Syracuse,NY	interview	NS
Larson (1964)	422 clergy	NE states	44% return	clergy under 45 more likely to counsel than refer
Binkley (1976)	54 clergy (United Meth.)	Southern California	63% return	NS
Good (1978)	25 clergy	Rural NY	50% return	NS
Gilbert (1981)	74 clergy (Assembly of God)	West Texas	67% return	NS
Elkins (1983)	107 clergy (United Meth.)	Middle Tenn.	37% return	NS
clergy total education				
Bentz (1967)	100 clergy	Florida	interview	more educated were more likely to refer
Stayton (1967)	63 clergy	Boston	–	NS
Good (1978)	25 clergy	Rural NY	50% return	NS[2]
Gilbert (1981)	74 clergy (Assembly of God)	West Texas	67% return	NS[2]
Beals (1982)	36 clergy	Columbus, OH	27% return	NS
Elkins (1983)	107 clergy (United Meth.)	Middle Tenn.	37% return	more educated were more likely to refer
clergy counselling-related education				
Stayton (1967)	63 clergy	Boston	?% return	the more counselling education, the more referrals
Bentz (1967)	100 clergy	Florida	interview	the more counselling education, the more referrals
Kevin (1976)	94 clergy	Austin, TX	69% return	the more counselling education, the more referrals
Binkley (1976)	54 clergy (United Meth.)	Southern California	63% return	more hours of clinical training significantly related to low referral activity
Good (1978)	25 clergy	Rural NY	50% return	NS[2]
Winett (1979)	48 clergy	Lexington, KY	42% return	counselling educated referred more to mental health centres NS to private practitioners
Gilbert (1981)	74 clergy	West Texas	67% return	NS (seminary counselling and psychology courses) more referral with more counselling workshops attended
Elkins (1983)	107 clergy (United Meth.)	Middle Tenn.	37% return	the more counselling education, the more referrals
clergy theological orientation				
Cumming and Harrington (1963)	59 churches	Syracuse, NY	interview	fundamentals referred less than others
Stayton (1967)	63 clergy	Boston	–	NS
Good (1978)	25 clergy	Rural NY	50% return	liberals referred more than conservatives
Gilbert (1981)	74 clergy (Assembly of God)	West Texas	67% return	NS
Elkins (1983)	107 clergy (United Meth.)	Southern California	37% return	NS

Notes: 1 When a 'percent return' is given, the data were collected by mail questionnaire.
2 Although non-significant, there was a trend in the appropriate direction. Larger N may have produced significance.

An interesting relationship between referral and education is the specific education which is related to the counselling role of the clergy. These studies, also summarised in table two, tend to again have fairly small samples from limited geographical areas although the return rates are somewhat higher than for some of the other research. Most of the studies indicate that more education regarding counselling and psychology produces a higher referral rate. The one study finding a non-significant trend in that direction can be assumed to be non-significant because the N is so extremely small. Gilbert (1981) may bear further investigation since it suggested some unique interaction between education and the particular denomination studied or an inter-action between age and the type of educational experience.

Binkley (1976) is the major exception to the general trend in the section on special education in table two, but note the nature of the variable used. Education in general counselling or psychology was not the variable; instead hours of 'clinical training' was investigated. Pastoral Clinical Education is a programme designed to increase the level of competence among pastors to do the counselling themselves. Hence these people should feel more capable of counselling with those whom other clergy, due to their own lack of direct training in clinical techniques, referred to other professionals. The general conclusion is that some education in psychology and counselling in general leads to a greater appreciation of the fellow professionals and therefore to more referrals, but the training of clergy in counselling techniques them-selves may produce more of an 'equal professional' feeling so that the total number of referrals is actually less.

Training could be specifically designed to educate about the referral process, but that appears uncommon. Virkler (1979) noted that 45% of the clergy in that study were not trained in how to identify cases where referral was appropriate, 55% reported no training in identifying avail-able sources to which referrals could be made, 63% reported a lack of ability to evaluate the quality of mental health resources available, and 56% reported having no training in how to help parishioners make the transition from them to a referral source. Such training could, in theory, be helpful but it appears few have received it. In two studies (Binkley, 1976; Good, 1978) training increased some direct or indirect referral activity although Beals (1982) found no significant difference.

The relationship found with the degree of counselling and psychol-ogy education and the increased offering of such courses in recent years suggests an interpretation of the occasional finding that younger clergy refer more than older. This relationship to age may be the func-tion of availability of the courses during training of the younger clergy. The Gilbert (1981) results might suggest that older clergy who refer more also attend counselling workshops since such courses may not have been available to them while in seminary.

Clergy have generally been grouped together in most studies as if they were interchangeable, and yet the host of denominations testifies to the major differences in approaches toward religion and the role of clergy that can be taken within our society. Hence the theological orientation as well as the denominational structure and definition of the clergy roles may be important. Unfortunately, only a few studies have even investigated current theological orientation. As summarised in table two, the results are mixed, with an occasional study finding the more conservative pastors less likely to refer than the more liberal pastors. Perhaps further investigation with studies more oriented towards the theology of the pastoral role would be helpful in this area.

Clergy setting and its impact upon referral

Clergy work within a particular situation, primarily congregations. These congregations systematically vary on a host of variables such as organisational differences, ethnicity, and geographical area. One would expect some of these variables to influence referral rates but only two have been investigated so far and been found to be significant. The research on congregational income and the size of the congregation is summarised in table three.

The results on size of congregation are mixed, although there is a tendency for clergy in larger churches to refer more than those in smaller churches. This may be due to other variables which are more directly related to clergy but show up indirectly in congregational size, including the sophistication of the clergy, the differential role of the clergy in larger versus smaller churches, and the location of larger churches. One could hypothesise that the larger churches draw the more sophisticated clergy who would be more likely to have training in counselling and psychology and hence refer more often than those in the smaller churches. One could also hypothesise that such churches are more likely to be located in metropolitan areas with multiple mental health resources to which people could be referred, than would be found in the case of the smaller churches. Another hypothesis would be that the pastor has more parishioners with the result being more restricted time for counselling and less of a feeling of personal involvement and caretaking for each particular parishioner, and hence more referral. The studies finding no significant relationship may be because of areas where mental health resources have a shorter history of availability. The data on congregational income are suggestive that more referrals take place with higher income congregations (that is, among those who can afford it).

Presenting problems

The problems parishioners present to clergy are also expected to be important for the manner in which clergy interact with other mental health professionals. The studies in this area, summarised in table four, are from either clients' reports themselves or from reports from

Table 3: Clergy setting

study	sample	location	method[1]	data
congregational size				
Cumming and Harrington (1963)	59 churches	Syracuse, NY	interview	larger churches referred significantly more
Binkley (1976)	54 clergy (United Meth.)	Southern California	63% return	larger referred significantly more
Kevin (1976)	94 clergy	Austin, TX	69% return	larger referred significantly more
Good (1978	25 clergy	Rural NY	50% return	NS[2]
Gilbert (1981)	74 clergy (Assembly of God)	West Texas	67% return	NS[2]
Elkins (1983)	107 clergy (United Meth.)	Middle Tenn.	37% return	NS[2]
congregational income				
Cumming and Harrington (1963)	59 churches	Syracuse, NY	interview	middle class churches had significantly higher referral activity
Kevin (1976)	95 clergy	Austin, TX	69% return	trend: higher income refer more

Notes: 1 When a 'percent return' is given, data were collected by mail questionnaire.
　　　2 NS: larger churches did not refer significantly more than smaller churches.

clergy. As the table indicates, clergy face a wide gamut of emotional problems. The most frequently reported issues are family-related which, including marital problems and other family problems, account for approximately half of their counselling load. The same result is found whether it is based upon client report or clergy report.

Outside of identifying major problems brought to clergy, integrating these studies is problematic. Different diagnostic labels for emotional distress has led to considerable confusion about which presenting problems clergy see as well as which they refer. Categories used in the research range from the over-simplified ones such as those we are using in table four to the Cumming and Harrington (1963) detailed listing of over 40 types of problems, many of which use technical terms. Despite this variety, it is apparent that clergy see a wide range of problems but over half the problems they face revolve around family-related issues.

The summarisation of data dealing with presenting problems becomes even more confusing when referral is included in the research. Two major research approaches to this problem have been used: retrospective data gathering and vignettes. The retrospective data gathering approach finds obvious mental disease, probably including psychotic and severe neurotic ideation or behaviour, to be the most often referred (Sandler, 1966; Bentz, 1967), but it is difficult to know the referral rate relative to the base rate of occurrence in the ioners.

Table 4: Presenting problems

study	sample	design[1]	read data as:	marital	sexual	child	family	work/social	situational crisis	personal adjustment	obvious mental disease	faith
client report								data				
Gurin et al. (1960)	national N = 345	interview	% N citing problem	42	–	12	5	6	14	19	–	–
Bell et al. (1976)	SE states N = 234	interview	% N citing problem	15	–	–	24	4	19	7	–	17
Veroff et al. (1981)	national N = 580	interview	% N citing problem	40	–	10	3	4	22	22	–	–
clergy report												
Gurin et al. (1960)	national N = 345	interview	% N citing problem	47	–	8	6	5	9	20	–	–
Sandler (1966)	Memphis N = 232	39% return	rank order	1	4	6/7	–	5	–	2	8	3
Bentz (1967)	Florida N = 100	interview	% N citing problem	–	*	*	50%	*	*	*	–	*
Hong and Wiehe	St Louis N = 61 (Lutheran)	57% return	% N citing problem	38	–	0	18	–	–	40	–	–
Morris et al. (1976)	SE states N = 178	64% return	F = frequently O = occasionally R = rarely	F	O	–	F	O	R	O	–	F
Veroff (1981)	national	interview	% N citing problem	45	–	8	4	4	23	15	–	–

Notes: 1 When a 'percent return' is given, data were collected by mail questionnaire.
– Category not used in study.
* Also occurred.

(When vignettes are used to research referral rate, a short case parish history is provided and clergy are asked what they would do with it. These studies often have both psychologists and clergy rate the degree to which they should be referred and hence will be discussed further below.)

Clergy-psychologist interactions

The research on clergy-psychologists' interactions has used several approaches. First is the vignette approach, an indirect form whereby the opinion of the two groups is solicited on the same cases as presented by the vignettes (Larson, 1964; Kevin, 1976; Matthews, 1976). It is difficult to summarise these studies because they each used different types of vignettes. Some typical results include Larson's finding that 29% of the clergy would suggest referring a person described as a violent male paranoid, whereas only 6% of the clergy would suggest referral for a women with sexual and marital problems. Kevin generally found that vignettes involving values and grief needed less referral by clergy and less need for a mental health professional. In these studies it can be generally concluded that clergy saw their role as providing at least major assistance in addition to referral while psychiatrists, for example, advised referral with limited or no continued assistance from the clergy. In light of this, it is interesting to note that Beals (1976) found one third of his sample seeing clergy and mental health professionals concurrently. In general the psychologists and clergy saw referral necessary in similar cases.

A second approach to the possible interaction of clergy and psychologist considers the acquaintance between clergy and mental health professionals. Logically, such acquaintance would seem to encourage active referrals and the research generally confirms this logic. While operational definitions of 'acquaintance' vary, four studies have reported significant correlations between high referral rates and acquaintance with a mental health professional (Kevin, 1976; Good, 1978; Binkley, 1976; Bentz, 1967). This particular variable may also underlie some of the findings noted earlier; for example, Bentz (1967) reported that more educated pastors were more acquainted with more mental health professionals as well as referring more. One would suspect that the actual acquaintance may be a more powerful causative agent than the education *per se*.

A third approach is to consider the awareness of clergy of mental health resources, but the limited research does not seem conclusive in this area. It does seem that most studies find the overwhelming majority of clergy are aware of basic mental health resources. This includes not only clergy in Florida (Bentz, 1967) but also West Texas Assembly of God clergy (Gilbert, 1981) and those in Lexington, Kentucky (Winett, 1979).

A fourth approach examines to which mental health professionals referrals are made. These studies are summarised in table five. The

Table 5: Use of mental health resources

study	sample	location	design	type						
				psychologist	psychiatrist	social worker	pastoral counsellor	marriage family counsellor	agency	other
A. 'do you refer to . . .?'										
Bentz (1967)	100 clergy	Florida	interview	27%	44%	–[1]	–	–	47%	(MD) 75%
Hong & Wiehe (1974)	61 clergy (Lutheran)	St Louis	57% return[2]	52%	36%	52%	41%	–	–	–
B. 'to whom do you refer most . . .?'										
Piedmont (1968)	212 clergy	St Louis	44% return	8%	33%	27%	16%	–	–	(hospital)9%
C. 'percentage of referrals to . . .' (high vs. low referrers)										
Binkley[3] (1976)	54 clergy (United Meth.)	Southern California	low referrals 63%, N = 26	6.3%	6.3%	9.2%	.8%	6.9%	9.6%	–
			high referrals N = 28	18.9%	6.6%	2.0%	7.8%	40.2%	23.5%	–
Good (1978)	25 clergy	rural NY	low referrals 50%, N = 9	0%	–[4]	–	36%	0%	18%	(MD)46%
			high referrals N = 13	15%	–	–	15%	11%	22%	18%

Notes: 1 – = Not used in study.
2 When a 'percent return' is given, data were collected by mail questionnaire.
3 All categories except psychiatrist were significantly different for high vs low referring clergy. X^2 Test of Independence (df = 5), p - .05).
4 Psychologist and psychiatrist referrals were combined.

studies vary considerably in their conclusions, which may be a function of the visibility of different professionals in different communities or some other as yet unidentified variables.

The last approach to studying the interaction of disciplines is to consider the question of reciprocity. Indeed, while the explicit purpose of this article is to examine the clergy-psychologists' relationship, a glance back at the tables shows that practically all of the research has been unidirectional: from clergy to psychologists. The studies allowing bidirectional referral (Cumming and Harrington, 1963; Bell, 1976; Bentz, 1967; Beals, 1982; Good, 1978; Binkley, 1976) report that clergy refer more clients to others than are referred to them, but little systematic investigation has been done in this area. Perhaps more striking than the unidirectionality of referral is the fact that the clergy show considerable discontent both with the lack of reciprocity and, in addition, with the lack of feedback on referrals that are given. And even when some feedback is given, many pastors report that it comes only upon their explicit request. For example, in Beals' (1982) study, two-thirds of the clergy reported no feedback from referrals, and there was a significant correlation between feedback received and both clergy satisfaction with referrals and clergy referral activity. High referring clergy either report more feedback, although they saw even that as being too limited (Good, 1978), or more often requested feedback from either the parishioner or the professional to whom referral was made (Binkley, 1976).

This last line of research on reciprocity of referral may mean that the definition of roles as equal professionals with different areas of expertise may be a critical variable in referrals as well as in broader relationships. The research is currently divided on this issue. Beals (1982) found that 79% of the mental health professionals in this study reported that they would consult with or refer to clergy if religious ideation were involved. However, this result may be because of the wording of the question and because it has such a great latitude, involving both consultation and referral, as well as being limited to the religious in an explicit, direct way. The results of Larson (1964) and Kevin (1976) are more consistent with the discontent noted earlier. Larson found clergy believing their role is to provide major assistance to the person in need, whereas the mental health professional saw the clergy role as of limited assistance and referral. Kevin (1976) found psychologists had a relatively low regard for the need of intervention by clergy and were generally not involved in exchanging referrals with clergy. The unidirectionality of the referral process seen so far does indeed seem consistent with previously cited studies which report that referrals from mental health professionals to clergy are much lower than vice versa, but clergy view this as problematic. Hence it appears that appropriate role definitions between the professions needs to be developed so that the professions have mutually compatible expectations and models for interaction.

Conclusion

From the literature reviewed above, it is apparent that low referral rates between psychologists and clergy stem in part from viewing clergy as 'gatekeepers' for the mental health profession. While there may be some interaction between referral rates and other descriptive variables examined, clergy seemed to voice the most discontent with the unequal relationship as perceived from lack of communication and reciprocity between the professionals. Further articles in this series will more closely evaluate the 'gatekeeper' model and seek new possibilities for the referral relationship between psychologists and clergy (Gorsuch and Meylink, 1988; Meylink, 1988).

Notes

1. In this review, it will become apparent that we do not intend to treat all studies as equal. Some of the studies are more limited and specific than are others, particularly regarding the size and type of sample. While all the studies will be tabled, the discussion of the tables will stress those studies which appear to us to be the most sound. Preference will be given to large national samples, for example, over small ad hoc samples. While differences such as samples are obvious from the way we have drawn up the tables, there are other more subtle differences among the studies, particularly in the definition of the variables. Unfortunately, in the social sciences everyone feels free to write their own items and these seldom match those used by any other investigator. Hence the degree to which the differences in studies arise – because, for example, of the differences in the way the questions were posed or differences in the regions where the studies were conducted – is unknown. Problems such as these preclude a more formal meta-analysis. The fact that several major conclusions do seem to replicate, despite such diversity in the research, is encouraging.

2. Several attempts have been made to better define theological or philosophical perceptions of clergy role as it relates to their counselling function (Clark and Thomas, 1979; Kevin, 1976; Beals, 1982; Rumberger and Rogers, 1982). Because of the diversity of approach, these will not be discussed here. Another body of literature indicates the importance of counselling by rating pastors give to it, the number of hours spent in this activity, and their counselling case load. Such studies underscore the fact that clergy do counsel and that they define that quite explicitly as part of their role (for example Meile, 1974).

References

Beals, K A (1982) A descriptive study of the religious and philosophical beliefs and referral practices of clergy and secular mental health professionals, unpublished doctoral dissertation, Boston University School of Theology.

Bell, R A, Morris, R R, Holzer, C E III, and Warheit, G J (1976) 'The clergy as a mental health resource: part I,' *Journal of Pastoral Care*, 30, pp. 103–115.

Bentz, W K (1967) 'The relationship between educational background and the referral role of ministers,' *Sociology and Social Research*, 51, pp. 199–208.

Binkley, J G (1976) Factors related to referral for psychotherapy by clergy, unpublished doctoral dissertation, California School of Professional Psychology.

Clark, S A and Thomas, A H (1979) 'Counseling and the clergy: perceptions of roles,' *Journal of Psychology and Theology*, 7, pp. 48–56.

Cumming, E and Harrington, C (1963) 'Clergyman as counselor,' *American Journal of Sociology*, 69, pp. 234–243.

Elkins, D E (1983) Factors influencing psychological referral practices of ministers of the Tennessee annual conference of the United Methodist Church, unpublished doctoral dissertation, George Peabody College for Teachers of Vanderbilt University.

Gilbert, M G (1981) 'The decision of assemblies of God pastors to counsel or refer,' *Journal of Psychology and Theology*, 9, pp. 250–256.

Good, A (1978) Short term intervention to improve referral practices of local clergy, unpublished doctoral dissertation, Lancaster Theological Seminary.

Gorsuch, R and Meylink, W D (1988) 'Toward a co-professional model of clergy-psychologist referral,' *Journal of Psychology and Christianity*, 7, 3, pp. 22–31.

Gurin, G, Veroff, J and Feld, S (1960) *Americans View their Mental Health: a nationwide interview survey*, New York, Basic Books.

Hong, B A and Wiehe, V R (1974) 'Referral patterns of clergy,' *Journal of Psychology and Theology*, 2, pp. 291-297.

Inman, D J and Bascue, L O (1983) 'Referral sources of psychologists in private practice,' *Psychological Reports*, 52, pp. 856-866.

Joint Commission on Mental Illness and Health (1961) *Action for Mental Health*, New York, Basic Books.

Kevin, R C (1976) Factors influencing the judgment and referral of mental health presenting problems by clergy and psychologists, unpublished doctoral dissertation, University of Texas at Austin.

Larson, R F (1964) 'Clerical and psychiatric conceptions of the clergyman's role in the therapeutic setting,' *Social Problems*, 11, pp. 419-428.

Mannino, F V, Rooney, H L and Hassler, F R (1967) 'A survey of clergy referrals to a mental health clinic,' *Journal of Religion and Health*, 6, pp. 66-73.

Matthews, S D (1976) Clinical judgment in parish ministers, pastoral counselors, and clinical psychologists, unpublished doctoral dissertation, Adelphi University.

Meile, R L (1974) 'Referral network: brokers and providers,' *American Journal of Mental Deficiency*, 78, pp. 404-408.

Meylink, W D (1988) 'Impact of referral training of psychologists on the clergy-psychologist professional interaction,' *Journal of Psychology and Christianity*, 7, 3, pp. 55-64.

Morris, R R, Bell, R A, and Holzer, C E III (1976) 'The clergy as mental health resource: part II,' *Journal of Pastoral Care*, 30, pp. 108-115.

Piedmont, E B (1968) 'Referrals and reciprocity: psychiatrists, general practitioners, and clergymen,' *Journal of Health and Social Behavior*, 9, pp. 29-41.

Rumberger, D J and Rogers, M L (1982) 'Pastoral openness to interaction with a private Christian counseling service,' *Journal of Psychology and Theology*, 10, pp. 337-345.

Sandler, N H (1966) 'Attitudes of ministers toward psychiatry,' *Journal of Religion and Health*, 5, pp. 47-60.

Stayton, W R (1967) Ministers' attitudes toward and practice of referral to mental health services, unpublished doctoral dissertation, Boston University.

Tryon, G S (1983) 'How full-time practitioners market their services: a national survey,' *Psychotherapy in Private Practice*, 1, pp. 91-100.

Veroff, J, Kulka, R A and Douwan, E (1981) *Mental Health in America*, New York, Basic Books.

Virkler, H A (1979) 'Counseling demands, procedures, and preparation of parish ministers: a descriptive study,' *Journal of Psychology and Theology*, 7, pp. 271-280.

Winett, R A, Majors, J S and Stewart, G (1979) 'Mental health treatment and referral practices of clergy and physician caregivers,' *Journal of Community Psychology*, 7, pp. 318-323.

Acknowledgements

The publisher and editors would like to acknowledge the following permissions to reproduce copyright material. All possible attempts have been made to contact copyright holders and to acknowledge their copyright correctly. We are grateful to: *Ageing and Society*, for L J Francis and D W Lankshear, 'Ageing Anglican clergy and performance indicators in the rural church, compared with the suburban church,' 13, 339–363, 1993; *Baptist Quarterly*, for E C Lehman Jr, 'Reactions to women in ministry: a survey of English Baptist church members,' 31, 302–320, 1986; *British Journal of General Practice*, for A W Jones, 'A survey of general practitioners' attitudes to the involvement of clergy in patient care,' 40, 280–283, 1990; *Educational Gerontology*, for J K Gulledge, 'Gerontological knowledge among clergy: implications for seminary training,' 18, 637–644, 1992; *Journal for the Scientific Study of Religion*, for M J Verdieck, J J Shields and D R Hoge, 'Role commitment processes revisited: American Catholic priests 1970 and 1985,' 27, 524–535, 1988; *Journal of Clinical Psychology*, for C A Rayburn, L J Richmond and L Rogers, 'Men, women and religion: stress within leadership roles,' 42, 540–546, 1986 (© 1986, Clinical Psychology Publishing Co., Inc., Brandon, VT 05733 USA. All rights reserved. Reproduced by permission of the publisher); *Journal of Pastoral Psychotherapy*, for H W Stone, 'A 25 year study of the changes in those who enter ministry,' 2, 13–26, 1989 (© By the Haworth Press, Inc. All rights reserved. Reprinted with permission. For copies of this work, contact Marianne Arnold at the Haworth Document Delivery Service [Telephone 1-800-3-HAWORTH; 10 Alice Street, Binghamton, NY 13904]. For other questions concerning rights and permissions contact Wanda Latour at the above address); *Journal of Psychology and Christianity*, for W D Meylink and R L Gorsuch, 'Relationship between clergy and psychologists: the empirical data,' 7, 56–72, 1988; *Journal of Psychology and Theology*, for W M Goldsmith and B N Ekhardt, 'Personality factors of men and women pastoral candidates, part 2: sex role preferences,' 12, 211–221, 1984, for D Winger and B Hunsberger, 'Clergy counselling practices, Christian orthodoxy and problem solving styles,' 16, 41–48, 1988, for A Nauss, 'Leadership styles of effective ministry,' 17, 59–67, 1989, for G Domino, 'Clergy's knowledge of psychopathology,' 18, 32–39, 1990, for H W Stone, 'Seminary dropouts: a study of predictability,' 18, 270–278, 1990, for B B Benda and F A DiBlasio, 'Clergy marriages: a multivariate model of marital adjustment,' 20, 367–375, 1992 (the copyright is held by *Journal of Psychology and Theology*); *Journal of Religious Gerontology*, for J L

Goodwin and M Y T Chen, 'From pastor to pensioner: a study of retired Canadian Protestant clergy from the continuity perspective,' 7, 3, 69–79, 1991; *Pastoral Psychology*, for C Burdsal, R Newton, J Burdsal and K Yates, 'On the examination of the role of the Episcopalian priest in the pastoral ministry,' 32, 58–71, 1983, for P J Keddy, P Erdberg and S D Sammon, 'The psychological assessment of Catholic clergy and religious referred for residential treatment,' 38, 147–159, 1990, for J Patrick, 'Assessment of narcissistic psychopathology in the clergy,' 38, 173–180, 1990, for S W Cardwell, 'Why women fail/succeed in ministry: psychological factors,' 30, 153–162, 1982; *Pastoral Sciences*, for H W Stone, 'Predicting ministerial effectiveness,' 8, 81–97, 1989; *Personality and Individual Differences*, for L J Francis and R Rodger, 'The influence of personality on clergy role prioritisation, role influences, conflict and dissatisfaction with ministry,' 16, 947–957, 1994; *Psychological Reports*, for D L Ostrander, C S Henry and C C Hendrix, 'The Stressors of Clergy Children Inventory: reliability and validity,' 67, 787–794, 1990 (© *Psychological Reports* 1990); *Review of Religious Research*, for R L Dudley and D Cummings, 'Factors related to pastoral morale in the Seventh-day Adventist Church,' 24, 127–137, 1982, for H N Malony and L F Majovski, 'The role of psychological assessment in predicting ministerial effectiveness,' 28,29–39, 1986, for L Stevens, 'Different voice, different voices: Anglican women in ministry,' 30, 262–275, 1989; *Sociological Analysis* (the official journal of the Association for the Sociology of Religion, now continued as *Sociology of Religion*), for J H Fichter, 'The myth of clergy burnout,' 45, 373–382, 1984 (© Association for the Sociology of Religion 1984), for L A Young and R A Schoenherr, 'The changing age distribution and theological attitudes of Catholic priests revisited,' 53, 73–87, 1992 (© Association for the Sociology of Religion, 1992); *Sociological Review*, for A Aldridge, 'Slaves to no sect: the Anglican clergy and liturgical change,' 34, 357–380, 1986; *Sociology*, for A Bryman, 'The value of re-studies in sociology: the case of clergy and ministers, 1971 to 1985,' 23, 31–53, 1989; *Sociology of Religion* (the official journal of the Association for the Sociology of Religion, formerly *Sociological Analysis*), for E C Lehman Jr, 'Gender and ministry style: things not what they seem,' 54, 1–11, 1993 (© Association for the Sociology of Religion, 1993); *Work and Stress*, for P J Dewe, 'New Zealand ministers of religion: identifying sources of stress and coping strategies,' 1, 351–363, 1987.

Name Index

Subject Index